Dear Student:

Included free with this edition of Lesikar's Basic Business Communication is our new Student Workbook on CD-ROM !!

(over there to be exact)

Compiled with the help of the authors, the CD is an interactive study guide which helps you prepare for exams or tests your knowledge after reading a chapter. You'll find multiple choice and true/false self-quizzes for every chapter, and the ability to get corrections and feedback from the web. Now, I'm sure I don't have to tell you that this is not the end-all and be-all of studying, but it should help you at least prepare.

If you get a moment between chapters, email me a note on what you think of it. If you have suggestions for improvement, I can be reached at **christine_scheid@mcgraw-hill.com.**

Thanks and have a good semester!

Christine Scheid

Christine Scheid
Development Editor

P.S. Be sure and check out our website for information and updates at: www.mhhe.com/lesikar.

EIGHTH EDITION

Lesikar's
Basic Business Communication

Raymond V. Lesikar
EMERITUS, LOUISIANA STATE UNIVERSITY

John D. Pettit, Jr.

Marie E. Flatley
SAN DIEGO STATE UNIVERSITY

McGraw Hill Irwin
McGraw-Hill

Boston   Burr Ridge, IL   Dubuque, IA   Madison, WI   New York   San Francisco
St. Louis   Bangkok   Bogotá   Caracas   Lisbon   London   Madrid
Mexico City   Milan   New Delhi   Seoul   Singapore   Sydney   Taipei   Toronto

Irwin/McGraw-Hill

A Division of The **McGraw·Hill** *Companies*

LESIKAR'S BASIC BUSINESS COMMUNICATION

This book is printed on acid-free paper.

international   1 2 3 4 5 6 7 8 9 0 VNH/VNH 9 3 2 1 0 9 8
domestic   2 3 4 5 6 7 8 9 0 VNH/VNH 9 3 2 1 0 9

ISBN 0-07-292990-1
ISBN 0-07-561942-3 (package)

Vice president and Editorial director: *Michael W. Junior*
Publisher: *Craig S. Beytien*
Sponsoring editor: *Karen M. Mellon*
Developmental editor: *Christine Scheid/Maryellen Krammer*
Marketing manager: *Ellen Cleary*
Project manager: *Paula M. Buschman*
Senior production supervisor: *Melonie Salvati*
Designer: *Kay Fulton*
Senior photo research coordinator: *Keri Johnson*
Photo researcher: *Charlotte Goldman*
Compositor: *ElectraGraphics, Inc.*
Typeface: *10/12 Times Roman*
Printer: *Von Hoffmann Press, Inc.*

Library of Congress Cataloging-in-Publication Data

Lesikar, Raymond Vincent.
    Lesikar's basic business communication/Raymond V. Lesikar, John
D. Pettit, Jr., Marie E. Flatley. — 8th ed.
      p. cm.
    Includes bibliographical references and index.
    ISBN 0-07-292990-1
    1. Commercial correspondence. 2. English language—Business
English. 3. Business communication. I. Pettit, John D. Jr.
II. Flatley, Marie Elizabeth. III. Title
HF5721.L37 1999
651.7'4—dc21   98-21173

INTERNATIONAL EDITION

When ordering the title, use ISBN 0-07-115819-7

http://www.mhhe.com

To those dear ones, both here and departed, whose love and encouragement are a part of this book. *R.V.L.*

To my father, J. Douglas "Doug" Pettit whose memory gives special meaning to my work and my life. *J.D.P., Jr.*

To my father and niece Megan who write clear, concise, and interesting email messages. *M.E.F.*

John D. Pettit, Jr.

Dr. John D. Pettit, Jr.'s career spans 35 years and includes teaching business communication and other business courses at several universities: Mississippi State University, Louisiana State University, Texas Tech University, University of North Texas, Wichita State University, and Austin Peay State University. He has contributed three books (in multiple editions) and numerous refereed publications and research paper presentations to the communication field.

Dr. Pettit earned his Ph.D. degree in management from Louisiana State University and his B.B.A and M.B.A degrees from the University of North Texas. He provides consulting and training for national and international organizations in business communication and management.

Dr. Pettit is a Fellow, former President, and former Executive Director of the Association for Business Communication; a former President and member of the Southwestern Federation of Administrative Disciplines; a member of the Academy of Management; and biographied in the Marquis publications of *Who's Who in the South and Southwest; Who's Who in America;* and *Who's Who in the World.*

Marie E. Flatley

Marie E. Flatley is a Professor of Information and Decision Systems at San Diego State University, where she teaches various courses in business communication. She received her B.B.A., M.A., and Ph.D. from the University of Iowa. In addition, she has done postgraduate study in AACSB sponsored programs at the University of Minnesota and Indiana University.

Marie is active in numerous professional organizations, including the Association for Business Communication, California Business Education Association, Delta Pi Epsilon, and the National Business Education Association. She has served as Associate Editor for the *Journal for Business Communication* and Editor for the *NABTE Review.* Currently, she is a member of the editorial board for the *Delta Pi Epsilon Journal.* Also, she is a Distinguished Member of the Association of Business Communication.

Her current research interests involve using technology to assist with the communication process. And she is currently writing a monograph for Delta Pi Epsilon on electronic communication.

Raymond V. Lesikar

Dr. Raymond V. Lesikar has served on the faculties of the University of North Texas, Louisiana State University at Baton Rouge, The University of Texas at Austin, and Texas Christian University. He served also as a visiting professor at the University of International Business and Economics, Beijing, China. His contributions to the literature include six books and numerous articles.

Dr. Lesikar has been active in consulting, serving over 80 companies and organizations. He is a Fellow, Distinguished Member and former president of the Association for Business Communication. In addition, he has served ABC in many capacities over the years. He also holds membership in the Southwest Federation of Administrative Disciplines and is a former president of the Southwest Social Science Association. His distinguished teaching career was highlighted by his service as major professor for 23 recipients of the doctoral degree.

This eighth edition continues our efforts to produce the most (1) authoritative, (2) thorough, (3) technologically current, (4) learnable, and (5) teachable book in the field. We are modestly confident that we have succeeded. What we have done to meet these five goals is summarized as follows.

AUTHORITATIVE

Our efforts to present the subject matter authoritatively involved a thorough review of the field. The information presented and procedures recommended are not just our ideas and preferences, though we support them. They represent the mainstream of business communication thought developed by researchers, teachers, and practitioners over the years.

THOROUGH

We worked diligently to cover the subject thoroughly. The content of the earlier editions was based on the results of two extensive surveys of business communication teachers. In this edition we supplemented the results of those surveys with suggestions from the highly competent professionals who reviewed the book. And we implemented the research findings and suggestions we heard from colleagues at professional meetings. The result is a book whose content has been developed and approved by experts in the field. As well as we can determine, this edition covers every topic that today's business communication leaders say it should have.

TECHNOLOGICALLY CURRENT

Because the computer has affected business communication in so many ways, we worked this subject into the book wherever applicable. Where technology is integral to the way business communicates today, we integrated it into the text discussion. In those cases where technology helps students perform special tasks, we presented it in boxes. We believe these efforts will enable students to exploit the power of the computer in saving time and improving work quality.

LEARNABLE

As in earlier editions, we worked hard to make the book serve the student in every practical way. Our goal was to make the learning experience easy and interesting. Our efforts led us to implement the following features, all of which have proved to be highly successful in preceding editions:

Readable writing. The writing is in plain, everyday English—the kind the book instructs the students to use.

Chapter objectives. Placed at the beginning of all chapters, clearly worded objectives emphasize the learning goals and are tied in to the chapter summaries.

Introductory situations. A realistic description of a business scenario introduces the student to each topic, providing context for discussion and examples.

Preliminary outlines of messages. To simplify and clarify the instructions for writing the basic message types, outlines of message plans precede the discussions.

Margin notes. Summaries of content appear in the margins to help students emphasize main points and to review text highlights.

Specialized report topics. Lists of research topics by major business disciplines are available for teachers who prefer to assign reports in the student's area of specialization.

Communications in brief. Boxes containing anecdotal communication messages add interest and make points throughout the book.

Abundant real business illustrations. Both good and bad examples with explanatory criticisms show the student how to apply the text instructions.

Cartoons. Carefully selected cartoons emphasize key points and add interest.

Photographs. Full-color photographs throughout the text emphasize key points and add interest to content. Teaching captions enhance the textual material.

Computer and Internet applications. Computer and Internet applications have been integrated throughout the book wherever appropriate—into topics such as readability analysis, graphics, research methods, and formatting.

Computer use suggestions. For students who want to know more about how useful computers can be in business communication, pertinent suggestions appear in boxes.

Chapter summaries by chapter objectives. Ending summaries in fast-reading outline form and by chapter objectives enable students to recall text highlights.

Critical thinking problems. Fresh, contemporary, in-depth business cases are included for all message and report types—more than in any competing text.

Critical thinking exercises. Challenging exercises test the student's understanding of text content.

Critical thinking questions. End-of-chapter questions emphasize text concepts and provide material for classroom discussion.

New cases. As in past editions, the realistic and thorough case problems are new.

In this edition, we have added an exciting new learning tool:

CD-ROM study guide. This supplement to the text is designed to reinforce the text instructions in the student's mind by providing interactive exercises with immediate feedback.

TEACHABLE

Perhaps more than anything we can do to help the teacher teach is to help the student learn. The features designed to provide such help are listed above. But there are additional things we can do to help the teacher teach. We worked very hard to develop these teaching tools; and we think we were successful. We sincerely believe the following list of features created for this edition are the most useful and effective ever assembled for a business communication textbook.

Instructor's resource box. Assembled for the course and where appropriate in file folders by chapters, the following support material is available for easy use with each lecture:

    Sample syllabi and grading systems
    Summary teaching notes
    Teaching suggestions
    Illustrated discussion guides for the slides/transparencies
    Answers to end-of-chapter critical thought questions
    Answers to end-of-chapter critical thinking exercises
    Sample solutions to cases
    Case problems from the previous edition (online)

Instructor's manual. The material in the Instructor's Resource Box is also available in this bound manual.

Transparency package. Fifty four-color acetates are included.

PowerPoint slides. Complete full-chapter slide shows are available for the entire text. These colorful slides provide summaries of key points, additional examples, and examples to critique.

Grading checklists. Lists of likely errors keyed to marking symbols are available for messages and reports. Similarly, symbols for marking errors of grammatical and punctuation correctness are available. They help the teacher in the grading process and provide the students with explanations of their errors.

The Irwin/McGraw-Hill Business Communication Video Series. This series consists of self-contained, informative segments covering such topics as writing correctly and the power of listening. Presented in a clear and engaging style, every segment holds students' interest while presenting the techniques for sharpening their communication skills. (Contact your Irwin/McGraw-Hill representative for more information.)

Test bank. This comprehensive collection of objective questions covers all chapters.

Computerized testing software. This advanced test generator enables the teacher to build and restructure tests to meet specific preferences.

Tele-Test. Customized exam preparation is furnished by the publisher.

Web site. A new web site fully supports the text. It includes a database of cases, new web cases that entail using web resources to write solutions, an author-selected collection of annotated links to relevant web sites organized by topic, a continually updated and enhanced technology chapter, and other active learning material.

ORGANIZATION OF THE BOOK

In response to reviewers' suggestions, we made minor organization changes. We moved coverage of claims and orders to Chapter 5 so that direct-order messages are in one chapter. Within this chapter we changed the order of inquiries and responses, placing inquiries first. These changes did little to alter the basic organization plan that has characterized this book through seven successful editions.

Part I begins with an introductory summary of the role of communication in the organization, including a description of the process of human communication.

Part II is a review of the basic techniques of writing. Here the emphasis is on clear writing and the effect of words.

Part III covers the basic patterns of business messages, beginning with the most common direct and indirect ones.

Part IV applies the contents of the preceding two parts to other forms of business messages (persuasion, sales, collections, memorandums, email, and job-search).

Part V concentrates on report writing. Although the emphasis is on the shorter report forms, the long, analytical reports also receive complete coverage.

Part VI reviews the other forms of business communication. Included here are communication activities such as participating in meetings, interviewing, telephoning, dictating, and listening.

Part VII comprises a four-chapter group of special communication topics—technology-assisted communication, cross-cultural communication, correctness, and business research methods. Because teachers use them in different ways and in different sequences, these topics are placed in this final part so that they can be used in the sequence and way that best fit each teacher's needs.

ADDITIONS TO CONTENT

As with previous editions, we thoroughly updated this edition. We expanded coverage wherever we and our reviewers thought it would improve content. Although not an addition in the true sense, we used the word *message* in place of *letter* in most places. Our purpose was to use a word more consistent with the additional means of communication (fax, email) brought about by technology. Our most significant additions or expansions are the following:

Etiquette. Throughout the book we emphasized the need for good business etiquette. Places where this emphasis is given are marked with a special icon.

Ethics. We continued our emphasis of ethics, expanding it wherever we saw a meaningful possibility.

Email. We added coverage of email. Although this rapidly expanding communication medium appears to be developing without direction, we tried to give it the meaningful content necessary in a college textbook.

Listening. Emphasizing active listening, we greatly expanded this major communication topic.

Paralanguage. To this little-understood part of human communication we gave added coverage.

Documentation. Because of the explosive growth of electronic information sources, we thoroughly revised and updated our coverage of documenting them.

Continually updated technology chapter. In addition to the updated chapter in the text, we make available each semester an updated version on our web site at www.mhhe.com/lesikar. Not only will this chapter contain up-to-date material, but it will also take full advantage of the medium through enhancements found by the icons ( ) placed in the text.

Online information gathering. Chapter 19 (Business Research Methods) updates and expands previous coverage of using the Internet to gather information. Additionally, it includes a discussion of channels, push technology, and personalized filters.

ACKNOWLEDGMENTS

Any comprehensive work such as this must owe credit to a multitude of people. Certainly, we should acknowledge the contributions of the pioneers in the business communication field, especially those whose teachings have become a part of our thinking. We should acknowledge also those colleagues in the field who served as reviewers for this edition. They are primarily responsible for the improvements that have been made. Although all identification was removed from the reviews given us, we were told that these people served as reviewers:

Bertee Adkins, *Eastern Kentucky University*

J. Douglas Andrews, *University of Southern California*

Mary Kay Boyd, *Florida Atlantic University*

Barbara Hagler, *Southern Illinois University*

Larry Honl, *University of Wisconsin–Eau Claire*

Robert Insley, *University of North Texas*

Richard Lacy, *California State University–Fresno*

Betty Schroeder, *Northern Illinois University*

Without exception, their work was good and helpful.

Because this eighth edition has evolved from all the previous editions, we also acknowledge those who contributed to those editions. They include:

Barbara Alpern, *Walsh College*

Frank Andera, *Central Michigan University*

Dan Armstrong, *Oregon State University*

Joan Beam, *Ferris State University*

James Bell, *Southwest Texas State University*

Peter Bracher, *Wright State University*

Stuart Brown, *New Mexico State University*

John J. Brugaletta, *California State University–Fullerton*

Dwight Bullard, *Middle Tennessee State University*

Connie Jo Clark, *Lane Community College*

Andrea Corbett, *University of Lowell*

Ben Crane, *Temple University*

Joan Feague, *Baker College*

Phyllis Howren, *University of North Carolina*

Carol L. Huber, *Skagit Valley College*

Robert Insley, *University of North Texas*

Edna Jellesed, *Lane Community College*

Pamela Johnson, *California State University–Chico*

Edwina Jordan, *Illinois Central College*

Shelby Kipplen, *Michael Owens Technical College*

Suzanne Lambert, *Broward Community College*

Jon N. Loff, *Allegheny Community College*

Charles Marsh, *University of Kansas*

Ethel A. Martin, *Glendale Community College*

Judy F. McCain, *Indiana University*

Mary Miller, *Ashland University*

Evelyn Morris, *Mesa Community College*

Frank E. Nelson, *Eastern Washington State College*

Julia Newcomer, *Texas Woman's University*

Rita Thomas Noel, *Western Carolina University*

Dolores Osborn, *Central Washington University*

Doris Phillips, *University of Mississippi*

Marilyn Price, *Kirkwood Community College*

Carolyn Rainey, *Southeast Missouri State University*

David Ramsey, *Southeastern Louisiana University*

Diane Reep, *University of Akron*

Elizabeth Regimbal, *Cardinal Stritch College*

Deborah Roebuck, *Kennesaw State College*

Jim Rucker, *Fort Hays State University*

Tim Sabin, *Portland Community College*

Barbara Shaw, *University of Mississippi*

Cheryl Shearer, *Oxnard College*

Douglas H. Shepherd, *State University of New York*

Gay Gibley, *University of Hawaii at Manoa*

C. Douglas Spitler, *University of Nebraska–Lincoln*

Lila B. Stair, *Florida State University*

Jerry Sullivan, *University of Washington*

Phyllis Taufen, *Gonzaga University*

Sandy Thomas, *Kansas City Kansas Community College*

Ruth Walsh, *University of South Florida*

George Walters, *Emporia State University*

Kathy Wessel, *South Suburban College*

James J. Weston, *California State University–Sacramento*

Michael Wunsch, *Northern Arizona University*

In addition, over the life of this book many of our professional colleagues have made a variety of inputs. Most of these were made orally at professional meetings. Our memories will not permit us to acknowledge these colleagues individually. Nevertheless, we are grateful to all of them.

Finally, on our respective home fronts, we acknowledge the support of our loved ones. Marie acknowledges husband Len Deftos and her immediate family. John acknowledges wife Suzanne and his family. Ray acknowledges all his family members, both present and departed, who have provided love and inspiration over the years. Without the support of all these dear people this book would not exist.

Raymond V. Lesikar
John D. Pettit, Jr.
Marie E. Flatley

CONTENTS IN BRIEF

PART 3

Basic Patterns of Business Messages

PART 4

Applications to Specific Situations

CHAPTER 7

Indirectness in Persuasion and Sales Messages 160

CHAPTER 8

Pattern Variations in Collections, Memorandums, and Email 186

PART 5

Fundamentals of Report Writing

PART **6**

Other Forms of Business Communication

PART **7**

Special Topics in Business Communication

CHAPTER **19**

Business Research Methods 537

APPENDIXES

Introduction

1 Communication in the Workplace

1

Communication in the Workplace

Upon completing this chapter, you will understand the role of communication in business. To achieve this goal, you should be able to

1 Explain the importance of communication to you and to business.

2 Describe the three main forms of communication in the business organization.

3 Describe the formal and informal communication networks in the business organization.

4 Explain the process of communication among people.

5 Explain three basic truths about communication.

6 Describe the plan of this book.

THE ROLE OF COMMUNICATION IN BUSINESS

Your work in business will involve communication—a lot of it—because communication is a major and essential part of the work of business.

■ Communication is important to business

THE IMPORTANCE OF COMMUNICATION SKILLS TO YOU

Because communication is so important in business, businesses want and need people with good communication skills. Evidence of the importance that business gives to communication skills comes from a nationwide survey of corporate recruiters.[1] The recruiters ranked four communication skills (writing, speaking, listening, and interpersonal communicating) in the top five criteria for selecting employees. A similar study, this one concerning MBA applicants, concluded that 85 percent of the recruiters hold communication skills to be the most important of the skills sought.[2] In yet another study, this one of 500 undergraduate and graduate business students, business communication was ranked first among all core business courses.[3] It held this ranking for both immediate importance and importance 10 years later.

■ Business needs good communicators,

Unfortunately, business's need for employees with good communication skills is all too often not fulfilled. Most employees, even the college trained, do not communicate well. Among the studies that support this observation, perhaps the most notable reports that one of the four major criticisms of today's college-trained people is their "poor communication and interpersonal skills." This study further reports that the shortcomings are in "both oral and, especially, written communication."[4]

■ but most people do not communicate well.

The communication shortcomings of employees and the importance of communication in business explain why you should work to improve your communication skills. Whatever position you have in business, your performance will be judged largely by your ability to communicate. If you perform (and communicate) well, you are likely to be rewarded with advancement. And the higher you advance, the more you will need your communication ability. The evidence is clear: Improving your communication skills improves your chances for success in business.

■ By improving your communication ability, you improve your chances for success.

WHY BUSINESS NEEDS TO COMMUNICATE

To understand how important communication is to business, note how much communication business requires. Take, for example, a pharmaceutical manufacturer. Throughout the company workers send and receive information. They process information with computers, write messages, fill out forms, give and receive orders, and talk over the telephone. More specifically, salespeople receive instructions and information from the home office and send back orders and weekly summaries of their activities. Executives use letters and telephone calls to initiate business with customers and other companies and respond to incoming letters and calls. Production supervisors receive work orders, issue instructions, and submit production summaries. Research specialists receive problems to investigate and later communicate their findings to management. Similar activities occur in every niche of the company. Everywhere workers receive and send information as they conduct their work.

■ Communication is vital to every part of business.

Oral communication is a major part of this information flow. So, too, are various types of forms and records, as well as the storage and retrieval facilities provided by computers. Yet another major part consists of various forms of written communication—letters, email messages, memorandums, and reports.

■ Communication takes many forms: oral, written, and computer.

---

[1] C. M. Ray, John J. Stallard, and C. S. Hunt, *Journal of Education for Business* (January–February 1994), pp. 41–44.

[2] Karen O. Dowd and Jeanne Liedtka, "What Corporations Seek in MBA Hires: A Survey," *Selections* 10, no. 2 (Winter 1994), pp. 34–39.

[3] Jean C. Swanson, David B. Meinhert, and Neil E. Swanson, "Business Communications: A Highly Valued Core Course in Business Administration," *Journal of Education for Business,* April 1994, p. 237.

[4] Lyman W. Porter and Lawrence E. McKibbon, *Management Education and Development: Drift or Thrust into the 21st Century?* New York: McGraw-Hill, 1988, p. 103.

Some Quotes on Communication by Real-World Businesspeople

Communication is *the* most important part of my job as a systems analyst and project manager.

Cindy Marzolf, systems analyst
Qualcomm

Good communication skills are necessary in any job, but especially in positions that involve interactions with clients and company management. You must be able to clearly, concisely, and eloquently convey information and ideas to these people.

Greg P. Tesone, Investment Banking Analyst
CEA Montgomery Media L.L.C.

It continues to amaze me that with the technology available today I continue to receive correspondence with errors. These errors have a significant impact on my perceptions of the individual, the company, and the product or service.

Mike Rook, Procurement Project Manager
Office Products Division
Hewlett-Packard

Writing and speaking skills have proven invaluable to me. I continually write letters to vendors and partners and memos to people within the company. I also write research reports detailing results of studies, and I use my speaking skills to present these results.

Nancy Bray, Marketing Research Associate
Group Voyagers, Inc.

Communication has a direct effect on productivity. If it is clear, people know what is expected and work gets done efficiently.

Rosemary Lenaghan, Controller
Catholic Charities, Diocese of Springfield in Illinois

- All organized effort, including the work of business, requires communication.

All of this communicating goes on in business because communication is essential to the organized effort involved in business. Communication enables human beings to work together. In a business, it is the vehicle through which management performs its basic functions. Managers direct through communication, coordinate through communication, and staff, plan, and control through communication.

MAIN FORMS OF COMMUNICATION IN BUSINESS

The importance of communication in business becomes even more apparent when we consider the communication activities of an organization from an overall point of view. These activities fall into three broad categories: internal operational, external operational, and personal.

- There are three categories of communication in business:

- (1) Internal operational—the communicating done in conducting work within a business,

INTERNAL-OPERATIONAL COMMUNICATION. All the communication that occurs in conducting work within a business is classified as internal operational. This is the communication among the business's workers that is done to implement the business's operating plan. By *operating plan* we mean the procedure that the business has developed to do whatever it was formed to do—for example, to manufacture products, provide a service, or sell goods.

- such as giving orders, assembling reports, writing memorandums, and communicating by computers.

Internal-operational communication takes many forms. It includes the orders and instructions that supervisors give workers, as well as oral exchanges among workers about work matters. It includes reports and records that workers prepare concerning sales, production, inventories, finance, maintenance, and so on. It includes the memorandums, email messages, and reports that workers write in carrying out their assignments.

Much of this internal-operational communication is performed on computer networks. Workers send electronic mail through networks to others throughout the business, whether located down the hall, across the street, or around the world. As you will learn in Chapter 16, the computer also assists the business writer and speaker in many other aspects of communication.

EXTERNAL-OPERATIONAL COMMUNICATION. The work-related communicating that a business does with people and groups outside the business is external-operational communication. This is the business's communication with its publics—suppliers, service companies, customers, and the general public.

■ (2) External operational—work-related communication with people outside the business,

External-operational communication includes all of the business's efforts at direct selling—salespeople's "spiels," descriptive brochures, telephone callbacks, follow-up service calls, and the like. It also includes the advertising the business does, for what is advertising but communication with potential customers? Radio and television messages, newspaper and magazine advertising, and point-of-purchase display material obviously play a role in the business's plan to achieve its work objective. Also in this category is all that a business does to improve its public relations, including its planned publicity, the civic-mindedness of its management, the courtesy of its employees, and the condition of its physical plant. And of very special importance to our study of communication, this category includes all the messages that workers write in carrying out their assignments.

■ such as personal selling, telephoning, advertising, and letter writing.

This public relations category includes a topic very important to us in our study of busi-

■ Letters display a company's etiquette.

"Gentlemen, It's only a suggestion but just remember who made it."
(*From* The Wall Street Journal, *with permission of Cartoon Features Syndicate.*)

In large businesses, much of the work done involves internal-operational communication.

ness communication—business messages. As we shall see, business messages do more than communicate information. They take the place of human contact. Thus they have the effect of human contact. The clarity, warmth, and understanding they display also send a message. The positiveness of this message is what we refer to as good business etiquette. And good business etiquette contributes greatly to a company's good image.

■ Both internal and external communications are vital to business success.

The importance of external-operational communication to a business hardly requires supporting comment. Every business is dependent on outside people and groups for its success. And because the success of a business depends on its ability to satisfy customers' needs, it must communicate effectively with its customers. In today's complex business society, businesses depend on each other in the production and distribution of goods and services. This interdependence requires communication. Like internal communication, external communication is vital to business success.

■ (3) Personal communication—non-business-related exchanges of information and feelings among people.

PERSONAL COMMUNICATION. Not all the communication that occurs in business is operational. In fact, much of it is without purpose as far as the business is concerned. Such communication is called personal.

Personal communication is the exchange of information and feelings in which we human beings engage whenever we come together. We are social animals. We have a need to communicate, and we will communicate even when we have little or nothing to say.

■ Personal communication affects worker attitudes.

We spend much of our time with friends in communication. Even total strangers are likely to communicate when they are placed together, as on an airplane flight, in a waiting room, or at a ball game. Such personal communication also occurs at the workplace, and it is a part of the communication activity of any business. Although not a part of the business's plan of operation, personal communication can have a significant effect on the success of that plan. This effect is a result of the influence that personal communication can have on the attitudes of the workers.

■ And attitudes affect worker performance.

The workers' attitudes toward the business, each other, and their assignments directly affect their willingness to work. And the nature of conversation in a work situation affects attitudes. In a work situation where heated words and flaming tempers are often present, the workers are not likely to make their usual productive efforts. However, a rollicking, jovial work situation is likely to have an equally bad effect on productivity. Somewhere between these extremes lies the ideal productive attitude.

Also affecting the workers' attitudes is the extent of personal communication permitted. Absolute denial of personal communication could lead to emotional upset, for most of us hold dear our right to communicate. On the other hand, excessive personal communication could interfere with the work done. Again, the middle ground is probably the best.

■ The extent of personal communication permitted affects worker attitudes.

COMMUNICATION NETWORK OF THE ORGANIZATION

Looking over all of a business's communication (internal, external, and personal), we see an extremely complex network of information flow. We see an organization feeding on a continuous supply of information. More specifically, we see dozens, hundreds, or even thousands of individuals engaging in untold numbers of communication events throughout each workday.

■ Information flow in a business forms a complex network.

Most of the information flow of operational communication is downward and follows the formal lines of organization (from the top administrators down to the workers). This is so because most of the information, instructions, orders, and such needed to achieve the business's objectives originate at the top and must be communicated to the workers. However, most companies recognize the need for more upward communication. They have found that administrators need to be better informed of the status of things at the bottom. They have also found that information from the lower levels can be important in achieving company work goals.

■ The flow is mainly downward, but upward communication is also important.

THE FORMAL NETWORK.   In simplified form, information flow in a modern business is much like the network of arteries and veins in the body. Just as the body has arteries, the business has major, well-established channels of information flow. These are the formal channels—the main lines of operational communication. Through these channels flows the bulk of the communication that the business needs to operate. Specifically, the flow includes the movements of information by reports, memorandums, records, and such within the organization; of orders, instructions, and messages down the authority structure; of working information through the organization's computer network; and of externally directed letters, sales presentations, advertising, and publicity. These main channels should not just happen; they should be carefully thought out and changed as the needs of the business change.

■ The main (formal) lines of flow are like the network of arteries in the body.

THE INFORMAL NETWORK.   Parallel to the formal network lies the informal network, a secondary network consisting primarily of personal communication (see Figure 1–1). Just as the formal network is like the arteries, the informal one is like the veins. It comprises the thousands upon thousands of personal communications that occur in a business.

■ The secondary (informal) network is like the veins.

FIGURE 1–1 Formal and Informal Communication Networks in a Division of a Small Manufacturing Company

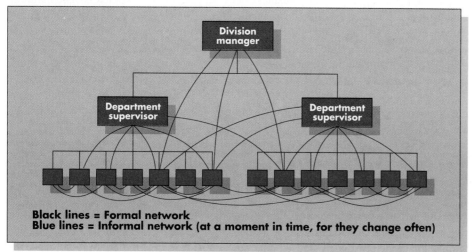

| The informal communication network of a business consists of all the communication of its employees whenever they get together.

Such communications follow no set pattern; they form an ever-changing and infinitely complex structure linking all the members of the organization.

The complexity of this informal network, especially in larger organizations, cannot be overemphasized. Typically, it is really not a single network but a complex relationship of smaller networks consisting of groups of people. The relationship is made even more complex by the fact that these people may belong to more than one group and that group memberships and the links between and among groups are continually changing. Truly, the informal network in a large organization is so complex as to defy description.

Known as the *grapevine* in management literature, this communication network is far more effective than a first impression might indicate. Certainly, it carries much gossip and rumor, for this is the nature of human conversation. And it is as fickle and inaccurate as the human beings who are a part of it. Even so, the grapevine usually carries far more information than the formal communication system; and on many matters it is more effective in determining the course of an organization. Wise managers recognize the presence of the grapevine. They give the talk leaders the information that will do the most good for the organization. That is, they keep in touch with the grapevine and turn it into a constructive tool.

VARIATION IN COMMUNICATION ACTIVITY BY BUSINESS

Just how much communicating a business does depends on several factors. The nature of the business is one. For example, insurance companies have a great need to communicate with their customers, especially through letters and mailing pieces, whereas housecleaning service companies have little such need. The business's operating plan affects the amount of internal communication. Relatively simple businesses, such as repair services, require far less communication than complex businesses, such as automobile manufacturers. Also, the people who make up a business affect its volume of communication. Every human being is unique. Each has unique communication needs and abilities. Thus, varying combinations of people will produce varying needs for communication.

THE PROCESS OF HUMAN COMMUNICATION

Although we may view the communication of a business as a network of information flow, we must keep in mind that a business organization consists of people and that the communication in the organization occurs among people. Thus, it is important to our basic un-

▌In many small businesses, little need for operational communication exists. Much of the communicating done is with customers.

derstanding of business communication to know how communication among people occurs. The following review of the human communication process will give you that knowledge.

THE BEGINNING: A MESSAGE SENT

To describe the communication process, we will use a situation involving two people—Marci and Kevin (see Figure 1–2). Although the steps described may suggest that Kevin and Marci are communicating in separate actions, the actions occur simultaneously. As one is sending, the other is receiving. Our description begins with Marci communicating a message to Kevin. Her message could be in any of a number of forms—gestures, facial expressions, drawings, or, more likely, written or spoken words. Whatever the form, Marci sends the message to Kevin.

■ The process begins when Marci sends a message to Kevin.

ENTRY IN THE SENSORY WORLD

Marci's message then enters Kevin's sensory world. By *sensory world* we mean all that surrounds a person that the senses (sight, hearing, smell, taste, touch) can detect. As we will see, Kevin's sensory world contains more than Marci's message.

■ The message enters Kevin's sensory world,

DETECTION BY THE SENSES

From his sensory world Kevin picks up stimuli (messages) through his senses. We must note, however, that Kevin's senses cannot detect *all* that exists in the world around him. Just how much they can detect depends on a number of factors. One is the ability of his senses. As you know, not all eyes see equally well and not all ears hear equally well. And so it is with the other senses. Another factor is Kevin's mental alertness. There are times when he is keenly alert to all that his senses can detect, and there are times when he is dull—in a stupor, a daydream, or the like. Furthermore, Kevin's cultural background has sensitized him more to some stimuli than to others. Yet another limiting factor is Kevin's will. In varying degrees, the mind is able to tune in or tune out events in the sensory world. In a noisy room full of people, for example, the conversation of a single person can be selected and the other voices ignored.

■ where his senses may detect it.

When Kevin's senses pick up Marci's message, they relay it to his brain—that is, as much or as little of the message as they detect. But Marci's message may not be all that

■ What Kevin's senses detect, they send to his brain,

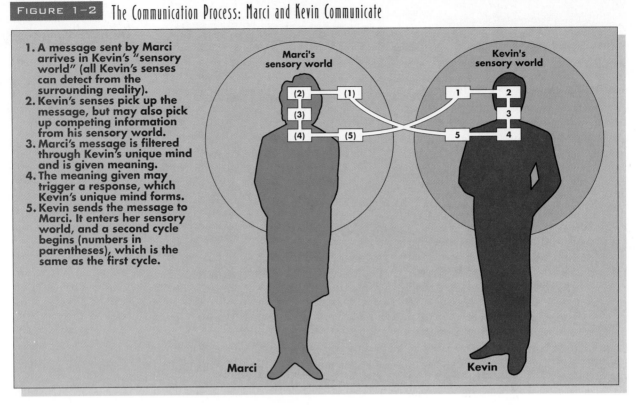

FIGURE 1-2 The Communication Process: Marci and Kevin Communicate

1. A message sent by Marci arrives in Kevin's "sensory world" (all Kevin's senses can detect from the surrounding reality).
2. Kevin's senses pick up the message, but may also pick up competing information from his sensory world.
3. Marci's message is filtered through Kevin's unique mind and is given meaning.
4. The meaning given may trigger a response, which Kevin's unique mind forms.
5. Kevin sends the message to Marci. It enters her sensory world, and a second cycle begins (numbers in parentheses), which is the same as the first cycle.

Marci's sensory world

Kevin's sensory world

Marci

Kevin

Kevin's senses pick up. In addition to Marci's message, his sensory world may contain outside noises, movements of objects, facial expressions, and the like. In fact, his senses are continually picking up messages from the world around him. Marci's message is just the primary one at the moment. The others are there, and they might interfere with Marci's message.

THE FILTERING PROCESS

■ where it goes through a filtering process.

When Marci's message gets to Kevin's brain, it goes through a sort of filtering process. Through that process Kevin's brain gives meaning to Marci's message. In other words, the message is filtered through the contents of Kevin's mind. Those contents include all his experience, knowledge, biases, emotions, cultural background—in fact, all Kevin is and has been. Obviously, no two people have precisely identical filters, for no two people have minds with precisely the same contents.

■ Because minds differ, message meanings differ.

Because people's filters differ, the meanings they give to comparable messages may differ. Thus, the meaning Kevin gives Marci's message may not be precisely the same as the one that someone else would give it. And it may not be the meaning Marci intended. For example, assume that Marci used the word *liberal* in her message. Now assume that Marci and Kevin have had sharply differing experiences with the word. To Marci the word is negative, for her experience has made her dislike things liberal. To Kevin the word is positive. Thus, the message Kevin receives from the word would not be precisely the message Marci sent. And so it could be with other words in Marci's message.

FORMATION AND SENDING OF THE RESPONSE

■ Kevin's mind reacts to the meaning, and he may respond.

After his mind has given meaning to Marci's message, Kevin may react to the message. If the meaning he received is sufficiently strong, he may react by communicating some form of response. This response may be through words, gestures, physical actions, or some other means.

When Kevin elects to communicate a response, through his mind he determines the general meaning that the response will take. This process involves the most complex workings of the mind, and we know little about it. There is evidence, however, that ability, here and throughout this stage, is related to one's intelligence and the extent that one permits the mind to react. Kevin's ability to evaluate filtered information and formulate meaning is also related to his ability with language. Ability with language equips one with a variety of symbols (words and other ways of expressing meaning). And the greater the number of symbols one possesses, the better one can be at selecting and using them.

■ Through his mind and its contents, Kevin determines the meaning of the response.

Kevin ends this stage of the communication process by forming a message. That is, he converts meanings into symbols (mainly words), and then he sends these symbols to Marci. He may send them in a number of ways—as spoken words, written words, gestures, movements, facial expressions, diagrams on paper, and so on.

■ Kevin forms a message and sends it.

THE CYCLE REPEATED

When Kevin sends his message to Marci, one cycle of the communication process ends. Now a second cycle begins. This one involves Marci rather than Kevin, but the process is the same. Kevin's message enters Marci's sensory world. Her senses pick it up and send it through her nervous system to her brain. There her unique mental filter influences the meaning she gives Kevin's message. This filtered meaning may also bring about a response. If it does, Marci, through her mind, selects the symbols for her response. Then she sends them to Kevin, and another cycle of communication begins. The process may continue, cycle after cycle, as long as Marci and Kevin want to communicate.

■ Then the cycle is repeated.

THE COMMUNICATION PROCESS AND WRITTEN COMMUNICATION

Although our description of the communication process illustrates face-to-face, oral communication, it also fits written communication. But there are some differences. Perhaps the most significant difference is that written communication is more likely to involve creative effort. It is more likely to be thought out, and it may even begin in the mind rather than as a reaction to a message received.

■ Written communication differs from oral communication in that it (1) is more likely to involve creative effort,

A second difference is the time between cycles. In face-to-face communication, cycles occur fast, often in rapid succession. In written communication, some delay occurs. How long the delay will be varies. Fax messages may be read a few minutes after they are transmitted, letters in a few days, reports perhaps in days, weeks, or months. Because they provide a record, written messages may communicate over extremely long time periods.

■ (2) has longer cycles, and

A third difference is that written communication usually involves a limited number of cycles and oral communication usually involves many. In fact, some written communica-

■ (3) usually has fewer cycles.

A Sure Way of Getting a Response

In oral communication the cycles can go on indefinitely. In sharp contrast, written communication may end after a single cycle. How one imaginative mother used a written communication to assure a second cycle makes a classic story.

The mother was having difficulty in getting her college-student son to answer her letters. She wrote regularly but rarely received a reply. In desperation, she resorted to psychology. She wrote the usual letter filled with news from home. Then she ended with a reference to an enclosed check and instructions to "use it as you like." She mailed the letter, but she did not include the check.

In short order the son responded. His letter was filled with the kind of information mothers like to hear. At the end was a thank-you for the check, "which must have been forgotten, so please send it."

The son got the check, the mother got a letter, and, of course, a second communication cycle occurred.

tion is one-cycle communication. That is, a message is sent and received, but none is returned.

SOME BASIC TRUTHS ABOUT COMMUNICATION

- The communication process reveals some basic truths.

Analysis of the communication process brings out three underlying truths that will help us understand its complexity.

- Because our mental filters differ, meanings sent may differ from meanings received.

MEANINGS SENT ARE NOT ALWAYS RECEIVED. The first underlying truth is that the meanings transmitted are not necessarily the meanings received. No two minds have identical filters. No two minds have identical storehouses of words, gestures, facial expressions, or any of the other symbol forms. And no two minds attach exactly the same meanings to all the symbols they have in common. Because of these differences in minds, errors in communication are bound to occur.

- Meanings are in the mind—not in symbols.

MEANING IS IN THE MIND. A second underlying truth is that meaning is in the mind—not in the words or other symbols used. How accurately one conveys meaning in symbols depends on how skillful one is in choosing symbols and on how skillful the person receiving the symbols is in interpreting the meaning intended. Thus, you should look beyond the symbols used. You should consider the communication abilities of those with whom you want to communicate. When they receive your messages, they do not look at the symbols alone. They also look for the meanings they think you intended.

- Because symbols are imperfect and people differ in their ability to communicate, communication is far from perfect.

THE SYMBOLS OF COMMUNICATION ARE IMPERFECT. The third underlying truth is that the symbols used in communication are imperfect. One reason for this is that the symbols we use, especially words, are at best crude substitutes for the real thing. For example, the word *man* can refer to billions of human beings of whom no two are precisely alike. The word *dog* stands for any one of countless animals that vary sharply in size, shape, color, and every other visible aspect. The word *house* can refer equally well to structures ranging from shanties to palatial mansions. The verb *run* conveys only the most general part of an action; it ignores countless variations in speed, grace, and style. These illustrations are not exceptions; they are the rule. Words simply cannot account for the infinite variations of reality.

Communication is also imperfect because communicators vary in their ability to convey thoughts. Some find it very difficult to select symbols that express their simplest thoughts. Variations in ability to communicate obviously lead to variations in the precision with which thoughts are expressed.

- Communication across cultures is especially difficult.

Communication across cultures is especially imperfect, for often there are no equivalent words in the cultures. For example, usually there is no precise translation for our jargon in other cultures. Words such as *condo, computer virus,* and *yuppie* are not likely to have equivalents in every other culture. Similarly, other cultures have specialized words unique and necessary to them that we do not have. For instance, the Eskimo have many words for *snow,* each describing a unique type. Obviously, such distinctions are vital to their existence. We can get along very well with the one word. As you will see in Chapter 17, this subject is so vital to today's business communication that an entire chapter is devoted to it.

- Even so, we communicate reasonably well.

Although the foregoing comments bring to light the difficulties, complexities, and limitations of communication, on the whole we human beings do a fairly good job of communicating. Still, miscommunication often occurs. And people who attach precise meanings to every word, who believe that meanings intended are meanings received, and who are not able to select symbols well are likely to experience more than their share.

RESULTING STRESS ON ADAPTATION

- The communication process shows the need for adaptation—an underlying principle in our study of communication.

Understanding the communication process can help you become a better communicator. The process shows that communication is a unique event—that every mind is different from every other mind. No two of us know the same words; and no two of us know equal amounts about all subjects. Obviously, such differences make communication difficult.

Unless the words (or other symbols) used in a message have the same meanings in the minds of both the sender and the recipient, communication suffers. Communication scholars have tried to solve this problem by stressing the adaptation of messages to the minds of their recipients. By *adaptation* we mean fitting the message to the recipients—using words and other symbols that they understand. As you will see, adaptation is the foundation for our review of communication principles in the pages ahead.

THE GOAL, PLAN, AND PHILOSOPHY OF THIS BOOK

The preceding discussion shows that communication is important to business, that it is performed in various and complex ways, and that it is imprecise. These observations suggest that communicating in business is not to be taken lightly. If you want to excel at it, you must develop your communication skills. Helping you do this is the goal of this book.

■ The goal of this book is to help you improve your communication skills.

THE PLAN: SITUATIONS, SOLUTIONS, SUMMARIES

To achieve this goal, the book introduces each major topic through a business communication situation that realistically places you in the business world. Each situation describes a possible communication problem. Then the following material instructs you on how to solve the problem. For your study convenience, summaries of the text material appear in the margins. A general summary by chapter objectives appears at the end of each chapter.

■ The book introduces topics by situations—then it shows solutions. Summaries help your study.

THE PHILOSOPHY: COMMUNICATE TO COMMUNICATE

In presenting this subject matter, the book takes a practical, realistic approach. That is, it views business communication as having one primary goal—to communicate.

Although this statement may appear elementary, it has significant meaning. All too often other goals creep in. For example, communicators sometimes seek to impress—perhaps by using big words and involved sentences. Or they seek to entertain with a clever choice of words. Good business communicators rarely have these goals. They primarily seek to communicate. They use words and sentences that communicate clearly and quickly. If the message has any difficulty, the reason is that the subject matter is difficult. In no way should the words and the sentence structures add to the difficulty.

■ Successful communication is the purpose of communicating.

■ Some writers have other goals (to impress, to entertain). Business communicators should seek only to communicate.

AN UNDERLYING RULE: ETHICAL COMMUNICATION

In the pages ahead, you will see how to achieve business goals through communication. In all cases, our emphasis will be only on achieving legitimate business goals. We say this because you will also see how words can be selected to achieve effects ranging from one extreme to the other. Always our emphasis will be on achieving effects that are consistent with honorable goals. More specifically, we will emphasize communicating in a friendly, clear, and fair manner. Nothing we present should be interpreted to suggest unethical behavior. Keep in mind this stress on ethics as you continue your study.

■ We stress only ethical communication.

SUMMARY BY CHAPTER OBJECTIVES

1. Business needs and rewards people who can communicate, for communication is vital to business operations.
   • But good communicators are scarce.
   • So, if you can improve your communication skills, you increase your value to business and business will reward you.
2. Communicating in business falls into three categories:
   • The communicating a business does to implement its operating plan (its procedure for doing what it was formed to do) is called *internal-operational* communication.

1 Explain the importance of communication to you and to business.

2 Describe the three main forms of communication in the business organization.

- The communicating a business does with outsiders (suppliers, other businesses, customers, and such) is called *external-operational* communication.
- Informal exchanges of information not related to operations are called *personal* communication.

3. The flow of communication in a business organization forms a complex and ever-changing network. Information continually flows from person to person—upward, downward, and laterally.
   - The communicating that follows the formal structure of the business forms the *formal* network. Primarily, operational information flows through this network.
   - The flow of personal communication forms the *informal* network.

4. The human communication process is as follows:
   - A message arrives in one's sensory world (all that one can detect with the senses).
   - The senses pick up the message and relay it to the brain.
   - The brain filters the message through all its contents (knowledge, emotions, biases, and such) and gives it a unique meaning.
   - This meaning may trigger a response, which the mind then forms.
   - The person then sends (by voice, marks on paper, gestures, or such) this message into the sensory world of another person.
   - Within this person the process described above is repeated (another cycle begins).
   - The process continues, cycle after cycle, as long as the people involved care to communicate.

5. The communication process reveals these truths:
   - Meanings sent are not always received (our mental filters differ).
   - Meaning is in the mind—not in the symbols (mainly words) used.
   - The symbols we use are imperfect, primarily because the reality they describe is so complex.

6. The plan of this book is to introduce you to the primary types of business communication problems through realistic situations.
   - You are placed in a business communication situation.
   - Then you are shown how to handle it.
   - And always the emphasis is on ethics.

CRITICAL THINKING QUESTIONS

1. Is the ability to communicate more important to the successful performance of a supervisor's job than to that of a company president's job? Defend your answer.

2. Make a list of types of companies requiring extensive communication. Then make a list of types of companies requiring little communication. What explains the difference in these two groups?

3. List the types of external-operational and internal-operational communication that occur in an organization with which you are familiar (school, fraternity, church, or such).

4. Identify the types of technology used primarily in internal- and external-operational communication to transmit messages. Explain what you think might account for the differences.

5. Discuss the question of how much personal communication should be permitted in a business organization. Defend your view.

6. Describe the network of communication in an organization with which you are familiar (preferably a simple one). Discuss and explain.

7. Describe what is in your sensory world at this moment. Contrast the parts that are usually in your awareness with the parts that are usually not in your awareness.

8. Using the model for the communication process as a base, explain how people reading or hearing the same message can disagree on its meaning.

9. Give an example of a simple statement that could be misunderstood. Explain why. Then revise the statement for more precise understanding.

CRITICAL THINKING EXERCISES

1. Megan Cabot is one of 12 workers in Department X. She has strong leadership qualities, and all her co-workers look up to her. She dominates conversations with them and expresses strong viewpoints on most matters. Although she is a good worker, her dominating personality has caused problems for you, the new supervisor of Department X. Today you directed your subordinates to change a certain work procedure. The change is one that has proven superior wherever it has been tried. Soon after giving the directive, you noticed the workers talking in a group, with Megan the obvious leader. In a few minutes she appeared in your office. "We've thought it over," she said. "Your production change won't work." Explain what is happening. How will you handle the situation?

2. After noticing that some workers were starting work late and finishing early, a department head wrote this memorandum to subordinates: It is apparent that many of you are not giving the company a full day's work. Thus, the following procedures are implemented immediately:

   a. After you clock in, you will proceed to your workstations and will be ready to begin work promptly at the start of the work period.

   b. You will not take a coffee break or consume coffee on the job at the beginning of the work period. You will wait until your designated break times.

   c. You will not participate in social gatherings at any time during the workday except during designated break periods.

   d. You will terminate work activities no earlier than 10 minutes prior to the end of the work period. You will use the 10 minutes to put up equipment, clean equipment, and police the work area.

   e. You will not queue up at the time clock prior to the end of the work period.

   The memorandum was not well received by the workers. In fact, it led to considerable anger, misunderstanding, and confusion. Using the model of communication as a base, analyze the memorandum and explain the probable causes of the difficulties.

3. After being introduced to a candidate for the presidency of their company, two workers had the following discussion. One worker is Scott, a college-age man who is holding a full-time job while going to school part-time. The other is Will, an old-timer—a self-made man and master craftsman.

   Scott: I like the candidate. He appears young, energetic, and bright.

   Will: He's young all right. Too young! Too bright! That fancy Harvard degree won't help him here. Why, I'll bet he hasn't spent one day in a working-man's shoes.

   Scott: Now that's not fair. He was trained to be an administrator, and he has had experience as an administrator—high-level experience. You don't need experience as a soldier to be a general.

   Will: Don't tell me what this company needs. I've spent 40 years here. I know. I was here when old J.P. (the company founder) was president. He started as a machinist and worked to the top. Best president any company could have. We loved the man. He knew the business and he knew the work we do.

   Scott: But that doesn't happen today. Administrators have to be trained for administration. They have to know administration, finance, marketing—the whole business field. You don't get that in the shop.

   Will: All you kids think that knowledge only comes from books. You can't substitute book sense for experience and common sense. I've been here 40 years, son. I know.

   The dialogue continued to accelerate and soon led to angry words. Neither Scott nor Will changed positions. Analyze the dialogue using the model of communication as the base.

2

Fundamentals of Business Writing

2

Adaptation and the Selection of Words

Upon completing this chapter, you will be able to adapt your language to specific readers and to select the most effective words for use in business communication. To reach this goal, you should be able to

1 Explain the role of adaptation in selecting words that communicate.

2 Simplify writing by selecting short and familiar words.

3 Use technical words appropriately.

4 Discuss the differences in the strength of words and select the words that communicate your message best.

5 Write concretely and stress active voice.

6 Write with clarity and precision by avoiding camouflaged verbs, by selecting the right words, and by using idioms correctly.

7 Use words that do not discriminate.

Choosing Words that Communicate

As a means of introducing yourself to business communication, place yourself in a hypothetical situation. You are the office manager of a manufacturing company. You have before you a memorandum from Max Schwartz, one of your assistants. Following your instructions, Max investigated your company's use of available space. He has summarized his findings in a memorandum report.

At first glance you are impressed with Max's report and with his ability. But after reading the report, you are not sure just what his investigation uncovered. Here is a typical paragraph:

In the interest of ensuring maximum utilization of the subterranean components of the building currently not apportioned to operations departments, it is recommended that an evaluation of requisites for storage space be initiated. Subject review should be initiated at the earliest practicable opportunity and should be conducted by administrative personnel not affiliated with operative departments.

Max's problem is altogether too commonplace in business. His words, though properly used, do not communicate quickly and easily. This and the following chapter show you what you can do about writing like this.

THE BASIC NEED FOR ADAPTATION

The study of clear writing logically begins with adaptation. By *adaptation* we mean fitting the message to the specific reader. Obviously, readers do not all have the same ability to understand a message. They do not all have the same vocabulary, the same knowledge of the subject, or the same mentality. Thus, to communicate clearly you should first know the person with whom you wish to communicate. You should form your message to fit that person's mind. This approach not only helps you communicate but also is the basis of good business etiquette. Making your message easy to understand is simply good business manners.

- For writing to be clear, it must be adapted to the reader.

VISUALIZING THE READER

In adapting your message, you begin by visualizing your reader. That is, you form a mental picture of what he or she is like. You imagine what the reader knows about the subject, what his or her educational level is, and how he or she thinks. In general, you consider whatever you believe could have some effect on your reader's understanding of your message. With this in mind, you form the message.

- Adaptation begins with visualizing the reader—imagining what he or she knows, feels, thinks, and such.

TECHNIQUE OF ADAPTING

In many business situations, adapting to your reader means writing on a level lower than the one you would normally use. For example, you will sometimes need to communicate with people whose educational level is below your own. Or you may need to communicate with people of your educational level who simply do not know much about the subject of your message.

To illustrate, assume that you need to write a memorandum to a group of less-educated workers. You know that their vocabularies are limited. If you are to reach them, you will have to use simple words. If you do not, you will not communicate. On the other hand, if you had to write the same message to a group of highly educated people, you would have a wider choice of words. These people have larger vocabularies than the first group. In either case, however, you would select words that the intended readers understand.

- Often you will need to write at levels lower than your own.

- In writing to less-educated workers, for example, you may need to simplify. You may write differently for highly educated people.

ADAPTATION ILLUSTRATED

The following paragraphs from two company annual reports illustrate the basic principle of adaptation. The writer of the first report apparently viewed the readers as people who were not well informed in finance.

Last year your company's total sales were $117,400,000, which was slightly higher than the $109,800,000 total for the year before. After deducting for all expenses, we had $4,593,000 left over for profits, compared with $2,830,000 for 1998. Because of these increased profits, we were able to increase your annual dividend payments per share from the 50 cents paid over the last 10 years.

The writer of the second report saw the readers as being well informed in finance. Perhaps this writer believed the typical reader would come from the ranks of stockbrokers, financial managers, financial analysts, and bankers. So this writer adapted the annual report to these readers with language like this:

The corporation's investments and advances in three unconsolidated subsidiaries (all in the development stage) and in 50 percent–owned companies was $42,200,000 on December 31, 1995, and the excess of the investments in certain companies over net asset value at dates of acquisition was $1,760,000. The corporation's equity in the net assets as of December 31, 1998, was $41,800,000 and in the results of operations for the years ended December 31, 1995 and 1996, was $1,350,000 and $887,500, respectively. Dividend income was $750,000 and $388,000 for the years 1998 and 1995, respectively.

Which writer was right? Perhaps both. Perhaps neither. The answer depends on what the stockholders of each company were really like. Both examples illustrate the technique of adaptation. They use different words for different audiences, which is what you should try to do.

ADAPTING TO MULTIPLE READERS

- If you write for one person in a group, you may miss the others.

Adapting your message to one reader is easy. But how do you adapt when you are communicating with two or more readers? What if your intended readers vary widely in education, knowledge of the subject, and so on? Writing to the level of the best-educated and best-informed persons would miss those at lower levels. Adapting your message to the lowest level runs the risk of insulting the intelligence of those at higher levels.

- To communicate with all of them, write for the lowest member of the group.

The answer is obvious. You have to adapt to the lowest level you need to reach. Not doing so would result in not communicating with that level. Of course, by writing for readers at the lowest level, you run the risk of offending those at higher levels. You can minimize this risk by taking care not to talk down. For example, you can carefully work in "as you know" and similar expressions to imply that you know the reader knows what you are writing about.

COMMUNICATION IN BRIEF

A Classic Case of Adaptation

There is a story told around Washington about a not-too-bright inventor who wrote the Bureau of Standards that he had made a great discovery: Hydrochloric acid is good for cleaning clogged drains.

He got this response: "The efficacy of hydrochloric acid is indisputable, but the corrosive residue is incompatible with metallic permanence."

Believing that these big words indicated agreement, this not-so-bright inventor wrote back telling how pleased he was that the bureau liked his discovery.

The bureaucrat tried again: "We cannot assume responsibility for the production of toxic residue with hydrochloric acid and suggest alternative procedure."

The inventor was even more gratified. He again expressed his appreciation to the bureau for agreeing with him.

This time the bureaucrat got the message. He replied in words any inventor would be certain to understand: "Don't use hydrochloric acid. It'll eat hell out of pipes."

In talking to a child, we naturally adapt the language to the child. Similarly, in business communication we need to adapt the language to the reader.

GOVERNING ROLE OF ADAPTATION

The preceding discussion shows that adaptation is basic to communication. In fact, it is so basic that you will need to apply it to all the writing and speaking instructions in the pages ahead. For example, much of what will be said about writing techniques will stress simplicity—using simple words, short sentences, and short paragraphs. You will need to think of simplicity in terms of adaptation. Specifically, you will need to keep in mind that what is simple for one person may not be simple for another. Only if you keep in mind the logical use of adaptation will you fully understand the intended meaning of the writing instructions.

- Adaptation underlies all that will be said about writing. Apply it to the other writing instructions.

SUGGESTIONS FOR SELECTING WORDS

A major part of adaptation is selecting the right words. These are the words that communicate best—that have correct and clear meanings *in the reader's mind.*

Selecting the right words depends on your ability to use language, your knowledge of the reader, and your good judgment. Few hard-and-fast rules apply. Still, you should keep in mind the suggestions presented in the following paragraphs. As you review them, remember that you must use them with good judgment. You must consider them in light of the need to adapt the message to your reader or readers.

As you will see, most of the suggestions support simplicity in writing. This approach is justified by three good reasons. The first is that many of us tend to write at too difficult a level. Instead of being ourselves, we change character when we write. Rather than being friendly, normal people, we become cold and stiff. We work to use big words and complex structures. Winston Churchill referred to this tendency when he made his classic remark: "Little men use big words; big men use little words." We would do well to follow the example of this big man.

The second reason for simplicity is that the writer usually knows the subject of the message better than the reader. Thus, the two are not equally equipped to communicate on the matter. If the writer does not work at reducing the message to the reader's level, communication will be difficult.

The third reason for simplicity is that convincing research supports it. According to the research of such experts as Gunning, Dale, Chall, and Flesch, writing slightly below the reader's level of understanding communicates best.

- Selecting the right words is a part of adaptation. Following are some suggestions to help you select such words.

- These suggestions stress simplicity for three reasons: (1) many people tend to write at a difficult level;

- (2) the writer usually knows the subject better than the reader; and

- (3) the results of research support simplicity.

A Case of Short, Familiar Words

In the Lord's Prayer, you will find 66 words—48 are of one syllable, a percentage of 72.

In "All the world's a stage" (Shakespeare's *As You Like It*), there are 212 words—150 are of one syllable, a percentage of 70.

In Abraham Lincoln's Gettysburg Address, there are 268 words—196 are of one syllable, a percentage of 73.

USE FAMILIAR WORDS

- Familiar words communicate. Use them. Use your judgment in determining what words are familiar.

The foremost suggestion for word selection is to use familiar words. These are the everyday words—the words with sharp and clear meanings in the mind. Because words that are familiar to some people may be unfamiliar to others, you will need to select familiar words with care. You have no choice but to rely on your judgment.

Specifically, using familiar words means using the language that most of us use in everyday conversation. We should avoid the stiff, more difficult words that do not communicate so precisely or quickly. For example, instead of using the more unfamiliar word *endeavor*, use *try*. Instead of using *terminate*, use *end*. Prefer *use* to *utilize*, *do* to *perform*, *begin* to *initiate*, *find out* to *ascertain*, *stop* to *discontinue*, and *show* to *demonstrate*.

- Difficult words are not all bad. Use them when they fit your needs and are understood.

The suggestion to use familiar words does not rule out some use of more difficult words. You should use them whenever their meanings fit your purpose best and your readers understand them clearly. The mistake that many of us make is to overwork the more difficult words. We use so much that they interfere with our communication. A good suggestion is to use the simplest words that carry the meaning without offending the readers' intelligence. Perhaps the best suggestion is to write the words you would use in face-to-face communication with your readers.

The following contrasting examples illustrate the communication advantages of familiar words over less familiar ones.[1] As you read the examples, consider the effect on communication of an entire letter or report written in the styles illustrated.

Unfamiliar Words	Familiar Words
This machine has a tendency to develop excessive and unpleasant audio symptoms when operating at elevated temperatures.	This machine tends to get noisy when it runs hot.
Ms. Smith's idiosyncrasies supply adequate justification for terminating her employment status.	Ms. Smith's peculiar ways justify firing her.
This antiquated mechanism is ineffectual for an accelerated assembly-line operation.	This old robot will not work on a fast assembly line.
The most operative assembly-line configuration is a unidirectional flow.	The most efficient assembly-line design is a one-way flow.
The conclusion ascertained from a perusal of pertinent data is that a lucrative market exists for the product.	The data studied show that the product is in good demand.
Company operations for the preceding accounting period terminated with a substantial deficit.	The company lost much money last year.

An example supporting the use of familiar words came from Cape Kennedy while scientists were conducting research in preparation for long spaceflights. In one experiment, a monkey was placed in a simulated spaceship with enough food to last many days. With an unlimited supply of food available, the monkey simply ate too much and died. A scientist used these words to record the incident: "One monkey succumbed unexpectedly ap-

---

[1] For some of these examples, we are indebted to students and friends who gave them to us over the years.

parently as a result of an untoward response to a change in feeding regimen." Most readers of the report missed the message. Why didn't the scientist report in everyday language, "One monkey died because it ate too much"?

Another real-life example involved President Franklin D. Roosevelt. Across his desk came a memorandum advising federal workers to do the following in the event of an air raid:

Such preparations shall be made as will completely obscure all federal buildings and nonfederal buildings occupied by the federal government during an air raid for any period of time from visibility by reason of internal or external illumination. Such obscuration may be obtained either by blackout construction or by termination of the illumination.

Irked by the heavy wording, FDR sent this memorandum to the author:

Tell them that in buildings where they have to keep the work going to put something over the windows; and, in buildings where they can let the work stop for a while, turn out the lights.

In this and the preceding examples, the familiar words are clearly better. Readers understand them.

CHOOSE SHORT WORDS

According to studies of readability, short words generally communicate better than long words. Of course, part of the explanation is that short words tend to be familiar words. But there is another explanation: A heavy use of long words—even long words that are understood—leaves an impression of difficulty that hinders communication.

- Generally, short words communicate better.

The suggestion that short words be chosen does not mean that all short words are easy and all long words are hard. Many exceptions exist. Few people know such one-syllable words as *gybe, verd,* and *id.* Even children know such long words as *hippopotamus, automobile,* and *bicycle.* On the whole, however, word length and word difficulty are related. Thus, you should concentrate on short words and use long words with caution. Use a long word only when you think your readers know it.

- Some exceptions exist.

This point is illustrated by many of the examples presented to support the use of familiar words. But the following illustrations give it additional support. In some of them, the long-word versions are likely to be understood by more highly educated readers. Even so, the heavy proportion of hard words clouds the message. Without question, the short-word versions communicate better. Note that the long words and their short replacements are in italics.

Long Words	**Short Words**
The decision was *predicated* on the *assumption* that an *abundance* of *monetary* funds was *forthcoming.*	The decision was *based* on the *belief* that there *would be more money.*
They *acceded* to the *proposition* to *terminate* business.	They *agreed* to *quit* business.
During the *preceding* year the company *operated* at a *financial deficit.*	*Last year* the company *lost money.*
Prior to *accelerating productive operation,* the supervisor inspected the machinery.	Before *speeding up* production, the supervisor inspected the machinery.
Definitive action was *effected subsequent* to the reporting date.	*Final* action was *taken after* the reporting date.
The *unanimity* of current forecasts is not *incontrovertible* evidence of an *impending* business acceleration.	*Agreement* of the forecasts is not *proof* that business *will get better.*
This *antiquated merchandising* strategy is *ineffectual* in *contemporary* business *operations.*	This *old sales* strategy *will not work* in *today's* business.

Mark Twain understood the value of using short words when he made this often-quoted statement: "I never use a word like *metropolis* when I can get the same price for *city.*" One bureaucrat who did not understand the principle created a position to improve

Technical Language?

When an ordinary person wants to give someone an orange, he or she would merely say, "I give you this orange." But when a lawyer does it, the words are something like this: "Know all persons by these present that I hereby give, grant, bargain, sell, release, convey, transfer, and quitclaim all my right, title, interest, benefit, and use whatever in, of, and concerning this chattel, otherwise known as an orange, or *Citrus orantium,* together with all the appurtenances thereto of skin, pulp, pip, rind, seeds, and juice, to have and to hold the said orange together with its skin, pulp, pip, rind, seeds, and juice for his own use and behoof, to himself and his heirs, in fee simple forever, free from all liens, encumbrances, easements, limitations, restraints, or conditions whatsoever, any and all prior deeds, transfers, or other documents whatsoever, now or anywhere made, to the contrary notwithstanding, with full power to bite, cut, suck, or otherwise eat the said orange or to give away the same, with or without its skin, pulp, pip, rind, seeds, or juice."

communication and gave it the title of Coordinator for the Obliteration of Proliferation of Obfuscation!

USE TECHNICAL WORDS AND ACRONYMS WITH CAUTION

- All fields have technical words.

Every field of business—accounting, information systems, finance—has its technical language. This language can be so complex that in some cases specialized dictionaries are compiled. Such dictionaries exist for computers, law, finance, and other business specialties. There are even dictionaries for subareas such as databases, desktop publishing, and real estate.

- These words are useful when you communicate with people in your field. But they do not communicate with outsiders. Use them with caution.

As you work in your chosen field, you will learn its technical words and acronyms. In time you will use these terms freely in communicating with people in your field. This is as it should be, for such terms are useful. Frequently, one such word will communicate a concept that would otherwise take dozens of words to describe.

A problem comes about, however, when you use technical terms with people outside your field. Because these words are everyday words to you, you tend to forget that not everyone knows them. The result is miscommunication. You can avoid such miscommunication by using technical words with extreme caution. Use them only when your readers know them.

- Some examples are *covered employment, cerebral vascular accident, annuity, bobtail.* These words are well known to people in special fields, but not to most outsiders.

Examples of misuse of technical writing are easy to find. To a worker in the Social Security Administration, the words *covered employment* commonly mean employment covered by social security. To some outsiders, however, they could mean working under a roof. When a physician uses the words *cerebral vascular accident* with other physicians, they understand. Most people would get little meaning from these words, but they could understand a *little stroke. Annuity* has a clear meaning to someone in insurance. A *contract that guarantees an income for a specified period* would have more meaning to uninformed outsiders. Computer specialists know *C++* and Java to be popular programming languages; but these words may have different meanings for others. To a trucker *bobtail* means a tractor cab without trailer. Nontruckers might get other meanings from that word—or perhaps no meaning at all.

- Use initials cautiously. Spell out and define as needed.

Initials (including acronyms) should be used with caution, too. While some initials, such as IBM, are widely recognized, others, such as CIM (computer integrated manufacturing), are not. Not only might your readers not know certain initials, they might confuse them with others. For example, if you saw IRA, you might think of the Irish Republican Army, and someone else might think of individual retirement account. And your instructor might think of a committee named Instructionally Related Activities. If you have any question as to whether your reader is familiar with the initials, the best practice is to spell out the words the first time you use them and follow them with the initials. Also, if you are writing a long document with several pages between where you defined initials originally and where you use them again, it is courteous to your reader to spell out again.

Probably the most troublesome technical language is that of the legal profession. Legal terms have too often worked their way into business communication. The result has been to add unnecessary words as well as words not understood by many business readers. Such words also produce a dull and formal effect.

Among the legal words that may add little real meaning are *thereto, therein, whereas, herewith,* and *herein.* For example, "the land adjacent thereto" can be written "the adjacent land" without loss in meaning. In addition, legal wordings such as *cease and desist* and *bequeath and devise* contain needless repetition.

Some legal words can be replaced with plain words. *Despite* can replace *notwithstanding. Ipso facto, sub judice,* and other such Latin phrases can be replaced by plain language with the same meaning.

Your technical language may not be any of the ones illustrated here, but you will have one. You will need to be careful not to use it when you write to people who do not understand it.

Select Words with the Right Strength and Vigor

In a way, words are like people; they have personalities. Some words are strong and vigorous. Some are weak and dull. And some fall between these extremes. Good writers know these differences, and they consider them carefully. They use the words that do the best job of carrying the intended meaning. As a rule, they make the stronger words stand out.

Selecting words with just the right personalities requires that you learn language well—that you learn to distinguish shades of difference in the meanings of words. For example, you should recognize that *tycoon* is stronger than *eminently successful businessperson,* that *bear market* is stronger than *generally declining market,* that *boom* is stronger than *a period of business prosperity,* and that *mother* is stronger than *female parent.*

You will not always want the strongest and most vigorous words. Sometimes, for good reason, you will choose weaker ones. The word *bill* is strong. Because it has a harsh meaning in some minds, you may prefer *statement* in some instances. The same goes for *debt* and *obligation, die* and *passed on, spit* and *saliva, labor boss* and *union official,* and *fired* and *dismissed.*

In selecting the stronger words, you should keep in mind that the verb is the strongest part of speech. Second is the noun. Verbs are action words, and action carries interest. Nouns are the doers of action—the heroes of the sentence. Thus, they also attract attention.

Adjectives and adverbs are weak words. They add length and distract from the key words, the nouns and the verbs. As Voltaire wrote, "The adjective is the enemy of the noun." In addition, adjectives and adverbs are judgment words. As we will see, objectivity—which is opposed to judgment—is a requirement of much business communication. But you should know that adjectives and adverbs are among the weaker words, and you should use them sparingly.

Use Concrete Language

Good business communication is marked by words that form sharp and clear meanings in the mind. These are the concrete words. You should prefer them in your writing.

Concrete is the opposite of abstract. Abstract words are vague. In contrast, concrete words stand for things the reader can see, feel, taste, or smell. Concrete words hold interest, for they refer to the reader's experience.

Among the concrete words are those that stand for things that exist in the real world. Included are such nouns as *chair, desk, computer, road, automobile,* and *flowers.* Also included are words that stand for creatures and things: *John Jordan, Mary Stanley, Mickey Mouse, Spot,* the *Metropolitan Life Building,* and *Mulberry Street.*

- Legal language has worked its way into business writing.

- Words like *thereto, herewith,* and *ipso facto* are examples.

- Replace legal language with plain words.

- Words have personalities. Select the stronger ones.

- To select words wisely, you should consider shades of difference in meanings.

- Sometimes weaker words serve your purpose best.

- Verbs are the strongest words. Nouns are second.

- Adjectives and adverbs are weak words. They involve judgment. Use them sparingly.

- Use concrete words.

- Concrete words are specific words.

- They stand for things that exist in the real world: *deck, chair, road.*

Abstract nouns have general meanings: *administration, negotiation.*

Concreteness also means exactness: *a 53 percent loss, the odor of decaying fish.*

Abstract nouns, on the other hand, cover broad meanings—concepts, ideas, and the like. Their meanings are general, as in these examples: *administration, negotiation, wealth, inconsistency, loyalty, compatibility, conservation, discrimination, incompetence,* and *communication.* Note how difficult it is to visualize what these words stand for.

Concreteness also involves how we put words together. Exact or specific wordings are concrete; vague and general wordings are abstract. For example, take the case of a researcher who must report the odor of a newly developed cleaning agent. The researcher could use such general words as "It has an offensive, nauseating odor." Now note how much more concrete language communicates: "It has the odor of decaying fish." The second example is concrete because it recalls an exact odor from memory. Notice the difference in communication effect in these contrasting pairs of wordings:

Abstract	Concrete
A significant loss	A 53 percent loss
Good attendance record	100 percent attendance record
The leading company	First among 3,212 competitors
The majority	62 percent
In the near future	By noon Thursday
A labor-saving robot	Does the work of seven workers
Light in weight	Featherlight
Substantial amount	$3,517,000

Now let us see the difference concreteness makes in the clarity of longer passages. Here is an example of abstract wording:

It is imperative that the firm practice extreme conservatism in operating expenditures during the coming biennium. The firm's past operating performance has been ineffectual for the reason that a preponderance of administrative assignments has been delegated to personnel who were ill-equipped to perform in these capacities. Recently instituted administrative changes stressing experience in operating economies have rectified this condition.

Written for concreteness, this message might read as follows:

We must reduce operating expenses at least $2 million during 1998–99. Our $1,350,000 deficit for 1996–97 was caused by the inexperience of our two chief administrators, Mr. Sartan and Mr. Ross. We have replaced them with Ms. Pharr and Mr. Kunz, who have had 13 and 17 years, respectively, of successful experience in operations management.

Another illustration of concreteness is the story of the foreign nation that competed strenuously with the United States in an international automobile show. In one category, only automobiles from these two countries were entered. One would surely win first place, the other second. The U.S. automobile won. The government-controlled press of the losing country gave this report to its people: "In worldwide competition, our excellent entry was judged to be second. The entry from the United States was rated next to last." The words sound concrete—*second, next to last.* But they omitted one fact needed for ethical concreteness—that only two automobiles were entered.

USE THE ACTIVE VOICE

Prefer the active voice to the passive voice.

In active voice, the subject does the action. In passive voice, it receives the action.

Active voice is stronger and shorter.

You should prefer the active voice to the passive voice. Active voice produces stronger, livelier writing. It emphasizes the action, and it usually saves words.

In active voice, as you will recall, the subject does the action. In passive voice, the subject receives the action. For example, the sentence "The auditor inspected the books" is in active voice. In passive voice, the sentence would read: "The books were inspected by the auditor."

These two sentences show the advantages of active voice. Clearly, the active-voice sentence is stronger. In it the doer of action acts, and the verb is short and clear. In the passive-voice sentence, the extra helping word *were* dulls the action. In addition, placing the doer of the action (*auditor*) in a prepositional phrase presents the information indirectly rather than directly. Note also that the active-voice sentence is shorter.

For further proof of the advantages of active over passive voice, compare the following sentences:

Passive	**Active**
The results were reported in our July 9 letter.	We reported the results in our July 9 letter.
This policy has been supported by our union.	Our union supported this policy.
The new process is believed to be superior by the investigators.	The investigators believe that the new process is superior.
The policy was enforced by the committee.	The committee enforced the policy.
The office will be inspected by Mr. Hall.	Mr. Hall will inspect the office.
A gain of 30.1 percent was reported for hardware sales.	Hardware sales gained 30.1 percent.
It is desired by the director that this problem be brought before the board.	The director desires that the secretary bring this problem before the board.
A complete reorganization of the administration was effected by the president.	The president completely reorganized the administration.

The suggestion that active voice be preferred does not mean passive voice is incorrect or you should never use it. Passive voice is correct, and it has a place. The problem is that many writers tend to overuse it, especially in report writing. Writing is more interesting and communicates better when it uses active voice.

Passive voice has a place. It is not incorrect.

Your decision on whether to use active or passive voice is not simply a matter of choice. Sometimes passive voice is preferable. For example, when identifying the doer of the action is unimportant to the message, passive voice properly de-emphasizes the doer.

Passive is better when the doer of the action is not important.

Advertising is often criticized for its effect on price.

Petroleum is refined in Texas.

Passive voice may enable you to avoid accusing your reader of an action:

Passive helps avoid accusing the reader.

The damage was caused by exposing the material to sunlight.

The color desired was not specified in your order.

Passive voice may also be preferable when the performer is unknown, as in these examples:

Passive is better when the performer is not known.

During the past year, the equipment has been sabotaged seven times.

Anonymous complaints have been received.

Yet another situation in which passive voice may be preferable is one in which the writer does not want to name the performer:

It is also better when the writer prefers not to name the performer.

The interviews were conducted on weekdays between noon and 6 PM.

Two complaints have been made about you.

In other instances, passive voice is preferable for reasons of style.

AVOID OVERUSE OF CAMOUFLAGED VERBS

An awkward construction that should be avoided is the camouflaged verb. When a verb is camouflaged, the verb describing the action in a sentence is changed into a noun. Then action words have to be added. For example, suppose you want to write a sentence in which *eliminate* is the action to be expressed. If you change *eliminate* into its noun form, *elimination,* you must add action words—perhaps *was effected*—to have a sentence. Your sentence might then be: "Elimination of the surplus was effected by the staff." The sentence is indirect and passive. You could have avoided the camouflaged construction with a sentence using the verb *eliminate:* "The staff eliminated the surplus."

Avoid camouflaged verbs. You camouflage a verb by changing it to a noun form and then adding action words.

■ For example, if *cancel* becomes *cancellation*, you must add "to effect a" to have action.

Here are two more examples. If we take the good action word *cancel* and make it into a noun, *cancellation,* we would have to say something like "to effect a cancellation" to communicate the action. If we change *consider* to *consideration,* we would have to say "give consideration to." So it would be with the following examples:

Action Verb	Noun Form	Wording of Camouflaged Verb
acquire	acquisition	make an acquisition
appear	appearance	make an appearance
apply	application	make an application
appraise	appraisal	make an appraisal
assist	assistance	give assistance to
cancel	cancellation	make a cancellation
commit	commitment	make a commitment
discuss	discussion	have a discussion
investigate	investigation	make an investigation
judge	judgment	make a judgment
liquidate	liquidation	effect a liquidation
reconcile	reconciliation	make a reconciliation
record	recording	make a recording

Note the differences in overall effect in these contrasting sentences:

Camouflaged Verb	Clear Verb Form
Amortization of the account *was effected* by the staff.	The staff *amortized* the account.
Control of the water *was not possible.*	They *could not control* the water.
The new policy *involved the standardization of* the procedures.	The new policy *standardized* the procedures.
Application of the mixture *was accomplished.*	They *applied* the mixture.
We must *bring about a reconciliation of* our differences.	We must *reconcile* our differences.
The *establishment* of a rehabilitation center *has been accomplished* by the company.	The company *has established* a rehabilitation center.

■ Avoid camouflaged verbs by (1) writing concretely and (2) preferring active voice. To comply with these suggestions, (1) make subjects persons or things and (2) write sentences in normal order.

From these illustrations you can see that our suggestion on camouflaged verbs overlaps our two preceding suggestions. First, camouflaged verbs are abstract nouns. We suggested that you prefer concrete words over abstract words. Second, camouflaged verbs frequently require passive voice. We suggested that you prefer active voice.

You can comply with these related suggestions by following two helpful writing hints. The first is to make the subjects of most sentences either persons or things. For example, rather than write "consideration was given to . . . ," you should write "we considered . . . ." The second is to write most sentences in normal order (subject, verb, object), with the doer of the action as the subject. Involved, strained, passive structures often result from attempts at other orders.

SELECT WORDS FOR PRECISE MEANINGS

■ Writing requires a knowledge of language.

Obviously, writing requires some knowledge of language. In fact, the greater your knowledge of language, the better you are likely to write. Unfortunately, all too many of us treat language routinely. We use the first words that come to mind. We use words without thinking of the meanings they convey. We use words we are not sure of. The result is vague writing.

■ You should study language and learn the shades of difference in the meanings of similar words.

If you want to be a good writer, you will need to study words carefully. You will need to learn their precise meanings, especially the shades of difference in the meanings of similar words. For example, *weary, tired, pooped, fagged out,* and *exhausted* all refer to the same thing. Yet in most minds there are differences in the meaning of these words. In a

Disraeli versus Gladstone: A Classic Illustration of Word Precision

Illustrating word precision are excerpts from a spirited debate in Parliament between the nimble-tongued Benjamin Disraeli and his arch adversary, William Gladstone. At the height of a particularly bitter argument, Gladstone asked Disraeli to define two words he had used in his attack on Gladstone's position: *misfortune* and *calamity*. Taking full advantage of the situation, Disraeli responded, "If you were to fall into the River Thames, Mr. Gladstone, that would be a misfortune. If someone were to pull you out, that would be a calamity."

rather formal message, *weary* would certainly be more acceptable than *pooped* or *fagged out*. Similarly, *fired, dismissed, canned, separated,* and *discharged* refer to the same action but have different shades of meaning. So it is with each of the following groups of words:

die, decease, pass on, croak, kick the bucket, check out, expire, go to one's reward

money, funds, cash, dough, bread, finances

boy, youth, young man, lad, shaver, stripling

fight, brawl, fracas, battle royal, donnybrook

thin, slender, skinny, slight, wispy, lean, willowy, rangy, spindly, lanky, wiry

ill, sick, poorly, weak, delicate, cachectic, unwell, peaked, indisposed, out of sorts

Knowledge of language also enables you to use words that carry the meanings you want to communicate. For example, *fewer* and *less* mean the same to some people. But careful users select *fewer* to mean "smaller numbers of items" and *less* to mean "reduced value, degree, or quantity." The verbs *affect* and *effect* are often used as synonyms. But those who know language select *affect* when they mean "to influence" and *effect* when they mean "to bring to pass." They use *feel* to express physical contact, perception, or such—not as a substitute for *believe* or *think*. Similarly, careful writers use *continual* to mean "repeated but broken succession" and *continuous* to mean "unbroken succession." They write *farther* to express geographic distance and *further* to indicate "more, in addition." They know that *learn* means "to acquire knowledge" and *teach* means "to impart knowledge."

■ You should learn the specific meanings of other words.

In your effort to be a precise writer, you should use correct idiom. By *idiom* we mean the way things are said in a language. Much of our idiom has little rhyme or reason, but if we want to be understood, we should follow it. For example, what is the logic in the word *up* in the sentence "Look up her name in the directory"? There really is none. This is just the wording we have developed to cover this meaning. "Independent of" is good idiomatic usage; "independent from" is not. What is the justification? Similarly, you "agree to" a proposal, but you "agree with" a person. You are "careful about" an affair, but you are "careful with" your money. Here are some additional illustrations:

■ Use correct idiom. Idiom is the way ideas are expressed in a language.

Faulty Idiom	Correct Idiom
authority about	authority on
comply to	comply with
different than	different from
enamored with	enamored of
equally as bad	equally bad
in accordance to	in accordance with
in search for	in search of
listen at	listen to
possessed with ability	possessed of ability
seldom or ever	seldom if ever
superior than	superior to

■ There is little reason to some idioms, but violations offend the reader. ·

SUGGESTIONS FOR NONDISCRIMINATORY WRITING

■ Avoid words that discriminate against sex, race, nationality, age, or disability.

Although discriminatory words are not directly related to writing clarity, our review of word selection would not be complete without some mention of them. By discriminatory words we mean words that do not treat all people equally and with respect. More specifically, they are words that refer negatively to groups of people, such as by sex, race, nationality, age, or disability. Such words run contrary to acceptable views of fair play and human decency. They do not promote good business etiquette, and thus have no place in business communication.

■ We often use discriminatory words without bad intent.

Many discriminatory words are a part of the vocabularies we have acquired from our environments. We often use them innocently, not realizing how they affect others. We can eliminate discriminatory words from our vocabularies by examining them carefully and placing ourselves in the shoes of those to whom they refer. The following review of the major forms of discriminatory words should help you achieve this goal.

AVOID SEXIST WORDS

All too prevalent in today's business communication are sexist words—words that discriminate against a person because of his or her sex. Although this form of discrimination can be against men, most instances involve discrimination against women. The reason is that many of our words suggest male superiority. This condition is easily explained: Our language developed in a male-dominated society. For reasons of fair play, you would do well to avoid sexist words. Suggestions for avoiding some of the more troublesome sexist words follow.

■ Avoid using the masculine pronouns (he, him, his) for both sexes.

MASCULINE PRONOUNS FOR BOTH SEXES.   Perhaps the most troublesome sexist words are the masculine pronouns (*he, his, him*) when they are used to refer to both sexes, as in this example: "The typical State University student eats *his* lunch at the cafeteria." Assuming that State is coeducational, the use of *his* suggests male supremacy. Historically, of course, the word *his* has been classified as generic—that is, it can refer to both sexes. But many modern-day businesspeople do not agree and are offended by the use of the masculine pronoun in this way.

■ You can do this (1) by rewording the sentence;

You can avoid the use of masculine pronouns in such cases in three ways. First, you can reword the sentence to eliminate the offending word. Thus, the illustration above could be reworded as follows: "The typical State University student eats lunch at the cafeteria." Here are other examples:

Sexist	**Nonsexist**
If a customer pays promptly, *he* is placed on our preferred list.	A customer who pays promptly is placed on our preferred list.
When an unauthorized employee enters the security area, *he* is subject to dismissal.	An employee who enters the security area is subject to dismissal.
A supervisor is not responsible for such losses if *he* is not negligent.	A supervisor who is not negligent is not responsible for such losses.
When a customer needs service, it is *his* right to ask for it.	A customer who needs service has the right to ask for it.

■ (2) by making the reference plural,

A second way to avoid sexist use of the masculine pronoun is to make the reference plural. Fortunately, the English language has plural pronouns (*their, them, they*) that refer to both sexes. Making the references plural in the examples given above, we have these nonsexist revisions:

■ as illustrated here;

If customers pay promptly, *they* are placed on our preferred list.

When unauthorized employees enter the security area, *they* are subject to dismissal.

Supervisors are not responsible for such losses if *they* are not negligent.

When customers need service, *they* have the right to ask for it.

In business today, men and women, the young and the old, and people of all races work side by side in roles of mutual respect. It would be unfair to use words that discriminate against any of them.

A third way to avoid sexist use of *he, his,* or *him* is to substitute any of a number of neutral expressions. The most common are *he or she, he/she, s/he, you, one,* and *person.* Using neutral expressions in the problem sentences, we have these revisions:

If a customer pays promptly, *he or she* is placed on our preferred list.

When an unauthorized employee enters the security area, *he/she* is subject to dismissal.

A supervisor is not responsible for such losses if *s/he* is not negligent.

When *one* needs service, *one* has the right to ask for it.

You should use such expressions with caution, however. They tend to be somewhat awkward, particularly if they are used often. For this reason, many skilled writers do not use some of them. If you use them, you should pay attention to their effect on the flow of your words. Certainly, you should avoid sentences like this one: "To make an employee feel he/she is doing well by complimenting her/him insincerely confuses her/him later when he/she sees his/her co-workers promoted ahead of him/her."

WORDS DERIVED FROM MASCULINE WORDS.   As we have noted, our culture was male dominated when our language developed. Because of this, many of our words are masculine even though they do not refer exclusively to men. Take *chairman,* for example. This word can refer to both sexes, yet it does not sound that way. More appropriate and less offensive substitutes are *chair, presiding officer, moderator,* and *chairperson.* Similarly, *salesman* suggests a man, but many women work in sales. *Salesperson, salesclerk,* or *sales representative* would be better. Other sexist words and nonsexist substitutes are as follows:

Sexist	Nonsexist
man-made	manufactured, of human origin
manpower	personnel, workers
congressman	representative, member of Congress
businessman	business executive, businessperson
mailman	letter carrier, mail carrier
policeman	police officer
fireman	fire fighter

- or (3) by substituting neutral expressions,

- as in these examples.

- Neutral expressions can be awkward; so use them with caution.

- Avoid words suggesting male dominance,

- such as these examples.

■ DILBERT © (*United Feature Syndicate. Reprinted by permission.*)

Sexist	Nonsexist
fisherman	fisher
cameraman	camera operator

■ But not all man-sounding words are sexist.

Many words with *man, his,* and the like in them have nonsexist origins. Among such words are *manufacture, management, history,* and *manipulate.* Also, some clearly sexist words are hard to avoid. *Freshperson,* for example, would not serve as a substitute for *freshman.* And *personhole* is an illogical substitute for *manhole.*

■ Do not use words that lower the status of women.

WORDS THAT LOWER WOMEN'S STATUS. Thoughtless writers and speakers use expressions belittling the status of women. You should avoid such expressions. To illustrate, male executives sometimes refer to their female secretaries as *my girl,* as in this sentence: "I'll have my girl take care of this matter." Of course, *secretary* would be a better choice. Then there are the many female forms for words that refer to work roles. In this group are *lady lawyer, authoress, sculptress,* and *poetess.* You should refer to women in these work roles by the same words that you would use for men: *lawyer, author, sculptor, poet.*

Examples of sexist words could go on and on. But not all of them would be as clear as those given above, for the issue is somewhat complex and confusing. In deciding which words to avoid and which to use, you will have to rely on your best judgment. Remember that your goal should be to use words that are fair and that do not offend.

AVOID WORDS THAT STEREOTYPE BY RACE OR NATIONALITY

■ Words depicting minorities in a stereotyped way are unfair and untrue.

Words that stereotype all members of a group by race or nationality are especially unfair. Members of any minority vary widely in all characteristics. Thus, it is unfair to suggest that Jews are miserly, that Italians are Mafia members, that Hispanics are lazy, that African Americans can do only menial jobs, and so on. Unfair references to minorities are sometimes subtle and not intended, as in this example: "We conducted the first marketing tests in the ghetto areas of the city. Using a sample of 200 African-American families, we . . . ." These words unfairly suggest that only African-Americans are ghetto dwellers.

■ Words that present members of minorities as exceptions to stereotypes are also unfair.

Also unfair are words suggesting that a minority member has struggled to achieve something that is taken for granted in the majority group. Usually well intended, words of this kind can carry subtle discriminatory messages. For example, a reference to a "neatly dressed Hispanic man" may suggest that he is an exception to the rule—that most Hispanics are not neatly dressed, but here is one who is. So can references to "a generous Jew," "an energetic Puerto Rican," "a hardworking African American," and "a Chinese manager."

■ Eliminate such references to minorities by treating all people equally and by being sensitive to the effects of your words.

Eliminating unfair references to minority groups from your communication requires two basic steps. First, you must consciously treat all people equally, without regard to their minority status. You should refer to minority membership only in those rare cases in which it is a vital part of the message to be communicated. Second, you must be sensitive to the effects of your words. Specifically, you should ask yourself how those words would affect you if you were a member of the minorities to which they are addressed. You should evaluate your word choices from the viewpoints of others.

AVOID WORDS THAT STEREOTYPE BY AGE

Your sensitivity in not discriminating by sex should also be extended to include by age—both against the old and the young. While those over 55 might be retired from their first jobs, many lead lives that are far from the sedentary roles in which they are sometimes depicted. They also are not necessarily feeble, forgetful, or forsaken. While some do not mind being called *senior citizens,* others do. Be sensitive with terms such as *mature, elderly,* and *golden ager,* also. Some even abhor *oldster* as much as the young detest *youngster.* The young are often called *teenagers* or *adolescents* when *young person, young man,* and *young woman* are much fairer. Some slang terms show lack of sensitivity, too—words such as *brat, retard,* and *dummy.* Even harsher are *juvenile delinquent, truant,* and *runaway,* for these labels are often put on the young based on one behavior over a short time period. Presenting both the old and young objectively is only fair.

Words that label people as old or young can arouse negative reactions.

As we have suggested, use labels only when relevant, and use positive terms when possible. In describing the old, be sensitive to terms such as *spry,* which on the surface might be well intended but can also imply a negative connotation. Present both groups fairly and objectively when you write about them.

AVOID WORDS THAT TYPECAST THOSE WITH DISABILITIES

People with disabilities are likely to be sensitive to discriminatory words. While television shows those with disabilities competing in the Special Olympics, often exceeding the performance of an average person, common sense tells us not to stereotype these people. However, sometimes we do anyway. Just as with age, we need to avoid derogatory labels and apologetic or patronizing behavior. For example, instead of describing one as *deaf and dumb,* use *deaf.* Avoid slang terms such as *fits, spells, attacks;* use *seizures, epilepsy,* or other objective terms. Terms such as *crippled* and *retarded* should be avoided since they degrade in most cases. Work to develop a nonbiased attitude, and show it through carefully chosen words.

Disabled people are sensitive to words that describe their disabilities.

IN CONCLUSION ABOUT WORDS

The preceding review of suggestions for selecting words is not complete. You will find more—much more—in the pages ahead. But you now have in mind the basics of word selection. The remaining are refinements of these basics.

More about words appears in the following pages.

As you move along, you should view these basics as work tools. Unfortunately, the tendency is to view them as rules to memorize and give back to the instructor on an examination. Although a good examination grade is a commendable goal, the long-run value of these tools is their use in your writing. So do yourself a favor. Resolve to keep these basics in mind every time you write. Consciously use them. The results will make you glad you did.

The preceding suggestions are realistic ways to improve your writing. Use them.

SUMMARY BY CHAPTER OBJECTIVES

1. To communicate clearly, you must adapt to your reader.
   - Adapting means using words the reader understands.
   - It also involves following the suggestions below.
2. Select words that your reader understands.
   - These are the familiar words (words like *old* instead of *antiquated*).

1 Explain the role of adaptation in selecting words that communicate.

2 Simplify writing by selecting short and familiar words.

- They are also the short words (*agreed to quit* rather than *acceded to the proposition to terminate*).

3. Use technical words with caution.
   - For example, use *a little stroke* rather than *a cerebral vascular accident*.
   - However, technical words are appropriate among technical people.

4. Select words with adequate strength and vigor.
   - Develop a feeling for the personalities of words.
   - Understand that words like *bear market* are stronger than *generally declining market*.

5. Prefer the concrete words and active voice.
   - Concrete words are the specific ones. For example, *57 percent majority* is more concrete than *majority*.
   - In active voice, the subject acts; in passive voice, it receives the action. For example, use *we reported the results* rather than *the results were reported by us*.
   - Active voice is stronger, more vigorous, and more interesting. But passive voice is correct and has a place in writing.

6. Write more clearly and precisely by following these suggestions:
   - Avoid overuse of camouflaged verbs—making a noun of the logical verb and then having to add a verb (*appear* rather than *make an appearance*).
   - Select words for their precise meanings (involves studying words to detect shades of difference in meaning—for example, differences in *fight, brawl, fracas, donnybrook, battle royal*).
   - Also, learn the specific ways that words are used in our culture (called *idiom*).

7. Avoid discriminatory words.
   - Do not use words that discriminate against women. (For example, using *he, him,* or *his,* to refer to both sexes and words such as *fireman, postman, lady lawyer,* and *authoress.*)

   - Do not use words that suggest stereotyped roles of race or nationality (African Americans and menial jobs, Italians and the Mafia), for such words are unfair and untrue.
   - Do not use words that discriminate against age or disability.

CRITICAL THINKING QUESTIONS

1. A fellow student says, "So I'm not a good writer. But I have other places to put my study time. I'm a management major. I'll have secretaries to handle my writing for me." Give this student your best advice, including the reasoning behind it.

2. Evaluate this comment: "Simplifying writing so that stupid readers can understand it is for the birds! Why not challenge readers? Why not give them new words to learn—expand their minds?"

3. Explain how you would apply the basic principle of adaptation to each of the following writing assignments:
   a. An editorial in a company newspaper.
   b. A memorandum to Joan Branch, a supervisor of an assembly department, concerning a change in assembly operations.
   c. A report to the chief engineer on a technical topic in the engineer's field.
   d. A letter to a laborer explaining pension benefits.
   e. A letter to company stockholders explaining a change in company manufacturing policy.

4. "Some short words are hard, and some long words are easy. Thus, the suggestion to prefer short words doesn't make sense." Discuss.

5. "As technical language typically consists of acronyms and long, hard words, it contributes to miscommunication. Thus, it should be avoided in all business communication." Discuss.

6. Using examples other than those in the book, discuss differences in word strength. Be sure to comment on strength differences in the parts of speech (nouns, verbs, adjectives, adverbs).

7. Define and give examples of active and passive voice. Explain when each should be used.

8. Discuss this statement: "When I use *he, him,* or *his* as a generic, I am not discriminating against women. For many years these words have been accepted as generic. They refer to both sexes, and that's the meaning I have in mind when I use them."

9. List synonyms (words with similar meanings) for each of the following words. Then explain the differences in shades of meaning as you see them.
   a. fat   f. understand
   b. skinny   g. dog
   c. old   h. misfortune
   d. tell   i. inquire
   e. happiness   j. stop

10. Discuss this statement: "The boss scolded Susan in a grandfatherly manner."

CRITICAL THINKING EXERCISES

USING SIMPLE WORDS

Instructions, Sentences 1–20: Assume that your readers are at about the 10th-grade level in education. Revise these sentences for easy communication to this audience.

1. We must terminate all deficit financing.

2. The most operative assembly-line configuration is a unidirectional flow.

3. A proportionate tax consumes a determinate apportionment of one's monetary flow.

4. Business has an inordinate influence on governmental operations.

5. It is imperative that consumers be unrestrained in determining their preferences.

6. Mr. Sanchez terminated John's employment as a consequence of his ineffectual performance.

7. Our expectations are that there will be increments in commodity value.

8. This antiquated mechanism is ineffectual for an accelerated assembly-line operation.

9. The preponderance of the businesspeople we consulted envision signs of improvement from the current siege of economic stagnation.

10. If liquidation becomes mandatory, we shall dispose of these assets first.

11. Recent stock acquisitions have accentuated the company's current financial crisis.

12. Mr. Coward will serve as intermediary in the pending labor-management parley.

13. Ms. Smith's idiosyncrasies supply adequate justification for terminating her employment.

14. Requisites for employment by this company have been enhanced.

15. The unanimity of current forecasts is not incontrovertible evidence of an impending business acceleration.

16. People's propensity to consume is insatiable.

17. The company must desist from its deficit financing immediately.

18. This antiquated merchandising strategy is ineffectual in contemporary business operations.

19. Percentage return on common stockholders' equity averaged 23.1 for the year.

20. The company's retained earnings last year exceeded $2,500,000.

Instructions: Exercise 21 concerns adaptation and technical language. As you must find your own sentences for it, this exercise differs from the others.

21. From one of your textbooks, select a paragraph (at least 150 words long) that would be difficult for a student less advanced in the subject than you. Rewrite the paragraph so that this student can understand it easily.

CRITICAL THINKING EXERCISES

Instructions, Sentences 22–58: Revise these sentences to make them conform to the writing suggestions discussed in the book. They are grouped by the suggestion they illustrate.

USING STRONG, VIGOROUS WORDS

22. I have an idea in mind of how we can enhance our savings.
23. Ms. Jordan possesses qualities that are characteristic of an autocratic executive.
24. Many people came into the store during the period of the promotion.
25. We are obligated to protect the well-being of the hired employees.
26. Companies promoting their products in the medium of the newspaper are advised to produce verbal messages in accord with the audience level of the general consuming public.

SELECTING CONCRETE WORDS

27. We have found that young men are best for this work.
28. She makes good grades.
29. John lost a fortune in Las Vegas.
30. If we don't receive the goods soon, we will cancel.
31. Profits last year were exorbitant.
32. Some years ago she made good money.
33. His grade on the aptitude test was not high.
34. Here is a product with very little markup.
35. The cost of the online database search was reasonable.
36. We will need some new equipment soon.

LIMITING USE OF PASSIVE VOICE

37. Our action is based on the assumption that the competition will be taken by surprise.
38. It is believed by the typical union member that his or her welfare is not considered to be important by management.
39. We are serviced by the Bratton Company.
40. Our safety is the responsibility of management.
41. You were directed by your supervisor to complete this assignment by noon.
42. It is believed by the writer that this company policy is wrong.
43. The union was represented by Cecil Chambers.
44. These reports are prepared by the salespeople every Friday.

45. Success of this project is the responsibility of the research department.
46. Our decision is based on the belief that the national economy will be improved.

AVOIDING CAMOUFLAGED VERBS

47. It was my duty to make a determination of the damages.
48. Harold made a recommendation that we fire Mr. Schultz.
49. We will make her give an accounting of her activities.
50. We will ask him to bring about a change in his work routine.
51. This new equipment will result in a saving in maintenance.
52. Will you please make an adjustment for this defect?
53. Implementation of the plan was effected by the crew.
54. Acceptance of all orders must be made by the chief.
55. A committee performs the function of determining the award.
56. Adaptation to the new conditions was performed easily by all new personnel.
57. Verification of the amount is made daily by the auditor.
58. The president tried to effect a reconciliation of the two groups.

SELECTING PRECISE WORDS

Instructions, Sentences 59–70: Following is an exercise in word precision. Explain the differences in meaning for the word choices shown. Point out any words that are wrongly used.

59. Performance during the fourth quarter was (average) (mediocre).
60. This merchandise is (old) (antique) (secondhand) (used).
61. The machine ran (continually) (continuously).
62. The mechanic is a (woman) (lady) (female person).
63. His action (implies) (infers) that he accepts the criticism.
64. Her performance on the job was (good) (topnotch) (excellent) (superior).
65. On July 1 the company will (become bankrupt) (close its door) (go under) (fail).
66. The staff members (think) (understand) (know) the results were satisfactory.
67. Before buying any material, we (compare) (contrast) it with competing products.

68. I cannot (resist) (oppose) her appointment.
69. Did you (verify) (confirm) these figures?
70. This is an (effective) (effectual) (efficient) plan.

USING PROPER IDIOM

Instructions, Sentences 71–80: These sentences use faulty and correct idioms. Make any changes you think are necessary.

71. The purchasing officer has gone in search for a substitute product.
72. Our office has become independent from the Dallas office.
73. This strike was different than the one in 1992.
74. This letter is equally as bad.
75. She is an authority about mutual funds.
76. When the sale is over with, we will restock.
77. Our truck collided against the wall.
78. We have been in search for a qualified supervisor since August.
79. Murphy was equal to the task.
80. Apparently, the clock fell off the shelf.

AVOIDING DISCRIMINATORY LANGUAGE

Instructions, Sentences 81–90: Change these sentences to avoid discriminatory language.

81. Any worker who ignores this rule will have his salary reduced.
82. The typical postman rarely makes mistakes in delivering his mail.
83. A good executive plans his daily activities.
84. The committee consisted of a businessman, a lawyer, and a lady doctor.
85. A good secretary screens all telephone calls for her boss and arranges his schedule.
86. An efficient salesman organizes his calls and manages his time.
87. Our company was represented by two sales representatives, one Hispanic engineer, and one senior citizen.
88. Three people applied for the job, including two well-groomed black women.
89. Handicap parking spaces are strictly for use by the crippled.
90. He didn't act like a Mexican.

Construction of Clear Sentences and Paragraphs

Upon completing this chapter, you will be able to construct clear sentences and paragraphs by emphasizing adaptation, short sentences, and effective paragraph design. To reach this goal, you should be able to

1 Explain the role of adaptation in writing clear sentences.

2 Write short, clear sentences by limiting sentence content and economizing words.

3 Design sentences that give the right emphasis to content.

4 Employ unity and clarity in writing effective sentences.

5 Compose paragraphs that are short and unified, use topic sentences effectively, show movement, and communicate clearly.

Writing Sentences and Paragraphs that Communicate

Continuing in your role as Max Schwartz's boss (preceding chapter), you conclude that not all his writing problems involve word choice. True, his words detract from the readability of his writing. But something else is wrong. His sentences just do not convey sharp, clear meanings. Although grammatically correct, they appear to be needlessly complex and heavy. His long and involved paragraphs also cause you concern.

What you have seen in Max's writing are problems concerning two other determinants of readability—the sentence and the paragraph. As you will learn in the pages ahead, these two writing units play major roles in communicating. This chapter will show you (and Max) how to construct sentences and paragraphs that produce readable writing.

FOUNDATION OF ADAPTATION

As you have seen, choosing the right words is basic to clear communication. Equally basic is the task of arranging those words into clear sentences. Like choosing words, constructing clear sentences involves adaptation to the minds of the intended readers.

- Sentences should be adapted to readers.

Fitting sentences to the minds of readers requires the reader analysis we discussed in the preceding chapter. You should simply study your readers to find out what they are like—what they know, how they think, and such. Then construct sentences that will communicate with them. Good business etiquette requires that you follow this procedure.

In general, this procedure involves using the simpler sentence structures to reach people with lower communication abilities and people not knowledgeable about the subject. It involves using the more complex sentence structures only when they are appropriate, usually when communicating with knowledgeable people. As we will see, even with knowledgeable people, simplicity is sometimes needed for the best communication effect.

- Use the simpler sentence structures for those less able to understand; use the more complex structures when appropriate.

In adapting sentences, you should aim a little below the level of your reader. Readability research tells us that writing communicates best when it does not tax the mind. Thus, some simplification is best for all readers. Keep this point in mind as you read through the rest of this chapter.

EMPHASIS ON SHORT SENTENCES

Writing simpler sentences largely means writing shorter sentences. Readability research tells us that the more words and the more relationships there are in a sentence, the greater is the possibility for misunderstanding. Apparently, the mind can hold only so much information at one time. Thus, to give it too much information is to risk miscommunication.

- Short sentences communicate better because of mind limitations.

What constitutes a short, readable sentence is related to the reader's ability. Readability studies show that writing intended to communicate with the middle-level adult reader should average about 16 to 18 words per sentence. For more advanced readers, the average may be higher. For less advanced readers, it should be lower.

- Short means about 16–18 words for middle-level readers.

This emphasis on short sentences does not mean that you should never use long sentences. You may use them occasionally, and you should—if you construct them clearly. Longer sentences are sometimes useful in subordinating information and in increasing interest by adding variety. The information needed to complete a thought sometimes requires a long sentence. What you should be concerned about is the average length of your sentences.

- Sometimes longer sentences are justified.

The following sentence from an employee handbook illustrates the effect of long sentences on communication:

When an employee has changed from one job to another job, the new corresponding coverages will be effective as of the date the change occurs, provided, however, if due to a physical disability or infirmity as a result of advanced age, an employee is changed from one job to another job and such change results in the employee's new job rate coming within a lower hourly job-rate bracket in the table, the employee may, at the discretion of

Grammar Checkers Help Writers Evaluate Length

Grammar checkers are useful in helping you evaluate length. They report the average sentence length as well as the number of sentences in paragraphs. They will also tell you the number of paragraphs, sentences, words, and syllables or characters in a document or the selected part of a document.

In the accompanying example, the software identified long sentences as any with more than 18 words. While it did find three long sentences, the average of 18.23 words per sentence is probably in the acceptable range. Therefore, the writer of this document should not feel compelled to shorten the long sentences if they are clear. However, the writer should examine the long sentences for the opportunity to improve clarity.

Basic Counts - C:\Data\PROFESS\BCQ_NetMeeting2.wpd (unmodified)

COUNTS:

Syllables	1562	Short sentences	10
Words	857	Long sentences	3
Sentences	47	Simple sentences	19
Paragraphs	16	Big words	193

AVERAGES:

Syllables per word	1.82
Words per sentence	18.23
Sentences per paragraph	2.93

Readability... Flagged... Close Help

---

the company, continue the amount of group term life insurance and the amount of accidental death and dismemberment insurance that the employee had prior to such change.

The chances are that you did not get a clear message from this sentence when you first read it. The explanation is not in the words used; you probably know them all. Neither is it in the ideas presented; they are relatively simple. The obvious explanation is the length of the sentence. So many words and relationships are in the sentence that they cause confusion. The result is vague communication at best—complete miscommunication at worst.

■ Short sentences are achieved in two ways.

You can write short, simple sentences in two basic ways: (1) by limiting sentence content, and (2) by using words economically. The following pages contain specific suggestions for doing this.

LIMITING SENTENCE CONTENT

■ Limiting content is one way to make short sentences.

Limiting sentence content is largely a matter of mentally selecting thought units and making separate sentences of most of them. Sometimes, of course, you should combine thoughts into one sentence, but only when you have good reason. You have good reason, for example, when thoughts are closely related or when you want to de-emphasize content. The advantage of limiting sentence content is evident from the following contrasting examples:

Long and Hard to Understand

This letter is being distributed with enrollment confirmation sheets, which are to serve as a final check on the correctness of the registration of students and are to be used later when obtaining semester grades from the regline system, which are to be available two weeks after the term officially ends.

Short and Clear

This letter is being distributed with enrollment confirmation sheets. It will serve now as a final check on student registration. Later, the codes on it will be used to access course grades through the regline system; the grades will be available two weeks after the term officially ends.

Long and Hard to Understand

Some authorities in human resources object to expanding normal salary ranges to include a trainee rate because they fear that through oversight or prejudice probationers may be kept at the minimum rate longer than is warranted and because they fear that it would encourage the spread from the minimum to maximum rate range.

Regardless of their seniority or union affiliation, all employees who hope to be promoted are expected to continue their education either by enrolling in the special courses to be offered by the company, which are scheduled to be given after working hours beginning next Wednesday, or by taking approved online courses selected from a list, which may be seen in the training office.

Short and Clear

Some authorities in human resources object to expanding the normal salary range to include a trainee rate for two reasons. First, they fear that through oversight or prejudice probationers may be kept at the minimum rate longer than is warranted. Second, they fear that expansion would increase the spread between the minimum and the maximum rate range.

Regardless of their seniority or union affiliation, all employees who hope to be promoted are expected to continue their education in either of two ways. (1) They may enroll in special courses to be given by the company. (2) They may take approved online courses selected from the list in the training office.

Without question, the long sentences in the examples are hard to understand, and the shorter versions are easy to understand. In each case, the difference is primarily in sentence length. Clearly, the shorter sentences communicate better. They give more emphasis to content and to organization of the subject matter.

However, you can overdo the writing of short sentences. A succession of short sentences can give the impression of elementary writing and draw attention from the content of the sentences to their choppiness. You should avoid these effects by varying the length and order of your sentences. But you should keep the length of your sentences within the grasp of your readers.

> ■ Avoid overdoing this suggestion. Too many short sentences give a choppy effect.

ECONOMIZING ON WORDS

A second basic technique of shortening sentences is to use words economically. Anything you write can be expressed in many ways, some shorter than others. In general, the shorter wordings save the reader time and are clearer and more interesting.

> ■ Another way to shorten sentences is through word economy.

A Marathon Sentence (308 Words) from U.S. Government Regulations

That no person in the classified civil service of the United States shall be removed therefrom except for such cause as will promote the efficiency of said service and for reasons given in writing, and the person whose removal is sought shall have notice of the same and of any charges preferred against him, and be furnished with a copy thereof, and also be allowed a reasonable time for personally answering the same in writing; and affidavits in support thereof; but no examination of witnesses nor any trial or hearing shall be required except in the discretion of the officer making the removal; and copies of charges, notice of hearing, answer, reasons for removal, and of the order of removal shall be made a part of the records of the proper department or office, as shall also the reasons for reduction in rank or compensation; and the copies of the same shall be furnished to the person affected upon request, and the Civil Service Commission also shall, upon request, be furnished copies of the same: *Provided, however,* that membership in any society, association, club, or other form of organization of postal employees not affiliated with any outside organization imposing an obligation or duty upon them to engage in any strike, or proposing to assist them in any strike, against the United States, having for its objects, among other things, improvements in the condition of labor of its members, including hours of labor and compensation therefore and leave of absence, by any person or groups of persons in said postal service, or the presenting by any such person or groups of persons of any grievance or grievances to the Congress or any Member thereof shall not constitute or be cause for reduction in rank or compensation or removal of such person or groups of persons from said service.

Economizing on words generally means seeking shorter ways of saying things. Once you try to economize, you will probably find that your present writing is wasteful and that you use uneconomical wordings.

To help you recognize these uneconomical wordings, a brief review of them follows. This review does not cover all the possibilities for wasteful writing, but it does cover many troublesome problems.

CLUTTERING PHRASES.   An often used uneconomical wording is the cluttering phrase. This is a phrase that can be replaced by shorter wording without loss of meaning. The little savings achieved in this way add up.

Here is an example of a cluttering phrase:

In the event that payment is not made by January, operations will cease.

The phrase *in the event that* is uneconomical. The little word *if* can substitute for it without loss of meaning:

If payment is not made by January, operations will cease.

Similarly, the phrase that begins the following sentence adds unnecessary length:

In spite of the fact that they received help, they failed to exceed the quota.

Although makes an economical substitute:

Although they received help, they failed to exceed the quota.

You probably use many cluttering phrases. The following partial list (with suggested substitutions) should help you cut down on them:

Cluttering Phrase	Shorter Substitution
Along the lines of	Like
At the present time	Now
For the purpose of	For
For the reason that	Because, since
In accordance with	By
In the amount of	For
In the meantime	Meanwhile
In the near future	Soon
In the neighborhood of	About
In very few cases	Seldom
In view of the fact that	Since, because
On the basis of	By

RHYMES WITH ORANGE

■ *Reprinted with special permission of King Features Syndicate.*

With the advent of computers, the way business messages are composed has changed, but the mental process involved remains unchanged. One still must select words and build sentences that form precise meanings in the minds of readers.

Cluttering Phrase	Shorter Substitution
On the occasion of	On
With regard to, with reference to	About
With a view to	To

SURPLUS WORDS.   To write economically, eliminate words that add nothing to sentence meaning. As with cluttering phrases, we often use meaningless extra words as a matter of habit. Eliminating these surplus words sometimes requires recasting a sentence, but sometimes they can just be left out.

- Eliminate surplus words.

The following is an example of surplus wording from a business report:

It will be noted that the records for the past years show a steady increase in special appropriations.

The beginning words add nothing to the meaning of the sentence. Notice how dropping them makes the sentence stronger—and without loss of meaning:

The records for the past years show a steady increase in special appropriations.

Here is a second example:

His performance was good enough *to enable* him to qualify for the promotion.

The words *to enable* add nothing and can be dropped:

His performance was good enough to qualify him for the promotion.

The following sentences further illustrate the use of surplus words. In each case, the surplus words can be eliminated without changing the meaning.

Contains Surplus Words	Eliminates Surplus Words
He ordered desks *that are of the* executive type.	He ordered executive-type desks.
There are four rules *that* should be observed.	Four rules should be observed.
In addition to these defects, numerous other defects mar the operating procedure.	Numerous other defects mar the operating procedure.
The machines *that were* damaged by the fire were repaired.	The machines damaged by the fire were repaired.
By *the* keeping of production records, they found the error.	By keeping production records, they found the error.

Contains Surplus Words	Eliminates Surplus Words
In the period between April and June, we detected the problem.	Between April and June we detected the problem.
I am prepared to report *to the effect* that sales increased.	I am prepared to report that sales increased.

■ Avoid roundabout ways of saying things.

ROUNDABOUT CONSTRUCTIONS.   As we have noted, you can write anything in many ways. Some of the ways are direct. Some cover the same ground in a roundabout way. Usually the direct ways are shorter and communicate better.

This sentence illustrates roundabout construction:

The department budget *can be observed to be decreasing* each *new* year.

Do the words *can be observed to be decreasing* get to the point? Is the idea of *observing* essential? Is *new* needed? A more direct and better sentence is this one:

The department budget decreases each year.

Here is another roundabout sentence:

The union *is involved in the task of reviewing* the seniority provision of the contract.

Now if the union is *involved in the task of reviewing,* it is really *reviewing.* The sentence should be written in these direct words:

The union *is reviewing* the seniority provision of the contract.

The following sentence pairs further illustrate the advantages of short, direct wording over roundabout wording:

Roundabout	Direct
The president *is of the opinion that* the tax was paid.	The president *believes* the tax was paid.
It is essential that the income be used to retire the debt.	The income *must* be used to retire the debt.
Reference is made to your May 10 report *in which you concluded* that the warranty is worthless.	Your May 10 report *concluded* that the warranty is worthless.
The supervisors *should take appropriate action to determine* whether the time cards are being inspected.	The supervisors *should determine* whether the time cards are being inspected.
The price increase *will afford* the company *an opportunity* to retire the debt.	The price *will enable* the company to retire the debt.
During the time she was employed by this company, Ms. Carr was absent once.	*While* employed by this company, Ms. Carr was absent once.
He criticized everyone he *came in contact with.*	He criticized everyone he *met.*

■ Repeat words only for effect and emphasis.

UNNECESSARY REPETITION OF WORDS OR IDEAS.   Repeating words obviously adds to sentence length. Such repetition sometimes serves a purpose, as when it is used for emphasis or special effect. But all too often it is without purpose, as this sentence illustrates:

We have not received your payment covering invoices covering June and July purchases.

It would be better to write the sentence like this:

We have not received your payment covering invoices for June and July purchases.

Another example is this one:

He stated that he believes that we are responsible.

The following sentence eliminates one of the *that*s:

He stated that he believes we are responsible.

How My Business Is Doing, as Expressed by:

An astronomer: "My business is looking up."
A cigarmaker: "Mine is going up in smoke."
An author: "Mine is all write."
A tailor: "Mine is just sew, sew."
A farmer: "Mine is growing."
An electric company worker: "Mine is light."
A ragpicker: "Mine is picking up."
An optician: "Mine is looking better."

Repetitions of ideas through the use of different words that mean the same thing (*free gift, true fact, past history*) also add to sentence length. Known as redundancies, such repetitions are illogical and can rarely be defended. Note the redundancy in this sentence:

■ Avoid repetitions of ideas (redundancies).

The provision of Section 5 provides for a union shop.

The duplication, of course, is in the meaning of *provides*. By definition, a *provision* provides. So the repetition serves no purpose. The following sentence is better:

Section 5 provides for a union shop.

You often hear this expression:

In my opinion, I think the plan is sound.

Do not *in my opinion* and *I think* express the same thought? Could you possibly think in an opinion other than your own? The following sentence makes better sense:

I think the plan is sound.

Here are other examples of redundancies and ways to eliminate them:

Needless Repetition	**Repetition Eliminated**
Please *endorse your name on the back of* this check.	Please *endorse* this check.
We must *assemble together* at 10:30 AM *in the morning.*	We must *assemble* at 10:30 AM.
Our new model is *longer in length* than the old one.	Our new model is *longer* than the old one.
If you are not satisfied, *return it back* to us.	If you are not satisfied, *return* it to us.
Tod Wilson is the *present incumbent.*	Tod Wilson is the *incumbent.*
One should know the *basic fundamentals* of clear writing.	One should know the *fundamentals* of clear writing.
The *consensus of opinion* is that the tax is unfair.	The *consensus* is that the tax is unfair.
By acting now, we can finish *sooner than if we wait until a later date.*	By acting now, we can finish *sooner.*
At the present time, we *are* conducting two clinics.	We *are* conducting two clinics.
As a matter of interest, I am interested in learning your procedure.	I am *interested* in learning your procedure.
We should *plan in advance for the future.*	We should *plan.*

DETERMINING EMPHASIS IN SENTENCE DESIGN

The sentences you write should give the right emphasis to content. Any written business communication contains a number of items of information, not all of which are equally important. Some are very important, such as a conclusion in a report or the objective in a let-

■ You should give every item its due emphasis.

■ Short sentences emphasize contents.

ter. Others are relatively unimportant. Your task as writer is to form your sentences to communicate the importance of each item.

Sentence length affects emphasis. Short, simple sentences carry more emphasis than long, involved ones. They stand out and call attention to their contents. Thus, they give the reader a single message without the interference of related or supporting information.

■ Long sentences de-emphasize contents.

Longer sentences give less emphasis to their contents. When a sentence contains two or more ideas, the ideas share emphasis. How they share it depends on how the sentence is constructed. If two ideas are presented equally (in independent clauses, for example), they get about equal emphasis. But if they are not presented equally (for example, in an independent and a dependent clause), one gets more emphasis than the other.

To illustrate the varying emphasis you can give information, consider this example. You have two items of information to write. One is that the company lost money last year. The other is that its sales volume reached a record high. You could present the information in at least three ways. First, you could give both items equal emphasis by placing them in separate short sentences:

The company lost money last year. The loss occurred in spite of record sales.

Second, you could present the two items in the same sentence with emphasis on the lost money.

Although the company enjoyed record sales last year, it lost money.

Third, you could present the two items in one sentence with emphasis on the sales increase:

The company enjoyed record sales last year, although it lost money.

■ Determining emphasis is a matter of good judgment.

Which way would you choose? The answer depends on how much emphasis each item deserves. You should think the matter through and follow your best judgment. But the point is clear: Your choice makes a difference.

The following paragraphs illustrate the importance of thinking logically to determine emphasis. In the first, each item of information gets the emphasis of a short sentence and none stands out. However, the items are not equally important and do not deserve equal emphasis. Notice, also, the choppy effect that the succession of short sentences produces.

The main building was inspected on October 1. Mr. George Wills inspected the building. Mr. Wills is a vice president of the company. He found that the building has 6,500 square feet of floor space. He also found that it has 2,400 square feet of storage space. The new store must have a minimum of 6,000 square feet of floor space. It must have 2,000 square feet of storage space. Thus, the main building exceeds the space requirements for the new store. Therefore, Mr. Wills concluded that the main building is adequate for the company's needs.

In the next paragraph, some of the items are subordinated, but not logically. The really important information does not receive the emphasis it deserves. Logically, these two points should stand out: (1) the building is large enough, and (2) storage space exceeds minimum requirements. But they do not stand out in this version:

Mr. George Wills, who inspected the main building on October 1, is a vice president of the company. His inspection, which supports the conclusion that the building is large enough for the proposed store, uncovered these facts. The building has 6,500 square feet of floor space and 2,400 square feet of storage space, which is more than the minimum requirement of 6,000 and 2,000 square feet, respectively, of floor and storage space.

The third paragraph shows good emphasis of the important points. The short beginning sentence emphasizes the conclusion. The supporting facts that the building exceeds the minimum floor and storage space requirements receive main-clause emphasis. The less important facts, such as the reference to George Wills, are treated subordinately. Also, the most important facts are placed at the points of emphasis—the beginning and ending.

The main building is large enough for the new store. This conclusion, reached by Vice President George Wills following his October 1 inspection of the building, is based on these facts: The building's 6,500 square feet of floor space exceed the minimum requirement by 500 square feet. The 2,400 square feet of storage space exceed the minimum requirement by 400 square feet.

The preceding illustrations show how sentence construction can determine emphasis. You can make items stand out, you can treat them equally, or you can de-emphasize them. The choices are yours. But what you do must be the result of good, sound thinking and not simply a matter of chance.

GIVING THE SENTENCES UNITY

Good sentences have unity. For a sentence to have unity, all of its parts must combine to form one clear thought. In other words, all the things put in a sentence should have a good reason for being together.

■ All parts of a sentence should concern one thought.

Violations of unity in sentence construction fall into three categories: (1) unrelated ideas, (2) excessive detail, and (3) illogical constructions.

■ There are three causes of unity error.

UNRELATED IDEAS.   Placing unrelated ideas in a sentence is the most obvious violation of unity. Putting two or more ideas in a sentence is not grammatically wrong, but the ideas must have a reason for being together. They must combine to complete the single goal of the sentence.

■ First, placing unrelated ideas in a sentence violates unity.

You can give unity to sentences that contain unrelated ideas in three basic ways: (1) You can put the ideas in separate sentences. (2) You can make one of the ideas subordinate to the other. (3) You can add words that show how the ideas are related. The first two of these techniques are illustrated by the revisions of the following sentence:

■ You can avoid this error by (1) putting unrelated ideas in separate sentences, (2) subordinating an idea, or (3) adding words that show relationship.

Mr. Jordan is our sales manager, and he has a degree in law.

Perhaps the two ideas are related, but the words do not tell how. A better arrangement is to put each in a separate sentence:

Mr. Jordan is our sales manager. He has a law degree.

Or the two ideas could be kept in one sentence by subordinating one to the other. In this way, the main clause provides the unity of the sentence.

Mr. Jordan, our sales manager, has a law degree.

Adding words to show the relationship of ideas is illustrated in the revision of the following example:

■ Modern executives often are extremely busy. They want and need their incoming messages to communicate easily and quickly.

Our production increased in January, and our equipment is wearing out.

The sentence has two ideas that seem unrelated. One way of improving it is to make a separate sentence of each idea. A closer look reveals, however, that the two ideas really are related. The words just do not show how. Thus, the sentence could be revised to show how:

Even though our equipment is wearing out, our production increased in January.

The following contrasting pairs of sentences further illustrate the technique:

Unrelated	**Improved**
Our territory is the southern half of the state, and our salespeople cannot cover it thoroughly.	Our territory is the southern half of the state. Our salespeople cannot cover it thoroughly.
Operation of the press is simple, but no machine will work well unless it is maintained.	Operation of the press is simple, but, like any machine, it will not work well unless it is maintained.
We concentrate on energy-saving products, and 70 percent of our business comes from them.	As a result of our concentration on energy-saving products, 70 percent of our business comes from them.

■ Excessive detail is another cause of lack of unity. If the detail is important, put it in a separate sentence. This means using short sentences.

EXCESSIVE DETAIL.   Putting too much detail into one sentence tends to hide the central thought. If the detail is important, you should put it in a separate sentence.

This suggestion strengthens another given earlier in the chapter—the suggestion that you use short sentences. Obviously, short sentences cannot have much detail. Long sentences—full of detail—definitely lead to lack of unity, as illustrated in these contrasting examples:

Excessive Detail	**Improved**
Our New York offices, considered plush in the 1980s, but now badly in need of renovation, as is the case with most offices that have not been maintained, have been abandoned.	Considered plush in the 1980s, our New York offices have not been maintained properly. As they badly need repair, we have abandoned them.
We have attempted to trace the Plytec insulation you ordered from us October 1, and about which you inquired in your October 10 letter, but we have not yet been able to locate it, although we are sending you a rush shipment immediately.	We are sending you a rush shipment of Plytec insulation immediately. Following your October 10 inquiry, we attempted to trace your October 1 order. We were unable to locate it.
In 1997, when I, a small-town girl from a middle-class family, began my studies at Darden University, which is widely recognized for its information systems program, I set my goal for a career with a major consulting firm.	A small-town girl from a middle-class family, I entered Darden University in 1997. I selected Darden because of its widely recognized information systems program. From the beginning, my goal was a career with a major consulting firm.

■ Illogical constructions can rob a sentence of unity.

ILLOGICAL CONSTRUCTIONS.   Illogical constructions destroy sentence unity. These constructions result primarily from illogical thinking. Illogical thinking is too complex for meaningful study here, but a few typical examples should acquaint you with the possibilities. Then, by thinking logically, you should be able to reduce illogical constructions in your writing.

■ Active and passive voice in the same sentence can violate unity.

The first example contains two main thoughts in two correct clauses. But one clause is in active voice *(we cut),* and the other is in passive voice *(quality was reduced).*

First we cut prices, and then quality was reduced.

We achieve unity by making both clauses active, as in this example:

First we cut prices, and then we reduced quality.

■ So can mixed constructions.

The mixed constructions of the following sentence do not make a clear and logical thought. The technical explanation is that the beginning clause belongs with a complex sentence, while the last part is the predicate of a simple sentence.

Because our salespeople are inexperienced caused us to miss our quota.

Revised for good logic, the sentence might read:

The inexperience of our salespeople caused us to miss our quota.

These sentences further illustrate the point:

Illogical Construction	Improved
Job rotation is when you train people by moving them from job to job.	Job rotation is a training method in which people are moved from job to job.
Knowing that she objected to the price was the reason we permitted her to return the goods.	Because we knew she objected to the price, we permitted her to return the goods.
I never knew an executive who was interested in helping workers who had got into problems that caused them to worry.	I never knew an executive who was interested in helping worried workers with their problems.
My education was completed in 1998, and then I began work as a sales representative for Microsoft.	I completed my education in 1998 and then began work as a sales representative for Microsoft.

ARRANGING SENTENCES FOR CLARITY

As you know, various rules of grammar govern the structure of sentences. You know, for example, that modifying words must follow a definite sequence—that altering the sequence changes meaning. "A venetian blind" means one thing. "A blind Venetian" means quite another. Long-established rules of usage determine the meaning.

Many such rules exist. Established by centuries of use, these rules are not merely arbitrary requirements. Rather, they are based on custom and on logical relationships between words. In general, they are based on the need for clear communication.

Take the rule concerning dangling modifiers. Dangling modifiers confuse meaning by modifying the wrong words. On the surface, this sentence appears correct: "Believing that the price would drop, our purchasing agents were instructed not to buy." But the sentence is correct only if the purchasing agents did the believing—which is not the case. The modifying phrase dangles, and the intended meaning was probably this: "Believing that the price would drop, we instructed our purchasing agents not to buy."

Other rules of grammar also help to make writing clear. Unparallel constructions leave wrong impressions. Pronouns that do not clearly refer to a definite preceding word are vague and confusing. Subject-verb disagreements confuse the reader. The list goes on and on. The rules of grammar are useful in writing clear sentences. You should know them and follow them. You will want to study Chapter 18 for a review of these rules and complete the diagnostic exercise at the chapter end for feedback on your understanding of them.

CARE IN PARAGRAPH DESIGN

Paragraphing is also important to clear communication. Paragraphs show the reader where topics begin and end, thus helping organize information in the reader's mind. Paragraphs also help make ideas stand out.

How one should design paragraphs is hard to explain, for the procedure is largely mental. Designing paragraphs requires the ability to organize and relate information. It involves the use of logic and imagination. But we can say little that would help you in these activities. The best we can do is give the following points on paragraph structure.

GIVING THE PARAGRAPHS UNITY

Like sentences, paragraphs should have unity. When applied to paragraph structure, unity means that a paragraph builds around a single topic or idea. Thus, everything you include in a paragraph should develop this topic or idea. When you have finished the paragraph, you should be able to say, "Everything in this paragraph belongs together because every part concerns every other part."

Marginal notes:
- Clear writing requires that you follow the established rules of grammar.
- These rules are based on custom and logical relationships.
- For example, dangling modifiers confuse meaning.
- So do unparallel constructions, pronouns without antecedents, and subject-verb disagreements.
- Paragraphing shows and emphasizes organization.
- It involves logical thinking.
- The contents of a paragraph should concern one topic or idea (unity).

■ But unity can vary in breadth. Paragraph unity concerns a narrow topic.

Unity is not always easy to determine. As all of a letter or a report may concern a single topic, one could say that the whole letter or report has unity. One could say the same about a major division of a report or a long paper. Obviously, paragraph unity concerns smaller units than these. Generally, it concerns the next largest unit of thought above a sentence.

A violation of unity is illustrated in the following paragraph from an application letter. As the goal of the paragraph is to summarize the applicant's coursework, all the sentences should pertain to coursework. By shifting to personal qualities, the third sentence violates paragraph unity. Taking this sentence out would correct the fault.

At the university I studied all the basic accounting courses as well as specialized courses in petroleum, fiduciary, and systems. I also took specialized coursework in the behavioral areas, with emphasis on human relations. Realizing the value of human relations in business, I also actively participated in organizations, such as Sigma Nu (social fraternity), Delta Sigma Pi (professional fraternity), YMCA, and Men's Glee Club. I selected my elective coursework to round out my general business education. Among my electives were courses in investments, advanced business report writing, financial policy, and management information systems. A glance at my résumé will show you the additional courses that round out my training.

KEEPING PARAGRAPHS SHORT

■ Generally, paragraphs should be short.

■ Short paragraphs show organization better than long ones.

■ Most readers prefer to read short paragraphs.

As a general rule, you should keep your paragraphs short. This suggestion overlaps the suggestion about unity, for if your paragraphs have unity, they will be short.

As noted earlier, paragraphs help the reader follow the writer's organization plan. Writing marked by short paragraphs identifies more of the details of that plan. In addition, such writing is inviting to the eye. People simply prefer to read writing with frequent paragraph breaks.

This last point is easily proved by illustration. Assume you have a choice of reading either of two business reports on the same subject. One report has long paragraphs. Its pages appear solid with type. The second report has short paragraphs and thus provides frequent rest stops. You can see the rest stops at first glance. Now, which would you choose? No doubt, you would prefer the report with short paragraphs. It is more inviting, and it appears less difficult. Perhaps the difference is largely psychological, but it is a very real difference.

■ About eight lines is a good average length.

How long a paragraph should be depends on its contents—on what must be included to achieve unity. Readability research has suggested an average length of eight lines for longer papers such as reports. Shorter paragraphs are appropriate for letters.

■ But length can and should vary with need.

Keep in mind that these suggestions concern only an average. Some good paragraphs may be quite long—well over the average. Some paragraphs can be very short—as short as one line. One-line paragraphs are an especially appropriate means of emphasizing major points in business messages. A one-line paragraph may be all that is needed for a goodwill closing comment.

■ A good practice is to question paragraphs over 12 lines.

A good rule to follow is to question the unity of all long paragraphs—say, those longer than 12 lines. If after looking over such a paragraph you conclude that it has unity, leave it as it is. But you will sometimes find more than one topic. When you do, make each topic into a separate paragraph.

MAKING GOOD USE OF TOPIC SENTENCES

■ Topic sentences can help make good paragraphs. But not every paragraph must have a topic sentence.

One good way of organizing paragraphs is to use topic sentences. The topic sentence expresses the main idea of a paragraph, and the remaining sentences build around and support it. In a sense, the topic sentence serves as a headline for the paragraph, and all the other sentences supply the story. Not every paragraph must have a topic sentence. Some paragraphs, for example, introduce ideas, relate succeeding items, or present an assortment of facts that lead to no conclusion. The central thought of such paragraphs is difficult to put into a single sentence. Even so, you should use topic sentences whenever you can. You should use them especially in writing reports that discuss a number of topics and subtopics. Using topic sentences forces you to find the central idea of each paragraph and helps you check paragraph unity.

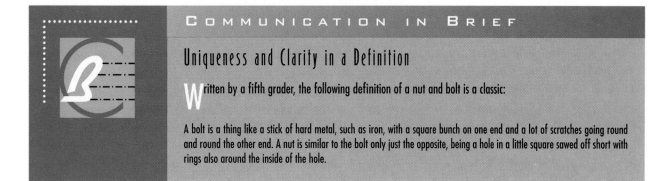

How a topic sentence should fit into a paragraph depends primarily on the subject matter and the writer's plan. Some subject matter develops best if details are presented first and then followed by a conclusion or a summary statement (the topic sentence). Other subject matter develops best if it is introduced by the conclusion or the summary statement. Yet other arrangements are possible. You must make the decision, and you should base it on your best judgment. Your judgment should be helped, however, by a knowledge of the paragraph arrangements most commonly used.

Placement of the topic sentence depends on the writer's plan.

TOPIC SENTENCE FIRST.   The most common paragraph arrangement begins with the topic sentence and continues with the supporting material. As this arrangement fits most units of business information, you should find it useful. In fact, the arrangement is so appropriate for business information that one company's writing manual suggests that it be used for virtually all paragraphs.

The topic sentence can come first.

To illustrate the writing of a paragraph in which the topic sentence comes first, take a paragraph reporting on economists' replies to a survey question asking their view of business activity for the coming year. The facts to be presented are these: 13 percent of the economists expected an increase; 28 percent expected little or no change; 59 percent expected a downturn; 87 percent of those who expected a downturn thought it would come in the first quarter. The obvious conclusion—and the subject for the topic sentence—is that the majority expected a decline in the first quarter. Following this reasoning, we would develop a paragraph like this:

A majority of the economists consulted think that business activity will drop during the first quarter of next year. Of the 185 economists interviewed, 13 percent looked for continued increases in business activity, and 28 percent anticipated little or no change from the present high level. The remaining 59 percent looked for a recession. Of this group, nearly all (87 percent) believed that the downturn would occur during the first quarter of the year.

TOPIC SENTENCE AT END.   The second most common paragraph arrangement places the topic sentence at the end, usually as a conclusion. Paragraphs of this kind usually present the supporting details first, and from these details they lead readers to the conclusion. Such paragraphs often begin with what may appear to be a topic sentence. But the final sentence covers their real meat, as in this illustration:

It can come last.

The significant role of inventories in the economic picture should not be overlooked. At present, inventories represent 3.8 months' supply. Their dollar value is the highest in history. If considered in relation to increased sales, however, they are not excessive. In fact, they are well within the range generally believed to be safe. *Thus, inventories are not likely to cause a downward swing in the economy.*

TOPIC SENTENCE WITHIN THE PARAGRAPH.   A third arrangement places the topic sentence somewhere within the paragraph. This arrangement is rarely used, for good reason. It does not emphasize the topic sentence, although the topic sentence usually deserves emphasis. Still, you can sometimes justify using this arrangement for special effect, as in this example:

Or it can come in the middle.

Numerous materials have been used in manufacturing this part. And many have shown quite satisfactory results. *Material 329, however, is superior to them all.* When built with material 329, the part is almost twice as strong as when built with the next best material. It is also three ounces lighter. Most important, it is cheaper than any of the other products.

LEAVING OUT UNNECESSARY DETAIL

- In writing paragraphs, leave out unnecessary information.

- But deciding what to include is a matter of judgment.

You should include in your paragraphs only the information needed. The chances are that you have more information than the reader needs. Thus, a part of your communication task is to select what you need and discard what you do not need.

What you need, of course, is a matter of judgment. You can judge best by putting yourself in your reader's place. Ask yourself questions such as these: How will the information be used? What information will be used? What will not be used? Then make your decisions. If you follow this procedure, you will probably leave out much that you originally intended to use.

The following paragraph from a memorandum to maintenance workers presents excessive information.

In reviewing the personnel history form you filled out last week, I found an error that needs to be corrected. The section titled "work history" has blank lines for three items of information. The first is for dates employed. The second is for company name. And the third is for type of work performed. On your form you wrote company name only, and it extended across all three blanks. You did not indicate years employed or your duties. This information is important. It is reviewed by your supervisors every time you are considered for promotion or for a pay increase. Therefore, it must be completed. I request that you come by my office and complete this form at your earliest convenience.

The message says much more than the reader needs to know. The goal is to have the reader come to the office, and everything else is of questionable value. Even if some explanation is desirable, would it not be better to explain at the office? This revised memorandum is better:

Please come by my office at your earliest convenience to correct an error in the personnel form you filled out last week.

GIVING THE PARAGRAPHS MOVEMENT

- Each paragraph should move an additional step toward the goal.

Good writing has movement. Movement is the writing quality that takes the reader toward the goal in definite and logical steps, without side trips and backward shifts.

The progress is steadily forward—step by step. The sentences move step by step to reach the paragraph goal, and the paragraphs move step by step to reach the overall goal.

Perhaps movement is best explained by example:

Three reasons justify moving from the Crowton site. First, the building rock in the Crowton area is questionable. The failure of recent geologic explorations in the area appears to confirm suspicions that the Crowton deposits are nearly exhausted. Second, the distances from the Crowton site to major consumption areas make transportation costs unusually high. Obviously, any savings in transportation costs will add to company profits. Third, the obsolescence of much of the equipment at the Crowton plant makes this an ideal time for relocation. The old equipment at the Crowton plant could be scrapped.

The flow of thought in this paragraph is orderly. The first sentence sets up the paragraph structure, and the parts of that structure follow.

SUMMARY BY CHAPTER OBJECTIVES

1. Writing that communicates uses words that the reader understands and sentence structures that organize the message clearly in the reader's mind. It is writing that is *adapted* to the reader.

   1 Explain the role of adaptation in writing clear sentences.

2. In general, you should use short sentences, especially when adapting to readers with low reading ability. Do this in two ways:
   - Limit sentence content by breaking up those that are too long.
   - Use words economically by following these specific suggestions:
     —Avoid cluttering phrases (*if* rather than *in the event that*).
     —Eliminate surplus words—words that contribute nothing (*It will be noted that*).
     —Avoid roundabout ways of saying things (*decreases* rather than *can be observed to be decreasing*).
     —Avoid unnecessary repetition (*In my opinion, I think*).

   2 Write short, clear sentences by limiting sentence content and economizing on words.

3. Give every item you communicate the emphasis it deserves by following these suggestions:
   - Use short sentences to emphasize points.
   - Combine points in longer sentences to de-emphasize them.
   - But how you combine points (by equal treatment, by subordination) determines the emphasis given.

   3 Design sentences that give the right emphasis to content.

4. Achieve unity and clarity in your sentences.
   - Make certain all the information in a sentence belongs together—that it forms a unit. These suggestions help:
     —Eliminate excessive detail.
     —Combine only related thoughts.
     —Avoid illogical constructions.
   - Ensure clarity by following the conventional rules of writing (standards of punctuation, grammar, and such).

   4 Employ unity and clarity in writing effective sentences.

5. Design your paragraphs for clear communication by following these standards:
   - Give the paragraphs unity.
   - Keep the paragraphs short.
   - Use topic sentences effectively, usually at the beginning but sometimes within and at the end of the paragraph.
   - Leave out unessential details.
   - Give the paragraphs movement.

   5 Compose paragraphs that are short and unified, use topic sentences effectively, show movement, and communicate clearly.

CRITICAL THINKING QUESTIONS

1. How are sentence length and sentence design related to adaptation?
2. Discuss this comment: "Long, involved sentences tend to be difficult to understand. Therefore, the shorter the sentence, the better."
3. What is the effect of sentence length on emphasis?
4. How can unity apply equally well to a sentence, to a paragraph, and to longer units of writing?
5. What are the principal causes of lack of unity in sentences?
6. Discuss this comment: "Words carry the message. They would carry the same meanings with or without paragraphing. Therefore, paragraphing has no effect on communication."
7. Defend the use of short paragraphs in report writing.
8. "Topic sentences merely repeat what the other sentences in the paragraph say. As they serve only to add length, they should be eliminated." Discuss.

CRITICAL THINKING EXERCISES

Instructions, Sentences 1–8: Break up these sentences into shorter, more readable sentences.

1. Records were set by both the New York Stock Exchange Composite Index, which closed at 493.24, up 1.65 points, topping its previous high of 491.59, set Wednesday, and Standard & Poor's Industrial Average, which finished at 1133.71, up 2.20, smashing its all-time record of 1131.51, also set in the prior session.
2. Dealers attributed the rate decline to several factors, including expectations that the U.S. Treasury will choose to pay off rather than refinance some $4 billion of government obligations that fall due next month, an action that would absorb even further the available supplies of short-term government securities, leaving more funds chasing skimpier stocks of the securities.
3. If you report your income on a fiscal-year basis ending in 1998, you may not take credit for any tax withheld on your calendar-year 1998 earnings, inasmuch as your taxable year began in 1997, although you may include, as a part of your withholding tax credits against your fiscal 1999 tax liability, the amount of tax withheld during 1998.
4. The Consumer Education Committee is assigned the duties of keeping informed of the qualities of all consumer goods and services, especially of their strengths and shortcomings, of gathering all pertinent information on dealers' sales practices, with emphasis on practices involving honest and reasonable fairness, and of publicizing any of the information collected that may be helpful in educating the consumer.
5. The upswing in business activity that began in 1998 is expected to continue and possibly accelerate in 1999, and gross domestic product should rise by $661 billion, representing an 8 percent increase over 1998, which is significantly higher than the modest 5 percent increase of 1997.
6. As you will not get this part of medicare automatically, even if you are covered by social security, you must sign up for it and pay $7.75 per month, which the government will match, if you want your physician's bills to be covered.
7. Students with approved excused absences from any of the hour examinations have the option of taking a special makeup examination to be given during dead week or of using their average grade on their examinations in the course as their grade for the work missed.
8. Although we have not definitely determined the causes for the decline in sales volume for the month, we know that during this period construction on the street adjacent to the store severely limited traffic flow and that because of resignations in the advertising department promotion efforts dropped well below normal.

Instructions, Sentences 9–38: Revise the following sentences for more economical wording.

9. In view of the fact that we financed the experiment, we were entitled to some profit.
10. We will deliver the goods in the near future.
11. Mr. Watts outlined his development plans on the occasion of his acceptance of the presidency.
12. I will talk to him with regard to the new policy.
13. The candidates who had the most money won.
14. There are many obligations that we must meet.
15. We purchased coats that are lined with rabbit fur.
16. Mary is of the conviction that service has improved.
17. Sales can be detected to have improved over last year.
18. It is essential that we take the actions that are necessary to correct the problem.
19. The chairperson is engaged in the activities of preparing the program.
20. Martin is engaged in the process of revising the application.
21. You should study all new innovations in your field.
22. In all probability, we are likely to suffer a loss this quarter.
23. The requirements for the job require a minimum of three years of experience.
24. In spite of the fact that the bill remains unpaid, they placed another order.
25. We expect to deliver the goods in the event that we receive the money.

26. In accordance with their plans, company officials sold the machinery.

27. This policy exists for the purpose of preventing dishonesty.

28. The salespeople who were most successful received the best rewards.

29. The reader will note that this area ranks in the top 5 percent in per capita income.

30. Our new coats are made of a fabric that is of the wrinkle-resistant variety.

31. Our office is charged with the task of counting supplies not used in production.

32. Their salespeople are of the conviction that service is obsolete.

33. Losses caused by the strike exceeded the amount of $640,000.

34. This condition can be assumed to be critical.

35. Our goal is to effect a change concerning the overtime pay rate.

36. Mr. Wilson replaced the old antiquated machinery with new machinery.

37. We must keep this information from transpiring to others.

38. The consensus of opinion of this group is that Wellington was wrong.

Instructions, Paragraphs 39–43: Rewrite the following paragraphs in two ways to show different placement of the topic sentence and variations in emphasis of contents. Point out the differences in meaning in each of your paragraphs.

39. Jennifer has a good knowledge of office procedures. She works hard. She has performed her job well. She is pleasant most of the time, but she has a bad temper, which has led to many personal problems with the work group. Although I cannot recommend her for promotion, I approve a 5 percent raise for her.

40. Last year our sales increased 7 percent in California and 9 percent in Arizona. Nevada had the highest increase, with 14 percent. Although all states in the western region enjoyed increases, Oregon recorded only a 2 percent gain. Sales in Washington increased 3 percent.

41. I majored in marketing at Darden University and received a B.S. degree in 1998. Among the marketing courses I took were marketing strategy, promotion, marketing research, marketing management, and consumer behavior. These and other courses prepared me specifically for a career in retailing. Included, also, was a one-semester internship in retailing with Macy's Department Stores.

42. Our records show that Penn motors cost more than Oslo motors. The Penns have less breakdown time. They cost more to repair. I recommend that we buy Penn motors the next time we replace worn-out motors. The longer working life offsets Penn's cost disadvantage. So does its better record for breakdown.

43. Recently China ordered a large quantity of wheat from the United States. Likewise, Germany ordered a large quantity. Other countries continued to order heavily, resulting in a dramatic improvement in the outlook for wheat farming. Increased demand by Eastern European countries also contributed to the improved outlook.

Writing for Effect

4

Upon completing this chapter, you will be able to write business communications that emphasize key points and have a positive effect on human relations. To reach this goal, you should be able to

1 Explain the need for effect in writing business messages.

2 Use a conversational style that eliminates the old language of business and "rubber stamps."

3 Use the you-viewpoint to foster goodwill.

4 Employ positive language to achieve goodwill and other desired effects.

5 Explain the techniques of achieving courtesy.

6 Use the four major techniques for emphasis in writing.

7 Write documents that flow smoothly through the use of a logical order helped by the four major transitional devices.

Conveying Business Etiquette through Emphasis on Human Relations

To prepare yourself for this chapter, once again play the role of Max Schwartz's supervisor. As you review Max's work, you note that he writes more than reports. Like many people in office positions, he writes more letters and memos than anything else.

The fact that he writes many letters and memos causes you to think. What if he writes letters the way he writes reports? These documents go outside the company and are read by customers, fellow businesspeople, and others. Because poorly written documents would give bad impressions of the company, you decide to review Max's documents. Typical of what you find is this letter denying a request for an adjustment:

Dear Mr. Morley:

Your Dec. 3d complaint was received and contents noted. After reviewing the facts, I regret to report that I must refuse your claim. If you will read the warranty brochure, you will see that the shelving you bought is designed for light loads—a maximum of 800 pounds. You should have bought the heavy-duty product.

I regret the damage this mistake caused you and trust that you will see our position. Hoping to be of service to you in the future, I remain,

Sincerely yours,

In this letter you detect more than just the readability problem you saw in Max's reports—you see serious problems. The words are not polite. Instead of showing concern for the reader, they are blunt, tactless, and unfriendly. Overall, they leave a bad impression in the reader's mind—the impression of a writer, and a business, unconcerned about the needs for good business etiquette.

BUSINESS ETIQUETTE AND THE NEED FOR EFFECT

As noted in the preceding chapters, clarity will be your major concern in much of the writing you do in business. It will be your major concern in most of the writing you do to communicate within the organization—reports, memorandums, email, messages, proposals, and so on. In such writing, your primary concern will be to communicate information. Whatever you do to communicate information quickly and easily will be appropriate.

■ Written communication within a business primarily requires clarity.

When you write letters, however, you will be concerned about communicating more than information. The information in the letters will be important, of course. In fact, it will probably be the most important part. But you will also need to communicate certain effects—primarily effects that display your good business etiquette.

■ Letter writing requires clarity and planned effect. The goodwill effect is valuable to business.

One effect you will need to communicate is the goodwill effect. Building goodwill through written messages is good business practice. Wise business leaders know that the success of their business is affected by what people think about the business. They know that what people think about a business is influenced by their human contact with that business—the services they receive, how they are treated, the manners (etiquette) displayed, and such. The written word is a major form of human contact.

The goodwill effect in messages is not desirable for business reasons alone. It is, quite simply, the effect most of us want in our relations with people. The things we do and say to create goodwill are the things we enjoy doing and saying. They are friendly, courteous things that make relations between people enjoyable. Most of us would want to do and say them even if they were not profitable. Clearly, they display the good manners of business practice. They display good business etiquette.

■ Most people enjoy building goodwill.

As you read the following chapters, you will see that other effects sometimes ensure the success of written messages. For example, in writing to persuade a reader to accept an unfavorable decision, you can use the techniques of persuasion. In applying for a job, you can use writing techniques that emphasize your qualifications. And in telling bad news,

■ For their success, letters and memos often require other effects.

you can use techniques that play down the unhappy parts. These are but a few of the effects that you may find helpful in writing.

Getting such effects in letters is largely a matter of skillful writing and of understanding how people respond to words. It involves keeping certain attitudes in mind and using certain writing techniques to work them into your documents. The following review of these attitudes and techniques should help you get the effects you need.

- Getting the desired effects is a matter of writing skill and of understanding people.

CONVERSATIONAL STYLE

One technique that helps build the goodwill effect is to write in conversational language. By conversational language we mean language that resembles conversation. It is warm and natural. Such language leaves an impression that people like. It is also the language we use most and understand best. Because it is easily understood, it is good business etiquette to use it.

- Writing in conversational language has a favorable effect.

RESISTING THE TENDENCY TO BE FORMAL

Writing conversationally is not as easy as you might think, because most of us tend to write formally. When faced with a writing task, we change character. Instead of writing in friendly, conversational language, we write in stiff and stilted words. We seek the big word, the difficult word. The result is a cold and unnatural style—one that doesn't produce the goodwill effect you want your messages to have. The following examples illustrate this problem and how to correct it.

- Writing in conversational language is not easy, for we tend to be stiff and formal.

Stiff and Dull	**Conversational**
Reference is made to your May 7 email, in which you describe the approved procedure for initiating a claim.	Please refer to your May 7 email, in which you tell how to file a claim.
Enclosed herewith is the brochure about which you make inquiry.	Enclosed is the brochure you asked about.
In reply to your July 11 letter, please be informed that your adherence to instructions outlined therein will greatly facilitate attainment of our objective.	By following the procedures you listed in your July 11 letter, you will help us reach our goal.
This is in reply to your letter of December 1, expressing concern that you do not have a high school diploma and asking if a GED would suffice as prerequisite for the TAA Training Program.	The GED you mention in your December 1 letter qualifies you for the TAA Training Program.
I shall be most pleased to avail myself of your kind suggestion when and if prices decline.	I'll gladly follow your suggestion if the price falls.

AVOIDING THE OLD LANGUAGE OF BUSINESS

Adding to our natural difficulty in writing business messages conversationally are some deep-rooted historical influences. Unfortunately, the early English business writers borrowed heavily from the formal language of the law and from the flowery language of the nobility. From these two sources they developed a style of writing that became known as the "language of business." It was a cold, stiff, and unnatural style. But it was generally accepted throughout the English-speaking world. The following expressions typify this style:

- The early English business writers developed an unnatural style for letters. This "language of business" was influenced by legal language and the language of the nobility.

In Openings	**In Contents**	**In Closings**
Your letter of the 7th inst. received and contents duly noted	Please be advised	Thanking you in advance
	Said matter	Trusting this will meet with your favor
We beg to advise	In due course	We beg to remain
In compliance with yours of even date	Inst., prox., ult.	Anticipating your favorable response
Your esteemed favor at hand	Kind favor	Assuring you of our cooperation

A Poem: The Old Language of Business

We beg to advise and wish to state
That yours has arrived of recent date.
We have it before us, its contents noted.
Herewith enclosed, the prices we quoted.
Regarding the matter, and due to the fact
That up until now your order we've lacked,
We hope you will not delay it unduly
And beg to remain yours very truly,

Anonymous

In Openings

This is to inform you

We have before us

Responding to yours of even date

Yours of the 10th ultimo to hand

Your favor received

In Contents

Kind order

Re:

In re

Said matter

Deem it advisable

Wherein you state as per our letter

In reply wish to state

Attached hereto

In Closings

Hoping to receive

I am, Dear Sir, yours respectfully

Trusting to be favored by your further orders, we are, Gentlemen, yours faithfully

---

This style of writing business letters reached a peak in the late 1800s, and it was still in much use in the early years of the 19th century. A typical business letter of this period would begin something like this: "Yours of the 7th inst. received and contents duly noted. In reply wish to state. . . ." It would end something like this: "Hoping to hear from you at your earliest convenience, I remain, Yours Sincerely . . ." The text between these parts would be equally stiff and unnatural. Further illustrating writing in the old language of business is this model letter from a leading letter book of the day:

Gentlemen,

We have to thank you for yours of the 28th inst., enclosing cheque for $95.12 in payment of our invoice of the 17th inst. Formal receipt enclosed herewith. Trusting to be favored with your further orders,

We are, Gentlemen,
Yours faithfully,[1]

Although the old language of business has faded away, some of its expressions remain with us. These include "enclosed please find," "please be advised," "this is to inform," "deem it advisable," and "take the liberty." You should not use them. Perhaps the most common remnants of the old language of business are the dangling closes (endings that trail off into the signature). Typical examples are "trusting to hear from you," "thanking you in advance, I remain," and "hoping to hear from you." These closes may express sincere feeling, but they belong to the past. You should leave them there.

- This style reached a peak in the late 1800s. "Yours of the 7th inst. received and contents duly noted" typifies this manner of writing.

- The old language of business has faded away, but some of its expressions remain (*please be advised, enclosed please find*). Do not use them.

---

[1] *Pitman's Mercantile Correspondence* (London: Sir Isaac Pitman & Sons, n.d.), p. 18.

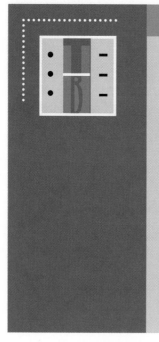

Grammar Checkers Help Identify Clichés

While not perfect, some grammar checkers will help writers identify clichés that creep into their writing. The checker here illustrates that it found a cliché, identified it as a cliché, and provided two suggestions for correcting it. Although the programs can help, writers still need to be able to identify the trite and overused expressions the software misses. Also, writers need to be able to recast sentences for clarity and sincerity.

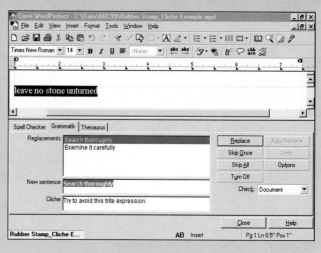

CUTTING OUT "RUBBER STAMPS"

■ Rubber stamps are expressions used by habit every time a certain type of situation occurs.

Rubber stamps (also called *clichés*) are expressions used by habit every time a certain type of situation occurs. They are used without thought and do not fit the present situation exclusively. As the term indicates, they are used much as you would use a rubber stamp.

■ They give the effect of routine treatment. It is better to use words written for the present case.

Because they are used routinely, rubber stamps communicate the effect of routine treatment, which is not likely to impress readers favorably. Such treatment tells readers that the writer has no special concern for them—that the present case is being handled in the same way as others. In contrast, words specially selected for this case are likely to impress. They show the writer's concern for and interest in the readers. Clearly, specially selected wording is the better choice for producing a goodwill effect. Some examples of rubber stamps you have no doubt heard before are listed below. These phrases, while once quite appropriate, have become stale with overuse.

a blessing in disguise

as good as gold

back against the wall

call the shots

last but not least

learning the ropes

leave no stone unturned

to add insult to injury

■ Expressions from the old language of business are rubber stamps. Some new ones exist.

Expressions from the old language of business account for many of the rubber stamps now in use. But modern business writers have developed many more. A widely used one is the "thank you for your letter" form of opening sentence. Its intent may be sincere, but its overuse makes it routine. Also overused is the "if I can be of any further assistance, do not hesitate to call on me" type of close. Other examples of modern business-letter rubber stamps are the following:

I am happy to be able to answer your letter.

I have received your letter.

This will acknowledge receipt of . . . .

According to our records . . . .

This is to inform you that . . . .

In accordance with your instructions . . . .

You do not need to know all the rubber stamps to stop using them. You do not even need to be able to recognize them. You only need to write in the language of good conversation, for these worn-out expressions are not a part of most conversational vocabularies. If you use rubber stamps at all, probably you learned them from reading other people's writings.

■ You can avoid rubber stamps by writing in your conversational vocabulary.

PROOF THROUGH CONTRASTING EXAMPLES

The advantages of conversational writing over writing marked by old business language and rubber stamps are best proved by example. As you read the following contrasting sentences, note the overall effects of the words. The goodwill advantages of conversational writing are obvious.

Dull and Stiff	**Friendly and Conversational**
This is to advise that we deem it a great pleasure to approve subject of your request as per letter of the 12th inst.	Yes, you certainly may use the equipment you asked about in your letter of August 12.
Pursuant to this matter, I wish to state that the aforementioned provisions are unmistakably clear.	These contract provisions are clear on this point.
This will acknowledge receipt of your May 10th order for four dozen Hunt slacks. Please be advised that they will be shipped in accordance with your instructions by Green Arrow Motor Freight on May 16.	Four dozen Hunt slacks should reach your store by the 18th. As you instructed, they were shipped today by Green Arrow Motor Freight.
The undersigned wishes to advise that the aforementioned contract is at hand.	I have the contract.
Please be advised that you should sign the form before the 1st.	You should sign the form before the 1st.
Hoping this meets with your approval	I hope you approve.
Submitted herewith is your notification of our compliance with subject standards.	Attached is notification of our compliance with the standards.
Assuring you of our continued cooperation, we remain	We will continue to cooperate.
Thanking you in advance	I'll sincerely appreciate . . . .

In face-to-face communication, words, voice, facial expressions, gestures, and such combine to determine the effect of the message. In writing, the printed word alone must do the job.

Dull and Stiff	**Friendly and Conversational**
Herewith enclosed please find	Enclosed is . . . .
I deem it advisable	I suggest . . . .
I herewith hand you	Here is . . . .
Kindly advise at an early date.	Please let me know soon.

YOU-VIEWPOINT

■ The you-viewpoint produces goodwill and influences people favorably.

■ The you-viewpoint emphasizes the reader's interests. It is an attitude of mind involving more than the use of *you* and *yours.*

Writing from the you-viewpoint (also called *you-attitude*) is another technique for building goodwill in written messages. As you will see in following chapters, it focuses interest on the reader. Thus, it is a technique for persuasion and for influencing people favorably. It is fundamental in the practice of business etiquette.

In a broad sense, you-viewpoint writing emphasizes the reader's interests and concerns. It emphasizes *you* and *your* and de-emphasizes *we* and *our.* But it is more than a matter of just using second-person pronouns. *You* and *your* can appear prominently in sentences that emphasize the we-viewpoint, as in this example: "If you do not pay by the 15th, you must pay a penalty." Likewise, *we* and *mine* can appear in sentences that emphasize the you-viewpoint, as in this example: "We will do whatever we can to protect your investment." The point is that the you-viewpoint is an attitude of mind. It is the attitude that places the reader in the center of things. Sometimes it just involves being friendly and treating people in the way they like to be treated. Sometimes it involves skillfully handling people with carefully chosen words to make a desired impression. It involves all these things and more.

THE YOU-VIEWPOINT ILLUSTRATED

Although the you-viewpoint involves much more than word selection, examples of word selection help explain the technique. First, take the case of a person writing to present good news. This person could write from a self-centered point of view, beginning with such words as "I am happy to report . . ." Or he or she could begin with the you-viewpoint words "You will be happy to know . . .". The messages are much the same, but the effects are different.

Next, take the case of a writer who must inform the reader that a request for credit has been approved. A we-viewpoint beginning could take this form: "We are pleased to have your new account." Some readers might view these words favorably. But some would sense a self-centered writer concerned primarily with making money. A you-viewpoint beginning would go something like this: "Your new charge account is now open for your convenience."

The third case is that of an advertising copywriter who must describe the merits of a razor. Advertising copywriters know the value of the you-viewpoint perhaps better than any other group. So no advertising copywriter would write anything like this: "We make Willett razors in three weights—light, medium, and heavy." An advertising copywriter would probably bring the reader into the center of things and write about the product in reader-satisfaction language: "So that you can choose the one razor that is just right for your beard, Willett makes razors for you in three weights—light, medium, and heavy."

■ Even a bad-news situation can benefit from you-viewpoint wording.

The you-viewpoint can even be used in bad-news messages. For example, take the case of an executive who must say no to a professor's request for help on a research project. The bad news is made especially bad when it is presented in we-viewpoint words: "We cannot comply with your request to use our office personnel on your project, for it would cost us more than we can afford." A skilled writer using the you-viewpoint would look at the situation from this reader's point of view, find an explanation likely to satisfy this reader, and present the explanation in you-viewpoint language. The you-viewpoint response might take this form: "As a business professor well acquainted with the need for economizing in all phases of office operations, you will understand why we must limit our personnel to work in our office."

The following contrasting examples demonstrate the different effects that changes in viewpoint produce. With a bit of imagination, you should be able to supply information on the situations they cover.

We-Viewpoint	You-Viewpoint
We are happy to have your order for Hewlett-Packard products, which we are sending today by UPS.	Your selection of Hewlett-Packard products should reach you by Saturday, as they were shipped by UPS today.
We sell the Forever cutlery set for the low price of $4 each and suggest a retail price of $6.50.	You can reap a $2.50 profit on each Forever set you sell at $6.50, for your cost is only $4.
Our policy prohibits us from permitting outside groups to use our equipment except on a cash-rental basis.	As your tax dollar pays our office expense, you will appreciate our policy of cutting operating costs by renting our equipment.
We have been quite tolerant of your past-due account and must now demand payment.	If you are to continue to enjoy the benefits of credit buying, you must clear your account now.
We have received your report of May 1.	Thank you for your report of May 1.
So that we may complete our file records on you, we ask that you submit to us your January report.	So that your file records may be completed, please send us your January report.
We have shipped the two dozen Crown desk sets you ordered.	Your two dozen Crown desk sets should reach you with this letter.
We require that you sign the sales slip before we will charge to your account.	For your protection, you are charged only after you have signed the sales slip.

A POINT OF CONTROVERSY

The you-viewpoint has been a matter of some controversy. Its critics point out two major shortcomings: (1) it is insincere and (2) it is manipulative. In either event, they argue, the technique is dishonest. It is better, they say, to just "tell it as it is."

These arguments have some merit. Without question, the you-viewpoint can be used to the point of being insincere; and it can be obvious flattery. Those who favor the technique argue that insincerity and flattery need not—in fact, should not—be the result of you-viewpoint effort. The objective is to treat people courteously—the way they like to be treated. People like to be singled out for attention. They are naturally more interested in themselves than in the writer. Overuse of the technique, the defenders argue, does not justify not using it. Their argument is supported by research showing that a majority of personality types, especially the friendlier and more sensitive, react favorably to you-viewpoint treatment.[2] A minority, mainly the less sensitive and harsher personalities, are less susceptible. A more recent research study compared readers' responses to a case written to determine the effect of the you-attitude. The study evaluated the readers' perception of the writer's tone, commitment to comply to the message, and satisfaction. It found support for using the you-viewpoint.[3]

On the matter of manipulative use of the you-viewpoint, we must again concede a point. It is a technique of persuasion, and persuasion may have bad as well as good goals. Supporters of the you-viewpoint argue that it is bad goals and not the techniques used to reach them that should be condemned. Persuasion techniques used to reach good goals are good.

The correct approach appears to lie somewhere between the extremes. You do not have to use the you-viewpoint exclusively or eliminate it. You can take a middle ground. You can use the you-viewpoint when it is friendly and sincere and when your goals are good. In such cases, using the you-viewpoint is "telling it as it is"—or at least as it should be. With this position in mind, we apply the technique in the following chapters.

■ Some say that the you-viewpoint is insincere and manipulative. It can be insincere, but it need not be. Using the you-viewpoint is just being courteous. Research supports its use.

■ The you-viewpoint can manipulate. But condemn the goal, not the technique.

■ A middle-ground approach is best. Use the you-viewpoint when it is the right thing to do.

---

[2] Sam J. Bruno, "The Effects of Personality Traits on the Perception of Written Mass Communication," doctoral dissertation, Louisiana State University, Baton Rouge, 1971.

[3] Annette N. Shelby and Lamar Reinsch, Jr., "Positive Emphasis and You-Attitude: An Empirical Study," *Journal of Business Communication,* October 1995, p. 319.

ACCENT ON POSITIVE LANGUAGE

■ Of the many ways of saying anything, each has a unique meaning.

Whether your written message achieves its goal will often depend on the words you use. As you know, one can say anything in many ways, and each way conveys a different meaning. Much of the difference lies in the meanings of words.

Effects of Words

■ Positive words are usually best for message goals, especially when persuasion and goodwill are needed.

Positive words are usually best for achieving your message goals. This is not to say that negative words have no place in business writing. Such words are strong and give emphasis, and you will sometimes want to use them. But your need will usually be for positive words, for such words are more likely to produce the effects you seek. When your goal is to change someone's position, for example, positive words are most likely to do the job. They tend to put the reader in the right frame of mind, and they emphasize the pleasant aspects of the goal. They also create the goodwill atmosphere we seek in most letters.

■ Negative words stir up resistance and hurt goodwill.

Negative words tend to produce the opposite effects. They may stir up your reader's resistance to your goals, and they are likely to be highly destructive of goodwill. Thus, to reach your writing goals, you will need to study carefully the negativeness and positiveness of your words. You will need to select the words that are most appropriate in each case.

■ So beware of strongly negative words (*mistake, problem*), words that deny (*no, do not*), and ugly words (*itch, guts*).

In doing this you should generally be wary of strongly negative words. These words convey unhappy and unpleasant thoughts, and such thoughts usually detract from your goal. They include such words as *mistake, problem, error, damage, loss,* and *failure.* There are also words that deny—words such as *no, do not, refuse,* and *stop.* And there are words whose sounds or meanings have unpleasant effects. Examples would differ from person to person, but many would probably agree on these: *itch, guts, scratch, grime, sloppy, sticky, bloody,* and *nauseous.* Or how about *gummy, slimy, bilious,* and *soggy?* Run these negative words through your mind and think about the meanings they produce. You should find it easy to see that they tend to work against most of the goals you may have in your messages.

Examples of Word Choice

To illustrate your positive-to-negative word choices in handling written messages, take the case of a company executive who had to deny a local civic group's request to use the company's meeting facilities. To soften the refusal, the executive could let the group use a conference room, which might be somewhat small for its purpose. The executive came up with this totally negative response:

We *regret* to inform you that we *cannot* permit you to use our clubhouse for your meeting, as the Ladies Investment Club asked for it first. We can, however, let you use our conference room, but it seats *only* 60.

The negative words are italicized. First, the positively intended message "We *regret* to inform you" is an unmistakable sign of coming bad news. *"Cannot* permit" contains an unnecessarily harsh meaning. And notice how the good-news part of the message is handicapped by the limiting word *only.*

Had the executive searched for more positive ways of covering the same situation, he or she might have written:

Although the Ladies Investment Club has reserved the clubhouse for Saturday, we can instead offer you our conference room, which seats 60.

Not a single negative word appears in this version. Both approaches achieve the primary objective of denying a request, but their effects on the reader differ sharply. There is no question as to which approach does the better job of building and holding goodwill.

For a second illustration, take the case of a correspondent who must write a letter granting the claim of a woman for cosmetics damaged in transit. Granting the claim, of course, is the most positive ending that such a situation can have. Even though this customer has had a somewhat unhappy experience, she is receiving what she wants. The negative language of an unskilled writer, however, can so vividly recall the unhappy aspects of the problem that the happy solution is moved to the background. As this negative version of the message illustrates, the effect is to damage the reader's goodwill:

We received your claim in which you contend that we were responsible for *damage* to three cases of Estée Lauder lotion. We assure you that we sincerely *regret* the *problems* this has caused you. Even though we feel in all sincerity that your receiving clerks may have been *negligent*, we will assume the *blame* and replace the *damaged* merchandise.

Obviously, this version grants the claim grudgingly, and the company would profit from such an approach only if there were extenuating circumstances. The phrase "in which you contend" clearly implies some doubt about the legitimacy of the claim. Even the sincerely intended expression of regret only recalls to the reader's mind the event that caused all the trouble. And the negatives *blame* and *damage* only strengthen the recollection. Certainly, this approach is not conducive to goodwill.

In the following version of the same message, the writer refers only to positive aspects of the situation—what can be done to settle the problem. The job is done without using a negative word and without mentioning the situation being corrected or suspicions concerning the honesty of the claim. The goodwill effect of this approach is likely to maintain business relations with the reader:

Three cases of Estée Lauder lotion are on their way to you by Mercury Freight and should be on your sales floor by Saturday.

For additional illustrations, compare the differing results obtained from these contrasting positive-negative versions of letter messages (italics mark the negative words):

Negative	Positive
You *failed* to give us the fabric specifications of the chair you ordered.	So that you may have the one chair you want, will you please check your choice of fabric on the enclosed card?
Smoking is *not* permitted anywhere except in the lobby.	Smoking is permitted in the lobby only.
We *cannot* deliver until Friday.	We can deliver the goods on Friday.
Chock-O-Nuts do not have that *gummy, runny* coating that makes some candies *stick* together when they get hot.	The rich chocolate coating of Chock-O-Nuts stays crispy good throughout the summer months.
You were *wrong* in your conclusion, for paragraph 3 of our agreement clearly states	You will agree after reading paragraph 3 of our agreement that . . . .
We *regret* that we *overlooked* your coverage on this equipment and apologize for the *trouble* and *concern* it must have caused you.	You were quite right in believing that you have coverage on the equipment. We appreciate your calling the matter to our attention.
We *regret* to inform you that we must deny your request for credit.	For the time being, we can serve you on a cash basis only.
You should have known that the camera lens *cannot* be cleaned with tissue, for it is clearly explained in the instructions.	The instructions explain why the camera lens should be cleaned only with a nonscratch cloth.
Your May 7 *complaint* about our remote control is *not* supported by the evidence.	Review of the situation described in your May 7 letter explains what happened when you used the remote control.

COURTESY

A major contributor to goodwill in business documents is courtesy. By courtesy we mean treating people with respect and friendly human concern. Used in business messages, courtesy is the foundation of business etiquette. It produces friendly relations between people. The result is a better human climate for solving business problems and doing business.

Developing courtesy in a message involves a variety of specific techniques. First, it involves the three discussed previously: writing in conversational language, employing the you-viewpoint, and choosing words for positive effect. It also involves other techniques.

■ Courtesy is a major contributor to goodwill in business documents.

■ Courtesy involves the preceding goodwill techniques.

COMMUNICATION IN BRIEF

A French General's Justification of Politeness

Once, at a diplomatic function, the great World War I leader Marshal Foch was maneuvered into a position in which he had to defend French politeness.

"There is nothing in it but wind," Foch's critic sneered.

"There is nothing in a tire but wind," the marshal responded politely, "but it makes riding in a car very smooth and pleasant."

SINGLING OUT YOUR READER

It also involves writing directly for the one reader.

One of the other techniques is to single out and write directly to your reader. Messages that appear routine have a cold, impersonal effect. On the other hand, messages that appear to be written for one reader tend to make the reader feel important and appreciated.

This means writing for the one situation.

To single out your reader in a message, you should write for the one situation. What you say throughout the document should make it clear that the reader is getting individual treatment. For example, a message granting a professor permission to quote company material in the professor's book could end with "We wish you the best of success on the book." This specially adapted comment is better than one that fits any similar case: "If we can be of further assistance, please let us know." Using the reader's name in the message text is another good way to show that the reader is being given special treatment. We can gain the reader's favor by occasionally making such references as "You are correct, Mr. Brock" or "As you know, Ms. Smith."

REFRAINING FROM PREACHING

The effect of courtesy is helped by not preaching (lecturing).

You can help give your documents a courteous effect by not preaching—that is, by avoiding the tone of a lecture or a sermon. Except in the rare cases in which the reader looks up to the writer, a preaching tone hurts goodwill. We human beings like to be treated as equals. We do not want to be bossed or talked down to. Thus, writing that suggests unequal writer-reader relations is likely to make the reader unhappy.

Usually preaching is not intended. It often results from efforts to persuade.

Preaching is usually not intended. It often occurs when the writer is trying to convince the reader of something, as in this example:

You must take advantage of savings like this if you are to be successful. The pennies you save pile up. In time you will have dollars.

It is insulting to tell the reader something quite elementary as if it were not known. Such obvious information should be omitted.

Elementary, flat, and obvious statements often sound preachy.

Likewise, flat statements of the obvious fall into the preachy category. Statements like "Rapid inventory turnover means greater profits" are obvious to the experienced retailer and would probably produce negative reactions. So would most statements including such phrases as "you need," "you want," "you should," and "you must," for they tend to talk down to the reader.

Another form of preachiness takes this obvious question-and-answer pattern: "Would you like to make a deal that would make you a 38 percent profit? Of course you would!" What intelligent and self-respecting retailer would not be offended by this approach?

DOING MORE THAN IS EXPECTED

Doing more than necessary builds goodwill.

One sure way to gain goodwill is to do a little bit more than you have to do for your reader. We are all aware of how helpful little extra acts are in other areas of our personal relationships. Too many of us, however, do not use them in our messages. Perhaps in the mistaken belief that we are being concise, we include only the barest essentials in our messages. The result is brusque, hurried treatment, which is inconsistent with our efforts to build goodwill.

The writer of a letter refusing a request for use of company equipment, for example, needs only to say no to accomplish the primary goal. This answer, of course, is blunt and totally without courtesy. A goodwill-conscious writer would explain and justify the refusal, perhaps suggesting alternative steps that the reader might take. A wholesaler's brief extra sentence to wish a retailer good luck on a coming promotion is worth the effort. So are an insurance agent's few words of congratulations in a letter to a policyholder who has earned some distinction.

Likewise, a salesperson uses good judgment in an acknowledgment letter that includes helpful suggestions about using the goods ordered. And in messages to customers a writer for a sales organization can justifiably include a few words about new merchandise received, new services provided, price reductions, and so on.

To those who say that these suggestions are inconsistent with the need for conciseness, we must answer that the information we speak of is needed to build goodwill. Conciseness concerns the number of words needed to say what you must say. It never involves leaving out information vital to any of your objectives. On the other hand, nothing we have said should be interpreted to mean that any kind or amount of extra information is justified. You must take care to use only the extra information you need to reach your goal.

■ As the extras add length, they appear not to be concise. But conciseness means word economy—not leaving out essentials.

AVOIDING ANGER

Expressing anger in messages—letting off steam—may sometimes help you emotionally. But anger helps achieve the goal of a message only when that goal is to anger the reader. The effect of angry words is to make the reader angry. With both writer and reader angry, the two are not likely to get together on whatever the message is about.

To illustrate the effect of anger, take the case of an insurance company correspondent who must write a letter telling a policyholder that the policyholder has made a mistake in interpreting the policy and is not covered on the matter in question. The correspondent, feeling that any fool should be able to read the policy, might respond in these angry words:

■ Rarely is anger justified in messages. It destroys goodwill.

If you had read Section IV of your policy, you would know that you are not covered on accidents that occur on water.

One might argue that these words "tell it as it is"—that what they say is true. Even so, they show anger and lack tact. Their obvious effect is to make the reader angry. A more tactful writer would refer courteously to the point of misunderstanding:

As a review of Section IV of your policy indicates, you are covered on accidents that occur on the grounds of your residence only.

Most of the comments made in anger do not provide needed information but merely serve to let the writer blow off steam. Such comments take many forms—sarcasm, insults, exclamations. You can see from the following examples that you should not use them in your letters:

No doubt, you expect us to hold your hand.

I cannot understand your negligence.

This is the third time you have permitted your account to be delinquent.

We will not tolerate this condition.

Your careless attitude has caused us a loss in sales.

We have had it!

We have no intention of permitting this condition to continue.

The language used in a letter communicates more than the message. It tells how friendly, how formal, how careful the writer is—and more.

BEING SINCERE

- Efforts to be courteous must be sincere.

Courteous treatment is sincere treatment. If your messages are to be effective, people must believe you. You must convince them that you mean what you say and that your efforts to be courteous and friendly are well intended. That is, your messages must have the quality of sincerity.

- Sincerity results from believing in the techniques of courtesy.

The best way of getting sincerity into your writing is to believe in the techniques you use. If you honestly want to be courteous, if you honestly believe that you-viewpoint treatment leads to harmonious relations, and if you honestly think that tactful treatment spares your reader's sensitive feelings, you are likely to apply these techniques sincerely. Your sincerity will show in your writing.

- The goodwill effort can be overdone. Too much you-viewpoint sounds insincere.

OVERDOING THE GOODWILL TECHNIQUES. There are, however, two major areas that you might alertly check. The first is the overdoing of your goodwill techniques. Perhaps through insincerity or as a result of overzealous effort, the goodwill techniques are frequently overdone. For example, you can easily refer too often to your reader by name in your efforts to write to the one person. Also, as shown in the following example, you-viewpoint effort can go beyond the bounds of reason.

So that you may be able to buy Kantrell equipment at an extremely low price and sell it at a tremendous profit, we now offer you the complete line at a 50 percent price reduction.

The following example, included in a form letter from the company president to a new charge customer, has a touch of unbelievability:

I was delighted today to see your name listed among Morgan's new charge customers.

Or how about this one, taken from an adjustment letter of a large department store?

We are extremely pleased to be able to help you and want you to know that your satisfaction means more than anything to us.

- Exaggerated statements are obviously insincere.

AVOIDING EXAGGERATION. The second area that you should check is exaggerated statements. It is easy to see through most exaggerated statements; thus, they can give a mark of insincerity to your message. Exaggerations are overstatements of facts. Although some exaggeration is conventional in sales writing, even here bounds of propriety exist. The following examples clearly overstep these bounds:

Already thousands of new customers are beating paths to the doors of Martin dealers.

Never has there been, nor will there be, a fan as smooth running and whispering quiet as the North Wind.

Everywhere coffee drinkers meet, they are talking about the amazing whiteness Cafree gives their teeth.

Many exaggerated statements involve the use of superlatives. All of us use them, but only rarely do they fit the reality about which we communicate. Words like *greatest, most amazing, finest, healthiest,* and *strongest* are seldom appropriate. Other strong words may have similar effects—for example, *extraordinary, stupendous, delicious, more than happy, sensational, terrific, revolutionary, colossal,* and *perfection.* Such words cause us to question; we rarely believe them.

■ Superlatives (*greatest, finest, strongest*) often suggest exaggeration.

THE ROLE OF EMPHASIS

Getting desired effects in writing often involves giving proper emphasis to the items in the message. Every message contains a number of facts, ideas, and so on that must be presented. Some of these items are more important than others. For example, the main goal of a message is very important. Supporting explanations and incidental facts are less important. A part of your job as a writer is to determine the importance of each item and to give each item the emphasis it deserves.

■ Emphasis also determines effect. Every item communicated should get the proper emphasis.

To give each item in your message proper emphasis, you must use certain techniques. By far the most useful are these four: position, space, structure, and mechanical devices. The following paragraphs explain each.

■ There are four basic emphasis techniques.

EMPHASIS BY POSITION

The beginnings and endings of a writing unit carry more emphasis than the center parts. This rule of emphasis applies whether the unit is the message, a paragraph of the message, or a sentence within the paragraph. We do not know why this is so. Some authorities think that the reader's fresh mental energy explains beginning emphasis. Some say that the last parts stand out because they are the most recent in the reader's mind. Whatever the explanation, research has suggested that this emphasis technique works.

■ Position determines emphasis. Beginnings and endings carry emphasis.

In the message as a whole, the beginning and the closing are the major emphasis positions. Thus, you must be especially mindful of what you put in these places. The beginnings and endings of the internal paragraphs are secondary emphasis positions. Your de-

"Has it ever occurred to you, Leland, that maybe you're too negative?" (*From* The Wall Street Journal, *with permission of Cartoon Features Syndicate.*)

sign of each paragraph should take this into account. To a lesser extent, the first and last words of each sentence carry more emphasis than the middle ones. Even in your sentence design, you can help determine the emphasis that your reader will give the points in your message. In summary, your organizational plan should place the points you want to stand out in these beginning and ending positions. You should bury the points you do not want to emphasize between these positions.

■ The first and last sentences of a message, the first and last sentences of a paragraph, and the first and last words of a sentence all carry more emphasis than the middle parts.

SPACE AND EMPHASIS

■ The more space a topic is given, the more emphasis the topic receives.

The more you say about something, the more emphasis you give it; and the less you say about something, the less emphasis you give it. If your message devotes a full paragraph to one point and a scant sentence to another, the first point receives more emphasis. To give the desired effect in your message, you will need to say just enough about each item of information you present.

SENTENCE STRUCTURE AND EMPHASIS

■ Sentence structure determines emphasis. Short, simple sentences emphasize content; long, involved ones do not.

As we noted in Chapter 3, short, simple sentences call attention to their content and long, involved ones do not. In applying this emphasis technique to your writing, carefully consider the possible sentence arrangements of your information. Place the more important information in short, simple sentences so that it will not have to compete with other information for the reader's attention. Combine the less important information, taking care that the relationships are logical. In your combination sentences, place the more important material in independent clauses and the less important information in subordinate structures.

MECHANICAL MEANS OF EMPHASIS

■ Mechanical devices (underscore, color, diagrams, and the like) also give emphasis to content.

Perhaps the most obvious emphasis techniques are those that use mechanical devices. By *mechanical devices* we mean any of the things that we can do physically to give the printed word emphasis. The most common of these devices are the underscore, quotation marks, italics, boldface type, and solid capitals. Lines, arrows, and diagrams can also call attention to certain parts. So can color, special type, and drawings. These techniques are infrequently used in business documents, with the possible exception of sales letters.

COHERENCE

■ Messages should be coherent. The relationships of parts should be clear.

Your documents are composed of independent bits of information. But these bits of information do not communicate the whole message. A part of the message is told in the relationships of the facts presented. Thus, to communicate your message successfully, you must do more than communicate facts. You must also make the relationships clear. Making these relationships clear is the task of giving coherence to your message.

■ Presenting information in logical order helps coherence.

The best thing you can do to give your message coherence is to arrange its information in a logical order—an order appropriate for the strategy of the one case. So important is this matter to message writing that it is the primary topic of discussion in following chapters. Thus, we will postpone discussion of this vital part of coherence. But logical organization is usually not enough. Various techniques are needed to bridge or tie together the information presented. These techniques are known as *transitional devices*. We will discuss the four major ones: tie-in sentences, repetition of key words, use of pronouns, and use of transitional words.

TIE-IN SENTENCES

■ Sentences can be designed to tie together succeeding thoughts.

By structuring your message so that one idea sets up the next, you can skillfully relate the ideas. That is, you can design the sentences to tie in two successive ideas. Notice in the following example how a job applicant tied together the first two sentences of the letter:

As a result of increasing demand for precision instruments in the Bloomington boom area, won't you soon need another experienced and trained salesperson to call on your technical accounts there?

With seven successful years of selling Morris instruments and a degree in civil engineering, I believe I have the qualifications to do this job.

Now substitute the following sentence for the second sentence above and note the abrupt shift it makes.

I am 32 years of age, married, and interested in exploring the possibilities of employment with you.

For another case, compare the contrasting examples of the sentence that follows the first sentence of a message refusing an adjustment on a trenching machine. As you can see, the strategy of the initial sentence is to set up the introduction of additional information that will clear the company of responsibility.

The Initial Sentence

Your objective review of the facts concerning the operation of your Atkins Model L trencher is evidence that you are one who wants to consider all the facts in a case.

Good Tie-In	Abrupt Shift
In this same spirit of friendly objectivity, we are confident that you will want to consider some additional information we have assembled.	We have found some additional information you will want to consider.

REPETITION OF KEY WORDS

By repeating key words from one sentence to the next, you can make smooth connections of successive ideas. The following successive sentences illustrate this transitional device (key words in italics). The sentences come from a letter refusing a request to present a lecture series for an advertising clinic.

■ Repetition of key words connects thoughts.

Because your advertising clinic is so well planned, I am confident that it can provide a really *valuable* service to practitioners in the community. To be truly *valuable*, I think you will agree, the program must be given the *time* a thorough preparation requires. As my *time* for the coming weeks is heavily committed, you will need to find someone who is in a better position to do justice to your program.

USE OF PRONOUNS

Because pronouns refer to words previously used, they make good transitions between ideas. So use them from time to time in forming idea connections. Especially use the demonstrative pronouns (*this, that, these, those*) and their adjective forms, for these words clearly relate ideas. The following examples (demonstrative pronouns in italics) illustrate this technique:

■ Pronouns connect with the words they relate to.

Ever since the introduction of our Model V 10 years ago, consumers have suggested only one possible improvement—voice controls. During all *this* time, making *this* improvement has been the objective of Atkins research personnel. Now we proudly report that *these* efforts have been successful.

TRANSITIONAL WORDS

When you talk in everyday conversation, you connect many of your thoughts with transitional words. But when you write, more than likely you do not use them enough. So be alert for places that need to be connected or related. Whenever sharp shifts or breaks in thought flow occur, consider using transitional words.

■ Use transitional words in your writing.

Among the commonly used transitional words are *in addition, besides, in spite of, in contrast, however, likewise, thus, therefore, for example,* and *also.* A more extensive list ap-

■ Transitional words tell the thought connection between following ideas.

pears in Chapter 10, where we review transition in report writing. That these words bridge thoughts is easy to see, for each gives a clue to the nature of the connection between what has been said and what will be said next. *In addition,* for example, tells the reader that what is to be discussed next builds on what has been discussed. *However* clearly shows a contrast in ideas. *Likewise* tells that what has been said resembles what will be said.

A WORD OF CAUTION

■ Do not use transitional words arbitrarily. Make them appear natural.

The preceding discussion does not suggest that you should use these transitional devices arbitrarily. Much of your subject matter will flow smoothly without them. When you use them, however, use them naturally so that they blend in with your writing.

SUMMARY BY CHAPTER OBJECTIVES

1 Explain the need for effect in writing business messages.

1. Although clarity is a major concern in all business writing, in letters and memos you will also be concerned with effect.
   - Specifically, you will need to communicate the effect of goodwill, for it is profitable in business to do so.
   - Sometimes you will need to communicate effects that help you persuade, sell, or the like.
   - To achieve these effects, you will need to heed the following advice.

2 Use a conversational style that eliminates the old language of business and "rubber stamps."

2. Write messages in a conversational style (language that sounds like people talking).
   - Such a style requires that you resist the tendency to be formal.
   - It requires that you avoid words from the old language of business (*thanking you in advance, please be advised*).
   - It requires that you avoid the so-called rubber stamps—words used routinely and without thought (*this is to inform, in accordance with*).

3 Use the you-viewpoint to foster goodwill.

3. In your messages, you will need to emphasize the you-viewpoint (*you will be happy to know . . . rather than I am happy to report . . .*).
   - But be careful not to be or appear to be insincere.
   - And do not use the you-viewpoint to manipulate the reader.

4 Employ positive language to achieve goodwill and other desired effects.

4. You should understand the negative and positive meanings of words.
   - Negative words have unpleasant meanings (*We cannot deliver until Friday*).
   - Positive words have pleasant meanings (*We can deliver Friday*).
   - Select those negative and positive words that achieve the best effect for your goal.

5 Explain the techniques of achieving courtesy.

5. You should strive for courtesy in your messages by doing the following:
   - Practice the goodwill techniques discussed above.
   - Single out your reader (write for the one person).
   - Avoid preaching or talking down.
   - Avoid displays of anger.
   - Be sincere (avoiding exaggeration and overdoing the goodwill techniques).

6 Use the four major techniques for emphasis in writing.

6. Use the four major techniques for emphasis in writing.
   - Determine the items of information the message will contain.
   - Give each item the emphasis it deserves.
   - Show emphasis in these ways:
     —By position (beginnings and endings receive prime emphasis).
     —By space (the greater the space devoted to a topic, the greater is the emphasis).
     —By sentence structure (short sentences emphasize more than longer ones).
     —By mechanical means (color, underscore, boldface, and such).

7 Write documents that flow smoothly through the use of a logical order helped by the four major transitional devices.

7. You should write messages that flow smoothly.
   - Present the information in logical order—so that one thought sets up the next.
   - Help show the relationships of thoughts by using these transitional devices:
     —Tie-in sentences.
     —Word repetitions.
     —Pronouns.
     —Transitional words.

CRITICAL THINKING QUESTIONS

1. Discuss this comment: "Getting the goodwill effect in letters requires extra effort. It takes extra time, and time costs money."

2. "Our normal conversation is filled with error. Typically, it is crude and awkward. So why make our writing sound conversational?" Discuss.

3. "If a company really wants to impress the readers of its messages, the messages should be formal and should be written in dignified language that displays knowledge." Discuss.

4. After reading a message filled with expressions from the old language of business, a young administrative trainee made this remark: "I'm keeping this one for reference. It sounds so businesslike!" Evaluate this comment.

5. "If you can find words, sentences, or phrases that cover a general situation, why not use them every time that general situation comes about? Using such rubber stamps would save time, and in business time is money." Discuss.

6. Discuss this comment: "The you-viewpoint is insincere and deceitful."

7. Evaluate this comment: "It's hard to argue against courtesy. But businesspeople don't have time to spend extra effort on it. Anyway, they want their documents to go straight to the point—without wasting words and without sugar coating."

8. "I use the words that communicate the message best. I don't care whether they are negative or positive." Discuss.

9. "I like letter writers who shoot straight. When they are happy, you know it. When they are angry, they let you know." Discuss.

10. A writer wants to include a certain negative point in a message and to give it little emphasis. Discuss each of the four basic emphasis techniques as they relate to what can be done.

11. Using illustrations other than those in the text, discuss and illustrate the four major transitional devices.

CRITICAL THINKING EXERCISES

Instructions: Rewrite Sentences 1–16 in conversational style.

1. I hereby acknowledge receipt of your July 7 favor.

2. Anticipating your reply by return mail, I remain . . . .

3. Attached please find receipt requested in your May 1st inquiry.

4. We take pleasure in advising that subject contract is hereby canceled.

5. You are hereby advised to endorse subject proposal and return same to the undersigned.

6. I shall appreciate the pleasure of your reply.

7. Referring to yours of May 7, I wish to state that this office has no record of a sale.

8. This is to advise that henceforth all invoices will be submitted in duplicate.

9. Agreeable to yours of the 24th inst., we have consulted our actuarial department to ascertain the status of subject policy.

10. Kindly be advised that permission is hereby granted to delay remittance until the 12th.

11. In conclusion would state that, up to this writing, said account has not been profitable.

12. Replying to your letter of the 3rd would state that we deem it a great pleasure to accept your kind offer to serve on the committee.

13. I beg to advise that, with regard to above invoice, this office finds that partial payment of $312 was submitted on delivery date.

14. In replying to your esteemed favor of the 7th, I submit under separate cover the report you requested.

15. In reply to your letter of May 10, please be informed that this office heretofore has generously supported funding activities of your organization.

16. Kindly advise the undersigned as to your availability for participation in the program.

Instructions, Sentences 17–32: Write you-viewpoint sentences to cover each of the situations described.

17. Company policy requires that you must submit the warranty agreement within two weeks of sale.

18. We will be pleased to deliver your order by the 12th.

19. We have worked for 37 years to build the best lawn mowers for our customers.

20. Today we are shipping the goods you ordered February 3.

21. (From an application letter) I have seven years of successful experience selling office machinery.

22. (From a memorandum to employees) We take pleasure in announcing that, effective today, the Company will give a 20 percent discount on all purchases made by employees.

23. Kraff files are made in three widths—one for every standard size of record.

24. We are happy to report approval of your application for membership.

25. Items desired should be checked on the enclosed order form.

26. Our long experience in the book business has enabled us to provide the best customer service possible.

27. So that we can sell at discount prices, we cannot permit returns of merchandise.

28. We invite you to buy from the enclosed catalog.

29. Tony's Red Beans have an exciting spicy taste.

30. We give a 2 percent discount when payment is made within 10 days.

31. I am pleased to inform you that I can grant your request for payment of travel expenses.

32. We can permit you to attend classes on company time only when the course is related to your work assignment.

Instructions, Sentences 33–48: Underscore all negative words in these sentences. Then rewrite the sentences for positive effect. Use your imagination to supply situation information when necessary.

33. Your misunderstanding of our January 7 letter caused you to make this mistake.

34. We hope this delay has not inconvenienced you. If you will be patient, we will get the order to you as soon as our supply is replenished.

35. We regret that we must call your attention to our policy of prohibiting refunds for merchandise bought at discount.

36. Your negligence in this matter caused the damage to the equipment.

37. You cannot visit the plant except on Saturdays.

38. We are disappointed to learn from your July 7 letter that you are having trouble with our Model 7 motor.

39. Tuff-Boy work clothing is not made from cloth that shrinks or fades.

40. Our Stone-skin material won't do the job unless it is reinforced.

41. Even though you were late in paying the bill, we did not disallow the discount.

42. We were sorry to learn of the disappointing service you have had from our sales force, but we feel we have corrected all mistakes with recent personnel changes.

43. We have received your complaint of the 7th in which you claim that our product was defective, and have thoroughly investigated the matter.

44. I regret the necessity of calling your attention to our letter of May 1.

45. We have received your undated letter, which you sent to the wrong office.

46. Old New Orleans pralines are not the gummy kind that stick to your teeth.

47. I regret to have to say that I will be unable to speak at your conference, as I have a prior commitment.

48. Do not walk on the grass.

Instructions, Numbers 49 and 50: The answers to these questions should come from letter examples to be found in following chapters.

49. Find examples of each of the four major emphasis techniques discussed in this chapter.

50. Find examples of each of the four transitional devices discussed in this chapter.

Basic Patterns
of Business Letters

5

Directness in Good News and Neutral Situations

Upon completing this chapter, you will be able to write direct-order messages effectively. To reach this goal, you should be able to

1 Describe the process of writing business messages.

2 Write clear, well-structured routine requests for information.

3 Compose orderly and thorough inquiries about prospective employees that show respect for human rights.

4 Write direct, orderly, and friendly answers to inquiries.

5 Phrase personnel evaluations that fairly present the essential facts.

6 Compose adjustment grants that regain any lost confidence.

7 Write order acknowledgments that cover problems and build goodwill.

8 Write claims that objectively and courteously explain the facts.

9 Write orders that systematically present the essential information.

THE PROCESS OF WRITING

■ We now take up business messages (primarily letters).

With this chapter you will begin writing business messages. Primarily, these messages are letters. But, because today's technology permits other communication forms (fax, e-mail), throughout this part of the book we emphasize the term *message*. Wherever it appears more precise to do so, however, we use the more specific word *letter*.

■ Following is a review of the process of writing.

As you write business messages, you should keep in mind what is involved in the process of writing. You should know the process and follow the process guidelines. The following brief review of the process should guide you in your efforts.

PLANNING THE MESSAGE

■ Begin by planning.

Your first step in writing a business message should involve planning. This is the prewriting stage—the stage in which you think through your writing project and develop a plan for doing it.

■ Determine the objective of the message.

First, you determine the objective of the message—what the message must do. Must it report information, acknowledge an order, ask for something, request payment of a bill, evaluate an applicant, or what?

■ Predict how the reader will react.

Next you predict the reader's likely reaction to your objective. Will that reaction be positive, negative, or somewhere in between? Of course, you cannot be certain of how the reader will react. You can only apply your knowledge of the reader to the situation and use your best judgment. Your prediction will determine the plan of the message you write.

GATHERING AND COLLECTING THE FACTS

■ Get the information (facts) you need.

The next step in writing a business message is to get all the information you will need. In a business situation, this means finding past correspondence; consulting with other employees; getting sales records, warranties, product descriptions, and inventory records—in fact, doing whatever is necessary to inform yourself fully of the situation. Without all the information you need, you may make costly mistakes. Moreover, if you do not have all the information you need, you will have to look for it in the midst of your writing. This can break your train of thought and cause you to lose time.

In a classroom situation, the write-up of the problem is likely to contain the information you need. So you will need to study the problem carefully, making certain that you understand all the information.

ANALYZING AND ORGANIZING INFORMATION

■ Select the message plan. Use direct order for favorable reactions.

If you predict the reader will react to your message positively, or even neutrally, you will usually organize the message in a direct plan. That is, you will get to your objective right away—at the beginning. In positive situations, you are likely to have no need for opening explanations or introductory remarks, for these would only delay achieving your objective. You simply start with the objective of the letter. This plan, commonly called the *direct order*, is easy to use. Fortunately, it is appropriate for most business messages.

■ Use indirect order for unfavorable reactions.

If you predict that your message will produce a negative reaction, you should usually write it in indirect order. *Indirect order* is the opposite of direct order. This plan gets to the objective after preparing the reader to receive it. As you will see in Chapter 6, such a message typically requires a more skillful use of strategy and word choice than does one written in direct order.

WRITING THE MESSAGE

■ Then write the message, striving for clarity and effect.

After you have the plan in mind, you write the message. You should write it in the clear and effective manner discussed in the preceding chapters—choosing words the reader understands, constructing sentences that present their contents clearly, using words that create just the right effect. You should carefully follow the text instructions for the message you are writing. In addition, you should present it in good format (as described in Appendix B). The product of this effort is a first draft. As you will see, the process does not end here.

REWRITING YOUR WORK

In actual business practice, your first draft may well be the final draft, for often time will not permit additional work on the document. But now you are in a learning situation. You are preparing for the time when you will not have time. Your efforts now should be directed toward improving your writing skills—toward learning writing techniques that can become reflexive in the years ahead when you will write under time pressures. Even so, when you reach the stage of your career when you must write under time pressures, you would be wise to employ as many of the following suggestions as time will permit.

When time permits, review your work.

After completing your first draft, you should review it carefully. Look at each word. Is it the right one? Would another one be more precise? Are there better, more concise ways of structuring your sentence? Did you say what you mean? Could someone read other meanings into your words? Is your organization the best for the situation? What we are suggesting is that you be your own critic. Challenge what you have done. Look for alternatives. Then, after you have conducted a thorough and critical review, make any changes that you think will improve your work.

Then revise it.

Input from others can also help you refine your writing. As you know, it is often difficult to find errors or weaknesses in your own work; yet others seem to find them easily. Thus, if your instructor permits or encourages any input from associates, consider it. Receive criticisms with an open mind, objectively evaluating them and using that which meets your review. Unfortunately, most of us are thin-skinned about such criticisms, and we tend to be defensive when they are made. You should resist this tendency.

Get input from others,

The most valuable input may be the written comments your instructor makes about the work submitted. Perhaps this input comes too late to benefit your grades. But it does not come too late to benefit your learning. You would be wise to take these comments and revise a final time, ending with your best possible product.

including your instructor.

EDITING AND PRESENTING THE FINAL DOCUMENT

After you have made all the changes you think are needed, you should construct the final draft. Here you become a proofreader, looking for errors of spelling, punctuation, and grammar. Probably you will use software analyzers to help you with this task. Then you determine that the format is appropriate. In general, you make certain the final document represents your very best standards—that it will reflect favorably on you and (in later years) your company. Then you present the message. This final message is the best you are capable of writing, and you have learned in the process of writing it.

Then process, edit, and proof the final draft.

PLAN OF THE PRESENTATION

Routine inquiries are messages seeking information that recipients are likely to give freely. Such messages will probably encounter little or no negative reaction. First we view in detail the techniques for handling a general type of inquiry. Then we review in a summary way a more specific type: an inquiry about personnel.

First we review inquiries.

In similar fashion we cover routine response messages. These are favorable answers to the inquiries businesses receive. Our study of routine responses begins with a thorough review of a general form of this message—one giving the information requested. Then we cover three similar but more specific types—responses to inquiries about personnel, favorable responses to claims (adjustments), and order acknowledgements. Because these types have much in common, our coverage of them is brief. We emphasize mainly special considerations and differences.

Then we cover various types of responses.

Next we review two somewhat different direct messages—claims and orders. As you will see, their uniqueness justifies a somewhat detailed coverage.

Finally we describe two unique direct types.

Routine Inquiries

Introduce yourself to routine inquiries by assuming you are the assistant to the vice president for administration of Pinnacle Manufacturing Company. Pinnacle is a small manufacturer of an assortment of high-quality products. Because the company is small, your duties involve helping your boss cover a wide assortment of activities. Many of your assignments involve writing messages.

Today you must write a request for information that the Pinnacle executives need in selecting a site for the company's expansion plant. As a member of this team, your boss has been assigned the task of finding suitable sites as well as certain basic information about each site. Of course, your boss has delegated much of this work to you.

Already you have found a number of possible locations. An advertisement you found in the classified section of today's *Wall Street Journal* may produce another. The advertisement describes a 120-acre tract on the Mississippi River 12 miles upstream from New Orleans. The location and price are right. So now you must get the other information the executives need. Does the land have deep frontage on the river? What about the terrain? Is the land well drained? How accessible is it by public roads? Your task is to write the letter that will get the information Pinnacle needs. If the answers are favorable, the executives probably will want to inspect the tract.

ROUTINE INQUIRIES

- Messages asking for information are routine.

- In such messages, there is usually no need to delay the request.

- An exception occurs if negative reader reaction is likely.

- Thus, the first step in planning the inquiry is to determine the reader's probable reaction.

Messages that ask for information are among the most common in business. Businesses need information from each other. They consider requests for information routine, and they cooperate in exchanging information.

Because businesses usually cooperate in such situations, you can write most requests for information in the direct order. That order saves time for both you and the reader. It gets right down to business without delaying explanation or description.

Directness is not preferred in some situations. As you will see in Chapter 6, directness may be inappropriate when the reader is expected to respond unfavorably. In such cases, you may need to use the indirect order to explain or persuade.

From the preceding discussion, you can see that before writing a request for information you must determine how your reader will receive the message. If you believe the reader will not consider the request routine, you should use indirect order. But if you think

▌Answering inquiry letters that do not include adequate explanation can be frustrating.

the reader will consider the request routine, you should use direct order. Of course, you could write such messages, as well as the others covered in this chapter, in the indirect order and get the job done. But because the indirect order is slow and takes more time, it is inconsistent with the needs of business in such situations. It does not conform to the practice of good business etiquette. As a general rule, you should be direct except when there is good reason not to be. The direct order recommended in this case follows these steps:

- Begin directly with the objective—either a specific question that sets up the entire message or a general request for information.
- Include necessary explanation—wherever it fits.
- If a number of questions are involved, give them structure.
- End with goodwill words adapted to the individual case.

This plan is discussed and explained in the following pages.

■ Then follow this general plan.

BEGINNING WITH THE OBJECTIVE

Because you normally have no reason to waste time in routine inquiries, for reasons of business etiquette you should begin them with the objective of the message. Since your objective is to ask for information, you can start with a question. A question beginning moves fast—the way most people want their work to go. Also, questions command attention and are therefore likely to communicate better than other sentence forms.

The direct beginning of an inquiry can be either of two basic types. First, it can be a specific question that sets up the information wanted. If your objective is to ask a number of questions, the beginning would be one that covers these questions. For example, if your objective is to get answers to specific questions about test results of a company's product, you might begin with these words:

Will you please send me test results showing how Duro-Press withstands high temperatures and exposure to sunlight?

In the body of the message you would include the precise questions concerning temperatures and exposure to sunlight. For example, you might ask questions such as these:

What is the effect when subjected to constant temperatures between 80 and 90 degrees?

What is the effect when subjected to long periods of below-freezing temperatures?

What is the effect of long exposure to direct sunlight?

The second type of beginning is a general request for information. This sentence meets the requirement:

Will you please answer the following questions about your new Duro-Press fabric?

The "will you" here and in the preceding example may appear unnecessary. The basic message would not change if the words were eliminated. In the minds of some authorities, however, including them softens the request and is worth the additional length.

Perhaps both of these direct approaches appear illogical to some. Our minds have been conditioned to the indirect approach that old-style writers have used over the years. Such writers typically begin with an explanation and follow the explanation with the questions. Clearly, this approach is slower and less businesslike. Contrasting examples on following pages illustrate the point.

■ When a favorable response is likely, you should begin with the request.

■ You may use either of two types of question beginnings: (1) a specific question that sets up the information wanted or

■ (2) a general request for information.

■ Either question beginning is better that the explanation-first plan.

INFORMING AND EXPLAINING ADEQUATELY

To help your reader answer your questions, you may need to include explanation or information. If you do not explain enough or if you misjudge the reader's knowledge, you make the reader's task difficult. For example, answers to questions about a computer often depend on the specific needs or characteristics of the company that will use it. The best-informed computer expert cannot answer such questions without knowing the facts of the company concerned.

■ Somewhere in the message, explain enough to enable the reader to answer.

How One Might Write a Routine Inquiry

Suppose one wants to write a routine inquiry, say, to find out about a merger. Here is how the message might read when written by a

12-year-old public school student: "What gives on this merger?"

21-year-old college graduate: "Kindly inform me on current general economic and specific pertinent industrial factors relating to the scheduled amalgamated proposals."

40-year-old junior executive: "J.P.—Please contact me and put me in the picture regarding the mooted merger. I have nothing in my portfolio on it. Sincerely, W.J."

55-year-old member of the board, with private secretary: "Without prejudice to our position vis-à-vis future developments either planned or in the stage of actual activating, the undersigned would appreciate any generally informative matter together with any pertinent program-planning data specific to any merger plans that may or may not have been advanced in quarters not necessarily germane to the assigned field of the undersigned."

65-year-old executive, now boss of the company and very busy: "What gives on this merger?"

■ Place the explanation anywhere it fits logically.

Where and how you include the necessary explanatory information depend on the nature of your message. Usually, a good place for general explanatory material that fits the entire message is following the direct opening sentence. Here it helps reduce any startling effect that a direct opening question might have. It often fits logically into this place, serving as a qualifying or justifying sentence for the message. In messages that ask more than one question, you will sometimes need to include explanatory material with the questions. If this is the case, the explanation fits best with the questions to which it pertains. Such messages may alternate questions and explanations.

STRUCTURING THE QUESTIONS

■ If the inquiry involves just one question, begin with it.

If your inquiry involves just one question, you can achieve your primary objective with the first sentence. After any necessary explanation and a few words of friendly closing comment, your message is done. If you must ask a number of questions, however, you will need to consider their organization.

■ If it involves more than one, make each stand out. Do this by (1) placing each question in a separate sentence,

Whatever you do, you will need to make your questions stand out. You can do this in a number of ways. First, you can make each question a separate sentence with a bullet, a symbol (for example, ●, ○, ■) used to call attention to a particular item. Combining two or more questions in a sentence de-emphasizes each and invites the reader's mind to overlook some.

■ (2) structuring the questions in separate paragraphs,

Second, you can give each question a separate paragraph, whenever this practice is logical. It is logical when your explanation and other comments about each question justify a paragraph.

■ (3) ordering or ranking the questions, and

Third, you can order or rank your questions with numbers. By using words (*first, second, third,* etc.), numerals (1, 2, 3, etc.), or letters (*a, b, c,* etc.), you make the questions stand out. Also, you provide the reader with a convenient check and reference guide to answering.

■ (4) using the question form of sentence.

Fourth, you can structure your questions in question form. True questions stand out. Sentences that merely hint at a need for information do not attract much attention. The "It would be nice if you would tell me . . ." and "I would like to know . . ." types are really not questions. They do not ask—they merely suggest. The questions that stand out are those written in question form: "Will you please tell me . . . ?" "How much would one be able to save . . . ?" "How many contract problems have you had . . . ?"

■ But take caution in asking questions that produce *yes* or *no* answers.

You may want to avoid questions that can be answered with a simple *yes* or *no.* An obvious exception, of course, would be when you really want a simple *yes* or *no* answer. For example, the question "Is the chair available in blue?" may not be what you really want to know. A better wording probably is "In what colors is the chair available?" Often you'll find that you can combine a yes/no question and its explanation to get a better, more concise question. To illustrate, the wording "Does the program run on an IBM? We have a ThinkPad 770" could be improved with "What models does the program run on?" or "Does the program run on the ThinkPad 770?"

ENDING WITH GOODWILL

Because it is the natural thing for friendly people to do, you should end routine inquiry messages with some appropriate, friendly comment. This is how you would end a face-to-face communication with the reader, and there is no reason to do otherwise in writing. Ending your message after the final question is like turning your back on someone after a conversation without saying good-bye. Such an abrupt ending would register negative meanings in your reader's mind and would defeat your goodwill efforts. Clearly, it would not be good business etiquette.

■ End with a friendly comment.

The facts of the case determine just what you should say in the close to make a goodwill impression. Your message will receive a more positive reaction if you use words selected specifically for the one case. Such general closes as "A prompt reply will be appreciated" and "Thank you in advance for your answer" are positive, for they express a friendly thank-you. And there is nothing wrong with a thank-you sincerely expressed here or elsewhere in business writing. The problem is in the routine, rubber-stamp nature of many expressions including it. A more positive reaction results from an individually tailored expression such as, "If you will get this refrigeration data to me by Friday, I will be very grateful."

■ When possible, make the close fit the one case.

CONTRASTING INQUIRY EXAMPLES

Illustrating bad and good techniques are the following two routine inquiry letters about land for a possible Pinnacle plant site. The first example follows the old-style indirect pattern. The second is direct. These examples include only the texts of the letters; but the ex-

■ The following examples show bad and good inquiries.

---

amples that follow show complete letters (on letterhead paper and with inside address, salutation, complimentary close, signature, and such) along with handwritten comments pointing out highlights. These two illustration forms are used throughout the business messages portion of this book.

THE OLD-STYLE INDIRECT LETTER.　The less effective letter begins slowly and gives obvious information. Even if one thinks that this information needs to be communicated, it does not deserve the emphasis of the opening sentence. The second sentence does refer to the objective of the letter, but it is not in the interest-gaining form of a question. The information wanted is covered hastily in the middle paragraph. There are no questions—just hints of needs for information. The items of information wanted do not stand out but are listed in rapid succession. They are not in separate sentences. The close is friendly, but old style. "By return mail" originated in the days when sailing ships shuttled mail across the seas.

■ First is the bad example. Its indirect beginning makes it slow.

Dear Mr. Piper:

We have seen your advertisement for a 120-acre tract on the Mississippi River in the July 1 *Wall Street Journal*. In reply we are writing you for additional information concerning said property.

We would be pleased to know the depth of frontage on the river, quality of drainage, including high and low elevations, and the availability of public roads to the property.

If the information you supply us is favorable to our needs, we will be pleased to inspect the property. Hoping to hear from you by return mail, I am,

Sincerely,

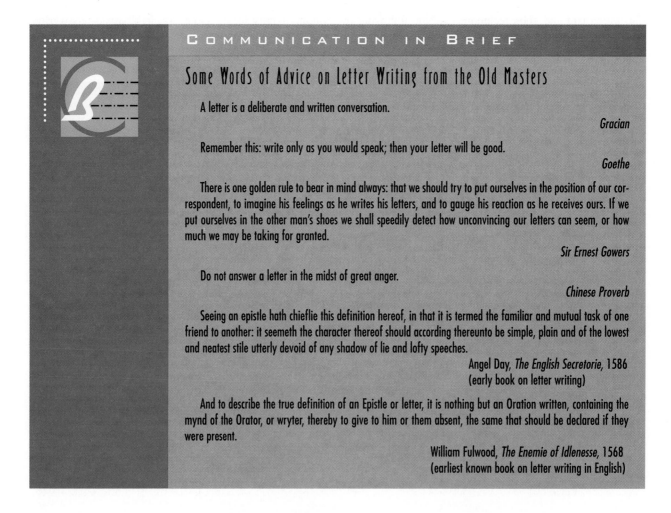

COMMUNICATION IN BRIEF

Some Words of Advice on Letter Writing from the Old Masters

A letter is a deliberate and written conversation.

Gracian

Remember this: write only as you would speak; then your letter will be good.

Goethe

There is one golden rule to bear in mind always: that we should try to put ourselves in the position of our correspondent, to imagine his feelings as he writes his letters, and to gauge his reaction as he receives ours. If we put ourselves in the other man's shoes we shall speedily detect how unconvincing our letters can seem, or how much we may be taking for granted.

Sir Ernest Gowers

Do not answer a letter in the midst of great anger.

Chinese Proverb

Seeing an epistle hath chieflie this definition hereof, in that it is termed the familiar and mutual task of one friend to another: it seemeth the character thereof should according thereunto be simple, plain and of the lowest and neatest stile utterly devoid of any shadow of lie and lofty speeches.

Angel Day, The English Secretorie, 1586
(early book on letter writing)

And to describe the true definition of an Epistle or letter, it is nothing but an Oration written, containing the mynd of the Orator, or wryter, thereby to give to him or them absent, the same that should be declared if they were present.

William Fulwood, The Enemie of Idlenesse, 1568
(earliest known book on letter writing in English)

This letter to a hotel inquires about convention accommodations for a professional association. In selecting a hotel, the organization's officers need answers to specific questions. The letter covers these questions.

Public Affairs

Merck & Co., Inc.
One Merck Drive
P.O. Box 100, WS1A-46
Whitehouse Station NJ 08889

MERCK

July 17, 1998

Ms. Connie Briggs, Manager
Lakefront Hotel
10017 Lakefront Boulevard
Chicago, IL 60613

Dear Ms. Briggs:

Direct—a courteous general request that sets up the specific question

Will you please help Merck decide whether we can meet at the Lakefront? Merck has selected your city for its 1999 meeting, which will be held August 16, 17, and 18. In addition to the Lakefront, the convention committee is considering the De Lane and the White House. In making our decision, we need the information requested in the following questions.

Explanation of situation provides background information

Specific questions with explanations where needed

Can you accommodate a group such as ours on these dates? Probably about 600 employees will attend, and they will need about 400 rooms.

What are your convention rates? We need assurance of having available a minimum of 450 rooms, and we could guarantee 400. Would you be willing to reserve for us the rooms we would require?

What are your charges for conference rooms? We will need eight for each of the three days, and each should have a minimum capacity of 60. On the 18th, for the one-half-hour business meeting, we will need a large assembly room with a capacity of at least 500. Can you meet these requirements?

Questions stand out—in separate paragraphs

Also, will you please send me your menu selections and prices for group dinners? On the 17th we plan our presidential dinner. About 500 can be expected for this event.

As convention plans must be announced in the next issue of our bulletin, may we have your response right away? We look forward to the possibility of being with you in 1997.

Individually tailored goodwill close

Sincerely,

Patti Wolff

Patti Wolff, Chair
Site Selection Committee

tr

∙∙

CASE ILLUSTRATION   Routine Inquiries. (Getting Information about a Training Program)
This letter is from a company training director to the director of a management-training program. The company training director has received literature on the program but needs additional information. The letter seeks this information.

J

SORBET

September 21, 1999

Ms. Katherine O. Hrozek
Director
Moissant Training Institute
1771 Poindexter Drive
Albany, NY 12224

Dear Ms. Hrozek:

Direct—a general request sets up the specific question

Please send me the additional information we need in determining whether to send some of our executives to your Western Management Institute. We have your illustrated brochure and the schedule you mailed August 17. Specifically, we need the answers to these questions:

Reference to brochure tells what writer knows—helps reader in responding

1. What are your quantity discount rates? We could send about six executives each session.

2. At what background level is your program geared? We have engineers, accountants, scientists, and business administrators. Most have college degrees. Some do not.

Numbered questions stand out—helps reader in responding

3. Can college credit be given for the course? Some of our executives are working on degrees and want credit.

Explanations worked into questions where needed

4. What are the names and addresses of training directors of companies that have sent executives to the program?

We will appreciate having your answers for our October 3 staff meeting. We look forward to the possibility of sending our executives to you in the years ahead.

Favorable forward look makes good will close

Sincerely,

Ronald I Dupre

Ronald I. Dupre
Director of Training

po

THE DIRECT AND EFFECTIVE LETTER.   The second example begins directly by asking for information. As the reader will welcome the inquiry, no need exists for delaying explanation. Because the direct opening may have a startling effect, explanatory information that justifies the inquiry follows. Next come the remaining questions, with explanations worked in wherever they help the readers in answering. The letter closes with a courteous request for quick handling. In addition, the close suggests the good news of possible quick action on the property.

Dear Mr. Piper:

■ This direct and orderly letter is better.

Will you please answer the following questions about the 120-acre tract you advertised in the July 1 *Wall Street Journal?* We are seeking such a site for a new plant, and it appears that your property could meet our needs.

- How deep is the frontage on the river at its shallowest and deepest points?
- What are drainage conditions on the land? A written description of the tract terrain should answer this question. In your description, please include a contour map showing minimum and maximum elevations.
- What is the composition and condition of the existing access road?

If your answers indicate that the site meets our needs, we will want to inspect the property. Since we must move fast on the building project, may I have your answers soon?

Sincerely,

INTRODUCTORY
SITUATION

Inquiries about People

From time to time, your work at Pinnacle involves investigating applicants for employment. Of course, in your position you do no hiring. The Human Resources Department conducts initial interviews, administers aptitude tests, and performs all the other screening tasks. Then it refers the best applicants to the executives in charge of the jobs to be filled. The executives, including your boss, make the final decisions.

This morning Human Resources sent your boss a Mr. Rowe W. Hart, who is applying for the vacant position of office manager. Mr. Hart appears to be well qualified—good test scores and employment record. After talking with Hart, your boss thinks that he is bright and personable. Because your boss believes that he cannot judge ability from a single interview, he has asked you to follow your usual practice of writing the applicant's references for their evaluations. In Hart's case, the best possibility appears to be Ms. Alice Borders, who was his immediate supervisor for three years.

Your task now is to write Ms. Borders a letter that will get the information you need. The following discussion and illustrations show you how.

INQUIRIES ABOUT PEOPLE

Messages asking for information about people are a special form of routine inquiry. Normally, they should follow this general plan:

■ Begin directly, with a general question seeking information or a specific question that sets up the entire message.

■ Explain the situation.

■ Cover the additional questions systematically, with explanations as needed.

■ End with adapted goodwill words.

■ Messages asking questions about people should follow this general plan.

■ The message involves two special considerations.

■ 1. Respect human rights, both legal and moral.

As you can see from this outline, the plan for the inquiry about personnel is virtually the same as that for the routine inquiry. But writing the message involves two special considerations, which is why we review this message separately.

First is the need to respect the rights of the people involved. Good business etiquette requires it. These rights are both legal and moral. In fact, because of the legal aspects, some companies do not permit their employees to correspond about personnel. Those companies

■ Answering inquiries about people requires the most careful thought, for the lives and rights of human beings are affected.

that do permit such exchanges of information should try to protect the rights of the people involved.

■ Ask only for information related to the job.

When you write these messages, for legal as well as ethical reasons, you should ask only questions related to the job. Specifically, you should avoid questions about the applicant's race, religion, sex, age, pregnancy, and marital situation.[1] Even questions about the applicant's citizenship status and arrest and conviction record are better not asked. So are questions about mental and physical handicaps and organization (especially union) memberships.

■ Stress fact, write for business use and when authorized, and treat confidentially.

In protecting these rights, you must seek truth and act in good faith. You should ask only for information you need for business purposes. You should ask only when the subject has authorized the inquiry. You should hold any information received in confidence. And you would do well to include these points in your message, either in words or by implication.

■ 2. Structure the questions around the job.

A second concern in writing this message is the need to structure the questions around the job involved. Specifically, the information you seek should be determined by your needs. What you need is information that will tell you whether the subject is qualified for the one job involved. Thus, you should analyze the job to determine the information you should have in selecting a person to do it. The questions you would ask about an applicant for a sales job, for example, would be quite different from those you would ask about an applicant for an accounting position.

EXAMPLES IN CONTRAST

■ Following are good and bad examples of a personnel inquiry.

In applying the preceding instructions to Rowe Hart's application for the position of office manager at Pinnacle, assume that analysis of the applicant and the job tells you that you should ask four questions. First, is Hart capable of handling the responsibilities involved? Second, does he know the work? Third, how hard a worker is he? Fourth, is he morally responsible? Now, how would you arrange these questions and the necessary explanation in a letter?

A SCANT AND HURRIED EXAMPLE.   The first letter example shows a not-so-good effort. The opening is indirect. The explanation in the opening is important, but does it deserve the emphasis that the beginning position gives it? Although the question part gives

---

[1] As required by the following acts and court cases relating to them: Wagner Act of 1935, Immigration and Nationality Act of 1952, Civil Rights Act of 1964, Vocational Rehabilitation Act of 1973, Age Discrimination Act of 1975, and Pregnancy Discrimination Act of 1978.

"First the good news—if I cure you, I'll become world famous." (*From* The Wall Street Journal, *with permission of Cartoon Features Syndicate.*)

the appearance of conciseness, it is actually scant. It includes no explanation. It does not even mention what kind of position Hart is being considered for. The items of information wanted do not stand out. In fact, they are not even worded as questions but are run together in a single declarative sentence. Though courteous, the closing words are old style.

Dear Ms. Borders:

Mr. Rowe W. Hart has applied to us for employment and has given your name as a reference. He indicates that he worked under your supervision during the period 1993–98.

We would be most appreciative if you would give us your evaluation of Mr. Hart. We are especially interested in his ability to handle responsibility, knowledge of office procedures, work habits, and morals.

Thanking you in advance for your courtesy, I remain,

Sincerely yours,

■ This bad one is slow and scant.

AN ORDERLY AND THOROUGH EXAMPLE.   The next example gives evidence of good analysis of the job and the applicant. The letter begins directly with an opening question that serves as a topic sentence. The beginning also includes helpful explanation. But this part is not given unnecessary emphasis, as was done in the preceding example. Then the letter presents the specific questions. Worded separately and in question form, each stands out and is easy to answer. Worked in with each question is explanation that will help the reader understand the work for which Hart is being considered. The close is courteous and tailored for the one case. Note also, throughout the letter, the concern for the rights of the people involved. Clearly, the inquiry is authorized, is for business purposes only, and will be treated confidentially.

Dear Ms. Borders:

Will you help me evaluate Mr. Rowe W. Hart for the position of office manager? In authorizing this inquiry, Mr. Hart indicated that he worked for you from 1993 to 1998. Your candid answers to the following questions will help me determine whether Mr. Hart is the right person for this job.

What is your evaluation of Mr. Hart's leadership ability, including human-relations skills? Our office has a staff of 11.

How well can Mr. Hart manage a rapidly expanding office system? Ours is a growing company. The person who manages our office will not only need to know good office procedures but will also need to know how to adapt them to changing conditions.

What is your evaluation of Mr. Hart's stamina and drive? The position he seeks often involves working under heavy pressure.

■ This good example show careful study of the job and the applicant.

This is the case of a freight-line executive who is looking for a manager for one of the company's branches. The top applicant is a shipping clerk for a furniture company. With the applicant's permission, the executive has written this letter to the applicant's employer.

ARROW FREIGHT

7171 INDIGO LAKE RD.
AUSTIN, TX 78710
512-212-8908
Fax: 512-212-8904

February 17, 1998

Mr. Amos T. Dodgson, Manager
Easterbrook Furniture, Inc.
3970 Burnham Avenue
Seattle, WA 98125

Dear Mr. Dodgson:

Direct-interest-gaining question tells reader what is needed

Will you do George Barton and me the favor of providing an evaluative report on him? He is an assistant shipping clerk with you who wants to manage a branch office for us. He has authorized this inquiry.

Explanation softens possible startling effect of opening

Human rights respected

Bullets make questions stand out—questions cover work to be done

• How well does he know packing and hauling techniques?

• How do you judge his administrative ability to run an office of one secretary and a work force of six?

• What is your appraisal of his ability to meet customers and generally build goodwill with the community?

• What do you know about his honesty and integrity? Our managers are solely responsible for their branch's assets—equipment as well as all receipts.

Explanation as needed

• As a final question, is there anything else you can tell me that might indicate whether Mr. Barton is the right person for our job?

I will be grateful for your answers. Of course, what you report will be held in strict confidence.

Friendly close and respect for human rights

Sincerely,

Mary E. Caperton

Mary E. Caperton
Manager

det

What is your evaluation of Mr. Hart's moral reliability? Our office manager is responsible for much of our company equipment as well as some company funds.

We will, of course, hold your answers in strict confidence. And we will appreciate whatever help you are able to give Mr. Hart and us.

Sincerely,

GENERAL FAVORABLE RESPONSES

When you answer inquiries favorably, your primary goal is to tell your readers what they want to know. Because their reactions to this goal will be favorable, you should use the direct order. The direct plan recommended below generally follows these steps:

- Begin with the answer, or state that you are complying with the request.
- Identify the correspondence being answered either incidentally or in a subject line.
- Continue to give what is wanted in orderly arrangement.
- If negative information is involved, give it proper emphasis.
- Consider including extras.
- End with a friendly, adapted comment.

> ■ Favorable reader reaction justifies this direct plan for the response.

BEGINNING WITH THE ANSWER

Using the direct order means giving readers what they want at the beginning. What they want are the answers to their questions. Thus, you should begin by answering. When a response involves answering a single question, you begin by answering that question. When it involves answering two or more questions, one good plan is to begin by answering one of them—preferably the most important. In the Chem-Treat case, this opening would get the response off to a fast start:

Yes, you can use Chem-Treat to prevent mildew.

> ■ Begin by answering. If there is one question, answer it; if there is more than one, answer the most important.

An alternative possibility is to begin by stating that you are giving the reader what he or she wants—that you are complying with the request. Actually, this approach is really not direct, for it delays giving the information requested. But it is a favorable beginning, and it does not run the risk of sounding abrupt, which is a criticism of direct beginnings. These examples illustrate this type of beginning:

The following information should tell you what you need to know about Chem-Treat.

Here are the answers to your questions about Chem-Treat.

> ■ Or begin by saying that you are complying with the request.

Either of these beginnings is an improvement over the indirect beginnings that are used all too often in business. Overworked indirect beginnings such as "Your April 3 inquiry has been received" and "I am writing in response to your letter" do little to accomplish the goal of the message. They also give obvious information. Although acceptable because of its courtesy, even the "Thank you for your April 7 inquiry" delays getting to the objective of answering.

IDENTIFYING THE CORRESPONDENCE BEING ANSWERED

Even though the indirect examples in the preceding paragraph have shortcomings, they do something desirable. They identify the message being answered. This identification information is useful for filing purposes. It also helps the reader recall or find the message being answered.

One good way of identifying the message being answered is to refer to it in the text of your letter. You should make such references incidentally, for they usually do not deserve strong emphasis. Illustrating this technique is the phrase "as requested in your April 3 letter."

Another good way of identifying the message being answered is the use of a *subject line,* a mechanical device usually placed in letters after the salutation. Although not needed in most letters, the subject line is useful in responses. Typically, the subject line contains an identifying term such as *Subject:, About:, or Re:,* followed by appropriate descriptive words. The words identify the nature of the message and the situation. For example, for the inquiry about Chem-Treat, these subject lines would be appropriate:

Subject: Your April 3 inquiry about Chem-Treat

Re: Your April 3 inquiry concerning Chem-Treat

LOGICALLY ARRANGING THE ANSWERS

If you are answering just one question, you have little to do after handling that question in the opening. You answer it as completely as the situation requires, and you present whatever explanation or other information you need to do so. Then you are ready to close the message.

If, on the other hand, you are answering two or more questions, the body of your message becomes a series of answers. As in all clear writing, you should work for a logical order, perhaps answering the questions in the order your reader used in asking them. You may even number your answers, especially if your reader numbered the questions. Or you may decide to arrange your answers by paragraphs so that each stands out clearly.

COMMUNICATION IN BRIEF

How Routine Responses Were Written in the Late 1800s

The following model letter for answering routine inquiries appears on page 75 of O. R. Palmer's *Type-Writing and Business Correspondence.* Published in 1896, the book was a leader in its field.

Dear Sirs:

Your favor of Dec. 18th, enclosing blue prints for tank, received. In reply thereto we beg to submit the following:

[*Here was a listing of materials for the tank.*]

Trusting that our price may be satisfactory to you, and that we shall be favored with your order, we beg to remain,

Very truly yours,

SKILLFUL HANDLING OF NEGATIVES

When your response concerns some bad news along with the good news, you may need to handle the bad news with care. Bad news stands out. Unless you are careful, it is likely to receive more emphasis than it deserves. Sometimes you will need to subordinate the bad news and emphasize the good news.

In giving proper emphasis to the good- and bad-news parts, you should use the techniques discussed in Chapter 4, especially position. That is, you should place the good news in positions of high emphasis—at paragraph beginnings and endings and at the beginning and ending of the message as a whole. You should place the bad news in secondary positions. In addition, you should use space emphasis to your advantage. This means giving less space to bad-news parts and more space to good-news parts. You should also select words and build sentences that communicate the effect you want. Generally, this means using happy and pleasant words and avoiding unpleasant and sad words. Your overall goal should be to present the information in your response so that your readers get just the right effect.

■ Emphasize favorable responses; subordinate unfavorable responses.

■ Place favorable responses at beginnings and ends. Give them more space. Use words skillfully to emphasize them.

CONSIDERATION OF EXTRAS

For the best in goodwill effect and for reasons of etiquette, you should consider including extras with your answers. These are the things you say and do that are not actually required. Examples are a comment or question showing an interest in the reader's problem, some additional information that may prove valuable, and a suggestion for use of the information supplied. In fact, extras can be anything that does more than skim the surface with hurried, routine answers. Such extras frequently make the difference between success and failure in the goodwill effort.

■ The little extra things you do for the reader will build goodwill.

Illustrations of how extras can be used to strengthen the goodwill effects of a message are as broad as the imagination. A business executive answering a college professor's request for information on company operations could supplement the requested information with suggestions of other sources. A technical writer could amplify highly technical answers with simpler explanations. In the Chem-Treat problem, additional information (say, how much surface area a gallon covers) would be helpful. Such extras genuinely serve readers and serve as evidence of good etiquette.

CORDIALITY IN THE CLOSE

As in most routine business writing situations, you should end routine responses with friendly, cordial words that make clear your willing attitude. As much as is practical, your words should be adapted to the one case. For example, you might close the Chem-Treat letter with these words:

■ End with friendly words adapted to the one case.

If I can help you further in deciding whether Chem-Treat will meet your needs, please write me again.

Or an executive answering a graduate student's questions concerning a thesis project could use this paragraph:

If I can give you any more of the information you need for your study of executive behavior, please write me. I wish you the best of luck on the project.

Notice that both of the examples above close with an offer of further help. Not only does this increase cordiality in the close, but it also signals the readers that all of their concerns have already been addressed. Using terms such as *further, additional,* and *any more* tells the reader the writer is willing to do a little extra if needed.

CONTRASTING ILLUSTRATIONS

Contrasting letters in answer to the Chem-Treat inquiry illustrate the techniques of answering routine inquiries. The first letter violates many of the standards set in this and earlier chapters. The second meets the requirements of a good business letter. Its cordiality gives evidence of good business etiquette.

■ Following are bad and good examples of response letters.

CASE ILLUSTRATION Routine Response Letters (Favorable Response to a Professor's Request)

This letter responds to a professor's request for production records that will be used in a research project. The writer is giving the information wanted but must restrict its use.

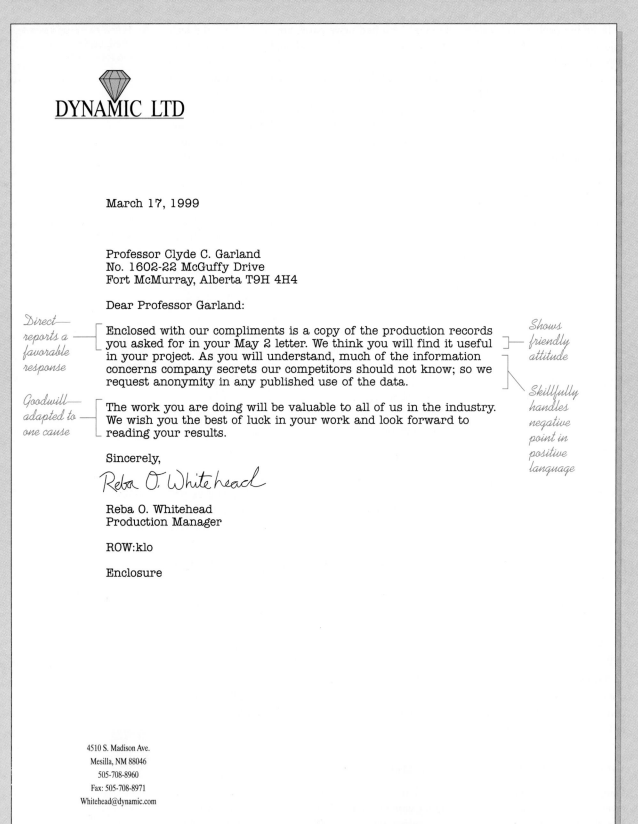

DYNAMIC LTD

March 17, 1999

Professor Clyde C. Garland
No. 1602-22 McGuffy Drive
Fort McMurray, Alberta T9H 4H4

Dear Professor Garland:

Direct reports a favorable response

Enclosed with our compliments is a copy of the production records you asked for in your May 2 letter. We think you will find it useful in your project. As you will understand, much of the information concerns company secrets our competitors should not know; so we request anonymity in any published use of the data.

Shows friendly attitude

Skillfully handles negative point in positive language

Goodwill adapted to one cause

The work you are doing will be valuable to all of us in the industry. We wish you the best of luck in your work and look forward to reading your results.

Sincerely,

Reba O. Whitehead

Reba O. Whitehead
Production Manager

ROW:klo

Enclosure

4510 S. Madison Ave.
Mesilla, NM 88046
505-708-8960
Fax: 505-708-8971
Whitehead@dynamic.com

CASE ILLUSTRATION · Routine Response Letters. (A Request for Detailed Information)

Answering an inquiry about a company's experience with a word processing center, this letter numbers the answers as the questions were numbered in the inquiry. The opening appropriately sets up the numbered answers with a statement that indicates a favorable response.

PROBST
INDUSTRIES

August 7, 1999

Ms. Ida Casey, Office Manager
Liberty Insurance Company
1165 Second Ave.
Des Moines, IA 50318-9631

Dear Ms. Casey:

Direct—tells that writer is complying

Following is the information about our telecommuting center you requested in your August 3 email. For your convenience, I have numbered my responses to correspond with the sequence you used.

Sets up listing

Orderly listing of answers

1. Our executives have mixed feelings about the effectiveness of the center. At the beginning, majority opinion was negative; but it appears now that most of the antagonism has subsided.

2. The center definitely has saved us money. Rental costs in the suburbs are much less than downtown costs; savings are estimated at nearly $6,000 monthly.

3. The changeover did create a morale problem among those remaining downtown even after we assured them that their workloads would not increase.

4. We created our center at the request of several sales representatives who had read about other companies setting up similar telecommuting centers. We pilot-tested the program in one territory for a year using volunteers before we implemented it companywide.

5. We are quite willing to share our center operating procedures with you. I am enclosing a copy of our procedures directive, which describes center operations in detail.

Complete yet concise answers

Friendly—adapted to the one case

If after reviewing this information you have any other questions, please write me again. And if you feel that an inspection of our operation would help, you are welcome to visit us. I wish you the best of luck in implementing your center.

This extra builds good-will

Sincerely,

David M. Earp

David M. Earp
Office Manager

Enclosure

AN INDIRECT AND HURRIED RESPONSE.   The not-so-good letter begins indirectly with an obvious statement referring to receipt of the inquiry. Though well intended, the second sentence continues to delay the answers. The second paragraph begins to give the information sought, but it emphasizes the most negative answer by position and by wording. This answer is followed by hurried and routine answers to the other questions asked. Only the barest information is presented. The close belongs to the language of business in great-grandfather's day.

■ The poor one is indirect and ineffective.

Dear Ms. Motley:

I have received your April 3 letter, in which you inquire about our Chem-Treat paint. I want you to know that we appreciate your interest and will welcome your business.

In response to your question about how many coats are needed to cover new surfaces, I regret to report that two are usually required. The paint is mildewproof. We do guarantee it. It has been well tested in our laboratories. It is safe to use as directed.

Hoping to hear from you again, I remain
                                    Yours sincerely,

EFFECTIVENESS IN DIRECT RESPONSE.   The better letter uses a subject line to identify the inquiry. Thus, it frees the text from the need to cover this detail. The letter begins directly, with the most favorable answer. Then it presents the other answers, giving each the emphasis and positive language it deserves. It subordinates the one negative answer, by position, volume of treatment, and structure. More pleasant information follows the negative answer. The close is goodwill talk, with some subtle selling strategy thrown in. "We know that you'll enjoy the long-lasting beauty of this mildewproof paint" points positively to purchase and successful use of the product.

Dear Ms. Motley:

■ This direct letter does a better job.

Subject: Your April 3 inquiry about Chem-Treat.

Yes, Chem-Treat paint will prevent mildew or we will give you back your money. We know it works, because we have tested it under all common conditions. In every case, it proved successful.

When you carefully follow the directions on each can, Chem-Treat paint is guaranteed safe. As the directions state, you should use Chem-Treat only in a well-ventilated room—never in a closed, unvented area.

One gallon of Chem-Treat is usually enough for one-coat coverage of 500 square feet of previously painted surface. For the best results on new surfaces, you will want to apply two coats. For such surfaces, you should figure about 200 square feet per gallon for a good heavy coating that will give you five years or more of beautiful protection.

We sincerely appreciate your interest in Chem-Treat, Ms. Motley. We know that you'll enjoy the long-lasting beauty of this mildewproof paint.

                                    Sincerely,

COMMUNICATION IN BRIEF

Skillful (?) Handling of a Complaint

A traveling man once spent a sleepless night in a hotel room, tormented by the sight of cockroaches walking over the ceiling, walls, and floor. Upon returning home, he indignantly protested the condition in a letter to the hotel management. Some days later, to his delight, he received a masterfully written response. It complimented him for reporting the condition, and it assured him that the matter would be corrected—that such a thing would never happen again. The man was satisfied, and his confidence in the hotel was restored. His satisfaction vanished, however, when he discovered an interoffice memo that had been accidentally inserted into the envelope. The memo said, "Send this nut the cockroach letter."

Personnel Evaluations

A request for an evaluation of a Pinnacle employee is the next item you take from your incoming messages. The writer, Ms. Mary Brooking, president, Red Arrow Transport, Inc., wants information about George Adams, Pinnacle's assistant shipping clerk. Ms. Brooking is considering Adams for the position of manager of a Red Arrow branch office. In her letter she asks some specific questions about him and about his ability to do the job. Because Adams works under the supervision of your office, he listed you as a reference.

You are well acquainted with Adams and his work. Just last week he came by your office to tell you that he was looking at an employment opportunity that offered advancement—something that Pinnacle, unfortunately, could not offer soon. Everything you have observed in his work supports your opinion that he is industrious and capable. He knows the shipping business, and he is an able supervisor. He tends to stick to his own ideas too strongly, and this has caused some friction with his superiors—you included. But you feel that this tendency reflects his independence and self-reliance, qualities that may be desirable in a branch manager with no immediate supervisors on the grounds.

Because you believe that Adams has earned the position he seeks, you want to write a letter that will help him. But because you are an honest person, you will report truthfully. Thus, you will write a letter that will be fair to all concerned—to Adams, to Ms. Brooking, and to you.

PERSONNEL EVALUATIONS

When you receive a request to evaluate a former employee, company policy may prohibit you from answering. For legal reasons, many companies do not permit such messages. But if you do write such a message, you should organize it in the direct order. The justification for the direct order is that the message is favorable, since you are doing what the reader requested. It is favorable regardless of whether it contains positive or negative information about the employee because the reader is getting the information requested. As described in the following paragraphs, this procedure will produce a good direct-order message:

- Personnel evaluations satisfy the reader. Thus, they justify the direct order, as outlined in this general plan.

- Begin by (1) answering a question or (2) saying that you are complying with the request.
- Refer to the inquiry incidentally or in a subject line.
- Report systematically, giving each item proper emphasis, taking care to be fair, and stressing fact rather than opinion.
- End with an adapted goodwill comment.

GENERAL PLAN OF PERSONNEL EVALUATIONS

As you can see, the plan for this message type is much like the plan previously discussed. You begin it either with an answer to one of the questions asked, as in this example:

Mr. Chester Bazzar, the subject of your May 11 inquiry, worked under my supervision for four months in 1996.

- Begin directly, either with significant information requested

Or you begin it with a statement indicating that you are complying with the request:

As you requested in your May 8 letter, here is my evaluation of Mr. Carlton I. Bowes.

- or a statement saying you are complying.

Somewhere in or near the beginning, you refer to the message being answered by incidental reference or in a subject line. Then you give the information requested in some orderly and logical fashion. In doing this, you may choose to organize around the questions asked. You may even number the responses, especially if the questions were numbered in the inquiry. Finally, you close with some appropriate, friendly words.

- Refer to the inquiry, present the information requested, and end with goodwill.

SPECIAL NEED FOR FAIR REPORTING

The one unique concern in writing this message is the need to report the information fairly—to present an accurate picture. It is important because what you write affects the lives of people. Presenting your information too positively would be unfair to your reader.

- It is especially important to present a true picture.

CASE ILLUSTRATION Personnel Evaluation Letters (Evaluation of a Good Worker)

Evaluating a well-qualified office worker with no significant deficiencies, this letter presents its information systematically. The opening comment is general; but by informing the reader of a favorable response, it has the effect of directness.

McMILLAN, INC.
WHOLESALE GROCERY

May 16, 1999

Mr. Brooke I. Crump, Manager
Bennett-Bond Instruments, Inc.
11731 Alvin Boulevard
Arlington, TX 76010

Dear Mr. Crump:

Identifies subject and inquiry letter

Subject: Report on Ms. Patricia Heine, requested by you May 10

Direct—tells that writer is complying

Following are my answers to your questions about Ms. Heine. For your convenience, I have arranged them in the numbered sequence used in your letter.

Numbering systematically arranges the answers for the reader's convenience

1. Ms. Heine worked for us from January 1996 to June 1998.

2. For the first six months, Ms. Heine worked as an administrative trainee. Her assignments rotated through the major departments of the company. Following the training period, she was placed in charge of customer services, where she remained until she left the company. On this assignment she demonstrated good administrative ability and a practical knowledge of dealing with people.

3. In all her assignments I found Ms. Heine a very capable worker. She worked hard, and she demonstrated good administrative potential. In fact, I had selected her to be groomed for a position of administrative responsibility.

Answers are complete, yet concise

4. I found Ms. Heine a most personable young woman. She got along with all her associates. I believe she is a person of integrity and good morals.

5. Ms. Heine left us for a higher paying job—one she felt offered her faster advancement. We wanted her to stay with us.

Summary of evaluation in a recommendation

I have a high regard for Ms. Heine. I recommend her to you for any work for which her experience has prepared her.

Goodwill ending

I am pleased to give you this confidential report on Ms. Heine.

Sincerely,

Mary L. Lamme

Mary L. Lamme
Office Manager

MLL:tt

1313 N. Palm Ave.
Palm Harbor, FL 34683
305-465-3200
Facsimile: 305-465-3256

Presenting it too negatively would be unfair to the applicant. Good business etiquette demands that you report fairly and accurately.

In conveying an accurate picture, you should carefully distinguish between facts and opinions. For the most part, you should report facts. But sometimes a reader wants your opinions. If you present opinions, you should clearly label them as such. You should support all opinions with facts.

■ Prefer facts to opinions.

Conveying an accurate picture of the subject also involves giving the facts proper emphasis. Even if every fact you present is true, the report could be unfair. The reason is that negative points stand out. They overshadow positive points. Thus, sometimes you may need to subordinate the negative points. Not to do so would be to give them more emphasis than they deserve.

■ Proper emphasis may require subordination.

This suggestion for subordinating negative points does not mean you should hide shortcomings or communicate wrong information. Quite the contrary. If the subject has a bad work record, you should report this. Purely and simply, your task is to communicate an accurate picture.

■ But subordination does not mean altering truth.

For legal reasons, sometimes you will need to leave out certain information. In the United States, laws and court decisions have affected the exchange of information about job applicants. Reports about an applicant's age, race, religion, sex, marital status, and pregnancy are generally prohibited. So are reports about an applicant's criminal record, citizenship, organization memberships, and mental and physical handicaps. Exceptions may be made in the rare cases in which such information is clearly related to the job.

■ Abide by legal requirements regarding information that may be reported.

EXAMPLES IN CONTRAST

Illustrating good and bad technique in personnel evaluations are the following contrasting letters about George Adams.

A SLOW, DISORGANIZED, AND UNFAIR REPORT.   The weaker letter begins indirectly—and with some obvious information. The first words are wasted. The letter shows little concern for proper emphasis. Note that the main negative point (the personality problem) receives a major position of emphasis (at a paragraph beginning). Even the information about the applicant's future at Pinnacle (which does not reflect on his abilities) gets negative treatment. The organization is jumbled. Information about personal qualities and about job performance, for example, appears in two different paragraphs. The close is an attempt at goodwill, but the words are timeworn rubber stamps.

Dear Ms. Brooking:

I have received your May 10 letter in which you ask for my evaluation of Mr. George Adams. In reply I wish to say that I am pleased to be able to help you in this instance.

■ This bad example violates the techniques emphasized.

Probably Mr. Adams's greatest weakness is his inability to get along with his superiors. He has his own ideas, and he sticks to them tenaciously. Even so, he has a good work record with us. He has been with us since 1988.

Mr. Adams is a first assistant in our shipping department. He is thoroughly familiar with rate scales and general routing procedure. He gets along well with his co-workers and is a very personable young man. In his work he has some supervisory responsibilities, which he has performed well. He is probably seeking other work because there is little likelihood that we will promote him.

Mr. Adams's main assignment with us has placed him in charge of our car and truck loadings. He has done a good job here, resulting in significant savings in shipping damages. We have found him a very honest, straightforward, and dependable person.

Trusting that you will hold this report in confidence, I remain

Sincerely,

GOOD ORGANIZATION AND FAIRNESS IN DIRECT REPORT.   The better letter begins directly, reporting a significant point in the first sentence. Use of the subject line frees the text of the need to identify the inquiry, which makes for a faster-moving beginning. The text presents the information in logical order, with like things being placed together. The words present the information fairly. The major negative point is presented almost positively, which is how it should be viewed in regard to the job concerned. The letter closes with an appropriate goodwill comment.

■ Directness, good organization, and correct emphasis mark this good letter.

Dear Ms. Brooking:

Subject: Your May 10 inquiry about George Adams

Mr. Adams has been our assistant shipping clerk since March 1988 and has steadily improved in usefulness to our company. We want to keep him with us as long as he wants to stay. But with things as they are, it will apparently be some time before we can offer him a promotion that would match the branch managership for which you are considering him.

Of course, I am glad to give you in confidence a report on his service with us. As first assistant, he has substituted at the head clerk's desk and is thus familiar with problems of rate scales and routing. His main assignment, however, is to supervise the car and truck loadings. By making a careful study of this work, he has reduced our shipping damages noticeably within the last year. This job also places him in direct charge of the labor force, which varies from 6 to 10 workers. He has proved to be a good boss.

We have always found Mr. Adams honest, straightforward, and dependable. He is a man of strong convictions. He has his own ideas and backs them up. He is resourceful and works well without direction.

I recommend Mr. Adams to you highly. If you need additional information about him, please write me again.

Sincerely,

ADJUSTMENT GRANTS

■ Good news in adjustment grants justifies directness, as in this general plan.

When you can grant an adjustment, the situation is a happy one for your customer. You are correcting an error. You are doing what you were asked to do. As in other positive situations, a message written in the direct order is appropriate. The direct-order plan recommended below follows these general steps:

■ Begin directly—with the good news.

■ Incidentally identify the correspondence that you are answering.

■ Avoid negatives that recall the problem.

■ Regain lost confidence through explanation or corrective action.

■ End with a friendly, positive comment.

In most face-to-face business relations, people communicate with courteous directness. You should write most business letters this way.

SPECIAL NEEDS OF ADJUSTMENT GRANTS

This plan has much in common with the message types already discussed. You begin directly with the good-news answer. You refer to the correspondence you are answering. And you close on a friendly note. But because the situation stems from an unhappy experience, you have two special needs. One is the need to overcome the negative impressions the experience leading to the adjustment has formed in the reader's mind. The other is the need to regain any confidence in your company, its products, or its service the reader may have lost from the experience.

■ Follow the good-news pattern, but consider two special needs.

NEED TO OVERCOME NEGATIVE IMPRESSIONS. To understand the first need, just place yourself in the reader's shoes. As the reader sees it, something bad has happened—goods have been damaged, equipment has failed, or sales have been lost. The experience has not been pleasant. Granting the claim will take care of much of the problem, but some negative thoughts may remain. You need to work to overcome any such thoughts.

■ Negative impressions remain; so overcome them.

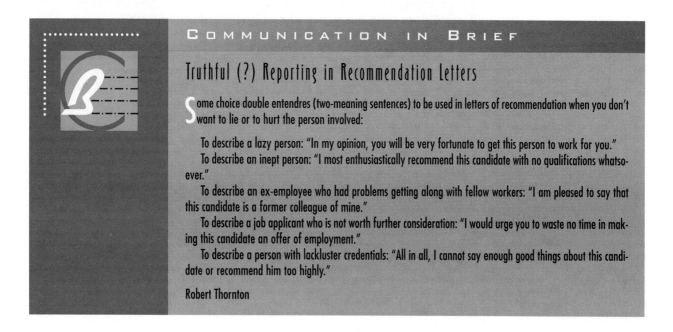

COMMUNICATION IN BRIEF

Truthful (?) Reporting in Recommendation Letters

Some choice double entendres (two-meaning sentences) to be used in letters of recommendation when you don't want to lie or to hurt the person involved:

To describe a lazy person: "In my opinion, you will be very fortunate to get this person to work for you."

To describe an inept person: "I most enthusiastically recommend this candidate with no qualifications whatsoever."

To describe an ex-employee who had problems getting along with fellow workers: "I am pleased to say that this candidate is a former colleague of mine."

To describe a job applicant who is not worth further consideration: "I would urge you to waste no time in making this candidate an offer of employment."

To describe a person with lackluster credentials: "All in all, I cannot say enough good things about this candidate or recommend him too highly."

Robert Thornton

You can attempt to do this using words that produce positive effects. For example, in the opening you can do more than just give the affirmative answer. You can add goodwill, as in this example:

The enclosed check for $89.77 is our way of proving to you that we value your satisfaction highly.

Throughout the message you should avoid words that recall unnecessarily the bad situation you are correcting. You especially want to avoid the negative words that could be used to describe what went wrong—words such as *mistake, trouble, damage, broken,* and *loss.* Even general words such as *problem, difficulty,* and *misunderstanding* can create unpleasant connotations.

Also negative are the apologies often included in these messages. Even though well intended, the somewhat conventional "we sincerely regret the inconvenience caused you . . . ." type of comment is of questionable value. It emphasizes the negative happenings for which the apology is made. If you sincerely believe that you owe an apology, or that one is expected, you can choose to apologize and risk the negative effect. In most instances, however, your efforts to correct the problem show adequate concern for your reader's interests.

NEED TO REGAIN LOST CONFIDENCE.   Except in cases in which the cause of the difficulty is routine or incidental, you also will need to regain the reader's lost confidence. Just what you must do and how you must do it depend on the facts of the situation. You will need to survey the situation to see what they are. If something can be done to correct a bad procedure or a product defect, you should do it. Then you should tell your reader what has been done as convincingly and positively as you can. If what went wrong was a rare, unavoidable event, you should explain this. Sometimes you will need to explain how a product should be used or cared for. Sometimes you will need to resell the product.

CONTRASTING ADJUSTMENTS

The techniques previously discussed are illustrated by the following adjustment letters. The first, with its indirect order and grudging tone, is ineffective. The directness and positiveness of the second clearly make it the better letter.

A SLOW AND NEGATIVE TREATMENT.   The ineffective letter begins with an obvious comment about receiving the claim. It recalls vividly what went wrong and then painfully explains what happened. As a result, the good news is delayed for an additional paragraph. Finally, after two delaying paragraphs, the letter gets to the good news. Though well intended, the close leaves the reader with a reminder of the trouble.

Dear Ms. Watson:

We have received your May 1 claim reporting that our shipment of Fireboy extinguishers arrived in badly damaged condition. We regret the inconvenience caused you and can understand your unhappiness.

Following our standard practice, we investigated the situation thoroughly. Apparently, the fault was in our failure to check the seals carefully. As a result, the fluid escaped in transit, damaging the exteriors of the fire extinguishers. We have taken corrective measures to assure that future shipments will be more carefully checked.

I am pleased to report that we are sending a replacement order. It will be shipped today by Red Line Motor Freight and should reach you by Saturday.

Again, we regret all the trouble caused you.

Sincerely,

THE DIRECT AND POSITIVE TECHNIQUE.   The better letter uses a subject line to identify the transaction. The opening words tell the reader what she most wants to hear in a positive way that adds to the goodwill tone of the message. With reader-viewpoint ex-

• •

CASE ILLUSTRATION Adjustment Grant Letters (Explaining a Human Error)

This letter grants the action requested in the claim of a customer who received sterling flatware that was monogrammed incorrectly. The writer has no excuse, for human error was to blame. His explanation is positive and convincing.

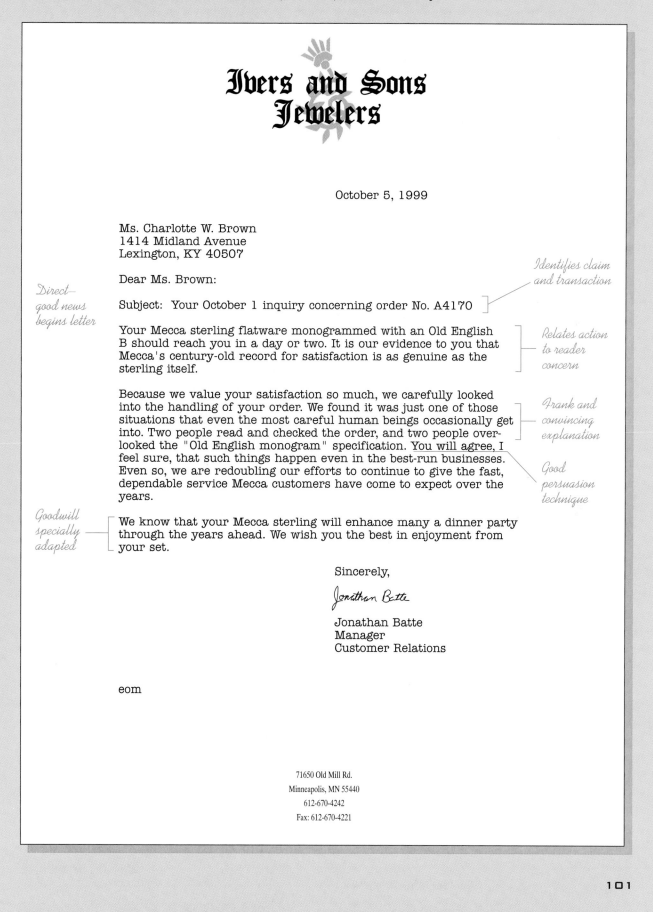

Ivers and Sons Jewelers

October 5, 1999

Ms. Charlotte W. Brown
1414 Midland Avenue
Lexington, KY 40507

Dear Ms. Brown:

Identifies claim and transaction

Direct—good news begins letter

Subject: Your October 1 inquiry concerning order No. A4170

Your Mecca sterling flatware monogrammed with an Old English B should reach you in a day or two. It is our evidence to you that Mecca's century-old record for satisfaction is as genuine as the sterling itself.

Relates action to reader concern

Because we value your satisfaction so much, we carefully looked into the handling of your order. We found it was just one of those situations that even the most careful human beings occasionally get into. Two people read and checked the order, and two people overlooked the "Old English monogram" specification. You will agree, I feel sure, that such things happen even in the best-run businesses. Even so, we are redoubling our efforts to continue to give the fast, dependable service Mecca customers have come to expect over the years.

Frank and convincing explanation

Good persuasion technique

Goodwill specially adapted

We know that your Mecca sterling will enhance many a dinner party through the years ahead. We wish you the best in enjoyment from your set.

Sincerely,

Jonathan Batte

Jonathan Batte
Manager
Customer Relations

eom

71650 Old Mill Rd.
Minneapolis, MN 55440
612-670-4242
Fax: 612-670-4221

planation, the letter then reviews what happened. Without a single negative word, it makes clear what caused the problem and what has been done to prevent its recurrence. After handling the essential matter of disposing of the damaged merchandise, the letter closes with positive resale talk far removed from the problem.

■ This better letter is direct and positive.

Dear Ms. Watson:

Subject: Your May 1 report on invoice 1348

Two dozen new and thoroughly tested Fireboy extinguishers should reach your sales floor in time for your Saturday promotion. They were shipped early today by Red Line Motor Freight.

Because your satisfaction with our service is important to us, we have thoroughly checked all the Fireboys in stock. In the past, we have assumed that all of them were checked for tight seals at the factory. We learned, thanks to you, that we must now systematically check each one. We have set up a system of checks as part of our normal handling procedure.

When you receive the new Fireboys, will you please return the original group by motor freight? We will pay all transportation charges.

As you may know, the new Fireboys have practically revolutionized the extinguisher field. Their compact size and efficiency have made them the top seller in only three months. We are confident they will play their part in the success of your sale.

Sincerely,

INTRODUCTORY SITUATION — Order Acknowledgments

The next work you take from your in-basket is an order for paints and painting supplies. It is from Mr. Orville Chapman of the Central City Paint Company, a new customer whom Pinnacle has been trying to attract for months. You usually acknowledge orders with routine messages, but this case is different. You feel the need to welcome this new customer and to cultivate him for future sales.

After checking your warehouse and making certain that the goods will be on the way to Chapman today, you are ready to write him a special letter of acknowledgment.

ORDER ACKNOWLEDGMENTS

■ Businesses usually acknowledge orders with form notes, but they sometimes use letters.

As the description of the preceding situation implies, acknowledgments are sent to let people who order goods know the status of their orders. Most acknowledgments are routine. They simply tell when the goods are being shipped. Many companies use form messages for such situations. Some use printed, standard notes with checkoff or write-in blanks. But individually written acknowledgments are sometimes justified, especially with new accounts or large orders.

■ Acknowledgment letters build goodwill, as shown in this general plan.

Skillfully composed acknowledgments can do more than acknowledge orders, though this task remains their primary goal. These messages can also build goodwill and show good business etiquette. Through a warm, personal, human tone, they can reach out and give a hearty handshake. They can make the reader feel good about doing business with a company that cares. They can make the reader want to continue doing business with that company. To maintain this goodwill for repeat customers, you will want to revise your form acknowledgments on a regular basis. If your company offers goods or services that are consumed often, you'll need to revise these messages more frequently than a business offering durable goods or services.

The sequence below illustrates how you should approach such messages.

■ Give status of order, acknowledging incidentally.

■ Include some goodwill—sales talk, reselling, or such.

■ Include a thank-you.

- Report frankly or handle tactfully problems with vague or back orders.
- Close with adapted, friendly comment.

FAVORABLE RESPONSE PATTERN WITH GOODWILL EMPHASIS

In writing the acknowledgment message outlined above, you emphasize goodwill building throughout. Your direct opening can begin this goal by emphasizing receiving the goods rather than sending them, as in this example:

> The Protect-O paints and supplies you ordered April 4 should reach you by Wednesday. They are leaving our Walden warehouse today by Blue Darter Motor Freight.

In addition, when the situation permits, you can include a warm expression of thanks for the order. When you are acknowledging a first order, a warm welcome can enhance your goodwill message. When such information is of service, you can even include some words about new products or services. And you can end the goodwill message with friendly talk in the close—perhaps a specially adapted forward look to continued business relations.

> ■ Directly acknowledge the order.

NEED FOR TACT IN SHIPMENT DELAYS

Sometimes the task of acknowledging is complicated by your inability to send the goods requested right away. You could be out of them; or perhaps the reader did not give you all the information you need to send the goods. In either case, a delay is involved. In some cases, delays are routine and expected and do not pose a serious problem. In others, they are likely to lead to major disappointments. When this is the case, you will need to use tact.

Using tact involves minimizing the negative effect of the message. In the case of a vague order, for example, you should handle the information you need without appearing to accuse the reader of giving insufficient information. To illustrate, you gain nothing by

> ■ When goods must be delayed, handle this news tactfully.

> ■ In vague orders, request the needed information positively.

Emphasize receipt of the items in back orders.

writing "You failed to specify the color of umbrellas you want." But you gain goodwill and practice good etiquette by writing "So that we can send you precisely the umbrellas you want, please check your choice of colors on the enclosed card." This sentence handles the matter positively and makes the action easy to take. It shows mannerly etiquette.

Similarly, you can handle back-order information tactfully by emphasizing the positive part of the message. For example, instead of writing "We can't ship the Crescent City pralines until the 9th," you can write "We will rush the Crescent City pralines to you as soon as our stock is replenished by a shipment due May 9." If the back-order period is longer than the customer expects or longer than the 30 days allowed by law, you may choose to give your customer an alternative. You could offer a substitute product or service. Giving the customer a choice builds goodwill. A more complete discussion of how to handle such negative news is provided in Chapter 6.

CONTRASTING ACKNOWLEDGMENTS

Following are contrasting examples.

The following two letters show bad and good technique in acknowledging Mr. Chapman's order. As you would expect, the good version follows the plan described in the preceding paragraphs.

SLOW ROUTE TO A FAVORABLE MESSAGE.   The bad example begins indirectly, emphasizing receipt of the order. Although intended to produce goodwill, the second sentence further delays telling what the reader wants most to hear. Moreover, the letter is written from the writer's point of view (note the *we*-emphasis).

This one is bad.

Dear Mr. Chapman:

Your April 4 order for $1,743.30 worth of Protect-O paints and supplies has been received. We are pleased to have this nice order and hope that it marks the beginning of a long relationship.

As you instructed, we will bill you for this amount. We are shipping the goods today by Blue Darter Motor Freight.

We look forward to your future orders.

Sincerely,

FAST-MOVING PRESENTATION OF THE GOOD NEWS.   The better letter begins directly, telling Mr. Chapman that he is getting what he wants. The remainder of the letter is customer welcome and subtle selling. Notice the good use of reader emphasis and positive language. The letter closes with a note of appreciation and a friendly, forward look.

This letter is better.

Dear Mr. Chapman:

Your selection of Protect-O paints and supplies should reach you by Wednesday, for the shipment left today by Blue Darter Motor Freight. As you requested, we are sending you an invoice for $1,743.30, including sales tax.

Because this is your first order from us, I welcome you to the Protect-O circle of dealers. Our representative, Ms. Cindy Wooley, will call from time to time to offer whatever assistance she can. She is a highly competent technical adviser on paint and painting.

Here in the home plant we will also do what we can to help you profit from Protect-O products. We'll do our best to give you the most efficient service. And we'll continue to develop the best possible paints—like our new Chem-Treat line. As you will see from the enclosed brochure, Chem-Treat is a real breakthrough in mildew protection.

We genuinely appreciate your order, Mr. Chapman. We are determined to serve you well in the years ahead.

Sincerely,

This letter concerns an order that cannot be handled exactly as the customer would like. Some items are being sent, but one must be placed on back order and one cannot be shipped because the customer did not give the information needed. The letter skillfully handles the negative points.

LOWE'S
Companies, Inc.

One of the "100 Best Companies to Work for in America"

October 7, 1999

Mr. Fred K. Fletcher, President
Fletcher Machine Works
4772 Worth Road
Detroit, MI 48201

Dear Mr. Fletcher:

Direct—tells about goods being sent

By noon tomorrow, your three new Baskin motors and one Dawson 110 compressor should reach your Meadowbrook shops. As you requested, we marked them for your West Side loading dock and sent them by Warren Motor Express.

Positive emphasis on delivery

Negative information presented with you-viewpoint emphasis

So that we can be certain of sending you the one handcart for your special uses, will you please review the enclosed description of the two models available? As you will see, the Model M is our heavy-duty design; but its extra weight is not justified for all jobs. When you have made your choice, please mark it on the enclosed card and mail the card to us. We'll send your choice to you as soon as we know it.

Helpful explanation—aids reader in making choice

Tactful—emphasis on receipt of goods

Your three dozen 317 T-clamps should reach you by the 13th. As you may know, these very popular clamps have been in short supply for some time now; but we have been promised a limited order by the 11th. We are marking three dozen for rush shipment to you.

We are always pleased to do business with Fletcher Machine Works and will continue to serve you with quality industrial equipment.

Friendly forward look

Sincerely,

Shannon E. Kurrus

Shannon E. Kurrus
Sales Manager

SEK:bim
Enclosure

𝓗allmark
Cards

June 10, 1999

Ms. Virginia T. Wells, Owner
Wells Farm Store
1317 Cameron Road
Magnolia, MS 39652

Direct reports handling of order

Dear Ms. Wells:

The assorted Hallmark Products you ordered June 7 should reach you by June 14. They were shipped this morning by United Parcel Service. As you specified, we will add the $785.40 charge to your account.

Emphasis on receipt of goods

Method of payment covered

Friendly close

We sincerely appreciate your order, Ms. Wells. We look forward to the privilege of serving you again.

Sincerely,

Victor V. Potts

Victor V. Potts
Sales Manager

ccs

HALLMARK CARDS, INCORPORATED · KANSAS CITY, MISSOURI 64141 · (816) 274-5111

Claims

Occasionally something goes wrong with the goods and services Pinnacle buys. When this happens in your area of responsibility, your job is to look after Pinnacle's interests. Today it happened. You received by motor freight an order for two dozen fire extinguishers. All of them were damaged. Leaking acid had ruined their finish. Pinnacle cannot accept them. You must write the seller, explaining what happened and getting the seller to correct the situation. In other words, you have to write a claim letter. Because the local fire marshal has ordered Pinnacle to have the fire extinguishers in place by next Monday, you must act fast.

The facts of the case tell you that this is not a routine letter. The news in claim messages is bad—bad for the writer and bad for the reader. How best to handle claim situations certainly requires careful thought. The following discussion should guide your thinking when you must handle claims.

CLAIMS

When something goes wrong between a business and its customers, usually someone begins an effort to correct the situation. Typically, the offended party calls the matter to the attention of those responsible. In other words, he or she makes a claim. The claim can be made in person, by telephone, or by written message. Our concern here is how to make it by written message. The following pages discuss a plan for handling claims by writing. In summary form, the plan is as follows:

- Begin directly. Tell what is wrong.
- Identify the situation (invoice number, product information, etc.) in the text or in a subject line.
- Present enough of the facts to permit a decision.
- Seek corrective action.
- End positively—friendly but firm.

Claims are written to collect for damages. They should follow this plan.

USING DIRECTNESS FOR BAD NEWS

Claim situations are bad-news situations. Goods have been damaged or lost, a product has failed to perform, or service has been bad. The situation is unhappy for both writer and reader.

As you know, usually bad-news situations are handled in indirect order. But claims are exceptions—for two good reasons. First, businesspeople want to know when something is wrong with their products or services so they can correct the matter. Thus, there is no reason for delay or gentle treatment. Second, as we have noted, directness lends strength, and strength in a claim enhances the likelihood of success.

A claim concerns a particular transaction, item of merchandise, or service call. So that your reader will quickly know exactly what your claim is about, you will have to include the necessary identification information and place it somewhere near the beginning. What you include depends on what is needed in each case—invoice number, order number or date, serial number of product, and so on.

You can handle the identification information incidentally or in a subject line. By incidental handling we mean working it into the message in a subordinate way. Handling it in a subject line involves using the mechanical device described and illustrated in Appendix B. Because a direct beginning is appropriate in the claim, the subject line may begin this directness, for it actually begins the message. The following example illustrates good wording and content for a subject line:

Subject: Damaged condition of fire extinguishers on arrival, your invoice No. C13144

Use directness for this bad-news because . . .

(1) the reader wants to know and (2) it adds strength.

Identify the transaction involved.

Do this incidentally or in a subject line.

In this letter a hotel manager presents a claim about defective carpeting. She makes the claim directly and forcefully—yet politely. She explains the problem clearly and emphasizes the effect of the damage.

CHARLES HOTEL

September 17, 1999

Mr. Luther R. Ferguson, President
Rich Carpet, Inc.
13171 Industrial Boulevard
Seattle, WA 98107

Clearly states problem and identifies transaction

Dear Mr. Ferguson:

Direct statement of problem

Subject: Color fading of your Kota-Tuff carpeting, your invoice 3147 dated January 3, 1995.

Emphasis on effect

The Kota-Tuff carpeting you installed for us last January has faded badly and is an eyesore in our hotel pool area. As you can see in the enclosed photograph, the original forest green color now is spotted with rings of varying shades of white and green. The spotting is especially heavy in areas adjacent to the pool. Probably water has caused the damage. But your written warranty says that the color will "withstand the effects of sun and water."

Explains nature and extent of defect

Establishes case firmly

Suggests solution

Because the product clearly has not lived up to the warranty, we ask that you replace the Kota-Tuff with a more suitable carpeting. If you are unable to find a satisfactory carpeting, we request a refund of the full purchase price, including installation.

Justifies claim

I will appreciate your usual promptness in correcting this problem.

Sincerely,

Luella E. Dabbs

Luella E. Dabbs
Manager

tos
Enclosure (photograph)

2-201 East 15th Street
North Vancouver, BC V7M 1S2
604-678-9080
FAX: 604-678-9076

STATING THE PROBLEM DIRECTLY

A good claim is a combination of courtesy and firmness. You begin by stating the problem clearly. And you include all information necessary for judging it. Sometimes it lends strength to the claim if you explain the consequences of what happened. A broken machine, for example, may have stopped an entire assembly line; or damaged merchandise may have caused a loss in sales. The following beginning sentence illustrates this point:

> The Model H freezer (Serial No. 713129) that we bought from you last September suddenly quit working, ruining $517 of frozen foods in the process.

■ Begin by stating the claim clearly, including all essential information.

EXPLAINING THE FACTS

Your next logical step is to present the supporting facts. Do this in a straightforward manner. Include all the facts needed to judge the legitimacy of your claim. And do this frankly and respectfully, avoiding words that suggest anger or mistrust. Your goal is to present the situation objectively, letting the facts justify your case.

■ Present the facts that justify the claim—objectively and without anger.

GIVING CHOICE IN CORRECTING ERROR

The facts you present should prove your claim. So your next step is to follow logically with the handling of the claim. How you handle the claim, however, is a matter for you to decide.

One way of handling the claim is to state specifically the action you want taken—return of money, free repairs, new merchandise. Another is to leave the decision to the reader. Because most businesspeople want to do the right thing for their customers, often this choice is the better one.

■ Next, handle the claim.

■ Either state what you want or let the reader decide.

OVERCOMING NEGATIVENESS WITH A FRIENDLY CLOSE

Your final friendly words should remove all doubt about your cordial attitude. For added strength, when strength is needed to support a claim, you could express appreciation for what you seek. This suggestion does not support use of the timeworn "Thanking you in advance." Instead, say something like "I would be grateful if you could get the new merchandise to me in time for my Friday sale." Whatever final words you choose, they should clearly show that yours is a firm yet cordial request in accord with the practice of good business etiquette.

■ Your closing words should show your cordial attitude.

CONTRASTING EXAMPLES OF CLAIM LETTERS

The following two letters show contrasting ways of handling Pinnacle's fire extinguisher problem. The first is slow and harsh. The second is courteous, yet to the point and firm.

■ The following contrasting letters show good and bad handling of a claim.

A SLOW AND HARSH LETTER. The first letter starts slowly with a long explanation of the situation. Some of the details in the beginning sentence are helpful, but they do not deserve the emphasis that this position gives them. The problem is not described until the second paragraph. The wording here is clear but much too strong. The words are angry and insulting, and they talk down to the reader. Such words are more likely to produce resistance than acceptance. The negative writing continues into the close, leaving a bad final impression.

Dear Ms. Golby:

As your records will show, on December 7 we ordered 24 Fireboy extinguishers (our Order No. 7135). The units were shipped to us by Red Arrow Freight (your Invoice No. 715C) and arrived at our loading docks December 15.

At the time of delivery, our shipping and receiving supervisor noticed that all the boxes were soaked with fluid. Further inspection showed that your workers had been negligent in check-

■ This bad one is slow and harsh.

ing the cap screws. As a result of their negligence, acid leaked and destroyed the chrome finish on all the units.

It is hard for me to understand a shipping system that permits such errors to take place. Pinnacle does not accept these fire extinguishers. Further, we want these damaged units taken off our hands and replaced with good ones. Because we will be inspected by the fire marshal Monday, we further insist that the replacements reach us by that date.

Respectfully,

A FIRM YET COURTEOUS LETTER.   The second letter follows the plan suggested in preceding paragraphs. A subject line quickly identifies the situation. The letter begins with a clear statement of the problem. Next, in a tone that shows firmness without anger, it tells what went wrong. Then it requests a specific remedy and asks what to do with the damaged goods. The ending uses subtle persuasion by implying confidence in the reader. The words used here leave no doubt about continued friendship.

■ This better letter closely follows text suggestions.

Dear Ms. Golby:

Subject: Acid leakage of Fireboy extinguishers, your Invoice No. 715C

The condition of the 24 Fireboy extinguishers received today has affected their ability to function.

At the time of delivery, the condition of your shipment was called to the attention of the Red Arrow Freight Company driver by our shipping and receiving supervisor. Upon inspection, we found all the boxes thoroughly soaked with fluid. Further inspection revealed that at least six of the extinguishers had leaked acid from the cap screws. As a result, the chrome finish of all the units had been badly damaged.

Because we are under orders from the fire marshal to have this equipment in our plant by Monday, please get the 24 replacement units to us by that date. Also, will you please instruct me what I should do with the defective units?

I am aware, of course, that situations like this will occur in spite of all precautions. And I am confident that you will replace the extinguishers with your usual courtesy.

Sincerely,

INTRODUCTORY SITUATION

Orders

In your position at Pinnacle, you receive this month's *Business Administrator* in the morning mail. As usual, this professional journal is filled with articles useful to workers who want to advance into administration. One of the articles lists the 10 most valuable books for administrators. You are impressed. You want these books for your personal library.

You might be able to get the books by looking for them at local bookstores, but this procedure would take more time than you can spare. You decide instead to order them from the publishers. Since you do not have these publishers' order forms, you will have to order in writing. The article gives publisher names along with the prices and necessary descriptions of the books. A business directory in the company library contains the publishers' addresses.

One of the orders you write will be to Business Books, Inc., publisher of three of the books you want. You are ready to write the order. But how do you organize it? What information do you include? The answers to these questions appear in the following discussion.

ORDERS

■ Rarely will you write an order.

Because most orders are now placed orally, made on the web, or made on order forms, order messages are not often written. When you must write an order, however, you would do well to use the plan that the following pages discuss in detail:

Tables Help Writers Organize Data for Easy Reading

Setting up tables within a document is now an easy task. Most word processors have a tables feature that allows writers to create tables as well as import spreadsheet and database files. In both instances, you can arrange information in columns and rows, in-serting detail in the cells. Headings can be formatted and formulas can be entered in the cells. The table you see here could be one the writer created for use in an order letter for computer supplies.

Item Number	Description	Quantity	Unit Price	Total Price
53-5698	Iomega Zip 100 MB Zip Drive-External	1	$149.95	$149.95
17-1121	3-pack 100 MB Iomega Disks	2	$ 41.95	$ 83.90
02-7821	Zip Disk Labels (25 pack)	1	$ 6.99	$ 6.99
02-7621	25-pin parallel 6 foot cable	1	$ 10.95	$ 10.95
		Total		$ 251.79

Organizing information with tables makes it eas-ier for both the writer and reader. The writer will be sure to include all information since the headings prompt for complete detail; the reader will be able to extract the needed information both quickly and ac-curately.

- Begin directly—with clear authorization.
- Systematically and consistently arrange items with identifying facts (number, units, catalog number, name, description points, unit price, total price).
- Cover shipping instructions and manner of payment.
- End with goodwill comment.

> But when you write one, follow this plan.

DIRECTLY AUTHORIZING THE ORDER

The preceding plan follows the direct arrangement appropriate for good-news messages. Clearly, an order is good news to the reader. This good news is best presented in words that authorize, such as "Please send me . . ." Anything less direct, such as "I would like to have . . ." falls short of authorization.

> Begin orders directly with a clear authorization.

SPECIFICALLY COVERING THE SALE

The remainder of the message is an exercise in clear, orderly, and complete coverage of the details the reader needs. There is no one best arrangement for these details, but you should be consistent in whatever you do. A good plan is to begin with the number and units needed and to follow with this arrangement of the remaining items:

> Identify the goods ordered clearly and in an orderly way.

- Identifying number (catalog number, ISBN, model number).
- Basic name (including trade names and brands when helpful).
- Unit price.
- Total price.

In finished form, the information might read like this:

3 dozen	No. 712AC, Woolsey Claw hammer, drop-forged head, hickory handle, 13 inches overall length, 16 ounces, at $44.74 per dozen	$134.22

A business manager's small mail order for office supplies is illustrated in this letter. The items ordered require a detailed description, which the writer provides in an orderly way.

Pioneer Insurance Company

1717 West 17th St.
Stockton, CA 95202

202-552-8989
FAX: 209-552-8943

November 7, 1999

Tells how to

Ms. Viola Green, Sales Manager
The Office Warehouse
1735 Townsend Street
San Francisco, CA 94107

Dear Ms. Green:

Qualifies prices quoted

Direct authorization — Please send me the office supplies listed below by prepaid parcel post at the address above. I am ordering from your September 7 price list.

Orderly listing of details

Items stand out

10 reams	No. 321A, Scroll bond paper, white, 25%-rag, 8 1/2 by 11 inches, 20-pound, @ 3.25	$32.50
4 boxes	No. 106B, laser paper, 8 1/2 by 11 inches, 20-lb, @ $5.40	21.60
5 dozen	No. 1171A, printer cartridges, @ $10.50	52.50
5 each	No. 215H, copy stands, Luddell model K, 26 inches high, black, @ $9.60	48.00
	TOTAL	$154.60

Prices stand out

Courteous yet forceful urge for prompt action — Please charge the amount to me on the usual 2/10, n/60 terms. Because our supplies of these items are nearly depleted, I will appreciate any rush service you can give this order.

Payment method covered

Sincerely,

Clovis S. Rosenbaum

Clovis S. Rosenbaum
Manager

eme

In addition to describing the items ordered, you need to include other vital information—shipping instructions, method of payment, and anything else necessary for filling the order. You may work some of this information into the beginning, following the authorization statement. You may include the remainder with your closing remarks.

■ Cover all the information needed—shipping instruction, payments, and the like.

CLOSING WITH A FRIENDLY COMMENT

As you would do in other direct-style messages, end this one with an appropriate friendly comment. If there is need for urgency, this information might well go with these goodwill words. If possible, make them fit the one case, as in this example:

■ Close with friendly words.

Since we have promised to make our first delivery on the 17th, would you please get these supplies to us by the 13th at the latest? We will sincerely appreciate your promptness.

CONTRASTING ORDERS

The following contrasting letters for the case described earlier show good and bad ways of ordering books.

■ The following two examples are of bad and good order letters.

A SLOW AND DISORDERLY ORDER.   The letter showing bad technique begins indirectly. The first sentence is useless and merely delays the main message. This message comes in the second sentence, but it is more a suggestion than an authorization. The information on the books is not orderly, and the format does not display it clearly. Neither the number of books wanted nor their prices stand out. One has to look for this information. The book titles are clear and will probably lead the reader to the right books. But edition numbers have been omitted, and this information could be important. Also, the items are ordered inconsistently. Payment details appear in the close, but they are vague and incomplete. The letter's abrupt ending will produce little goodwill.

Dear Sales Manager:

■ This bad one is slow and disorderly.

Information I have indicates that your company is the publisher of three books I would like for my personal library. I would sincerely appreciate it if you would be so kind as to send them to me. They are as follows:

Basic Management, price $26.95, by Alonzo Bevins, 1 copy.
Clear Writing for Business, price $21.95, by Mildred Knauth, 1 copy.
Managing Organizations, 2 copies, by Hugo W. Bass, price $25.95.

I have enclosed a check in the amount of $100.80. I will pay any additional charges.

Sincerely,

A DIRECT AND ORDERLY ORDER.   The second letter avoids the faults of the first. It begins with a direct authorization to ship goods. Then it lists the books wanted in an orderly fashion. The numbers and units stand out. Clear identification information appears in the center position. Extensions in the right-hand column emphasize the price information, including the total cost. In the close, the remaining matter of additional charges is handled. Although the closing goodwill words are somewhat routine, they are appropriate for this routine situation.

Dear Sales Manager:

■ This good order letter is fast and efficient.

Please send me the following books:

1 copy Alonzo Bevins, Basic Management, 2nd ed., 1998, @ $26.95 . . . . . $ 26.95
1 copy Mildred Knauth, Clear Writing for Business, 1999, @ $21.95 . . . . . 21.95
2 copies Hugo W. Bass, Managing Organizations, 3rd ed., 1999, @ $25.95   51.90
Total . $100.80

The enclosed check for $100.80 covers your 1999 list prices for the books. If prices have increased and/or if I owe shipping charges or sales taxes, please bill me for the additional amount. Or, if you prefer, I will pay on delivery.

I will appreciate your promptness in handling this order.

Sincerely,

OTHER DIRECT MESSAGE SITUATIONS

■ Other direct message situations occur.

In the preceding pages, we have covered the most common direct message situations. Others occur, of course. You should be able to handle them with the techniques that have been explained and illustrated.

■ You should be able to handle them by applying the techniques covered in this chapter

In handling such situations, remember that whenever possible, you should get to the goal of the message right away. You should cover any other information needed in good logical order. You should carefully choose words that convey just the right meaning. More specifically, you should consider the value of using the you-viewpoint, and you should weigh carefully the differences in meaning conveyed by the positiveness or negativeness of your words. As in all cordial human contacts, you should end your message with appropriate and friendly goodwill words.

SUMMARY BY CHAPTER OBJECTIVES

1 Describe the process of writing business messages.

1. The process of writing business messages begins with planning.
   - Begin by determining the objective of the letter (what it must do).
   - Next, predict the reader's probable reaction to the objective.
   - Then assemble all the information you will need.
   - Select the message plan (direct order if positive or neutral reaction; indirect order if negative reaction).
   - Write the message, applying your knowledge of conciseness, readable writing, and effect of words.
   - Review your work critically, seeking ways of improving it.
   - Get input from others.
   - Evaluate all inputs.
   - Revise, using your best judgment. This end product is an improved message, and you have had a profitable learning experience.

2 Write clear, well-structured routine requests for information.

2. The routine inquiry is a basic direct-order message.
   - Begin it with a request—either (1) a request for specific information wanted or (2) a general request for information.
   - Somewhere in the message explain enough to enable the reader to answer.
   - If the inquiry involves more than one question, make each stand out—perhaps as separate sentences or separate paragraphs.
   - Consider numbering the questions.
   - And word them as questions.
   - End with an appropriate friendly comment.

3 Compose orderly and thorough inquiries about prospective employees that show respect for human rights.

3. Inquiries about people follow much the same order as described above.
   - But they require special care, since they concern the moral and legal rights of people.
   - So seek truth, and act in good faith.
   - Also, adapt your questions to the one applicant and the one situation rather than follow a routine.

4 Write direct, orderly, and friendly answers to inquiries.

4. When responding to inquiries favorably, you should begin directly.
   - If the response contains only one answer, begin with it.
   - If it contains more than one answer, begin with a major one or a general statement indicating you are answering.
   - Identify the message being answered early, perhaps in a subject line.
   - Arrange your answers (if more than one) logically.
   - And make them stand out.
   - If both good- and bad-news answers are involved, give each answer the emphasis it deserves, perhaps by subordinating the negative.
   - For extra goodwill effect, consider doing more than was asked.
   - End with appropriate cordiality.

5. Handle personnel evaluations directly.
  - Do so even if they contain negative information, for you are doing what the reader asked.
  - You have two logical choices for beginning the message.
    — You can begin by answering a question asked, preferably one deserving the emphasis of the opening position.
    — You can begin with a statement indicating you are complying with the request.
  - Refer to the message you are answering early in your message (perhaps in the subject line).
  - Present the information in a logical order, making each answer stand out.
    — Numbering the responses is one way of doing this.
    — Arranging answers by paragraphs also helps.
  - Report fairly and truthfully.
    — Stress facts and avoid opinions.
    — Give each item the emphasis it deserves.
  - End with appropriate friendly comment.

5 Phrase personnel evaluations that fairly present the essential facts.

6. As messages granting adjustments are positive responses, write them in the direct order.
  - But they differ from other direct-order messages in that they involve a negative situation.
    — Something has gone wrong.
    — You are correcting that wrong.
    — But you should also overcome the negative image in the reader's mind.
  - You do this by first telling the good news—what you are doing to correct the wrong.
  - In the opening and throughout, emphasize the positive.
  - Avoid the negative—words like *trouble, damage,* and *broken.*
  - Try to regain the reader's lost confidence, maybe with explanation or with assurance of corrective measures taken.
  - End with a goodwill comment, avoiding words that recall what went wrong.

6 Compose adjustment grants that regain any lost confidence.

7. Write order acknowledgments in the form of a favorable response.
  - Handle most by form messages or notes.
  - But in special cases use individual messages.
  - Begin such messages directly, telling the status of the goods ordered.
  - In the remainder of the message, build goodwill, perhaps including some selling or reselling.
  - Include an expression of appreciation somewhere in the message.
  - End with an appropriate, friendly comment.

7 Write acknowledgments that cover problems and build goodwill.

8. Claims are a special case. Even though they carry bad news, they are best written in the direct order. The reason: the reader usually wants to correct the problem and requires only that the facts be presented; also, directness strengthens the claim. Follow this general plan:
  - Somewhere early in the message (in a subject line or incidentally in the first sentence) identify the transaction.
  - Then state what went wrong, perhaps with some interpretation of the effects.
  - Follow with a clear review of the facts, without showing anger.
  - You may want to suggest a remedy.
  - End with cordial words.

8 Write claims that fairly and courteously explain the facts.

9. Orders are best written in the direct order, as follows:
  - Begin with a direct authorization to ship.
  - Carefully and systematically identify the items you want (catalog number, basic name, descriptive points, unit price, total price, and so on).
  - Include all other information vital to the sale (shipping instructions, method of payment, time requirements).
  - End with friendly, appropriate words that fit the one case.

9 Write orders that systematically present the essential information.

CRITICAL THINKING QUESTIONS

1. When is the direct order appropriate in inquiries? When would you use the indirect order? Give examples.

2. "Explanations in inquiries merely add length and should be eliminated." Discuss.

3. What should the writer do to respect the rights of people in inquiries about them?

4. "In writing inquiries about people, I do not ask specific questions. Instead, I ask for 'everything you think I should know' about the person." Discuss this viewpoint.

5. Discuss why just reporting truthfully may not be enough in handling negative information in messages answering inquiries.

6. Defend a policy of doing more than asked in answering routine inquiries. Can the policy be carried too far?

7. What can acknowledgment messages do to build goodwill?

8. Discuss situations where each of the following forms of an order acknowledgment would be preferred: form letter, merged letter, and a special letter.

9. Discuss how problems (vague orders, back orders) should be handled in messages acknowledging orders.

10. Discuss the relationship of positive and negative words to fair treatment in employee evaluation letters.

11. Why is it usually advisable to do more than just grant the claim in an adjustment-grant message?

12. Usually bad-news messages are appropriately written in the indirect order. Why should claims be exceptions?

13. Justify the use of negative words in claims. Can they be overused? Discuss.

14. Discuss the relative directness of these beginnings of an order:
    a. "Please ship the following items. . . ."
    b. "I would like to have the following. . . ."
    c. "I need the following items. . . ."
    d. "I would appreciate your sending me the following items. . . ."
    e. "Can you send me the following items. . . ?"

CRITICAL THINKING EXERCISES

1. List your criticisms of this letter asking for information about an applicant for a job:

Dear Ms. Bentley:

Inez Becker has applied to us for a job as inventory clerk in our parts department. She listed you as a reference and claims that she worked for you as a records clerk in your parts department for the period May 1995 to August 1998. Because I am impressed with Ms. Becker, I would like to have your evaluation of her.

I am especially interested in her work ethic and how she gets along with other workers. I am curious about why she left the job with you. Also, please tell me whether you would hire her back if you had an opening. In addition, I would like to know about her honesty, character, and attitude.

Thank you in advance for your prompt response.

Sincerely, yours,

2. Point out the shortcomings in this response letter. The letter is a reply to an inquiry about a short course in business communication taught by a professor for the company's employees. The inquiry included five questions: (1) How did the professor perform? (2) What was the course format (length, meeting structure)? (3) What was the employee evaluation of the instruction? (4) Was the course adapted to the company and its technical employees? (5) Was homework assigned?

Dear Mr. Braden:

Your January 17 inquiry addressed to the Training Director has been referred to me for attention since we have no one with that title. I do have some training responsibilities and was the one who organized the in-house course in clear writing. You asked five questions about our course.

Concerning your question about the instructor, Professor Alonzo Britt, I can report that he did an acceptable job in the classroom. Some of the students, including this writer, felt that the emphasis was too much on grammar and punctuation, however. He did assign homework, but it was not excessive.

We had class two hours a day from 3:00 to 5:00 PM every Thursday for eight weeks. Usually the professor lectured the first hour. He is a good lecturer but sometimes talks over the heads of the students. This was the main complaint in the evaluations the students made at the end of the course, but they had many good comments to make also. Some did not like the content, which they said was not adapted to the needs of a technical worker. Overall, the professor got a rating of B— on a scale of A to F.

We think the course was good for our technical people, but it could have been better adapted to our needs and our people. I also think it was too long—about 10 hours (five meetings) would have been enough. Also, we think the professor spent too much time lecturing and not enough on application work in class.

Please be informed that the information about Professor Britt must be held in confidence.

Sincerely,

3. Point out the shortcomings in this letter granting a claim for a fax machine received in damaged condition. Inspection of the package revealed that the damage did not occur in transit.

Dear Ms. Orsag:

Your May 3 letter in which you claim that the Rigo FAX391 was received in damaged condition has been carefully considered. We inspect all our machines carefully before packing them, and we pack them carefully in strong boxes with Styrofoam supports that hold them snugly. Thus we cannot understand how the damage could have occurred.

Even so, we stand behind our product and will replace any that are damaged. However, we must ask that first you send us the defective one so we can inspect it. After your claim of damage has been verified, we will send you a new one.

We regret any inconvenience this situation may have caused you and assure you that problems like this rarely occur in our shipping department.

Sincerely,

4. List your criticisms of this letter inquiring about a convenience store advertised for sale:

Dear Mr. Meeks:

This is in response to your advertisement in the May 17 *Daily Bulletin* in which you describe a convenience store in Clark City that you want to sell. I am very much interested since I would like to relocate in that area. Before I drive down to see the property, I need some preliminary information. Most important is the question of financing. I am wondering whether you would be willing to finance up to $50,000 of the total if I could come up with the rest, and how much interest would you charge and for how long. I would also like to have the figures for your operations for the past two or three years, including gross sales, expenses, and profits. I need to know also the condition of the building, including such information as when built, improvements made, repairs needed, and so on.

Hoping that you can get these answers to me soon so we can do business.

Sincerely yours,

5. Criticize the following claim letter.

Dear Mr. Stanton:

For many years now I have bought your candies and have been pleased with them. However, last June 4 I ordered 48 boxes of your Swiss Decadance chocolates, and it appears you tried to push off some old stock on me. I have sold some of the boxes, and already three customers have returned the candy to me. The candy is rancid—obviously old. Probably the whole lot was bad and I now have a bunch of dissatisfied customers.

I have taken the remaining boxes off the shelves and will send them back to you—after I get my money back.

Sincerely,

CRITICAL THINKING PROBLEMS

ROUTINE INQUIRIES

1. As a junior executive with Granite Insurance, Inc., you have been assigned the task of designing a correspondence-improvement program for Granite's home-office personnel. As explained by your boss, Ms. Carolyn Damon, some of the correspondence going out on Granite's letterhead is embarrassing, to say the least. Some form of improvement program is badly needed. She wants you to think through the problem and propose a solution.

   As you begin your thinking, you recall that at a professional meeting a few weeks ago you heard Mr. Troy Bartosh talk about a program his company, Five Star Insurance, is conducting. You don't recall many of the specifics Troy mentioned, but you remember that he has been highly pleased with the results. So, before you propose anything, you want to pick Troy's brain. You'll write him right away.

   You haven't yet decided what you need to know, but a few thoughts run through your mind. Does Five Star use formal classes for the instruction? Clinics? Personal conferences? Who does the teaching? Is a critical evaluation of employee writing involved? Was a company manual prepared for the program? (If it was, maybe they will send you one.) Perhaps you'll want to know how much time the employees have to give to the program. And is this company time or the employees' free time? As you continue your thinking, other ideas come to mind. From this brainstorming session you will select the questions whose answers will help you design Granite's program.

   Now write the letter that will get you precisely what you need.

2. Play the role of training director for Megatronics, Inc., a manufacturer of various electronic products. From Ella Thurston, your counterpart at Westin Engineering, you have learned about an exciting new training film called *Leadership Style: A Historical Review.* As Ella explained, this film reviews the leadership styles of a number of leaders in history: Hannibal, Shaka (the Zulu chieftain), and Robert E. Lee, among others. She recalls also that the film was prepared by a Harvard business professor, although she didn't remember the name. She insisted that the film carries a modern message in spite of its historical base. She didn't remember much more, except that

she got it from Quality Training, Inc., a training source you often use.

You want to know more about this film, so you will address an inquiry to the Quality Training people, seeking more information on the film's content. (Perhaps they have a descriptive brochure they can send you.) You'll also ask about cost, both purchase and rental. Because you want something suitable for both upper and middle management, you'll need to know the level for which the film was prepared. Also, you'll want to know whether the film has an accompanying instructor's guide. There may be other questions, so think through the problem. Now write the letter that will get you the information you need.

3. In today's *Wall Street Journal* you saw an advertisement about some property that just might be what you have been looking for:

Rocky Mountain Lodge on 29 scenic acres of forest. Breathtaking mountain view. Running stream through property. Twenty-two rooms, 25 baths. Large kitchen, dining room, and lobby. Giant fireplace. Three service buildings. Two tennis courts. A steal at $2,450,000. P.O. Box 7413, Denver, CO 80209.

One of the industrial clients of your real estate business is seeking a building like this. The area and the price are right. But your client has some specific requirements that the advertisement doesn't cover. So you will write a letter to the advertiser to determine whether the place meets those requirements.

Your client wants a place that is easily accessible throughout the year by automobile. Because the building would be used as a corporate retreat and training center, two rooms suitable for meetings of up to 15 people would be needed. Then there should be at least 15 rooms suitable for bedrooms. It would be helpful if the advertiser could send you a picture of the place—or perhaps a brochure. Also, you'd like to know the real estate taxes on the property. And how old is the structure? You may think of other facts your client should know before inspecting the property. Now write the letter.

4. The current copy of *Environmental Design* magazine contains an eye-catching advertisement that whets your professional appetite. You are the manager of administration of Capital Institutional Services, Inc., with offices in Boston, New York, Seattle, Atlanta, Chicago, San Francisco, and Dallas. You provide tax, legal, and financial services to high-level individuals—primarily to top-middle and top income clients.

Because clients come to your offices to work with your professional staff, you indeed want to provide an office atmosphere consistent with client interests, tastes, and backgrounds. Thus, the Nouveau Art ad on page 90 of *Environmental Design,* which says the studio will provide art pieces for business offices for a fee, is the one that caught your eye. Nouveau Art might very well help in providing the decor and atmosphere you desire at Capital. The ad goes on to indicate that Nouveau Art will change art pieces

every six months to give each office an individual and cultured appearance. Office appearance is important not only to your clients but to your own staff as well.

But you have questions about how the service can relate to your office needs. First, you wonder about the types of art available—modern, portrait, oil, and such. And what type of advice does the company give with its fee? The ad is vague concerning the charge for the services, so you need to know the exact amount Nouveau Art would charge for all the offices you coordinate. Also, you want to know about the artists' backgrounds. Does Nouveau Art furnish brochures for the office if someone should inquire about pieces that are displayed? And who is responsible in case of theft, loss, or damage? Does art mean all art forms? Or which ones? Are sculptures available?

Write the message to be sent to Nouveau Art. You may add other facts to the case as long as it remains a direct-inquiry situation. Make sure the message is complete.

5. "That's what we need—managers who can make effective presentations!" you think as you notice an ad in the latest issue of *Executive Development* magazine.

From Power Presentations, Inc., the ad is aimed at people who feel a need to develop their oral communication ability in group presentations. The company offers a unique training program—one that can be taken on the manager's own time. It promises results and cites some amazing success stories resulting from the course. You are skeptical, but you will look into the matter before making a final judgement. Your first move is to write a letter to Power Presentations, Inc.

As the advertisement suggests, in your letter you will ask for the brochure, which describes the course in detail. And as the ad also suggests, you will ask specific questions.

One question you want answered concerns the videotape recordings mentioned in the advertisement. Apparently the videos are an integral part of the course. As you understand it, the students perform on tape, mail in the tape, then get critiques of their performance on audiocassette tapes and on personalized written forms. You assume that a camcorder and a VCR are necessary for the $495 cost, but you want to know exactly what equipment you will need. Your company will likely pick up one-half of the cost. Is there a discount offered if a certain number of managers agree to take the course?

It's your belief that people learn to give good presentations by actually giving them. Thus, you want a hands-on course. You are not interested in theoretical treatment of the speech process or senseless generalities. The course would need to be practical to be usable by your managers. Moreover, you want specific business applications. What are the qualifications of the people who will be providing the criticisms? What education and what experience have they had?

You are most interested in course validation as

well. But exaggerated claims and testimonials don't convince you. Does Power Presentations have scientific evidence to document their course? You want names and addresses of some satisfied users of the course, preferably from the same size and type as your organization.

Prepare the letter that will get you the information you need about the on-your-own presentation skills course from Power Presentation, Inc.

6. Your role today casts you as special publications editor for the International Association for Human Resources. In this role, your current assignment is to write a form letter with the objective of obtaining information for a book the association plans to publish. The title of the book will be *Leadership Skills for the 21st Century.*

The direct-inquiry letter will be sent to human resource managers in medium- to large-size companies throughout the United States. It will attempt to get these managers' ideas on what leadership techniques work for them. Because you feel that human resource managers will want to cooperate in the project, you decide to begin directly with the request. As you see it, what human resource manager would not like to comment on a subject like this?

But there is a catch: The association members voted against a questionnaire; they viewed it as a form too lacking in vitality. Besides, if your letter inspires your readers, they may write entire chunks of copy that can be directly used in the book. (That idea may be played up as a reward or reader benefit.)

Thus, you will present your request, explain how the idea originated, and outline pertinent topics about leadership on which you are seeking advice. You will want to mention that readers are free to comment on any leadership topic or technique they see fit, particularly if they have had unusual experiences with it. You will end the letter by acknowledging the reader's contribution to the executives and human resource administrators who will read the book.

Originality ranks high in this letter, so adapt your words strategically to the targeted group. Address your letter to one of the human resource managers on you mailing list. You will probably mail 6,000 copies of this letter throughout the nation. Some of the recipients will want to reply by e-mail, so give them permission to use your e-mail address listed on the association's letterhead.

(Note: This situation could be repeated for any number of timely topics such as how to plan, value systems of the workforce, how to motivate people, job design, and so on.)

7. Select an advertisement from *The Wall Street Journal* for a product a business might purchase. Then write a letter to the advertiser asking for the information the business would need before buying the product. So that your instructor may better evaluate your inquiry, clip or photocopy the advertisement and attach it to the letter. With your instructor's permission, you may also conduct this assignment using the World Wide

Web as a source of advertised products. (In this case, print the Web page on which you find the ad and attach it to your letter.)

(Note: Some instructors might want to use this problem for a specific product and have you find three advertisements for it. Write a form letter to the three companies to collect information so that you can compare products before purchasing one of them.)

8. Eureka! You think you've finally found it—the perfect gift for your parents. It's a trip to the Disney Institute in Orlando, Florida. It's a new concept in adult education, offering classes in culinary arts, home video, computer animation, and storytelling as well as sports, lifestyle choices, and many others. Appealing to those in the mainstream, these classes are not particularly lofty.

Unlike Disney's other properties, this one is targeted at adults (and children over 10) who find that learning new things enhances the quality of their life. One couple was elated to discover they could take courses in several types of culinary cuisines without having to travel to exotic places. And evenings offer both live entertainment and film screenings. Disney aims to blend education and entertainment into an enjoyable vacation experience.

The facilities at this new Disney property have also blended new designs with familiar features from their other properties. Customers will find soft, soothing pastels rather than stimulating colors and cartoon figures characteristic of other properties. Even the gift shops on the property stock very different items, such as organic-gardening supplies and self-help books. However, this new resort does have some of the amenities one expects from Disney—comfortable accommodations and friendly, clean-cut employees.

You've heard costs range from $400 to $1600 for three-day stays, so you realize you need to find out what these various price levels include. Write to James Andrews, Director of Marketing, asking questions that are important to you in deciding whether this would be a suitable gift for your parents. You might ask about the room facilities, proximity to shopping, and availability of other sporting and cultural events. Since this will be a gift, you might be interested in learning whether all costs are covered or if there will be additional charges for supplies and classroom materials.

Format your inquiry as either a fax sent to (407 934-2741 or a business letter sent to Mr. Andrews at The Disney Institute, 1901 Buena Vista Drive, Lake Buena Vista, FL 32830-1000.

9. Your graduation date is coming up, and a generous relative (you choose which one) wants to give you something special yet practical as a gift. You have learned in your business communication class and saw firsthand in other settings that color can enhance presentations and documents. And you've been thinking about getting a color printer since you know you'll be writing many reports and proposals once you start working. You have been evaluating ink-jet

printers that would fit your current budget, but your relative is willing to spend more. So when you saw the ad in today's paper for a Canon color laser printer, you went right to the Canon Web site to find out more.

You read press releases on the color laser printer and even reviewed the posted information on product features and specifications. It looks as if the Canon printer is unsurpassed in color quality, speed, and efficiency compared to other printers in its class. However, two of your most important question categories still need answers—cost and availability. You are also interested in knowing more about two features mentioned in the product description: web spooling and rip-while-printing. Write a message asking specific questions that will help you decide whether or not to suggest that your relative give you a Canon color laser printer for graduation.

Direct your inquiry to Rosemary Lenaghan, Marketing Manager. You may send it to her as a fax at (516) 354-1114 or as a letter to Canon U.S.A., Inc., Canon Plaza CPPD, Lake Success, NY 11042.

INQUIRIES ABOUT PEOPLE

10. Move the calendar ahead to the time of your graduation. With diploma in hand, you are making interviews with prospective employers. You have just come from what you think was a very productive one with a company you like and for a job you would like to have. During the interview you gave the interviewer a list of references, all professors you had in your major field of study. In each case, you asked the professor for permission to use her or his name in your job search. All agreed enthusiastically.

Now switch roles. You are the interviewer. Write a letter to one of the professors on the list asking the questions you believe are vital in this situation. Be careful to ask only for the information the professor can be expected to know.

11. Stephanie Paquette is your top candidate for the position of sales manager for the northwest division of Thurston-Tyson Industries, Inc., manufacturers of a wide assortment of industrial instruments. The job requires knowledge of industrial selling inside and out. The sales manager must know the market, the goods, promotion—the works. The job also requires good leadership ability, for the district sales force consists of seven salespeople who cover a five-state area. The sales manager must be computer literate, for the company is up-to-date in the use of current technology. Also, the manager must be a good desk worker, for the paper load is heavy.

As well as you can determine, Ms. Paquette has the necessary qualifications. Without question, she knows selling and industrial equipment. Her nine years of successful work with Caswell Manufacturing (a competitor) as a salesperson, speak for themselves. Whether she can do a good job supervising salespeople may be another matter. Perhaps you can learn more of what you need to know from Chester

Smaley, your counterpart at Caswell. She gave him as a reference. Consider carefully what Mr. Smaley can tell you. Then write the letter that will get this information for you. You are the national sales manager for Thurston-Tyson.

12. You are the administrative vice president for Granite Insurance, Inc. Of all the people you interviewed for the position of office manager at the home office, Ellie Koenig appears to be the best. You plan to hire her if her references support your observations.

The work of office manager requires a well-rounded and competent person. The office manager must know office management inside and out and be able to supervise a staff of nine. He or she must be well acquainted with computers and all the current technology, for yours is an up-to-date office. The person selected must be personable, for he or she is the one many policyholders talk to when they bring their problems to the company. Also, the office manager will have to be able to work well with both top management and the agents in the field, for at Granite this office is truly a service operation.

You think Ms. Koenig meets these requirements, but you would like some supporting information. So you will write her references to find the support you need. One of them is Mr. Wilhelm Becker, who was her immediate superior at Acton Distributors, where she worked as assistant to the president. (Becker, of course, is the president.) Write Becker a letter asking the questions you need answered before you can hire this applicant.

13. Your role today is that of administrator of the Gros Foundation. Begun by the late Ridley J. Gros, Sr., the foundation consists of approximately $120 million in various assets. Among them is Bending Oaks Plantation—the 175-year-old ancestral home of the Gros family. This palatial 55-room structure, along with its well-kept gardens and surrounding 1,400 acres of wilderness, is maintained by the Foundation and is open to the public during daytime hours.

For the past 40 years, maintenance of the gardens and grounds has been performed by the able Bernard Coda, who recently announced his retirement. So now you are looking for a replacement.

Among the applicants is Betty Ann McAlister, who reports 23 years of experience as a gardener with the Colonial City Parks Department. She appears to be the best qualified of the applicants, but you will verify your impressions through an inquiry to her former supervisor. On her application, Ms. McAlister identifies this person as Laquita Moran, the director. Ms. McAlister explained that she resigned from the Colonial City job because her family moved to your city so her husband, whose health was failing, could be admitted to the local Veterans Administration Hospital.

The person selected as caretaker of Bending Oaks Plantation must have expert gardening skills, of course. Because the caretaker works without direct supervision, he or she must also be self-motivated— and must take pride in maintaining a showplace. The estate has an elaborate security system; the caretaker is privy to its operations and has access to all of the house and grounds. Thus, he or she must be a highly respectable person and honest beyond question.

Now you must write the letter asking what Ms. Moran knows about Ms. McAlister's qualifications for the job. Make certain that you include all the appropriate questions.

14. Today's assignment calls for you to project yourself into the role of manager of Bonaventure Towers, a luxury high-rise condominium near Panama City, Florida. You are trying to hire an assistant manager who will take part of the workload off your shoulders. You may have located the right person in Courtney Casay, whom you have just interviewed. She indicated that she was most interested in relocating to the Florida panhandle area.

The job, as you envision it, would involve managing the physical plant, housekeeping, and security departments at the Bonaventure Towers. This means responsibility for 17 employees. The person selected would have to be available to handle special problems around the clock, seven days a week. Part of the compensation for the job would be a rent-free 2,400-square-foot condominium on-site. So the assistant manager would have to be culturally informed, discreet, and mature in order to be compatible with the guests and owners.

Ms. Casay's résumé indicates that she can meet these job requirements. She earned a bachelor of arts degree in hotel administration from Emory University. She began her career in sales and catering with a Chicago hotel chain. After three years there, she took a job with a Montreal hotel as night manager, indicating that she needed to move because of a divorce. She has no children. Her résumé lists a wide variety of hobbies and interests, including art leagues, symphony, tennis, and scuba diving.

Ms. Casay lists Professor Lynn Judd, her college advisor, as a reference; so you will write Professor Judd about Ms. Casay's qualifications for the job. Other than an internship that she completed with him, Professor Judd has limited knowledge of her work experience. But he can evaluate her personal characteristics and educational training. Write the professor a letter inquiring about the qualifications of Courtney Casay. Be specific in your questions so that the information you receive will be complete and relevant.

15. Today's email brought you an application from a terrific candidate for the open multimedia web analyst position at GE Information Services in Rockville, Maryland. As Steve Li, Director of Human Resources, you have been searching for just the right person to fill this position. You have been looking for someone with both technical skills and a college degree to work in a multifunctional team environment designing and developing Internet applications. The application letter and résumé you received today came from Amy Guetz in response to an announcement you posted on E-span just last week.

Amy's bachelor of science degree in information systems plus her summer jobs and work experience seem to qualify her for this position. Furthermore, her résumé pointed to her own home page, where she has demonstrated her design skills as well as a bit of Java script, too. Her degree program provided her with a working knowledge of UNIX, object-oriented programming, and telecommunications. She also selected Java as an elective, taking it in the summer along with working as an intern.

On the internship she gained hands-on experience with a variety of web projects. She created digital graphics and edited video using a variety of software programs. And she used Director, Premiere, Powerpoint, Video Spigot, and 3D on a regular basis. Additionally, her employers utilized her excellent written communication skills by asking her to script some short videos. In this internship she learned to juggle a variety of projects and meet deadlines in a fast-paced environment. Amy seems to be the perfect candidate for the position.

The reference sheet she included with her résumé includes the name and contact information for her internship sponsor. Since her good grades and degree make you believe she is academically qualified, you decide to check with her internship sponsor first for information on her interpersonal skills, learning ability, and integrity. Ask specific questions that will help you determine if she is a good team player yet also interested in her own professional development. Assure the reader that all responses will be held in strict confidence.

FAVORABLE RESPONSES

16. Assume the role of the owner of the Surf Kitchen, a popular restaurant on Padre Island, a resort area off the southern tip of Texas. Today you received a letter from Inez Chung, secretary for the Young Business Leaders Club at The University of Texas.

Ms. Chung states that her club members will be on Padre Island during the first week in March. As the finale of their trip, they want a dinner at your restaurant on March 5. Can you accommodate the group? She notes that there will be about 55 members present; so they would need a private room that would hold them all. Do you have one? She further explains that the group would be informally attired—and "perhaps a wee bit boisterous." Would that be acceptable? She asks also about menu selections and prices.

You would be pleased to have the group on the date requested. In fact, you will hold that date for them for two weeks. And, yes, you have a private dinning room that will take care of 55 people—up to 75, in fact. Informal attire is the rule at the your restaurant. On the possibility of boisterous behavior, you have absolutely no objection to a group's having fun. But there are, of course, limits. Any group must be held liable for any damages done. You can answer the question about menus and prices by sending a copy of your menu. You would discount prices 10 percent for a group this size. Of course, the usual 15 percent service charge would be added to the bill.

Now write the letter that will give Ms. Chung the information she needs.

17. As franchise manager for Southern Fried Chicken, Inc., answer the inquiry of Sean Starnes. Mr. Starnes explains in his letter that he has an ideal location for a franchise and has $150,000 in cash. However, he says he knows very little about how franchises work.

You certainly appreciate Mr. Starnes's inquiry, and you are very willing to respond. Southern Fried is trying to expand operations into all parts of the country, but it awards franchises only after very careful investigation. Company experts check proposed locations—a safety measure that has enabled the company to boast that not one of its outlets has failed. Total investments vary with the location, but they range from $300,000 to $500,000. A minimum of $125,000 cash is required. Southern Fried Chicken can assist in the financing, but normally the franchise owners handle the financing locally.

The franchise agreement requires that the basic foods be purchased from Southern Fried. This agreement ensures a quality product, and it saves money for all concerned. In general, the franchise owner is an independent operator; but the company does exercise some controls over such things as building appearance, sanitation, courtesy, and food quality. These controls, management thinks, are the reason for the company's success.

With this information in mind, write the letter that will hold Mr. Starnes's interest. The next step will be for him to send you a personal résumé and a financial statement, including bank references.

18. Assume the role of director of the Moissant Training Institute and answer the example letter on p. 84 of your textbook.

A review of the letter shows that Ms. Dupre wants the answer to four questions about your school. You can answer three of them positively, but the fourth must be answered somewhat negatively.

The negative answer is to the question about quantity discounts. You just do not make them. As a part of Moissant University, your program is planned to break even. Any cut in cost would be difficult to handle.

On the positive side, the course can carry five semester hours of elective credit in business administration. But to receive these credit hours, one must be admitted as a student to Moissant University prior to beginning the program. You are sending a brochure describing the university's admission policies and procedures.

There should be no problem for technically trained executives. In fact, the course is designed for them. You are delighted to send the names of companies that have sent executives to the program, and to include the names and addresses of those training directors from companies in the Albany area (make up this information). Of course, you will want to work a little to keep Ms. Dupre interested in your school.

19. Assume that you are your professor in this course and must answer a letter written by Ms. Diane Turner. An alumnus of your school, Diane writes this query: "When I studied business communication under you three years ago, you taught us that such expressions as 'enclosed herewith,' 'beg to advise,' 'in re,' and 'whereas' are out-of-date and therefore incorrect for use in business writing. Am I remembering and interpreting correctly? Are legal letters any different? My husband, an attorney, insists that such expressions are clear, readily understood, and in tone with legal correspondence. To prove his point, he brings home letters from other lawyers. . . . We would be very grateful if you would enlighten us on the subject—and at the same time settle a family debate."

Reluctant as you may be to mix in any family's domestic argument, you see here a chance to be of service to a man who might accept a logical idea if it were clearly presented and well defended; and certainly you should come to the aid of a former student. She has correctly remembered your teachings—and you tell her so from the beginning. You will note that you are well aware of the traditional use of legalistic language among lawyers. Perhaps this language has its place in legal documents, although many authorities question its use. But it has absolutely no place in correspondence between nonlawyers.

20. As Professor Noe Flores, you will say yes to the request you received from Tom Delanoy at Victory Manufacturing. You will gladly prepare the supervisor's handbook for the South American division of Victory, of which he is division manager.

You remember Tom from the two-week crash course he took from you at Le Grande University before his relocation from the United States to Buenos Aires. He lived with your family for two weeks, speaking and hearing only Spanish, while taking a course that has become popular with executive transfers to the southern hemisphere over the years. You taught him as much Spanish and South American culture as you could. Apparently, you did well with him judging by his compliments and his success as division manager.

After one year in his position, Tom wants you to help with the internal operations of his South American division by preparing a supervisor's handbook in Spanish. His request also asks about when you could complete the work and your professional fee. In his request, Tom mentions that he wants the handbook to cover how to report accidents, how to discipline, and other supervisory matters; so an on-site visit would seem imperative. He wants to know when you could come for a walk-through of his divisional operations.

You estimate that you can produce the handbook within two weeks of the time you complete the suggested tour of Victory's operations. For the next month, you have only one two-week study group scheduled, and you will hold open the following two-week period for writing the manual. You believe you could schedule a two-day visit to the company facilities to collect information and then spend the remainder of the two-week period producing the actual handbook. The job fascinates you, since you have not undertaken such a project before.

Your charge for the project will be $3,500 plus expenses for the on-site tour. Normally you receive $4,000 per person for a two-week instructional program. But the novelty of the project and your need for variety make the $3,500 fee reasonable. You'd like to try your hand at something different, and the thought of preparing the manual feels right to you. You do not feel that your university teaching and activities will interfere with the manual preparation, since midterms have just been completed and final exams are still two months away.

One thing does pop into your mind, however: your writing style in Spanish is a literary one. You wonder about the literary approach in a manual of the type you envision for Victory. You have looked over *Lesikar's Basic Business Communication,* eighth edition, which a colleague in the School of Business at Le Grande lent to you. You have reviewed Chapters 2, 3, and 4, and you will try to incorporate what you learned into the manual. You believe that you can do this even in Spanish. Using American business writing principles in another language would be interesting and challenging.

Prepare the letter to send immediately to Tom Delanoy. You want to nail down the dates so that you can begin to concentrate on the writing project. You will send the letter by email.

21. Today's mail brings a request from Carolyn Waters Reed, senior vice president for International Medical Benefits, Inc. She's concerned about the quality of a forthcoming planning retreat consisting of the president, five vice presidents, and her. At last year's retreat, there was more turf fighting than planning. Ms. Reed is determined to have a more productive retreat this year; the date is still six months away.

She wants you, a behavioral management consultant, to lead the two-day planning session. Before she makes a decision, she wants to know specifics about your availability, experience, fees, skills, background, and satisfied clients. You will answer her questions.

Yes, you have performed the role of process consultant many times—and successfully! Last year you conducted 250 days of training, although not all of it was as a processor. You offer most all behavioral management services, but your preferred specialties are group dynamics and process consulting.

You have been so successful at this type of activity that three years ago you wrote a book about your experiences titled *Making Meetings Work.* The book describes techniques that can help make groups more effective in their purposes. Actually, it's a study of your work involving unsuccessful and successful groups and the conditions that differ for each. You provide copies for clients when you contract for two or more days of training.

Throughout the past year, you have worked for some large, successful companies as a group processor. Chem Safe and Blair, Inc., are among them. And you know their training directors well. They wouldn't mind telling anyone about your work for them as long as confidential or competitive information is not exchanged. Ms. Reed can call or write them to get their experiences with your process techniques.

You believe that the two-day planning meeting is a good idea, especially if it is handled as a retreat. You prefer to work this way—away from the organization—so that you can concentrate more on the people personally. Your fee for such work is $4,000 per day plus expenses. You would gladly "walk through" the company operations before working with the executive team. Your fee for this activity is $1,500 plus expenses.

Because of the behavioral nature of your work, you believe that experience is the best indicator of expertise. That's how you stay current—by continually working with clients and testing out new ideas as they apply to ongoing groups. You did receive a degree in psychology from State University. When you graduated, you worked full-time in industry for five years. Then you went out on you own into the consulting market.

In essence, you are a self-made person whose hard work paid off. These qualities account for your success, and they are the ones with which most clients identify. You belong to the International Society for Training Directors and the Association for Human Resource Administrators. When you are in town, you attend their meetings.

Write a direct reply to Ms. Reed that will tell her what she wants to know about the work you can perform for International Medical Benefits.

22. Surf the Net and find a product or service that a business might want to get more information about before buying. If you select a product, it could be one for resale. Or it could be an industrial product, one consumed by a business.

Next, assume that you are an account representative for the manufacturer of this product. Make a list of questions that businesses would likely ask about the product or service. Then write a letter answering the questions. As you receive inquiries later on, you can draw on these answers to address other specifics questions you will be asked.

For this assignment, attach your list of questions and a copy of the product or service ad from the Net. These items will help your instructor evaluate your work.

23. As Cheryl Hollar of Yankee Dollar Computers, you must answer a letter you received from a prospective franchisee. You advertise regularly in *The Wall Street Journal* and encourage people to write to you for more information about your franchise operations. You are always on the alert for people with good entrepreneurial talent who will market your products effectively.

In her inquiry letter to you, Jackie Jankovich asks

about your Yankee Dollar operations. She is looking for a new direction in her career. After spending seven years as an account representative for a national financial services company, she now wants to consider other options. Among them is being her own boss.

With a bachelor of business administration degree in finance (minor in accounting) from State University, she appears to have identified a good location with good traffic flow and negligible competition. But her finances are weak; she has $30,000 in savings, $18,000 cash value in life insurance, and $24,000 in stock. She wants to know how the Yankee Dollar franchises work—how they help individual franchise owners, what controls they maintain, how they supply franchise outlets, and such. You will answer her questions.

Yankee Dollar is trying to expand its operations into all parts of the country and internationally. But franchises are awarded only after careful investigation. This is a safety factor, you feel, and explains why not one outlet has failed in the company's history.

Total investment in the operation normally ranges from $200,000 to $300,000, depending on local cost variations. A minimum of $75,000 in cash is required. The company can assist in finding financing, but usually the franchise owner handles such things locally.

A Yankee Dollar franchise agreement requires that the basic product line be purchased from the company. This requirement ensures a quality product; and it permits economies of scale, also. Each franchise owner is to a large extent an independent business operator; but the company does maintain some control for the best interest of all. There are certain requirements for the appearance of the building, store hours, price control, courtesy, and store personnel. Such requirements, Yankee Dollar feels, are good reasons for the phenomenal success of the firm.

With this information in mind, fill in the details for your complete answers. If this person is interested, her next step will be to send you a detailed personal résumé. Also, you will need a financial statement, including bank references.

(Note: With some adjustments, this situation can be adapted to other franchise operations. You can consult the franchise section of *The Wall Street Journal* for advertisements from many different kinds of franchise firms.)

24. As Troy Kubicek, Director of Customer Relations for Deere and Company, you recently received an inquiry from Linda Hittle, CFO of Wiedenbach USA, in Poway, California. She is considering recommending that her company purchase a John Deere Gator for use at their new company site. She told you that she recently read an article about the Gator vehicle produced by Deere and Company that won the Industrial Design Excellence Award from the Industrial Designers Society of America and *Business Week* magazine. She believes the vehicle looks like one her company would find useful in many ways in the new site but has several questions she needs answered first.

You, of course, are delighted with Ms. Hittle's interest in the Gator. She learned from the article that the vehicle was tested by army's elite Rapid Reactive Forces, and performed flawlessly in evacuating wounded soldiers from foxholes. And Deere's web site described it as ideal for carrying loads or roaming about in rugged places. She asked about its weight and its engine. She also asked if it would fit in a garage designed for the average car. You can report that it weighs just 1,400 pounds and will easily fit in a normal garage stall. Also, it is available with either a gasoline engine or a diesel-powered one. The newest diesel model comes with a three-cylinder, 18-horsepower engine that has slightly more power than the gasoline model.

For added goodwill, you have determined that the dealer nearest Ms. Hittle's mailing address is just four miles away. It is E-Z Equipment at 235 South Highway 101, Solana Beach, CA 92075. She can reach E-Z by phone at (619) 481-5563 or by fax at (619) 753-3102. Or she can call (800) 537-8233 to find other dealerships in her location carrying this vehicle.

PERSONNEL EVALUATIONS

25. It's not easy to write an accurate and fair evaluation of yourself, but that is your assignment. Specifically, your task is to assume the role of the professor whom you have listed as a reference in your application for the job of your choice from the company of your choice. (See problem 10 for background information.)

You (the professor) have just received a letter asking the right questions for an applicant (the real you) for the job involved. Now you (the professor) will respond. In this role, you will carefully evaluate the applicant's scholastic record, personality, character, relations with you—in short, everything you have learned about her or him. Then you will arrange this information as answers to the questions you were asked in the letter.

To help your instructor, write a list of these questions. Attach the list to your letter.

26. You are Chester Smally, national sales manager for the Caswell Manufacturing Company. Today you received a letter from your counterpart at Thurston-Tyson Industries, Inc., inquiring about your employee Stephanie Paquette. (See Problem 11 for background information.)

You have known for some time that Stephanie is looking for something better than the job she has with you, and you don't blame her. Her chances for advancement with you are blocked by senior people with long tenure. She is a superior salesperson, and you think she has the ability to organize and supervise a sales force. She is a good leader, and she is thoroughly familiar with the industrial market. She is skilled in using computers in her work, for your sales force takes advantage of all the latest technology.

On the matter of her ability behind the desk you

are not certain. You question whether she gives enough attention to details. Your supporting evidence for this view is that she rarely turns in her reports on time. But perhaps if she were given new responsibilities, she would change. She has always done the tasks she considers really necessary.

Using your imagination (within reason) to supply any other information you may need, write the letter that will cover Stephanie's qualifications for the job and be fair to all concerned.

27. In the role of Edjer Vander-Muelen, Garrison Industries, write a report on the job skills of Ms. Tom Bronkhorst, who has applied for the position of account representative with Bimmerle, Inc. Bimmerle indicates she is the best of six people who have applied for the job—at least on paper. Before proceeding, Bimmerle needs information from you about Ms. Bronkhorst's qualifications.

An account representative at Bimmerle, Inc., must have the best possible technical skills in everything from peripherals to updates of software programs. Not only do representatives need to have technical knowledge about computers, but they also must know how to adapt that knowledge to the needs of large and small businesses in diverse industries. And Bimmerle representatives must have interpersonal competencies to relate to the customers' different personalities.

Ms. Bronkhorst began work in your word processing division at Garrison Industries two years ago. Because of her educational background and work experience, you promoted her to assistant manager after a year. She has done well in that role, so you will write a favorable report about her.

Technically, Ms. Bronkhorst should do well in the job. She has received academic training in both mainframe and personal computers with internal and user languages. Her 3.3 GPA (4.0 system) attests to her mastery of the curriculum. In addition, her work experience in systems design and personal computer software has given her excellent technical and computer application knowledge. Indeed, it was her technical superiority that made you promote her to assistant manager in your word processing department. She supervises five entry-level clerks in the department and attends to their training and work, in addition to other matters that you delegate to her.

Personally, Ms. Bronkhorst is shy and somewhat timid. However, she adapts to others easily and quickly. She appears to work best when others (you!) structure her schedule and activities. Often she is reluctant to establish plans, preferring to have you take the initiative in most departmental issues. You wonder whether she could organize the work of an account representative. Perhaps she might. But you have seen only her dependence on others for structure—not her independent, aggressive side.

Moreover, the job of account representative would be a step down in status for Ms. Bronkhorst. She's an assistant manager and enjoys the connotation of that title. You do not know about the money involved in the job. But the security and status generally associated with account representatives would be less

than what she presently has with Bimmerle. She wants to be closer to her aging parents, but you wonder if that personal circumstance is a sufficient reason for her to take a new job.

From these points, it may seem that you are more negative than positive about Ms. Bronkhorst's "fit" for the job. But you are not. Actually, Ms. Bronkhorst is highly qualified. The negative parts are your opinions and inferences. Balance them with the facts and present an objective, properly proportioned picture of Ms. Bronkhorst's qualifications for the job. Remember: The report should be favorable.

28. As Thomas Burgess, senior auditor for McElroy and Slinger, CPAs, you are going to answer the questions asked of you in an inquiry about Eva Cavazos. She has applied to Capital Financial Services, Inc. (CFS), as an account representative for their college/university retirement and tax-deferred annuity program. They believe strongly in her potential but need the lowdown from you before they go forward in the process.

Capital Financial Services is looking for people to sell and service accounts to faculty and staff at three state and two private schools. Account people need versatility—ability to explain technical information in nontechnical terms, high energy, excellent interpersonal skills, and a sincere desire to provide individualized service, particularly after a sale. Competition with other firms authorized to provide similar services is keen and intense.

Your overall evaluation of Cavazos's job skills is good, and you will say so in your letter to Capital Financial Services. In the job area of accounting expertise, Ms. Cavazos's work for you was excellent. She handled all of the painstaking details that you assigned to her on field audits. Also, she never complained about the long hours, the travel, or the weekend work. Her stamina, energy, and technical competence seemed to grow with each audit performed. Primarily, she audited chemical manufacturing firms, since her previous work experience had been with such a company. As you remember, she was almost too eager to seek additional details and explanations even after samples of documents had revealed sufficient evidence.

In the area of personal skills and interpersonal abilities, you have a slightly negative point to report. In final audit reviews with clients, she often became irritated when people did not understand her explanations. Having to use different explanations and to answer questions about her statements put her slightly on edge. You talked with her about this behavior, and she willingly listened without angry reactions. She made direct efforts to improve this part of her personality, but she never completely overcame her uncomfortable reactions to needs for further explanations.

Among her peers and fellow auditors, however, she worked comfortably and easily. She demonstrated a high degree of self-motivation and job commitment. She carried out assignments faithfully, consistently, and creatively. In her work for CFS, you believe she would perform with the same professional commitment and high expertise that she did for you.

Using these facts, write a balanced, objective evaluation letter. Your evaluation of Munoz and her auditing work is good but not totally positive, so consider the emphasis and proportion that each category of information deserves in your writing effort. Also, watch the connotative meanings of your words.

29. You are the manager of technical services at Nationwide Casualty and Property Company. You open your mail today and are surprised to find an inquiry letter about Charles Brownlee, a systems analyst in your department. He has applied to Champion Insurance Company to become a manager of information services there. He would oversee 45 workers.

As manager of information services, Brownlee would face a demanding job. He would have to be technically current in all phases of computer operations, for the department provides data entry, maintenance and control of the databases, hardware operations, and systems design for the entire company. Also, the manager would need supervision skills in training and motivating employees, specifically, and in planning, organizing, and controlling, in general. And there would be liaison functions with other departments in the company— sales, underwriting, accounting, and such.

Because you have been impressed with Brownlee's technical expertise and professional potential over the last three years, you will write a favorable recommendation for him. He joined your company first as a data entry clerk. He quickly worked his way into programming and systems analysis. Before working at Nationwide Casualty and Property, he did software programming for a retailer. Indeed, you have been impressed with the intensity and diversity of his technical computer skills. In addition, the 29 employees in your department consider him their informal leader, attesting to his expert computer knowledge. If there is a problem, you seek out his advice; the employees in the department do the same.

In the area of general supervision, you must make inferences because you have not observed his managerial behavior directly. You know that he has military experience as a part of his personnel record. And he has worked diligently toward his MBA at night for the past five years. The impact of his education has not been apparent for your company since he has not had positions in which to use his integrative coursework experience. More than likely, the job of manager at Champion will use much more of his educational background.

Personally, Charles Brownlee is unassuming, quiet, and reserved. He has faithfully carried out whatever work assignments you have given him. Also, you know that he has taught basic courses at the local junior college for several semesters. You feel that Brownlee will have to be more deliberately assertive in his managerial role with Champion. His natural role that you have witnessed is that of obedient

follower. Working with other department managers will demand that he take a more solid stand than you have seen him take.

Despite the negatives, you will write a favorable evaluation of Brownlee for the Champion position. It will be good but objective as well.

30. As Kim Nguyen, program director for radio station WVAS in Chicago, you've received a request for information on a recent intern at your station from Tom McLaughlin, the station manager at Home Grown Music in Sycamore, Illinois. The intern, Terry Lenaghan, recently completed a full semester at your station as part of his school program in telecommunications and broadcasting, and you were delighted with his performance.

Tom asked you several questions about Terry's performance, ability, and interpersonal skills. Fortunately, you can speak highly for Terry in all these areas and give specific examples of each. Terry far exceeded your expectations for an intern. He had the usual qualities you would expect of a typical employee, such as honesty and reliability. But he also went out of his way to help others and to learn new skills. In fact, when you recently remodeled a studio, he was on hand on the weekend to help move and set up the equipment. He read manuals and helped set up the new equipment properly; it functioned perfectly the first time you turned it on. And he stayed around for the cleanup, too.

While his school has given him excellent training and his grades show he has mastered the course material, you have the feeling that his abilities are not yet fully challenged. He seems to learn new skills much faster than most of your current employees, and he seems to enjoy taking on new challenges. He is both articulate and creative. In fact, you felt confident enough in him to assign him to a couple of important teams: one was working on creating new programming concepts, and another was evaluating new equipment. While most interns would have been rather passive on such important teams, Terry contributed at those times when his insight into the questions at hand were unusually clear for a newcomer. Additionally, the team members seemed to welcome his contributions fully, and he got along beautifully with the wide variety of people on these teams.

Not only can you highly recommend Terry for a position in broadcasting at the Sycamore business (919 Dekalb Avenue, Sycamore, IL 60178), but you can also say that if he were to move to the Chicago area you would hire him immediately. He's the type of competent employee who is a joy to have on one's staff.

ADJUSTMENT GRANTS

31. Last week Mrs. Leona Hoecker came to your New York fashion salon, Margo's Creations. Because this old customer from Albany spends freely and expects much attention, three of your fashion creators hovered around her for four hours perfecting a gown for her to

wear to the governor's inaugural ball next week.

Today's mail brings in a harshly worded letter from Mrs. Hoecker. She reports that you sent her a size 9 creation. "I can't begin to get it on," she writes. She says she doesn't understand "how such incompetence could occur." If you can't get the gown she ordered to her by next Thursday, she wants you to credit her account for the $1,250 cost. She can get a new gown locally.

Quickly you check to see what happened. Sure enough, your employees got her measurements mixed up with those of another customer. The only reason for the mistake is the unexpected increase in business you have had lately. Your employees have been working long overtime hours.

Yes, you can and will get the gown to Mrs. Hoecker in time for the ball. Already your employees are working on it, and the gown will receive priority attention until completed. You guarantee delivery by Federal Express no later than next Wednesday.

Now you will write the letter that will tell Mrs. Hoecker what you will do, explain what happened, and keep her goodwill. Last year she spent more than $13,000 with you.

32. Play the role of sales manager for the Perfection Plus Wig Company and grant the claim of one of your good customers. This customer, the owner of the Wig Shop, writes that last month she ordered 12 of your Bonnie Bettie human-hair wigs at $945 each. Already, two of the three she sold have been returned. "The hair is not securely fixed," she states. "It comes out easily." She wants to return the wigs and get her money back—unless you can get me the quality wigs you have sent me in the past."

You were not surprised to get the letter. Just yesterday you learned that your production specialist had changed the production method without authorization. He had a novel idea for cutting down on the work time involved. The plan decreased production time—but decreased quality as well.

Now you must work to correct the damage that has been done. You have taken measures to make certain such errors won't happen again. You are calling in all Bonnie Bettie wigs from all your customers. And you are asking those customers to call in all they have sold and to replace them with good wigs. You will send these good wig replacements right away.

Write the letter that will handle The Wig Shop's claim and regain any lost confidence.

33. Your Crescent City Candy Company has been sending various candies to The Candyman's House in Birmingham, Alabama, on a monthly basis for the past 11 years. You were surprised today to get the following letter from the owner, Alice Buffington.

Dear _____:

Please credit my account in the amount of $336.40 for the 10 dozen boxes of Old New Orleans pecan rolls you sent me. The pecans are rancid. Already some of our customers have returned them. Probably others are disappointed in us, for we have sold almost

four boxes. I have taken them off the shelf. Please tell me what to do with the remaining packages. I ask that you give this matter your immediate attention.

Indeed you will give the matter your immediate attention. You quickly learn what happened. Last month you pulled 36 boxes of pecan rolls out of inventory because they were old (last year's crop). They were supposed to have been destroyed, but they weren't. Your shipping clerk made a mistake and filled Alice's order with these bad rolls. In defense of the shipping clerk, he has recently been working long overtime hours to handle a large number of new orders.

After conferring with your workers, you conclude that such a problem won't occur again. Any inventory to be destroyed will be disposed of immediately. You can promise that only the best, freshest candies will be sent in the future.

Of course, you will credit Alice's account for the full amount, as she requested. In addition, you'd like to satisfy her original need for candy. So you'll offer to send her the full amount, guaranteed to be fresh and delicious, with a 15 percent discount. You want very much to make sure this old customer remains a friend of the company.

34. You received a strongly worded claim letter today from Sara Sue Stone, executive assistant to the president of Coronado Industries. She indicated the 125 videocassettes you provided for their management and technical staff are defective. The videotapes were a one-hour presentation given by internationally known Dr. Morris E. Massey on communication and motivation at the company's executive planning retreat. The presentation was so inspiring that Coronado top management asked Massey for permission to duplicate the original video and distribute it throughout the organization. They contracted with you to produce 125 tapes at $32.50 per tape.

The letter states that certain parts of the audio are faulty and that the video fades in at least three places. Coronado has checked the original and it is OK. Thus, they believe the problem is with the videocassettes or the duplication procedure. The company wants new tapes or their money back within one week because they are currently beginning the implementation phase of their planning cycle. They also want your word that whatever happened won't occur again.

As you hurriedly check the facts of the case, you find that Coronado is correct in their claim that the tapes were defective. Even though the fault is not entirely yours, you will provide them with new ones. You will personally inspect these tapes before they are sent to make sure they are duplicated properly. So, yes, you will grant their claim.

In your first backtracking effort, you check with your machine maintenance people, and they report no slipping heads on the recorders or other such maintenance factors at the time of the Coronado job. Next, you check with your tape suppliers, and they shed some light on the problem. Two weeks before they delivered their last shipment of blank VX-L tapes to you, they had a small fire in one section of their warehouse. Some merchandise was damaged, and the cleanup crews thought they had removed all of the damaged items. Apparently, the damage went farther than was originally suspected. And you received some tapes that had been exposed to the intensive heat in the fire. At least this is the only logical explanation you can come up with at the moment. You can only hope you received just 125 defective tapes and not a larger number.

Your supplier will send you new tapes. But that is the least of your worries right now. You need to keep the Coronado account. Thus, you'll send them 125 newly taped copies of their original tape on TX-L quality videocassettes. And you will do so and have them delivered within the week as they prefer. In addition, you'll explain what happened with your supplier. You will work hard to keep Coronado sold on your reputation and quality work. They have had a bad experience with your company, so reassure them that such defective work is a one-time occurrence.

Let the distinctiveness of your writing speak for the individuality of your work and service. Write the adjustment letter to the executive assistant of Coronado Industries.

35. As vice president of sales for Smokey Ridge Chemical Supply, Inc., you are going to grant the claim submitted to you by the purchasing agent for Fun and Fitness Centers of America, Inc. Fun and Fitness reports that 14 of its 65 centers throughout the eastern United States have experienced plumbing problems as a result of swimming pool and hot tub chemicals you sold them. Central management orders the chemicals, which are shipped directly to each franchise.

The 14 pools and tubs, the purchasing agent claims, have had to be replumbed because of soaplike substances created by the combination of methylene chloride and chlorine used to keep pools and tubs clean and in good appearance. Clogging of the pool pipes has been reported on a regular basis over a two-week period by the various franchises. There could be other clogging reports if the trend continues. Fun and Fitness employees say they have followed the same instructions and proportions for adding the chemicals as they always have. Thus, the problem must be with the chemicals themselves.

If everything happened as this letter reports, something is indeed wrong. As you conduct an investigation of the case, you conclude that Fun and Fitness has every reason to be alarmed, because the fault is yours. If you are to keep this lucrative account, you are going to have to work hard to convince the Fun and Fitness management that such occurrences are not normal in the operating of your chemical supply business.

Back in the spring, your business agreed to hire three part-time clerical workers for the summer months through the Employment Strategy co-op program. The purpose of this program was to give economically disadvantaged minorities an opportunity to gain valuable work experience and to improve their job skills. Most of the workers are high school students who need summer employment. Along with their employment, however, came an increase in typing and filing errors. Even though you assigned more supervision to the co-op employees, the number of rework items increased.

Such was the case with Invoice #44723, the Fun and Fitness Centers' order. As the order was being entered into the computer by one of the student workers, the last two numbers were reversed on one of the chemical products that was ordered. *Item #3945* (methylene chloride) was entered rather than *Item #3954* (muriatic acid—a standard pool additive). When methylene chloride is mixed with other chlorine–based chemicals, the result can produce the soaplike substance that clogged the pipes of the pools and tubs. Fortunately, the compound is not toxic to humans, as the Fun and Fitness people feared; but it will clog pipes. Your chemical engineer confirms all these facts.

Your shipping personnel should have caught the error, but they did not. Part of their job is to double-check the logic of orders. But they often do not do so, as was the case with Invoice #44723. You are not happy with them, and you have told them so. At any rate, you will pay for the replumbing jobs. But you will need a complete billing from the plumbers indicating exactly what they did. Also, you want the Fun and Fitness people to return all the unused methylene chloride, if there is any. You are sending the muriatic acid based on their original order. It should arrive within five days.

The only thing left to do before you write the adjustment letter is to plan the resale part. How can you keep Fun and Fitness sold on your products and service? Think about it. Then write the letter that will grant the adjustment and explain what happened in such a manner that will lead naturally to the resale material concluding the letter.

36. As Robert Edwards, customer relations manager for the local Oldsmobile dealership, you received the following letter from Eleanor Braaten, one of your dealership's new customers. Everything she reports in her letter is consistent with the information you just reviewed on the General Motors Extranet this morning. In fact, General Motors posted new instructions for how to correct this known problem.

Dear Service Manager:

I am thoroughly disappointed with the ineffective windshield-wiper repair done last week on my six-month-old Intrigue.

Ever since the rainy season began, I've been having trouble with the windshield wipers. They work when I turn them on, but they also work sporadically by themselves. Sometimes I'm driving along and they suddenly wipe the windshield; this happens especially when I go over speed bumps or rough roads. Since it seems to happen intermittently, I've not been able to show your mechanic the problem until the wipers reach the point where they are on nearly all the time.

I've brought my car in twice; first, the repair was short-lived, and the second time it wasn't done at all. On a brand-new car, this mechanical problem is unacceptable. Your service people told me that they replaced the entire unit; if this is the case, the new unit is as defective as the original.

To become a thoroughly satisfied customer, I ask only that when I bring the car in for the third time that you get the repair done right. Please let me know when you will have someone who knows how to fix the problem so that I can bring the car in for repair at that time.

Sincerely,

Eleanor Braaten

Write Ms. Braaten granting the full, reasonable adjustment she seeks. Additionally, to rebuild goodwill for both your dealership and General Motors products, offer her a 10 percent discount on all service charges (including oil changes) for a full year as well as on any accessories available in your inventory. Assure her that General Motors is working to produce high-quality products and wants to keep her as a satisfied driver of a General Motors automobile. Send your adjustment letter to Ms. Braaten at 3733 Thirty-first Avenue, Rock Island, IL 61201-0825.

ACKNOWLEDGMENTS (VAGUE AND BACK ORDERS)

37. As Janet Baker, a supervisor in the newly created direct purchasing division of Compaq Computing, you have learned that one of your jobs is to contact potential buyers whose orders cannot be filled immediately as well as those whose orders are vague. Your job is to keep customers and retain their goodwill.

    Today's email brought a delightful order from Jane Adami. Jane told you she has been waiting for over a year to buy a complete computer system with a flat panel monitor at a reasonable price. She was delighted to see your new ad in the most recent issue of *PC World* and wants the system shipped to her immediately.

    Not only was she highly complimentary of the quality of your company's products, but she said she was delighted that Compaq has this system because she knows how good your service is. She said she can hardly wait to get the system that she has been talking to her friends about for so long. In fact, she reported that ever since Compaq joined with Mitsubishi Electric and Advanced Display Inc., she has been waiting for you to bring out the industry's leading system at one of the best prices available.

    Jane is definitely a customer you would like to

keep, not only because of her own enthusiasm for the product but also because of her positive word-of-mouth promotion of it. However, your production manager reported today that with all the current orders on hand, Jane's system could not be ready for at least six weeks. Apparently, your new pricing level released a pent-up demand for the product, and your supply on hand will not meet unusually large demand.

While you could send Jane a system immediately with a standard monitor, you can tell from her letter that she definitely wants the flat panel mode. You must let her know of the delay while reminding her of some of the reasons it is worth the six-week wait—good pricing, quality product, small footprint and flexibility, low power consumption, no screen emissions, and high-quality resolution with rich color. Write a response that will retain the order and Jane's goodwill.

38. As owner of Harmony Clothiers, you have a difficult situation to deal with today. Your advertisements in *Jubilee, Octave,* and *Close Harmony* appear to be paying off.

    Already you have received 11 orders for custom-made uniforms for men's glee clubs and quartets. The latest one, from the Hi Lo Harmoneers, is for 25 red blazers with black slacks. Appropriate sizes and other specifications are complete and in order.

    All is well except that you can't meet their requirements for delivery within 30 days. The problem is your backlog of work from prior orders, all of them requiring rush treatment. The best you can promise is delivery in 60 days.

    Write to the Hi Lo Harmoneers giving them the bad news. You may use your imagination to supply any facts you may need, but keep them logical. Convince the group that your blazers and slacks are worth waiting for.

39. As manager of the Crested Valley Country Club, a 6,820-yard, par 72 private golf and tennis club, you must write a letter to the Bruno Corporation. It seems that the sales manager wants to rent your facilities for a half day on July 30, for a two-team, best-ball golf tournament to be held during the company's annual sales meeting, which will be conducted at a nearby hotel. The sales manager's February 1 letter wants you to confirm his request right away.

    Yes, you do rent out your facilities one day per week—on Mondays, when the club is closed to its members for repairs, watering, and the like. But you have already booked another group to use the course that day—the Association for Nursing Home Administrators, which is meeting at a nearby luxury resort for its yearly convention. The resort, however, has no golf course. In fact, you have four groups on consecutive Mondays from the last week in July through the first three weeks in August who will be using your facilities; and you just can't bump any of them. The last weekend in August is reserved for your Labor Day tournament for the club members; the club is open that Monday for the holiday tournament.

    The first clear date you could arrange would be September 15. Would Bruno consider this date for its sales meeting? You have only one other day—October 17—open before December 1. Work hard (but without high pressure) to persuade the company to take the September date. Acknowledge this order and handle the back order for your facilities in a way that will win this account for Crested Valley Country Club.

40. Assume the role of the owner of Reader's Respite and answer a letter from avid reader Mrs. Linda Hardy. Mrs. Hardy has responded to your advertisement in the current edition of *Smithsonian* for books about important issues.

    Mrs. Hardy ordered three books. One of them you can send—*Zulu Covenant* by James Hickman, at $9.95 in paperback. The other two give you some problems.

    First is the order for *Vietnam: A Senseless Encounter*, by Helena Gonzalez. Ms. Gonzalez has written no book that you can locate by this title. She did, however, write *The Fall of Saigon* ($13.95) and *Cambodian Travesties* ($15.95). Both are available only in hardback. Your advertisement listed nothing by Ms. Gonzalez. In fact, Mrs. Hardy wrote in the *Vietnam* title on the form herself. You will have to know which book she wants before you can fill her order.

    Second, Mrs. Hardy requested *The People's Princess*, by Ronald Joseph and Gay Mongan, which has been so popular that you sold out of it last week. Another shipment is due from the publisher in two weeks, and you will send the book as soon as it arrives.

    Bill Mrs. Hardy for the $9.95 plus $2.00 shipping and handling charges and 7 percent sales tax. You will bill her for the other books similarly as you send them. Handle the situation tactfully, since people like Mrs. Hardy often become your bread-and-butter customers.

41. As sales manager for New England Timemasters, Inc., manufacturers of high-quality clocks, you have a rush order for eight of your Happy Hours wall clocks ($156 each) and five of your Old Reliable grandfather clocks ($876 each). The order is from The House of Clocks, one of your newest customers.

    You can send the Happy Hours clocks right away, but you will need more information before you can ship the Old Reliables. You make this clock in walnut, pecan, and oak. The House of Clocks specified no material preference. Also, they didn't say which dial face they wanted. Both arabic- and roman-numeral dials are available. You must get this missing information before you can send these clocks.

    Now write the letter that will straighten out this situation.

42. Play the role of sales manager for the Digi-lator Manufacturing Company, manufacturers of a combination digital watch and minicalculator (the Digi-lator) and other, related products. Last month you prematurely advertised your Digi-lator in leading industrial publications. The response has been terrific. Orders have been coming in well beyond expectations. Normally you would be happy about

such results, but this time you have a problem. You will not be able to fill these orders as soon as expected.

The reason for this problem is that your technical workers went on strike for a three-week period. Production stopped completely. Now that the strike has been settled, production is just barely starting again. You can begin sending the Digi-lators to some customers within a week, but other customers will have to wait longer. You will fill orders in the sequence in which they reached you.

One of your orders came from Dottie Darby, owner of Dottie's Jewelry, Inc. The order is for 12 Digi-lators at $48 each and 24 Sentinel minicalculators at $8.40 each. You can send the calculators right away from your inventory. But you can't promise Dottie delivery of the Digi-lators until three weeks from now.

Now write the letter that will tell Dottie what she needs to know and keep her happy with your products.

CLAIMS

43. You have been a busy person these past days getting your Furniture Warehouse ready for its annual spring sale. This is a traditional event in the area, and it attracts hundreds of local citizens. The prices are genuinely low, and the quality is uniformly high.

    Your efforts were running smoothly until today's delivery of Night-Right mattresses and box springs. Already you have advertised them for your sale—at the low price of $219 per set. You had ordered 60 sets. They arrived today, but 37 of them are badly soiled and faded. You think water damage is the problem, but you can't be certain. They weren't damaged in transit, for the heavy paper covering them shows no signs of mishandling.

    The mattresses are so much a part of your sale that you will write Night-Right immediately, seeking rapid replacement. The sale is just nine days away, and you want the goods by then. You will return the damaged products, but you don't intend to pay shipping charges. Now write the letter.

44. Today you learned the disappointing news that a mix-up occurred in the gifts your company, Electronics Supply, gave at Christmas to its prime customers. You had ordered 122 twelve-pound smoked turkeys from Smokehouse, Inc., to be given to customers named by your salespeople. At $48 each, delivered, you thought you had a good buy. But the news you learned today is that your salespeople are getting thank-you notes for four-pound packages of smoked sausage. As you recall, this package sells for around $16.

    Apparently, the Smokehouse people made a switch on you, probably inadvertently. Something has to be done about it. Besides the money, you are concerned about what your good customers may think. You have always given generously—certainly more than a $16 package of sausage.

    Now you will write a claim letter to Smokehouse. You will describe the problem, and you will say what you want Smokehouse to do about it. Even though Christmas is long past, you think the company should send the turkeys along with a letter of explanation. As you see it, the cost of the sausages should be Smokehouse's loss.

45. Positive publicity and advertising! Those are key elements in your job as marketing manager of Wilder Systems, wholesale distributors of computer hardware parts for personal computers. You need to keep your name constantly before your retail and industrial customers. You have done this over the years through gifts to your better accounts. Last winter, you ordered magazine subscriptions for some of your better customers early in the winter to be sent to them in the spring. You felt that a springtime gift would differentiate you from your competitors who gave Christmas remembrances.

This year you decided to have complimentary one-year subscriptions of *Golfer's Digest, Tennis,* and *Fisher's Havens* sent to your 167 largest established accounts. It was your idea that the publications, delivered each month, would provide the repetition you needed to establish your identity on a continuous basis. For $10.25 per year and with each issue carrying your name as the gift donor, the total amount you spent for the 167 subscriptions seemed like a true bargain. Based on your sales representatives' input to you, you ordered a golf, tennis, or fishing magazine, depending on the sporting interests of the owner of the business involved. All three magazines are published by Netsports, Inc.

You furnished a list of names with the appropriate order forms to Netsports, Inc., four months ago. Their acknowledgment letter assured you that the 167 orders would start with the April issues. Today is May 10 and still no one has received the complimentary subscriptions, Indeed, you are embarrassed. Your salespeople have told the customers of your intentions. And the customers are waiting expectantly for their magazines.

Thus, you will write a claim letter that will ask for an explanation of what went wrong and a refund of one-fourth of the price you paid for the subscriptions. You feel that Netsports, Inc., should write to each subscriber relieving you of any responsibility. And if they can't deliver right away, you want a full refund. The damage to your goodwill is evident, and the requests you are making are moderate in relation to your losses.

Write the claim letter rationally but firmly.

46. Last week when you saw your phone bill, you became steaming mad. You had received a telemarketing call from someone you assumed was from your phone company, offering various new long-distance plans. The new plan you thought you had signed up for didn't kick in—and those 200 "free" weekend long-distance minutes appeared as charges on your bill. You called the phone company immediately to report the error. However, the customer service person you talked with told you that the company had no such plan and that you must have misunderstood the telemarketer who contacted you.

A week later you are still upset but decide to take positive action. While you know that you heard and clearly understood the offer you accepted, you are concerned that you may have been the target of telemarketing scam. Although you don't blame the phone company (you select one), you do think it is in their best interests to know about it so they can take action to eliminate it. Also, you want to know that you can be assured that when someone calls your home representing the company, you are truly talking to one of their representatives.

Write your claim to the senior vice president of marketing explaining the problem in enough detail so some constructive action can be taken and asking for reassurance that future calls from the company will be legitimate ones.

47. As Len Deftos, a supervisor in information systems for Stevens Insurance Brokerage in Clearwater, Florida, you think the air quality in the building you and your staff occupy is causing declines in health and productivity. Not only are those with allergies complaining, but others are continually complaining of dry, itchy eyes; nose and throat irritation; headaches; fatigue; dizziness; and other flu-like symptoms. In your informal investigation, you have learned the building recycles its air to keep the heating and cooling costs down. And on another floor some extensive remodeling is under way possibly introducing off-gassing from new materials such as formaldehyde and other elements. Plus, the last tenant apparently moved out after experiencing similar symptoms.

While you realize it is more expensive to use fresh air, it may be worth it to the landlord in the long run to keep tenants. Fresh air is healthier because bacteria and mold are thinned out. But before you call for that action, you would like to let the landlord, Barbara DuBois, know the problem and ask her to have an indoor analysis completed. You called a couple of local companies recommended by the indoor environment division of the Environmental Protection Agency and have learned the analysis would cost between $1,200 and $2,000 for a building your size. Be sure to stress the importance of your claim, since as little as a 1 percent loss in productivity has a big impact on the work in a labor-intensive environment such as yours. Fax your claim to Ms. Dubois at (813) 399-2569.

ORDERS

48. As Juanita Martinez, owner of Juanita's Gift Shop, you are interested in several of the items described in the sales brochure sent you by the Elect-O-Matic Manufacturing Company. The brochure suggests that you buy the items from your local supplier, or if one isn't available, "write us directly." You don't know of any suppliers in your area that carry the Elect-O-Matic line, so you'll just order from the manufacturer. The prices quoted in the brochure would be the same, you assume. You want the following (you determine the selection of colors):

- Elect-O electric scissors. Lightweight. Cuts all nonmetal sheet materials up to ⅛ inch thick. Fingertip control. In white, beige, brown, or black. 8 ozs. $14.50 each. Order No. S-1228. (You want 12.)
- Elect-O flashlight. Batteries never need replacing. Just plug in regular outlet for recharging. In red, black, or beige. 10 ozs. $11.25 each. Order No. F-242. (You want 24.)
- Elect-O car vacuum. Plugs into cigarette lighter. Supersuction motor does heavy-duty job. 10-ft. cord included. In brown, black, or beige. 5 lbs. With attachments, $24.50. Without attachments, $20.25. Order No. V-272. (You want 8, all with attachments.)

Now write the letter. Cover shipping instructions. You will pay from their invoice. And ask for delivery within two weeks so that the goods will arrive before your spring promotion.

49. Select at least three items from an advertisement (or advertisements) in a newspaper, trade publication, or the like. Write a letter ordering these items. Make certain that you give all the information needed to complete the sale (size, color, weight, material, etc.). Take care to cover the cost portion, including shipping costs and manner of payment. And don't forget to give proper shipping instructions. For the benefit of your instructor, attach the advertisements to your letter.

50. As human resources director of Heizer Operations, Inc., one of your duties is to keep the company library current. You order books and statistical series in human resource management, and you also keep current the library's holdings of computer software packages.

Today, you have identified four such software packages from your team of human resource professionals. All of the packages are offered through Human Resources Research, Ltd., of Vancouver, British Columbia. You are going to write an order letter based on the following program package descriptions. These descriptions were passed along to you over the last months by members of your human resource department.

Compensation Administration. Cost—$8,015; uses stored mathematical formulas and statistical distribution patterns to create optimum individual salary levels from existing job factor point values or from vendor's job evaluation methodology; 20 percent discount if more than two programs ordered.

Executive Forecaster. Automates the succession process; searches database files and matches candidates to open positions; helps identify, develop, and track executive talent; outputs either in standard or custom reports or charts; $4,085; no discounts.

Talent Bank. Discount of 15 percent for two or more programs; decision-support software system for selecting individuals, screening talent pools, locating people to fill position openings, and developing career support; $5,035 each.

Career Management for Organizations. $100 annual update fee; five modules take user through career planning process—career development; assessing, gathering information; making decisions, taking actions; management reports; $7,000; discount for three or more programs; does not apply to update.

You have not done business with HRR before, but you will ask the company to bill you. HRR should pay shipping cost. You will order one of each of the first three programs listed and two of the last one. Also, to keep yourself and others current in the area of PC software packages in human resource management, you will order for your library the following updating service from HRR:

PC Software Packages for Human Resource Administration. J.D. Dunn, updated bimonthly; electronic directory of software for human resources; $85 for latest CD; $80 per year for supplemental service online.

51. As president of the Midwestern Association of Manufacturers, an industry trade group, you plan to visit Russia next year on a goodwill tour. Because you will be a guest of various countries in eastern Europe, you believe it would be appropriate to present gifts to certain dignitaries and key industrial leaders in the host cities. Thus, you decide on some unique works of art from the U.S. Southwest.

The source of your selection is a brochure you picked up while vacationing in New Mexico last summer. From it, you make the following selections for your tour:

Bronze-coated/plaster-base sculpture by Horace Battaglia; 12½ inches by 11 inches by 8 inches, edition 25, titled "Fast Gun," $39.90.

"The Rattlesnake" by Tonya Beauchamp, cold-cast bronze and resin finished in patina, 8 ¾ inches high, edition 40, $47.25.

Mike Mazzlo, 10 inches by 22 inches, "Trail Drive," wood base with bronze and powdered-plaster sculpture, edition 45, $33.35.

"Headin' Home," 11 inches by 8 inches, watercolor print, Michelle Zechmeister, $16.75.

You will order by letter 6 each of the first 2 items, 12 of the third, and 18 of the fourth from Joe Henry's Gallery, 651 Canyon Road, Taos, NM 24189. Send a check for $500 with your letter and ask that the gallery extend credit for the balance.

You want each sculpture boxed and labeled separately, and you'll pay handling charges of up to $2.50 for each one. Also, you'll need the order delivered to you by June 1, since you plan to leave by the middle of that month.

52. You always enjoy attending the meetings of the Association for Business Communication. Not only are you surrounded by professionals who truly enjoy and promote the importance of good communication skills in business, but you also learn from both the scholarly and the applied presentations. Today you heard a particularly good presentation by a Brigham Young University professor on the design of business

documents. In his presentation, he referred to a publication on document design, *Before & After,* that he highly recommended, giving those present ordering information, including the address and fax number.

He also had sample issues on hand from past volumes. You reviewed some of these samples closely after the presentation and have decided to order a subscription for $36 for one year as well as three of the back issues at $10 each. The specific issues you will order are the following: (1) volume 2, number 2, on characteristics of a good logo; (2) volume 4, number 4, on rules for designing efficient forms; and (3) volume 4, number 5, on designing a newsletter. Additionally, you are interested in learning about any other publications *Before & After* might have. Write the order that you will either fax to (916) 784-3880 or mail to PageLab, 18730 Sierra Gardens Drive, Roseville, CA 95661-2912.

Indirectness in Bad-News Messages

Upon completing this chapter, you will be able to write indirect responses to convey bad news. To reach this goal, you should be able to

1 Determine which situations require using the indirect order for the most effective response.

2 Use tact and courtesy in refusals of requests.

3 Write adjustment refusals that minimize and overcome bad impressions.

4 Compose tactful, yet clear, credit-refusals that foster goodwill.

INTRODUCTORY SITUATION

Refused Requests

As in Chapter 5, assume again the role of assistant to the Pinnacle vice president. Today your boss assigned you the task of responding to a request letter from the local chapter of the National Association of Peace Officers. This worthy organization has asked Pinnacle to contribute to a scholarship fund for certain needy children.

The request letter is persuasive. It points out that the scholarship fund is terribly short. As a result, the association is not able to take care of all the needy children. Many of them are the children of officers who were killed in the line of duty. You have been moved by the letter, and you would like to comply. But you cannot.

You cannot contribute now because Pinnacle policy does not permit it. Even though you do not like the effects of the policy in this case, you think the policy is good. Each year Pinnacle earmarks a fixed amount—all it can afford—for contributions. Then it doles out this amount to the causes that a committee of its executives considers the most worthy. Unfortunately, all the money earmarked for this year has already been given away. You will have to say no to the request, at least for now. You can offer to consider the association's cause next year.

Your letter must report the bad news, though it can hold out hope for the future. Because you like the association and because you want it to like Pinnacle, you will try to handle the situation delicately. The task will require your best strategy and your best writing skills.

SITUATIONS REQUIRING INDIRECTNESS

As explained in Chapter 5, when a message is primarily bad news, you should usually write in the indirect order. The indirect order is especially effective when you must say no or convey other disappointing news. The main reason for this approach is that negative messages are received more positively when an explanation precedes them. An explanation may even convince the reader that the writer's position is correct. In addition, an explanation cushions the shock of bad news. Not cushioning the shock makes the message unnecessarily harsh, and harshness destroys goodwill. It is not good business etiquette.

■ Usually bad-news messages should be in the indirect order.

You may want to use directness in some bad-news situations. If, for example, you think that your negative answer will be accepted routinely, you might choose directness. You also might choose directness if you know your reader well and feel that he or she will appreciate frankness. And you might choose directness anytime you are not concerned about goodwill. But such instances are not the rule. Usually you would be wise to use indirectness in refusals.

■ There are exceptions, as when the bad news is routine or when the reader prefers frankness.

The following pages analyze some common message situations that are usually best handled in the indirect order. As in the preceding chapter, the first situation is a common one—the refusal of a request. We cover it in detail. Then we cover two other common message types: the refusal of a request for adjustment and the refusal of credit. Since handling these two situations is similar to the handling of the first one, we cover them briefly. The focus here is on special considerations involving each type. We keep repetition to a minimum.

■ Following are typical message situations calling for the indirect order.

REFUSED REQUEST

Refusal of a request is definitely a bad-news message. Your reader has asked you for something, and you must say no. How bad the news is varies from case to case. Even so, it is hard to imagine a refusal that is good news. Because the news is bad, for reasons of good business etiquette you should usually write the request refusal in the indirect order.

■ Refusing a request calls for the indirect order

Your reason for refusing indirectly has been mentioned, but its importance warrants repeating it. In the refusal message you have two goals. The main one is to say no. The other is to maintain goodwill. You could achieve the first goal by simply saying no—plainly and directly. Maintaining goodwill, however, requires more. It requires that you convince your

■ In refusals you have two goals: (1) to refuse, and (2) to maintain goodwill. The first goal alone would be easy, but the second goal makes both goals hard.

Writing letters the old-fashioned way can be wasteful and inefficient. Today's progressive business writers enjoy the advantages of composing messages at the computer.

If you can compromise, let what you can do imply what you cannot do.

If you can make a compromise, you can use it to include your refusal. That is, by saying what you can do, you can imply clearly what you cannot do. For example, if you write "The best we can do is . . ." you make it clear that you cannot do what the reader has requested. Yet you do this in the most positive way that the situation will permit.

CLOSING WITH GOODWILL

End with a pleasant off-subject comment.

Even a skillfully handled refusal is the most negative part of your message. Because the news is disappointing, it is likely to put your reader in an unhappy frame of mind. That frame of mind works against your goodwill goal. To reach your goodwill goal, you must shift your reader's thoughts to more pleasant matters.

Adapt the close to the one case.

The best closing subject matter depends on the facts of the case, but it should be positive talk that fits the one situation. For example, if your refusal involves a counterproposal, you could say more about the counterproposal. Or you could make some friendly remark about the subject of the request as long as it does not remind the reader of the bad news. In fact, your closing subject matter could be almost any friendly remark that would be appropriate if you were handling the case face to face. The major requirement is that your ending words have a goodwill effect.

Avoid ending with the old, negative apologies.

Ruled out are the timeworn, negative apologies. "Again, may I say that I regret that we must refuse" is typical of these. Also ruled out are the equally timeworn appeals for understanding, such as "I sincerely hope that you understand why we must make this decision." Such words emphasize the bad news.

CONTRASTING REFUSALS

The advantage of the indirect order in refusal letters is evident from the following contrasting examples. Both refuse clearly. But only the letter that uses the indirect order gains reader goodwill.

HARSHNESS IN THE DIRECT REFUSAL. The first example states the bad news right away. This blunt treatment puts the reader in a bad frame of mind. The result is that the reader is less likely to accept the explanation that follows. The explanation is clear, but note the unnecessary use of negative words *(exhausted, regret, cannot consider)*. Note also how the closing words leave the reader with a strong reminder of the bad news.

Tact and strategy mark this refusal, in which an office manager turns down a textbook author's request. The author has asked for model letters that can be used as examples in a correspondence guidebook. The office manager reasons that complying with this request would take more time than he is willing or able to give.

G
GUARDIAN
INSURANCE
COMPANY

October 3, 1999

Dr. Ruth A. Howard
College of Business
Dorman University
1901 Finny Street
Calgary, Alberta T2M 2Y9

On-subject beginning— ties in with request

Dear Dr. Howard:

Sets up explanation

Your Correspondence Guidebook described in your September 21 letter should be a really practical aid to the business executive.

You-viewpoint explanation

The practical value of the book, as I see it, depends largely on the quality of its illustrations. Your book demands illustrations that meet all the criteria of good correspondence. But getting the quality of illustration you need will require careful checking by someone who knows good writing, and going through the thousands of letters in our records will take considerable time and skill. For this reason, I am sure you will understand why the best we can do is to make our files open to you or your staff. We would, of course, be happy to provide working space for you, and we assure you our very best cooperation. If you wish to use our files in this way, please let us know.

Refusal logically flows from explanation

Note positive wording of refusal

Goodwill close— off subject and pleasant

Please let us know, also, if we can help you further. We look forward to seeing your book.

Sincerely,

Raphael E. Pattillo

Raphael E. Pattillo
Office Manager

ced

334 N. Hampton St.
Stanley, NY 14561
716-773-4422
FAX 716-773-4416

WA
WILKERSON ASSOCIATES
Consultants to Management

January 20, 1999

Mr. Thelbert H. Gooch
Executive Director
Association of Professional Consultants
7112 Avondale Road
Phoenix, AZ 85017-8409

Dear Mr. Gooch:

On-subject beginning— compliment gains reader's favor

Your January 13 invitation to address the National Association of Administrators is a most distinct honor to me personally. I am well aware of the high quality of NAA's membership.

Sets up explanation

Offer of alternative shows concern— builds goodwill

Presenting a major paper to this quality group deserves a thorough and competent effort. Obviously, such an effort requires time. Because my time is fully committed to a writing project for the months ahead, I must suggest that you get someone who has the time to do the job right. May I recommend Ms. Paula Perkins of my staff? Paula is an outstanding speaker and an expert on women's issues in management.

Reasonable, convincing explanation

Goodwill close— adapted to this one case

If I can help you further in your efforts to get speakers, you can write me at Forrest@wa.com. I wish you good luck with the program.

Sincerely,

Forrest Y. Wilkerson

Forrest Y. Wilkerson
President

Dear Ms. Cangelosi:

We regret to inform you that we cannot grant your request for a donation to the association's scholarship fund.

So many requests for contributions are made of us that we have found it necessary to budget a definite amount each year for this purpose. Our budgeted funds for this year have been exhausted, so we simply cannot consider additional requests. However, we will be able to consider your request next year.

We deeply regret our inability to help you now and trust that you understand our position.

Sincerely,

■ This bad letter is harsh because of its directness.

TACT AND COURTESY IN AN INDIRECT REFUSAL.   The second example skillfully handles the negative message. Its opening words are on subject and neutral. They set up the explanation that follows. The clear and logical explanation ties in with the opening. Using no negative words, the explanation leads smoothly to the refusal. Note that the refusal is also handled without negative words and yet is clear. The friendly close fits the one case.

Dear Ms. Cangelosi:

Your efforts to build the scholarship fund for the association's needy children are most commendable. We wish you good success in your efforts to further this worthy cause.

We at Pinnacle are always willing to assist worthy causes whenever we can. That is why every January we budget for the year the maximum amount we believe we are able to contribute to such causes. Then we distribute that amount among the various deserving groups as far as it will go. Since our budgeted contributions for this year have already been made, we are placing your organization on our list for consideration next year.

We wish you the best of luck in your efforts to help educate the deserving children of the association's members.

Sincerely,

■ This letter using the indirect approach is better.

INTRODUCTORY SITUATION	Adjustment Refusals

Sometimes your job at Pinnacle involves handling an unhappy person. Today you have to do that, for the morning mail has brought a strong claim for adjustment on an order for Pinnacle's Do-Craft fabrics. The claim writer, Ms. Arlene Sanderson, explains that a Do-Craft fabric her upholstering company used on some outdoor furniture has faded badly in less than 10 months. She even includes sample cuts of the fabric to prove her point. She contends that the product is defective, and she wants her money back—all $2,517 of it.

Inspection of the fabric reveals that it has been subjected to strong sunlight for long periods. Do-Craft fabrics are for inside use only. Both the Pinnacle brochures on the product and the catalog description stress this point. In fact, you have difficulty understanding how Ms. Sanderson missed it when she ordered from the catalog. Anyway, as you see it, Pinnacle is not responsible and does not intend to refund the money. At the same time, it wants to keep Ms. Sanderson as a customer and friend. Now you must write the letter that will do just that. The following discussion tells you how.

ADJUSTMENT REFUSALS

Messages that refuse claims carry bad news. As with other bad-news messages, you should usually handle them indirectly. As we have seen, such an approach can be as positive as the situation permits as well as in accord with good business etiquette. The indi-

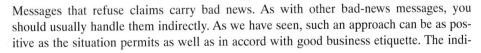

■ Messages refusing claims for adjustment are bad news.

On Controlling Anger in Letters: Some Words of Advice from Abraham Lincoln

An officer in the field had blundered badly, and Secretary of War Stanton was furious. "I feel that I must give this man a piece of my mind," he said to President Lincoln. "By all means, do so," said Lincoln. "Write him now while it's fresh on your mind. Make the words sting. Cut him up." Thus encouraged, Stanton wrote the letter, a masterpiece of angry words. He then pridefully took his letter to Lincoln.

After reading the letter, the president responded. "This is a good one," he said. "Now tear it up. You have freed your mind on the subject, and that is all that's necessary. You never want to send such letters. I never do."

rect approach is especially necessary when there is reason to be concerned about your reader's sensitive feelings. Of course, not all claims are refused. Most are legitimate, and most companies try hard to correct for legitimate damages. But some claims are not well founded. They may be based on wrong information, or they may be dishonest. In such cases a company is likely to say no.

DETERMINING THE BASIC STRATEGY

- Your first step is to determine your explanation and the strategy for presenting it.

Your first step in refusing a claim for adjustment is to decide how to explain your decision. Probably your best course is to base your explanation on the facts of the case. You should review them, and from your review determine precisely why a refusal is justified. Then, with these facts in mind, you should search for the best possible way of presenting your position. This mental effort requires that you think through the situation thoroughly—especially from your reader's point of view. It should end with the development of a strategy for presenting your case clearly and convincingly.

- Then present your strategy following this plan.

After you have determined what to say, you write the message. Although variations may be justified, usually you should follow this general order:

- Begin with words that are on subject, are neutral as to the decision, and set up your strategy.
- Present the strategy that explains or justifies, being factual and positive.
- Refuse clearly and positively, perhaps including a counterproposal.
- End with off-subject, friendly words.

APPLYING THE INDIRECT PLAN

- Follow the general plan for bad-news messages.

The above plan clearly is much like that for the refused request previously discussed. It should be, for a refused adjustment is really a special type of refused request. Both messages have the same need to identify the correspondence being answered near the beginning—either incidentally or in a neutral subject line. Likewise, both have the same need to begin with words that set up the strategy that will justify the refusal. And here lies the primary difference between this and other refused requests. The strategies you are likely to use are different.

- Set up your strategy in the opening, as in these examples.

As we have noted, the strategy you select should be based on the legitimate reason for your refusal and the facts of the case. Of the many strategies available to you, one is to begin on a point of common agreement and then explain how the case at hand is an exception. To illustrate, a case involving a claim for adjustment for failure of an air conditioner to perform properly might begin thus:

You are correct in believing that a two-ton Deep Kold window unit should cool the ordinary three-room apartment.

The following explanation will show that the apartment in question is not an ordinary apartment.

Another strategy is to build the case that the claim for adjustment goes beyond what can reasonably be expected. A beginning such as this one sets it up:

Assisting families to enjoy beautifully decorated homes at budget prices is one of our most satisfying goals. We do all we reasonably can to reach it.

The following explanation, of course, will show that the requested adjustment goes beyond what can be reasonably expected. Many such strategy possibilities are available to you.

- Avoid negatives in explaining and refusing.

Following comes the explanation that supports the refusal. Here you should use a minimum of negative language. Especially should you avoid words that question the reader's honesty. Such an effect would conflict with good business etiquette. And as in other refused request letters, you should follow the explanation with the refusal. Your refusal should be clearly worded, yet you want it to be as positive as the situation permits. For example, this one is clear, but it contains no negative language:

For reasons you will understand, we can pay only when our employees pack the goods.

If a compromise is in order, you might present it in positive language like this:

In view of these facts, the best we can do is repair the equipment at cost.

As in all bad-news messages, you should end this one with some appropriate, positive comment not directly related to the situation involved. You could write about new products or services, industry news, or such. Neither negative apologies nor words that recall the problem are appropriate here.

- Close positively and off subject.

CONTRASTING ADJUSTMENT REFUSAL LETTERS

Bad and good treatment of Pinnacle's refusal to give money back for the faded fabric are illustrated by the following two letters. The bad one, which is blunt and insulting, destroys goodwill. The good one, which uses the techniques described in the preceding paragraphs, stands a fair chance of keeping goodwill.

- The following examples show the value of the preceding plan.

COMMUNICATION IN BRIEF

A Not-So-Successful Refusal

Crusty old Mr. Whiffle bought an umbrella from a mail-order company. When the umbrella did not function to his requirements, Mr. Whiffle wrote the company a letter asking for his money back.

The mail-order company answered with a well-written letter of refusal.

Again Mr. Whiffle wrote, and again the company replied with a nicely written refusal.

Mr. Whiffle wrote a third time. The mail-order company refused a third time.

So angry was Mr. Whiffle that he boarded a bus, traveled to the home office of the mail-order company, and paid a visit to the company's adjustment correspondent. After a quick explanation of his purpose, Mr. Whiffle broke the umbrella over the adjustment correspondent's head. The correspondent then gave Mr. Whiffle his money.

"Now why didn't you do this before?" Mr. Whiffle asked. "You had all the evidence."

Replied the correspondent, "But you never explained it so clearly before."

BLUNTNESS IN A DIRECT REFUSAL.   The bad letter begins bluntly with a direct statement of the refusal. The language is negative (*regret, must reject, claim, refuse, damage, inconvenience*). The explanation is equally blunt. In addition, it is insulting ("It is difficult to understand how you failed. . . ."). It uses little tact, little you-viewpoint. Even the close is negative, for it recalls the bad news.

Dear Ms. Sanderson:

Subject: Your May 3 claim for damages

I regret to report that we must reject your request for money back on the faded Do-Craft fabric.

We must refuse because Do-Craft fabrics are not made for outside use. It is difficult for me to understand how you failed to notice this limitation. It was clearly stated in the catalog from which you ordered. It was even stamped on the back of every yard of fabric. Since we have been more than reasonable in trying to inform you, we cannot possibly be responsible.

We trust that you will understand our position. We regret very much the damage and inconvenience our product has caused you.

Sincerely,

TACT AND INDIRECT ORDER IN A COURTEOUS REFUSAL.   The good letter begins with friendly talk on a point of agreement that also sets up the explanation. Without accusations, anger, or negative words, it reviews the facts of the case, which free the company of blame. The refusal is clear, even though it is made by implication rather than by direct words. It is skillfully handled. It uses no negatives, and it does not receive undue emphasis. The close shifts to helpful suggestions that fit the one case. Friendliness and resale are evident throughout the letter but especially in the close.

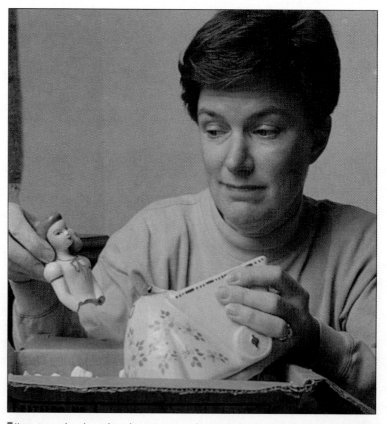

Happenings such as this are bitter disappointments to those involved. Letters about the matter should not recall this scene unnecessarily.

An out-of-town customer bought an expensive dress from the writer and mailed it back three weeks later, asking for a refund. The customer explained that the dress was not a good fit and that she really did not like it anymore. But perspiration stains on the dress proved that she had worn it. This letter skillfully presents the refusal.

MARIE'S
Fashions

103 BREAKER RD. HOUSTON, TX 77015 713-454-6778 Fax: 713-454-6771

February 19, 1999

Ms. Maud E. Krumpleman
117 Kyle Avenue E
College Station, TX 77840-2415

Dear Ms. Krumpleman:

On-subject opening—neutral point from claim letter

We understand your concern about the exclusive St. John's dress you returned February 15. As always, we are willing to do as much as we reasonably can to make things right.

Sets up explanation

Review of facts supports writer's position

What we can do in each instance is determined by the facts of the case. With returned clothing, we generally give refunds. Of course, to meet our obligations to our customers for quality merchandise, all returned clothing must be unquestionably new. As you know, our customers expect only the best from us, and we insist that they get it. Thus, because the perspiration stains on your dress would prevent its resale, we must consider the sale final. We are returning the dress to you. With it you will find a special alteration ticket which assures you of getting the best possible fit free of charge.

Good restraint—no accusations, no anger

Note positive language in refusal

Emphasis on what store can do helps restore goodwill

Friendly goodwill close

So, whenever it is convenient, please come by and let us alter this beautiful St. John's creation to your requirements. We look forward to serving you.

Sincerely,

Marie O. Mitchell

Marie O. Mitchell
President

dm

This better letter is indirect and tactful.

Dear Ms. Sanderson:

Subject: Your May 3 letter about Do-Craft fabric

Certainly, you have a right to expect the best possible service from Do-Craft fabrics. Every Do-Craft product is the result of years of experimentation. And we manufacture each yard under the most careful controls. We are determined that our products will do for you what we say they will do.

Because we do want our fabrics to please, we carefully ran the samples of Do-Craft Fabric 103 you sent us through our laboratory. Exhaustive tests show that each sample has been subjected to long periods in extreme sunlight. Since we have known from the beginning that Do-Craft fabrics cannot withstand exposure to sunlight, we have clearly noted this in all our advertising, in the catalog from which you ordered, and in a stamped reminder on the back of every yard of the fabric. Under the circumstances, all we can do concerning your request is suggest that you change to one of our outdoor fabrics. As you can see from our catalog, all of the fabrics in the 200 series are recommended for outdoor use.

You will probably also be interested in the new Duck Back cotton fabrics listed in our 500 series. These plastic-coated cotton fabrics are most economical, and they resist sun and rain remarkably well. If we can help you further in your selection, please contact us at service@pinnacle.com.

Sincerely,

INTRODUCTORY SITUATION

Credit Refusals

Although Chester Carter, your boss at Pinnacle, is in charge of the credit department, you do not normally get involved in credit work. But exceptions occur. Today, for example, the credit manager consulted with Chester about a request for credit from Bell Builders Supply Company, one of Pinnacle's long-time cash customers. The financial information Bell submitted with the request does not justify credit. Bell has more debt than it can afford, and still more debt would only make matters worse.

Because a refusal appears to be best for all concerned, Pinnacle will turn down Bell's request. The decision is fair, but it will not be good news to Bell. In fact, it might even end this firm's cash business with Pinnacle. Handling the situation is obviously a delicate task.

The importance of the case prompts Chester to ask you to write the refusal for his signature. A refusal from a top executive, Chester thinks, just might be effective. Now you are faced with the task of writing the message that will refuse the request yet keep the reader as a cash customer.

CREDIT REFUSALS

Because credit is personal, use tact in refusing it.

Some think tact is not necessary.

But treating people tactfully pleases us personally.

It also gains future customers for your business.

Messages that refuse credit are more negative than most refusals. The very nature of credit makes them so. Credit is tied to personal things, such as morals, acceptance in society, character, and integrity. So, unless skillfully handled, a credit refusal can be viewed as a personal insult. For the most positive results, such a refusal requires the indirect order and a strategy that demonstrates good business etiquette.

Some will argue that you need not be concerned about the reader's reactions in this situation. Since you are turning down the reader's business, why spend time trying to be tactful? Why not just say no quickly and let it go at that? If you will study the situation, the answer becomes obvious.

In the first place, being kind to people is personally pleasing to all of us. At least, it should be. The rewards in business are not all measured in dollars and cents. Other rewards exist, such as the good feelings that come from treating people with courtesy and respect.

In the second place, being kind to people is profitable in the long run. People who are refused credit still have needs. They are likely to satisfy those needs somewhere. They may have to buy for cash. If you are friendly to them, they just might buy from you. In addition, the fact that people are bad credit risks now does not mean that they will never be good credit risks. Many people who are good credit accounts today were bad risks at some time in the past. By not offending bad risks now, you may keep them as friends of your company until they become good risks.

DETERMINING THE STRATEGY

Your first step in writing a credit refusal message is to work out your explanation. That explanation will depend on the reason for the refusal. If you are refusing because the applicant is a bad moral risk, you have a very difficult assignment. You cannot just say bluntly that you are refusing because of bad character. Even people with low morals would bristle at this approach. In such cases, you might choose a roundabout approach. For example, you might imply the reason. Since the applicant knows his or her credit reputation, a mere hint should indicate that you also know it.

Begin by working out the refusal strategy. You can imply the reason with bad moral risks.

Some credit authorities in the United States prefer a more direct approach for bad moral risks, citing the Equal Credit Opportunity Act of 1975 as support. This act states that applicants refused credit are entitled to written explanation of the reasons for the refusal. One way of implementing this approach is to follow the refusal with an invitation to come in (or telephone) to discuss the reasons. This discussion could be followed by a written explanation, if the applicant wants it. Opponents of this approach argue that the applicants already know the facts—that very few of them would pursue the matter further.

But some authorities favor offering an explanation.

If you are refusing because your applicant's financial condition is weak, your task is easier. Weak finances are not a reflection on character, for instead of being related to personal qualities, they are related to such factors as illness, unemployment, and bad luck. Thus, with applicants whose finances are weak, you can talk about the subject more directly. You also can talk more hopefully about granting credit in the future. In actual practice, cases do not fit neatly into these two groups. But you should be able to adapt the suggestions that follow to the facts of each case.

Frank discussion is effective with weak financial risks.

In any case, as described below, your message should follow this general plan of organization:

Follow this organization plan.

- Begin with words that set up the strategy (explanation), are neutral as to the decision, and tie in with the application.
- Present the explanation.
- Refuse tactfully—to a bad moral risk, by implication; to a person with weak finances or in a weak economic environment, positively and with a look to the future.
- End with adapted goodwill words.

ADAPTING THE BAD-NEWS PLAN

You will recognize the pattern above as the same one suggested for the two preceding refusal situations. The opening sets up your strategy, it is neutral as to decision, and it is on subject. Again, the significant difference between this and the preceding refusals is in the strategies that can be used. In this case, the beginning words might refer to the order involved (if one accompanied the request), as in this example:

Following the bad-news pattern, set up strategy with on-subject and neutral words—perhaps a reference to an order accompanying the request.

Your January 22 order for Rock-Ware roofing shows good planning for the rush months ahead. As you will agree, it is good planning that marks the path of business success.

The strategy this opening sets up is to explain that well-managed businesses hold down indebtedness—something the reader needs to do.

A popular and appropriate strategy is to begin with a simple expression of gratefulness for the credit application and then lead into a courteous explanation and refusal. Although it is usually effective, the timeworn "Thank you for your application" variety is better replaced with different wording, such as this:

A thank-you for the request is appropriate and popular strategy.

We are sincerely grateful for your credit application and will do all that we reasonably can to help you get your business started.

"No."
(*From* The Wall Street Journal, *with permission of Cartoon Features Syndicate.*)

The following explanation will show that the facts of this case make granting credit something beyond what the writer can reasonably do.

■ Explanations to bad moral risks can be vague.

The explanation set up by the opening can be an additional point of difference. If you are refusing because of the reader's bad credit morals, you need to say little. Bad moral risks know their records. You need only to imply that you also know. For example, this sentence handles such an explanation well, and it also gives the answer.

Our review of your credit record requires that we serve you only on a cash basis at this time.

■ Explanations to weak financial risks with good morals can be more open.

Your explanation to applicants with good morals but weak finances can be more open financial discussions of the facts of the case. Even so, you should select your words carefully to avoid any unintended negative effect. In some cases, you might want to show concern for the reader's credit problem.

■ Refuse clearly and positively.

Whatever explanation you use, your words should lead to a clear but positive refusal. For a good moral risk with bad finances, this one does the job well:

Thus, for the best interest of both of us, we must postpone extending credit until your current assets-to-liabilities ratio reaches 2 to 1.

■ Close with positive, friendly words that fit the one case.

As in the other bad-news messages, you should end the credit refusal with words of goodwill. Preferably, avoid anything routine, and make the words fit the one case. A suggestion for cash buying or comments about merchandise or service can be effective. So can a forward look to whatever future relations appear appropriate. This closing meets these requirements:

As one of Meyers's cash customers, you will continue to receive the same courtesy, quality merchandise, and low prices we give to all our customers. We look forward to serving you soon.

CONTRASTING CREDIT REFUSAL ILLUSTRATIONS

■ The following letters contrast credit refusal techniques.

The following two contrasting letters refusing Bell's credit application clearly show the advantages of tactful indirect treatment. The bad letter does little other than refuse. The good one says no clearly, yet it works to build goodwill and cultivate cash sales.

HARSHNESS AS A RESULT OF TACTLESS TREATMENT.   The weaker letter does begin indirectly, but the opening subject matter does little to soften the bad news. This obvious subject matter hardly deserves the emphasis that the opening gives it. Next comes the refusal—without any preceding explanation. It uses negative words (*regret, do not meet, weak, deny*). Explanation follows, but it is scant. The appeal for a cash sale is weak. The closing words leave a bad picture in the reader's mind.

As the merge information in the address area indicates, this is a department store's form letter refusing credit to bad moral risks. Such stores ordinarily use form letters because they must handle credit on a mass basis. Because form letters must fit a variety of people and cases, they tend to be general.

DAYTON HUDSON CORPORATION

Date

«Title». «FirstName» «LastName»
«JobTitle»
«Company»
«Address 1»
«Address 2»
«City», «State» «PostalCode»

Dear «Title» «LastName»:

Favorable beginning contact—routine but appropriate

We sincerely appreciate your interest in an account with Dayton Hudson Corp. Whenever we can, we are always willing to serve you.

Sets up explanation

Positive suggestion of cash buying

In determining what we can do for you regarding your «RequestDate» request for credit, we made the routine check you authorized. The information we have received permits us to serve you only as a cash customer. But, as you know, cash buying here at Dayton Hudson's can mean real savings for you.

Explanation is clear and positive—implies that writer knows credit record

Positively worded refusal

We look forward to seeing you in the store again and serving you very soon.

Friendly closing words

Sincerely,

Cynthia R. Wunch

Cynthia R. Wunch
Credit Manager

hts

777 Nicollet Mall, Minneapolis, Minnesota 55402-2055

TARGET   MERVYN'S   DAYTON'S   HUDSON'S   MARSHALL FIELD'S

That College Touch in a Refusal

A merchant was finding it difficult to write a letter refusing an adjustment when in walked his college-student son.

"You're going to college," the merchant said to the boy. "Why don't you write this letter for me? This letter borders on fraud, but the guy spends good money with me. So use that college touch in turning him down."

The young man worked feverishly at his assignment. A short time later, he proudly handed his masterpiece to his dad.

"It has that college touch, all right," the merchant commented. "But since when do you spell *dirty* with a *u,* and why capitalize *rat*?"

■ This one is tactless.

Dear Mr. Bell:

We have received your May 3 order and accompanying request for credit.

After carefully reviewing the financial information you submitted, we regret to report that you do not meet our requirements for credit. It is our considered judgment that firms with your weak assets-to-liabilities ratio would be better off buying with cash. Thus, we encourage you to do so.

We would, of course, be pleased to serve you on a cash basis. In closing, let me assure you that we sincerely regret that we must deny you credit at this time.

Sincerely,

COURTESY AND TACT IN A CLEAR REFUSAL.   The better letter generally follows the plan outlined in preceding pages. Its on-subject, neutral opening sets up the explanation. The explanation is thorough and tactful. Throughout, the impression of genuine concern for the reader is clear. Perhaps the explanation of the values of cash buying would be out of place in some cases. In this case, however, the past relationship between reader and writer justifies it. The letter ends with pleasant words that look to the future.

■ This good letter refuses tactfully.

Dear Mr. Bell:

Your May 3 order for Pinnacle paints and supplies suggests that your company is continuing to make good progress.

To assure yourself of continued progress, we feel certain that you will want to follow the soundest business practices possible. As you may know, most financial experts say that maintaining a reasonable indebtedness is a must for sound growth. About a 2-to-1 ratio of current assets to liabilities is a good minimum, they say. In the belief that this minimum ratio is best for all concerned, we extend credit only when it is met. As soon as you reach this ratio, we would like to review your application again. Meanwhile, we will strive to meet your needs on a cash basis.

We appreciate your interest in Pinnacle paints and look forward to serving you.

Sincerely,

OTHER INDIRECT MESSAGES

■ Adapt the techniques of this chapter.

The types of indirect messages covered in preceding pages are the most common ones. There are others. Some of these (sales, collections, and job applications) are rather special types. They are covered in the following chapters. You should be able to handle all the other indirect types that you encounter by adapting the techniques explained and illustrated in this chapter.

1. When the main point of your message is bad news, use the indirect order.
   - But exceptions exist, as when you believe that the news will be received routinely.
   - Make exceptions also when you think the reader will appreciate directness.

1 Determine which situations require using the indirect order for the most effective response.

2. The refusal of a request is one bad-news situation that you will probably choose to treat indirectly.
   - In such situations, strive to achieve two main goals:
     —to refuse, and
     —to maintain goodwill.
   - Begin by thinking through the problem, looking for a logical explanation (or reasoning).
   - Write an opening that sets up this explanation.
   - Then present your explanation (reasoning), taking care to use convincing and positive language.
   - Refuse clearly yet positively.
   - Close with appropriate, friendly talk that does not recall the bad news.

2 Use tact and courtesy in refusals of requests.

3. Refusals of adjustments follow a similar pattern.
   - First, determine your explanation (reasoning) for refusing.
   - Begin with neutral words that set up your reasoning and do not give away the refusal.
   - Then present your reasoning, building your case convincingly.
   - Refuse clearly and positively.
   - Close with appropriate friendly talk that does not recall the refusal.

3 Write adjustment refusals that minimize the negative and overcome bad impressions.

4. Messages refusing credit are more negative than most other types of refusals, for the refusal is tied to personal things.
   - As with other types of refusals, begin by thinking through a strategy.
   - If you are refusing because of the applicant's bad credit character, use a roundabout approach.
   - If you are refusing because of the applicant's weak finances, be more direct.
   - In either case, choose opening words that set up your strategy, are neutral, and tie in with the request being answered.
   - To the bad moral risk, imply the facts rather than state them bluntly.
   - In refusals because of weak finances, look hopefully to credit in the future.
   - End all credit refusals with appropriate positive words, perhaps suggesting cash buying, customer services, or other appropriate topics.

4 Compose tactful yet clear credit refusals that foster goodwill.

CRITICAL THINKING QUESTIONS

1. Give examples of when directness is appropriate for responses giving negative (bad-news) information.

2. Writing in the indirect order usually requires more words than does writing in the direct order. Since conciseness is a virtue in writing, how can the indirect order be justified?

3. What strategy is best in a message refusing a request when the reasons for the refusal are strictly in the writer's best interests?

4. Apologies in refusals are negative, for they call attention to what you are refusing. Thus, you should avoid using them. Discuss.

5. An adjustment correspondent explained the refusal of an adjustment request by saying that company policy did not permit granting claims in such cases. Was this explanation adequate? Discuss.

6. Is there justification for positive writing in a message refusing credit? You are not going to sell to the reader, so why try to maintain goodwill?

7. Discuss the difference between refusing credit to a good moral risk with bad finances or in a poor economic environment and refusing credit to a bad moral risk.

CRITICAL THINKING EXERCISES

1. Point out shortcomings in the following letter from a sports celebrity declining an invitation to speak at the kickoff meeting for workers in a fund-raising campaign for a charity.

Dear Ms. Chung:

As much as I would like to, I must decline your request that I give your membership a free lecture next month. I receive many requests to give free lectures. I grant some of them, but I simply cannot do them all. Unfortunately, yours is one that I must decline.

I regret that I cannot serve you this time. If I can be of further service in the future, please call on me.

Sincerely yours,

2. Criticize the following letter refusing the claim for a defective riding lawn mower. The mower was purchased 15 months earlier. The purchaser has had difficulties with it for some time and submitted with the claim a statement from a local repair service

verifying the difficulties. The writer's reason for refusing is evident from the letter.

Dear Mr. Skinner:

Your May 12 claim of defective workmanship in your Model 227 Dandy Klipper riding mower has been reviewed. After considering the information received, I regret to report that we cannot refund the purchase price.

You have had the mower for 15 months, which is well beyond our one-year guarantee. Even though your repair person says that you had problems earlier, he is not one of our authorized repair people. If you will read the warranty you refer to in your letter, you will see that we honor the warranty only when our authorized repair people find defects. I think you will understand why we must follow this procedure.

If you will take the machine to the authorized service center in your area (La Rue Lawn and Garden Center), I am confident they can correct the defect at a reasonable charge.

If I can be of additional service, please contact me.

Sincerely,

CRITICAL THINKING PROBLEMS

REFUSED REQUESTS

1. As sales manager for Marcel Drago Fashions, Inc., manufacturers of a middle-priced line of women's clothing, you receive a letter from Carmen Medina, owner of Carmen's Dress Shop. Apparently, Carmen doesn't know much about her business. In fact, her letter states that she has been in the business only three months.

In her letter, Carmen explains that she bought more clothing from you than she can sell. She wants to return $2,655 of the purchases she made 10 weeks ago. You can't accept. It's just not the way this business operates. There is an element of risk in retailing styled merchandise, which is why buying must be done wisely. Manufacturers would not be in business long if they had to take care of their errors by discounting clothes at the end of the season. In

fact, the price structure is not designed to permit such sales.

As you see it, Carmen needs a lesson in retailing practices. Your explanation of your refusal will give it to her. And you will try to do it in such a way as to keep her business.

2. In the position of public relations director for the Wang-Burton Iron Works, answer a letter written by Ms. Monica Scruggs, a third-grade teacher from a nearby city. Ms. Scruggs has asked to bring her class of 25 students on a visit through your plant next Friday afternoon. She is certain "the Wang-Burton people won't mind." She promises that the children will be well behaved. She will bring two parents along to keep them in line.

Because of potential dangers throughout the plant, Wang-Burton management doesn't even permit adult groups to visit the production areas. There is too much that could go wrong. You know the kids will be disappointed, for Ms. Scruggs's letter tells how excited they are about it. As a compromise, you would be willing to visit this class and show a film on your operation. You would also give each child a little booklet that explains what you do. The booklet may be a little advanced for them, but your explanation should help make its contents clear.

Now write the letter that graciously handles this difficult assignment.

3. Assume that you are a student representative and chairperson of your school's campus traffic committee. The committee consists of three students and four faculty members. This group has just concluded a meeting at which it considered a request for open parking on campus from Action, a student group dedicated to promoting various student causes. *Open parking* means no parking privileges for anyone. Students, faculty, staff—all would be equal on a first-come, first-served basis.

After considering the pros and cons of the question in a four-hour session, the committee voted unanimously to retain the present system. This system gives parking priority to faculty, staff, and handicapped students. The current arrangement makes sense, the committee concluded. And they asked you to convey their reasoning in a letter that also conveys the decision.

4. As Nancy Bray, marketing director for a brand-new online magazine targeted for the business traveler, you have received a request today from one of your newest and potentially most profitable advertisers, Ford Motor Corporation. The request from Lee McLaughlin in Ford's advertising division is for advance warnings about controversial articles as well as those that favor Ford's competitors.

Frankly, you are quite surprised that Ford would make such a request after all the controversy Chrysler caused when it decided to pull its ads from ABC's "Ellen" after the star declared she was gay. And it seems that the public is putting out a loud cry for advertisers to downplay their role in influencing the media. Furthermore, the organization Magazine Publishers of America has come out against allowing advertisers to exert undue control over magazine content. In addition to these reasons, you wonder why a company would want to spend its time reviewing your magazine, which is designed to help business travelers.

In clearly refusing this request, you must work hard not only to keep the account but also to establish Ford's trust in your promise of exercising good judgment in your editorial practices.

5. As Perry Hansen, president of the Rock Island Bank, you received the following request from an employee, Carol Weissmann, in your urgent email folder today. Carol is requesting that her telecommuting be extended immediately to four days per week from the current two days, double what your company policy states. As a leader in offering flexible work schedules, you have long recognized that this time-related benefit

has indeed increased both employee morale and employee productivity.

Perry,

I'm interested in extending my telecommuting to four days per week beginning next month.

Not only have I been able to complete all the work assigned to me on a timely basis during the current two-day schedule, but it has helped my family immensely to have me home these days. In addition, being able to run errands that are hard to do during the regular workday schedule, we've been able to reduce our child care costs since I can now pick the baby up on a timely basis. Furthermore, now that the children are getting older, more flextime would allow me to attend their soccer games, take Susan to her ballet lessons and watch her perform, and spend time helping both with their homework after school. Occasionally, I've even attended day meetings with their teachers. And one of nicest reasons is that I can take floater holidays when my children are home from school for teacher in-service days and other reasons.

As you know from my past year's experience, I do complete my work in a timely fashion. Giving me this flexibility for two more days would greatly enhance my family life.

Carol

While you agree that Carol's performance on the two-day flextime plan has been satisfactory, you are not certain that extending it to four days would be beneficial to the bank. You know from the literature that managers like to see their staff working. In fact, Carol may be jeopardizing her own promotions and raises by reducing her visibility. Plus, she needs to share with her co-workers in the responsibility for other on-site tasks. Furthermore, none of her reasons for requesting the change point to any business advantage.

As a member of the state banking executive association, you have not heard of any competing banks that offer more than two days per week of telecommuting, nor do most of the businesses in the area. While you will refuse her request, you can suggest that if she can show how the bank will benefit from her telecommuting a third day every other week, you might consider that compromise on a trial basis. You recognize that retaining dependable employees is important; and while Carol didn't mention it, most flextime plans reduce both employee stress and absenteeism.

Even though you will reply to this request by e-mail, be sure to apply the bad-news approach, saying no clearly while retaining Carol's goodwill.

6. As manager of the Panama City Boat Show, you sent out a mass mailing last week in which you invited manufacturers of boats, boat motors, and such to rent exhibition space at the annual boat show. Today, the first responses came in.

One, from the High Seas Manufacturing Company, makes a request that you cannot grant. Thus, you must prepare a refusal that will say no but at the same time will retain the company's goodwill.

The High Seas sales manager wrote, "Enclosed is a check for display space at your boat show. We want our usual location at the main entrance. We have had this spot for 11 years; and as longtime supporters of your show, we believe we have earned this prime location." This request reminds you of why you have your job. Your predecessor, Edward Richter, was fired because of favoritism. To preclude favoritism at future shows, the board of directors instructed you to determine display location by lot—more specifically, by drawing location numbers from a box. That way, everyone has an equal chance of getting high-traffic locations.

In your refusal to High Seas, you will need to do more than say no. You will try to convince the sales manager that your decision is correct. As you write, remember that the High Seas people—"longtime supporters of your show"—have done nothing wrong and deserve only the most courteous treatment.

7. Assume you are 10 years into your career and you have far exceeded the goals you have set for yourself in your professional life. You have worked diligently at your profession, and you have appreciated the valuable education you received at your college. You have applied the skills that you acquired time and again. You are a proud and grateful alumnus.

Today's mail brings a sincere letter from your college's dean complimenting you on your professional achievement record. It also requests that you serve on a board of advisors that the dean is forming. The board will meet two times a year—once in the fall and once in the spring. Primarily, the board will advise the dean on curriculum matters and provide a forum for exchange of ideas between academia and the business world. Each meeting is planned to last one day; the first is scheduled for the first Friday in November. The spring date has yet to be set.

Although you are flattered by the dean's request, you will have to refuse to serve on the board. Your schedule just will not permit it right now. (Note: Assume reasons for refusing that are consistent with your professional demands—traveling for executives, sales meetings, planning sessions, training workshops, and audit preparation are examples of some reasons. There are certainly others. Make sure they are realistic; trumped-up excuses are easy to see through.)

Also, you suspect that the dean wants you to contribute to her private discretionary fund. Already you donate generously to the student scholarship fund of your academic department. So bring out that you have supported the school consistently over the years.

Write a tactful, pleasant, but firm refusal to the dean. Your career demands and professional schedule are just too great right now. Somewhere down the road, however, you might be willing to serve. So keep the door open for that possibility by retaining the dean's goodwill. She does many good things for the college.

8. Project yourself into the role of sales promotion director at Compdeck, Inc., and solve a difficult situation you are facing today. One of the largest, most prestigious automobile dealerships in the area—Carolu Motors—is having a big promotional event next month.

The sales manager, Billy Harris, has written you a most appealing persuasive letter. The dealership would be pleased if you would donate a Compdeck computer to be given away during the month-long promotion. Although Harris gave no specifics, the Satellite Pro from Toshiba with its 445 CDX, 133 MHz, pentium processor, and MMX technology comes quickly to mind. It's currently on sale nationally for $2,499. Harris noted that other major businesses have contributed items, such as washing machines, dryers, other home appliances, and lawn mowers.

And what's in it for you and Compdeck if you comply with the request? Harris indicates you could display your other products in the large dealership showroom throughout the month. Also, the donations would be advertised for a month in two major newspapers in the city.

All this sounds enticing; but from a dollar-and-cents standpoint, the much-needed publicity is just a little too high-priced. Besides, if you give products to this dealership, how could you say no to the many other requests you would certainly receive? You feel that you could really be creating problems for yourself if you said yes. Thus, you will write a polite no to Harris.

ADJUSTMENT REFUSALS

9. As sales manager of the Legends Hotel, you have received a claim letter from Justin Waggoner, convention chairperson for the National Sales Executives Association (NSEA). A week ago the NSEA held its annual convention at your hotel. It was a good meeting for all concerned, and ended with a president's dinner your staff carefully prepared and served. But Mr. Waggoner doesn't like the bill for 420 dinners at $24.50 each. "We sold only 377 tickets," he writes, "and didn't consume 420 meals."

Checking through your correspondence, you find that Waggoner estimated that 420 executives would attend the president's dinner. You asked him to give you a final count by noon of the day of the dinner. He didn't. So you prepared 420 meals. You watched much of the food go to waste.

Clearly the fault is not yours. You cannot grant Waggoner's claim. But you want to make him understand why you must refuse, and you want to keep him happy. You'd like to get the group back for another convention.

10. For this assignment, assume that you are the owner-manager of The Plant House. You must refuse a claim made by Peter Yang, an out-of-town contractor. Late last spring Mr. Yang worked out a deal with you to sell him plants for landscaping a subdivision he was building. The total sale amounted to $47,200, which included a 25 percent discount from your usual retail price.

Now Mr. Yang claims that a set of plants worth approximately $14,380 failed to survive. He wants replacement plants or his money back. You cannot give him either. The survival of plants depends as much on how they are planted and how they are cared for throughout the first month as on their condition at the time of sale. You know the plants were in good condition when you shipped them. Mr. Yang's employees did the planting and the caretaking; so the blame must fall on him.

Try to make Mr. Yang accept your decision as a just one. As a goodwill gesture, you can offer to replace the dead plants at cost, which you estimate to be $12,500.

11. It's election time in your state, and your printing company has enjoyed receiving some profitable jobs from the candidates. One in particular was a $31,500 order for posters for the Shelly Kelly for Governor organization.

Today you receive a letter from Patti Seidel, the Shelly Kelly campaign manager. She presents the claim that the posters were inferior in quality. "The colors are not as sharp and clear as the sample you showed us," she writes. "Since we don't have time to wait, we must use them. Yet we think a 20 percent adjustment is in order."

You don't intend to give the adjustment. It's not only because you're against Shelly Kelly, but you know the facts are on your side. Ms. Seidel selected an inferior cardboard for the job—against your advice. The sample posters she looked at were made on better quality cardboard. She could have had the quality she wants had she been willing to pay the additional 15 percent for the better cardboard.

Now you must write Ms. Seidel and refuse her claim. But you'll want to handle the matter diplomatically. Shelly Kelly could win the election.

12. You are the owner and manager of the Custom Foot shoe store. Your store was one of the first in the area to offer custom-made shoes for just slightly more than mass-produced shoes. In fact, you can provide these shoes for just $180 a pair, whereas comparable high-end, name-brand shoes typically sell for around $1,000.

Your customers choose from a variety of classic styles such as wing tips and loafers as well as from materials such as suede or leather. They are then measured precisely by an electronic scanner. Your store, like several others, has over 670 samples on hand for customers to try on in order to determine the fit they prefer, allowing the tightness to be individually designated too. Once the shoes have been selected, the customer puts down a deposit (as a contract acceptance) that is applied toward the purchase when the shoes are delivered, about three weeks later.

Today's mail brought the return of a pair from a customer you remember as being particularly pleased with her custom shoes. In fact, she told you she was planning to wear them at a special business function at the end of the month. This customer, Megan Adami, said she was returning the shoes because they didn't match the outfit she bought them to complete; she mentioned nothing about the price or fit. Also, when inspecting the shoes, you could clearly see they had been worn outdoors. Therefore, you must refuse

the adjustment she seeks. Clearly, you want to keep this customer's goodwill and future business, but once a customer has accepted a pair of your custom-made shoes you cannot accept a return except perhaps for faulty materials or workmanship.

Feel free to offer Megan a reasonable counterproposal. Or since you remember her clearly, perhaps you can list some occasions on which Megan might wear these shoes or offer ideas on outfits that might complement them. You can write Megan at 12271 Sixty-ninth Terrace North, Seminole, FL 33772.

13. The Computer Instructional Institute (CII) provides all types of computer training to those who want and need to update their skills. Primarily, it offers training to employees of businesses who would rather "farm out" their technical training than provide it themselves in-house. Ninety percent of CII's business is done this way.

As curriculum manager for the institute, you receive a letter today from Servando Perez, human resources manager for Innovative Security Systems. He wants you to refund the $2,700 he paid to send three employees to one of your most popular courses, Computer Basics, which covers word processing, spreadsheets, and database systems. The price of the three-day course was $900 per person. "They did not get anything from the course," writes Mr. Perez. "They can't do their work any better now than they could before they took your course."

To investigate the nature of his claim, you look at the course evaluations. Although you know that the evaluations are not good indicators of learning, the participants rated the course instructor and the course as "good" and "excellent" on all the dimensions on the forms. Also, on the assessment of exit skills acquired, each participant "graded out" at 80 percent or more of the proficiency offered in the course. Thus, you are convinced that the problem is not with the course, the instructor, or your institute. With these facts, you are going to have to refuse Mr. Perez's claim for adjustment.

Most studies indicate that it takes some time for the effects of the computer training to show in work efficiency. Perhaps Mr. Perez is expecting too much too soon. Also, you offered a "basics" course with emphasis on applications to general business situations. It might be that Innovative needs a more specialized system. Your course covered all of the topics that were sent in the course outline to participants right after their payments were received. Or it might be that the company needs to commit to some of the newer software programs you covered in the course, if they have not done so already. What system they use will depend on their organizational needs.

You consider all of these reasons—and perhaps others—as you begin to plan the adjustment refusal to Mr. Perez. He sends quite a few employees to you for technical computer training. So be sure to use good logic and tact in the letter. You will tell him no and keep him as a customer for CII.

14. As adjustment manager of Computers Plus, you must deny the claim of Polly Ann Powers. Ms. Powers sent you an irate claim letter asking for full money back for the Hewlett-Packard OfficeJet 500 Color All-in-One Machine she bought with her computer last month. It's a "four-in-one" unit—a color printer, fax, copier, and scanner. She asks for the return of the full purchase price of $557.50, including tax. Along with the letter, she returned the unit with instructions to "junk it."

When you inspect the machine, you find that it isn't working because apparently it received a heavy jolt of some kind or another. Even so, the broken parts can be replaced easily. You can't give Ms. Powers her money back, but you will repair the machine at cost, which is only $35.50. Your one-year guarantee doesn't cover damage from unusual or harsh treatment, which is clearly evident in this case.

Write the adjustment refusal that will keep Ms. Powers happy with your products and service.

CREDIT REFUSALS

15. Your credit check of the Gutierrez Mercantile Company told you something you didn't detect when you talked personally with Manuel O. Gutierrez about his credit application. In fact, after talking with him, you thought that the credit check would be routine and that the $14,380 order accompanying his request was certain to go through. But the credit check shows negative information. Without question, Mr. Gutierrez has extended his credit too far. For the past year he has been slow to pay. And his credit obligations are much too high.

So, even though you would like to have the sale, you must refuse. If you handle this situation delicately, perhaps he will become a good customer in time.

16. As owner of The Fashion Plate, a dress shop for the fashionable women in your city, you have the task of refusing the credit application of Ms. Bettie Applewhite. Ms. Applewhite is a paralegal employee of one of the major law firms in town. She makes a fair salary, but she spends more than she makes. Her record for payment in town is slow, and apparently it is getting slower. You must refuse.

Because Ms. Applewhite is a personable and basically honest woman, you will try hard to refuse tactfully. You would like to reduce the negative effect of the refusal and keep her as a cash customer. Because The Fashion Plate is a prestigious shop, you use no form letters. Each one is individually tailored to the one case.

17. As Janet Winger, the branch manager of a local credit union located near campus, you are responsible for refusing credit requests. The one you must write today is a bit difficult since the applicant has no credit rating rather than a bad one.

In your interview with Marina Munson, you learned that she has a degree in drama from your local university and is returning for a master's degree and teaching certificate. She apparently lived with friends during the last few years and has held some part-time jobs, a strategy that allowed her to save enough money for a down payment on a condo near campus. She reasons that she'd like to buy the condo rather than waste money on rent, and she has determined that the mortgage payment for the amount she wants to borrow would be equivalent to rent for comparable space. Additionally, she says she plans to get a roommate to split the costs.

Since Ms. Munson hasn't paid for rent, phone, or utilities in recent years and has no substantial work history, you must deny her request. She also has no credit card, so she cannot show that she has paid her bills on time in the past. However, she has shown that she is responsible by accumulating no debt and saving the down payment. And in a couple of years after she has completed her degree and taught awhile, she could be just the kind of customer your credit union would like to have. Your refusal will involve educating Ms. Munson on how to establish a good credit history. Also, you might suggest as an alternative that she get a co-signer who would pay the loan if she defaults; the co-signer must also undergo a credit check.

18. At Thetford's, a department store that targets middle- and upper-income customers as its market niche, the credit policy in the past has tended to be quite liberal. Because the store is located in a large metropolitan area and wants to enhance its image among its competitors and customers, this liberal policy worked well. But times have changed for Thetford's.

The past credit policy has increased collection efforts for the store. And these efforts have found only partial success in bringing in overdue accounts. As credit manager for the store, you want Thetford's image to be favorable to its buying publics, but not at the expense of creating problems in collecting past-due accounts. Extending credit to people who won't pay on time is like shooting yourself in the foot. Thus, you decide to tighten your policy in order to reduce the number of delinquent accounts with which the store must deal.

Assume that you are an assistant credit manager of Thetford's and you have been assigned the task of preparing a new credit refusal letter. Over the past month, in assessing those who have applied but don't qualify, you have found some of each type of account you remember from your college training—some "established people" going bad, some "new people" with inadequate financial resources, and a few "bad moral risks." You know that credit refusal letters to each one will vary in wording based on the reasons for denying credit.

Thus, you will select one type of account specified by your boss (the role to be filled by your instructor) and prepare a credit refusal letter for it. In all cases, you will need to be courteous and specific. Thetford's is quite conscious of its image, so watch out for needless negatives, trite wordings, and brusque treatments. You still want the cash business of the people who will receive the letter. And don't word it so that it sounds like a form letter.

Write the credit refusal letter in the most effective way possible for Thetford's. (Note: This case may be repeated for all types of credit risks being assessed.)

19. Nine months ago, Theresa Hargis hung out her shingle to practice law. She graduated 10th in her class of 275 from State University School of Law last year. Most agree that her potential for a productive and profitable legal practice in your city is good.

In starting her private practice, Ms. Hargis leased office space for a year, hired a secretary, and purchased new office furniture. All of these expenses were necessary for establishing her legal practice. Today, you receive a credit report on her for the $1,214.73 worth of personalized stationery, note pads, and business cards she ordered last week from your business, Pro Press. The reports show a definite late-pay record. Thus, you are going to refuse credit to this new attorney.

Ms. Hargis has paid her office rent 12 days late for the last four months. Her note payment on the office furniture has been erratic, averaging 8 to 15 days late over the last five months. What Ms. Hargis needs to do is to establish more clients and thus more income rather than more expenses. Moreover, the report shows that she still owes the local hospital money for the expenses incurred when she gave birth to her and her husband's first child six months ago.

There are many lawyers in the local area, so the competition for legal services is keen. You predict that in time Ms. Hargis will establish herself and become a profitable account for you. Now, however, she wants to overextend; and that could be disastrous financially. She needs to generate more business before taking on exorbitant operating expenses.

Write a credit refusal for this new account that needs more maturity. You can offer a 5 percent cash discount. Be tactful, however, because business from professional accounts such as this will prove profitable for you over the long run.

20. Assume that you are in your first full-time job after graduating from college six months ago. Right after you graduated, you received a mailing from MagnaCard asking you to apply for credit with the company.

MagnaCard is a national and international company; in fact, it is the most widely accepted symbol of "charge it" that presently exists. As explained in the letter you received, MagnaCard's credit policy is to grant credit to only the top-rated people who apply. They particularly favor young people like you—people on the way to becoming future top administrators and executives.

Today's mail brings you the following letter:

We at MagnaCard were glad to receive your recent credit application. Based on the information we have received about you, however, we respectfully regret to inform you that we must deny your request for credit with us.

Trusting that you will understand our position on this matter and hoping you have a good career, we remain.

Very truly yours,

MagnaCard

That's not the way I was taught to write negative letters when I was in college, you think to yourself; the letter is too blunt and tactless. Rewrite the form letter using a more personalized approach. You plan to send the letter to MagnaCard suggesting that they substitute your letter for the present one they send out.

4

Applications to Specific Situations

Indirectness in Persuasion and Sales Messages

Upon completing this chapter, you will be able to use persuasion effectively in making requests and composing sales messages. To reach this goal, you should be able to

1 Use imagination in writing skillful persuasive requests that begin indirectly, develop convincing reasoning, and close with goodwill and action.

2 Describe the choices available in determining the structure of a sales mailing.

3 Describe the preliminary steps of studying the product or service and selecting the appeals to use in a sales.

4 Discuss the choices of mechanics available to the sales writer.

5 Compose sales letters that gain attention, persuasively present appeals, and effectively drive for action.

NEED FOR INDIRECTNESS IN PERSUASION

Although messages in which you ask for something that your reader may be reluctant to give need not involve bad news, they are handled in the indirect order. For example, with a message requesting a favor that will require some personal sacrifice, your chances for success will be greater if you justify the request before making it. This approach, of course, follows the indirect order. Or, for another example, when you write a letter selling a product or service, your readers will usually resist your efforts. To succeed, therefore, you have to begin by convincing them that they need the product or service. This approach also follows the indirect order. Such indirect messages involving persuasion are the subject of this chapter.

■ Certain requests and sales messages are best written in the indirect order.

INTRODUCTORY SITUATION

Persuasive Requests

Introduce yourself to the next business message situation by returning to your hypothetical position at Pinnacle. As a potential executive, you spend some time working for the community. Pinnacle wants you to do this for the sake of good public relations. You want to do it because it is personally rewarding.

Currently, as chair of the fund-raising committee of the city's Junior Achievement program, you head all efforts to get financial support for the program from local businesspeople. You have a group of workers who will call on businesspeople. But personal calls take time, and there are many people to call on.

At its meeting today, the Junior Achievement board of directors discussed the problem of contacting businesspeople. One director suggested using a letter to sell them on giving money. The board accepted the idea with enthusiasm. With just as much enthusiasm, it gave you the assignment of writing the letter (for the president's signature).

As you view the assignment, it is not a routine letter-writing problem. Although the local businesspeople are probably generous, they are not likely to part with money without good reason. In fact, their first reaction to a request for money is likely to be negative. So you will need to overcome their resistance in order to persuade them. Your task is indeed challenging.

PERSUASIVE REQUESTS

Requests that are likely to be resisted require a slow, deliberate approach. The direct order suggested for routine requests (Chapter 5) just will not do the job. Persuasion is necessary. By *persuasion,* we mean reasoning with the reader—presenting facts and logic that support your case. In this approach, which is discussed in detail below, you should generally follow this indirect plan:

■ Requests that are likely to be resisted require persuasion.

■ Open with words that (1) set up the strategy and (2) gain attention.

■ Present the strategy (the persuasion), using persuasive language and you-viewpoint.

■ Make the request clearly and without negatives (1) either as the end of the message or (2) followed by words that recall the persuasive appeal.

■ Generally follow this indirect plan.

DETERMINING THE PERSUASION

Planning the persuasive request requires imagination. You begin by thinking of a strategy that will convince your reader. To do this, put yourself in your reader's shoes. Look at the request as the reader sees it, and determine the reader's objections. Think about what you can say to overcome those objections. From this thinking, you should develop your plan. Of course, the plan you develop and the words you select to implement it should fully support your need for good business etiquette.

■ The persuasion is planned to overcome reader objections.

Persuasive requests and sales letters arrive uninvited. They have goals that are likely to encounter reader resistance. Unless they gain the reader's attention at the beginning, they are likely to end up in a wastebasket.

■ Many persuasive appeals may be used—money rewards, personal benefits, and so on.

The specific plan you develop will depend on the facts of the case. You may be able to show that your reader stands to gain in time, money, or the like. Or you may be able to show that your reader will benefit in goodwill or prestige.

In some cases, you may persuade readers by appealing to their love of beauty, excitement, serenity, or the like. In other cases, you may be able to persuade readers by appealing to the pleasant feeling that comes from doing a good turn. Many other possibilities exist. You select the one that best fits your case.

GAINING ATTENTION IN THE OPENING

■ The opening sets the strategy and gains attention.

In the indirect messages previously discussed, the goal of the opening is to set up the explanation. The same goal exists in persuasion messages, but persuasion messages have an additional goal: to gain attention.

■ Attention is needed to get the reader in a mood to receive the persuasion.

The need to gain attention in the opening of persuasion messages is obvious. You are writing to a person who has not invited your message and probably does not agree with your goal. So you need to get that person into a receptive mood. An interesting beginning is a good step in this direction.

■ What you write to gain attention is limited only by your imagination.

Determining what will gain attention also requires imagination. It might be some statement that arouses mental activity, or it might be a statement offering or implying a reader benefit. Because questions arouse mental activity, they are often effective openings. The following examples indicate the possibilities.

From the cover letter of a questionnaire seeking the opinions of medical doctors:

What, in your opinion as a medical doctor, is the future of the private practice of medicine?

From a letter requesting contributions for orphaned children:

While you and I dined heartily last night, 31 orphans at San Pablo Mission had only dried beans to eat.

From a letter seeking the cooperation of business leaders in promoting a fair:

What would your profits be if 300,000 free-spending visitors came to our town during a single week?

PRESENTING THE PERSUASION

Following the opening, you should proceed with your goal of persuading. Your task here is a logical and orderly presentation of the reasoning you have selected.

As with any argument intended to convince, you should do more than merely list points. You should help convey the points with convincing words. Since you are trying to penetrate a neutral or resistant mind, you need to make good use of the you-viewpoint. You need to pay careful attention to the meanings of your words and the clarity of your expression. Because your reader may become impatient if you delay your objective, you need to make your words travel fast.

- Your persuasion follows.

- Present the points convincingly (selecting words for effect, using you-viewpoint, and the like).

MAKING THE REQUEST CLEARLY AND POSITIVELY

After you have done your persuading, move to the action you seek. You have prepared the reader for what you want. If you have done that well, the reader should be ready to accept your proposal.

Like negative points, your request requires care in word choice. You should avoid words that detract from the request. You should also avoid words that bring to mind images and ideas that might work against you. Words that bring to mind reasons for refusing are especially harmful, as in this example:

I am aware that businesspeople in your position have little free time to give, but will you please consider accepting an assignment to the board of directors of the Children's Fund?

The following positive tie-in with a major point in the persuasion strategy does a much better job:

Because your organizing skills are so desperately needed, will you please serve on the board of directors of the Children's Fund?

Whether your request should end your message will depend on the needs of the case. In some cases, you will profit by following the request with words of explanation. This procedure is especially effective when a long persuasion effort is needed. In such cases, you simply cannot present all your reasoning before stating your goal. On the other hand, you may end less involved presentations with the request. Even in this case, however, you may want to follow the request with a reminder of the appeal. As illustrated in the second example letter (p. 164), this procedure associates the request with the advantage that saying yes will give the reader.

- Follow the persuasion with the request.

- Word the request for best effect.

- Do not use a negative tone.

- Be positive.

- The request can end the message or be followed by more persuasion.

- Ending with a reminder of the appeal is also good.

CONTRASTING PERSUASION LETTERS

The persuasive request is illustrated by contrasting letters that ask businesspeople to donate to Junior Achievement. The first letter is direct and weak in persuasion; the second

- The following letters illustrate good and bad persuasion efforts.

letter is indirect and persuasive. The second letter, which follows the approach described above, produced better results.

OBVIOUS FAILURE IN DIRECTNESS.   The weaker letter begins with the request. Because the request is opposed to the reader's wishes, the direct beginning is likely to get a negative reaction. In addition, the comments about how much to give tend to lecture rather than suggest. Some explanation follows, but it is weak and scant. In general, the letter is poorly written. It has little of the you-viewpoint writing that is effective in persuasion. Perhaps its greatest fault is that the persuasion comes too late. The old-style close is a weak reminder of the action requested.

■ This bad letter has no persuasion strategy.

Dear Mr. Williams:

Will you please donate to the local Junior Achievement program? We have set $50 as a fair minimum for businesses to give. But larger amounts would be appreciated.

The organization badly needs your support. Currently, about 900 young people will not get to participate in Junior Achievement activities unless more money is raised. Junior Achievement is a most worthwhile organization. As a business leader, you should be willing to support it.

If you do not already know about Junior Achievement, let me explain. Junior Achievement is an organization for high school youngsters. They work with local business executives to form small businesses. They operate the businesses. In the process, they learn about our economic system. This is a good thing, and it deserves our help.

Hoping to receive your generous donation by return mail, I am,

Sincerely,

SKILLFUL PERSUASION IN AN INDIRECT ORDER.   The next letter shows good imagination. It follows the indirect pattern described above. Its opening has strong interest appeal and sets up the persuasion strategy. Notice the effective use of you-viewpoint throughout. Not until the reader has been sold on the merits of the request does the letter ask the question. It does this clearly and directly. The final words leave the reader thinking about a major benefit that a yes answer will give.

■ This better letter uses good persuasion strategy.

Dear Mr. Williams:

Right now—right here in our city—620 teenage youngsters are running 37 corporations. The kids run the whole show, their only adult help being advice from some of your business associates who work with them. Last September they applied for a charter and elected officers. They selected products for manufacture—antifreeze, candles, and chairs, to name a few. They issued stock—and they sold it, too. With the proceeds from stock sales, they set up a production operation. Now they are producing and marketing their products. This May they will liquidate their companies and account to their stockholders for their profits or losses.

You, as a public-spirited citizen, will quickly see the merits of the Junior Achievement program. You know the value of such realistic experience to the kids—how it teaches them the operations of business and how it sells them on the merits of our American system of free enterprise. You can see, also, that it's an exciting and wholesome program, the kind we need more of to combat delinquency. After you have considered these points and others you will find in the enclosed brochure, I know you will see that Junior Achievement is a good thing.

Like all good things, Junior Achievement needs all of us behind it. During the 13 years the program has been in our city, it has had enthusiastic support from local business leaders. But with over 900 students on the waiting list, our plans for next year call for expansion. That's why I ask that you help make the program available to more youngsters by contributing $50 (it's deductible). Please make your check payable to Junior Achievement, and send it right away. You will be doing a good service for the kids in our town.

Sincerely,

In this letter a trade publication editor seeks information from an executive for an article on desirable job application procedures. The request involves time and effort for the executive. Thus, persuasion is necessary.

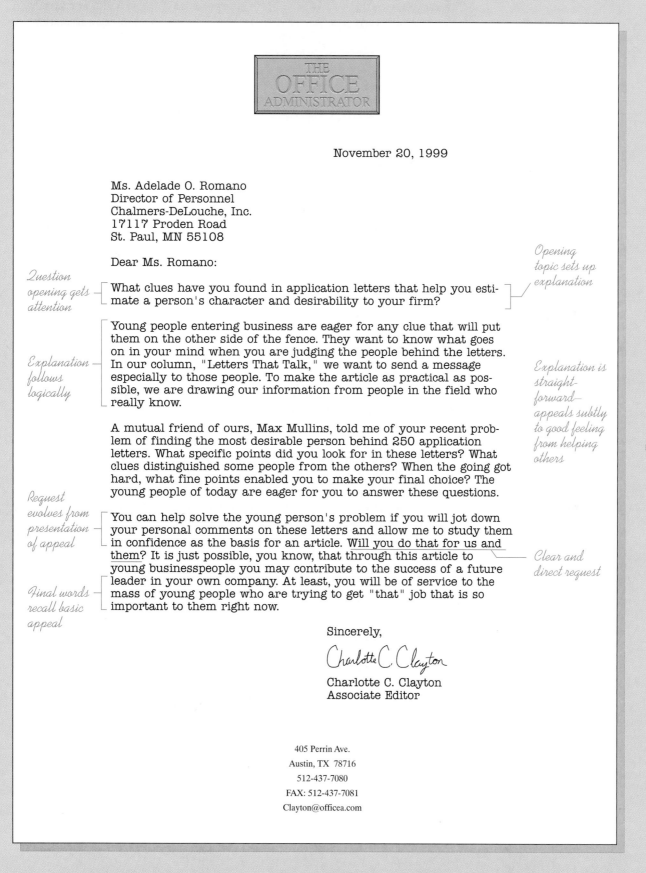

THE
OFFICE
ADMINISTRATOR

November 20, 1999

Ms. Adelade O. Romano
Director of Personnel
Chalmers-DeLouche, Inc.
17117 Proden Road
St. Paul, MN 55108

Dear Ms. Romano:

Question opening gets attention

What clues have you found in application letters that help you estimate a person's character and desirability to your firm?

Opening topic sets up explanation

Explanation follows logically

Young people entering business are eager for any clue that will put them on the other side of the fence. They want to know what goes on in your mind when you are judging the people behind the letters. In our column, "Letters That Talk," we want to send a message especially to those people. To make the article as practical as possible, we are drawing our information from people in the field who really know.

Explanation is straight-forward—appeals subtly to good feeling from helping others

A mutual friend of ours, Max Mullins, told me of your recent problem of finding the most desirable person behind 250 application letters. What specific points did you look for in these letters? What clues distinguished some people from the others? When the going got hard, what fine points enabled you to make your final choice? The young people of today are eager for you to answer these questions.

Request evolves from presentation of appeal

You can help solve the young person's problem if you will jot down your personal comments on these letters and allow me to study them in confidence as the basis for an article. Will you do that for us and them? It is just possible, you know, that through this article to young businesspeople you may contribute to the success of a future leader in your own company. At least, you will be of service to the mass of young people who are trying to get "that" job that is so important to them right now.

Clear and direct request

Final words recall basic appeal

Sincerely,

Charlotte C. Clayton

Charlotte C. Clayton
Associate Editor

405 Perrin Ave.
Austin, TX 78716
512-437-7080
FAX: 512-437-7081
Clayton@officea.com

Sales Messages

Introduce yourself to the next message type by assuming the role of Anthony A. Killshaw, a successful restaurant consultant. Over the past 28 years, you have acquired an expert knowledge of restaurant operations. You have made a science of virtually every area of restaurant activity—menu design, food control, purchasing, kitchen organization, service. You have also perfected a simple system for data gathering and analysis that quickly gets to the heart of most operations' problems. Testimonials from a number of satisfied clients prove that the system works.

Knowing that your system works is one thing. Getting this knowledge to enough prospective clients is another. So you have decided to publicize your work by writing restaurant managers and telling them about what you have to offer.

At the moment, your plan for selling your services by mail is hazy. But your direct-mail package will probably consist of a basic letter, a printed brochure, and a form to be checked by prospective customers. The letter will carry the major message, and the brochure will cover the details. The recipients will be the major restaurant operations that are on the roster of the American Restaurant Association.

Because sales writing requires special skills, you have decided to use the help of a local advertising agency—one with good direct-mail experience. However, you have a pretty good idea of what you want, so you will not leave the work entirely up to the agency's personnel. You will tell them what you want included, and you will have the final word on what is acceptable.

VALUE OF SALES WRITING

- Professionals usually do the sales writing; so why study the subject?

Probably you will never write sales messages—real ones, that is. In business, professional writers usually write them. These professionals achieve their status by practicing long and hard, and usually they are blessed with a special talent for writing. Why, then, you might ask, should you study sales writing?

- The answer: Knowing selling techniques helps you in writing other types of messages.

The answer is that even an amateurish effort to write sales messages gives you knowledge of selling techniques that will help you in many of your other activities. Especially will it will help you in writing other business messages, for in a sense most of them involve selling something—an idea, a line of reasoning, your company, yourself.

- It also helps in your daily life, for much of what you do involves selling.

Even in your daily life you will find good use for selling techniques. From time to time, all of us are called on to sell something. If we are employed in selling goods and services, our sales efforts will, of course, be frequent. In other areas of business, our sales efforts may consist only of selling such intangibles as an idea, our own competence, or the goodwill of the firm. In all such cases, we use selling techniques. Thus, sales writing and selling techniques are more valuable to you than you might think. After you have studied the remainder of this chapter, you should see why.

PRELIMINARY EFFORTS

- Usually brochures, leaflets, a letter, and such combine to form a sales mailing.

As you probably know from experience, most direct-mail sales efforts consist of a number of pieces. Typically, brochures, leaflets, foldouts, a letter, and so on combine to form a coordinated message. But usually a letter is the main piece. It carries the main message, and the other pieces carry the supporting details.

- But our emphasis will be on the letter.

The following discussion emphasizes the letter, for it would be beyond the scope of this book to cover more. But much of what is said about the letter applies to other forms of sales literature. After you have studied the following material, you should have a general idea of how to sell by mail.

KNOWING THE PRODUCT OR SERVICE AND THE READER

Before you can begin writing, you must know about the product or service you are selling. You simply cannot sell most goods and services unless you know them and can tell the prospects what they need to know. Before prospects buy a product, they may want to know how it is made, how it works, what it will do, and what it will not do. Clearly, a first step in sales writing is careful study of your product or service.

In addition, you should know your readers. In particular, you should know about their needs for the product or service. Anything else you know about them can help—their economic status, age, nationality, education, and culture. The more you know about your readers, the better you will be able to adapt your sales message.

In large businesses, a marketing research department or agency typically gathers information about prospective customers. If you do not have such help, you will need to gather this information on your own. If time does not permit you to do the necessary research, you may have to follow your best logic. For example, the nature of a product can tell you something about its likely buyers. Industrial equipment would probably be bought by people with technical backgrounds. Expensive French perfumes and cosmetics would probably be bought by people in high-income brackets. Burial insurance would appeal to older members of the lower economic strata. If you are purchasing a mailing list, you usually receive basic demographics such as age, sex, race, education, income, and marital status of those on the list. Sometimes you know more—interests, spending range, consumption patterns, and such.

- Begin work on a sales message by studying the product or service to be sold.

- Also, study your readers.

- Research can help you learn about prospective customers. If research is not possible, use your best logic.

DETERMINING THE APPEAL

With your product or service and your prospects in mind, you are ready to create the sales letter. This involves selecting and presenting basic appeals. By *appeals,* we mean the strategies you use to present a product or service to the reader. You could, for example, present a product's beauty or its taste qualities. You could stress that a product will provide hours of fun or that it will make one more attractive to the opposite sex. Or you could present a product through an appeal to profits, savings, or durability.

For convenience in studying appeals, we can divide them into two broad groups. In one group are emotional efforts to persuade. Such efforts affect how we feel, taste, smell, hear, and see. They also include strategies that arouse us through love, anger, pride, fear, and enjoyment. In the other group are rational appeals. These are appeals to reason—to the thinking mind. Such appeals include strategies based on saving money, making money, doing a job better, and getting better use from a product.

In any given case, many appeals are available to you. You should consider those that fit your product or service and those that fit your readers best. Such products as perfume, style merchandise, candy, and fine food lend themselves to emotional appeals. On the other

- Next, decide on what appeals and strategies to use.

- Appeals may be emotional (to the feelings) or rational (to the reason).

- Select the appeals that fit the product and the prospects.

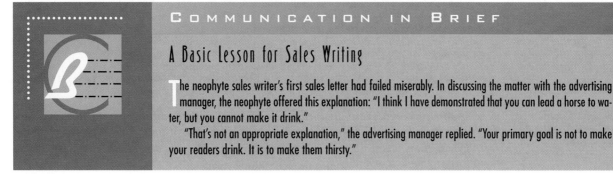

COMMUNICATION IN BRIEF

A Basic Lesson for Sales Writing

The neophyte sales writer's first sales letter had failed miserably. In discussing the matter with the advertising manager, the neophyte offered this explanation: "I think I have demonstrated that you can lead a horse to water, but you cannot make it drink."

"That's not an appropriate explanation," the advertising manager replied. "Your primary goal is not to make your readers drink. It is to make them thirsty."

hand, such products as automobile tires, tools, and industrial equipment are best sold through rational appeals. Automobile tires, for example, are not bought because they are pretty but because they are durable, because they grip the road, and because they are safe. Sometimes the appeals can be combined to support each other.

■ The prospects' uses of the product often determine which appeal is best.

How the buyer will use the product may be a major basis for selecting a sales strategy. Cosmetics might well be sold to the final user through emotional appeals. Selling cosmetics to a retailer (who is primarily interested in reselling them) would require rational appeals. A retailer would be interested in their emotional qualities only to the extent that these make customers buy. A retailer's main questions about the product are: Will it sell? What turnover can I expect? How much money will it make for me?

STRUCTURE OF THE SALES LETTER

■ Writing sales letters involves imagination.

After selecting the appeal, you should write the sales letter. At this point, your imagination comes into the picture. Writing sales letters is as creative as writing short stories, plays, and novels. In addition to imagination, it involves applied psychology and skillful word use. There are as many different ways of handling a sales letter as there are ideas. The only sure measure of the effectiveness of each way is the sales that the letter brings in.

■ Sales-letter plans vary in practice, but this plan is used most often.

Because sales letters can vary greatly, it is hard to describe their order. But you should usually follow this conventional pattern:

- Gain favorable attention in the opening.
- Create desire by presenting the appeal, emphasizing supporting facts, and emphasizing reader viewpoint.
- Include all necessary information—using a coordinated sales package (brochures, leaflets, and such).
- Drive for the sale by urging action now and recalling the main appeal.
- Possibly add a postscript.

This pattern is similar to the classic AIDA model (attention, interest, desire, action) developed almost a century ago. The techniques used in developing this pattern are discussed below. As you study them, bear in mind that in actual practice only your imagination will limit the possibilities open to you.

DETERMINING LETTER MECHANICS

■ The makeup of sales letters differs somewhat from that of ordinary letters. For example, sales letters may use impersonal salutations, headlines for inside addresses, and attention-gaining devices.

A part of your effort in planning a sales letter is to determine its makeup. The physical arrangements of sales letters may differ in many ways from those of ordinary business letters. With few exceptions, sales letters are mass-produced rather than individually processed. They may use individually processed inside addresses. This effective technique is often replaced by impersonal salutations, such as "Dear Students," "Dear Homeowner," or "Dear Sir." One technique eliminates the salutation and inside address and places the beginning words of the letter in the form of these parts. As shown below, this arrangement gives the letter what appears at first glance to be a normal layout.

IT'S GREAT FOR PENICILLIN,
BUT YOU CAN DO WITHOUT IT
ON YOUR ROOF . . . .

We're referring to roof fungus, which, like penicillin, is a moldlike growth. However, the similarity ends there. Unlike penicillin, roof fungus serves . . . .

■ Mechanical techniques help gain attention and build an effective appeal.

Sales letters may use a variety of mechanical techniques to gain attention. Pictures, lines, diagrams, and cartoons are common. So is the use of different ink colors. Such devices as coins, stamps, sandpaper, rubber bands, pencils, and paper clips have been affixed to sales letters to gain interest and help put over the appeal. One letter, for example, was mailed on scorched pages to emphasize the theme of "some hot news about fire insurance." A letter with a small pencil glued to the page used the theme that "the point of the pencil is to make it easy to order" a certain magazine. As you can see, the imaginative possibilities in sales writing are boundless.

The opening of the sales letter has one basic requirement. It must gain attention. If it does not, it fails. The reason is apparent. Because sales letters are sent without invitation, they are not likely to be received favorably. In fact, they may even be unwanted. Unless the first words of a sales letter overcome the barrier and gain attention, the letter goes into the wastebasket.

■ The basic requirement of the opening is to gain attention.

Your plan for gaining attention is a part of your creative effort. But the method you use should assist in presenting the sales message. That is, it should help set up your strategy. It should not just gain attention for attention's sake. Attention is easy to gain if nothing else is needed. A small explosion set off when the reader opens the envelope would gain attention. So would an electric shock or a miniature stink bomb. But these methods would not be likely to assist the selling.

■ The opening should also set up the strategy.

One of the most effective attention-gaining techniques is a statement or question that introduces a need that the product will satisfy. For example, a rational-appeal letter to a retailer would clearly tap his or her strong needs with these opening words:

■ Rational appeals stress logic.

Here is a proven best-seller—and with a 12 percent greater profit.

Another rational-appeal beginning is the first sentence of a letter seeking to place metered personal computers in hotel lobbies:

Can you use an employee who not only works free of charge but also pays you for the privilege of serving your clientele 24 hours a day?

Yet another rational-appeal beginning is this opening device from a letter selling a trade publication to business executives:

How to move more products,
Win more customers,
And make more money
. . . for less than $1 a week

This paragraph of a letter selling a fishing vacation at a lake resort illustrates a need-fulfilling beginning of an emotional-appeal approach:

■ Emotional appeals evoke feelings.

Your line hums as it whirs through the air. Your lure splashes and dances across the smooth surface of the clear water as you reel. From the depth you see the silver streak of a striking bass. You feel a sharp tug. And the battle is on!

As you can see, the paragraph casts an emotional spell, which is what emotional selling should do. It puts a rod in the reader's hand, and it takes the reader through the thrills of the sport. To a reader addicted to fishing, the need is clearly established. Now the reader will listen to see how the need can be fulfilled.

As was mentioned previously, gimmicks are sometimes used to gain attention. But a gimmick is effective only if it supports the theme of the letter. One company made effective use of a penny affixed to the top of a letter with these words:

■ Gimmicks can gain attention and emphasize a theme.

Most pennies won't buy much today, but this penny can save you untold worry and money—and bring you new *peace of mind*.

A paper manufacturer fastened small samples of sandpaper, corrugated aluminum, and smooth glossy paper to the top of a letter that began with these words:

You've seen the ads—
you've heard the talk—
now feel for yourself what we mean by *level-smooth*.

The use of a story is another opening approach. Most people like to read stories, and if you can start one interestingly, your reader should want to read the rest of it. Here is the attention-catching beginning of a masterpiece used by Boys Town to sell sponsor memberships:

A knock at the door, a swirl of snow over the threshold—and standing in the warm glow of the hall light was little Joe. His thin jacket was drawn tightly around his small body. "I'm here, Father. I'm here for an education," he blurted out.

Thus far, the attention-gaining techniques illustrated have been short. But longer ones have been used—and used effectively. In fact, a technique currently popular in direct-mail selling is to place a digest of the sales message at the beginning—usually before the salutation. The strategy is to quickly communicate the full impact of the sales message before the reader loses interest. If any of the points presented arouse interest, the reader is likely to continue reading.

Illustrating this technique is the beginning of a letter selling subscriptions to *Change*. These lines appeared before the salutation, which was followed by four pages of text.

A quick way to determine whether you should read this letter:

If you are involved in or influenced by higher education—and you simply don't have the time to read copiously in order to "keep up"—this letter is important. Because it offers you a money-shortcut (plus a *free gift* and a money-back guarantee).

As a subscriber to CHANGE, the leading magazine of higher learning, you'll have facts and feelings at your fingertips—to help *you* form opinions. On today's topics: tenure, professors' unions, open admissions, the outlook for new PhDs . . . On just about any subject that concerns academe and you.

CHANGE has the largest readership of any journal among academic people. To find out why 100,000 people now read CHANGE every month, take three minutes to read the following letter.

PRESENTING THE SALES MATERIAL

After your attention-gaining opening has set up your sales strategy, you develop that strategy. What you do in this part of the letter is the product of the thinking and planning that you did at the beginning. In general, however, you should show a need and present your product or service as fulfilling that need.

The plan of your sales message will vary with your imagination. But it is likely to follow certain general patterns determined by your choice of appeals. If you select an emotional appeal, for example, your opening has probably established an emotional atmosphere that you will continue to develop. Thus, you will sell your product based on its effects on your reader's senses. You will describe the appearance, texture, aroma, and taste of your product so vividly that your reader will mentally see it, feel it—and want it. In general, you will seek to create an emotional need for your product.

If you select a rational appeal, your sales description is likely to be based on factual material. You should describe your product based on what it can do for your reader rather than how it appeals to the senses. You should write matter-of-factly about such qualities as durability, savings, profits, and ease of operation. Differences in these two sharply contrasting types of appeals are shown in the illustrations near the end of the chapter.

The writing that carries your sales message can be quite different from your normal business writing. Sales writing usually is highly conversational, fast moving, and aggressive. It even uses techniques that are incorrect or inappropriate in other forms of business writing—sentence fragments, one-sentence paragraphs, folksy language, and such. It uses mechanical emphasis devices (underscore, capitalization, boldface, italics, exclamation marks, color) to a high degree. It uses all kinds of graphics and graphic devices as well as a variety of type sizes and fonts. Its paragraphing often appears choppy. Apparently, the direct-mail professionals believe that whatever will help sell is appropriate.

STRESSING THE YOU-VIEWPOINT

In no area of business communication is the you-viewpoint more important than in sales writing. We human beings are selfish creatures. We are persuaded best through self-interest. Thus, in sales writing you should base your sales points on reader interest. You should liberally use and imply the pronoun *you* throughout the sales letter. To do so is not only good for persuasion, but also promotes good business etiquette.

The techniques of you-viewpoint writing in sales letters are best described through illustration. For example, assume you are writing a sales letter to a retailer. One point you want to make is that the manufacturer will help sell the product with an advertising campaign. You could write this information in a matter-of-fact way: "Star mixers will be advertised in *Ladies' Home Journal* for the next three issues." Or you could write it based on what the advertising means to the reader: "Your customers will read about the new Star mixer in the next three issues of *Ladies' Home Journal.*" For another example, you could quote prices in routine words such as "a four-ounce bottle costs $2.25, and you can sell it for $3.50." But you would emphasize the readers' interest with words like these: "You can sell the four-ounce size for $3.50 and make a 55 percent profit on your $2.25 cost." Using the you-viewpoint along with an explicit interpretation of how the facts benefit the reader will strengthen the persuasiveness. The following examples further illustrate the value of this technique:

MATTER-OF-FACT STATEMENTS	YOU-VIEWPOINT STATEMENTS
We make Aristocrat hosiery in three colors.	You may choose from three lovely shades.
The Regal has a touch as light as a feather.	You'll like Regal's featherlight touch.
Lime-Fizz tastes fresh and exciting.	You'll enjoy the fresh, exciting taste of Lime-Fizz.
Baker's Dozen is packaged in a rectangular box with a bright bull's-eye design.	Baker's Dozen's new rectangular package fits compactly on your shelf, and its bright bull's-eye design is sure to catch the eyes of your customers.

CHOOSING WORDS CAREFULLY

In persuasive messages, your attention to word choice is extremely important, for it can influence whether the reader acts on your request. Try putting yourself clearly in your reader's place as you select words for your message. Some words, while closely related in meaning, have clearly different emotional effects. For example, the word *selection* implies a choice while the word *preference* implies a first choice. Here are some examples where a single adjective changes the effect of a sentence:

■ Consider the effect of your words.

You'll enjoy the sensation our hot salsa gives you.
You'll enjoy the sensation our fiery salsa gives you.
You'll enjoy the sensation our burning salsa gives you.

Framing your requests in the positive is also a proven persuasive technique. Readers will clearly opt for solutions to problems that avoid negatives. Here are some examples.

ORIGINAL WORDING	POSITIVE WORDING
Reorganization Plan A will cause 10 percent of the staff to lose their jobs.	Reorganization Plan A will retain 90 percent of the workforce.
Our new laser paper keeps the wasted paper from smudged copies to less than 2 percent.	Our new laser paper provides smudge-free copies more than 98 percent of the time.

INCLUDING ALL NECESSARY INFORMATION

Of course, the information you present and how you present it are matters for your best judgment. But you must make sure that you present enough information to complete the sale. You should leave none of your reader's questions unanswered. Nor should you fail to overcome any likely objections. You must work to include all such basic information in your letter, and you should make it clear and convincing.

In your effort to include all necessary information, you can choose from a variety of enclosures—booklets, brochures, leaflets, and the like. When you use such enclosures, you should take care to coordinate all the parts. All the parts in the mailing should form a unified sales message. As a general rule, you should use the letter to carry your basic sales message. This means your letter should not shift a major portion of your sales effort to an enclosure. Instead, you should use enclosures mainly to supplement the letter. The enclosures might cover descriptions, price lists, diagrams, and pictures—in fact, all helpful in-

■ Give enough information to sell. Answer all questions; overcome all objections.

■ Coordinate the sales letter with accompanying booklets, brochures, and leaflets. But make the letter carry the main sales message. Enclosures should serve as supplements.

formation that does not fit easily into the letter. To ensure that all the parts in the mailing fit into a unified effort, you would be wise to direct your reader's attention to each of them. You can do this best through incidental references at appropriate places in the letter (for example, by saying "as shown on page 3 of the enclosed booklet" or "see page 7 of the enclosed brochure").

DRIVING FOR THE SALE

■ End with a drive for the sale.

After you have caught your reader's interest in your product or service, the next logical step is to drive for the sale. After all, this is what you have been working for all along. It is a natural conclusion to the sales effort you have made.

■ In strong selling efforts, a command is effective. For milder efforts, a request is appropriate. Take the reader through the motions.

How you should word your drive for the sale depends on your strategy. If your selling effort is strong, your drive for action may also be strong. It may even be worded as a command. ("Order your copy today—while it's on your mind.") If you use a milder selling effort, you could use a direct question. ("Won't you please send us your order today?") In any event, the drive for action should be specific and clear. In no way should it resemble a hint. For best effect, it should take the reader through the motions of whatever he or she must do. Here are some examples:

Just check your preferences on the enclosed stamped and addressed order form. Then drop it in the mail today!

Won't you please permit us to deliver your Tabor recorder on approval? The number is 1-800-348-8821. Order it now, while you're thinking about it.

Mail the enclosed card today—and see how right the *Atlantic* is for you!

Visit our web site today to place your order for your custom-made PC.

URGING THE ACTION

■ Urge action now.

Because readers who have been persuaded sometimes put things off, you should urge immediate action. "Do it now" and "Act today" are versions of this technique. You can make the technique especially effective if you tie it in with a practical reason for doing it now. Here are some examples:

. . . to take advantage of this three-day offer.

. . . so that you can be ready for the Christmas rush.

. . . so that you will be the first in your community.

RECALLING THE APPEAL

■ Recalling the appeal in the final words is good technique.

Yet another effective technique for the close of a sales letter is to use a few words that recall the basic appeal. Associating the action with the benefits that the reader will gain by taking it adds strength to your sales effort. Illustrating this technique is a letter selling

❙ As in this *National Geographic* example, most sales mailings consist of a letter and a coordinated group of support pieces.

Maxell videotapes to retailers. After building its sales effort, the letter asks for action and then follows the action request with these words:

. . . and start taking your profits from the fast-selling Maxell videotape.

Another illustration is a letter selling a fishing resort vacation that follows its action words with a reminder of the joys described earlier.

It's your reservation for a week of battle with the fightingest bass in the Southland.

ADDING A POSTSCRIPT

Unlike other business letters where a postscript (P.S.) appears like an afterthought, a sales letter can use a postscript as a part of its design. It can be used effectively in a number of ways—to urge the reader to act, to emphasize the major appeal, to invite attention to other enclosures, to suggest that the reader pass along the sales message, and so on. Postscripts effectively used by professionals include the following:

▪ Postscripts are acceptable and effective.

PS: Don't forget! If ever you think that *Action* is not for you, we'll give you every cent of your money back. We are that confident that *Action* will become one of your favorite magazines.

PS: Hurry! Save while this special money-saving offer lasts.

PS: Our little magazine makes a distinctive and appreciated gift. Know someone who's having a birthday soon?

EVALUATING CONTRASTING EXAMPLES

The following two letters show good and bad efforts to sell Killshaw's restaurant consulting services. Clearly the bad letter is the work of an amateur and the better one was written by a professional.

▪ Following are bad and good letters.

WEAKNESS IN AN ILLOGICAL PLAN. The amateur's letter begins with a dull statement about the consultant's services that is little more than an announcement of what the consultant does. Then, as a continuation of the opening, it offers the services to the reader. Such openings do little to gain attention or build desire. Next comes a routine, I-viewpoint review of the consultant's services. The explanation of the specific services offered is

CASE ILLUSTRATION **Sales Letters (Using Emotional Appeal to Sell New Orleans)**

Sent to a select group of young business and professional people, this letter takes the readers through the experiences that they will enjoy if they accept the offer.

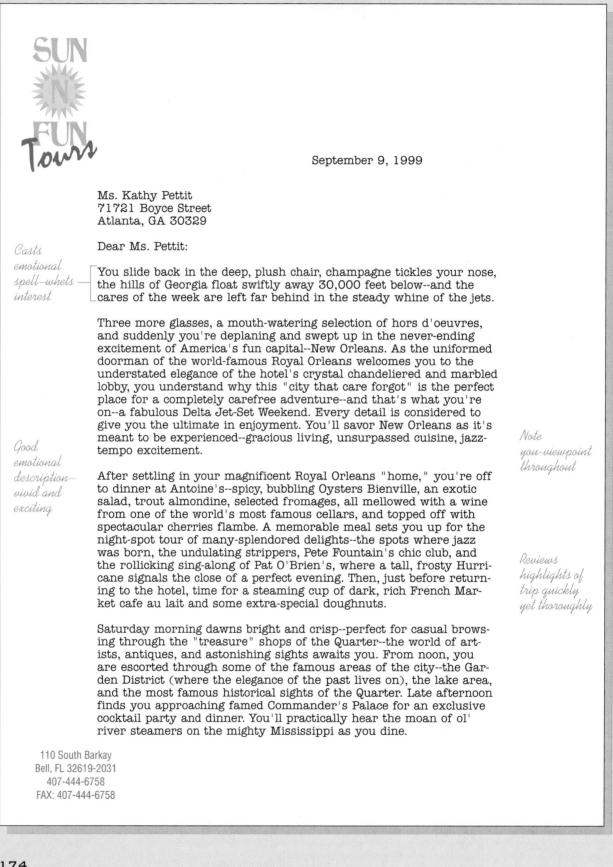

SUN
N
FUN
Tours

September 9, 1999

Ms. Kathy Pettit
71721 Boyce Street
Atlanta, GA 30329

Dear Ms. Pettit:

Casts emotional spell—whets interest

You slide back in the deep, plush chair, champagne tickles your nose, the hills of Georgia float swiftly away 30,000 feet below--and the cares of the week are left far behind in the steady whine of the jets.

Three more glasses, a mouth-watering selection of hors d'oeuvres, and suddenly you're deplaning and swept up in the never-ending excitement of America's fun capital--New Orleans. As the uniformed doorman of the world-famous Royal Orleans welcomes you to the understated elegance of the hotel's crystal chandeliered and marbled lobby, you understand why this "city that care forgot" is the perfect place for a completely carefree adventure--and that's what you're on--a fabulous Delta Jet-Set Weekend. Every detail is considered to give you the ultimate in enjoyment. You'll savor New Orleans as it's meant to be experienced--gracious living, unsurpassed cuisine, jazz-tempo excitement.

Note you-viewpoint throughout

Good emotional description— vivid and exciting

After settling in your magnificent Royal Orleans "home," you're off to dinner at Antoine's--spicy, bubbling Oysters Bienville, an exotic salad, trout almondine, selected fromages, all mellowed with a wine from one of the world's most famous cellars, and topped off with spectacular cherries flambe. A memorable meal sets you up for the night-spot tour of many-splendored delights--the spots where jazz was born, the undulating strippers, Pete Fountain's chic club, and the rollicking sing-along of Pat O'Brien's, where a tall, frosty Hurricane signals the close of a perfect evening. Then, just before returning to the hotel, time for a steaming cup of dark, rich French Market cafe au lait and some extra-special doughnuts.

Reviews highlights of trip quickly yet thoroughly

Saturday morning dawns bright and crisp--perfect for casual browsing through the "treasure" shops of the Quarter--the world of artists, antiques, and astonishing sights awaits you. From noon, you are escorted through some of the famous areas of the city--the Garden District (where the elegance of the past lives on), the lake area, and the most famous historical sights of the Quarter. Late afternoon finds you approaching famed Commander's Palace for an exclusive cocktail party and dinner. You'll practically hear the moan of ol' river steamers on the mighty Mississippi as you dine.

110 South Barkay
Bell, FL 32619-2031
407-444-6758
FAX: 407-444-6758

Ms. Kathy Pettit
September 9, 1999
Page 2

Night ends back in the Quarter--with the particular pleasure of your
choice. But don't sleep too late Sunday! Unforgettable "breakfast at
Brennan's" begins at 11 a.m., and two hours later you'll know why
it is the most famous breakfast in the world! Wrap up your relaxed
visit with shopping in the afternoon; then the mighty Delta jet
whisks you back to Atlanta by 7 p.m. This perfect weekend can be
yours for the very special price of only $375, which includes trans-
portation, lodging, and noted meals. For double occupancy, the price
per person is only $335. Such a special vacation will be more fun
with friends, so get them in on this bargain--you owe yourself the
pleasures of a Jet-Set Weekend in America's fun capital.

*Tells how
need can be
satisfied—
gives details*

This Jet-Set Weekend to dream about becomes a reality starting
right now--a free call to the Delta Hostell at 800-491-6700 confirms
your reservation to escape to the fun, the food, and the fantasy of
New Orleans, city of excitement. The city is swinging--waiting for
you!

*Perhaps the
action would
be more
effective if it
were more
direct, but it
is persuasive*

*The final
words link
the action
with the
main appeal*

Sincerely,

Mary Massey

Mary Massey
Travel Consultant

P.S. Check out our web site at http://www.sun_n_fun.com/ for some
sights and sounds you'll experience on this fabulous Jet-Set
Weekend.

This letter selling a service on the World Wide Web capitalizes on the company's unique name. The letter is especially noteworthy for its concise and convincing presentation of benefits.

The Monster Board
Careers on the Web

The main message appears in this attention position:

Fill job openings **cheaper, smarter, faster** than ever before
(and get **one job posting free** during our introductory special)

The attention-getting name invites further reading

Dear Hiring Manager:

The Monster Board?

OK, I admit, it's an odd name for the greatest recruitment tool since the want ad.

But when I first had the idea—to connect millions of job seekers with job openings on the Internet—I knew it was a <u>monstrous</u> idea. Hence the name. And now that we're recognized as the best in the business, we'll always be The Monster Board.

What is it, exactly?

The Monster Board is an "employment opportunities" job site on the World Wide Web. It attracts millions of job seekers because they can browse through over 50,000 job openings.

A preliminary explanation presents a concise description of the service

They don't have to wade through them all, of course. They can search by job title, location, or keyword. So no matter how many positions are listed, The Monster Board matches the right candidate to the right jobs, every time.

What's in it for you, the employer? Plenty.

A specific listing of the benefits the service provides is presented in convincing language

- **More candidates.** The Monster Board is sought out by nearly 1 million job hunters every month—over 1,500 per hour! (and we have the audited figures to prove it).

- **Better candidates.** Satisfied customers report high quality responses unmatched by traditional media.

- **Hard-to-find candidates.** The Monster Board draws the curious-but-currently-employed, who aren't reading the want ads but can't resist running a quick, personalized job search on The Monster Board.

The result?

Simply put, recruiting on The Monster Board is:

Cheaper - It costs only $150 for a 60-day job posting. But that's not all—you can give your company a high profile with an online brochure, banner ad, or career fair. Whatever Monster solution you choose, you'll <u>fill positions at a lower cost per hire.</u>

Smarter - You'll <u>get better results for less effort.</u> Start by letting us do recruitment advertising for you. We'll spend millions this year alone, driving great candidates to The Monster Board to see your job openings.

Faster - Send job listings right from your desktop and get immediate results once they're posted. <u>Spend less time sorting resumes and more time interviewing</u> high quality, pre-qualified candidates.

This listing relates the major advantages of the service to the reader's needs— in you-viewpoint language

Best of all, it's quick and easy.

Whether you want all the bells and whistles or a simple job posting, our helpful, savvy staff will work with you to create a custom solution for your business.

And you don't need to be online - you don't even need a computer - to recruit on the Internet. If you don't have an e-mail address, our Monster staff will fax the resumes we receive on your behalf.

More qualified candidates. Less work for you. What could be better?

A FREE JOB POSTING.

An incentive gives strength to the drive for action

I realize you may be skeptical about this at first, so I want to give you a little extra incentive to try something new. During our introductory period, <u>when you buy one job posting for $150, we'll give you a second one FREE!</u> (The free job posting must be ordered at the same time as the paid job posting. One to a customer.)

Take the first step to ending your hiring headaches. Try the tremendously successful recruitment service with a funny name: The Monster Board. You can contact us via phone, fax, mail or e-mail. All the details are on the reply card, along with the I.D. number you'll need to order your free job.

Sincerely,

Jeff Taylor
Founder, The Monster Board

P.S. If you're still skeptical, take a quick look at what other hiring managers have to say about their experiences on The Monster Board in our brochure. It's hard to argue with that kind of success. And it's hard to turn down a free job posting. Call us at 1-800-MONSTER and select option 1!

A postscript directs attention to supporting evidence in an enclosed brochure little better. Although the message tells what the consultant can do, it is dull. The drive for action is more a hint than a request. The closing words do suggest a benefit for the reader, but the effort is too little too late.

■ The bad letter is amateurish. It does little more than announce that services are available.

Dear Ms. Collins:

You have probably heard in the trade about the services I provide to restaurant management. I am now pleased to be able to offer these services to you.

From 28 years of experience, I have learned the details of restaurant management. I know what food costs should be. I know how to find other cost problems, be they the buying end or the selling end. I know how to design menu offerings for the most profitability. I have studied kitchen operations and organization. And I know how the service must be conducted for best results.

From all this knowledge, I have perfected a simple system for analyzing a restaurant and finding its weaknesses. This I do primarily from guest checks, invoices, and a few other records. As explained in the enclosed brochure, my system finds the trouble spots. It shows exactly where to correct all problems.

I can provide you with the benefits of my system for only $1,500—$700 now and $800 when you receive my final report on your operations. If you will fill out and mail in the enclosed form, I will show you how to make more money.

Sincerely,

SKILLFUL PRESENTATION OF A RATIONAL APPEAL.   The better letter follows the conventional sales pattern described in the preceding pages. Its appeal is rational, which is justified in this case. The opening quotation attracts attention. It holds interest for a restaurant manager. Thus, the chances of getting the prospect to read further are good. The following sentences explain the service quickly—and interestingly. Then, in good you-viewpoint writing, the reader learns what he or she will get from the service. This part is loaded with reader benefit (profits, efficiency, cost cutting). Next, after the selling has been done, the letter drives for action. The final words tie in the action with its main benefit—making money.

■ Following the conventional pattern, the better letter uses good strategy and technique.

Dear Ms. Collins:

"Killshaw is adding $15,000 a year to my restaurant's profits!"

With these words, Bill Summers, owner of Boston's famed Pirate's Cove, joined the hundreds of restaurant owners who will point to proof in dollars in assuring you that I have a plan that can add to your profits.

My time-proven plan to help you add to your profits is a product of 28 years of intensive research, study, and consulting work with restaurants all over the nation. I found that where food costs exceed 40 percent, staggering amounts slip through restaurant managers' fingers. Then I tracked down the causes of these losses. I can find these trouble spots in your business—and I'll prove this to you in extra income dollars!

To make these extra profits, all you do is send me, for a 30-day period, your guest checks, bills, and a few other items I'll tell you about later. After these items have undergone my proven method of analysis, I will write you an eye-opening report that will tell you how much money your restaurant should make and how to make it.

From the report, you will learn in detail just what items are causing your higher food costs. And you will learn how to correct them. Even your menu will receive thorough treatment. You will know what "best-sellers" are paying their way—what "poor movers" are eating into your profits. All in all, you'll get practical suggestions that will show you how to cut costs, build volume, and pocket a net 10 to 20 percent of sales.

For a more detailed explanation of this service, you'll want to read the enclosed information sheet. Then won't you let me prove to you, as I have to so many others, that I can add money to your income this year? This added profit can be yours for the modest investment of $1,500 ($700 now and the other $800 when our profit plan report is submitted). Just fill out the enclosed form, and place it along with your check in the addressed and stamped envelope that is provided for your convenience.

That extra $25,000 or more will make you glad you did!

Sincerely,

USING A SECOND LETTER IN THE MAILING

A currently popular way of adding strength to the sales effort is to use a second letter (or note or memorandum) as a part of the mailing. This second letter is usually headed with a boldly displayed message saying something like "Don't read this unless you've decided not to buy." Apparently, the technique is effective. At least, direct-mail professionals seem to think it is, for they use it widely. An example of such a message follows.

Accompanying a letter selling subscriptions to a magazine, *The Texas Fisherman,* this second message reviews the main sales message of the letter. As you can see, it is really another sales letter. It even ends with a drive for action, and it has a postscript that intensifies the drive. This mailing was highly successful. Perhaps the second message contributed to its success.

■ A second letter is often a part of the mailing.

DON'T READ THIS UNLESS YOU HAVE DECIDED NOT TO CLAIM YOUR *FREE TEXAS SALTWATER BIG 3 BOOK.*

■ Here is an example of a second letter.

Frankly, I'm puzzled.

I just don't understand why every fisherman and boat owner in Texas doesn't run—not walk—to the nearest mailbox and return the enclosed FREE BOOK CERTIFICATE.

Here's a guidebook that will bring you better times and better catches each and every time you head for that big beautiful Gulf. PLUS, you get a money-saving bargain on a subscription to THE TEXAS FISHERMAN—the news monthly that Texas outdoorsmen swear by. Month after month you'll be in on all the latest tips about where the big ones are biting. Each issue sports super-big photographs of fishermen grinning their heads off, holding up the catch for the day.

And Dave Ellison is there each month telling you the latest there is about boating. Plus many other boating articles every month. Over 34,000 Texas boaters and fishermen are subscribing now. And the yearly renewal rate is just fantastic!

But those 34,000 aren't important this morning. The important person to me today is YOU. I want YOU as a new subscriber—because I know you'll find more helpful advice here than in any other publication in the state today.

Do yourself a favor. Send off your FREE BOOK CERTIFICATE now, today, while you're thinking about it. Have more fun and catch more fish!

Sincerely for better fishing and boating,

Bob Gray, Publisher

P.S. Please hurry! We have only a limited supply of this FREE BOOK. Get yours now!

SUMMARY BY CHAPTER OBJECTIVES

1. Requests that are likely to be resisted require an indirect, persuasive approach.
   • Such an approach involves developing a strategy—a plan for persuading.
   • Your opening words should set up this strategy and gain attention.
   • Follow with convincing persuasion.
   • Then make the request—clearly yet positively.
   • The request can end the letter, or more persuasion can follow (whichever you think is appropriate).
2. Sales letters are a special type of persuasive request.
   • Typically, a sales mailing contains a number of pieces—brochures, reply forms, and such.
   • But our emphasis is on the sales letter, which usually is the main item in the mailing.

1 Use imagination in writing skillful persuasive requests that begin indirectly, use convincing reasoning, and close with goodwill and action.

2 Describe the choices available in determining the structure of a sales mailing.

3 Describe the preliminary steps of studying the product or service and selecting the appeals to use in a sales letter.

4 Discuss the choices of mechanics available to the sales writer.

5 Compose sales letters that gain attention, persuasively present appeals, and effectively drive for action.

3. Begin work on the sales letter by studying the product or service to be sold. Also, study your prospects, using marketing research information if available.
   - Then select an appropriate appeal (or appeals).
   - Appeals fall into two broad groups: emotional and rational.
     —Emotional appeals play on our senses (taste, hearing, and so on) and our feelings (love, anger, fear, and the like).
     —Rational appeals address the rational mind (thrift, durability, efficiency, and such).
   - Select the appeals that fit the product and prospects.

4. Before beginning to write, you determine the mechanics of the mailing.
   - Sales letters may use impersonal salutations (Dear Student), headlines rather than inside addresses, pictures, lines, and such to gain attention.
   - Your imagination is the major limitation on what you can choose to do.

5. Although innovations are frequently used, most sales letters follow this traditional plan:
   - The opening seeks to gain attention and set up the sales presentation.
   - The sales message follows.
   - In emotional selling, the words establish an emotional atmosphere and build an emotional need for the product or service.
   - In rational selling, the appeal is to the thinking mind, using facts and logical reasoning.
   - Throughout the letter, emphasis is on good sales language and the you-viewpoint.
   - All the information necessary for a sale (prices, terms, choices, and the like) is included in the letter, though references are made to details in the enclosures (brochures, leaflets, and so on).
   - Next comes a drive for a sale.
     —It may be a strong drive, even a command, if a strong sales effort is used.
     —It may be a direct question if a milder effort is desired.
     —In either case, the action words are specific and clear, frequently urging action *now*.
     —Taking the action may be associated with the benefits to be gained.
     —Postscripts often are included to convey a final sales message.

TECHNOLOGY IN BRIEF

Clipart Helps Business Writers Add Interest to Sales Letters

Sales letters and their supplements often include art that increases visual appeal as well as attracts attention to documents. Today's business writers need not be artists to use good art in their documents since word processing software includes graphic libraries as well as providing some basic drawing tools. And most programs accept a variety of graphics from other sources. Some readily available sources of prepared graphics include the following:

- Graphics bundled with presentation, spreadsheet, and word processing programs.
- Clip art from both commercial and shareware sources, which can be bought off the shelf or downloaded from the Internet.
- Scanned graphics from printed sources.

Here is a sampling of a variety of graphics easily combined with text in documents.

CRITICAL THINKING QUESTIONS

1. Explain why a persuasive request is usually written in the indirect order. Could the direct order ever be used for such messages? Discuss.

2. What is the role of the you-viewpoint in persuasive requests?

3. Discuss the relationship between a persuasive request and a sales message.

4. What appeals would be appropriate for the following products when they are being sold to consumers?
   a. Shaving cream.
   b. Carpenter's tools.
   c. Fresh vegetables.
   d. Software.
   e. Lubricating oil.
   f. Ladies' dresses.
   g. Perfume.
   h. Fancy candy.
   i. CD players.
   j. Hand soap.

5. With what products would you use strong negative appeals? Positive appeals?

6. When could you justify addressing sales letters to "occupant"? When to each reader by name?

7. Rarely should a sales letter exceed a page in length. Discuss this statement.

8. Should the traditional sales-letter organization discussed in the text ever be altered? Discuss.

9. Discuss the relationship between the sales letter and its accompanying printed brochures, leaflets, and the like.

10. When do you think a strong drive for action is appropriate in a sales letter? When do you think a weak drive is appropriate?

CRITICAL THINKING EXERCISES

1. Criticize the persuasive request letter below. It was written by the membership chairperson of a chapter of the Service Corps of Retired Executives (SCORE), a service organization consisting of retired executives who donate their managerial talents to small businesses in the area. The recipients of the letter are recently retired executives.

   Dear Ms. Petersen:
   As membership chair it is my privilege to invite you to join the Bay City chapter of the Small Business Advisory Service. We need you, and you need us.
   We are a volunteer, not-for-profit organization. We are retired business executives who give free advice and assistance to struggling small businesses. There is a great demand for our services in Bay City, which is why we are conducting this special membership drive. As I said before, we need you. The work is hard and the hours can be long, but it is satisfying.
   Please find enclosed a self-addressed envelope and a membership card. Fill out the card and return it to me in the envelope. We meet the first Monday of every month (8:30 at the Chamber of Commerce office). This is the fun part—strictly social. A lot of nice people belong.
   I'll see you there Monday!

   Sincerely yours,

2. Criticize the sales letter below. It was written to people on a mailing list of fishing enthusiasts. The writer, a professional game fisher, is selling his book by direct mail. The nature of the book is evident from the letter.

   Have you ever thought
   why the pros catch fish
   and you can't?

   They have secrets. I am a pro, and I know these secrets. I have written them and published them in my book, *The Bible of Fishing*.
   This 240-page book sells for only $29.95, including shipping costs, and it is worth every penny of the price. It tells where to fish in all kinds of weather and how the seasons affect fishing. It tells about which lures to use under every condition. I describe how to improve casting and how to set the hook and reel them in. There is even a chapter on night fishing.

   I have personally fished just about every lake and stream in this area for over forty years and I tell the secrets of each. I have one chapter on how to find fish without expensive fish-finding equipment. In the book I also explain how to determine how deep to fish and how water temperature affects where the fish are. I also have a chapter on selecting the contents of your tackle box.
   The book also has an extensive appendix. Included in it is a description of all the game fish in the area—with color photographs. Also in the appendix is a glossary which covers the most common lures, rods, reels, and other fishing equipment.
   The book lives up to its name. It is a bible for fishing. You must have it! Fill out the enclosed card and send it to me in the enclosed stamped and addressed envelope. Include your check for $29.95 (no cash or credit cards, please). Do it today!

   Sincerely yours,

3. Criticize each of the following parts of sales letters. The product or service being sold and the part identification are indicated in the headings.

   Letter Openings

   Product or service: a color fax machine
   a. Now you can fax in color!
   b. Here is a full-color fax that will revolutionize the industry.
   c. If you are a manufacturer, ad agency, architect, designer, engineer, or anyone who works with color images, the Statz Color Fax can improve the way you do business.

   Product or service: a financial consulting service
   d. Would you hire yourself to manage your portfolio?
   e. Are you satisfied with the income your portfolio earned last year?
   f. Dimmitt-Hawes Financial Services has helped its clients make money for over a half century.

   Parts of Sales Presentations

   Product or service: a paging service
   a. Span-Comm Messaging is the only paging service that provides service coast to coast.
   b. Span-Comm Messaging is the only paging service

that gives you the freedom to go coast to coast and still receive text messages.

c. Span-Comm Messaging gives you coast-to-coast service.

Product or service: a color fax machine

d. The Statz Color Fax is extraordinary. It produces copies that are indistinguishable from the originals.

e. The extraordinary Statz Color Fax produces copies identical to the originals.

f. Every image the Statz Color Fax produces is so extraordinary you may not be able to tell a fax from an original.

Product or service: Vermont smoked hams

g. You won't find a better-tasting ham than the old-fashioned Corncob Smoked Ham we make up here on the farm in Vermont.

h. Our Corncob Smoked Ham is tender and delicious.

i. You'll love this smoky-delicious Corncob Smoked Ham.

Product or service: a unique mattress

j. Control Comfort's unique air support system lets you control the feel and firmness of your bed simply by pushing a button.

k. The button control adjusts the feel and firmness of Control Comfort's air support system.

l. Just by pushing a button you can get your choice of feel and firmness in Control Comfort's air support system.

Action Endings

Product or service: an innovative writing instrument

a. To receive your personal Airflo pen you have but to sign the enclosed card and return it to us.

b. You can experience the writing satisfaction of this remarkable writing instrument by just filling out and returning the enclosed card.

c. Don't put it off! Now, while it's on your mind, sign and return the enclosed card.

Product or service: a news magazine

d. To begin receiving your copies of *Today's World,* simply fill out and return the enclosed card.

e. For your convenience, a subscription card is enclosed. It is your ticket to receiving *Today's World.*

f. If you agree that *Today's World* is the best of the news magazines, just sign and return the enclosed card.

CRITICAL THINKING PROBLEMS

PERSUASIVE REQUESTS

1. Play the role of a member of your student government. From time to time the organization has tried to get faculty members to deposit their old examinations in the library so that all students can have access to them before tests. In general, these efforts have met with little success. Looking over the letters used in the past to persuade faculty members to cooperate, you conclude that these letters just might explain the failure. They are poorly done—blunt, tactless, and without convincing argument.

   After you point out the shortcomings of these letters, the other members of the student government call your hand. "If you think you can do better," they tell you, "you are welcome to it!" You know that you can, so you accept the challenge.

   Now you must think through the situation carefully. In your mind you build a line of reasoning that will be likely to convince the professors that they should cooperate. Then you will present your thinking in the form of a letter. Your final product will be sent to all faculty members under the signature of your student government president, Rob Ruiz.

2. Now that you are a successful businessperson, you find yourself involved in civic work. Your current involvement is with the United Givers Association. You are the chairperson of this year's money-raising drive for your area.

   On the 21st of next month, the organization will hold its kickoff rally, an inspirational meeting of all campaign workers in the district. For it, you want a keynote speaker who can build enthusiasm as well as one whose name will add prestige to the affair. The first name that comes to mind is the mayor (or another community leader your instructor may designate) of your city.

   It is your job to write this person a letter that will persuade him or her to participate. There is no pay, of course—only the rewarding feeling one gets for doing something good. (You may fill in any details you need—time, place, etc.)

3. In your job as an advertising copywriter, you have been given the assignment of writing a letter for the local chapter of the Hire an Ex-convict (HEXCON) organization. The goal of this organization is to help ex-convicts find employment upon their release from prison.

   The assignment interests you, for you believe in HEXCON's goal. You know that a job is the first requirement for successful rehabilitation. You also know how difficult it is for these unfortunate people to find jobs. So you will do your very best on this assignment.

   Specifically, your assignment involves writing a letter that will be sent to local business leaders. In the letter you will build a case for hiring ex-convicts. Of course, you will have to think through the situation first. Then you develop your strategy. You will present this strategy to the executives in your most artful and persuasive language.

   Write the letter for the signature of Donna Prather, who is president of the local chapter of HEXCON.

Enclose an addressed card on which the readers can indicate their willingness to cooperate. Association members will call on them later to work out hiring details.

4. As Lisa Miller, a purchasing agent for the McLaughlin Body Company in Moline, Illinois, you work hard to get good suppliers for the company. While your work involves some travel and visits to suppliers, the majority of your time is spent in the company office. Therefore, you are concerned with both its impact on you and its impact on those suppliers who visit your office.

   In the past few weeks you have been thinking about a book review you read in *Business Week* along with something one of your suppliers mentioned. The review of the book *The Mozart Effect* discussed how the author had brought together various medical studies relating to the impact of music on people's performance—both mental and physical. The author concluded that music affects people's moods and can enhance both creativity and spatial reasoning. In fact, perhaps that is why one anatomy professor at the University of Washington medical school plays 10 to 15 minutes of Mozart every class period. Perhaps increased spatial reasoning would help in the plant, too, by reducing misjudgments related to the line movement. Furthermore, the review noted that one study found that students who sing or play musical instruments score up to 51 points higher on the Scholastic Aptitude Test (SAT) than the national average. And music's positive influence on the body was documented in reducing anxiety, cancer, blood pressure, pain, and more.

   Last week one of your suppliers, Butch Trevor, phoned; he commented negatively on the radio station that played while he was waiting on hold for you. Apparently, he was forced to listen to a certain radio talk show while waiting and found it a bit disconcerting, putting him in a bad frame of mind just before he talked with you. After speaking with Trevor, you investigated to see who was responsible for deciding what gets piped in to both the building and the phone system. To your surprise, you learned that there is no set policy and that the current practice is to let the person who turns on the system select the station.

   Since you now know that music can affect performance, you have decided to write a persuasive request to Thomas McLaughlin, CEO, asking him to set criteria for the music that is piped in to the building and phone system. You will want to stress the benefits that might accrue to the company for making thoughtful selections.

5. You have recently read in the *New York Times* and heard on the major television network news shows that the Senate turned down a formal request from Wyoming's Senator Michael B. Enzi to use his laptop computer in the Senate chamber. It seems to you that tradition is winning over common sense, so you decide to write to your own senators, persuading them to vote for this reasonable request.

   While the senator from Wyoming may have argued that his staff is smaller than those of senators from larger states, you believe all members of the Senate could be more efficient with laptops at their disposal. They could have easy and quick access to all kinds of documents, not only saving trees but saving everyone's time, and reducing the need to dig through briefcases and stacks of paper. Senators could use the laptops to find accurate, up-to-date information and specific facts. And if they used an intranet, they could send and receive messages quickly from their own staff.

   Furthermore, the laptop keyboards could be of the quiet, squishy type that cause no distracting noise. And neither the central processing units nor the screens of laptops have the noisy fans that desktops sometimes have. Also, you could require that speakers be turned off or that headphones be used.

   You firmly believe that computer technology would enable the Senate to be more efficient, putting your tax dollars to their best use. Write the senators of your state, calling for their support of the initiative to use laptops in the Senate chamber.

6. As Webmaster for Skyland Corporation, Inc., you must persuade the 3,425 employees of the company to meet the deadlines for your quarterly update of the Skyland web page. The home page's buttons give mostly information about the company. But one of them is more personal—The Skyland Family. In this part, you feature the human side of your enterprise, such as births of children and grandchildren, community honors and involvement, graduations, weddings, and other activities of a personal nature.

   Over the past year, you have noticed that fewer and fewer people report such personal things to you. And those who do miss the publication cutoff dates. You have sent reminder notices to employees over the local area network (LAN), and you have sent special messages to supervisors. But the situation has not improved.

   Your company, Skyland Corporation, is a large conglomerate with a diverse product-service mix. The corporation consists of a division that produces dairy products and chipped ice, another division that operates drive-in convenience stores, and another division that focuses on international operations. And these are only the more prominent ventures. The idea for the inclusion of The Skyland Family on the Web site is to show that the diversity of the product line and the number of employees in no way indicate that management is unconcerned about its employees. Too, it is good public relations to show that there are many corporate citizens within the workforce. Thus, you depend vitally on reports of personal incidentals to give the "family touch" to your Web site.

   Originally, you published personal information as "The Skyland Family Newsletter," a printed house organ. But that was before electronic media. Now you include this information on your web page.

   Put on your persuasive-thinking cap and prepare a message that will request employees to turn in their personal happenings to you on time—that's 30 days before the end of each quarter. After this date, you are designing and editing copy, arranging layout, and planning for publication. Also, you need more people to report events to you. Surely there are more things happening that your workforce can report to you as news. You have designed a form for reporting the personal events, which you will include with your message.

About 75 percent of your workforce has direct computer access. You will send the message to these workers through the LAN. For those who do not have such direct access, you will include a letter with their paychecks. This dual-media delivery will not, however, affect the appeals you select or the persuasive message you send.

7. For over a year, the Edge City Society of Management Development (SMD) has given serious thought to ethics in business. Because of that concern, the society's board of directors decided to sponsor a short course titled "Ethics in Business." The board selected three distinguished people to teach the course: Dr. Marilynn Price of Antoine University, an internationally recognized authority on ethics; George Highfield, chief financial officer of Financial Industries, Inc., a leading advocate of improved ethics in management; and Jack Hagar, a well-known consultant and motivational speaker on the subject of ethics.

You, the newly appointed director of the short-course program, think that your three teachers are extremely good. Now all you need is managers to hear what they have to say. You plan to appeal to the top executives of the companies in the area to send their middle and senior managers to the sessions. There will be no charge, for SMD is paying the expenses.

The three-hour course will be offered at three times—the first three Fridays of next month from 7:00 to 10:00 PM. The sessions will be held at the Crescent Hotel Conference Room A. You will ask for first, second, and third choice of dates for the managers who attend so that you can balance each session.

You haven't decided yet what persuasive appeal you will you use. So now you will think through the situation, looking for the best strategy. Then you will put that strategy in your best persuasive language. Address the persuasive request letter to Melanie Megandorf, the first chief executive on your list.

SALES LETTERS

8. As a writer of direct-mail copy, you have been hired by your favorite bank to write a sales letter. This letter will be sent to new citizens of the city to get them to do their banking with your bank.

Because you need to know your product before you sell it, you will first learn things about your bank—the advantages it offers, interest rates, special services provided, and the like. Then, with this information gathered, you'll arrange it strategically and present it so convincingly that a new citizen will want to use the bank's services.

You will enclose a special introduction card with each letter. The card will entitle the bearer to a valuable gift (a leather-bound checkbook holder and a supply of 200 personalized checks). The letters will be addressed individually to the new citizens.

9. As a copywriter with the Sands-Eckhardt Advertising Agency, you must write a sales letter for the Mirror Bay Hotel. Located on the Mississippi Gulf coast, this is truly one of the nation's better resort hotels. It provides just about everything a vacationer would want—golfing on a beautiful 18-hole course, tennis on 10 clay courts, a marina with a wide assortment of rental boats, deep-sea fishing on the hotel's own *Southern Belle,* and fishing off the hotel's pier. Bicycles can be rented, and there are miles of hiking trails in the area. Then, for those who like swimming, there is a broad, sandy beach as well as the hotel's beautiful pool. To top it off, there is the excellent food that has earned the dining room a four-star rating from the International Gourmet Association. Truly, Mirror Bay is a wonderful spot.

The full facilities of the club are available at reasonable rates. The prices begin at $260 per day per couple and range upward to $445. Singles prices range from $185 to $345. The price includes room, breakfast, and dinner. Golf, tennis, bicycles, boating, and deep-sea fishing cost extra. If you need additional information, supply it with your logical imagination; but make certain that you do nothing to change the basic facts.

The letter will go to a select group of professional people in surrounding states.

10. Today's sales role casts you as marketing manager for a professional sports team (football, baseball, men's or women's basketball, hockey, soccer, or such—your or your instructor's choice). At present, you are concerned about season-ticket sales for the coming season. They are well below sales for previous years, and you intend to do something about it.

One thing you will do is write a sales letter to the people who bought season tickets last year but did not this year. Because you have their addresses, you feel that a good sales letter might be an effective way of reaching a proven group of season-ticket buyers.

You will begin your work on the letter by thinking through why so many people didn't renew their season tickets. Was it the team's performance? The local economic situation? The price of the tickets? The facilities? Attitudes toward the owners, the coaching staff, or the players? You will explore all possible reasons.

When you have completed this task, you'll think about what you can say to counter these reasons. In other words, you will develop the best possible strategy to overcome any negative ideas your readers may have. In addition, you'll do what you can to get the readers excited about the coming season; and that means you will have to use the you-viewpoint, positive emphasis, and other persuasive techniques. Even if you don't sell any season tickets, perhaps the interest you kindle will bring your readers to more of the games.

For prices and other information about tickets, use

actual information about the team you have selected. Most teams have web pages that contain such information. You will download, print, and attach the information to your letter. But you will not use any text from the sources in your letter, which will be much more targeted and specific than the general information you find.

You will assume that a brochure accompanies your letter that has all the details needed, including a return envelope and an order form. Your letter will be computer processed and merged with your list. Address the one you write to the first person on the list, Kimber Lawson.

(Note: This case can also be adapted to college sports activities or to performing arts series—symphony, opera, theater, etc.)

11. Six years ago, you started your Fitness Plus Center to cater to health-minded people of all ages and professions. From a modest beginning that included a 4,500-square-foot building and two exercise instructors, you have recently purchased a 35-acre plot of land on which you have constructed a guest lodge and facilities for all types of aerobic and fitness activities.

What you must do now, however, is advertise the availability of your newly developed facilities. One of the segments of the market you want to tap is the business professional. You are going to write a direct-mail letter to this group, selling them on one or more of your wellness packages: (1) the 3-day Fitness Weekend; (2) the 7-day Total Fitness Program; (3) the 13-day Program for Total Wellness; and (4) the individualized Corporate Well-Being Program.

Most business professionals know the importance of good health. It improves their productivity as well as their lifestyle. And that's exactly what your fitness/wellness programs offer—improved self-concept, lifestyle, and individual performance for practicing business professionals. For a business, lower insurance rates, decreased turnover, and other economic benefits are possible.

Your programs are based on the medical research of Kenneth H. Cooper, M.D., the man who started Americans exercising aerobically. Participants enjoy a supportive live-in environment that offers the best medically supervised and individualized wellness program available. They can relax in the quiet, luxurious lodge nestled among the remote 35 acres

dotted with the finest medical and exercise facilities. The individualized Corporate Well-Being Program includes these features:

1. Comprehensive physical exam and evaluation.
2. Supervised exercise and fitness classes.
3. Weight-control and nutrition classes.
4. Stress-reduction sessions.
5. Smoking-cessation instruction.

By signing up for one of the programs at the Fitness Plus Retreat Center, business professionals can come to where "The Path to Good Health Begins." Costs are as follows: 13-day package, $3,500; 7-day package, $2,000; 3-day package, $1,000. Individualized corporate programs are available and are priced per company after a thorough needs analysis.

Prepare the letter that will sell your new facilities and the fitness/wellness programs to one of the professionals on your list.

12. Select a brochure, advertisement, or other item containing information on a product or service that can be sold to business executives by direct mail. You may use printed or electronic (Internet, CD-ROM) sources as the basis for your search. The information you collect should be detailed enough to enable you to write a sales letter from it. You may assume that this information will accompany the letter in the form of a brochure.

Examine the material in the item carefully and work out the best possible plan for selling the product or service to the business executives on your mailing list. You will need to identify the objections that might be associated with buying the product or service and list the ways to overcome these objections. A careful selection of appeals should begin your sales strategy. Then, write the letter that will put your sales strategy into action. Take special care to use words and techniques that will be most effective with your special group of readers.

For class purposes, attach the product or service information that you collected to your letter. Be careful that your letter accurately presents the product or service. And be especially careful not to borrow the language of the information you are attaching to your letter. (Be original.) Address the letter to any executive on your mailing list.

8

Pattern Variations in Collections, Memorandums, and Email

Upon completing this chapter, you will be able to write effective collection messages, memorandums, and email. To reach this goal, you should be able to

1 Design a series of collection messages according to the credit risk involved and standard practice in the field of business.

2 Write effective messages for each of the stages in the collection series: early, middle, and last-resort.

3 Explain the variations in the form of memorandum stationery.

4 Discuss the wide range of formality used in memorandums.

5 Describe the primary differences between memorandums and letters written for similar situations.

6 Write clear and effective memorandums for routine inquiries, routine responses, policies and directives, bad-news messages, persuasive messages, and messages to file.

7 Understand the phenomenal growth and nature of email.

8 Follow conventional procedures and organize and write clear email messages.

Collection Letters

Play the role of credit manager of Macy's Department Store. Like most credit managers, you have the assignment of handling all credit accounts. Your department is responsible for approving (or disapproving) all credit requests. After a credit account has been established, you keep records of credit sales, send out statements of what is owed, and record payments as they come in. For the most part, your duties are routine and pleasant.

You have one duty, however, that is less routine and less pleasant. It is the duty of collecting money from credit customers who do not pay on time. Most customers pay regularly, of course, but there are always some who do not. Getting delinquent customers to pay usually involves contacting them by mail. First, you send notices, which serve mainly as reminders. Then, if the reminders do not work, you send letters. *Collection letters*, as they are called, are the subject of this discussion.

DIFFERENCES AND SIMILARITIES IN OTHER MESSAGE SITUATIONS

As we have noted, if you know the techniques and patterns covered in previous chapters, you should be able to adapt them to other situations. In this chapter we cover some of the more important of these situations. Specifically, we cover collections, memorandums, and email. Much of this coverage will support what you have already learned, but you will find some exceptions.

■ The techniques previously studied apply to other situations, with some exceptions.

THE COLLECTION SERIES

When your customers do not pay their bills on time, you must try to collect. They owe you money, so you have every right to ask them to pay. And when they do not pay, you have every right to take action to get your money. Even so, good business etiquette requires that you proceed along this route with courtesy and respect. The following discussion shows you how businesses generally do this.

■ Collection efforts are defensible, but they should use good etiquette.

If you follow business practice, you will use letters in your efforts. You could use other ways—the telephone, personal visits, or collection agencies. And fax and email are likely to be used more and more in the future. But for the present, letters are the most common way. Thus, the following discussion emphasizes them.

■ Letters are commonly used to collect.

Of course, modern technology plays a significant role in collections. In addition to their use in maintaining purchase and payment records, computers are used to flag delinquent accounts. And they are used to generate collection messages. How to compose these messages is the subject of the following discussion.

■ Computers also are used in the process.

COLLECTING THROUGH A SERIES OF EFFORTS

Before learning techniques used in writing collection letters, you should know how businesses usually collect past-due bills. Typically, their collection efforts consist of a series of steps. Each step is a contact (usually by mail) with the delinquent customer. In a first step, the bill is sent with a due date specified. If this bill is not paid, a second bill may be sent—maybe even a third. Sometimes, for added strength, reminder words such as "Please," "May we remind you," or "You have probably forgotten" are added to a past-due bill. These reminders may be in various forms—printed enclosures, stickers, or stamped words.

■ The typical collection procedure consists of a number of progressively stronger efforts. The first are reminders.

If the reminders fail to bring in the money, the efforts get stronger. Messages (usually letters) are sent—in series, each one progressively more forceful. How many messages are sent depends on company policy. When the buildup fails to bring in the money, a final

■ Next comes a series of persuasive messages, ending with a final, threatening message.

FIGURE 8.1 Diagram of the Collection Procedure

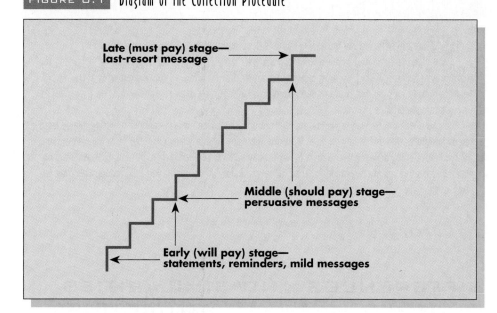

Note: The number of steps depends on the policy of the firm.

message ends the effort. Additional action through collection agencies or the courts may follow.

In a sense, the buildup of collection efforts resembles a stairway (see Figure 8.1). Each step represents a collection effort. The first steps are called *early-stage* collection efforts. These are mainly reminders. The assumption at this stage is that the debtors *will* pay and that the company need only remind them.

Following the early (will-pay) stage comes the middle stage of collection. Here the company's attitude is that debtors have to be convinced they *should* pay. This is truly a persuasion stage. The company's goal is to sell the debtors on the idea of paying, while retaining goodwill. This stage comprises the bulk of most collection series.

After all persuasive efforts to collect have failed, the messages must stop. Thus, a final stage must end the collection message series. In this stage the debtors have to be convinced that they *must* pay. This last-resort stage consists of just one message. Because this message is so different from the others, it justifies being treated as a stage in itself.

DETERMINING THE COLLECTION SERIES

The number of and time intervals between collection efforts vary by company. The choices made are influenced by two factors: the class of credit risk and standard practice in the field.

Typically, companies evaluate the degree of credit risk involved. They move slowly with good risks and fast with poor risks. Thus, a collection series for good risks might extend over several messages, only a few with poor risks. Businesses with a wide range of risks among their customers might classify them into groups and use different series of messages for each group.

Collection efforts between businesses illustrate how standard practice influences collection efforts. Businesses expect and generally receive payments from each other on time. Thus, when payment between businesses is slow, collection efforts typically move fast. Also, credit dealings between businesses are generally viewed as more impersonal than credit dealings between a business and an individual. As a result, collection efforts between businesses are more matter-of-fact and firm.

■ The series resembles a stairway.

■ The number of and time intervals between collection efforts are influenced by degree of risk and practice in the field.

■ Collection efforts between businesses are usually short and fast.

Careful screening of credit applicants can greatly reduce the need for collection letters.

Bill-paying time can be a frustrating experience for many people. Often the collection efforts of creditors compete for attention. Those that stand out from the rest are the ones most likely to bring in payment

INTRODUCTORY SITUATION   Reminder Messages

At the moment, your work at Macy's Department Store involves trying to collect from some good credit customers who are behind in paying their bills. All of them passed Macy's credit investigation at one time or another, but now they are delinquent. You must do something about it.

All the people in the group you are concerned about have open accounts. As is Macy's practice, you billed them on the due date and a month later. Another month later, you billed them a third time—this time with a printed reminder. Today you are ready to take a stronger step—to remind them in a letter.

Because Macy's has so many customers, you will use a form letter. You know that most large businesses do this, but you will work hard to make your form letter sound as individually tailored as possible. This means you will try to make it read like an individual letter and not like a form letter. You do not want to offend these customers. After all, they were at one time a very select group.

EARLY-STAGE COLLECTIONS

■ The early stage of collection begins with reminders of the bill.

As long as you believe that your credit customers intend to pay, you should handle them tactfully. At first, you can simply send duplicates of the original bill, as suggested earlier. If these reminders do not bring in payment, you will need to send a first collection message. This will usually be an early-stage message. Although such messages vary in organization, most of them follow this plan:

■ Most early-stage messages are written this way.

■ Begin directly with a reminder of the past-due bill.

■ Include some goodwill material—comments showing benefits of paying and confidence that the debtor will pay.

■ End with a friendly, forward-looking, goodwill comment.

WRITING REMINDER MESSAGES

■ Such messages remind directly and are short and courteous.

As noted previously, the most common early-stage messages are direct reminders of bills past due. Such messages are usually short—sometimes only two or three sentences. They remind the debtor forthrightly of the past-due account. They soften the force of the directness by conveying the underlying impression that the debtor will pay. They are courteous throughout, and they do not lecture or talk down. Because the account is not long past due, they rarely use persuasive language urging payment.

■ But there are exceptions.

Not all first messages follow this pattern. Typically these exceptions subtly combine mild persuasion with a straightforward request for payment. As you will note from the *Business Week* Case Illustration (p. 191), these messages are a mild form of middle-stage collection effort.

CONTRASTING REMINDER MESSAGES

■ Following are good and bad examples of an early-stage letter.

The following two messages (both form letters) show bad and good ways of reminding Macy's delinquent customers of their debts. Both letters do the job of reminding, but the better one is more courteous.

AN UNNECESSARILY HARSH FIRST LETTER.   The bad letter begins bluntly—and negatively. Its words are too harsh for this stage of the collection effort. The close contains the most positive wording in the letter, but such dangling expressions belong to the distant past.

This letter subtly persuades by first establishing an obligation for benefits received. Then it asks that the reader pay for these benefits. It ends with friendly, forward-looking words.

BusinessWeek

Beyond news. Intelligence.

Persuasion through establishing benefits received

Dear Subscriber:

When you agreed to try <u>Business Week</u>, you probably gave some thought to the benefits our magazine might bring you—such as keeping you up-to-date on the latest business news . . . and showing you how to deal more profitably with your personal business affairs.

Courteous request for payment

We hope you are finding <u>Business Week</u> to be a valuable resource as over 7 million readers do. So please take a moment now to send us payment for your subscription if you haven't already done so.

A wish for enjoyment of the benefits

By taking care of the enclosed invoice <u>right</u> <u>now</u>, you can be sure of uninterrupted delivery of valuable business information that will help you prepare for a successful career in our fast-changing marketplace.

An urge to act with a forward look

Sincerely,

J. DiMarco

L. DiMarco
Manager
Subscriber Marketing

P.S. If your payment has already been sent, please accept our thanks.

A Division of The McGraw·Hill Companies

1221 Avenue of the Americas, New York, New York 10020-1095

•••

CASE ILLUSTRATION **Early-Stage Collection Letters (A Retailer's First Form Letter)**

Written for customers with good past records, this direct-style letter reminds about the past-due bill and subtly persuades the reader to pay.

TECH CENTER STORES, INC.

Date

FIELD(Personal Title) FIELD(First Name) FIELD(Initial). FIELD() FIELD(Last Name)
FIELD (Street Address)
FIELD(City), FIELD(State) FIELD(Zip Code)

Dear FIELD(Personal Title) FIELD(Last Name):

Direct— clear yet courteous

Your payment of the FIELD(Balance Due) now FIELD(Months Late) months past due on your account has not yet reached us. In view of your good record, we are confident you will want to clear your account by sending us your check right away. For your convenience, we are enclosing a return-addressed envelope.

Subtle persuasion

Goodwill close— a friendly forward look

We appreciate your past business, and we look forward to serving you again.

Sincerely,

Hilda Brand

Hilda Brand

enclosure

240 N. Berlin St.
Hamlin, TX 79520
915-676-5890
FAX: 915-676-5891

Dear Mr. Beloit:

You have not responded to the last two statements we sent you and are now two months past due on your account. Thus, I am sending you yet another statement (enclosed). I urge you to pay immediately and protect your credit record.

Thanking you in advance for your payment.

Sincerely,

Enclosure

A COURTEOUS REMINDER TO PAY.   The better letter directly reminds the reader of the past-due bill, but it does so with courtesy and tact. It gives the reader a face-saving explanation (that he or she forgot). It includes the subtle suggestion that paying is something the reader will want to do. Appropriate goodwill comments end the letter.

Dear Mr. Beloit:

This is just a friendly reminder that your account with us shows $317.90 now two months past due. If you're like me, you'll appreciate having the matter called to your attention.

Macy's genuinely appreciates your business. We look forward to serving you in the years ahead.

Sincerely,

■ This bad letter is too harsh for the early stage.

■ This letter is better.

INTRODUCTORY SITUATION

A Series of Persuasive Collection Messages

Back at your credit manager's desk at Macy's Department Store, you have analyzed the results of your reminders. On the whole, you are satisfied. Many of the delinquent customers came through. As you expected, however, some ignored your message. Now you will have to take stronger measures.

Following a convention established by many companies over long years of experience, you will now send stronger messages. These messages will attempt to persuade—to show why the debtors *should pay*. Each message will be stronger than the last. Of course, the collection efforts stop when a debtor pays. But you will continue sending messages to debtors who do not pay. You will stop the buildup when you think there is little chance that the debtor will respond.

The big task before you now is to compose messages that will bring in the money. Obviously, this is no routine job. As the following pages show, it takes the very best in strategy and in persuasive wording.

MIDDLE-STAGE COLLECTIONS

If your reminders do not collect the money, you will need to send stronger messages to convince debtors that they *should* pay. Here your procedure is to select a basic appeal and then to present this appeal convincingly. That is, you persuade. Thus, you use the persuasion techniques described in Chapter 7.

■ When reminders fail, you should use persuasive messages.

ANALYZING THE STRATEGY

As in other cases requiring persuasion, the readers' wishes run contrary to yours. You want them to pay. They have shown by ignoring your reminders that at best they are not eager to pay. Thus, they are not likely to favorably receive your persuasive message to collect. More than likely, they do not want to hear from you at all. In such situations, you must gain reader attention at the beginning. If you do not, the odds of getting your message across are slim.

In persuading debtors to pay, you should use strategy. As in other persuasion cases, you should begin by looking at the situation as the other person sees it. Then you should select appeals that will work with that particular person.

■ Debtors do not receive such messages favorably.

■ Persuading debtors to pay requires strategy.

Although the available appeals differ and may be applied with overlapping variations, they generally fall into the following categories:

- Pride—appeals to the reader's concern for self and what others think.
- Ethics—appeals to "doing the right thing."
- Self-interest—emphasizes why it is best for the reader to pay.
- Fear—stresses the bad things that could happen by not paying.

After selecting an appeal, you should develop it. That is, you should think out the reasoning that will persuade the reader to pay. Then you should present this reasoning with whatever strength is appropriate for the stage of your collection effort. Although such messages vary in organization, this is the most common plan for presenting them:

- Begin with attention-gaining words that set up the appeal.
- Present the appeal using you-viewpoint adaptation and persuasive language.
- Request payment. (You may end here.)
- Consider ending with words recalling the appeal.

GAINING ATTENTION IN THE OPENING

The middle-stage persuasion message is not invited. It is probably not even wanted. Thus, your first words have a special need to gain attention. Since your debtors have received your reminders, they know that they owe you. More than likely, most of them intend to pay when it is convenient. They may quickly label your message as just another dun and put it aside. If this message is to have a chance of succeeding, it must gain attention right away.

To gain attention, you will need to find some interesting opening words. Whatever words you select, they should help set up your basic appeal. The possibilities are limited only by the imagination.

One successful late middle-stage letter began with the question, "When they ask about you, what should we tell them?" These personal words clearly gain attention, and they set up a discussion of the dire consequences of losing credit. Another beginning got the reader's attention with these words: "How would you write to a good friend on an embarrassing subject?" This personal and interesting question sets up a discussion of a topic that relates to friendship—to the reader's moral obligation to a friend.

PERSUASIVELY PRESENTING THE APPEAL

Following the persuasive strategy previously discussed, you next present the appeal your opening has set up. Because your opening words set up the appeal, the shift at this point should be smooth and natural.

As in all persuasive writing, your task here is to adapt to the reader's point of view. More specifically, you persuade—you sell—you convince. Your words should carry just the right degree of force for the particular stage of collection you are in. Early in the series you persuade mildly; toward the end you persuade forcefully. But do not forget that effective persuasion does not insult, talk down, lecture, or show anger. Instead, in the spirit of good business etiquette, it is caring and friendly. Keep in mind also that throughout this stage of the collection series you hope to collect, to maintain cordial relations, and perhaps even to continue doing business with the debtor.

CLOSING WITH A REQUEST FOR PAYMENT

After you have made your persuasive appeal, the logical follow-up is to ask for the payment. You should ask directly, in words that do not merely hint at payment but form a clear question. "Will you please write a check for $77.88 today and mail it to us right away?" meets this requirement. "We would appreciate your writing and sending your check for $77.88" does not.

In collection letters, as in sales letters, a closing reminder of a benefit resulting from the

A Most Effective Collection Appeal?

Back in the 1870s, a little peddler arrived in a western mining town with little more than a mule, a wagon, and a wagonload of assorted merchandise. He had no sooner turned onto Main Street than the mule balked.

Calmly, the little peddler spoke: "This is once. Now giddap!" The mule didn't move.

Again the peddler spoke: "This is twice. Now giddap!" The mule didn't move.

A third time the peddler spoke: "This is the third time. Now giddap!" The mule didn't move.

The little peddler calmly walked to the back of the wagon, got his rifle, walked up to the mule, and in front of half the people in town shot the mule dead.

Without a mule, the little peddler could go no place, so he started a store in the town. It prospered, and in time people began to buy on credit. A few got a little behind in their payments. The little man just mailed them their bills. Across the bottom of each bill he wrote, "This is once."

He never had any trouble collecting.

action strengthens the appeal. For example, a letter stressing the advantages of a prompt-pay record for a business could end with these words:

> Will you please write out and mail a check for the $275.30 right now while you're thinking about it? It's your best insurance for keeping your invaluable prompt-pay record.

■ Linking payment with a benefit to be gained is good.

CONTRASTING FORM COLLECTION LETTERS

The following examples are a contrasting series of middle-stage letters for the situation described at the beginning of this section. The letters, which include exact amounts owed, appear to be individually prepared; this is one benefit of today's word processing and database software's merge features. The letters in the first series are not very good. Those in the second series are much better.

■ Following are a series of good and a series of bad middle-stage letters.

POOR WRITING AND WEAK APPEAL IN A BAD SERIES.   Letters like those in the first series are used all too often in business. Such letters have little appeal. What little they have does not form a logical buildup in strength throughout the series. In addition, these letters are all poorly written. And they do not practice good etiquette. Actual tests have shown them to be far less effective than the letters that follow the plan given in preceding pages.[1]

Flaws in the first letter are obvious. Its direct beginning is too harsh for this stage, and its I-viewpoint development of the appeal to the value of a good credit rating is hurried, lecturing, and generally ineffective. It includes also a second appeal—an appeal to shame. As you know, mixing appeals can be dangerous.

Dear Mr. Benoit:

I was very much disappointed to learn that you still have not paid your past-due account of $247.81, now 75 days past due. I have contacted you several times in regard to this matter and have endeavored in every way to persuade you to pay this honest obligation.

I had hoped to make you see that your credit depended on payment of your bills. However, it would appear that this phase of the matter does not interest you, and we are compelled to draw our own conclusions.

I am not in a position to devote much time to any one account, and your continued neglect will only cause us all a great deal of unpleasantness. I therefore urge you to give this matter your prompt attention.

Sincerely,

■ This bad one has weak appeal and is harsh.

---

[1] The letters in these two series were tested through a Baton Rouge, Louisiana, department store. The second (good) series proved to be almost twice as effective as the first (bad) series.

Illustrating courteous firmness, this early-middle-stage letter was produced from a customized template developed for use with word processing software. The individually adapted parts were merged.

B&SI

September 17, 1999

Mr. Fulton M. Folts, President
Folts Furniture, Inc.
4217 Pemberton Road
North Attleboro, MA 02763

Dear Mr. Folts:

Good interest value

Opening sets up discussion of appeal

"Sure pay" as a credit record means sterling integrity, as you know.

"Prompt pay" means all that and more. It means alert business management.

You have both records, and we appreciate your account because you do. The record is worth a lot to you in the trade.

Appeal is strong— concise

The only way to keep a "prompt pay" standing is to pay promptly-- every time. And since your payment of $1,358.38, now 45 days overdue, is slipping over the margin, we'd like to see you send a check right away and clear it up. Then we could happily regard the lapse as a temporary matter and keep your credit record in the preferred accounts, where it belongs.

Reference to goods bought and not paid for is subtle persuasion

Whether or not you have enjoyed much stove-selling weather, you were certainly foresightful in getting your stock early. Those Firefly Reflectors are worth more now than they were when you bought them. Definitely, it was a good deal for you.

Good drive for payment— recalls advantage reader gains by paying

Won't you make it a good deal for us, too? You can do so by sending us your check for $1,358.38 in the enclosed addressed envelope. Do it now and keep your "prompt pay" reputation.

Sincerely,

Shannon O Tatum

Shannon O. Tatum
Credit Manager

1380 Fulton Dr.
Madison, WI 53707
608-890-4567
FAX: 608-890-4556

•••

CASE ILLUSTRATION Middle-Stage Collection Letters (A Strong Negative Appeal for Payment)

The negativeness of this letter to a department store customer is justified because the customer has ignored two notices and three letters. The previous letters stressed the advantages of paying. Now it is time to stress the disadvantages of not paying.

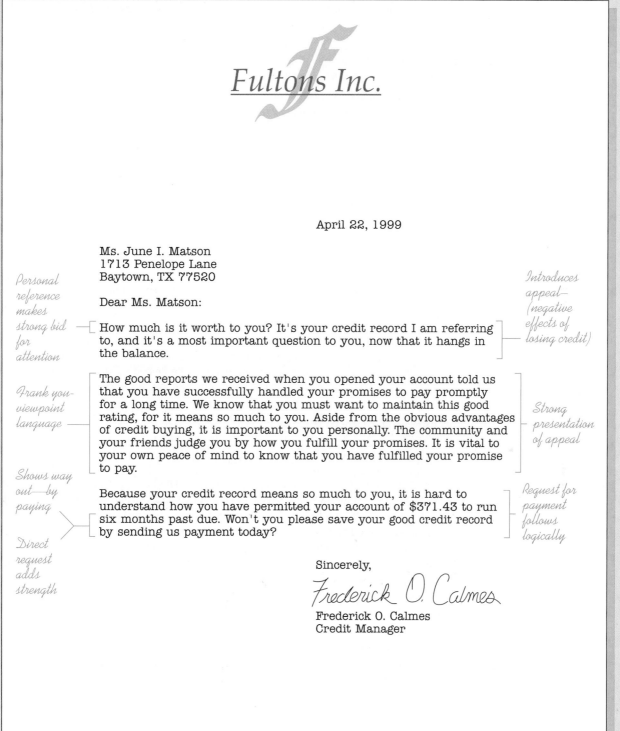

Personal reference makes strong bid for attention

Frank you-viewpoint language

Shows way out by paying

Direct request adds strength

Fultons Inc.

April 22, 1999

Ms. June I. Matson
1713 Penelope Lane
Baytown, TX 77520

Dear Ms. Matson:

How much is it worth to you? It's your credit record I am referring to, and it's a most important question to you, now that it hangs in the balance.

The good reports we received when you opened your account told us that you have successfully handled your promises to pay promptly for a long time. We know that you must want to maintain this good rating, for it means so much to you. Aside from the obvious advantages of credit buying, it is important to you personally. The community and your friends judge you by how you fulfill your promises. It is vital to your own peace of mind to know that you have fulfilled your promise to pay.

Because your credit record means so much to you, it is hard to understand how you have permitted your account of $371.43 to run six months past due. Won't you please save your good credit record by sending us payment today?

Sincerely,

Frederick O. Calmes

Frederick O. Calmes
Credit Manager

Introduces appeal— (negative effects of losing credit)

Strong presentation of appeal

Request for payment follows logically

3317 AVONDALE AVENUE • LIVONIA, MI 48151 • 313-678-9900 • FAX: 313-678-

The second letter also is written with I-viewpoint emphasis. Its heavily negative words give the effect of directness, and they give away the objective before any persuading can be done. The tone is negative throughout.

Dear Mr. Benoit:

■ This bad one is typical of letters often used in business.

Because you have ignored our last letter, I must insist that you pay the $247.81, now 60 days past due on your account.

I cannot understand why you are permitting your credit record to be ruined. Your credit record is valuable to you, and you should want to protect it. You can protect your credit record only by paying your bills on time.

You will agree that we have made every effort to cooperate with you. We have been patient and have a right to expect you to meet your end of the bargain.

I will look forward to your immediate payment.

Sincerely,

The third letter attempts to shame the reader, and its negative language probably invites anger more than it persuades. Also, its negative review of last-resort action possibilities is premature for middle-stage collection letters.

Dear Mr. Benoit:

■ This harshly worded letter invites anger.

I have notified you on many previous occasions that your account with us is in arrears. Apparently, you have chosen to ignore all our notices. Once again, I appeal to your better judgment and request that you make payment. The amount owed is $247.81, now 90 days past due.

My time is valuable to this concern; therefore I cannot devote too much attention to any one account. Your continued failure to heed my requests will force me to take drastic action. I can do one of two things. I can report you to the Retailers Credit Bureau, in which event your credit would be severely injured. Or I can turn this matter over to our attorney for legal action.

I am expecting payment by return mail.

Sincerely,

■ Gradual buildup of strength is evident in the following better series.

BUILDUP OF APPEAL IN A GOOD SERIES.   The better series generally follows the instructions given in preceding pages. Each letter contains strong persuasion. Although each letter in the series is stronger than the preceding one, no anger or lecturing tone is evident. The words are calm and reasonable throughout the series.

The first letter begins with an interesting question. The you-viewpoint of the question gives it extra attention value. The letter then moves into a presentation of the fair-play appeal, which it develops skillfully. The writing is strong yet positive. The closing request for money flows logically from the persuasion. Notice how the suggestion of urgency strengthens the request.

Dear Mr. Benoit:

■ Good use of the fair-play appeal is shown here.

How would you write to a good friend on a somewhat embarrassing subject? That's the question we must answer now, and we're not sure that we know just how to go about it. You see, you are that friend; and the subject is your overdue account.

As you recall, some time ago you wanted something we had, and we were happy to let you have it simply on your promise to pay 30 days later. We are happy to have served you. But it's only fair, isn't it, that now you should fulfill your end of the agreement?

So, in all fairness, will you please send us your check for $247.81? Because your account is 60 days past due, please do it right away. An addressed envelope is enclosed for your convenience.

Sincerely,

Some Classic Responses to Collection Letters

"What would your neighbors think if we repossessed your car?" the collection letter read.

"I have taken the matter up with them," the delinquent debtor responded. "They think it would be a lousy trick."

Crotchety old Mr. Crump received the following collection message from the big-city department store: "We are surprised that we haven't received any money from you."

The old gentleman responded, "No need to be surprised. I haven't sent any."

Obviously annoyed by strong collection letters, a retailer responded with these choice words: "I am doing the best I can. Every month I place my bills in a hat. Then I draw out bills and pay them until my money runs out. If you don't stop pestering me with your collection letters, you won't even get in the hat next month."

A retailer ordered a carload of refrigerators before paying for the last order. The manufacturer responded with a collection message saying that the goods could not be sent until payment was made for the last order.

"Unable to wait so long," the retailer replied. "Cancel order."

The collection letter was terse: "Please remit the amount you owe us right away."

The response was quick and equally terse: "The amount we owe you is $145.20."

The second letter in the good series begins with an attention-gaining exclamation. The opening words set up an appeal to the reader's pride in having a prompt-pay record. Then the letter develops the appeal convincingly. The request for money logically follows the appeal. The final words link the action with the reward it will bring the reader.

Dear Mr. Benoit:

You don't belong in that group!

Every day Macy's deals with hundreds of charge customers. More than 99 percent of them come through with their obligations to pay. We mark them as "prompt pay," and the doors to credit buying are opened to them all over town. Less than 1 percent don't pay right away. Of course, they sometimes have good reasons, and most of them explain their reasons to us. And we work something out. But a few allow their good credit records to tarnish.

Somehow, you have permitted your account to place your name in this last group. We don't think it belongs there. Won't you please remove it by writing us a check for $247.81, now 75 days past due? This would place you in the group in which you belong. You can use the addressed envelope or drop it by our store office. We're open 9–9, Monday–Saturday.

Sincerely,

■ This letter skillfully uses an appeal to pride.

The third letter in the series also has a strong attention-gaining opening. The following explanation builds the case convincingly. It is more negative than the explanation used in the two preceding letters. For the first time in the series, the message contains more talk about the consequences of not paying than the advantages of paying. But letters at this stage of the series can afford to be somewhat negative. After describing the consequences of not paying, the letter shows how paying will allow the reader to avoid them. The final words link the action with a benefit it will give the reader.

Dear Mr. Benoit:

What should we report about you?

As you may know, all members of the Capital Credit Bureau must report their long-past-due accounts for distribution to the members. At the moment, your own account hangs in the balance. And we are wondering whether we will be forced to report it. We are concerned because what we must say will mean so much to you personally.

■ Frankness and conviction make this letter effective.

A slow-pay record would just about ruin the good credit reputation you have built over the years. You wouldn't find it easy to buy on credit from Capital Bureau members (and this includes just about every credit-granting business in town). Your credit privileges would probably be cut off completely. It would take you long years to regain the good reputation you now enjoy.

So won't you please avoid all this by mailing a check for $247.81, now 90 days past due? It would stop the bad report and save your credit record.

Sincerely,

| INTRODUCTORY SITUATION | Last-Resort Collection Letters |

Assume now that the middle-stage collection letters you wrote for Macy's Department Store brought in money from most of the delinquent accounts. As is usually the case, however, they did not work with every debtor. Your problem now is to deal with these delinquents.

You think that you have given the delinquents every reasonable chance to pay, that the time has come to end the collection effort. So you will write a final letter. In it you will tell the debtors that unless they pay this time, you will turn the accounts over to a local collection agency. The agency will assist in collecting, and it will report the bad credit records to other businesses. You will also tell the debtors how this action will affect them. Then you will give them one last chance to pay. You do not like to do this, but the debtors have left you no other choice.

The message will have to be strong, because it is the last one. The following section tells you how to write this message.

LAST-RESORT MESSAGES

- Collection series end with a final (last-resort) message.

- They threaten some last-resort action (reporting to credit bureau, taking to court).

Hard as you may try, your collection messages will not bring in all of the money. Some debtors will ignore your most persuasive efforts. Because you cannot continue your collection efforts indefinitely, you will need to take last-resort action with these debtors. You will use the final message in the collection series to inform them of this action.

A number of last-resort actions are available to you. One of the most common is to report the account to some credit interchange group, such as a local credit bureau. Another is to sell the account to a collection agency empowered with full authority to take legal steps if necessary. Yet another is to take the delinquent to court. You will need to decide what action is best in your case. In making your decision, you should consider the standard practices in your field of business, the nature and amount of the account, and the image of your firm.

FRANK & ERNEST by BOB THAVES

FRANK & ERNEST © (*United Feature Syndicate. Reprinted by permission.*)

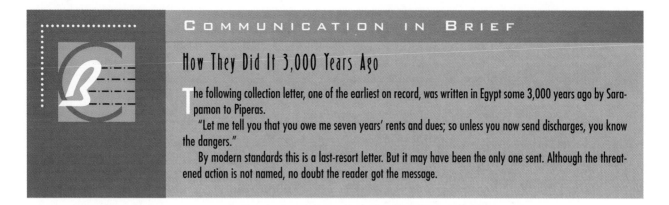

COMMUNICATION IN BRIEF

How They Did It 3,000 Years Ago

The following collection letter, one of the earliest on record, was written in Egypt some 3,000 years ago by Sara-pamon to Piperas.

"Let me tell you that you owe me seven years' rents and dues; so unless you now send discharges, you know the dangers."

By modern standards this is a last-resort letter. But it may have been the only one sent. Although the threatened action is not named, no doubt the reader got the message.

In planning last-resort strategy, you should keep in mind that laws govern collection procedures and that more laws of this kind are likely to be enacted. Currently, a few states have debt-collection laws, and federal legislation controls some areas of debt. The state laws are numerous and varied, but they generally protect consumers from extreme abuses. The federal laws prohibit using language that threatens garnishment of wages, taking possession of property, and involving the consumer's employer and bank. As far as we can determine, the practices suggested in the following pages are in accord with current U.S. legislation.

- You should know the laws governing collections.

JUSTIFYING DIRECTNESS

Clearly, the final message in the collection series conveys bad news. And usually indirectness is appropriate for such situations. This case, however, is an exception. We recommend directness for this message, and for good reason.

- This bad-news message logically is presented in direct order.

As you have learned, directness lends strength. You have reached the point in the collection series where strength is justified. You did not use directness throughout the middle stage because you were concerned with keeping goodwill. You wanted to salvage the account. Now you are more interested in collecting money. Thus, you can justify using the following time-tested direct plan for presenting the last-resort message:

- Directness adds strength, which is appropriate in this case.

- Begin by stating what you are doing, and why.
- Persuade by explaining the effects of this action—firmly, clearly, and without anger.
- Give the reader a last chance to pay by setting a deadline and urging that it be met.
- Perhaps end by associating paying with avoiding the effects of the action that will be taken if payment is not made.

- This time-tested plan is effective.

PRESENTING THE ACTION DIRECTLY

You begin the last-resort message with a clear statement of your action. That is, you tell right away what you are going to do. Such direct openings are strong, and they gain attention. In addition, you might consider bringing in facts that justify the action. Of course, the reader probably knows these facts very well. Even so, mentioning them may hold down a defensive reaction by the debtor. Something like this would do the job:

- Begin the message with the threat of action. It is good to justify the action.

Your failure to pay the $378.40, now seven months past due on your account, leaves us no choice but to report you to the Omaha Credit Bureau.

INTERPRETING THE ACTION

Your explanation of the effects of the action on the debtor comes next. This is your last effort to persuade. In developing the persuasion, you should place yourself in the reader's position to see how last-resort action will affect him or her. It may, for example, mean the end of credit buying, court costs, loss of prestige, and personal embarrassment. Whatever the effects, you should select those most appropriate in the one case. Then you should decide how to present them convincingly.

- Then explain the effects of the action on the debtor. Use you-viewpoint.

Describing the effects of your action requires your best writing skills. You will especially need to watch the tone of your words. You need not be as tactful as you were in earlier messages, but you will need to avoid showing anger. As you know, anger invites resistance. So, instead of showing anger, let your words show concern for the debtor's problem. You wish things had not turned out this way, but the debtor's actions leave you no choice.

Offering a Last Chance in the Close

After describing the effects of the last-resort action, you should give the debtor a last chance to pay. Thus, your close should set a deadline for payment or perhaps for other arrangements. You should urge the debtor to meet this deadline. As in other persuasive efforts, your final words might well recall what the debtor will gain (or avoid) by paying. The following close meets these requirements well:

We will report you to the Capital Credit Bureau on the 15th. So won't you please help yourself by sending us your check for $129.90 by that date? It's the one way you can save your credit reputation.

Contrasting Last-Resort Messages

Illustrating a final effort are the following two messages—both letters. Both are strong. But for reasons explained below, the second one clearly is superior.

WEAKNESS IN AN ANGRY LETTER.   The indirect order in the first letter is the letter's greatest weakness. In addition, because they invite resistance, the angry words tend to reduce effectiveness. Also, the threat of action comes late—far from the beginning position of emphasis. Nowhere in the letter is there explanation of the effects of the action.

Dear Ms. Benoit:

We can no longer tolerate your complete disregard of your long-past-due account. We have written you repeatedly, but you have not shown the courtesy of an acknowledgment. Therefore, we must now turn over your account to the Capital Credit Bureau.

We will give you one week from the date of this letter to make payment of the $3,251.49, now 120 days past due. If payment is not received by May 3, we will take action.

Sincerely,

STRENGTH IN A CALM YET FIRM APPEAL.   The better letter gets right down to business with a clear statement of the action that will be taken. Then it moves into a convincing interpretation of this action. Notice the you-viewpoint—how the words emphasize the effects on the one reader. Although the message is negative, the overall tone is wholesome. There is no evidence of anger. The close, a final recall of the disadvantages of not paying, leaves the action in the reader's hands.

Dear Ms. Benoit:

Your failure to respond to our previous attempts to collect your 120-days-overdue account of $3,251.49 leaves us no choice but to turn your account over to the Capital Credit Bureau for collection. This is an action we had hoped not to take, for it is unpleasant for both of us—particularly for you.

For you it means that you would be forced by the courts to pay the amount of your bill—plus court costs. In addition to being expensive, legal action may be embarrassing to you. Also, your credit record could be permanently injured.

Both of us want to avoid these bad effects of legal action. We'll do our part by holding off action for seven days after the date of this letter. To do your part, you must pay us before that date. It's all up to you, for only you can save your credit record and the embarrassment of court action.

Sincerely,

Sent after seven unsuccessful efforts to collect, this form letter was made to appear personally written by working in specific facts of the one case.

FANNINS
DEPARTMENT

3423 S. Longfell Rd.   Jayess, MS 39641   601-565-4000   FAX: 601-565-4012

July 10, 1999

Mr. Tyrone H. Perry
409-87 Wicker Street
Bellsville, Ontario K8P 3Z1

Dear Mr. Perry:

Direct statement gets attention

Your failure to answer any of our seven requests for payment of the $3,317.10, now 10 months past due, leaves us no choice but to take you to court for collection. We sincerely want to avoid this action, for it would be unpleasant for both of us. It would be especially unpleasant for you.

Although strong, shows no anger— only concern for the reader

For you it would mean that you would be forced to pay. You would pay not only the $3,317.10 you owe, but also court costs. In addition, you would pay attorneys' fees.

Also, legal action would be embarrassing to you. It produces the kind of information people talk about. Your friends would pick it up. So would other businesspeople. Results might well be an end to your credit buying. And your credit reputation would be injured permanently.

Explanation of effects of action is strong and convincing

Strong appeal for payment in terms of reader benefit

You can avoid the effects of court action only by paying before the 17th, the day we shall turn your account over to our attorney. Won't you please help yourself by mailing your check in the enclosed, pre-addressed envelope by that date? It's the only way you can avoid the cost and embarrassment of going to court.

Links payment with benefits to be gained

Sincerely,

Crystal O. Charles

Crystal O. Charles
Credit Manager

Enclosure

Memorandums

To introduce yourself to memorandums, go back to your hypothetical position with Pinnacle. Much of your work involves communicating with fellow employees. Of course, oral communication serves your needs most of the time, for the bulk of your communicating is with people near you or easily reached by telephone. But sometimes you must communicate within the organization in writing, especially if the person you want to reach is unavailable or in another location or if you want a permanent record of your communication. Writing the formal letters discussed in preceding chapters hardly seems appropriate in intracompany communication, for such communication tends to be informal. In intracompany communication, instead of writing a letter, you would probably write an email message or a memorandum, which is really an in-house letter. As you will see, the contents of these messages are much like those of letters except that these messages have a different physical arrangement and tend to be more informal. How to write them is the subject of this discussion.

THE NATURE OF MEMORANDUMS

- Memorandums are letters sent within the company.

The instructions presented in the preceding chapters also apply to both printed and electronic memorandums (commonly called memos). Memorandums, of course, are letters written inside the organization, though some companies use them in outside communication. Memorandums are primarily the written messages exchanged by employees in the daily conduct of their work. As you will see in Chapter 11, some memorandums communicate factual, problem-related information and are classified as reports. Those not classified as reports are the memorandums that concern us here. Nevertheless, much of the following discussion applies to both types.

Variations in Form

- Most large companies use printed memorandum stationery with *Date, To, From,* and *Subject* headings.

Most large companies have stationery printed especially for memorandums. Sometimes, the word *Memorandum* appears at the top in large, heavy type. But some companies prefer other titles, such as *Interoffice Correspondence, Office Memo,* or *Interoffice Communication.* Below this main heading come the specific headings common to all memorandums: *Date, To, From, Subject* (though not necessarily in this order). This simple arrangement is displayed in Figure 8.2. Because memorandums are often short, some companies use 5 × 8½-inch stationery for them as well as the conventional 8½ × 11-inch size. As Figure 8.3 shows, memorandums are usually initialed by the writer rather than signed.

- Some larger companies have additional headings (*Department, Plant, Territory, Store Number,* and such).

Large organizations, especially those with a number of locations and departments, often include additional information on their memorandum stationery. *Department, Plant, Location, Territory, Store Number,* and *Copies to* are examples (see Figure 8.4). Since in some companies memorandums are often addressed to more than one reader, the heading *To* may be followed by enough space to list a number of names.

- Memorandums are processed in various ways: individual typing, templates or macros, email.

Not all companies use printed memorandum stationery for processing memorandums. In some the memorandums are individually printed. In others, memorandums are created through the use of templates or macros (a word processing feature that prompts you for heading information and formats the document). In addition, many companies have memorandums structured in their email system (see Figure 8.2).

Wide Range of Formality

- Memorandums vary widely in formality.

Because memorandums usually are messages sent and received by people who work with and know one another, they tend to be informal. Even so, their degree of formality ranges from one extreme to the other. At one end are the casual handwritten notes that workers exchange. At the other are the formal messages written by lower ranking workers to their top administrators. The typical memorandum falls somewhere between these extremes.

FIGURE 8.2 Typical Electronic Mail Screens

SIMILARITIES AND DIFFERENCES IN MEMORANDUMS AND LETTERS

As we have noted, the order and techniques for writing memorandums are much the same as those for writing letters. The reason is that the situations for both are similar. Some memorandums ask for or give routine information; thus, they are appropriately written in the same order and use the same techniques as letters that do the same. That's also true for memorandums that communicate negative messages and memorandums that seek to persuade. The explanation, of course, is that in a very real sense memorandums are letters. They differ from letters primarily in that they are written to people within an organization rather than to people outside the organization.

Although memorandums are internal letters, they differ from letters in two major ways. First, memorandums are more likely to be written in the direct order. Most letters also are direct, but an even greater percentage of memorandums are direct. Most memorandums are direct because they concern work information, and such information rarely requires preliminary explanation, justification, or persuasion strategies.

The second major difference is that usually the writers of memorandums have less need to be concerned about the effect of their words. That is, tactfulness, negativeness–positiveness, you-viewpoint, or such usually are not major concerns. This is not to say that rudeness and harshness are acceptable—that the practice of good business etiquette does not apply to relations between employees. It simply means that people working together in business situations typically want and expect clear, straightforward communication. They are not personally involved in the message; so there is little need to be concerned about their sensitivity to the wording.

■ Because the situations involved are similar, the techniques for writing memos and letters are similar.

■ Memorandums differ from letters in two major ways: (1) They are more likely to be direct.

■ (2) They are less likely to involve concern about word effect.

FIGURE 8.3 Illustration of Good Form for the Memorandum Not on Printed Stationery

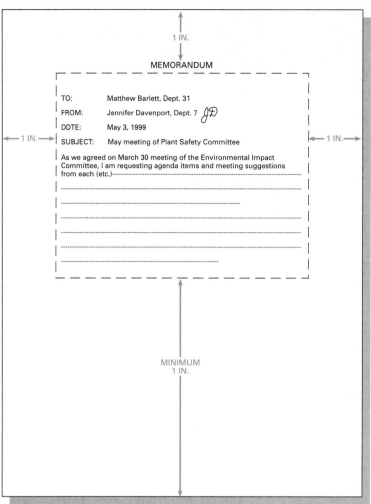

MEMORANDUMS ILLUSTRATED

■ Look for the similarities and differences in the following examples.

The similarities and differences between memorandums and letters are clearly evident from examples. In the following pages, we present examples of the basic types of memorandums, and we make pertinent comments about each. First, we look at the direct-order forms—the direct inquiry and the direct response. Next, we review a policy memorandum (also called *directive*), which is a direct-order message that has no comparable letter type. We then inspect the less common indirect forms—those conveying negative messages. And finally we cover a unique message—the memorandum to file. Other forms of memorandums exist, but they are rare.

DIRECT MEMORANDUMS—ROUTINE INQUIRIES

■ The direct-inquiry memorandum follows the pattern of the direct-inquiry letter.

The following direct-inquiry memorandum clearly follows the plan of a direct-inquiry letter. It begins directly. Then it systematically covers the vital bits of information. Note the logic of its organization and the straightforward and clear communication. Although its words are courteous, there is no need for delicacy to avoid offending the reader. Perhaps its close lacks the outgoing friendliness of a good letter, but it is courteous.

PENNY-WISE STORES, INC.

MEMORANDUM

To: **Date:**

                              From:

Store: **Store:**

At: **At:**

Territory: **Territory:**

Copies to:

Subject: Form for in-house letters (memos)

This is an illustration of our memorandum stationery. It should be used for all written communications within the organization.

Notice that the memorandum uses no form of salutation. Neither does it have any form of complimentary close. The writer does not need to sign the message. He or she needs only to initial after the typed name in the heading.

Notice also that the message is single-spaced with double spacing between paragraphs.

DATE: April 1, 1999
TO: Remigo Ruiz
FROM: Becky Pharr
SUBJECT: Request for cost information concerning meeting at Timber Creek Lodge

As we discussed in my office today, please get the necessary cost information for conducting our annual sales meeting at the Timber Creek Lodge, Timber Creek Village, Colorado. Our meeting will begin on the morning of Monday, June 5; so we should arrange to arrive on the 4th. We will leave after a brief morning session on June 9.

> ■ The memorandum begins directly— with the objective. The necessary explanation follows.

Specifically, I want the following information:

> ■ Then the specific information needed is listed in logical order.

- Travel costs for all 43 participants, including air travel to Denver and ground travel between the airport and the lodge. I have listed the name and home stations of the 43 participants on the attached sheet.
- Room and board costs for the five-day period, including cost with and without dinner at the lodge. As you know, we are considering the possibility of allowing participants to purchase dinners at nearby restaurants.
- Costs for recreational facilities at the lodge.
- Costs for meeting rooms and meeting equipment (projectors, lecterns, and such). We will need a room large enough to accommodate our 43 participants.

I'd like to have the information by April 15. If you need additional information, please contact me at x3715 or Pharr@yahoo.com.

> ■ The memorandum ends with courteous words.

Memos form a significant part of the communications used to coordinate the work in production units such as this.

DIRECT MEMORANDUMS—ROUTINE RESPONSES

- This memorandum should be direct, orderly, and clearly worded.

The illustration selected for a routine-response memorandum is the answer to the preceding example. Like the comparable letter, this memorandum begins directly. Then it presents its contents in an orderly way, arranging them by general topics. Because the situation involves no personal feelings on the part of the communicants, the emphasis is on clear and factual writing.

DATE: April 14, 1999
TO: Becky Pharr
FROM: Remigo Ruiz
SUBJECT: Cost information for sales meeting at Timber Creek Lodge

- This example meets the requirements. It begins directly.

As you requested in your April 1 memo, here are the cost details for conducting our annual sales meeting at Timber Creek Lodge June 4–9.

- Then it presents the information— concisely and in good order.

Round-trip air transportation for our 43 representatives from their homes to Denver would be $19,312 (see schedule attached). Ground transportation from Denver to Timber Creek Lodge could be by chartered bus or by rental car. The White Transport Company would provide round-trip bus transportation from the airport to the lodge for $25 per person, for a total of $1,075. Automobile rental costs for a midsize vehicle for the five-day meeting would be approximately $235 per vehicle, for unlimited mileage. At one vehicle for every four people, we would need 11 automobiles, for a total cost of $2,585. The advantage of automobile rental is that the participants would have transportation throughout the week, although the lodge provides limited shuttle service to Timber Creek Village.

Private room accommodations at the lodge, including breakfast and lunch, would be $125 per day per person, or $625 for the entire meeting. The total for our 43 attendees would be $26,825. Dinners at the lodge could be included for an additional $12 per person per day, making the per person total $685 and the total for all participants $29,405. However, several quality restaurants are in Timber Creek Village, which is less than a mile away. We would probably need to budget about $15 each for dinner away from the lodge. The lodge reports that its meeting room will easily accommodate our 43 participants. For a group the size of ours, the lodge would provide the meeting room, projectors, lecterns, and such without additional charge. The lodge's recreational facilities (golf, tennis, swimming) would also be available without additional charge, except for equipment rentals.

- It ends courteously.

You will find the lodge's current descriptive information at <timbercreek.com>. It should answer other questions you may have. If you need additional information in making your decision, I'd be pleased to get it for you.

Enclosure

DIRECT MEMORANDUMS—POLICY MEMORANDUMS AND DIRECTIVES

Internal written messages giving work rules, procedures, instructions, and the like are common in most large organizations. Called *policies* and *directives,* these messages from administrators to subordinates may be written as memorandums, though they sometimes take other forms. In general, such messages are formal documents and are more important than most internal communications. They are often compiled in policy manuals—perhaps kept in loose-leaf form in a notebook and updated as new memorandums are issued.

■ Company policies and directives may be written in memorandum form.

Policy memorandums and directives are more formally written than most internal communications because of their official nature. Typically, they follow the direct order. They begin with a topic (thesis) statement that repeats the subject-line information and includes the additional information needed to identify the specific situation. The remainder of the message consists of a logical, orderly arrangement of the rules and procedures covered. So that they stand out, the rules and procedures are often numbered or arranged in outline form.

■ They should be somewhat formal, direct, clearly written, and well organized.

The following memo exemplifies the good qualities of a policy memorandum. It begins directly with words that tell the nature of the message. Then it clearly outlines the steps to be taken. It ends with an appeal for compliance. Although the wording lacks the warmth that would be appropriate in a letter, it conveys the firmness necessary in this situation. Even so, the words are respectful and cordial.

■ The following example is direct, orderly, and firm.

DATE: June 10, 1999
TO: All Employees
FROM: Terry Boedeker, President
SUBJECT: Energy conservation

To help us keep costs low, the following conservation measures are effective immediately:

■ The beginning is direct and immediately identifies the situation.

- Thermostats will be set to maintain temperatures of 78 degrees Fahrenheit throughout the air-conditioning season.
- Air conditioners will be shut off in all buildings at 4 PM Monday through Friday.
- Air conditioners will be started as late as possible each morning so as to have the buildings at the appropriate temperature within 30 minutes after the start of the workday.
- Lighting levels will be reduced to approximately 50 to 60 footcandles in all work areas. Corridor lighting will be reduced to 5 to 10 foot candles.
- Outside lighting levels will be reduced as much as possible without compromising safety and security.

■ Clear writing and listing result in good readability.

In addition, will each of you help in conservation areas under your control? Specifically, I ask that you do the following:

■ Separate listing of other measures gives order and enhances understanding.

- Turn off lights not required in performing work.
- Keep windows closed when the cooling system is operating.
- Turn off all computer monitors and printers at the end of the day.

I am confident that these measures will reduce our energy use significantly. Your efforts to follow them will be greatly appreciated.

■ Closing personal remarks add to effectiveness.

INDIRECT (BAD-NEWS) MEMORANDUMS

Memorandums that convey bad news are not rare in business. What is rare are bad-news memorandums that require indirect, diplomatic treatment. As we have noted, most memorandums communicate information of little personal concern to the people involved. Thus, most memorandums can be written in the direct order and with little or no concern for tactful handling. But there are exceptions—memorandums carrying bad news that concerns the reader personally. It is memorandums of this relatively rare type that we will now illustrate.

■ Although rare, memorandums refusing personal requests are occasionally written.

Like the indirect-letter situations reviewed previously, such personal bad-news messages require tactful handling. This means treating them indirectly—paving the way for the bad news with explanation, justification, or such. It means watching words carefully,

■ They should be handled indirectly and tactfully.

Businesses with multiple locations send many of their memos by fax or email.

trying to emphasize the positive over the negative. It means writing from the reader's point of view with consideration for his or her best interests. These and other points discussed with respect to indirect letters also apply to this type of memorandum.

Illustrating this memorandum type is the following memorandum. It follows closely the plan and techniques recommended for bad-news letters. Note especially the concern for the reader's feelings and skillful use of strategy and words to soften the effect of the bad news.

■ The following memorandum illustrates such handling.

DATE: May 24, 1999
TO: Jerry Cunningham
FROM: Albert A. Morton
SUBJECT: Your request for change in vacation dates to July 8–21

■ Subject line identifies without suggesting bad news.

■ This example begins indirectly and pleasantly, leading to the explanation.

Your reasons for requesting a change in vacation dates are quite reasonable and certainly deserve consideration.

■ The explanation is positively worded, clear, and convincing.

In evaluating them, I must consider more than merit. I must also follow the rules in the contract agreement between the company and the union. These rules specify that no more than 10 percent of any department's workers can be on vacation at one time. This means a maximum of two for your department. The contract also specifies that seniority will determine vacation priorities.

■ The refusal follows, in the positive form of an alternative vacation time.

In addition to you, both Rita Gann (18 years) and Kim Wong (14 years) have requested vacations for July 8–21. Because both of them have more service than you (10 years), the best I can do for you is give you the July 22–August 4 period. These dates would permit you to do at least some of the things outlined in your request.

■ The ending is positive and friendly.

Please consider these dates. Then let me know whether they are satisfactory. I assure you that I'll do whatever I am permitted to help you with your vacation planning.

INDIRECT (PERSUASIVE) MEMORANDUMS

Although persuasive memorandums are rare, those that are written are likely to be highly important. Usually they concern a company project, proposal, or such that involves employee participation (a fund drive, company function, or safety campaign). In general, they follow the pattern of the persuasive letter. They present a persuasion strategy designed to move the reader to accept whatever is being promoted. Their pattern is indirect, beginning with attention-gaining words that set up the persuasion strategy. Then they present this persuasion strategy, leading to the request for action.

    The following memorandum uses all these techniques, just as they would be used in a letter of the same type.

DATE: August 22, 1999
TO: All Employees
FROM: Cindy VanVoorhes
            Training Director
SUBJECT: Your professional development

Do you know any of these people—Monica Chavez, Hal Worley, Michael Tong, Pam Hawley, Stephanie Tomacek, Rudy Garcia?

They are your fellow employees, and they have two things in common. One, they were recently promoted to highly responsible positions. Two, they have all been participants in our Corporate Training Program.

As you may know, the Corporate Training Program is Gaston Petroleum's way of helping you develop professionally—completely at Gaston's expense. Through the program Gaston pays all costs (tuition, fees, and books) of your participation in the night and on-line programs at City Tech.

All you need to do is follow an approved curriculum designed to help you professionally and satisfactorily meet course requirements (grade of C or better). It's as simple as that. You study. You learn. Gaston pays. And you benefit professionally—maybe through promotion.

I'd like to tell you more about how the Corporate Training Program can help you. Just drop by my office (20A, Human Resources Suite) any time during work hours. I'll give you the details. Although I won't be able to promise you a promotion, I will promise to help you grow professionally.

THE MEMORANDUM TO FILE

Memorandums are often written for the writer's file. Such *memorandums to file* are a means of making a record of events, activities, and such and of retaining this information for future use. For example, an executive who is having difficulties with an errant subordinate might record the subordinate's errors in memorandums as they occur and address the memorandums to file. Later, the executive could review these memorandums in building a case for disciplinary action. Or an executive who participates with other executives in a meeting at which no record is kept might record the events of the meeting in a memorandum addressed to file. The information would then be stored for future reference.

    The following memorandum illustrates the second case. Here, copies might be routed to all the participants both for personal use and for confirmation of the events of the meeting.

DATE: October 19, 1999
TO: FILE
FROM: Cindy Boros
SUBJECT: Meeting on problems with in-house training program

On October 17, 1999, Charles Davidson, Diane Kennedy, and Peter Dominguez met in my office to review the progress of our on-line management training program.

Diane and Peter reported that their employees expressed strong dissatisfaction with the first course conducted. Charles and I reported less negative (although not entirely positive)

- Persuasive memos are rare. They follow the pattern of a persuasive letter.

- Following is such a memorandum.

- Use of familiar names gains attention and sets up the persuasion.

- Explanation of the program is persuasive.

- After the persuasion the readers are told what they must do to reap the benefits.

- The ending reemphasizes the major benefit.

- Executives write memorandums to their files as records and reminders.

- The direct beginning identifies the particulars.

- A concise summary of the event follows.

experiences from our employees. The evidence submitted clearly suggested that the course was "over the heads" of the participants, though the subject matter, we concluded, was not too difficult for the employees involved.

■ This part emphasizes the achievements.

We also agreed that in selecting the next course we will carefully consider the levels of subject matter and instruction. In addition, we agreed that I will monitor the instruction throughout the next course.

INTRODUCTORY SITUATION

Email

As in preceding chapters, play the role of your hypothetical position with Pinnacle Manufacturing Company. Like most businesses today, Pinnacle uses current technology wherever practical. The personal computer on your desk links you with all the administrative employees at your plant, with the representatives out in the field, and with key people at the companies with which Pinnacle has business dealings. When you must communicate with someone in any of these groups, you have three primary choices. You can use the telephone, you can write memorandums or letters, or you can use your PC to send email messages. How best to organize and write these email messages is the primary subject of the following section.

THE GROWTH AND NATURE OF EMAIL

■ Recent growth of email has been phenomenal.

The rapid growth of email has been the most exciting business communication development in recent years. In just a short time email has emerged as a mainstream form of business communication. It has become especially important within large organizations, primarily those with multiple installations and/or those with employees in widespread locations. Email has gained in importance in communication between organizations, also. In fact, its growth continues at a rapid rate—25 percent increase per year according to one source.[2]

■ It has grown because it

The reasons for this rapid growth are the advantages email has over other communication forms, especially over its principal competitor, the telephone. Among the reasons, the following are most significant:

■ eliminates "telephone tag,"

- Email eliminates "telephone tag"—the problem of trying to contact busy people who are not always available for telephone calls. (Messages sent to them can be stored in their electronic mailboxes until they are ready to read them.)

■ saves time,

- Conversely, email saves the time of these busy people. They are spared the interruptions of telephone calls.

■ facilitates fast decisions, and

- Email can speed up the process of making business decisions, because it permits rapid exchanges from all involved in the decisions.

■ is cheap.

- Email is cheap. It permits unlimited use at no more than the cost of an Internet connection.

■ Email messages range from formal to informal.

A review of email writing is complicated by the fact that email messages are extremely diverse. They run the range from highly informal to formal. The informal messages often resemble face-to-face oral communication; some even sound like chitchat that occurs between acquaintances or friends. Email messages are often written in a fast-pitched environment with little time for deliberation. At the opposite extreme are those written at a leisurely pace. Because of this diversity, explaining how to write email messages is difficult. We have no choice but to take a middle-ground approach. With intelligent adaptation, you should be able to apply the pointers we present to any of your email writing needs in business.

[2] David Angell and Brent Heslop, *Elements of Email Style* (Reading, MA: Addison-Wesley, 1994), p. 1.

CONSTRUCTION OF EMAIL MESSAGES

Much of what you do in constructing email messages is standardized, especially the mechanical parts pertaining to structure. But the second part of your effort, writing the message, is far from standardized. Although the following review covers both, the writing receives the greater emphasis. It is here that you are likely to need the most help.

INCLUDING THE PREFATORY ELEMENTS

Although the various email systems differ somewhat, the elements are standardized. They include the following parts:

- **To:** Here is placed the email address of the recipients.
- **Cc:** If someone other than the prime recipient is to receive a *courtesy copy,* his or her address goes here.
- **Bcc:** This line stands for *blind courtesy copy.* The recipient's message will not show this information; that is, he or she will not know who else is receiving a copy of the message.
- **Subject:** This line describes the message as precisely as the situation permits. The reader should get from it a clear idea of what the message is about.
- **Attachments:** In this area you can enter a file that you desire to send along with the message. As will be emphasized later, you should make certain that what you attach is really needed.
- **The message:** The information you are sending goes here. How to write it is the subject of much of the following discussion.

■ These standard parts precede the message.

BEGINNING THE MESSAGE

Typically, email messages begin with the recipient's name. If writer and reader are acquainted, first name only is the rule. If not, the specific situation may determine the first words. A "friendly generic greeting such as *Greetings*"[3] is appropriate for a group of people with whom you communicate. Use of the recipient's full name also is acceptable. The salutations commonly used in letters (Dear Sir, Gentlemen, Dear Mr., Dear Ms.) are rarely used in email. When writing to someone or a group you do not know, it is appropriate to identify yourself early in the message. This identification may include your purpose and your company. Your title and position may also be helpful.

■ Begin with the recipient's name or a greeting. Identify yourself if necessary.

ORGANIZING THE CONTENTS

Even though email messages often are written under time pressure, you would do well to organize them carefully. For most short, informative messages, a "top-down" order is appropriate. This plan, used in newspaper writing, involves presenting the most important material first. The remaining information follows in descending order of importance. Such an arrangement permits a busy reader to get the essential facts without reading the entire message. Many writers routinely follow this practice.

The longer and more complex messages follow a variety of organization patterns. For those messages resembling a business letter, you may choose to borrow from your knowledge of letter-writing strategies. For example, a negative message may benefit from an indirect plan. A persuasive message may appropriately use a sales strategy. Some long email messages may resemble business reports. You should use your knowledge of report presentation in organizing them (see Chapters 10–12). Even headings are appropriate in very long messages.

■ Organize short messages by presenting information in descending order of importance.

■ Organize complex messages as their contents suggest.

WRITING THE MESSAGE

Instructions for writing email messages are much the same as those given in Chapters 2, 3, and 4 for other types of messages. For the purpose of email writing, we may group the

■ Use these techniques in writing the message.

---

[3] *Ibid.,* p. 22.

more important of these instructions under three heads: conciseness, clarity, and courtesy. A fourth, correctness (covered in Chapter 18), is equally vital. Each of these important qualities for email writing are briefly reviewed in following paragraphs.

CONCISENESS. As we have mentioned, email often is written by busy people for busy people. In the best interests of all concerned, email messages should be as short as complete coverage of the subject matter will permit. This means culling the information available and using only that which is essential. It means also that the information remaining should be worded concisely. In the words of one email authority, "Short messages are better, even—especially—the important ones.[4]

Frequently in email communication, a need exists to refer to previous email messages. The easiest way, of course, is to tell your mailer to include the entire message. Unless the entire message is needed, however, this practice adds length. It is better either to paraphrase the essentials from the original or to quote the selected parts that cover the essentials. All quoted material should be distinguished from your own words by the sign > at the beginning and the sign < at the end of the quoted part. Another technique is to place three of these signs (>>>) at the beginning of all parts you write and three of these signs (<<<) at the beginning of all parts you are quoting from previous messages.

CLARITY. Especially important in email writing is clarity of wording. As suggested in Chapters 2 and 3, you should know and practice the techniques of readable writing. You should select words that quickly create clear meanings. Typically, these are the short, familiar ones. You should strive for concreteness, vigor, and precision. Your sentences should be short, and so should your paragraphs. In fact, all of the advice given in Chapters 2 and 3 is applicable to the writing of clear email messages.

ETIQUETTE. It goes without saying that good business etiquette should be practiced in all business relations. We all want to receive courteous and fair treatment. In fact, this is the way we human beings prefer to act. Even so, the current literature has much to say about anger among email participants. "Flaming," as the practice of sending abusive or offensive language is called, has no place in business. Good business etiquette should prevail. Throughout the preceding chapters, especially in Chapter 4, we have emphasized the techniques of showing good business etiquette. As you will recall, Chapter 4 emphasized the effect of your words. The skillful use of positive language and you-viewpoint can also be effective in email. So can the use of conversational language. Nondiscriminatory language also helps, as can emphasis on sincerity. In fact, virtually all the instructions given on goodwill building apply here. Also in the interest of good business etiquette, you will want to let your reader know when no response is required to your email message.

CORRECTNESS. One would think that the need for correctness in email writing would be universally accepted. Unfortunately, such is not the case. Because of the fast pace of email communication, some practitioners argue that "getting the message out there" is the important goal—that style need not be a matter of concern. In the view of one in this group, "You should not add stylistic and grammatical refinements to your email messages because they'll slow you down.[5]

We cannot accept this view. *How* one communicates is very much a part of the message. Bad spelling, illogical punctuation, awkward wording, and such stand out like sore thumbs. Such errors reflect on the writer. And they can reflect on the credibility of the message. If one knows correctness, it is easy enough to get it right the first time. What is the logic of doing something wrong when you know better? Clearly, an error-filled message strongly suggests the writer's ignorance.

To avoid any such suggestion of ignorance, you should follow the grammatical and punctuation instructions presented in Chapter 18. And you should follow the basic

---

[4] Bill Howard, "Making Order Out of Email Chaos," *PC Magazine,* May 27, 1997, p. 95.

[5] Guy Kawasaki, as quoted in Angell and Heslop, *E-mail Style,* p. 3.

Marginal notes:

■ Cut nonessentials and write concisely.

■ Minimize references to previous communications.

■ Use the techniques of clear writing.

■ Be courteous, as suggested in preceding chapters.

■ Write correctly. Some critics disagree.

■ Correctness is a part of the message.

instructions for using words, constructing sentences, and designing paragraphs presented in the writing chapters. Before pressing the Send button, proofread your message carefully.

CLOSING THE MESSAGE

Most email messages end with just the writer's name—the first name alone if the recipient knows the writer. But in some messages, a closing statement may be appropriate. "Thanks" and "Regards" are popular. So are the acronyms THX (thanks) and TTFN (ta-ta for now) The conventional complimentary closes (sincerely yours, yours truly, cordially yours) so common in letters are rarely used in email.

> ■ End with your name or a closing statement.

Today most email software has a signature feature that will automatically attach a signature file to a message. Some programs even allow the writer to set up an alternative signature, giving users the flexibility to choose between a standard, the alternate, and none attached at all. Writers sometimes set up a formal full signature in one file and an informal signature in another. The important point to remember is to close with a signature that gives the reader the information he or she needs to know.

USING EMPHASIS DEVICES

When you write email messages, you may find that certain elements of style are missing either on your system or on your readers' systems. While most of the current versions of Windows and Macintosh email programs support mechanical devices such as underscoring, font variations, italics, bold, and color, some older or mainframe-based systems do not. Email writers have attempted to overcome the limitations of these older systems by developing alternative means of showing emphasis. To show underscoring, they use the sign _ at the beginning of the words needing underscoring. They use asterisks (*) before and after words to show boldface. Solid capital letters are another means of emphasis, although some critics believe this practice is greatly overused. In the words of one critic, "TOO MANY CAPITALS GIVE THE APPEARANCE OF SHOUTING."[6] A sign they use to emphasize items in a list is the bullet. Since there is no standardized bullet character that will display on all computers, many writers of email use substitute characters. One is the asterisk (*) followed by a tab space. Another is the dash (—) followed by a tab space.

> ■ Email has limited use of emphasis devices. These substitutes have been developed.

USING INITIALISMS CAUTIOUSLY

Probably as a result of the early informal development of email, a somewhat standardized system of initialisms has developed. Their purpose has been to cut message length and to save the writer's time. In spite of these apparent advantages, you would be wise to use them cautiously. They have meaning only if readers know them. Even so, you should be acquainted with the more widely used ones, such as those below.[7] You are likely to find others created by your email correspondents.

> ■ Initialisms have been developed to save time. But use them cautiously.

BTW	by the way
FYI	for your information
FAQ	frequently asked question
FWIW	for what it's worth
IMHO	in my humble opinion
TTFN	ta-ta for now
TIA	thanks in advance

---

[6] Cohen, L., *How to Improve Your Email Messages* [Online]. Available: http//galaxy.einet.net/editorsLanceCohen/How_to_improve_your_E_mail.html (1997).

[7] Linda Lamb and Jerry Peek, *Using Email Effectively* (Sebastopol, CA: O'Reilly and Associates, Inc., 1995), p. 107.

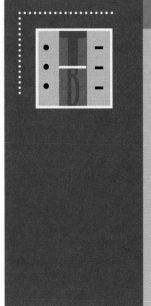

Using Good Email Etiquette Helps Writers Convey Intended Message

Using proper email etiquette is as easy as applying a bit of empathy to your messages: send only what you would want to receive. The following additional etiquette guides will help you consider a variety of issues when using email.

- Is your message really needed by the recipient(s)?
- Is your message for routine rather than sensitive messages?
- Are you sure your message is not spam (an annoying message sent repeatedly) or a chain letter?
- Have you carefully checked that your message is going where you want it to go?

- Has your wording avoided defamatory or libelous language?
- Have you complied with copyright laws and attributed sources accurately?
- Have you avoided humor and sarcasm your reader may not understand as intended?
- Have you proofread your message carefully?
- Is this a message you would not mind having distributed widely?
- Does your signature avoid offensive quotes or illustrations, especially those that are religious, political, or sexual?
- Are attached files a size that your recipient's system can handle?
- Are the files you are attaching virus free?

It is important to keep in mind that these practices and some of the other pointers given in this review apply only to current usage. Computers and their use are changing almost daily. The techniques of email writing also are likely to change over time.

SUMMARY BY CHAPTER OBJECTIVES

1 Design a series of collection messages according to the credit risk involved and standard practice in the field of business.

1. Collection messages are usually sent in a series.
   - First comes a reminder, usually a statement.
   - Next come persuasive messages.
   - The series ends with a last-resort message.
   - The number of messages in the series is influenced by credit risk and practice in the field.
     —Exclusive shops, for example, would be likely to use a longer, slower series than that used by stores catering to bad risks.
     —Some businesses classify customers into risk groups and treat each differently.
   - Typically, collection series between businesses are short and move fast.
   - The length and harshness of a series should reflect management's philosophy.

2 Write effective messages for each of the stages in the collection series: early, middle, and last-resort.

2. *Early.* Begin a collection series on the assumption that the reader *will* pay.
   - Your first message should be a short, courteous reminder of the past-due bill.
   - Such messages are typically direct, though the indirect order is effective sometimes.
   - These messages usually contain appropriate goodwill talk.
   Middle. Construct the middle-stage messages on the assumption that the reader *should* pay.
   - Thus, persuasion is needed.
   - Begin by selecting an appeal (fair play, pride, or such), and develop this appeal in words that convince.
   - Each succeeding message in this stage is stronger than the preceding one.
   - Since messages in this stage are not invited, begin them with attention-gaining words.
   - These words should set up your strategy (the appeal selected).
   - Then present the appeal, taking care to make it convincing and at the right strength for the collection stage involved.
   - But keep the tone friendly (no anger).

- End with a request for payment, perhaps linking payment with a benefit to be gained by paying.

Last-resort. After the buildup of middle-stage messages has failed, write a final message (last resort). The assumption here is that the reader must pay.
- Begin by selecting a last-resort action (reporting to a credit bureau, going to court).
- Write the message in direct order, telling what action you will take.
  —Use directness because it adds strength.
  —And make this last letter strong.
- Throughout, show concern rather than anger.
- Present the effects of this action in convincing words.
- Close with a last-chance offer of a deadline for paying before taking the action threatened.
- Consider a final recall of the appeal, associating it with the action.

3. Memorandums (letters written inside a company) usually are processed on special stationery.
   - Typically, *Memorandum* appears at the top and *Date, To, From,* and *Subject* follow.
   - Large organizations often include more information (for example, *Department, Plant, Location, Copies to, Store Number*).

3 Explain the variations in the form of memorandum stationery.

4. Most memorandums are informal, but they can be formal.
   - Simple inquiries, responses, and such from and to employees are informal.
   - Messages from employees to higher authorities in the organization are likely to be formal.

4 Discuss the wide range of formality used in memorandums.

5. The situations for writing memorandums and letters are much alike, but there are two differences.
   - Memorandums are more likely to be written in the direct order.
   - Memorandums frequently have less need for you-viewpoint and positive language.

5 Describe the primary differences between memorandums and letters written for similar situations.

6. Generally, write memorandums as you would a comparable letter.
   - Use the direct pattern for routine inquiries and responses, policy memorandums, and directives.
   - Use the direct pattern even for some bad-news messages—those that do not involve the reader personally.
   - Use indirectness for bad-news memorandums that personally involve the reader.
   - Use the indirect pattern for persuasive memorandums.
   - Use clear summaries of events, activities, and such in memorandums to file, which are written to assist the writer's memory.

6 Write clear and effective memorandums for routine inquiries, routine responses, policies and directives, bad-news messages, persuasive messages, and messages to file.

7. Today, email is a mainstream form of business communication.
   - It has grown because it
     —Eliminates "telephone tag."
     —Saves time.
     —Speeds up decision making.
     —Is cheap.
   - Email messages range from formal to informal.

7 Understand the phenomenal growth and nature of email

8. The way to write good email messages is as follows:
   - Use standardized prefatory parts.
   - Begin with recipient's name or a greeting.
   - Organize logically.
     —For short messages, present the information in descending order of importance.
     —For long messages, use the organization that best presents the information.
   - Make the message short.
   - Write clearly, following instructions in Chapters 2 and 3.
   - Be courteous.
   - Write correctly.
   - Close with your name or a closing statement.
   - Use asterisks, dashes, solid caps, and such, as needed, to show emphasis.
   - Sometimes initialisms are useful, but use them cautiously.

8 Follow conventional procedures and organize and write clear email messages.

CRITICAL THINKING QUESTIONS

1. "Only one test is meaningful in determining how good a collection message is: how well it brings in the money." Discuss.
2. Describe the collection series you would recommend for a store selling inexpensive clothing to high-risk customers. Explain your selection.
3. Describe the collection series you would recommend for an exclusive clothing store selling mainly to low risks. Explain your selection.
4. Most first reminders are written in the direct order. Middle-stage messages tend to be written in the indirect order. Discuss the reasons for these practices.
5. This book recommends cordiality throughout the collection procedure. What is the logic of this practice?
6. If the last-resort collection message is the strongest in the series and therefore the most likely to bring in the money, why not use it earlier?
7. Discuss the role of negative and positive wording and the you-viewpoint throughout the collection series.
8. Explain the logic of using negative words in memorandums that you would not use in letters carrying similar messages.
9. Although bad-news memorandums are not rare, indirect bad-news memorandums are. Explain.
10. Discuss and justify the wide range of formality used in memorandums.
11. Memorandums differ much more than letters in their physical makeup. Explain and discuss.
12. Discuss the special need for clear writing and adaptation in policy memorandums and directives.
13. *a.* Discuss the reasons for email's phenomenal growth.
    b. Is this growth likely to continue?
14. Some authorities say that concerns about correctness inhibit a person's email communication. Does this stand have merit? Discuss.

CRITICAL THINKING EXERCISES

Criticize the following form collection letters. They were written for a large department store for middle- to upper-income customers with good credit records at the time they were granted credit. The series consists of five letters.

1. *First letter (60 days past due)*

   Dear _____:

   Please be informed that your account with us shows an unpaid balance of $327.48, now 60 days past due. Surely there must be some mistake. I know you will correct the matter right away by mailing in your check. If there is some problem, please call me to make arrangements.

   Sincerely yours,

   Alice Blumberg, Credit Manager

2. *Third letter (120 days past due)*

   Dear _____:

   Because you have ignored my previous efforts to collect the $327.48, now four months past due, I must firmly call this matter to your attention.

   Perhaps you do not realize the seriousness of what you have done. Your credit rating is in jeopardy. You are in danger of losing a reputation that took a lifetime to build. And once your reputation is ruined, you will find it very difficult to regain it.

   I know you do not want this to happen. So please send us the amount owed right away. If there is a problem, at least call me or write me and explain so we can work out a payment plan. If we do not hear from you soon, we will take appropriate action.

   Sincerely yours,

   Alice Blumberg, Credit Manager

3. *Fifth letter (180 days past due)*

   Dear _____:

   I am extremely disappointed to find your name among our debtors who are a full six months past due in paying their honest obligations. In spite of the fact that I have repeatedly informed you of your obligation, you have completely ignored the matter. I will no longer be patient.

   Unless you pay the $327.48 you owe, we will take drastic action. We will go to court; and we can and will collect. Either you pay us by November 16 or I'll see you in court.

   Sincerely yours,

   Alice Blumberg, Credit Manager

4. Point out the weaknesses in this policy memorandum. The writer's objective is to establish a clear policy for hiring and firing employees.

   TO: All Administrators
   FROM: Ada H. Horton, President
   DATE: June 7, 1999
   SUBJECT: Hiring and terminating policies

   Since joining ElectroTech 16 years ago, I have witnessed every conceivable discrepancy in our employment policies, racism, sex discrimination, nepotism—you name it. It is time that you stop these practices. Henceforth you will rigidly adhere to the following rules.

   Do not consider race, religion, sex, or nationality because they have no relationship to job performance. When selecting new employees, make sure that all qualifications are considered. Do not consider physical ability or age. However, when the job requires it, you can consider physical ability to perform. For similar reasons you can consider age. Use the doctor's report for these decisions and do not make these evaluations yourself. Always hire the best applicant for the job.

When you have to reduce your force, do not play favorites as has sometimes been done in the past. Always discharge first the less competent. Job performance appraisals should determine which employees to discharge. When you have two or more with equal performance ratings, seniority should be used. Job terminations based on poor performance or for disciplinary reasons must be supported by evidence and must be approved in advance by our Human Resources Review Committee.

A personnel action memo is required every time we hire or fire. Send it to Human Resources explaining what was done and why. Include all supporting evidence upon which the decision was based.

5. Critique this memo informing an employee that she was not selected for promotion to a higher position in the organization.

TO: Alma DuPuis
FROM: Monty Duke
DATE: May 17, 1999
SUBJECT: Your application for position of human resources director

One of my most difficult assignments is having to tell a colleague that he or she did not get a promotion sought. But it is my duty to do so. Therefore I must report that you were not judged best qualified for the position of human resources director.

The committee recommended Don James. They considered Don to be best qualified because of his long and distinguished record with us. I am confident you would agree if you saw his credentials.

Although you were not selected, the committee wants you to know that they appreciate your interest in the position and your years of service to the company.

CRITICAL THINKING PROBLEMS

COLLECTIONS

ELECTRONICS DISTRIBUTORS, INC., SERIES

1. (*Early stage.*) The Electrotech Store, owned by Sid Sugarek, owes your company, Electronics Distributors, Inc., $5,187.40 for an assortment of electronic equipment. You sent this firm the original invoice 75 days ago with terms of 2/10, n/30. Thirty days later (on the due date), you sent the first formal notice; and 30 days after that, you sent the second formal notice.

   Today you are ready to try your first letter. You suspect that Mr. Sugarek needs to be reminded, but you will try to make the reminder a gentle one. This account has been a good one over the years.

2. (*Middle stage.*) It is now 21 days after your first letter to Sid Sugarek and his Electrotech Store. You have not received payment. So it is time to try again to collect the $5,187.40 now over two months past due.

   You will write a somewhat stronger letter this time. For a basic appeal you'll stress the value of a prompt-pay record. Because the customer is a valued one with a long history of profitable relations with you, you'll be careful not to insult or offend, but you will be strong enough to convince Mr. Sugarek that he should pay.

3. (*Middle stage.*) Your last letter to Sid Sugarek and his Electrotech Store didn't work. Now, another 15 days later, you will write again.

   This time you will try a stronger appeal. You will stress the fair-play theme—that is, you will emphasize how you did something for Mr. Sugarek when he needed it. Now it's only fair that he take care of his end of the bargain. Use your best persuasion to drive home the point, but remember, you are not yet ready for threatening talk.

4. (*Middle stage.*) Sid Sugarek and his Electrotech Store

still haven't paid. Fifteen days after you wrote to Mr. Sugarek stressing the fair-play appeal, you wrote again. Now, another 15 days later, you have to write yet another letter.

   In this letter you will use some negative appeal for the first time. You will talk about the danger of losing a good credit reputation. Even so, it won't be threatening; nor will it show anger. If this one does not bring in the money, the next letter will be the last one.

5. (*Last resort.*) After five futile attempts, you will try one more letter to collect from Sid Sugarek and his Electrotech Store. If Mr. Sugarek does not pay, you will turn over the case to your attorney for collection. Your letter will show Mr. Sugarek how essential it is that he pay. Not to do so would cost him heavily in court fees as well as in damage to his reputation. You will give Mr. Sugarek 15 days from today before you take final action.

LIPMAN AND ASSOCIATES SERIES

6. (*Early stage.*) Lipman and Associates, a management consulting firm, has had some difficulty collecting from the Poston Iron Works. About four months ago Dwight Poston came to Sean Lipman with serious operational problems. Mr. Lipman worked with Dwight Poston and his executives personally for four 9-hour days. He worked out Poston's problems; and Mr. Poston and the Poston people said they were well satisfied.

   After completing the job, Lipman and Associates billed Poston Iron Works $5,960 for services rendered ($150 per hour plus expenses). Thirty days later Mr. Poston had not paid, so Lipman sent a duplicate bill. Now an additional 30 days later Mr. Poston still hasn't paid.

   Sean Lipman thinks it is time to send a gentle reminder. Because he had very friendly relationships with Dwight Poston and his executives, Mr. Lipman will take the approach that payment has been overlooked and that a friendly reminder will be appreciated. Write the letter.

7. (*Middle stage.*) Sean Lipman is very disappointed that his reminder letter didn't bring in the Poston Iron Works money. Now, 30 days later, he will write a second letter. This one will stress the fair-play appeal (We've given you something you needed; now how about doing something for us). Write the letter for Sean Lipman.

8. (*Middle stage.*) Thirty days after sending the second letter to the Poston Iron Works, Sean Lipman had to write another letter. It didn't work. Now, 15 days later, he's ready to try his hand at letter writing again. If this letter doesn't work, the next letter will threaten last-resort action.

   This fourth letter will stress the advantages of keeping a good credit record. It will give convincing argument to support the appeal. Write the letter.

9. (*Last resort.*) Sean Lipman doesn't like to do it, but he feels that he must take last-resort action to collect the $5,960 Poston Iron Works owes his consulting firm. If Mr. Poston doesn't pay within 15 days, Lipman and Associates will take the matter to court. The letter will explain vividly the effects of this action. It makes Mr. Poston see that he has no choice but to pay. Write the letter for Mr. Lipman.

GALEN VICKI, D.D.S., SERIES

10. (*Early stage.*) Galen Vicki, D.D.S., M.S., practices orthodontics in a large city. Having begun his practice right after graduating from dental school, Dr. Vicki has established a standard procedure of payment for his patients, 90 percent of whom are referred to him by general dentists. First, Dr. Vicki evaluates the need for his services through a 30-minute interview and inspection. From this interview, he determines whether patients need braces and the extent and nature of the necessary services.

   Thereafter, other appointments are made to place the braces and adjust them periodically throughout the treatment period. After the first evaluation appointment, a contract is prepared and mailed to each patient indicating the total amount owed and the payment schedule. Standard treatment in the profession requires that one-fourth of the total amount be paid before any treatment is provided, with the balance of the amount owed paid in regular monthly payments for the duration of the treatment, due on the first of each month.

   Dr. Vicki has acquired a good number of patients in his relatively new practice. Most of them sign their contracts and pay the initial amounts; after three or four months, however, payments begin to lag and quickly become overdue. Thus, he requests that you design a collection series for him—one that will bring the accounts up-to-date without hurting the goodwill Dr. Vicki has with his patients.

   After talking with the doctor about contemporary collection practices, you design the following plan. When accounts are 30 days past due, you will send a statement. The next month you will send another statement, this one with a printed reminder saying "60 days past due." If these two statement notices do not bring results, you will send a form letter when the account is 90 days past due. Printed personally for each recipient, the letter will not use strong persuasion. It will emphasize as its central issue that payment probably has been overlooked. In addition, the letter will stress the quality of the professional care that the patient is receiving as a goodwill issue. Write this first-stage reminder letter to any one of Dr. Vicki's delinquent patients.

11. (*Middle stage.*) When the first letter does not bring in the money for Dr. Vicki, you will use a second letter. This one will be sent 30 days after the first. In addition to being later, the account is now larger, for another payment has become due.

    This will be a form letter that will attempt to persuade the clients that they "should pay." In it you will use the "fair is only fair" approach that you used for Dr. Vicki's early-stage debtors.

12. (*Late middle stage.*) If after another 30 days the fair-play letter described above does not work, you write a stronger letter. Also in the "should pay" category, this letter stresses the value of a good credit rating in the community. Because the next letter will be the last, you will make this one much stronger than the preceding one. Address it to any one of the good doctor's overdue accounts.

13. (*Last resort.*) When none of the previous efforts to collect for Dr. Vicki have worked, you send a final letter. It comes 30 days after the preceding effort, or 180 days after the account became due.

    This final letter talks about two actions. One is the termination of all services; that is, Dr. Vicki will no longer continue to provide the services for which money is owed. Second, Dr. Vicki will turn the account over to the MedCollect Agency with full authorization to collect, through the courts if necessary. You will talk about the consequences of these actions. Also, you will show how the debtor can avoid such collection efforts by paying before the deadline—15 days from the date of the letter.

THREE SIGMA MARKET RESEARCH, INC., SERIES

14. (*Early stage.*) As president of Three Sigma Market Research, Inc., your collection problem of the moment concerns the difficulty you are having getting the money owed you by Calhoun Home Development, Inc. Some six months ago, you met with the president of Calhoun, Carolyn Shelton, about the marketing research problem she was having with the development of Silver Leaves Estates, a 250-unit retirement village. You worked with Ms.

Shelton personally for four 8-hour days, and you conducted a market study that consumed 79 hours of employee time. Then you submitted the finished report to her. You were satisfied that your study gave the firm the information it needed for its project.

After submitting the report, you billed Calhoun $10,140 for services rendered. Thirty days later it had not paid; so you sent a duplicate bill. Now, an additional 31 days later, Calhoun Home Development still has not responded.

You feel it is time to send a gentle reminder. Because you had very cordial relations with Carolyn Shelton, you will take the approach that payment has been overlooked and that a friendly reminder will be appreciated. Write the letter.

15. (*Middle stage.*) You are disappointed that your reminder to Carolyn Shelton did not bring in the money. Now, 60 days later, you will write a second letter. This one will stress the fair-play appeal (We have given you something you needed; now how about doing something for us). You will prepare it so that the letter will include a 60:40 ratio of goodwill to persuasion.

16. (*Middle stage.*) Thirty days after sending the second letter to Calhoun Home Development, you wrote them another letter. It did not work. Now, 15 days later, you are ready to try your hand at writing to the company again. If this letter does not work, the next letter will announce last-resort action.

This fourth letter will stress the advantages of keeping a good credit report. And it will give convincing arguments to support the appeal. Keep the goodwill–persuasion ratio at about 35:65 as you prepare the letter.

17. (*Last resort.*) You do not like to do it, but you feel that you must take last-resort action to collect the $10,140 Calhoun Home Development owes you. If the firm does not pay within 15 days, you will take the matter to court. The letter will explain vividly the effects of this action. It will make Calhoun Home Development see that it has no choice but to pay. Prepare this last-resort letter.

18. (*Early stage.*) As Christen Chambers, co-owner of Chambers and Hornaday Design, you and your partner, Chad Hornaday, have been running a successful Web design business for three years. Actually, it started in college as a project for a small-business class. The success of the project led you to realize that not only did you and Chad have the talent and necessary skills to design Web sites for others, but that your ideas were good. In fact, with classmate Kevin Stamper as your main programmer, Chambers and Hornaday Design was profitable from the first month of operation.

Kevin's ability to quickly learn new cutting-edge technologies and employ them in your Web sites has given you a distinct competitive advantage in being able to present your firm as one on the forefront. Your ability to listen well to prospective clients and then show them that you can consistently provide exactly what they want has won you many new clients. Chad's good money management skills kept you in the black from the start. However, in examining your accounts last month, you and Chad noticed an increase in the percentage of late payers. In fact, one of your longest and best customers, a local charity group, has not paid in 60 days, even with two reminder letters.

Because you, Chad, and Kevin have all seen this charity on the local PBS station requesting funds, you know it is still active. In fact, the TV programming may have distracted the charity from paying its bills on time. Write a friendly letter persuading this client to pay. Remind the group members how useful the Web site is in helping them publicize their activities as well as bring in new pledges. You may even want to mention you saw them on PBS, giving out the Web site address to viewers and potential contributors.

19. (*Middle stage.*) Another 30 days have passed with no payment and no word from your client. However, you know the charity received lots of pledges during the TV fund drive, so you think you can persuade the members to pay now. Remind them that you have been providing the service for 90 days and it is only fair that they pay you for helping them be so successful in their drive. You may tell them how important you believe their cause is and even offer some ideas for ways your future services can enhance the number of people who visit their Web site. Make it clear that you expect them to pay, but work to maintain their goodwill.

20. (*Middle stage.*) You cannot believe it—no word from your client for another 30 days. While you still would like to keep this charity as a client and recognize that its funding cycles have wide swings, you still need to be paid for your services. In fact, your records show that, until now, the members paid on time from the first day they were clients. However, not only is their account four months past due but you have been continuing to support their Web page. Write a strong letter urging them to clear up their overdue account immediately. Give them good reasons why it is in their interest to pay you.

21. (*Last resort.*) Six months have passed without a single word or payment from the charity client. You are extremely disappointed with this nonaction and will write a last-resort letter. Chad tells you it is good business practice to continue to collect on nonprofits even though you do not like having to do it. However, rather than taking this group's members to court or even turning their account over to a collection agency, as you might with other clients, your actions will be serious but less severe. You will turn over their nonpayment record to the local credit agency as well as remove and stop supporting their Web site. Give them 15 days to pay you the full amount before you act. Try to express your sincere interest in doing business with them.

MEMORANDUMS

DIRECT MEMORANDUMS (INQUIRIES)

22. In your job at _____ (a nearby company of your choice) you are greatly disappointed in the writing ability of a number of your subordinates. Most are engineers well trained in their specialty areas. But their technical skills do not carry over to their writing. They need help.

    You believe that they (and perhaps others in other departments) could benefit from writing instruction. So you will write a memorandum to your training director to ask that the company sponsor a writing course. As you see it, the course should stress the basics of clear writing—word selection, sentence design, message organization, and such. It would even include the rudiments of grammar and punctuation, for you have noted many such problems in the writing of your people. You would recommend seven of your people for the program—more if there is room for them. But you suspect other departments would also want to send people.

    Although the training director might have other ideas, you will suggest that Professor _____ (your instructor) be hired to conduct the course. She (or he) has done this kind of work for other companies in the area and has an excellent reputation. You were a student in the professor's class a few years ago when you were with another company and can verify the quality of her (or his) teaching. Length of the course, expense, course design, and such would have to be worked out with the professor, but you will attach a copy of the syllabus the professor used in the 15-hour course you had with her (him).

    Now write the memorandum that will inform the training director of your needs.

23. For this assignment you are a trainee in the Department of Human Resources at the Montrose, Illinois, plant of Allied Industries. In recent months an increase in hiring has caused a major parking problem at the plant. There simply are not enough parking spaces to accommodate the plant's employees. And there is no short-run possibility for additional parking space. Something must be done, and soon.

    Your boss, Susan Bartosh, who is the director of human resources, has just returned from a meeting of company administrators. She tells you that the group addressed the parking problem and concluded that the best short-run solution would be to organize a car-pooling program. They devised the following plan:

    First, the plant manager will send all employees a persuasive message explaining the problem and seeking their cooperation. After this memorandum has been sent, your department will then send a memo to all department heads to get the information they need to start the program. As you expected, your boss assigned the letter writing task to you.

    As Ms. Bartosh explains, this memo will request that the department heads poll their employees to get the information your department needs. She isn't certain about all that should be requested, but she suggested the most obvious items in these words: "Certainly, you'll want the names of those already in car pools. They already are cooperating. And you'll want to know which of the remaining employees would be willing to form car pools and, if they are willing, whether they have preferences about who will be in their group. If they don't have group members in mind, we'll help them. For this task, you'll need the addresses of those willing to participate. You may need more information, so think through the problem. Then write the memo that will get the information you need. When the information comes in, you will be the one to form the groups."

    Now write the memo to the department heads, for Ms. Bartosh's signature, of course.

24. One year ago, the Employee Educational Support Program was begun at Wasson Industries. This program, which pays all tuition and book costs for employees wanting to further their education, was your brainchild. (You are the company's director of training.) You take pride in the program, but you don't yet know how effective it has been. Now you will try to get the information that will permit you to appraise the program's success.

    You will send a memorandum to the executive in charge of training at each of Wasson's 25 plants. You will ask each executive to summarize the educational activity under the program over the past year. Specifically, you'll need to know the number of employees who participated, the courses they studied, and their successes (or failures). Also, you need to know how much was spent for school charges and for other expenditures (books, fees, and such). Finally, you'd like to know the executive's personal assessment of the program. Does she or he think it is worthwhile? Can its continuation be justified?

    Although you will write the same memorandum to each of the 25 training executives, address this one to Hilda Nunez, the training director at the San Francisco plant.

25. You were surprised when you read recently that nearly 80 percent of all web sites provide access to databases. In addition, you also discovered that some of the most successful sites are those that provide for mass customization. For example, users answer a few questions about their needs, and the web site queries a database and provides a customized result.

    As Michael Deftos, director of your campus bookstore, you think such customization would help you compete effectively with the little book outlets around campus that seem to be skimming off your sales by offering low prices on textbooks for your university's large-volume classes. Not only is the campus bookstore a full-service store, supplying books and supplies for all university courses, but its profits go right back to the students through support of numerous campus projects. If students could enter their class lists and select the books they want for all their courses at one time, they might be more likely to purchase everything from you in one easy web interaction. Such a feature on your bookstore's web site might also generate sales of clothing and other items with the school's logo and mascot to students, alumni, and friends of the school.

Write a memo to the director of campus computer services, Ron Lycan, inquiring about implementing this kind of program on the bookstore's web site. Ask about costs, security, and recommendations for ongoing support. Ask other questions you have been wondering about, too. One that just crossed your mind concerns how quickly such a project could be up and running. Ask Ron for his response before the bookstore's advisory council meeting next Friday.

DIRECT MEMORANDUMS (RESPONSES)

26. Assume the role of Hilda Nunez at Wasson's San Francisco plant (see problem 24 for background details). You now have the information requested by the training director and will present it in memorandum form.

    So far, the educational program has moved slowly. Of the plant's 355 employees, 16 have taken advantage of the offer. The total cost to the company has been $12,874—$1,300 for fees, $9,980 for tuition, and $1,594 for books and supplies.

    Thirteen of the participants have completed 21 college courses without failure. Most (18) of the courses have been in business subjects (basic accounting, 6; management principles, 4; business communication, 4; basic finance, 2; and human resource management, 2). The remaining three were in history and English (2). Grades earned were A's, 7; B's, 5; and C's, 6. Two participants have taken trade school work in welding.

    Although the first year has been slow, you feel the program is gaining fast. In fact, during the past two weeks you have had a strong increase in questions and applications. In your mind, the program is a good means of developing administrators. Most of those enrolled have advancement goals in mind; and the courses they are taking will help them.

    Now write the memorandum that will give the training director the necessary information. You may supply any additional supporting facts needed as long as they are consistent with the information given above.

27. At its last meeting, the board of directors of _____ (a major company of your choice in your area) voted to sponsor three full-support scholarships to qualified children of employees. They determined the criteria and the selection process. And they decided on the school (your school was selected). Now they will need to determine the amount needed for the award. You, the administrative assistant to the chief executive officer, have been asked to get this information.

    What the board wants is a reasonable cost for nine months of support. This amount will include all school costs—tuition, fees, books, and such. Housing is a major item, for recipients will not be expected to live at home. Food, transportation, recreation, and incidentals also will be supported. In all cases, a modest amount will be allowed.

    Now it is your task to assemble this information by category. Costs of some items (tuition, fees) will be precise and easy to find. Most other costs will require some personal investigating and subjective estimating. You'll explain how you arrived at the estimates in your memo to the CEO.

28. Play the role of a department head at Magna-Tech Electronics and respond to a memorandum requiring you to recommend 10 percent of your workforce (rounded to the nearest whole number) for job termination. In recent months, business has been bad for the company—so bad that management decided that a reduction in force is in order. Thus, all department heads of the company received a request from the director of human resources telling them about the situation and asking them to respond by recommending who among their workers should be terminated.

    The memo indicated that you are to use job performance as the main criterion in justifying layoffs. If performance is difficult to measure, however, seniority can be used. If reductions in force would make it difficult to maintain a 10 percent reduction in production, an appeal for exception could be requested. In no case are age, sex, religion, race, or nationality to be used as criteria for layoffs.

    There are 13 workers in your department (shipping and storage). So, following the requirements of the memorandum, you will need to terminate only one.

    As you mentally review your 13 workers, you find the task both distasteful and difficult. All 13 are hardworking and efficient; not one of them deserves to be laid off. Since you must recommend one, however, you conclude that it will be either Merle Boyd or Martha Welch, both of whom have less seniority than any of the others. Merle has been on the job 13 months, and Martha 23. Both are hard workers, but Martha appears to have learned your storage and inventory procedures better than Merle, perhaps because she has been on the job longer.

    Both Martha and Merle have undergone one performance evaluation at Magna-Tech. Martha received the higher overall rating—88 percent as compared with Merle's 82. Although it's a subjective evaluation, you feel that Martha is also slightly better qualified because of her bright, outgoing personality and her willingness to work. Merle is a quiet person who doesn't often extend himself, though he has fulfilled every assignment satisfactorily.

    As pointed out in the memorandum outlining the procedure for recommending terminations, you have the right to appeal for exception if you have good reason. You believe you have good reason. For the past three months, your department has been unable to keep up with its work. You have asked for an additional shipping clerk. And now it appears that you will lose a worker rather than gain one. Perhaps other departments are experiencing a slowdown, but yours is not. Cutting a position would mean more expensive overtime. You could cut a position effectively only if production declined much more than it has.

In summary, your memorandum will have two messages. It will recommend who should be terminated, if someone must be. And it will appeal for an exception to the order requiring a reduction in the number of your workers.

29. Recently your company's chief financial officer, Michael McLaughlin, wrote you, as chief information officer, for ideas on ways to increase the security of your company's information. He reminded you that the value of this asset is growing more important all the time. However, he asked you not to address the external threats most people think of—hackers, competitors, or viruses—but the threats from internal sources. You were quite impressed that he recognized this recently acknowledged threat and were delighted that he asked for your recommendations.

After careful consideration, in your response you will recommend the following actions:

- Hire an external auditor to access the current system. Ask that the auditor be acquainted with both your industry and experienced with identifying internal problems.
- Write a policy that covers all who have access to your company's information. This should include all employees and temps as well as business partners and suppliers who access your extranet.
- Garner senior-level management support and educate top managers on the need for this policy.
- When distributing the policy to employees, provide training on the importance of protecting this valuable asset.
- Use tracking software to know who is logging on and off your computer systems and the frequency and times they are on the system. Pay attention to how many unauthorized users are attempting to log on to your system, too.
- Terminate access to your computer system immediately for all employees leaving your company. Remind them in their exit interviews of their obligation to keep company information confidential.

Be sure to thank Michael for his willingness to consult you, and offer to answer any other questions he may have.

DIRECT MEMORANDUMS (DIRECTIVES)

30. As assistant to the president of _____ (a large metropolitan bank of your choice), the president has asked you to write a directive in memorandum form prescribing a dress code for bank employees. The president wants two separate directives—one for men and one for women. (For class purposes, write the one for your sex.)

As you prepare to write this directive, you recall the president's instructions: "For years we have had an unwritten code specifying conservative dress and grooming for all employees who are visible to the public. Recently, however, more and more employees have strayed from this unwritten code. Every day I see our employees wearing some pretty far-out clothes, and some of their hairstyles and their use of cosmetics don't project the professional image of a bank. The situation appears to be getting worse. I want you to work up an appropriate set of dress and grooming standards that we can live with. Don't make them too stringent, but certainly rule out anything that would project a wrong image. Work up a first draft. Then we'll talk about it before we send it out."

Now you will begin to jot down the dress and grooming rules that you think will meet the president's requirements. When you have finished, write the memorandum that will convey them to the employees. You will deliver the directive in two ways—through email and on paper.

31. You are the director of human resources at the Hillsdale plant of Armstrong-Hundley, Inc., manufacturers of agricultural implements. Although the company's sales have been reasonably good, its profits have not. High operating costs at the outdated Hillsdale plant are largely to blame for the dismal profit picture. Top management has taken drastic action to correct this situation. It is closing the Hillsdale plant and shifting that plant's operations to the Jacksonville plant.

Employees at the Hillsdale plant may request transfer to the Jacksonville plant. As far as possible, the company will honor such requests. If more employees than can be accommodated request transfers, selections will be made on the basis of past performance and seniority. Armstrong-Hundley won't pay the expenses of transfer, such as moving expenses incurred by production workers, for there is no shortage of such workers in the Jacksonville area. However, the company will cover the moving expenses of administrators (department heads and up) and professionals (primarily engineers, human resource specialists, and accountants), because these people would be difficult to replace. The company can offer to help toward home sales, but selling a home should not be a problem in view of the current real estate boom in Hillsdale.

Your task now is to write a memorandum telling all department heads at the Hillsdale plant the facts of the company's decision. The memorandum will instruct them to call meetings of their employees at which they will explain what the company is doing and what the employees' options are. It will also tell the employees that they have one month to make their decisions. Information copies will go to the company's professionals and administrators. Assume that your memo will be distributed by email.

32. Play the role of an administrative trainee working as assistant to the plant manager of _____ (an area plant). Jonathan Dugan, your boss, has received a memo from a group of seven professionals (see

Problem 39 for additional information) requesting a change in employee parking. He likes the suggestion and has made preliminary plans to implement it.

In general, the new plan will assign all employees to specific parking lots. Middle managers; department heads; professionals (accountants, engineers, scientists, and such); and a few senior plant workers will be assigned to the 120 spaces in Lot A. This lot is at the plant entrance and is the most convenient. All other employees will be assigned to Lot B (390 spaces) and Lot C (512 spaces). Since Lot B is preferable to Lot C, assignments to Lot B will be based on seniority.

After lot assignments are made, the company will issue decals to be placed on windshields (upper left corner). These will identify lot assignments. All employees must fill out automobile registration cards, which will accompany the directive that will be sent to each employee. The cards will permit registration of a second car, if necessary. The cards must be returned within 15 days of the date of the directive. After all cards have been processed, lot assignments and decals will be sent to each employee. Plant security will be responsible for enforcing parking assignments.

Your boss has asked you to write the directive that will present all the information needed—for his signature, of course. If you think additional information is needed, you may supply it from your logical imagination; but be certain it is in keeping with the nature of the problem.

33. As Matt Lenaghan, manager for the local Target store, you know your company works hard to comply with all Occupational Safety and Health Administration (OSHA) standards. You both keep the required records and eliminate anything that would negatively affect the health and safety of your employees. However, this morning on your way to work, you heard on the radio a Department of Labor statistic on teen deaths and injuries in the workplace—70 teens are killed on the job and over 210,000 injured each year. Since you employ many teen workers part-time during both the Christmas season and summer vacations, you think it would be wise to increase the efforts your store makes to keep its teen workers safe.

Write a memo to all full-time employees encouraging them to help the teens they work with learn to recognize hazards and follow safe work practices. Remind them that the Fair Labor Standards Act not only limits the hours minors under 16 can work but also prohibits teens from driving a car or truck, operating heavy equipment, and using power tools. Let them know that the retail industry accounts for 51 percent of the teen injuries, so it is important that they stress safety with Target's teen workers.

Several steps can be taken to protect these teens, who are identified by their blue vests rather than the red ones worn by others. First, after training teens on a particular task, review the instructions to be certain they were understood clearly. Let teens know that if they have any questions, they should be sure to ask.

Second, explain and model the appropriate use of any safety equipment, and make sure that teens wear protective gear whenever needed. And finally, tell teens what accidents could happen and how they should handle them if they do.

In your memo, in addition to letting workers know what steps they can take, remind them that you welcome their ideas for improving the safety of both teens and other employees.

INDIRECT MEMORANDUMS (BAD NEWS)

34. As sales manager for Highfield Insurance Company, you must inform your salespeople that the boundaries of the company's sales districts are being revised. Your product is the insurance that borrowers from financial institutions can buy to cover payment of their loans in the event of their death. Your sales force sells the insurance to financial institutions, which in turn sell it to their customers.

In the past few years, you noticed that some of your salespeople make far more money than others, and you couldn't explain the differences by sales ability alone. So you looked into the matter carefully and found that the sales districts were far from equal in sales potential.

Perhaps their sales potential was nearly equal when they were formed, but much has happened since then. Some of the sales districts are now so large that their salespeople can work solely on the larger, more lucrative accounts and ignore the rest. The result, of course, is that Highfield is not served adequately in these districts.

You are therefore revising the district boundaries. You will reduce the size of the larger districts by as much as 50 percent. You will increase the size of some other districts. And you will add a few districts. The result, you feel, will be fair to both Highfield and the salespeople. You know, however, that some of the salespeople won't see it this way.

Now you must write a memorandum informing your salespeople of what you have done and why. You will write it in such a way that they will regard what you have done as fair even if they don't like it. In the memorandum, you will refer to an enclosure that describes the recipient's revised district.

35. Assume the role of the training director of _____ (the company chosen in Problem 22) and answer a memo from one of your department heads. The memo requests that you schedule a writing course for some of his or her employees. You always want to do all you can to honor such requests, for you like to see the department heads show interest in what you provide them. And normally you would eagerly provide the training they request. But this time you must make an exception. You can't comply with the request for the simple reason that your training budget is depleted. Heavy demands for specialized computer training have consumed all the funds for the year.

Even though you must refuse, you can offer some

hope. You can put the writing course in the hopper for consideration next year. And unless something unexpected occurs, you think it could be scheduled. There is also the possibility that someone within the company could teach the course at no additional expense. You will look through personnel records for such a person, and you'll put out the word to other administrators. Perhaps the department head who made the request can help in this search.

Write the memo that will give the answer. But try to present the bad news in a positive way. You don't want to discourage such an interest in training.

36. As the assistant to the training director of Moss Electronics, you have the sad assignment of sending a bad-news memo to Brad Tilden, a very nice and capable young employee. Last month Moss announced that it would grant a two-year leave with pay and cover all expenses for one qualified employee to pursue an MBA at a university of her or his choice.

Competition for the award was keen. Seventeen qualified employees applied. And after a process of elimination, two candidates remained: Brad Tilden and Monica Brashear. Both candidates had excellent credentials. The decision had to be based on a final interview with the selection committee, which had to make a subjective evaluation.

As chair of the selection committee, you thought Monica had a slight edge. The other committee members agreed with you. Even so, Brad is a competent and deserving young man. He has a bright future with the company.

Now you must write a memo to Brad that will inform him of the committee's decision. You will try hard to break the news gently. You want to keep him satisfied with his job and his company. Perhaps you can make him see that ranking in the final 2 out of a field of 17 is no small accomplishment.

37. As the office manager for a local Jacor radio station (you name one), you recently were asked by your boss to tell one of your radio-show hosts, Terry Patrick, that he could no longer come to work for a Jacor station dressed as he has been for the past few weeks.

What an unpleasant task! You know Terry will not be happy with the "new rule" for dress; but you also realize that it is in his best interest to know that management is unhappy. Since Terry has just been on the job three months, you think that one strategy for delivering this bad news is to educate him on the dress practices the Jacor management at this station expects. You know he has a terrific, upbeat personality; so you might even consider using a bit of creative humor that makes the point. And, of course, rather than standing behind company policy, you could give him several good reasons for changing. Explaining how Terry will benefit would be convincing, and some altruistic appeals would likely work well, too. Terry loves helping out at kids' sporting events as well as at the local boys' and girls' clubs. You could talk about the model he provides for young people both in his behavior and his dress.

In any case, be sure you deliver the bad news clearly so that he can make an informed choice on how to dress for work.

INDIRECT MEMORANDUMS (PERSUASIVE)

38. As director of employee relations for Anderson Foods, Inc., you are organizing an investment club in response to the requests of a small group of employees.

The goals of the club will be (1) to make money for the club's members and (2) to assist its members in learning about investing. Membership will be open to any interested employee. Members must invest at least $30 per month and will share in the club's assets on a basis proportionate to their investment. The club will meet monthly to discuss investment possibilities and will make its investment decisions by majority vote. Dr. Stanley Block, a finance professor at San Saba University, has agreed to serve as the club's advisor without compensation; and Charles Nixon, the company attorney, has agreed to help work up the club's charter.

You think the idea of an investment club is excellent, and you plan to join. To invest effectively, however, the club will need a large number of members. Thus, you will have to persuade employee to join. You will do this by sending a memo by email to all 464 Anderson employees.

Before your write the memo, you have some thinking to do. You must determine what appeals are likely to move employees to join the club. Should the appeal be to profit? To learning about investments? To the fellowship of group membership? To saving money? You'll think through all these possibilities— and more. For obvious reasons, you'll tell them when and where the first meeting will be held. (If you think you need additional information, you may supply it.)

39. Today at lunch you and six of your friends at work discussed the parking problem at your plant (select an area company). Unfortunately, all in the group voiced their disapproval of the current open parking rule. This rule gives every employee (except the plant manager and three other high-ranking executives) equal rights to parking spaces. Since most of you are professionals (accountants, scientists, engineers, department heads) who work 9 to 5, you get the spaces remaining after the 8:30-to-4:30 employees have taken their choices. Thus, you often have to park in distant lots.

After getting worked up in the discussion, the seven of you decided to present your case to the plant manager. And since you have a reputation as a skilled writer, the others elected you to compose the memo that will carry the message. But all seven will sign it.

As you begin your task, you think through the problem carefully. You will build a case that will logically support your goal. You'll take care not to give the impression that you are complaining "soreheads." Specifically, you'll ask for assigned parking lots for all employees with lot assignments based on status in the company. As you and your group see it, such assignments are earned and are not arbitrarily awarded.

Write the memo that you and your six friends will sign. Address it to Jonathan Dugan, Plant Manager.

40. You recently read a report by a senior research fellow at the Conference Board, a business research group, that described a growing trend in business appears to be sabbaticals—once the sole province of the teaching profession. Her report cited statistics that show at least 10 percent of large companies now offer some sort of paid leave and another 15 percent offer unpaid leaves of absence. Newer programs are being instituted that give four and eight weeks of paid leave to employees with 4 to 10 years of experience. Many of these leaves are often given to employees to perform some sort of community service that is beneficial to the company, too.

Your major reasons for wanting to implement a sabbatical at your company are to help curb turnover and to reward longevity. You realize that good employees are your most valuable assets. Not only do sabbaticals help reduce employee burnout, but they also boost productivity and morale. People who have taken sabbaticals report coming back to work with more energy and new ideas.

Write a persuasive memo to your boss, Paul Adami, suggesting that he propose this idea to the board of directors. In your persuasive efforts, you realize that you may have a few naysayers who believe such sabbaticals are nothing more than a paid vacation. In fact, some will probably argue that the company probably does not really need any employee who can be gone that long. Therefore, you clearly realize the importance of using an effective persuasive strategy.

41. Three months ago, you, the training director for Consummate Energy Company, were given an additional assignment—developing and running a fitness program for the company's 680 home-plant employees. You began this assignment by consulting with the fitness authorities at nearby Newton University. This was a good move, for Newton proved to have the answer to your needs.

First, Newton's administration will permit Consummate employees to use the Newton gymnasium and other athletic facilities (swimming pool, track, tennis courts, weight rooms, dressing rooms, and such) at the modest charge of $15 per month per participant if they restrict their use of these facilities to the period from 6:30 to 8:30 AM. (This is the only charge participants will pay.) Second, where needed, Newton's physical education specialists will assist the participants for a modest fee (Consummate will pay this). Third, Newton's fitness director has given you excellent help in working out a tentative program for your people. Now that you have the facilities and a tentative program, you must convince the employees that they should enroll. You will do this by means of a persuasive memo.

In the memo, you will announce the program and

try to sell it to the employees. Your persuasive appeal will bring out the primary ingredients of the program, emphasizing the choices that each participant can make. For those who like games, there will be basketball, tennis, racquetball, and volleyball. Runners and walkers can do their thing on indoor or outdoor tracks. Cindy Carmel, a widely recognized authority on aerobics, will conduct an aerobics group. Weight lifting will be supervised by Dr. Anthony Bienvenu, who will work out weight programs and provide instructions for those needing assistance. Swimmers and divers will have full use of Newton's heated Olympic-size pool and diving well. Such activities as gymnastics, dance, and calisthenics will be available if enough employees are interested in them. The format for each activity may be changed to fit the preferences of the participants. And efforts will be made to satisfy every employee preference.

In addition to describing activities and goals, you will use whatever strategy you think necessary to help sell the program. So you will think through the situation carefully. Then you will write the letter that will persuade employees to enroll. Don't forget to tell them how to sign up (you may determine specifics).

EMAIL MESSAGES

42. (*Direct inquiry.*) As Joan Marian, Director of Human Resources at Wiedenbach Incorporated, you have recently become very interested in having your company participate in online education. A good friend, Margaret Moen, told you that her company uses training from ZDNet University (http://www.zdu.com/) as a form of educational benefit. Employees who are preapproved are allowed to enroll in online continuing education classes. If they successfully complete the course, the company will cover all costs. While the tuition for these courses is rather inexpensive at $4.95 a month, the courses often require a book or special software program.

All classes are instructor-led and last four or eight weeks. They can be accessed anytime, allowing employees to take the courses from home or from work. Other features include office-hour chats with the instructor and use of online message boards. Online student lounges are available, where students can exchange tips, form study groups, and share problems and solutions. Sometimes special guests are also part of the classes.

This program sounds terrific to you, but you feel you need to know more before recommending that your company adopt this kind of educational program. Therefore, you decide to go to the ZDNet University web site to check it out yourself. While the site mentions costs, it does not talk about volume discounts or partnerships with companies. Also, as far as you can tell, it does mention quizzes, but it does not reveal how the authenticity of the user is verified. And as you peruse the sight, several other questions come to mind.

Write an email inquiry to the help desk using the questions form on the ZDNet site, asking all the questions you need answered before suggesting that your company participate in this kind of program.

43. (*Direct response.*) Today's email brought a request from your boss, Michael Rook, for cost-of-living comparisons for two job candidates your company may hire. One candidate might be moving to your area from San Diego, California, and the other from Moline, Illinois. He plans to offer both candidates $40,000 to be competitive with the job market in your area, but he wants to be armed with the information on cost of living when he makes the offers. Use at least two different web calculators to generate the numbers he wants and explain what each calculator includes. Some, for example, include various taxes and others do not. Respond to the request by email.

44. (*Directives.*) Your company seems to be doing all it can to promote wellness, since unplanned employee absenteeism can be very disruptive to your business. Not only do you have company-sponsored fitness programs, but you have worked closely with a nutritionist to design the menus in the company cafeteria that are both healthy and tasty. However, lately you have noticed that colds and the flu are spreading rampantly and repeatedly throughout your company.

Your employees seem reluctant to call in sick for several reasons. One major reason is the fear of retaliation from fellow employees for dumping their work on colleagues who are already overburdened. And in talking casually with employees, you have learned that they feel taking sick days may jeopardize their jobs, a fear that lingers from an earlier downsizing.

Although counterproductive because coming to work and infecting others hurts business, this behavior is consistent with national trends. A study by Commerce Clearing House (CCH), an Illinois provider of employment law information, found that unscheduled absenteeism is at its lowest rate in a decade.

While your objective is still to keep absenteeism rates low, you feel you must encourage supervisors to send sick employees home to keep these employees from spreading their cold and flu viruses to others. Instruct supervisors to send sick employees home directly or to the company nurse, who will decide whether the employee can stay or be sent home.

45. (*Indirect—bad news.*) As the manager of the local Safeway store, you have been evaluating your store's use of shelf space. In looking over sales data from the past three years, you have noticed a considerable growth in greeting card sales. This coincides with other reports you have read about the growth in sales of greeting cards in mass-related outlets such as drug and grocery stores.

Therefore, you invited representatives of both large and independent card companies to call on you to discuss the possibility of increasing their shelf space. Unfortunately, one representative apparently misunderstood your purpose. Today's email brought the following letter from the General Manager of Coloriginals, Inc., an independent cardmaker in Los Angeles.

[Your Name],

I am very disappointed to learn that the shelf space you promised us for our line of specialty greeting cards has not materialized.

Last month when I visited with you at your Safeway store in Mission Valley, we discussed increasing our shelf space 100 percent this year and another 50 percent next year. You viewed our line of hand-painted cards, noting that one particular card of a rose would be perfect for your parents' anniversary. You agreed that these crafted cards have much more appeal to your shoppers than computer-generated ones. And you were pleased to learn that these cards have a higher profit margin for you than those from the larger greeting card companies.

Please assure me that we still have this agreement and that the next time our representative visits your Mission Valley store she will find our cards prominently displayed. To order a complete line of our cards, please call us today at 1-888-555-1234 so we can ship them to you immediately. We look forward to providing your customers with quality, hand-painted cards, which will bring you a good return.

Candice Keller
General Manager

While you like the cards and the potential for profit, you have promised nothing. In fact, since you met with Ms. Keller last month, your current major supplier, Gibson Greetings, has asked you to hold off making any decision on shelf-space allocation. Gibson has received a surprise—an unsolicited buyout offer from American Greetings—and their shelf-space allocations were one of the major assets American Greetings was interested in acquiring. Since you have enjoyed a long and profitable relationship with Gibson, you have agreed to hold off on your decision until the buyout offer expires next month.

You must refuse Ms. Keller's request for an increase in shelf space at this time. However, to retain her goodwill you decide to offer a temporary compromise (you determine the compromise). Write an email message to her that will do so.

46. (*Indirect—persuasive.*) Send an email to all your employees, encouraging them to take part in the companywide program to recycle telephone books. Not only do you believe in eliminating waste, but you want to encourage your employees to help the environment, too. Remind them that all they need to do is to turn in their old phone books when they pick up their new ones this week. Tell them how fast, easy, and convenient it will be for them to do this before the end of the week while the telephone company's recycling bins are here.

9

Strategies in the Job-Search Process

Upon completing this chapter, you will be able to conduct an effective job search; compose effective job-application letters, résumés, and follow-up letters; and prepare for interviews. To reach these goals, you should be able to

1 Develop and use a network of contacts in your job search.

2 Assemble and evaluate information that will help you select a job.

3 Identify the sources that can lead you to an employer.

4 Compile traditional and electronic résumés that are strong, complete, and organized.

5 Write letters of application that skillfully sell your abilities.

6 Explain how you can participate effectively in an interview.

7 Write application follow-up letters that are appropriate, friendly, and positive.

8 Maintain your job-search skills.

The Job-Search Process

Introduce yourself to this chapter by assuming a role similar to one you are now playing. You are Jason Andrews, a student at Olympia University. In a few months, you will complete your studies for work in labor relations.

You believe that it is time to begin seeking the job for which those studies have been preparing you. But how do you do this? Where do you look? What does the search involve? How should you present yourself for the best results? The answers to these and related questions are reviewed in the following pages.

THE JOB SEARCH

- For success in job seeking, use the following procedures.

Of all the things you do in life, few are more important than getting a job. Whether it involves your first job or one further down your career path, job seeking is directly related to your success and your happiness. It is vital that you conduct the job search properly—that you prepare wisely and carefully and proceed diligently. The following review of job-search strategies should help you succeed.

BUILDING A NETWORK OF CONTACTS

- Begin the job search by building a network of contacts in this way:

You can begin the job search long before you are ready to find employment. In fact, you can do it now by building a network of contacts. More specifically, you can build relationships with people who can help you find work when you need it. Such people include classmates, professors, and businesspeople.

- (1) Broaden your circle of friends.

At present, your classmates are not likely to be holding positions in which they make or influence hiring decisions. But in the future, when you may want to make a career change, they may hold such positions. Right now, some of them may know people who can help you. The wider your circle of friends, the more likely you are to make employment contacts.

- (2) Know your professors.

Knowing your professors and making sure that they know you can also lead to employment contacts. Because professors often consult for business, they may know key executives and be able to help you contact them. Professors sometimes hear of position openings, and in such cases they can refer you to the hiring executives. Demonstrating your work ethic and your ability in the classroom is probably the best way to get your professors to know you and help you. Take advantage of opportunities to meet your professors outside the classroom, especially the professors in your major field.

- (3) Meet executives.

Obviously, meeting key business executives can also lead to employment contacts. You may already know some through family and friends. But broadening your relationships among businesspeople would be helpful. You can do this in various ways, but especially through college professional groups such as the Association for Information Technology Professionals, Delta Sigma Pi, and the Society for the Advancement of Management. By taking an active role in the organizations in your field of study, especially by working on program committees and by becoming an officer, you can get to know the executives who serve as guest speakers.

- (4) Make contacts through internships.

If your school offers internships, you can make good career contacts through them. But you should find the one that is best for you, that offers you the best training for your career objective. And by all means, do not regard an internship as just a job. Regard it as a foundation step in your career plan. The experience you gain and the contacts you make in an internship might lead to your first career position. In fact, if you perform well, your internship could turn into full-time employment.

- (5) Work with community organizations.

In addition to these more common ways of making contacts, you can use some less common ones. By working in community organizations (charities, community improvement groups, fund-raising groups), you can meet community leaders. By attending meetings of professional associations (every field has them), you can meet the leaders in your field. In fact, participation in virtually any activity that provides contacts with business leaders can open doors for you now and in the future.

IDENTIFYING APPROPRIATE JOBS

To find the right job, you need to investigate both internal and external factors. The best fit occurs when you have carefully looked at yourself—your education, personal qualities, experience, and any special qualifications. However, to be realistic, these internal qualities need to be analyzed in light of the external factors. Some of these factors may include the current and projected job market, economic needs, location preferences, and family needs.

- Look at both your internal and external factors.

ANALYZING YOURSELF.   When you are ready to search for a job, you should begin the effort by analyzing yourself. In a sense, you should look at yourself much as you would look at a product or service that is for sale. After all, when you seek employment, you are really selling your ability to work—to do things for an employer. A job is more than something that brings you money. It is something that gives equal benefits to both parties—you and your employer. Thus, you should think about the qualities you have that enable you to do the work that an employer needs to have done. This self-analysis should cover the following categories.

- Begin with a self-analysis covering these background areas:

EDUCATION.   The analysis might well begin with education. Perhaps you have already selected your career area such as accounting, finance, information systems, management, or marketing. If you have, your task is simplified, for your specialized curriculum has prepared you for your goal. Even so, you may be able to note special points—for example, electives that have given you special skills or that show something special about you (such as psychology courses that have improved your human-relations skills, communication courses that have improved your writing and speaking skills, or foreign language courses that have prepared you for international assignments).

- (1) Education. For specialized curricula, the career path is clear.

If you have pursued a more general curriculum (general business, liberal arts, or such), you will need to look at your studies closely to see what they have prepared you to do. Perhaps you will find an emphasis on computers, written communication, human relations, foreign languages—all of which are sorely needed by some businesses. Or perhaps you will conclude that your training has given you a strong general base from which to learn specific business skills.

- For general curricula, a career choice must be made.

In analyzing your education, you should look at the quality of your record—grades, honors, special recognitions. If your record is good, you can emphasize it. But what if your work was only mediocre? As we will point out later, you will need to shift the emphasis to your stronger sales points—your willingness to work, your personality, your experience. Or perhaps you can explain, for example, by noting that while working your way through school may have limited your academic performance, it gave you valuable business skills.

- Consider quality of educational record (grades, honors, courses taken).

"It says here in your resume that you're an experienced poofreader."

- (2) Personal qualities (people skills, leadership, and such).

PERSONAL QUALITIES.   Your self-analysis should also cover your personal qualities. Qualities that relate to working with people are especially important. Qualities that show leadership or teamwork ability are also important. And if you express yourself well in writing or speaking, note this, for good communication skills are valuable in most jobs.

Of course, you may not be the best judge of your personal qualities, for we do not always see ourselves as others see us. You may need to check with friends to see whether they agree with your assessments. You may also need to check your record for evidence supporting your assessments. For example, organization membership and participation in community activities are evidence of people and teamwork skills. Holding office in an organization is evidence of leadership ability. Participation on a debate team or college bowl is evidence of communication skills.

- (3) Work experience (with interpretations).

WORK EXPERIENCE.   If you have work experience, you should analyze it. Work experience in your major deserves emphasis. In fact, such work experience becomes more and more important as you move along in your career. Work experience not related to the job you seek can also tell something important about you—even if the work was part-time. Part-time work can show willingness and determination, especially if you have done it to finance your education. And almost any work experience can help develop your skills in dealing with people.

- (4) Special qualities (languages, communication skills, and such).

SPECIAL QUALIFICATIONS.   Your self-analysis should also include special qualifications that might be valuable to an employer. The ability to speak a foreign language can be very helpful for certain international businesses. Athletic participation, hobbies, and interests may also be helpful. To illustrate, athletic experience might be helpful for work for a sporting goods distributor, a hobby of automobile mechanics might be helpful for work with an automotive service company, and an interest in music might be helpful for work with a piano manufacturer.

- Combine internal and external factors.

ANALYZING OUTSIDE FACTORS.   After you have analyzed yourself, you need to combine this information with the work needs of business and other external influences. Your goal in this process is to give realistic direction to your search for employment. Where is the kind of work you are seeking available? Are you willing to move? Is such a move compatible with others in your life—your partner, your children, your parents? Does the location meet with your lifestyle needs? Although the availability of work may drive the answer to some of these questions, you should answer them as well as you can on the basis of what you know now and then conduct your job search accordingly. Finding just the right job should be one of the most important goals in your life.

FINDING YOUR EMPLOYER

- Search for potential employers by using these sources:

You can use a number of sources in your search for an employer with whom you will begin or continue your career. Your choice of sources will probably be influenced by the stage of your career.

- (1) your school's placement center,

PLACEMENT CENTERS.   If you are just beginning your career, one good possibility is the placement center at your school. Most large schools have placement centers, and these attract employers who are looking for suitable applicants. Many placement centers offer excellent job-search counseling and maintain databases on registrants containing school records, résumés, and recommendation letters for review by prospective employers. Most have directories listing the major companies with contact names and addresses.

- (2) your network of personal contacts,

NETWORK OF PERSONAL CONTACTS.   As has been noted, the personal contacts you make can be extremely helpful in your job search. In fact, according to some employment reports, personal contacts are the leading means of finding employees. Obviously, personal contacts are more likely to be a source of employment opportunities later in your career—when you may need to change jobs.

- (3) classified advertisements,

CLASSIFIED ADVERTISEMENTS.   Help-wanted advertisements in newspapers and professional journals, either online or in print provide good sources of employment op-

Web Page Résumés Can Work for You

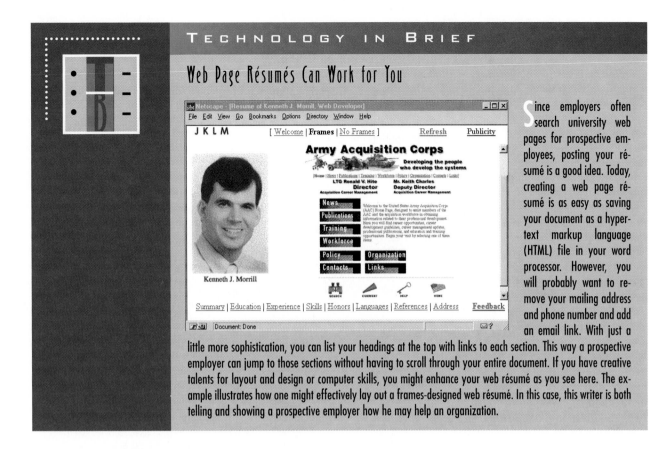

Since employers often search university web pages for prospective employees, posting your résumé is a good idea. Today, creating a web page résumé is as easy as saving your document as a hypertext markup language (HTML) file in your word processor. However, you will probably want to remove your mailing address and phone number and add an email link. With just a little more sophistication, you can list your headings at the top with links to each section. This way a prospective employer can jump to those sections without having to scroll through your entire document. If you have creative talents for layout and design or computer skills, you might enhance your web résumé as you see here. The example illustrates how one might effectively lay out a frames-designed web résumé. In this case, this writer is both telling and showing a prospective employer how he may help an organization.

portunities for many kinds of work. Many are limited, however, in the opportunities they provide for new college graduates. Classified ads are good sources for experienced workers who are seeking to improve their positions, and they are especially good sources for people who are conducting a major search for high-level positions. However, they are only a partial list of jobs available.

ONLINE DATABASES.   In addition to finding opportunities in classifieds, you will also find them in online databases. E-span, for example, lists jobs available throughout the country, with new opportunities posted regularly. Some companies even post job openings on the web. While many of these are posted on intranets, some companies open their systems to all interested job seekers. And, of course, there are some private online companies that will place your résumé and companies' jobs in databases that can be accessed for a fee. Furthermore, you could query users of newsgroups or listservs about job openings they know exist. All of these online systems are sources for job opportunities.

■ (4) online databases,

EMPLOYMENT AGENCIES.   Companies that specialize in finding jobs for employees can be useful. Of course, such companies charge for their services. The employer sometimes pays the charges, usually if qualified applicants are scarce. While employment agencies are commonly used to place experienced people in executive positions, they can also help job seekers gain temporary employment.

■ (5) employment agencies,

Temping can lead to permanent employment with a good fit. It allows the worker to get a feel for the company and the company to observe the worker before making a job commitment.

WEB PAGES.   To make yourself more visible to potential employers, you may want to consider posting your résumé to the web. Some employers actively search for new employees on university web pages. And most of today's word processors let you save your documents in hypertext markup language (HTML), creating a basic web page for you. It is a good idea to link your web page to your major department or to a business student

■ (6) web pages,

club, allowing more potential employers to find your résumé. With a little extra effort, you can create a web page that greatly expands on the printed résumé. You will need to put your web page address on your printed résumé.

(7) prospecting techniques.

PROSPECTING.   Some job seekers approach prospective employers directly, either by personal visit or by mail (or email). Personal visits are effective if the company has an employment office or if a personal contact can set up a visit. Mail contacts typically include a résumé and an application letter. The construction of these messages is covered later in the chapter.

Résumés and Application Letters

In your role as Jason Andrews, you consider yourself well qualified for a career in labor relations. You know the field from both personal experience and classroom study. You grew up in a working-class neighborhood. From an early age, you worked at a variety of jobs, the most important of which was a job as a shipping and receiving clerk. You were a truck driver and a member of the Teamsters for two years. Your college studies were especially designed to prepare you for a career in labor relations. You studied Olympia University's curriculum in industrial relations, and you carefully chose the electives that would give you the best possible preparation for this career. As evidenced by your grades, your preparation was good.

Now it is time to begin your career. Over the past weeks you followed good procedures in looking for employment (as reviewed in the preceding pages). Unfortunately, you had no success with the recruiters who visited your campus. Now you will send written applications to a select group of companies that you think might use a person with your skills. You have obtained the names of the executives you should reach at these companies. You will mail them the application package—résumé and application letter. The following discussion shows you how to prepare these documents for best results.

PREPARING THE APPLICATION DOCUMENTS

Pursue job openings by personal visit or by mail.

After your search has uncovered a job possibility, you pursue it. How you pursue it depends on the circumstances of the case. When it is convenient and appropriate to do so, you make contact in person. It is convenient when the distance is not great, and it is appropriate when the employer has invited such a contact. When a personal visit is not convenient and appropriate, you apply by mail, email, or fax.

You are likely to use résumés, application letters, and reference sheets in your job search.

Whether or not you apply in person, you are likely to use some written material. If you apply in person, probably you will take a résumé with you to leave as a record of your qualifications. If you do not apply in person, of course, the application is completely in writing. Typically, it consists of a résumé, a letter of application, and a reference sheet. At some point in your employment efforts, you are likely to use each of these documents.

Prepare them as you would prepare a sales mailing.

Preparing these documents is much like preparing a sales mailing. They all involve selling. You are selling a product or services—your ability to do work. The résumé and reference sheet are much like the supporting material that accompanies the sales letter. The application letter is much like the sales letter. These similarities should become obvious to you as you read the following pages.

Study the product (you) and the work.

As in preparing a sales mailing, you begin work on a written application for a job by studying what you are selling. And what you are selling is you. Then you study the work. Studying yourself involves taking personal inventory—the self-analysis discussed earlier in the chapter. You should begin by listing all the information about you that you believe an employer would want to know. Studying the work means learning as much as you can about the company—its plans, it policies, its operations. It also means learning the requirements of the work that the company wants done. Sometimes you can get this information through personal investigation. More often, you will have to develop it through logical thinking.

With this preliminary information assembled, you are ready to plan the application. First, you need to decide just what your application will consist of. Will it be just a letter; a letter and a résumé (also called a *vita, qualifications brief,* or *data sheet*) or a letter, résumé, and reference sheet? The résumé is a summary of background facts in list form. You will probably select the combination of letter and résumé, for this arrangement is likely to do the best job. Some people prefer to use the letter alone. When this is done, the letter usually contains much detail, for it must do the whole sales job. You will include the reference sheet when asked or when it supports your case.

■ Next, decide on whether to send a letter alone or with a résumé.

After you've decided to use the résumé, you must decide whether to use the traditional or electronic format. The traditional is used in face-to-face interviews where you know it will be used exclusively there. If you have reason to believe the company will store your résumé electronically, you should use the electronic formation. Some recommend preparing both formats. Constructing these forms are similar, but they differ in some very important ways.

■ Choose the traditional or electronic format.

CONSTRUCTING THE TRADITIONAL RÉSUMÉ

After deciding what your form will be, you construct the parts. Perhaps you will choose to begin with the résumé, for it is a logical next step from the self-analysis discussed above. In fact, the résumé is a formal arrangement of that analysis.

■ The résumé lists facts in some orderly way.

You will want to include in the résumé all background information you think the reader should have about you. This means including all the information that is reviewed in an accompanying letter plus supporting and incidental details. Designed for quick reading, the résumé lists facts that have been arranged for the best possible appearance. Rarely does it use sentences.

The arrangements of résumés differ widely, but the following procedures generally describe how most are written:

- Logically arrange information on education (institutions, dates, degrees, major field); information on employment (dates, places, firms, duties, accomplishments); personal details (memberships, interests, achievements, and such—but not religion, race, and sex); and special information derived from other information (achievements, qualifications, capabilities). Add a reference sheet as needed.
- Construct a heading for the entire résumé and subheadings for the parts.
- Include other vital information such as objectives and contact information.
- Arrange the data for best eye appeal, making the résumé balanced, not crowded, and not strung out.

■ Follow this plan in constructing a résumé.

SELECTING THE BACKGROUND FACTS.   Your first step in preparing the résumé is to review the background facts you have assembled about yourself and then to select the facts that you think will help your reader evaluate you. You should include all the information covered in the accompanying letter, for this is the most important information. In addition, you should include significant supporting details not covered in the accompanying letter to avoid cluttering it.

■ Begin by reviewing the background facts you have assembled. Select the facts that will help the reader evaluate you.

ARRANGING THE FACTS INTO GROUPS.   After selecting the facts you want to include, you should sort them into logical groups. Many grouping arrangements are possible. The most conventional is the three-part grouping of *Education, Experience,* and *Skills* or *Personal Qualities.* Another possibility is a grouping by job functions or skills, such as *Selling, Communicating,* and *Managing.* Yet another is an arrangement by time—perhaps listing the information in reverse chronological order to show a progression of training and experience. You may be able to work out other logical arrangements.

■ Sort the facts by conventional groups, job functions, time, or a combination.

You can also derive additional groups from the four conventional groups mentioned above. For example, you can have a group of *Achievements.* Such a group would consist of special accomplishments taken from your experience and education information. An-

■ Also, consider groups such as *Achievements* and *Qualifications.*

other possibility is to have a group consisting of information highlighting your major *Qualifications*. Here you would include information drawn from the areas of experience, education, and skills or personal qualities. Illustrations of and instructions for constructing groups such as these appear later in the chapter.

■ Write headings for the résumé and its parts.

CONSTRUCTING THE HEADINGS. With your information organized, a logical next step is to construct the headings (captions) for the résumé. Probably you will begin by constructing the main head—the one that covers the entire document.

■ Topic heads are most common.

The most widely used form of main head is the topic, which consists only of words that describe what follows. Your name is usually the main heading. It should be presented clearly; usually this means using larger and bolder type so that the name stands out from the rest of the résumé. If an employer remembers only one fact from your résumé, that fact should be your name. It can be presented in either all caps or caps and lowercase:

Terrence P. Lenaghan

The next level of headings might be *Objective, Education, Experience,* and *Skills.* These headings can be placed to the left or centered above the text that follows.

■ Talking heads interpret for the reader.

A second and less widely used form is the talking head. This form uses words that tell the nature of what follows. For example, instead of the topic head, *Education,* a talking head might read *Specialized Training in Accounting* or *Computer Software Program Skills Acquired.* Obviously, these heads add to the information covered. They help the reader interpret the facts that follow.

■ Distinguish the headings from the other information by font selection.

As you can see from the illustrations in the chapter, the headings are distinguished from the other information in the résumé by the use of different sizes and styles of type. The main head should appear to be the most important of all (larger and heavier). Headings for the groups of information should appear to be more important than the information under them. Good business etiquette requires that you choose heading forms carefully, making sure they are neither so heavy and large that they offend nor so light and small that they show no distinctions. Your goal is to choose forms that properly show the relative importance of the information and are pleasing to the eye.

■ Display your contact information prominently.

INCLUDING CONTACT INFORMATION. Your address and telephone number are the most likely means of contacting you. Thus, you should display them prominently somewhere in the résumé. You may also want to display your fax number, email address, or web page address. The most common location for displaying contact information is at the top, under the main head.

■ Anticipate changes in contact information.

When it is likely that your address or telephone number will change before the job search ends, you would be wise to include two addresses and numbers—one current and the other permanent. If you are a student, for example, your address at the time of applying for a job may change before the employer decides to contact you. Therefore, you may want to consider using an answering service so that you can receive your messages wherever you go.

■ Consider a statement of your objective.

INCLUDING A STATEMENT OF OBJECTIVE. Although not a category of background information, a statement of your objective is appropriate in the résumé. Headings such as *Career Objective, Job Objective,* or just *Objective* usually appear at the beginning.

■ However, note that some authorities oppose it.

Not all authorities agree on the value of including the objective, however. Recommending that they be omitted from today's résumés, some authorities suggest that the résumé should concentrate instead on skills, experience, and credentials. Some experts argue that the objective includes only obvious information that is clearly suggested by the remainder of the résumé. They argue also that an objective limits the applicant to a single position and eliminates consideration for other jobs that may be available.

■ Even so, probably you should use it.

Those favoring the use of a statement of objective reason that it helps the recruiter see quickly where the applicant might fit into the company. Since this argument appears to have greater support, at least for the moment, probably you should include the objective. But make an exception when your career goal is unclear and you are considering a variety of employment possibilities.

Primarily, your statement of objective should describe the work you seek. When you can, you should add to its effectiveness by including words that convey a long-term interest, as in this example:

Objective: A position in human resource management that will provide an opportunity for growth and advancement.

Another technique for enhancing the effectiveness of the objective statement is to include words that emphasize your major qualifications for the work, as in this example:

Objective: To apply 17 years of successful high-tech sales experience to selling quality products for an agile company.

Also, for a résumé tailored to fit a specific company, the wording can include the company name and exact job title the company uses:

Job Objective: Sales Representative for Johnson & Johnson leading to sales management.

PRESENTING THE INFORMATION.   The information you present under each heading will depend on your good judgment. You should list all the facts that you think are relevant. You will want to include enough information to enable the reader to judge your ability to do the work you seek.

Your coverage of work experience should identify completely the jobs you have held. A minimum coverage would include dates, places, firms, and responsibilities. If the work was part-time, you should say so without demeaning the skills you developed on the job. In describing your duties, you should select words that highlight what you did, especially the parts of this experience that qualify you for the work you seek. Such a description will reflect your practice of good business etiquette. For example, in describing a job as credit manager, you could write "Credit analyst for Federated Stores, St. Petersburg, Florida, 1997–99." But it would be more meaningful to give this fuller description: "Credit analyst for Federated Stores, St. Petersburg, Florida, 1997–99, supervising a staff of seven in processing credit applications and communications."

If your performance on a job shows your ability to do the work you seek, you should consider emphasizing your accomplishments in your job description. For example, an experienced marketer might write this description: "Marketing specialist for Colgate-Palmolive, 1996–99. Served in advisory role to company management. Developed marketing plan that increased profits 24 percent in two years." Or a successful advertising account executive might write this description: "Phillips-Ramsey Agency, San Diego, 1997–99. As account executive, developed successful campaigns for nine accounts and led development team in increasing agency volume 18 percent."

As you can see from the examples above, the job descriptions are strengthened by the use of action verbs. Verbs are the strongest of all words. If you choose them well, they will do much to sell your ability to do work. A list of the more widely used action verbs appears in Figure 9.1.

Because your education is likely to be your strongest selling point for your first job after college, you will probably cover it in some detail. (Education gets less and less emphasis in your applications as you gain experience.) At a minimum, your coverage of education should include institutions, dates, degrees, and areas of study. For some jobs, you may want to list specific courses, especially if you have little other information to present or if your coursework has uniquely prepared you for those jobs. If your grade-point average (GPA) is good, you may want to include it. Remember, for your résumé, you can compute your GPA in a way that works best for you as long as you label it accurately. For example, you may want to select just those courses in your major, labeling it Major GPA. Or if your last few years were your best ones, you may want to present your GPA for just that period. In any case, include GPA when it works favorably for you.

What personal information to list is a matter for your best judgment. In fact, the trend appears to be toward eliminating such information. If you do include personal information, you should probably omit race, religion, sex, age, and marital status because current laws prohibit hiring based on them. But not everyone agrees on this matter. Some authorities believe that at least some of these items should be included. They argue that the law only pro-

- The statement should cover the job you seek and more, as in these examples.

- List the facts under the headings.

- When covering work experience, at a minimum include dates, places, firms, and responsibilities.

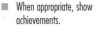

- When appropriate, show achievements.

- Use action verbs to strengthen the appeal.

- For education, include institutions, dates, degrees, and areas of study.

- For legal reasons, some personal information (on race, religion, sex) should probably not be listed.

FIGURE 9.1 A List of Action Verbs That Add Strength to Your Résumé

The underlined words are especially good for pointing out **accomplishments.**

Management skills
administered
analyzed
assigned
attained
chaired
consolidated
contracted
coordinated
delegated
developed
directed
evaluated
executed
improved
increased
organized
oversaw
planned
prioritized
produced
recommended
reviewed
scheduled
strengthened
supervised

Communication skills
addressed
arbitrated
arranged
authored
collaborated
convinced
corresponded
developed
directed
drafted
edited
enlisted
formulated
influenced

interpreted
lectured
mediated
moderated
negotiated
persuaded
promoted
publicized
reconciled
recruited
spoke
translated
wrote

Research skills
clarified
collected
critiqued
diagnosed
evaluated
examined
extracted
identified
inspected
interpreted
interviewed
investigated
organized
reviewed
summarized
surveyed
systematized

Technical skills
assembled
built
calculated
computed
configured
designed
devised
engineered
fabricated

installed
maintained
operated
overhauled
performed troubleshooting
programmed
remodeled
repaired
retrieved
solved
upgraded

Teaching skills
adapted
advised
clarified
coached
communicated
coordinated
demystified
developed
enabled
encouraged
evaluated
explained
facilitated
guided
informed
instructed
persuaded
set goals
stimulated
trained

Financial skills
administered
allocated
analyzed
appraised
audited
balanced
budgeted
calculated
computed

developed
forecast
managed
marketed
planned
projected
researched

Creative skills
acted
conceptualized
created
customized
designed
developed
directed
established
fashioned
founded
illustrated
initiated
instituted
integrated
introduced
invented
originated
performed
planned
revitalized
shaped

Helping skills
assessed
assisted
clarified
coached
counseled
demonstrated
diagnosed
educated
expedited
facilitated
guided
motivated

referred
rehabilitated
represented

Clerical or detail skills
approved
arranged
catalogued
classified
collected
compiled
executed
generated
implemented
inspected
monitored
operated
organized
prepared
processed
purchased
recorded
retrieved
screened
specified
systematized
tabulated
validated

More verbs for accomplishments
achieved
expanded
improved
pioneered
reduced (losses)
resolved (problems)
restored
spearheaded
transformed

Source: *The Damn Good Resume Guide* © 1996 by Yana Parker. Reprinted by permission of Ten Speed Press, Berkeley, California.

- Information on activities and interests tells about one's personal qualities.

- Consider listing references, but know that some authorities favor postponing using them.

hibits employers from considering such information in hiring—that it does not prohibit applicants from presenting the information. They reason that if such information helps you, you should use it. The illustrations shown in this chapter support both viewpoints.

Personal information that is generally appropriate includes all items that tell about your personal qualities. Information on your organization memberships, civic involvement, and social activities is evidence of experience and interest in working with people. Hobbies and athletic participation tell of your balance of interests. Such information can be quite useful to some employers, especially when personal qualities are important to the work involved.

Authorities disagree on whether to list references on the résumé. Some think that references should not be contacted until negotiations are further along. Others think that references should be listed because some employers want to check them early in the screening process. One recent study of human resource administrators in Fortune 500 organizations rated the importance of references on résumés of recent college graduates as the lowest of all major groupings—between not too important and somewhat important.[1] Clearly, both views have substantial support. You will have to make the choice based on your best knowledge of the situation.

When you do list someone as a reference, good business etiquette requires that you ask for permission first. While you plan to use only those who can speak highly of you, sometimes asking for your reference's permission beforehand helps that person prepare better. And, of course, it saves you from unexpected embarrassment such as a reference not remembering you, being out of town, or, worse yet, not having anything to say.

A commonly used tool is a separate reference sheet. When you use it, you close the résumé with a statement indicating references are available. Later, when the reader wants to check references, you give her or him this sheet. The type size and style of the main heading of this sheet should match that used in your résumé. It will say something like "References for [*your name*]." Below this heading is a listing of your references, beginning with the strongest one. In addition to solving the reference dilemma, use of this separate reference sheet allows you to change both the references and the ordering of them for each job. A sample reference sheet is shown in the example in Figure 9.5.

Sometimes you may have good reason not to list references, as when you are employed and want to keep the job search secret. If you choose not to list them, you should explain their absence. You can do this in the accompanying letter; or you can do it on the résumé by following the heading "References" with an explanation, such as "Will be furnished on request."

How many and what kinds of references to include will depend on your background. If you have an employment record, you should include one for every major job you have held—at least for recent years. You should include references related to the work you seek. If you base your application heavily on your education or your personal qualities, or both, you should include references who can vouch for these areas—professors, clergy, community leaders, and the like. Your goal is to list those people who can verify the points on which your appeal for the job is based. At a minimum, you should list three references. Five is a good maximum.

Your list of references should include accurate mailing addresses, with appropriate job titles. Complete addresses are important because the reader is likely to write the references. Also useful are telephone and fax numbers as well as email addresses. Job titles (officer manager, president, supervisor) are helpful because they show what the references are able to tell about you. It is good etiquette to include appropriate forms of address—Mr., Mrs., Ms., Dr., and so on.

ORGANIZING FOR STRENGTH.   After you have identified the information you want to include on your résumé, you will want to organize or group items to present yourself in the best possible light. Three strategies for organizing this information are the *reverse chronological approach,* the *functional* or *skills approach,* and the *accomplishments/achievements* or *highlights approach.*

The *reverse chronological* organizational layout (Figures 9.6 and 9.7), presents your education and work experience from the most recent to oldest. It emphasizes the order and time frame in which you have participated in these activities. It is particularly good for those who have progressed in an orderly and timely fashion through school and work.

A *functional* or *skills* layout (Figure 9.8) organizes around three to five areas particularly important to the job you want. Rather than forcing an employer to determine that you developed one skill on one job and another skill on another job, this organizational plan does that for the reader. It is particularly good for those who have had many jobs, for those who have taken nontraditional career paths, and for those who are changing fields. Creating this kind of résumé takes much work and careful analysis of both jobs and skills to show the reader that you are a good match for the position.

An *accomplishments/achievements* layout (Figure 9.9) presents a picture of you as a competent worker. It puts hard numbers and precise facts behind skills and traits you have.

----

[1] Kevin L. Hutchinson and Diane S. Brefka, "Personnel Administrators' Preferences for Resume Content: Ten Years After," *Business Communication Quarterly,* June 1997, pp. 71–72.

- Good etiquette requires that you get permission.

- Consider using a separate sheet for references.

- Select references that cover your background.

- Include accurate mailing addresses and job titles.

- Choose an organizational strategy that best presents your case.

- The reverse chronological approach is orderly.

- The functional or skills approach emphasizes relevant skills.

- The accomplishments/achievements approach shows you can perform.

FIGURE 9.2 Good Standard Typefaces for Scannable Resumes

Futura	**Courier**
Format for accuracy	Format for accuracy
Organize for strength	Organize for strength
Helvetica	**Century Schoolbook**
Format for accuracy	Format for accuracy
Organize for strength	Organize for strength
ITC Officina Sans	**Garamond**
Format for accuracy	Format for accuracy
Organize for strength	Organize for strength
Univers	**Times New Roman**
Format for accuracy	Format for accuracy
Organize for strength	Organize for strength

Refer back to Figure 9.1 for some good verb choices to use in describing accomplishments. Here is an example illustrating this arrangement in describing work done at a particular company:

Successfully managed the Austin store for two years in a period of economic decline with these results:

- Increased profits 37 percent.
- Reduced employee turnover 55 percent.
- Grew sales volume 12 percent.

> The highlights or summary approach shows you are a good fit for the position.

Information covered under a *Highlights* or *Summary* heading may include key points from the three conventional information groups—education, experience, and personal qualities. Typically, this layout emphasizes the applicant's most impressive background facts that pertain to the work sought, as in this example:

Highlights

- **Experienced:** three years of practical work as programmer/analyst in designing and developing financial software for the banking industry.
- **Highly trained:** B.S. degree with honors in computer science.
- **Self-motivated:** proven record of successful completion of independent work on major projects.

Although such items may overlap others in the resume, using them in a separate group emphasizes strengths. See an example of an accomplishments layout in Figure 9.9.

> List the information without use of personal pronouns (I, we, you).

> Use the same grammatical form for all equal-level headings and for the parts listed under each heading.

WRITING IMPERSONALLY AND CONSISTENTLY. Because the résumé is a listing of information, you should write without personal pronouns (no *I*'s, *we*'s, *you*'s). You should also write all equal-level headings and the parts under each heading in the same grammatical form. For example, if one major heading in the résumé is a noun phrase, all the other major headings should be noun phrases. The following four headings illustrate the point. All but the third (an adjective form) are noun phrases. The error can be corrected by making the third a noun phrase, as in the examples to the right:

Not Parallel	**Parallel**
Specialized study	Specialized study
Experience in promotion work	Experience in promotion work
Personal and physical	Personal and physical qualities
Qualified references	Qualified references

Illustrating grammatical inconsistency in the parts of a group are the following items:

Have good health

Active in sports

Ambitious

Inspection of these items shows that they do not fit the same understood words. The understood word for the first item is *I* and for the second and third, the understood words are *I am*. Any changes that make all three items fit the same understood words would correct the error.

MAKING THE FORM ATTRACTIVE.   The attractiveness of your résumé will say as much about you as the words. The appearance of the information that the reader sees plays a part in forming his or her judgment. A sloppy, poorly designed presentation may even ruin your chances of getting the job. Thus, you have no choice but to give your résumé and your application letter an attractive physical arrangement.

■ Make the résumé attractive.

Designing the résumé for eye appeal is no routine matter. There is no one best arrangement, but a good procedure is to approach the task as a book designer would. Your objective is to design an arrangement of type and space that appears good to the eye. You would do well to use the following general plan for arranging the résumé.

■ Design it as a book designer would. Use balance and space for eye appeal.

Margins look better if at least an inch of space is left at the top of the page and on the left and right sides of the page and if at least 1½ inches of space are left at the bottom of the page. Your listing of items by rows (columns) appears best if the items are short and if they can be set up in two uncrowded rows, one on the left side of the page and one on the right side. Longer items of information are more appropriately set up in lines extending across the page. In any event, you would do well to avoid long and narrow columns of data with large sections of wasted space on either side. Arrangements that give a heavy crowded effect also offend the eye. Extra spacing between subdivisions and indented patterns for subparts and carryover lines are especially pleasing to the eye.

■ Here are some suggestions on form.

While layout is important in showing your ability to organize and good spacing increases readability, design considerations such as font and paper selection affect attractiveness almost as much. Commercial designers say that type size for headings should be at least 14 points and for body text, 10 to 14 points. They also recommend using fewer than four font styles on a page. Some word processing software has a "make it fit" feature that allows the user to fit information on one page. It will automatically adjust font sizes to fit the page. Be sure the resulting type size is both appropriate and readable.

■ Choose fonts carefully.

Another factor affecting the appearance of your application documents is the paper you select. The paper should be appropriate for the job you seek. In business, erring on the conservative side is usually better; you do not want to be eliminated from consideration simply because the reader did not like the quality or color of the paper. The most traditional choice is white, 100 percent cotton, 20- to 24-lb. paper. Of course, reasonable variations can be appropriate.

■ Conservative paper usually is best.

CONTRASTING BAD AND GOOD EXAMPLES.   The résumés in Figures 9.3 and 9.4 are at opposing ends of the quality scale. The first one, scant in coverage and poorly arranged, does little to help the applicant. Clearly the second one is more complete and better arranged.

■ Figures 9.3 and 9.4 show bad and good form.

Weakness in Incompleteness and Bad Arrangements.   Shortcomings in the first example (Figure 9.3) are obvious. First, the form is not pleasing to the eye. The weight of the type is heavy on the left side of the page. Failure to indent carryover lines makes reading difficult.

This résumé also contains numerous errors in wording. Information headings are not parallel in grammatical form. All are in topic form except the first one. The items listed under *Personal* are not parallel either. Throughout, the résumé coverage is scant, leaving out many of the details needed to present the best impression of the applicant. Under *Experience,* little is said about specific tasks and skills in each job; and under *Education,* high school work is listed needlessly. The references are incomplete, omitting street addresses and job titles. Certainly, the résumé does not show good business etiquette.

Strength through Good Arrangement and Completeness.   The next résumé (Figure 9.4) appears better at first glance, and it gets even better as you read it. It is attractively arranged. The information is neither crowded nor strung out. The balance is good. Its content is also superior to that of the other example. Additional words show the quality of Mr. Andrews's work experience and education, and they emphasize points that make him suited for the work he seeks. This résumé excludes trivial personal information and has only the facts that tell something about Andrews's personal qualities. Complete mailing addresses permit the reader to contact the references easily. Job titles tell how each is qualified to evaluate the subject.

CONSTRUCTING THE ELECTRONIC RÉSUMÉ

> The electronic résumé should be constructed to be scanned accurately and retrieved when an appropriate position is being filled.

Although paper résumés are not obsolete, a recent addition to the job-search process is the electronic résumé. Today's electronic résumé is simply one that can be scanned into a database and retrieved when a position is being filled. Since the objective is getting your résumé reviewed in order to be interviewed, you should use the following strategies to improve your chances with the computer.

> Use keywords that describe precisely what you can do.

INCLUDING KEYWORDS.   One strategy, using keywords, is often recommended for use with electronic scanning software. These keywords are usually nouns or concrete words that describe skills and accomplishments precisely. Instead of listing a course in comparative programming, you would list the precise languages compared, such as Visual Basic, C++, and Java. Instead of saying you would like a job in information systems, you would name specific job titles such as systems analyst, network specialist, or application specialist. Using industry-specific terminology is highly recommended.

> Use keywords common to those an employer would use to retrieve your résumé.

One way to identify the keywords in your field is by reading ads, listening to recruiters, and listening to your professors. Start building a list of words you find used repeatedly. From this list, choose those words most appropriate for the kind of work you want to do. Amplify your use of abbreviations, acronyms, and jargon appropriate to the work you want to do.

> Use precise nouns on the electronic résumé.

CHOOSING WORDS CAREFULLY.   Unlike the traditional résumé, the electronic résumé is strengthened not by the use of action verbs but rather by the use of nouns. Informal studies have shown that those retrieving résumés from these databases tend to use precise nouns.

> Use both precise nouns and action verbs in the hybrid résumé.

For the hybrid résumé, one you use in face-to-face and scanning situations, you can combine the use of precise nouns with strong action verbs. The nouns will help ensure that the résumé gets pulled from the database, and the verbs help the face-to-face recruiter see the link to the kind of work you want to do.

> Be sure the font you use can be read easily by scanners.

PRESENTING THE INFORMATION.   Since you want your résumé to be read accurately, you will use a font most scanners can read without problem. Figure 9.2 shows some of these fonts. Most scanners can easily handle fonts between 10 and 14 points. Although many handle bold, when in doubt use all caps for emphasis rather than bold. Also, because italics often confuse scanners, avoid them. Underlining is best left out as well. It creates trouble with descending letters such as *g* or *y* when the line cuts through the letter. In fact, you should use all lines sparingly. Also, avoid graphics and shading wherever possible; they just confuse the software. Use white paper to maximize the contrast, and always print in the portrait mode. The Donald Zatyko résumé in Figure 9.10 is an electronic résumé generated by an online program from Resumix.

> Send your résumé by the medium that serves you best.

Today companies accept résumés by mail, fax, and email. Be sure to choose the format that serves you best. If a company asks for résumés by fax and email, they may prefer to capture them electronically. Others still prefer to see an applicant's ability to organize and layout a printed page. Some employers give the option to the sender. (See Figure 9.11 for a "hybrid" résumé.) Obviously, when speed gives you a competitive advantage, you'll choose the fax or email options. However, you do lose some control over the quality of the document. If you elect to print and send a scannable résumé, it is best not to fold it. Just mail it in a 9 × 12 envelope. For a little extra cost, you will help ensure that your résumé gets scanned accurately rather than wondering if your key words were on a fold that a scanner might have had difficulty reading.

WRITING THE APPLICATION LETTER

You should begin work on the application letter by fitting the facts from your background to the work you seek and arranging those facts in a logical order. Then you present them in much the same way that a sales writer would present the features of a product or service. Wherever logical, you adapt the points made to the reader's needs. Like those of sales letters, the organizational plans of application letters vary. However, the following procedure (discussed in detail below) is used in most successful efforts:

- Begin with words selected to gain attention appropriately and to set up the review of information.
- Present your qualifications, keeping like information together and adapting to the company and the job.
- Use good sales strategy, especially you-viewpoint and positive language.
- Drive for the appropriate action (request for interview, reference check, further correspondence).

GAINING ATTENTION IN THE OPENING. As in sales writing, the opening of the application letter has two requirements: It must gain attention, and it must set up the review of information that follows.

Gaining attention is especially important in prospecting letters (application letters that are not invited). Such letters are likely to reach busy executives who have many things to do other than read application letters. Unless the letters gain favorable attention right away, the executives probably will not read them. Even invited letters must gain attention because they will compete with other invited letters. Invited letters that stand out favorably from the beginning have a competitive advantage.

As the application letter is a creative effort, you should use your imagination in writing the opening. But the work you seek should guide your imagination. Take, for example, work that requires an outgoing personality and a vivid imagination such as sales or public relations. In such cases, you would do well to show these qualities in your opening words. At the opposite extreme is work of a conservative nature, such as accounting or banking. Openings in such cases should normally be more restrained.

In choosing the best opening for your case, you should consider whether you are prospecting or writing an invited letter. If the letter has been invited, your opening words should begin qualifying you for the work to be done. They should also refer incidentally to the invitation, as in this example:

Will an honor graduate in accounting with experience in managerial accounting qualify for the work you listed in today's *Times?*

In addition to fitting the work sought, your opening words should set up the review of qualifications. The preceding example meets this requirement well. It structures the review of qualifications around two areas—education and experience.

You can gain attention in the opening in many ways. One way is to use a topic that shows understanding of the reader's operation or of the work to be done. Employers are likely to be impressed by applicants who have made the effort to learn something about the company, as in this example:

Now that Taggart, Inc., has expanded operations to Central America, can you use a broadly trained business administration graduate who knows the language and culture of the region?

Another way is to make a statement or ask a question that focuses attention on a need of the reader that the writer seeks to fill. The following opening illustrates this approach:

Marginal notes:

- Writing the application letter involves matching your qualifications with the job.

- This plan for writing the letter has proved to be effective.

- Gain attention and set up the information review in the opening.

- Gaining attention in the opening makes the letter stand out.

- Use your imagination in writing the opening. Make the opening fit the job.

- An invited letter might refer to the job and the source of the invitation.

- You can gain attention by showing an understanding of the reader's operations.

• •

FIGURE 9.3 **Incompleteness and Bad Arrangement in a Traditional Résumé** This résumé presents Jason Andrews ineffectively (see "Introductory Situation to Résumés and Application Letters"). It is scant and poorly arranged.

RÉSUMÉ

JASON L. ANDREWS

3177 North Hawthorne Boulevard
Olympia, New York 12407

*Bad form —
Type heavily
weighted to
left*

Telephone?

Personal

Age: 27
Married
One child, age 1
5 ft. 11 in. tall
Interests: tennis, fishing, reading
Active in sports
Weight: 165 lbs.
Memberships: Delta Sigma Pi, Sigma Iota Epsilon, Methodist Church, Olympia
    Community League

*Not
parallel
and some
extraneous
information*

Experience

1993-97 Equipment repair, Davidson Electric, Olympia, NY
1991-93 Driver, Wayland Trucking Co., New York, NY
1989-91 Clerk, Kiawa Garment Co., New York, NY

*Scant
information
on work done*

Education

1993-97 Olympia University, Bachelor of Business Administration degree,
        major in labor relations, 24 semester hours in labor and management
        courses, a 3.7 grade-point average, 3.9 in major field.

Not needed —— 1990-93 C.H. Aldridge High School, New York, NY

References

Ms. June Rojas   Prof. Helen K. Robbins
Davidson Electric   Olympia University
Olympia, N.Y. 12509   Olympia, NY 12507

Mr. Todd Frankle   Prof. Carl Cueno
Wayland Trucking Co.   Olympia University
47723 Beecher   Olympia, NY 12507
New York, NY 10029

*Incomplete
addresses —
No job titles*

•••
FIGURE 9.4 Thoroughness and Good Arrangement in a Traditional Résumé This complete and reverse chronologically organized résumé presents Jason Andrews's case effectively (see "Introductory Situation to Resumes and Applications Letters").

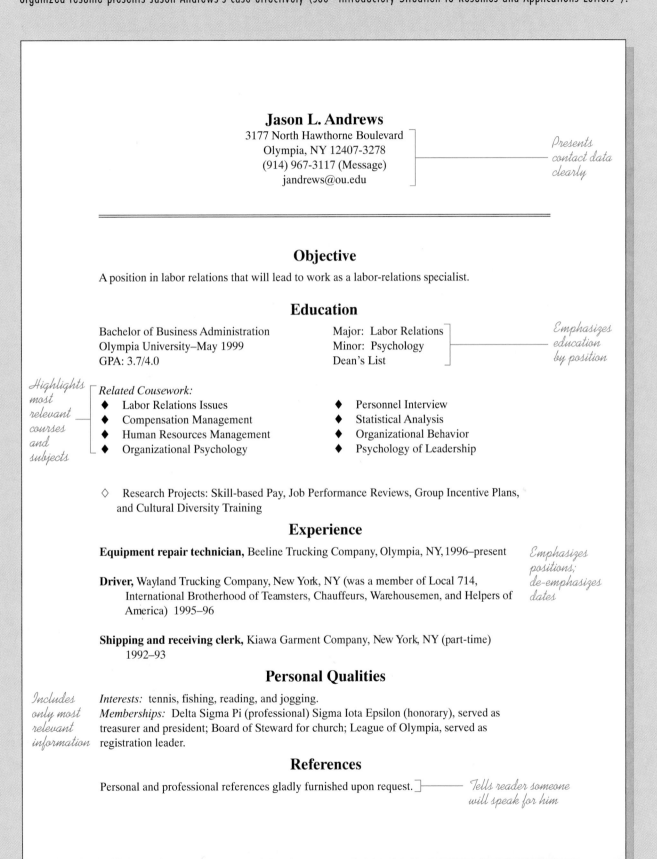

Jason L. Andrews
3177 North Hawthorne Boulevard
Olympia, NY 12407-3278
(914) 967-3117 (Message)
jandrews@ou.edu

Presents contact data clearly

Objective

A position in labor relations that will lead to work as a labor-relations specialist.

Education

Bachelor of Business Administration   Major: Labor Relations
Olympia University–May 1999   Minor: Psychology
GPA: 3.7/4.0   Dean's List

Emphasizes education by position

Highlights most relevant courses and subjects

Related Cousework:
- ◆ Labor Relations Issues
- ◆ Compensation Management
- ◆ Human Resources Management
- ◆ Organizational Psychology
- ◆ Personnel Interview
- ◆ Statistical Analysis
- ◆ Organizational Behavior
- ◆ Psychology of Leadership

◇ Research Projects: Skill-based Pay, Job Performance Reviews, Group Incentive Plans, and Cultural Diversity Training

Experience

Equipment repair technician, Beeline Trucking Company, Olympia, NY, 1996–present

Driver, Wayland Trucking Company, New York, NY (was a member of Local 714, International Brotherhood of Teamsters, Chauffeurs, Warehousemen, and Helpers of America) 1995–96

Shipping and receiving clerk, Kiawa Garment Company, New York, NY (part-time) 1992–93

Emphasizes positions; de-emphasizes dates

Personal Qualities

Includes only most relevant information

Interests: tennis, fishing, reading, and jogging.
Memberships: Delta Sigma Pi (professional) Sigma Iota Epsilon (honorary), served as treasurer and president; Board of Steward for church; League of Olympia, served as registration leader.

References

Personal and professional references gladly furnished upon request.

Tells reader someone will speak for him

•••

FIGURE 9.5 **Thoroughness and Good Arrangement for a Reference Sheet** This reference sheet presents Jason Andrews's references completely.

Jason L. Andrews
3177 North Hawthorne Boulevard
Olympia, NY 12407-3278
(914) 967-3117 (Message)
jandrews@ou.edu

Heading format matches résumé

Ms. June Rojas, Service Manager
Beeline Trucking Company
7114 East 71st Street
Olympia, NY 12509-4572
Telephone: (518) 342-1171
Fax: (518) 342-1200
Email: June.Rojas@beeline.com

Mr. Todd E. Frankle, Manager
Wayland Trucking Company
47723 Beecher Road
New York, NY 10029-0007
Telephone: (718) 466-9101
Fax: (718) 468-9100
Email: tfrankle@aol.com

Professor Helen K. Robbins
Department of Management
Olympia University
Olympia, NY 12507-0182
Telephone: (518) 392-6673
Fax: (518) 392-3675
Helen.Robbins@ou.edu

Professor Carol A. Cueno
Department of Psychology
Olympia University
Olympia, NY 12507-0234
Telephone: (518) 392-0723
Fax: (518) 392-7542
Email: Carol.Cueno@ou.edu

Complete information and balanced arrangement

FIGURE 9.6   Traditional Résumé Organized in Reverse Chronological Format

GIOVANNA GALLO

5476 Kiowa Drive #28 ✦ La Mesa, CA 91942
619-462-9363 (Home) ✦ 619-425-1389 (Work)
ggallo@sdsu.edu (E-mail) ✦ http://giovanna.home.page.aol.com

◆ OBJECTIVE

A challenging full-time Administrative Assistant position in a dynamic and progressive company where my creative talents and innovative capabilities can be efficiently utilized.

Employs a positive tone.

◆ EDUCATION

Degree:	Bachelor of Science, San Diego State University, December 1999
Major:	Business and Administration
Emphasis:	Information and Decision Systems
GPA:	3.7/4.0 with Honors
Computer Skills:	Windows, DOS, Macintosh operating systems
	MS Word ✦ Excel ✦ PowerPoint ✦ Access ✦ WordPerfect ✦ Lotus 1-2-3
Honors:	Dean's list, four semesters
	James W. Marshall Memorial Scholarship: 1998-1999

Uses concise layout of credentials.

◆ WORK EXPERIENCE

Administrative Assistant,
Austin Financial Services, San Diego, CA   *January 1998 to Present*

Emphasizes position held rather than place or date

✦ Coordinate the operations of the administrative and loan processing department. ✦ Interview prospective clients for the business. ✦ Recommend decisions on loan applications submitted to the company. ✦ Evaluate proposals for new operating equipment, computer software, and hardware. ✦ Prepare weekly payroll and payables. ✦ Write and compose reports and letters to administrative staff and clients. ✦ Implement organizational filing and retrieving systems. ✦ Organize monthly seminars for new and current employees. ✦ Schedule daily appointments for CEO and clients.

Uses descriptive action verbs.

Private Tutor, *Self-employed*   *August 1997 to Present*
✦ Tutor Math and Spanish for elementary, high school, and college students. ✦ Prepare weekly lessons for students of different ages and grades. ✦ Clarify students' educational questions. ✦ Record appointments and student information in a database system. ✦ Maintain a safe, clean, and enjoyable working environment.

Front Desk Manager, *Saddleback College, Orange, CA*   *January 1997 to December 1998*
✦ Communicated via telephone and in person with college students of different backgrounds and cultures. ✦ Performed heavy data entry and monthly payroll. ✦ Scheduled and rescheduled daily appointments for students and instructional assistants. ✦ Maintained an intricate filing system. ✦ Assisted students with set up and function of computers.

◆ REFERENCES

Available upon request   *Provides closure and says someone will speak for her.*

FIGURE 9.7 Traditional Résumé Organized in Reverse Chronological Format Presents the applicant's military experience and work history and highlights key skills, targeting Alamo.

Presents contact information clearly

George Español Oboza
10671 Penara Street • San Diego, California 92126 • (619) 689-2290 • 570-45-2209

Objective
To secure an entry-level management position with Alamo's Los Angeles Management Team

Uses precise, targeted objective

Education
San Diego State University
Bachelor of Science in Business Administration -- Emphasis: Management
May 1997

Military Experience
United States Naval Reserve
Hospital Corpsman (August 1990 to present)

Describes military experience in clear terms avoiding military jargon

Prepared personnel evaluation reports ✦ Updated navy and marine medical records ✦ Inoculated personnel ✦ Assisted with the company's plan-of-the-month mailers ✦ Supplied medical assistance to marines during field-combat exercises

Operation Desert Storm
Served at Camp Pendleton, California (February 1991 -- August 1991)

Coordinated medical officer's physical readiness reports, lab reports, and other administrative paperwork in a clinic environment ✦ Supervised junior personnel in clinic protocol ✦ Administratively processed home-bound, Camp Pendleton marines from the Gulf War ✦ Medically supervised combat-training exercises ✦ Inventoried medical supplies and placed orders on needed medicines ✦ Dispensed drugs ✦ Tested marines for sexually–transmitted diseases ✦ Prepared agar-plate cultures for pathological confirmation ✦ Drew blood from patients

Work History
San Diego Fire Department - Human Resources Division
Administrative Intern (January 1996 to October 1996)

Composed fire chief's public letters and commendation letters to fire fighters and administrative staff ✦ Served as liaison for fire fighters scheduled for respiratory-fitness examinations with Sharp Rees-Stealy clinics throughout San Diego ✦ Assisted the division secretary with various projects and reports ✦ Updated and maintained division's manuals and logs

7-Eleven
Clerk (February 1991 to February 1992 and June 1994 to July 1995)

Processed cash, check, and credit card sales ✦ Trained new clerks in store's operating procedures ✦ Serviced customers' requests and inquiries ✦ Stocked inventory

Summary of Skills
➤ *Skilled in customer service*
➤ *Strong in written communication*
➤ *Experienced in supervisorial duties*
➤ *Proficient in Windows 95, Word, and Access*

Emphasizes strongest points in special section with distinctive look

References
Furnished upon request

Carolynn C. Winship

12366 69th Terrace North
Seminole, FL 33772
(813) 399-2569
cwinship@usf.edu

Emphasizes tight organization through use of horizontal ruled lines

Objective   An accounting position with a CPA firm

Education

Emphasizes degree and GPA through placement

<u>Bachelor of Science</u>: University of South Florida, December 1998
Major: Business Administration
Emphasis: Accounting
GPA: 3.42 with Honors

Uses internal bullets to increase readability

<u>Accounting-Related Coursework</u>:
Financial Accounting ❖ Cost Accounting and Control ❖ Accounting Information Systems ❖ Auditing ❖ Concepts of Federal Income Taxation ❖ Financial Policy ❖ Communications for Business and Professions

<u>Activities</u>:
Vice-President of Finance, Beta Alpha Psi
Editor, Student Newsletter for Beta Alpha Psi
Member, Golden Key National Honors Society

Skills
Computer

Emphasizes key skills relevant to objective

- Assisted in installation of small business computerized accounting system using Quick Books Pro.
- Prepared tax returns for individuals in the VISA program using specialty tax software.
- Used Excel to design data input forms, analyze and interpret results of most functions, generate graphs, and create and use macros.

Accounting

- Developed financial statements and general ledger.
- Reconciled accounts for center serving over 1,300 clients.
- Prepared income, gift, and estate tax returns.
- Processed expense reports for 20 professional staff.
- Used Great Plains and Solomon IV.

Varies use of action verbs

Business
Communication

- Conducted client interviews and researched tax issues.
- Communicated both in written and verbal form with clients.
- Delivered several individual and team presentations on business cases, projects, and reports to business students.

Work History
Administrative
Assistant

<u>Disabled Student Services Center</u>, University of South Florida
Tampa Bay, FL, Spring 1997. Spring 1998.

Tax Assistant

<u>Rosemary Lenaghan, Certified Public Accountant</u>. Seminole, FL 1997.

References available upon request

249

Kim V. Nguyen

3733 31st Avenue
Rock Island, IL 61201
309-786-2575 (Voice Message)
knguyen@uichicago.edu
www.uichicago.edu/students/knguyen.htm

JOB TARGET   TRAINER/TRANSLATOR for an international high-tech company

HIGHLIGHTS OF QUALIFICATIONS

Emphasizes those qualifications most relevant to position sought

- Experienced in programming in C, Visual Basic, and Java.
- An enthusiastic team member/leader whose participation brings out the best in others.
- Excellent in analytical ability.
- Skilled in gathering data and interpreting it.
- Bilingual–English/Vietnamese.

EDUCATION

Presents the most important items here.

DEGREE	B.S. English–June 1999—University of Illinois at Chicago	
EMPHASIS	Education	MAJOR GPA–3.87/4.00
HONORS	Dean's List, four semesters	
	Chevron Scholarship, Fall 1998	
MEMBER	Mortar Board, Women's Golf Team	

EMPLOYMENT

DEERE & COMPANY, INC.   GOVERNOR JIM EDGAR CAMPAIGN
Student Intern, Summer 1998   Volunteer in Computer Services, Fall 1998

Several years' experience in the restaurant business including supervisory positions.

Identifies most significant places of work and de-emphasizes less important work

ACCOMPLISHMENTS

Presents only selected accomplishments from various work and volunteer experience that relates to position sought

- Designed and developed a database to keep track of financial donations.
- Managed hardware/software network.
- Coded new screens and reports; debugged and revised screen forms for easier entry.
- Developed online training program for executive use of NetMeeting.
- Provided computer support to virtual volunteers on election committee.

REFERENCES

Will gladly furnish personal and professional references on request.

Donald R. Zatyko

Home Address:
5476 Kiowa Drive #1
La Mesa CA 91942
(619) 469-4685
E-mail: zatyko@mail.sdsu.edu

Program creates format.

OBJECTIVE:

Challenging full-time position applying skills and experience in information systems and involving interests in future technologies.

EMPLOYMENT HISTORY:

5/97—8/97, Student Intern at Union Bank of California
Performed market research of bank needs and vendor options for purchase of Marketing Customer Information File (MCIF) system. Identified recent trends in data warehouse applications for financial institutions. Analyzed sales tracking process looking for ways to automate and improve accuracy.

User chooses words carefully and checks spelling.

9/92—1/96, Programmer/Analyst 2 at Huntington National Bank
Developed implementation strategies for Internet bank project. Presented design possibilities and document solutions for management. Enhanced reporting functions of item/image check processing. Installed, tested and maintained retail lockbox system.

8/96—12/97, Graduate Assistant at San Diego State University
Graduate Assistant for Professor of Business Communication. Other work experience includes advertising for small acccounting firm, LAN support for insurance sales start-up company, tax preparer at H&R Block.

EDUCATION:

MBA in Marketing, San Diego State University, 1997, GPA: 3.4
BSCIS in Computer Engineering, Ohio State University, 1992, GPA: 2.6

Writer uses industry-specific jargon and acronyms along with precise words.

ADDITIONAL SKILLS:

Designed and implemented web site for OSU Alumni Club of San Diego. Received Huntington's Master level certificate in General Banking by completing American Institute of Banking classes. Tutored high school students in math for state proficiency exam.

GREG TESONE

390 Sepulveda Blvd. #109
Los Angeles, CA 90049
310-472-7936 (H) 310-260-6077 (W)
E-mail: gtesone@ceam.com

Avoids italics and lines yet is pleasantly arranged for human reader.

OBJECTIVE

To leverage my financial background in an analyst position with an investment bank

EXPERIENCE

CEA•Montgomery Media L.L.C. (Investment Banking) Analyst; Santa Monica, CA; 1996—Present

Uses industry terminology and strong action verbs

- Worked extensively on business plan to raise capital for local Internet entertainment content developer by interviewing company officers, analyzing market information, building financial models, and contacting prospective investors
- Participated extensively in business development activities, including an early-stage buy-side acquisition search and several early-stage sell-side investor searches
- Helped design and build a database in Microsoft Access to store general, financial, and product data for companies, business contacts, and merger and acquisition activity

Montgomery & Associates (Strategy Consulting) Research Associate; Santa Monica, CA; 1995—96

- Performed extensive primary and secondary research; financial modeling; cost competitive analysis; competitive assessment and market entry; and segmentation, sizing, and distribution analysis primarily in the satellite communications area

EDUCATION

B.S. in Business Administration, Emphasis in Finance; **GPA: 3.68**
San Diego State University, May 1995

- **Honors:** Graduated Magna Cum Laude with Distinction in Finance; Made Dean's List Four Semesters; Undergraduate and Business School Honors Programs

Selects only most important items. Most will be eliminated as work experience grows.

- **Memberships:** Alpha Kappa Psi, Professional business fraternity; Finance and Investment Society, Campus club; Phi Kappa Phi, Honor society; Beta Gamma Sigma, Honor society

PERSONAL

Interests include golfing, camping, skiing, and traveling

REFERENCES

Available on request

Job boards on campus are a good place to look for announcements of job openings.

When was the last time you interviewed a young college graduate who wanted to sell and had successful sales experience?

If you seek more conservative work, you should use less imaginative openings. For example, a letter answering an advertisement for a beginning accountant might open with this sentence:

Because of my specialized training in accounting at State University and my practical experience in managerial cost-based accounting, I believe I have the qualifications you described in your *Journal* advertisement.

Sometimes one learns of a job possibility through a company employee. Mentioning the employee's name can gain attention, as in this opening sentence:

At the suggestion of Ms. Mary E. Adami of your staff, I am sending the following summary of my qualifications for work as your loan supervisor.

Many other possibilities exist. In the final analysis, you will have to use what you think will be best for the one case. But you should avoid the overworked beginnings that were popular a generation or two ago such as "This is to apply for . . ." and "Please consider this my application for . . ." Although the direct application these words make may be effective in some cases (as when answering an advertisement), the words are timeworn and dull.

- You can stress a need of the reader that you can fill.

- Use conservative openings for applications in a conservative field.

- Using an employee's name gains attention.

- Many opening possibilities exist, but avoid the old-style ones.

■ Present your qualifications. Fit them to the job.

■ You do this by studying the job. Use all available information sources.

■ Include education, experience, personal qualities, references.

■ The emphasis each of these areas deserves varies by job. So consider the job in determining emphasis.

■ Do not rely too heavily on the résumé. The application letter should carry all the major selling points.

■ In organizing the background facts, select the best of these orders: logical grouping, time, job requirements.

■ Use words that present your qualifications most favorably.

SELECTING CONTENT.   Following the opening, you should present the information that qualifies you to do the work. Begin this task by reviewing the job requirements. Then select the facts about you that qualify you for the job.

If your letter has been invited, you may learn about the job requirements from the source of the invitation. If you are answering an advertisement, study it for the employer's requirements. If you are following up an interview, review the interview for information about job requirements. If you are prospecting, your research and your logical analysis should guide you.

In any event, you are likely to present facts from three background areas: education, experience, and skills and/or personal details. You may also include a fourth—references. But references are not exactly background information. If you include references, they will probably go into the reference sheet.

How much you include from each of these areas and how much you emphasize each area should depend on the job and on your background. Most of the jobs you will seek as a new college graduate will have strong educational requirements. Thus, you should stress your education. When you apply for work after you have accumulated experience, you will probably need to stress experience. As the years go by, experience becomes more and more important—education, less and less important. Your personal characteristics are of some importance for some jobs, especially jobs that involve working with people.

If a résumé accompanies the application letter, you may rely on it too much. Remember that the letter does the selling and the résumé summarizes the significant details. Thus, the letter should contain the major points around which you build your case, and the résumé should include these points plus supporting details. As the two are parts of a team effort, somewhere in the letter you should refer the reader to the résumé.

ORGANIZING FOR CONVICTION.   You will want to present the information about yourself in the order that is best for you. In general, the plan you select is likely to follow one of three general orders. The most common order is a logical grouping of the information, such as education, skills and/or personal details, and experience. A second possibility is a time order. For example, you could present the information to show a year-by-year preparation for the work. A third possibility is an order based on the job requirements. For example, selling, communicating, and managing might be the requirements listed in an advertised job.

Merely presenting facts does not ensure conviction. You will also need to present the facts in words that make the most of your assets. You could say, for example, that you "held a position" as sales manager; but it is much more convincing to say that you "supervised a sales force of 14." Likewise, you do more for yourself by writing that you "earned a degree in business administration" than by writing that you "spent four years in college." And it is more effective to say that you "learned cost accounting" than to say that you "took a course in cost accounting."

You can also help your case by presenting your facts in reader-viewpoint language wherever this is practical. More specifically, you should work to interpret the facts based on their meaning for your reader and for the work to be done. For example, you could present a cold recital like this one:

I am 21 years old and have an interest in mechanical operations and processes. Last summer I worked in the production department of a container plant.

Or you could interpret the facts, fitting them to the one job:

The interest I have held in things mechanical over most of my 21 years would help me fit into one of your technical manufacturing operations. And last summer's experience in the production department of Miller Container Company is evidence that I can and will work hard.

Since you will be writing about yourself, you may find it difficult to avoid overusing I-references. But you should try. An overuse of I's sounds egotistical and places too much attention on the often repeated word. Also, such overuse is not good business etiquette. Some I's, however, should be used. The letter is personal. Stripping it of all I-references would rob it of its personal warmth. Thus, you should be concerned about the number of I-references. You want neither too many nor too few.

DRIVING FOR ACTION IN THE CLOSE.   The presentation of your qualifications should lead logically to the action that the close of the letter proposes. You should drive for whatever action is appropriate in your case. It could be a request for an interview, an invitation to engage in further correspondence (perhaps to answer the reader's questions), or an invitation to write references. Rarely would you want to ask for the job in a first letter. You are concerned mainly with opening the door to further negotiations.

Your action words should be clear and direct. Preferably, you should put them in question form. As in the sales letter, the request for action may be made more effective if it is followed by words recalling a benefit that the reader will get from taking the action. The following closes illustrate this technique, although some may think the second is overly aggressive:

The highlights of my training and experience show that I have been preparing for a career in human resources. May I now discuss beginning this career with you? You can reach me at 813-921-4113 or by email at ljdeftos@ucsd.edu to talk about how I can help in your human resource work.

I am very much interested in discussing with you how my skills will contribute to your company's bottom line. If I do not hear from you by Friday, October 22, I'll call on Monday to arrange a time for a mutually convenient meeting.

CONTRASTING APPLICATION LETTERS.   Illustrating bad and good techniques, the following two application letters present the qualifications of Jason L. Andrews, the job seeker described in the introductory situation at the beginning of the chapter. The first letter follows few of the suggestions given in the preceding pages, whereas the second letter is in general accord with these suggestions.

A Bland and Artless Presentation of Information.   The bad letter begins with an old-style opening. The first words stating that this is an application letter are of little interest. The following presentation of qualifications is a matter-of-fact, uninterpreted review of information. Little you-viewpoint is evident. In fact, most of the letter emphasizes the writer (note the I's). The information presented is scant. The closing action is little more than an I-viewpoint statement of the writer's availability.

| The job interview is the final examination of the application process. Appropriate grooming and relaxed, yet enthusiastic behavior are helpful to the applicant's success.

Dear Mr. Stark:

This bad one is dull and poorly written.

This is to apply for a position in labor relations with your company.

At present, I am completing my studies in labor at Olympia University and will graduate with a Bachelor of Business Administration degree with a major in labor relations this May. I have taken all the courses in labor relations available to me as well as other helpful courses such as statistics, organizational psychology, and human resource management.

I have had good working experience as a shipping and receiving clerk, truck driver, and repairer. Please see details on the enclosed résumé. I believe that I am well qualified for a position in labor relations and am considering working for a company of your size and description.

Because I must make a decision on my career soon, I request that you write me soon. For your information, I will be available for an interview on March 17 and 18.

Sincerely,

Skillful Selling of One's Ability to Work.   The better letter begins with an interesting question that sets the stage for the following presentation. The review of experience is interpreted by showing how the experience would help in performing the job sought. The review of education is similarly covered. Notice how the interpretations show that the writer knows what the job requires. Notice also that reader-viewpoint is stressed throughout. Even so, a moderate use of I's gives the letter a personal quality. The closing request for action is a clear, direct, and courteous question. The final words recall a main appeal of the letter.

Dear Mr. Stark:

This better letter follows textbook instructions.

Is there a place in your labor relations department for a person who is specially trained in the field and who knows working people and can talk with them on their level? My background, experience, and education have given me these unique qualifications.

All my life I have lived and worked with working people. I was born and reared by working parents in a poor section of New York City. While in high school, I worked mornings and evenings in New York's garment district, primarily as a shipping and receiving clerk. For two years, between high school and college, I worked full-time as a truck driver for Wayland Trucking and belonged to the Teamsters. Throughout my four years of college, I worked half-time as an equipment repairer for Davidson Electric. From these experiences, I have learned to understand labor. I speak labor's language, and working people understand and trust me.

My college studies at Olympia University were specially planned to prepare me for a career in labor relations. Pursuing a major in human resources, I studied courses in labor relations, labor law, human resource administration, organizational behavior, administrative management, business policy, and collective bargaining. In addition, I studied a wide assortment of supporting subjects: economics, business communication, information systems, industrial psychology, human relations, and operations management. My studies have given me the foundation of knowledge on which to learn the practical side of labor relations work. I plan to begin the practical side of my development in June after I receive the Bachelor of Business Administration degree with honors (3.7 grade point average on a basis of 4.0).

These brief facts and the information in my résumé describe my diligent efforts to prepare for a career in labor relations. May I now talk with you about beginning that career? You can reach me at 917-938-4449 to bring me to your office at your convenience to talk about how I could help in your labor relations work.

Sincerely,

HANDLING THE INTERVIEW

Your initial contact with a prospective employer can be by mail, email, phone, or a personal (face-to-face) visit. Even if you contact the employer by mail, a successful application will eventually involve a personal visit—or an *interview,* as we will call it. Much of the preceding parts of this chapter concerned the mail contact. Now our interest centers on the interview.

■ Apply for the job—by mail or visit.

In a sense, the interview is the key to the success of the application—the "final examination," so to speak. You should carefully prepare for the interview, as the job may be lost or won in it. The following review of employment interview highlights should help you understand how to deal with the interview in your job search. You will find additional information about interviewing in Chapter 14.

■ The interview is essential. For it, follow these procedures:

INVESTIGATING THE COMPANY.   Before arriving for an interview, you should learn what you can about the company—its products or services, its personnel, its business practices, its current activities, its management. Such knowledge will help you talk knowingly with the interviewer. And perhaps more important, the interviewer is likely to be impressed

■ (1) Find out what you can about the employer.

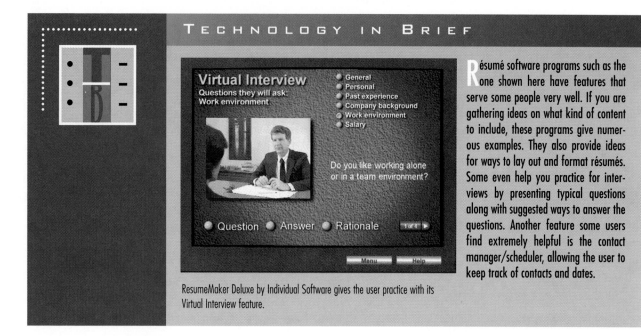

TECHNOLOGY IN BRIEF

Virtual Interview
Questions they will ask:
Work environment

● General
● Personal
● Past experience
● Company background
● Work environment
● Salary

Do you like working alone or in a team environment?

● Question ● Answer ● Rationale

Menu   Help

ResumeMaker Deluxe by Individual Software gives the user practice with its Virtual Interview feature.

Résumé software programs such as the one shown here have features that serve some people very well. If you are gathering ideas on what kind of content to include, these programs give numerous examples. They also provide ideas for ways to lay out and format résumés. Some even help you practice for interviews by presenting typical questions along with suggested ways to answer the questions. Another feature some users find extremely helpful is the contact manager/scheduler, allowing the user to keep track of contacts and dates.

Mary O. Mahoney
1718 Cranford Avenue
Rockwell, MD 20854
Voice: 301-594-6942
Fax: 301-594-1573
May 17, 1999

Mr. Nevil S. Shannon
Director of Personnel
Snowdon Industries, Inc.
1103 Boswell Circle
Baltimore, MD 21202

Dear Mr. Shannon:

Effective attention-getting question

Will you please review my qualifications for work in your administrative trainee program? I base my case on my training, work attitude, and personal skills.

Good organization plan set-up

Good interpretation of education

My training for administration consists primarily of four years of business administration study at State University. The Bachelor of Business Administration degree I will receive in June has given me a broad foundation of business knowledge. As a general business major, I studied all the functional fields (management, marketing, information systems, finance, accounting) as well as the other core business subjects (communications, statistics, law, economics, production, and personnel). I have the knowledge base that will enable me to be productive now. And I can build upon this base through practical experience.

Skillfully handles lack of experience

As I am seeking my first full-time job, I must use means other than work experience to prove my work attitude. My grade point record at State is evidence that I took my studies seriously and that I worked hard. My 3.3 overall average (4.0 basis) placed me in the top 10 percent of the graduating class. I also worked diligently in student associations. My efforts were recognized by the special assignments and leadership roles given me. I assure you that I would bring these work habits with me to Snowdon Industries.

Individually adapted

Good use of fact to back up personal qualities

Throughout college, I devoted time to the development of my personal skills. As an active member of the student chapter of the Society for the Advancement of Management, I served as treasurer and program chairperson. I participated in intramural golf and volleyball. And I was an active worker in the Young Republicans, serving as publicity chairperson for three years. All this experience has helped me to have the balance you seek in your administrative trainees.

Good ending message

These highlights and the additional evidence presented in the enclosed resume present my case for a career in administration. May I have an interview to continue my presentation? You can reach me at 301-764-0017. I could be in your office at your convenience to talk about working for Snowdon.

Clear request for action — flows logically from preceding presentation

Sincerely,

Mary O Mahoney

Mary O. Mahoney

Enclosure

Mildred E. Culpepper
2707 Green Street
Lincoln, NE 68505
Message: 402-594-6942
Fax: 402-594-1573
E-mail: mculpper@nsu.edu
April 17, 1999

Ms. Marlene O'Daniel
Vice President for Administration
Continental Insurance Company
3717 Donahue Street
Des Moines, IA 50316

Dear Ms. O'Daniel:

Gains attention with associate's name— opens door

Shows the writer knows the work in interpretations of experience

On the suggestion of Mr. Victor O. Krause of your staff, here is a summary of my qualifications for work as your communications specialist.

Presently I am in my fifth year as communications specialist for Atlas Insurance. Primarily my work consists of writing letters to Atlas policyholders. This work has made me a convert of business writing and it has sharpened my writing skills. And more important, it has taught me how to gain and keep customers for my company through writing.

Employs conservative style and tone

Additional experience working with businesspeople has given me an insight into the communication needs of business. This experience includes planning and presenting a communication improvement course for local civil service workers, a course in business writing for area business executives, and a course in bank communication for employees of Columbia National Bank.

Uses subtle you-viewpoint— implied from writer's understanding of work

My college training was certainly planned to prepare me for work in business writing. Advertising and public relations were my areas of concentration for my B.S. degree from Northern State University. As you will see in the enclosed résumé, I studied all available writing courses in my degree plan. I also studied writing through English and journalism.

References résumé

Brings review to a conclusion— fits qualification presented to the job

In summary, Ms. O'Daniel, my experience and my studies have equipped me for work as your communication specialist. I know business writing. I know how it should be practiced to benefit your company. May I have the privilege of discussing this matter with you personally? Please contact me at 402-786-2575 so that I can arrange to be in your office at any time convenient to you.

Moves appropriately for action

Sincerely,

Mildred E. Culpepper

Mildred E. Culpepper

Enc.

12713 Sanchez Drive
San Bernardino, CA
92405

Mr. Conrad W. Butler
Office Manager
Darden, Inc.
14316 Butterfield Road
San Francisco, CA 94129

Dear Mr. Butler:

Gains attention with question

Can Darden, Inc., use a hardworking State University business major who wants a career in office administration? My experience, education, and personal qualities qualify me well for this work.

Sets up rest of letter tightly

Justifies job search

My five years of work experience (see enclosed résumé) have taught me to do all phases of office work. For the past two years I have been in charge of payrolls at Gynes Manufacturing Company. As the administrator of payrolls, I have had to handle all types of office operations, including records management and general correspondence. Although I am happy on this job, it does not offer the career opportunity I seek with Darden.

Brings out highlights with review of experience

Complementing my work experience are my studies at Metropolitan Community College. In addition to studying the prescribed courses in my major field of business administration, I selected electives to help me in my career objective. And I believe I have succeeded. In spite of full-time employment through most of my time in college, I was awarded the Associate of Arts degree last May with a 3.3 grade-point average (4.0 basis). But most important of all, I learned from my studies how office work should be done.

Interprets positively

In addition, I have the personal qualities that would fit me harmoniously into your organization. I like people, and through experience I have learned how to work with them as both a team leader and a player.

Sets up action and uses adaption in concluding statement

My preparation has been designed to prepare me for work in office administration, Mr. Butler. So may I talk to you about working for Darden? Please call me at 714-399-2569 to arrange an interview.

Requests action clearly and appropriately

Sincerely,

Jimmy I. Goetz

Jimmy I.

Enc.

4407 Sunflower Drive
Phoenix, AZ 85017
July 8, 1999

Ms. Anita O. Alderson, Manager
Tompkins-Oderson Agency, Inc.
7403 Tamaron Street
Los Angeles, CA 90022

Dear Ms. Alderson:

Uses reader's words for good attention gainer.

Sound background in advertising. . . well trained. . . works well with others. . . .

These key words in your July 6 advertisement in the *Times* describe the person you want, and I believe I am that person.

Demonstrates ability to write advertising copy through writing style used.

Shows clearly what the writer can do on job through interpretation.

I have gained experience in every phase of retail advertising while working for the *Lancer*, our college newspaper. I sold advertising, planned layouts, and wrote copy. During the last two summers, I gained firsthand experience working in the advertising department of Wunder & Son. I wrote a lot of copy for Wunder, some of which I am enclosing for your inspection; you will find numerous other examples on my web page at http://www.msu.edu/home/mjanek.htm. I also did just about everything else there is to do in advertising work. I enjoyed it, and I learned from it. This experience clearly helps me fit in and contribute to the work in your office.

Shows strong determination through good interpretation.

In my concentrated curriculum at the university, I studied marketing with a specialization in advertising. I completed every course offered in advertising and related fields. My honor grades give some evidence that I worked hard and with sincerity. This educational background has definitely given me a firm foundation and stimulated my ability to be creative in working for you.

Understanding the importance of being able to get along well with people, I actively participated in Sigma Chi (social fraternity), the First Methodist Church, and Pi Tau Pi (honorary business fraternity). From the experience gained in these associations, I am confident that I can fit in well with the people in your advertising department.

Provides good evidence of social skills.

Leads smoothly to action.

As you can see from this description and the enclosed résumé, I am clearly qualified for a position in advertising. May I now meet with you to discuss this matter further? You can reach me at michael.janek@msu.edu or at 602-713-2199 to arrange a convenient time to talk about doing your advertising work.

Uses a clear and strong drive.

Sincerely,

Michael S. Janek
Michael S. Janek

enclosures

by the fact that you took the time to investigate the company. That effort might even place you above your competitors.

(2) Make a good appearance (conservative dress and grooming).

MAKING A GOOD APPEARANCE.   How you look to the interviewer is a part of your message. Thus, you should work to present just the right image. Interviewers differ to some extent on what that image is, but you would be wise to present a conservative appearance. This means avoiding faddish, offbeat styles, preferring the conservative, conventional business colors such as browns, blues, blacks, and grays. Remember that the interviewer wants to know whether you fit into the role you are seeking. You should appear to fit the part.

Some may argue that such an insistence on conformity in dress and grooming infringes on one's personal freedom. Perhaps it does. We will even concede that employers should not force such biases on you. But you will have to be realistic if you want a successful career. If the people who can determine your future have fixed views on matters of dress and grooming, it is good business etiquette to respect those views.

(3) Anticipate the questions; plan the answers.

ANTICIPATING QUESTIONS AND PREPARING ANSWERS.   You should be able to anticipate some of the questions that the interviewer will ask. Questions about your education (courses, grades, honors, and such) are usually asked. So are questions about work experience, interests, career goals, location preferences, and activities in organizations. You should prepare answers to these questions in advance. Your answers will then be thorough and correct, and your words will display poise and confidence. Your preparation will reflect your concern for good business etiquette.

Be prepared to handle standard questions,

In addition to general questions, interviewers often ask more complicated ones. Some of these are designed to test you—to learn your views, your interests, and your ability to deal with difficult problems. Others seek more specific information about your ability to handle the job in question. Although such questions are difficult to anticipate, you should be aware that they are likely to be asked. Following are questions of this kind that one experienced interviewer asks:

What can you do for us?

Would you be willing to relocate? To travel?

Do you prefer to work with people or alone?

How well has your performance in the classroom prepared you for this job?

What do you expect to be doing in 10 years? In 20 years?

What income goals do you have for those years (10 and 20 years ahead)?

Why should I rank you above the others I am interviewing?

Why did you choose _____ for your career?

How do you feel about working overtime? Nights? Weekends?

Did you do the best work you are capable of in college?

Is your college record a good measure of how you will perform on the job?

What are the qualities of the ideal boss?

What have you done that shows leadership potential? Teamwork potential?

What are your beginning salary expectations?

Sometimes interviewers will throw in tough or illegal questions to test your poise. These are naturally stressful, but being prepared for these kinds of questions will keep you cool and collected.[2] Here are some examples:

tough questions,

What is your greatest weakness?

With hindsight, how could you have improved your progress?

What kind of decisions are most difficult for you?

---

[2] Martin Yate, *Knock 'em Dead 1997* (Holbrook, MA: Adams Media Corp., 1997), pp. 168–84.

What is the worst thing you have heard about this company?

See this pen I'm holding? Sell it to me.

Tell me about a time when you put your foot in your mouth.

What kinds of people do you find it difficult to deal with?

What religion do you practice?

How old are you?

Are you married?

Do you plan to have children?

If you get through these types of questions, you might have some brainteasers or rid- | ■ brainteaser or critical thinking questions,
dles thrown your way. Most of those asking these questions are not necessarily looking for
the right answer but instead are judging your thinking and creativity skills. Be sure that
you reason aloud rather than sitting there silently so that you can show you are thinking.
Here are some real questions that have been asked in interviews and the companies that
have used them.[3]

How many barbers are there in Chicago? (McKinsey & Co.)

How many golf balls does it take to fill the swimming pool used at the Altanta Olympics? (Booz, Allen & Hamilton)

Why are manhole covers round? (Microsoft)

Why do Coke cans have an indent at the bottom? (Booz, Allen & Hamilton)

You and your neighbor, who aren't necessarily friends, are planning tag sales for the same day. You're both selling the exact
same used TV. You feel the TV will sell for $100. He insists on selling it at $40. What do you do?

Recently, the behavior interview style has become popular with campus recruiters. | ■ and behavioral questions.
Rather than just determine your qualifications for the job, interviewers are attempting to
verify if you can do the work. They ask questions about current situations since how you
behave now is likely to transfer to similar situations in another job. Here are a few examples of behavioral questions:

What major problem have you faced in group projects and how have you dealt with it?

Do you tend more toward following the rules or toward stretching them?

What do you think your performance review will say one year from now?

PUTTING YOURSELF AT EASE.   Perhaps it is easier to say than to do, but you should | ■ (4) Be at ease—calm, collected, confident.
be at ease throughout the interview. Remember that you are being inspected and that the
interviewer should see a calm and collected person. How to appear calm and collected is
not easy to explain. Certainly, it involves talking in a clear and strong voice. It also involves controlling your facial expressions and body movements. Developing such controls
requires self-discipline—working at it. You may find it helpful to convince yourself that
the stress experienced during an interview is normal. Or you may find it helpful to look at
the situation realistically—as merely a conversation between two human beings. Other approaches may work better for you. Use whatever approaches work. Your goal is to control
your emotions so that you present the best possible appearance to the interviewer.

HELPING CONTROL THE DIALOGUE.   Just answering the questions asked is often | ■ (5) Help bring out the questions that show your qualifications.
not enough. Not only are you being evaluated, but you are evaluating others as well. The
questions you ask and the comments you play off them should bring up what you want the
interviewer to know about you. Your self-analysis revealed the strong points in your background. Now you should make certain that those points come out in the interview.

How to bring up points about you that the interviewer does not ask is a matter for your | ■ Here are some examples of how to do it.
imagination. For example, a student seeking a job in advertising believed that a certain
class project should be brought to the interviewer's attention. So she asked, "Do you attach any importance to advertising campaigns done as class projects in your evaluation?"

---

[3] Nina Munk and Suzanne Oliver, "Think Fast!" *Forbes,* March 24, 1997, pp. 146–51.

The anticipated affirmative answer allowed her to show her successful project. For another example, a student who wanted to bring out his knowledge of the prospective employer's operations did so with this question: "Will your company's expansion at the Bakersfield plant create new job opportunities there?" How many questions of this sort you should ask will depend on your need to supplement your interviewer's questioning. Your goal should be to make certain that the interviewer gets all the information you consider important.

FOLLOWING UP AND ENDING THE APPLICATION

- Follow up the interview with thank-you, status-inquiry, job-acceptance, and job-rejection messages.

The interview is only an early step in the application process. A variety of other steps can follow. Conveying a brief thank-you message by letter, email, or telephone is an appropriate follow-up step. It shows good business etiquette, and because some of your competitors will not do this, it can give you an advantage. If you do not hear from the prospective employer within a reasonable time, it is appropriate to inquire by telephone, email, or letter about the status of your application. You should certainly do this if you are under a time limit on another employer's offer. The application process may end with no offer (frequently with no notification at all—a most discourteous way of handling applicants), with a rejection notice, or with an offer. How to handle these steps in writing is reviewed in the following paragraphs.

OTHER JOB-SEARCH LETTERS

- Getting a job can involve writing more than letters and résumés.

Getting a job can involve writing more than application letters and résumés. You should follow up an interview with a thank-you letter. After much time has passed, you may want to write a letter inquiring about the status of your application. You may need to write a letter accepting a job, refusing one, or resigning one.

From the preceding instructions, you should be able to write such letters. For this reason, the following review of them is brief.

- Good business etiquette requires that you write a thank-you letter following an interview.

- The typical order for such a letter is as follows: (1) expression of gratefulness, (2) appropriate comments fitting the situation, (3) any additional information needed, and (4) a goodwill close.

WRITING A THANK-YOU LETTER.   After an interview it is good business etiquette to write a thank-you letter. It is the courteous thing to do, whether or not you are interested in the job. If you are interested, the letter can help your case. It singles you out from the competition and shows your interest in the job.

Such letters are usually short. They begin with an expression of gratefulness. They say something about the interview, the job, or such. They take care of any additional business (such as submitting information requested). And they end on a goodwill note—perhaps a hopeful look to the next step in the negotiations. The following letter does these things:

Dear Mr. Hornaday:

I genuinely appreciate the time you gave me yesterday. You were most helpful. And you did a first-rate job of selling me on Graystone-Brune, Inc.

As you requested, I have enclosed samples of the advertising campaign I developed as a class project. If you need anything more, please let me know.

I look forward to the possibility of discussing employment with you soon.

Sincerely,

- When employers do not respond, you may write a follow-up letter. It follows the order of the routine inquiry letter.

CONSTRUCTING A FOLLOW-UP TO AN APPLICATION.   When a prospective employer is late in responding to an application, you may need to write a follow-up letter. Employers are often just slow, but sometimes they lose the application. Whatever the explanation, a follow-up letter may help to produce action.

Such a letter is a form of routine inquiry. As a reason for writing, it can use the need to make a job decision or some other good explanation. The following letter is an example:

Dear Mr. Terrado:

Because the time is approaching when I must make a job decision, will you please tell me the status of my employment application with you.

You may recall that you interviewed me in your office November 7. You wrote me November 12 indicating that I was among those you had selected for further consideration.

Barrow, Inc., remains one of the organizations I would like to consider in making my career decision. I will very much appreciate hearing from you by December 3.

Sincerely,

PLANNING THE JOB ACCEPTANCE.   Job acceptances in writing are merely favorable response letters with an extra amount of goodwill. Because the letter should begin directly, a yes answer in the beginning is appropriate. The remainder of the letter should contain a confirmation of the starting date and place and comments about the work, the company, the interview—whatever you would say if you were face to face with the reader. The letter need not be long. This one does the job well:

■ You may need to write a letter accepting a job. Write it as you would a favorable response letter.

Dear Ms. Garcia:

Yes, I accept your offer of employment. After my first interview with you, I was convinced that Allison-Caldwell was the organization for me. It is good to know that you think I am right for Allison-Caldwell.

Following your instructions, I will be in your Toronto headquarters on May 28 at 8:30 AM ready to work for you.

Sincerely,

WRITING A LETTER REFUSING A JOB.   Letters refusing a job offer follow the normal refusal pattern. One good technique is to begin with a friendly comment—perhaps something about past relations with the company. Next, explain and present the refusal in clear yet positive words. Then end with more friendly comment. This example illustrates the plan.

■ To refuse a job offer, use the normal refusal pattern (indirect).

Dear Mr. Chen:

Meeting you and the other people at Northern was a genuine pleasure. All that I saw and heard impressed me most favorably. I was especially impressed to receive the generous job offer that followed.

In considering the offer, I naturally gave some weight to these favorable impressions. Even though I have accepted a job with another firm, they remain strong in my mind.

Thank you for the time and the courteous treatment you gave me.

Sincerely,

WRITING A LETTER OF RESIGNATION.   At some point in your career you are likely to resign from one job to take another. When this happens, probably you will inform your employer of your resignation orally. But when you find it more practical or comfortable, you may choose to resign in writing. In some cases, you may do it both ways. As a matter of policy, some companies require a written resignation even after an oral resignation has been made. Or you may prefer to leave a letter of resignation following your oral announcement of it.

■ Job resignations are made in person, by letter, or both.

Your letter of resignation should be as positive as the circumstances permit. Even if your work experiences have not been pleasant, you will be wise to depart without a final display of anger. As an anonymous philosopher once explained, "When you write a resignation in anger, you write the best letter you will ever regret."

■ Make the letter as positive as circumstances permit.

The best resignation letters are written in the indirect order. The situation is negative; and, as you know, indirectness usually is advisable in such cases. But many are written in the direct order. They present the resignation right away, following it with expressions of gratitude, favorable comments about past working experiences, and the like. Either approach is acceptable. Even so, you would do well to use the indirect order, for it is more likely to build the goodwill and favorable thinking you want to leave behind you.

■ Preferably use indirect order, for the situation is negative.

The example below shows the indirect order, which is well known to you. It begins with a positive point—one that sets up the negative message. The negative message follows, clearly yet positively stated. The ending returns to positive words chosen to build goodwill and fit the case.

Dear Ms. Chambers:

Working as your assistant for the past five years has been a genuinely rewarding experience. Under your direction I have grown as an administrator. And I know you have given me a practical education in retailing.

As you may recall from our past discussions, I have been pursuing the same career goals that you held early in your career. Thus I am sure you will understand why I now submit my resignation to accept a store management position with Lawson's in Belle River. I would like my employment to end on the 31st; but I could stay a week or two longer if needed to help train my replacement.

I leave with only good memories of you and the other people with whom I worked. Thanks to all of you for a valuable contribution to my career.

Sincerely,

CONTINUING JOB-SEARCH ACTIVITIES

Keeping your attention on the job market alerts you to changes and opportunities in the field.

Some authorities recommend continuing your job search two weeks into a new job. It provides insurance if you should discover the new job isn't what you expected. However, continuously keeping your finger on the pulse of the job market is a good idea. Not only does it provide you with information about changes occurring in your field, but it also keeps you alert to better job opportunities as soon as they are announced.

Update your résumé regularly to reflect new accomplishments and skills.

MAINTAINING YOUR RÉSUMÉ.   While many people intend to keep their résumés up-to-date, they just do not make it a priority. Some others make it easy by updating as changes occur. And a few update their résumés at regularly designated times such as a birthday, New Year's Day, or even the anniversary of their employment. No matter what works best for you, updating your résumé as you gain new accomplishments and skills is important.

Keeping current in your professional reading brings many benefits.

READING JOB ADS/PROFESSIONAL JOURNALS.   Nearly as important as keeping your résumé updated is keeping up on your professional reading. Most trade or professional journals have job notices or bulletin boards you should check regularly. These ads give you insight into what skills are in demand, perhaps helping you choose assignments where you get the opportunity to develop new skills. Staying up-to-date in your field can be stimulating; it can provide both challenges and opportunities.

SUMMARY BY CHAPTER OBJECTIVES

1 Develop and use a network of contacts in your job search.

2 Assemble and evaluate information that will help you select a job.

3 Identify the sources that can lead you to an employer.

4 Compile traditional and electronic résumés that are strong, complete, and organized.

1. A good first step in your job search is to build a network of contacts.
   • Get to know people who might help you later—classmates, professors, business leaders, and such.
   • Use them to help you find a job.
2. When you are ready to find work, analyze yourself and outside factors.
   • Look at your education, personal qualities, and work experience.
   • From this review, determine what work you are qualified to do.
   • Then select the career that is right for you.
3. When you are ready to find a job, use the contact sources available to you.
   • Check university placement centers, personal contacts, advertisements, online sources, employment agencies, and web pages.
   • If these do not produce results, prospect by mail.
4. In your application efforts, you are likely to use résumés and application letters. Prepare them as you would written sales material.
   • First, study your product—you.

- Then study your prospect—the employer.
- From the information gained, construct the résumé, letter, and reference sheet.

In writing the résumé (a listing of your major background facts), you can choose from two types.

- The *traditional* type for face-to-face interviews.
- The *electronic* type for scanned résumés.

In preparing the traditional résumé, follow this procedure:

- List all the facts about you that an employer might want to know.
- Sort these facts into logical groups—*experience, education, personal qualities, references, achievements, highlights.*
- Put these facts in writing. As a minimum, include job experience (dates, places, firms, duties) and education (degrees, dates, fields of study). Use some personal information, but omit race, religion, sex, marital status, and age.
- Authorities disagree on whether to list references. If you list them, use complete mailing addresses and have one for each major job.
- Include other helpful information: address, telephone number, email address, web page address, and career objective.
- Write headings for the résumé and for each group of information; use either topic or talking headings.
- Organize for strength in reverse chronological, functional/skills, or accomplishment/highlights approach.
- Preferably write the résumé without personal pronouns, make the parts parallel grammatically, and use words that help sell your abilities.
- Present the information for good eye appeal, selecting fonts that show the importance of the headings and the information.

In preparing the electronic résumé, follow these procedures:

- Include industry-specific keywords.
- Choose precise nouns over action verbs.
- Present the information in a form read accurately by scanners.

5. As the application letter is a form of sales letter, plan it as you would a sales letter.

   5 Write letters of application that skillfully sell your abilities.

   - Study your product (you) and your prospect (the employer) and think out a strategy for presentation.
   - Begin with words that gain attention, begin applying for the job, and set up the presentation of your sales points.
   - Adapt the tone and content to the job you seek.
   - Present your qualifications, fitting them to the job you seek.
   - Choose words that enhance the information presented.
   - Drive for an appropriate action—an interview, further correspondence, reference checks.

6. Your major contact with a prospective employer is the interview. For best results, you should do the following:

   6 Explain how you can participate effectively in an interview.

   - Research the employer in advance so you can impress the interviewer.
   - Present a good appearance through appropriate dress and grooming.
   - Try to anticipate the interviewer's questions and to plan your answers.
   - Make a good impression by being at ease.
   - Help the interviewer establish a dialogue with questions and comments that enable you to present the best information about you.

7. You may need to write other letters in your search for a job.

   7 Write application follow-up letters that are appropriate, friendly, and positive.

   - Following the interview, a thank-you letter is appropriate.
   - Also appropriate is an inquiry about the status of an application.
   - You may also need to write letters accepting, rejecting, or resigning a job.
   - Write these letters much as you would the letters reviewed in preceding chapters: direct order for good news, indirect order for bad.

8. To learn information about the change occurring in their field and to be aware of better job opportunities, employees should

   8 Maintain your job-search skills.

   - Maintain their résumés.
   - Read both job ads and professional journals.

CRITICAL THINKING QUESTIONS

1. "Building a network of contacts to help one find jobs appears to be selfish. It involves acquiring friendships just to use them for one's personal benefit." Discuss this view.

2. Maryann Brennan followed a broad program of study in college and received a degree in general studies. She did her best work in English, especially in the writing courses. She also did well in history, sociology, and psychology. As much as she could, she avoided math and computer courses.

   Her overall grade point average of 3.7 (4.0 basis) placed her in the top 10 percent of her class. What advice would you give her as she begins her search for a career job?

3. Discuss the value of each of the sources for finding jobs to a finance major (*a*) right after graduation and (*b*) after 20 years of work in his or her specialty.

4. Assume that in an interview for the job you want, you are asked the questions listed in the text under the heading "Anticipating Questions." Answer these questions.

5. The most popular arrangement of résumé information is the three-part grouping: education, experience, and personal details. Describe three other arrangements. When would each be used?

6. Distinguish between the traditional résumé and the electronic résumé. When would each be most appropriate?

7. What is meant by *parallelism of headings?*

8. Describe the application letter and résumé you would write (*a*) immediately after graduation, (*b*) 10 years later, and (*c*) 25 years later. Point out similarities and differences, and defend your decision.

9. What differences would you suggest in the writing of application letters for jobs in (*a*) accounting, (*b*) banking, (*c*) advertising copy writing, (*d*) administration, (*e*) sales, (*f*) consulting, and (*g*) information systems?

10. Discuss the logic of beginning an application letter with these words: "This is to apply for . . ." and "Please consider this my application for the position of . . ."

11. "In writing job-application letters, just present the facts clearly and without analysis and interpretation. The facts alone will tell the employer whether he or she wants you." Discuss this viewpoint.

12. When should the drive for action in an application letter (*a*) request the job, (*b*) request an interview, and (*c*) request a reference check?

CRITICAL THINKING EXERCISES

1. Criticize the following résumé parts. (They are not from the same résumé.)

   a. Work Experience

1996–99	Employed as sales rep for Lloyd-Shanks Tool Company
1993–96	Office manager, Drago Plumbing Supply, Toronto
1991–93	Matson's Super Stores. I worked part time as sales clerk while attending college.

   b. References

   Mr. Carl T. Whitesides
   Sunrise Insurance, Inc.
   317 Forrest Lane
   Dover, DE 19901-6452

   Patricia Cullen
   Cullen and Cullen Realtors
   2001 Bowman Dr.
   Wilmington, DE 19804

   Rev. Troy A. Graham
   Asbury Methodist Church
   Hyattsville, MD 20783

   D. W. Boozer
   Boozer Industries
   Baltimore, MD 21202

   c. Education

1995	Graduated from Tippen H.S. (I was in top 10 percent of class.)
1999	B.S. from Brady University with major in marketing

1999 to present.	Enrolled part time in M.B.A. program at Waldon University

   d. Qualifications

   Know how to motivate a sales force. I have done it.
   Experienced in screening applicants and selecting salespeople.
   Know the pharmaceutical business from 11 years of experience.
   Knowledgeable of realistic quota setting and incentives.
   Proven leadership ability.

2. Criticize these sentences from application letters:

   Beginning Sentences

   a. Please consider this my application for any position for which my training and experience qualify me.

   b. Mr. Jerry Bono of your staff has told me about a vacancy in your loan department for which I would like to apply.

   c. I am that accountant you described in your advertisement in today's *Times-Record*.

   d. I want to work for you!

   Sentences Presenting Selling Points

   e. From 1995 to 1999 I attended Brady University where I took courses leading to a B.S. degree with a major in finance.

   f. I am highly skilled in trading corporate bonds as a result of three years spent in the New York office of Collins, Bragg, and Weaver.

g. For three years (1996–99) I was in the loan department at Bank One.
h. My two strongest qualifications for this job are my personality and gift of conversation.
   Sentences from Action Endings
i. I will call you on the 12th to arrange an interview.

j. If my qualifications meet your requirements it would be greatly appreciated if you would schedule an interview for me.
k. Please call to set up an interview. Do it now—while it is on your mind.

CRITICAL THINKING PROBLEMS

APPLICATIONS

1. Move the date to the time you will complete your education. You have successfully prepared yourself for the career of your choice, but the visiting recruiters have not yet offered you a job. Now you must look on your own. So you find the best job for which you believe you are qualified in the "Classified Advertisements" sections of the area newspapers. Write the application letter that will present your qualifications for this job. Attach the advertisement to the letter. (Assume that a résumé accompanies the letter.)

2. Write the résumé and reference sheet to accompany the letter for Problem 1.

3. Project yourself five years past your graduation date. During those years, you have had good experience working for the company of your choice in the field of your choice. (Use your imagination to supply this information.)

   Unfortunately, your progress hasn't been what you had expected. You think that you must look around for a better opportunity. Your search through the classified advertisements in your area newspapers, online, and *The Wall Street Journal* turns up one promising possibility (you find it). Write an application letter that skillfully presents your qualifications for this job. (You may make logical assumptions about your experience over the five-year period.) For class purposes, clip the advertisement to your letter.

4. Write the résumé and reference sheet to accompany the letter in Problem 3.

5. Assume you are in your last term of school and graduation is just around the corner. Your greatest interest is in finding work that you like and that would enable you to support yourself now and to support a family as you win promotions.

   No job of your choice is revealed in the want ads of newspapers and trade magazines. No placement bureau has provided anything to your liking. So you decide to do what any good salesperson does: survey the product (yourself) and the market (companies that could use a person who can do what you are prepared to do) and then advertise (send each of these companies a résumé with an application letter). This procedure sometimes creates a job where none existed before; and sometimes it establishes a basis for negotiations for the "big job" two, three, or five years after graduation. And very frequently, it puts you on the list for the good job that is not filled through advertising or from the company staff. Write the application letter.

6. Write the résumé and reference sheet to accompany the letter for Problem 5.

7. Move the calendar to your graduation date so that you're now ready to sell your working ability in the job market for as much as you can get and still hold your own. Besides canvassing likely firms with the help of prospecting letters and diligently following up family contacts, you've decided to look into anything that appears especially good in the ad columns of newspapers, on-line services, and magazines. The latest available issues of big-town publications and on-line services list the following jobs that you think you could handle. (You may change publication and place names to fit your section of the country.)

a. *Office manager.* Insurance company seeks personable, college-trained person to manage office of five employees. People skills and good communication ability a must. Knowledge of office procedures and word processing essential. Send application material to Human Resource Office, P.O. Box 7197, [your city] .

b. *Assistant Webmaster.* Outstanding information technology, organizational, and interpersonal skills are needed for work on company intranet, extranet, and Internet sites. Mastery of HTML coding, website design including graphic design, and client server technology is vital. Candidates must also possess excellent writing skills and the ability to effectively manage multiple projects while interfacing with company employees. A bachelor's degree with a background in information systems, marketing, or communications is required. Please send résumé to Megan Adami in Human Resources, 7165 North Main Street, [your city] , or fax it to 1-888-444-5047, or email it to megan_adami@cnet.com.

c. *Management trainee.* Fast-growing manufacturer in the food-processing industry has opening in its training program. Only high-energy, results-oriented people with good communication skills need apply. Opportunities for advancement to management positions based on performance. Applicants must demonstrate a professional image and possess skills in working with people. Computer literacy required. Apply to Human Resource Director, P.O. Box 9133, [your city] .

d. *Accounting majors.* International accounting firm seeks recent accounting graduates. Well-rounded study of accounting and computers essential. Some travel. Advancement based on performance. Communication and human-relations skills required. Must be a hard worker and willing to work long hours during peak periods. Excellent compensation and benefits. Apply to Accounting Director, P.O. Box 2985, [your city] .

e. *Staff accountant.* Successful candidate should have a B.S. in accounting and be proficient in Lotus and/or Excel. Would be responsible for performing account analysis for corporate accounts, assisting in consolidation of subsidiaries, and assisting in the preparation of annual and quarterly financial statements and financial reports for certain subsidiaries. Experience in the local environment or small business is desirable. If you are concerned with order, quality, and accuracy, please contact us by mail at Administrative Partner, Winship and Acord, P.C., 3013 Stonybrook Drive, [your city] , or by email at CWA@compuserve.com, or by fax at 1-217-399-2569.

f. *Network specialist.* The person in this position will support application services in all areas related to a production manufacturing environment. This includes covering the help desk, solving technical problems, and researching and generating solutions. Additionally, this person must be able to perform tape backups and restores as well as handle system administrative functions. Must be results oriented, able to work in a team environment, and work with minimal supervision. Must have good analytical skills along with effective interpersonal communication skills. A degree in information systems or computer science is preferred. Our company supports a drug-free workplace and requires that all offers of employment be contingent on satisfactory preemployment drug test results. Send your application documents to Director of Employment, Dept. IS-CS 123, [your city] .

g. *Technology analyst/consultant.* A fast-growing, highly regarded information technology assessment/consulting firm has a position for someone with expertise in client/server technology and object-oriented technology and/or related areas. Must have excellent written communications and interpersonal skills. Vendor or user organization experience is highly desirable. Position is in the Bay Area. Send or fax your résumé to director of human resources at 500 Airport Road, Suite 100, [your city] or 415-579-1022.

h. *Financial analyst.* An eastern-based investment firm is seeking an analyst to help with the evaluation of potential private equity investments and marketing of an existing and new leveraged buyout fund. Should have a bachelor's degree from a good school and some experience in banking. Ideal candidates will have strong analytical capabilities and excellent computer skills,

particularly spreadsheet, word processing, and database. Please fax résumé and cover letter to 203-869-1022.

i. *Professional services marketing.* International leader in management consulting needs qualified person to market professional services and products to existing and new accounts. With a group of polished professionals, sell services to business executives including business strategies and/or reengineering consulting. Excellent written and oral skills. Demonstrated ability to prepare/deliver winning engagement proposals and client presentations. Travel required. Must have business degree. Send letter and résumé to Human Resources Department, Box 11051, Chicago, IL 58641.

j. *Sales representative.* An international company providing specialized products for flight and machinery components seeks to expand its client base in the West Coast, Central, Northeast, and Southeast regions. Successful candidates will be poised, persuasive "closers" with some technical knowledge. Sales experience or utility maintenance experience is desirable. Good knowledge of these new territories is desirable. Send résumé to Box 1022, [your desirable city] .

k. *Client/server programmer.* The largest supplier of curriculum and support services seeks to expand its staff. Desirable candidates will have experience with PowerBuilder, Visual Basic, or C++; object-oriented analysis and design skills; GUI design experience; and a solid understanding of Windows 95 and NT. Applicants should be able to design, implement, and test systems, working on projects from inception to completion. Please send or fax résumé to the human relations coordinator at 825 Lincoln Blvd., [your city] , or 215-295-1022.

l. *Marketing professional.* An international, rapidly growing consumer and trade publisher is seeking a self-motivated individual to help us reach our goal of doubling revenues by the year 2005. Ideal candidate will be an innovative, results-oriented professional willing to take the challenge of developing new markets. Should be good at packaging and repackaging information products for a large and expanding customer base. We are looking for those with some experience, creative writing talent, leadership skills, good communications skills, and strong interpersonal skills. Sell yourself through your cover letter and résumé. Send to Thomas McLaughlin, corporate vice president, 2411 Blackhawk Road, [your city] , or fax to 619-681-1022.

m. *Executive administrative assistant.* Vice president of a Fortune 500 manufacturing company seeks a highly competent, personable, organized and dependable executive assistant. College degree desired. Must have excellent communication skills and thorough command of word processing and graphics programs. In addition to basic business knowledge in accounting, finance, marketing, and management an understanding of manufacturing in a global market would be desirable. Apply to director of human resources, P.O. Box 3733, [your city] .

n. *Graphic artist.* An employee-owned systems integration firm has an immediate need for a graphic artist. A bachelor's degree or an associate's degree with some experience desired. Must be proficient in CorelDraw, preferably in a Windows environment. Will prepare presentation and curriculum support graphics for government customer. Knowledge of project management software is a plus. Must have a work portfolio. Send résumé to the attention of KML, P.O. Box 900, [your city] .

o. *MIS specialist.* A local medical clinic is seeking an individual to manage a multisite, multiplatform computer system. Will be responsible for troubleshooting and coordinating problems in a Windows NT environment and writing reports for management. A background in the health care/medical field combined with a good knowledge of computing is highly desirable. Send résumé to [your city's name] Community Clinic, 1113 Henderson, [your city] .

p. *Financial manager.* Multispecialty medical group (60 doctors) needs dedicated professional to work in providing financial planning and control in growing organization. Join a team of financial specialists who bear responsibility for budgeting, general accounting, reimbursement, billing processes, and external reporting. Development of long and short range financial goals and evaluation of their impact on strategic objectives and service mission. Degree in accounting/finance. Technical and team skills needed. Competitive salary and benefits package. Send letter and résumé to Mount Renault Medical Group, Box 14871, New York, NY 00146.

q. *Accountant.* A major real estate developer and property management company seeks an accountant. Must have a bachelor's degree in accounting. Will assist in financial reporting, tax preparation, cash flow projections, and year-end audit workpaper preparation. Mastery of Excel is required as are good communication skills. Some work experience in accounting is desirable; internship experience in an accounting or real estate environment is also desirable. Send your résumé and cover letter to TPL, P.O. Box 613, [your city] .

r. *Accounting majors.* Multinational consumer electronics firm seeks entry-level accountant for work in its controller's division. This person must be knowledgeable in financial and cost accounting, internal auditing, budgeting, and capital investments. A multinational orientation, degree in accounting, and progress toward completion of CPA or CMA are a plus. Good communication skills (written and oral) and computer applications are required. Interested applicants should send letter and résumé to Box B.O. & L., [your city] .

s. *Bank examiner.* Federal Reserve Bank (nearest to your location) seeks positions for career-oriented individuals. Persons hired will conduct on-site examinations of foreign banks operating in the U.S. in their lending activities, derivative products, bank operations, and financial information. Applicants must possess a bachelor's degree in accounting, finance, or economics. Evidence of cross-cultural sensitivity and foreign language proficiency are preferred. Travel 30–50 percent of the time. Excellent oral/written skills and U.S. citizenship required. Apply with letter and résumé to Federal Reserve Board, Human Resources Department, [your region] .

t. *Proposal writer.* Global leader in high-technology asset management needs individual to prepare proposals for clients. Person selected must be a team player, thrive on high-tech challenges in fast-paced environment, and possess a state-of-the-art solution orientation. Excellent writing skills essential, along with BBA degree and experience with various hardware/software technologies. Job includes coordinating appropriate persons to define solutions and preparing program plans with cost estimation for clients. Send letter and résumé to Department SAS, [your city] .

u. *Assistant to operations manager.* Proven leader in the insurance industry seeks a highly motivated assistant to the operations manager of regional service center. Technical skills include proficiency in Microsoft Word, Excel, Powerpoint, Access, and other database applications. College training preferred with good people skills. Person selected must be able to develop and maintain effective working relationships with internal and external customers. Apply to H R Department, Box 7438, [your city] .

v. *Safety and health assistant.* World leader in battery manufacturing is looking for an individual to work in safety and health area of production plant and distribution center. The successful candidate will need to have a business or related degree and possess excellent organizational and people skills. Job duties involve administering health/safety programs, conducting training, and working with governmental agencies and regulatory personnel. Excellent opportunity for results-oriented individual seeking to work for a safe, attractive, and sanitary environment. Send letter and résumé to Box SH, [your city] .

w. *Account executive for display advertising.* State business journal invites applications for career-oriented individuals. Qualified candidates must be college graduates (business preferred) and have work background to demonstrate reliability and commitment. Job scope involves selling display advertising in creative ways for specialized business print and on-line publications. Applicants should be of high energy, aggressive, and creative. Send applications to Drawer HBD, [your city] .

x. *Financial consultant.* Large communications services company needs qualified person to provide communication-based utility automation consulting to electric utilities. Must have comprehensive financial management knowledge. Perform economic analyses on current and proposed projects; assist in development of budgets; evaluate budget to actual performance; prepare monthly reports. Demonstrated knowledge of strategic planning, valuation techniques, accounting principles, and economic forecasts. Must communicate well orally and in writing. Send letter and résumé to ALC Communications, Box 18135, Dallas, TX 78412.

y. *Executive personal assistant.* Innovative software development company is looking for a mature, detail-oriented person to assist the president with daily duties. Successful candidate will be computer literate; capable of working with little to no supervision; and able to thrive in a dynamic, fast-paced environment. Applicant must have good oral and written communication skills and be able to work with people and with current office technology. Excellent compensation and benefits. Great opportunity for advancement. Must be college graduate, preferably with degree in business and some MIS coursework. A career opportunity. Send letter and résumé to P.O. Box 1777, [your city] .

z. *Materials management trainee.* Progressive health food producer with 11 state-of-the-art manufacturing facilities and participative work environment needs materials management trainee. The position will help to manage master scheduling functions, production control, customer service, product distribution, and capacity planning. Business degree with production/operations management concentration and progress toward APICS Certification preferred. Excellent analytical, communication, and people management skills. Interested applicants should send letter and résumé to Box 7801, [your city] .

aa. *Convention services marketer.* Major international hotel organization needs trainees to work in its convention services division. Job activities include prospecting for clients, selling hotel facilities and services, negotiating contracts, servicing client needs, coordinating with intermediaries, and performing other activities for marketing planning/control. Individuals with degrees in marketing and with job experience in service industries preferred. High-energy, good visionary applicants will join team of success-oriented professionals. Qualified applicants should apply to Box SRD, [your city] .

bb. *Marketing trainees.* International leader in precious gemstone mining and processing seeks qualified persons to help build marketing program. Candidates must have ability to analyze market opportunities; research and select target markets; design market strategies; plan market programs; and organize, implement, and control marketing

effort. This position offers the right persons the opportunity to use education and skills in an exciting high-growth corporate environment. College education with emphasis in marketing plus career-minded orientation are essential. To be considered, send cover letter and résumé to Box 3355, [your city] .

cc. *Compensation analyst.* Large transportation company has an exciting and challenging opportunity for a junior-level compensation professional to support the corporate compensation program in the areas of job analysis, market pricing, merit/incentive programs, pay structures, and various compensation studies. The ideal candidate will have a college degree with demonstrated analytical skills in compensation analysis and job evaluation. Spreadsheet knowledge, strong communication/interpersonal skills, and ability to interact with senior-level management are essential. Interested applicants should apply by sending letter and résumé to Drawer OWG, [your city] .

dd. *Instruction assistant.* Airline Training and Consulting Group is seeking individuals to assist with instructional design and development. Job responsibilities include training and development of new instructors, developing and enhancing training courses in instructional design, and maintaining classroom and associated equipment. A college degree and a thorough knowledge of state-of-the-art learning technologies are a must. Individuals should possess people-enhancing skills. Send letter and résumé to Box 5551, [your city] .

ee. *Management trainee.* Excellent career opportunity with major HMO for recent college graduate, preferably with business major. Assignments will rotate through company operations. Member Services, Underwriting, Claims, Enrollment, etc. Qualified applicant will possess excellent oral and written communication skills, ability to exercise independent judgment, and good problem-solving ability. Must be geographically mobile. Ability to work with people important. Outstanding benefits. Competitive compensation and good working environment. Good advancement possibilities. Apply to P.O. Box 331, [your city] .

ff. *Assistant to cash and risk manager.* Leading manufacturer of videoconferencing systems looking for person who will be expected to replace manager upon retirement in three years. Work involves overseeing all aspects of cash management including investments, banking, foreign exchange, cash-flow forecasting, external leasing, and risk management. Applicant must have degree in finance or accounting. Good PC skills a requirement. Must be able to work with people and have good oral and written communication skills. Only hard workers need apply. Abovemarket compensation and good benefits. Apply to P.O. Box 8488, [your city] .

Concentrate on the ad describing the job you would like most or could do best—and then write an application letter that will get you that job. Your letter will first have to survive the siftings that eliminate dozens (sometimes hundreds) of applicants who lack the expected qualifications. Toward the end you'll be getting into strong competition in which small details may give you the little extra margin of superiority that will get you an interview and a chance to campaign further.

Study your ad for what it says and even more for what it implies. Weigh your own preparation even more thoroughly than you weigh the ad. You may imagine far enough ahead to assure completion of all the courses that are blocked out for your degree. You may build up your case a bit on what you actually have. Sort out the things that line you up for the *one* job, organize them strategically, and then present them. Assume that you've attached a résumé.

8. Write the résumé and reference sheet to accompany the letter for Problem 7.

9. You are looking ahead to your graduation soon. You've decided to begin to look for jobs on-line. Tap into a system that you know posts jobs in your major (such as E-span) or a corporate web site that posts job openings. Browse through the jobs until you see one that appeals to you and for which you'll be qualified when you graduate. Print (or save) a copy of the ad so you'll have it handy when you write your résumé and letter of application. Address the points covered in the ad and tell them that you learned about the position from a particular online system. If you are transmitting your response online, be sure to place your strongest points on the first few screens.

PART

5

Fundamentals
of Report Writing

C H A P T E R

10

Basics
of Report Writing

Upon completing this chapter, you will be able to prepare well-organized, objective reports. To reach this goal, you should be able to

1 State a problem clearly in writing.

2 List the factors involved in a problem.

3 Explain the common errors in interpreting and develop attitudes and practices conducive to good interpreting.

4 Organize information in outline form, using time, place, quantity, factor, or a combination of these as bases for division.

5 Construct topic or talking headings that outline reports logically and meaningfully.

6 Write reports that are clear, objective, consistent in time viewpoint, smoothly connected, and interesting.

7 Prepare reports collaboratively.

Report Writing

Introduce yourself to the subject of report writing by assuming the role of administrative assistant to the president of Technicraft, Inc. Much of your work at this large manufacturing company involves getting information for your boss. Yesterday, for example, you looked into the question of excessive time spent by office workers on coffee breaks. A few days earlier, you worked on an assignment to determine the causes of unrest in one of the production departments. Before that assignment you investigated a supervisor's recommendation to change a production process. You could continue the list indefinitely, for investigating problems is a part of your work.

So is report writing, for you must write a report on each of your investigations. You write these reports for good reasons. Written reports make permanent records. Thus, those who need the information contained in these reports can review and study them at their convenience. Written reports can also be routed to a number of readers with a minimum of effort. Unquestionably, such reports are convenient and efficient means of transmitting information.

Your report-writing work is not unique in your job. In fact, report writing is common in virtually all operations of the company. Sometimes reports are written by individuals. Increasingly, however, they are prepared in collaboration with others. For example, the engineers often report on the technical problems they encounter. The accountants regularly report to management on the company's financial operations. From time to time, production people report on various aspects of operations. The salespeople regularly report on marketing matters. And so it is throughout the company. Such reporting is vital to your company's operations—as it is to the operations of all companies. Organizations require information for many reasons. In a sense, they feed on information. Reports supply them with a vital portion of the information they need.[1]

This chapter and the following two chapters describe the structure and writing of this vital form of business communication.

How often you write reports in the years ahead will depend on the size of the organization you work for. If you work for a very small organization (say, one with fewer than 10 employees), you will probably write only a few. But if you work for a midsize or larger organization, you are likely to write many. In fact, the larger the organization, the more reports you are likely to write. The explanation is obvious. The larger the organization, the greater is its complexity; and the greater the complexity, the greater is the need for information to manage the organization. As reports supply much of the information needed, the demand for them is great.

- Reports are vital to larger organizations. You will probably write them.

DEFINING REPORTS

You probably have a good idea of what reports are. Even so, you would be likely to have a hard time defining them. Even scholars of the subject cannot agree, for their definitions range from one extreme to the other. Some define reports to include almost any presentation of information; others limit reports to only the most formal presentations. For our purposes, this middle-ground definition is best: *A business report is an orderly and objective communication of factual information that serves a business purpose.*

- A business report is an orderly and objective communication of factual information that serves a business purpose.

The key words in this definition deserve emphasis. As an *orderly* communication, a report is prepared carefully. Thus, care in preparation distinguishes reports from casual exchanges of information. The *objective* quality of a report is its unbiased approach. Reports seek truth. They avoid human biases. The word *communication* is broad in meaning. It covers all ways of transmitting meaning—speaking, writing, drawing, and such. The basic ingredient of reports is *factual information*. Factual information is based on events, records, data, and the like. Not all reports are business reports. Research scientists,

- The key words are *orderly, objective, communication, factual information,* and *serves a business purpose.*

---

1 The following review of report writing is condensed from Raymond V. Lesikar and John D. Pettit, Jr., *Report Writing for Business,* 10th ed. (Burr Ridge, IL: Irwin/McGraw-Hill, 1998).

Report writing requires hard work and clear thinking in every stage of the process. To determine the problem and to gather facts, you will need to consult many sources of information.

medical doctors, ministers, students, and many others write them. To be classified as a business report, a report must *serve a business purpose.*

This definition is specific enough to be meaningful, yet broad enough to take into account the variations in reports. For example, some reports (information reports) do nothing more than present facts. Others (analytical reports) go a step further by including interpretations, sometimes accompanied by conclusions and recommendations. There are reports that are highly formal both in writing style and in physical appearance. And there are reports that show a high degree of informality. Our definition permits all of these variations.

DETERMINING THE REPORT PURPOSE

- Work on a report begins with a business need (problem).

Your work on a report logically begins with a need, which we refer to generally as the *problem* in the following discussion. Someone or some group (usually your superiors) needs information for a business purpose. Perhaps the need is for information only; perhaps it is for information and analysis; or perhaps it is for information, analysis, and recommendations. Whatever the case, someone with a need (problem) will authorize you to do the work. Usually the work will be authorized orally. But it could be authorized in a letter or a memorandum.

- Your first task is to get the problem clearly in mind.

After you have been assigned a report problem, your first task should be to get your problem clearly in mind. Elementary and basic as this task may appear, all too often it is done haphazardly. And all too often a report fails to reach its goal because of such haphazardness.

THE PRELIMINARY INVESTIGATION

- To do this, you should begin by gathering all the information you need to understand the problem.

Getting your problem clearly in mind is largely a matter of gathering all the information needed to understand it and then applying your best logic to it. Gathering the right information involves many things, depending on the problem. It may mean gathering material from company files, talking over the problem with experts, searching through printed sources, and discussing the problem with those who authorized the report. In general, you should continue this preliminary investigation until you have the information you need to understand your problem.

NEED FOR A CLEAR STATEMENT OF THE PROBLEM

After you understand your problem, your next step is to state it clearly. Writing the problem statement is good practice for several reasons. A written statement is preserved permanently. Thus, you may refer to it time and again. In addition, a written statement can be reviewed, approved, and evaluated by people whose assistance may be valuable. Most important of all, putting the problem in writing forces you to think it through.

■ Then you should express the problem clearly, preferably in writing.

The problem statement normally takes one of three forms: infinitive phrase, question, or declarative statement. To illustrate each, we will use the problem of determining why sales at a certain store have declined:

■ The problem statement may be (1) an infinitive phrase, (2) a question, or (3) a declarative statement.

1. *Infinitive phrase:* "To determine the causes of decreasing sales at Store X."
2. *Question:* "What are the causes of decreasing sales at Store X?"
3. *Declarative statement:* "Store X sales are decreasing, and management wants to know why."

These three forms are grammatical structures with which to state a report problem. As such, crystal-clear thinking must precede any grammatical statement, for clear problem statements are only as good as the thinking that guides them. Accordingly, one form is not better than another. You may use any of the three forms for stating the report problem. All of them should give a problem statement with equal clarity and with the same intended meaning.

■ One form is not superior to the others.

One way to make sure you have the problem clearly in mind is to state it in one form (say the infinitive phrase) and then state it again in another form (say the question form). No differences in meanings should exist between the two problem statements. If there are differences, you should rethink the report problem for clarity before you proceed further in the report process.

■ State the problem in several forms. The meaning should be the same.

DETERMINING THE FACTORS

After stating the problem, you determine what needs to be done to solve it. Specifically, you look for the factors of the problem. That is, you determine what subject areas you must look into to solve the problem.

■ Next, you should determine the factors of the problem.

Problem factors may be of three types. First, they may be subtopics of the overall topic about which the report is concerned. Second, they may be hypotheses that must be tested. Third, in problems that involve comparisons, they may be the bases on which the comparisons are made.

■ The factors may be subtopics of the overall topic, hypotheses, or bases for comparison.

USE OF SUBTOPICS IN INFORMATION REPORTS

If the problem concerns a need for information, your mental effort should produce the main areas about which information is needed. Illustrating this type of situation is the problem of preparing a report that reviews Company X's activities during the past quarter. Clearly, this is an informational report problem—that is, it requires no analysis, no conclusion, no recommendation. It only requires that information be presented. The mental effort in this case is concerned simply with determining which subdivisions of the overall topic should be covered. After thoroughly evaluating the possibilities, you might come up with something like this analysis:

■ Subtopics of the overall topic are the factors in information reports.

Problem statement: To review operations of Company X from January 1 through March 31.

Subtopics
1. Production
2. Sales and promotion
3. Financial status

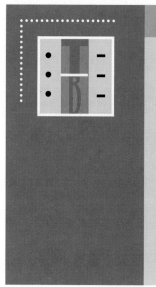

Styles or Tags: A Useful Formatting Feature

Anytime you find a need to repeatedly use the same formatting codes, *styles* or *tags* is a feature you will want to use. Although the feature is called styles in word processing and tags in desktop publishing, the two do essentially the same thing. When writing reports is a regular part of your job, you can create styles or tags to help you format titles, headings, body text, bibliography items, and any other parts that you use repeatedly.

In addition, you can create a library of styles to use across all your documents. Not only will using these styles ensure consistency within your report, but also your reports will be consistent over time. And you will save yourself the time and effort of having to look up the formatting you used the last time you wrote a similar report. If you decide to change the look of your report, you can edit the style instead of having to search through your entire document for all the individual formatting codes. Or you could simply delete the current style and apply a new one.

Styles and tags are easy both to create and to use. Once you have set them up, you reap rewards every time you use them.

4. Plant and equipment
5. Product development
6. Human resources

HYPOTHESES FOR PROBLEMS REQUIRING SOLUTION

> Hypotheses (possible explanations of the problem) may be the factors in problems requiring solution.

Some problems concern why something bad is happening and perhaps how to correct it. In analyzing problems of this kind, you should seek explanations or solutions. Such explanations or solutions are termed *hypotheses*. Once formulated, hypotheses are tested, and their applicability to the problem is either proved or disproved.

To illustrate, assume that you have the problem of determining why sales at a certain store have declined. In preparing this problem for investigation, you would think of the possible explanations (hypotheses) for the decline. Your task would be one of studying, weighing, and selecting, and you would come up with such explanations as these:

> For example, these hypotheses could be suggested to explain a store's loss in sales.

Problem statement: Sales at the Milltown store have declined, and management wants to know why.

Hypotheses:
1. Activities of the competition have caused the decline.
2. Changes in the economy of the area have caused the decline.
3. Merchandising deficiencies have caused the decline.
4. Changes in the environment (population shifts, political actions, etc.) have caused the decline.

In the investigation that follows, you would test these hypotheses. You might find that one, two, or all apply. Or you might find that none is valid. If so, you would have to advance additional hypotheses for further evaluation.

BASES OF COMPARISON IN EVALUATION STUDIES

> For evaluation problems, the bases for evaluating are the factors.

When the problem concerns evaluating something, either singularly or in comparison with other things, you should look for the bases for the evaluation. That is, you should determine what characteristics you will evaluate. In some cases, the procedure may concern more than naming the characteristics. It may also include the criteria to be used in evaluating them.

> This illustration shows the bases for comparing factory locations.

Illustrating this technique is the problem of a company that seeks to determine which of three cities would be best for a new factory. Such a problem obviously involves a comparison of the cities. The bases for comparison are the factors that determine success for the type of factory involved. After careful mental search for these factors, you might come up with a plan such as this:

Problem statement: To determine whether Y Company's new factory should be built in City A, City B, or City C.

Comparison bases:
1. Availability of labor
2. Abundance of raw material
3. Tax structure
4. Transportation facilities
5. Nearness to markets
6. Energy sources
7. Community attitude

NEED FOR SUBBREAKDOWN

Each of the factors selected for investigation may have factors of its own. In the last illustration, for example, the comparison of transportation in the three cities may well be covered by such subdivisions as water, rail, truck, and air. Labor may be compared by using such categories as skilled labor and unskilled labor. Breakdowns of this kind may go still further. Skilled labor may be broken down by specific skills: machinists, plumbers, pipefitters, welders, and such. The subdivisions could go on and on. Make them as long as they are helpful.

■ The factors sometimes have factors of their own. That is, they may also be broken down.

GATHERING THE INFORMATION NEEDED

For most business problems, you will need to conduct a personal investigation. A production problem, for example, might require gathering and reviewing the company's production records. A sales problem might require collecting information through discussions with customers and sales personnel. A computer problem might require talking to both end users and programmers. A purchasing problem might require getting sales literature, finding prices, compiling performance statistics, and so on. Such a personal investigation usually requires knowledge of your field of work, which is probably why you were assigned the problem.

■ The next step is to conduct the research needed. A personal investigation is usually appropriate.

Some business problems require a more formal type of research, such as an experiment or a survey. The experiment is the basic technique of the sciences. Business uses experiments primarily in the laboratory, although experiments have some nonlaboratory applications in marketing. Surveys are more likely to be used in business, especially in marketing problems. If you are called on to use experiments or surveys, it will probably be because your training has prepared you to use them. If you should need these techniques in this course, you will find them summarized in Chapter 19.

■ Experiments or surveys are sometimes needed.

In some cases, you may use library research to find the information you need. Perhaps you have a good working knowledge of the techniques of library research. If you do not, you will find these techniques also summarized in Chapter 19. To present facts from library sources in reports, you will need to use still other techniques—constructing a bibliography, citing references, quoting, paraphrasing, and so on. These techniques are covered in Appendix E.

■ Sometimes library research is used.

With the computer, you can search for electronically stored information. By using the Internet, a worldwide collection of networks, you can connect to information sources throughout the world. For example, you can work with others at different locations, you can access databases, you can use larger computers to help in your research, or you can browse any number of library catalogs. As noted in Chapter 16, the Internet is a vital source for information gathering in business reports. Information quality varies widely on the Internet, however. You should make sure the sources you consult are reliable.

■ The Internet gives you access to many information sources. Quality may vary.

In any event, your task is to apply whatever research techniques are required to get the information you need for your problem. When you have gathered that information, you are ready for the next step in report preparation.

■ Apply the research techniques needed for the problem.

Interpreting facts requires playing the role of a judge. To get to the truth, you must rise above the ordinary person and think without bias, prejudice, and emotion. You should consider all sides of a problem in your search for the truth.

INTERPRETING THE FINDINGS

- Next, apply the information collected to the problem. Interpret it.

- Interpreting is mental. You can profit from the following advice.

With your research done, you are ready to prepare your findings for presentation. Good business etiquette requires that you perform this task with your readers' convenience in mind. If your readers will want only the facts you have found, you need only organize by subtopics of the subject. But if your readers will want an analysis of the data with application to the problem, you must do much more. You must interpret the information as it affects the problem. Applying and interpreting your findings is obviously a mental process. Thus, we can give you only limited advice on how to do it. But even though this advice is limited, you can profit by following it.

ADVICE FOR AVOIDING HUMAN ERROR

- Avoid human error by remembering these fundamentals:
- 1. Report the facts as they are.

- 2. Do not think that conclusions are always necessary.

- 3. Do not interpret a lack of evidence as proof to the contrary.
- 4. Do not compare noncomparable data.

- 5. Do not draw illogical cause-effect conclusions.

- 6. Beware of unreliable and unrepresentative data.

- 7. Do not oversimplify.

The first advice is to avoid certain human tendencies that lead to error in interpretation. Foremost among these are the following:

1. Report the facts as they are. Do nothing to make them more or less exciting. Adding color to interpretations to make the report more interesting amounts to bias.

2. Do not think that conclusions are always necessary. When the facts do not support a conclusion, you should conclude that there is no conclusion. All too often report writers think that if they do not conclude, they have failed in their investigation.

3. Do not interpret a lack of evidence as proof to the contrary. The fact that you cannot prove something is true does not mean that it is false.

4. Do not compare noncomparable data. When you look for relationships between sets of data, make sure they have similarities—that you do not have apples and oranges.

5. Do not draw illogical cause-effect conclusions. Just because two sets of data appear to affect each other does not mean they actually do. Use your good logic to determine whether a cause-effect relationship is likely.

6. Beware of unreliable and unrepresentative data. Much of the information to be found in secondary sources is incorrect to some extent. The causes are many: collection error, biased research, recording mistakes. Beware especially of data collected by groups that advocate a position (political organizations, groups supporting social issues, and other special interest groups). Make sure the sources you uncover are reliable. And remember that the interpretations you make are no better than the data you interpret.

7. Do not oversimplify. Most business problems are complex, and all too often we neglect some important parts of them.

■ You're right. This report does make you look like a fool. (*Vietor's Funny Business.*)

APPROPRIATE ATTITUDES AND PRACTICES

In addition to being alert to the most likely causes of error, you can improve your interpretation of findings by adopting the following attitudes and practices:

1. Maintain a judicial attitude. Play the role of a judge as you interpret. Look at all sides of every issue without emotion or prejudice. Your primary objective is to uncover truth.

2. Consult with others. It is rare indeed when one mind is better than two or more. Thus, you can profit by talking over your interpretations with others.

3. Test your interpretations. Unfortunately, the means of testing are subjective and involve the thinking process. Even so, testing is helpful and can help you avoid major error. Two tests are available to you.

First is the test of experience. In applying this test, you use the underlying theme in all scientific methods—reason. You ponder each interpretation you make, asking yourself, "Does this appear reasonable in light of all I know or have experienced?"

Second is the negative test, which is an application of the critical viewpoint. You begin by making the interpretation that is directly opposite your initial one. Next, you examine the opposite interpretation carefully in light of all available evidence, perhaps even building a case for it. Then you compare the two interpretations and retain the one that is more strongly supported.

STATISTICAL TOOLS IN INTERPRETATION

In most cases, the information you gather is quantitative—that is, expressed in numbers. Such data in their raw form usually are voluminous, consisting of tens, hundreds, even thousands of figures. To use these figures intelligently, you must first find ways of simplifying them so that your reader can grasp their general meaning. Statistical techniques provide many methods for analyzing data. By knowing them, you can improve your ability to interpret. Although a thorough review of statistical techniques is beyond the scope of this book, you should know the more commonly used methods described in the following paragraphs.

Possibly of greatest use to you in writing reports are *descriptive statistics*—measures of central tendency, dispersion, ratios and probability. Measures of central tendency—the mean, median, and mode—will help you find a common value of a series that appropriately describes a whole. The measures of dispersion—ranges, variances, and standard deviations—should help you describe the spread of a series. Ratios (which express one quantity as a multiple of another) and probabilities (which determine how many times something will likely occur out of the total number of possibilities) can also help you convey common meaning in data analysis. Inferential and other statistical approaches are also useful but go beyond these basic elements. You will find descriptions of these and other useful techniques in any standard statistics textbook.

A word of caution, however: Your job as an analyst is to help your reader interpret the

■ Adopt the following attitudes and practices:

■ 1. Maintain a judicial attitude.

■ 2. Consult with others.

■ 3. Test your interpretations.

■ Use the test of experience—reason.

■ Use the negative test—question your interpretations.

■ Statistics permit you to examine a set of facts.

■ Descriptive statistics should help the most.

information. Sometimes unexplained statistical calculations—even if elementary to you—may confuse the reader. Thus, you must explain your statistical techniques explicitly. You must remember that statistics are a help to interpretation, not a replacement for it. Whatever you do to reduce the volume of data deserves careful explanation so that the reader will receive the intended meaning.

ORGANIZING THE REPORT INFORMATION

When you have finished interpreting your information, you know the message of your report. Now you are ready to organize this message for presentation. Your goal here is to present the information in the order that communicates best to your readers. In the interest of good business etiquette, you want not just what is easiest for you but what will best serve your readers. Organizing the report message, of course, is the procedure of constructing the outline. As you know, an outline is the plan for the writing task that follows. It is to you, the writer, what the blueprint is to the construction engineer or what the pattern is to the dressmaker. Constructing an outline forces you to think before you write. When you do this, your writing is likely to benefit.

Although your plan may be written or mental, using a written plan would be advisable for all but the shortest problems. In a longer report, the outline forms the basis for the table of contents. Also, in most long reports, and even in some short ones, the outline topics may be used as guides to the reader by placing them within the text as headings to the material they cover.

In constructing your outline, you probably will use either the conventional or the decimal symbol system to mark the levels. The conventional system uses Roman numerals to show the major headings and letters of the alphabet and Arabic numbers to show the lesser headings, as illustrated here:

Conventional System

   I. First-level heading
      A. Second level, first part
      B. Second level, second part
         1. Third level, first part
         2. Third level, second part
            a. Fourth level
               (1) Fifth level
                  (a) Sixth level
  II. First-level heading
      A. Second level, first part
      B. Second level, second part
      Etc.

The decimal system uses whole numbers to show the major sections. Whole numbers followed by decimals and additional digits show subsections. That is, the digits to the right of the decimal show each successive step in the outline. Illustration best explains this system:

Decimal System

1.0 First-level heading
    1.1 Second level, first part
    1.2 Second level, second part
        1.2.1 Third level, first part
        1.2.2 Third level, second part
            1.2.2.1 Fourth level, first part
            1.2.2.2 Fourth level, second part

2.0 First-level heading
    2.1 Second level, first part
    2.2 Second level, second part
    Etc.

Whatever system you use, when you begin producing the final report you also will show differences in the levels of headings by placement and form (font, size, or style). The placement and form options available to you are reviewed in Appendix B.

THE NATURE AND EXTENT OF OUTLINING

In general, you should build the outline around the objective of the report and the information you have gathered to meet that objective. With the objective and your information in mind, you build the structure of the report mentally. In this process, you shift facts and ideas about until the most workable order becomes clear. That order is the one that presents the findings in the clearest and most meaningful way.

■ The outline is designed to meet the objective of the report.

How much work you will have to do at this stage varies by problem. In some cases, you may have little to do, for you may have determined the order of the report in preceding steps. For example, the problem factors that you determined early in the investigation may also be the main heads of your outline. Or perhaps you worked out an order for presenting your research findings when you analyzed and interpreted them. In all likelihood, when you reach the stage of consciously constructing the outline, you will find that you have already done some of the work. Even so, there will probably be much to do. In doing it, you would be wise to use the general procedure described in the following paragraphs.

■ When you reach the outlining stage, you have probably done some of the work.

INTRODUCTORY AND CONCLUDING PARTS

Outlining is concerned mainly with the part of the report commonly called the *body*. The body is the part of the report that presents the information gathered, with analyses and interpretations where needed. It is usually preceded by an introduction, which is common in all but the shortest reports. And it is usually followed by an ending section, which may be a summary, a conclusion, a recommendation, or some combination of the three. The introduction and the ending section are parts of the outline, of course, but the following discussion does not concern them. The structure and content of these parts are discussed where appropriate in following chapters.

■ The following discussion of outlining deals with the body of the report. Assume that an introduction and a conclusion will be added.

ORGANIZATION BY DIVISION

The outlining procedure described in the following pages is based on the idea that outlining is a process of dividing. The subject you are dividing is all the information (facts) you have gathered and interpreted. Thus, you begin the task of organizing by looking over that information for some logical way of dividing it into comparable parts. When you find a way, you divide it. This process gives you the major outline parts indicated in Figure 10.1 by the Roman numeral captions (II, III, IV, and so on).

■ You may view outlining as a process of division. First, you divide the whole into parts.

In short reports, one division may be enough. Long reports, however, may require that each part in the first division be divided. The parts in the second division are identified by capital letter headings (A, B, C). You may have to divide a third time (for the 1, 2, 3 outline parts). In fact, you may continue to subdivide as long as it is practical to do so. Each division makes a step in the outline.

■ Then you divide the parts into subparts. You may subdivide further.

DIVISION BY CONVENTIONAL RELATIONSHIPS

In dividing your information into subparts, you have to find a way of dividing that will produce approximately equal parts. Time, place, quantity, and factor are the general bases for these divisions.

■ Time, place, quantity, and factor are the bases for the process of division.

Whenever the information you have to present has some time aspect, consider organiz-

Software Tools Assist the Writer in Both Identifying Factors and Outlining

Inspiration is a productivity tool aimed at helping business executives create and outline business documents.

The example shown here demonstrates how individuals or groups can brainstorm the factors of a report that investigates which laser printers a product design department should purchase. Using either the diagram or outline view (or both), a report writer would list as many ideas as possible. Later, the items and relationships can be rearranged by dragging and moving pointers.

The software will update the outline symbols as changes are made. Users can toggle between the views to work with the mode that is best for them.

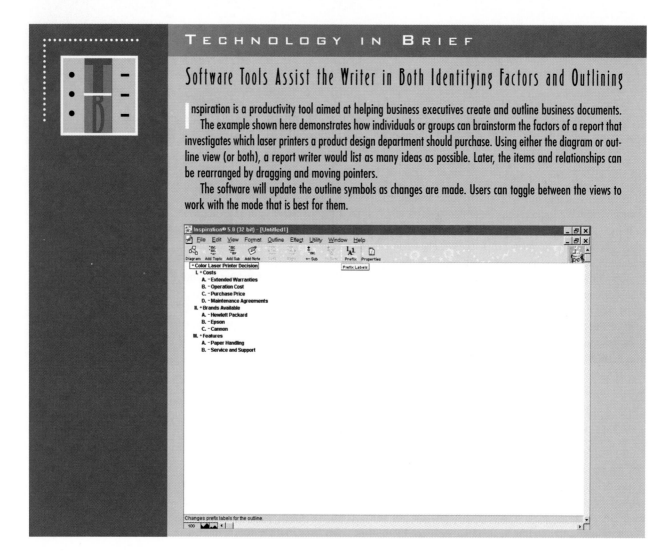

When the information has a time basis, division by time is possible.

ing it by *time*. In such an organization, the divisions are periods of time. These time periods usually follow a sequence. Although a past-to-present or present-to-past sequence is the rule, variations are possible. The periods you select need not be equal in duration, but they should be about equal in importance.

A report on the progress of a research committee illustrates this possibility. The period covered by this report might be broken down into the following comparable subperiods:

The period of orientation, May–July
Planning the project, August
Implementation of the research plan, September–November

The happenings within each period might next be arranged in order of occurrence. Close inspection might reveal additional division possibilities.

If the information you have collected has some relation to geographic location, you may use a *place* division. Ideally, this division would be such that the areas are nearly equal in importance.

When the information is related to geographic location, a place division is possible.

A report on the U.S. sales program of a national manufacturer illustrates a division by place. The information in this problem might be broken down by these major geographic areas:

New England

Atlantic Seaboard

South

Southwest

FIGURE 10.1 Procedure for Constructing an Outline by Process of Division

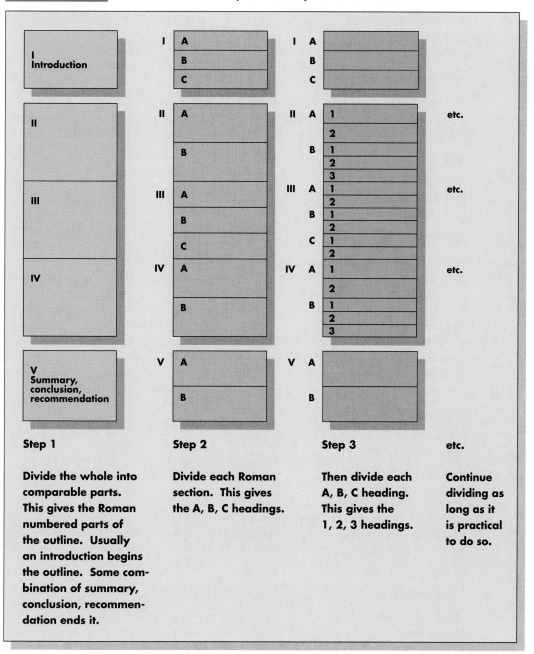

Step 1

Divide the whole into comparable parts. This gives the Roman numbered parts of the outline. Usually an introduction begins the outline. Some combination of summary, conclusion, recommendation ends it.

Step 2

Divide each Roman section. This gives the A, B, C headings.

Step 3

Then divide each A, B, C heading. This gives the 1, 2, 3 headings.

etc.

Continue dividing as long as it is practical to do so.

Source: Raymond V. Lesikar and John D. Pettit, Jr., *Report Writing for Business,* 10th ed. (Burr Ridge, IL: Irwin/McGraw-Hill, 1998).

Midwest

Rocky Mountains

Pacific Coast

Another illustration of organization by place is a report on the productivity of a company with a number of manufacturing plants. A major division of the report might be devoted to each of the plants. The information for each plant might be broken down further, this time by sections, departments, divisions, or the like.

Quantity divisions are possible for information that has quantitative values. To illustrate, an analysis of the buying habits of potential customers could be divided by such income groups as the following:

■ Division based on quantity is possible when the information has a number base.

Under $30,000

$30,000 to under $45,000

$45,000 to under $60,000

$60,000 to under $85,000

$85,000 to under $100,000

$100,000 and over

Another example of division on a quantitative basis is a report of a survey of men's preferences for shoes, in which an organization by age groups might be used to show variations in preference by ages. Perhaps the following division would be appropriate:

Youths, under 18

Young adults, 18–30

Adults, 31–50

Senior adults, 51–70

Elder adults, over 70

Factor breakdowns are less easily seen than the preceding three possibilities. Problems often have few or no time, place, or quantity aspects. Instead, they require that certain information areas be investigated. Such areas may consist of questions that must be answered in solving a problem, or of subjects that must be investigated and applied to the problem.

An example of a division by factors is a report that seeks to determine which of three cities is the best as the location of a new office for property management. In arriving at this decision, one would need to compare the three cities based on the factors affecting the office location. Thus, the following organization of this problem would be a possibility:

Location accessibility

Rent

Parking

Convenience to current customers

Facilities

Another illustration of organization by factors is a report advising a manufacturer whether to begin production of a new product. The solution of this problem will be reached by careful consideration of the factors involved. Among the more likely factors are these:

Production feasibility

Financial considerations

Strength of competition

Consumer demand

Marketing considerations

COMBINATION AND MULTIPLE DIVISION POSSIBILITIES

Not all division possibilities are clearly time, place, quantity, or factor. In some instances, combinations of these bases of division are possible. In a report on the progress of a sales organization, for example, the information collected could be arranged by a combination of quantity and place:

Areas of high sales activity

Areas of moderate sales activity

Areas of low sales activity

Although less logical, the following combination of time and quantity is also a possibility:

- Factors (areas to be investigated) are a fourth basis for dividing information.

- Combinations of time, place, quantity, and factor are sometimes logical.

Periods of low sales

Periods of moderate sales

Periods of high sales

Some problems can be organized in more than one way. For example, take the problem of determining the best of three cities for locating a new manufacturing plant. It could be organized by cities or by the bases of comparison. Organized by cities, the bases of comparison would probably be the second-level headings:

■ Multiple organization possibilities can occur.

II. City A
   A. Availability of workers
   B. Transportation facilities
   C. Public support and cooperation
   D. Availability of raw materials
   E. Taxation
   F. Sources of power
III. City B
   A. Availability of workers
   B. And so on
IV. City C
   A. Availability of workers
   B. And so on

■ This plant-location problem is organized by place.

Organized by bases of comparison, cities would probably be the second-level headings:

II. Availability of workers
   A. City A
   B. City B
   C. City C
III. Transportation facilities
   A. City A
   B. City B
   C. City C
IV. Public support and cooperation
   A. City A
   B. City B
   C. City C

■ Here, it is organized by factors (the bases of comparison).

At first glance, both plans appear logical. Close inspection, however, shows that organization by cities separates information that has to be compared. For example, three different parts of the report must be examined to find out which city has the best worker availability. In the second outline, the information that has to be compared is close together. You can determine which city has the best worker availability after reading only one section of the report.

Nevertheless, these two plans show that some problems can be organized in more than one way. In such cases, you must compare the possibilities carefully to find the one that best presents the report information.

■ The second plan is better because it makes comparison easy.

WORDING OF THE OUTLINE

The outline in its finished form is the table of contents. Its parts serve as headings to the sections of the report (which is why we refer to these parts as *headings* in the following discussion). Since the outline is an important part of the report, you should construct its final wording carefully. In this regard, you should consider the conventional principles of construction reviewed in the following pages.

■ When the outline will appear in the report, take care in its wording.

TOPIC OR TALKING HEADINGS.   In selecting the wording for outline headings, you have a choice of two general forms—topic headings and talking headings. *Topic headings*

■ You may use topic or talking headings. Topic headings give only the subject of discussion.

are short constructions, frequently consisting of one or two words. They merely identify the topic of discussion. Here is a segment of a topic-heading outline:

II. Present armor unit
    A. Description and output
    B. Cost
    C. Deficiencies
III. Replacement effects
    A. Space
    B. Boiler setting
    C. Additional accessories
    D. Fuel

■ Talking headings identify the subject and tell what is said about it.

Like topic headings, *talking headings* (or *popular headings* as they are sometimes called) identify the subject matter covered. But they go a step further. They also indicate what is said about the subject. In other words, talking headings summarize the material they cover, as in this illustration:

II. Operation analyses of armor unit
    A. Recent lag in overall output
    B. Increase in cost of operation
    C. Inability to deliver necessary steam
III. Consideration of replacement effects
    A. Greater space requirements
    B. Need for higher boiler setting
    C. Efficiency possibilities of accessories
    D. Practicability of firing two fuels

The following report outline is made up of headings that talk:

I. Orientation to the problem
    A. Authorization by board action
    B. Problem of locating a woolen mill
    C. Use of miscellaneous government data
    D. Factors as bases of problem solution
II. Community attitudes toward the woolen industry
    A. Favorable reaction of all towns to new mill
    B. Mixed attitudes of all towns toward labor policy
III. Labor supply and prevailing wage rates
    A. Lead of San Marcos in unskilled labor
    B. Concentration of skilled workers in San Marcos
    C. Generally confused pattern of wage rates
IV. Nearness to the raw wool supply
    A. Location of Ballinger, Coleman, and San Marcos in the wool area
    B. Relatively low production near Big Spring and Littlefield
V. Availability of utilities
    A. Inadequate water supply for all towns but San Marcos
    B. Unlimited supply of natural gas for all towns
    C. Electric rate advantage of San Marcos and Coleman
    D. General adequacy of all towns for waste disposal
VI. Adequacy of existing transportation systems
    A. Surface transportation advantages of San Marcos and Ballinger
    B. General equality of airway connections
VII. A final weighting of the factors
    A. Selection of San Marcos as first choice
    B. Recommendation of Ballinger as second choice
    C. Lack of advantages in Big Spring, Coleman, and Littlefield

This report outline is made up of topic headings:

I. Introduction
   A. Authorization
   B. Purpose
   C. Sources
   D. Preview
II. Community attitudes
   A. Plant location
   B. Labor policy
III. Factors of labor
   A. Unskilled workers
   B. Skilled workers
   C. Wage rates
IV. Raw wool supply
   A. Adequate areas
   B. Inadequate areas
V. Utilities
   A. Water
   B. Natural gas
   C. Electricity
   D. Waste disposal
VI. Transportation
   A. Surface
   B. Air
VII. Conclusions
   A. First choice
   B. Alternative choice
   C. Other possibilities

PARALLELISM OF CONSTRUCTION.   As a general rule, you should write headings at each level of the outline in the same grammatical form. In other words, equal-level headings should be parallel in structure. This rule is not an exercise in grammar; its purpose is to show similarity. As you will recall from the discussion of conventional relationships of data, equal-level headings are divided consistently using time, place, quantity, factor, or combinations. You want to show consistently such equal-level divisions through parallel headings. For example, if the heading for Roman numeral I is a noun phrase, all other Roman numeral headings should be noun phrases. If the heading for A under I is a sentence, the A, B, C headings throughout the outline should be sentences. However, authorities also permit varying the form from one part to another (example: sentences for A, B, and C under II and noun phrases for A, B, and C under III).

The following segment of an outline illustrates violations of parallelism:

A. Machine output is lagging (sentence).
B. Increase in cost of operations (noun phrase)
C. Unable to deliver necessary steam (decapitated sentence)

You may correct this violation in any of three ways—by making the headings all sentences, all noun phrases, or all decapitated sentences. If you desire all noun phrases, you could construct such headings as these:

A. Lag in machine output
B. Increase in cost of operations
C. Inability to deliver necessary steam

Or you could make all the headings sentences, like this:

A. Machine output is lagging.
B. Cost of operations is increasing.
C. Boiler cannot deliver necessary steam.

■ Headings making up a level of division should be parallel grammatically.

CONCISENESS IN WORDING. Your talking captions should be the shortest possible word arrangement that can also meet the talking requirement. Although the following captions talk well, their excessive lengths obviously affect their roles in communicating the report information:

Personal appearance enhancement is the most desirable feature of contact lenses that wearers report.

The drawback of contacts mentioned by most people who can't wear them is that they are difficult to put on.

More comfort is the most desired improvement suggested by wearers and nonwearers of contact lenses.

Obviously, the captions contain too much information. Just what should be left out, however, is not easily determined. Much depends on the analysis the writers have given the material and what they have determined to be most significant. One analysis, for example, would support these revised captions:

Personal appearance most desirable feature

Difficulty of eye placement prime criticism

Comfort most desired improvement

VARIETY OF EXPRESSION. In the report outline, as in all other forms of writing, you should use a variety of expressions. You should not overwork words, for repeating words too frequently makes for monotonous writing; and monotonous writing is not pleasing to the reader. The following outline excerpt illustrates this point:

A. Chemical production in Texas
B. Chemical production in California
C. Chemical production in Louisiana

As a rule, if you make the headings talk well, there is little chance of monotonous repetition. Since your successive sections would probably not be presenting similar or identical information, headings really descriptive of the material they cover would not be likely to use the same words. The headings in the preceding example can be improved simply by making them talk:

A. Texas leads in chemical production.
B. California holds runner-up position.
C. Rapidly gaining Louisiana ranks third.

WRITING THE REPORT

After you have collected and organized your information, you are ready to begin writing. Much of what you should do in writing the report was covered in the review of clear writing techniques in Chapters 2 and 3. All of these techniques apply to report writing, and you would do well to keep them in mind as you write. As in all the business messages discussed previously, in report writing you have an obligation to communicate as easily, as clearly, and as quickly as possible. Good business etiquette demands that you do so. Your reader's time is valuable to his or her understanding of your message, and his or her understanding is vital to work performance.

You can further help your reader to receive the report message clearly by giving your report some specific characteristics of well-written reports. These characteristics are objectivity, consistency in time viewpoint, transition, and interest. We review each of them in the following pages.

REQUIREMENT OF OBJECTIVITY

Good report writing presents facts and logical interpretation of facts. It avoids presenting the writer's opinions, biases, and attitudes. In other words, it is objective.

You can make your report objective by putting aside your prejudices and biases, by approaching the problem with an open mind and looking at all sides of every issue, and by fairly reviewing and interpreting the information you have uncovered. Your role should be much like that of a fair-minded judge presiding over a court of law. You will leave no stone unturned in your search for truth.

OBJECTIVITY AS A BASIS FOR BELIEVABILITY.   An objective report has an ingredient that is essential to good report writing—believability. Biased writing in artfully deceptive language may at first glance be believable. But if bias is evident at any place in a report, the reader will be suspicious of the entire report. Maintaining objectivity is therefore the only sure way to make report writing believable.

■ Objective writing is believable.

OBJECTIVITY AND THE QUESTION OF IMPERSONAL VERSUS PERSONAL WRITING.   Recognizing the need for objectivity, the early report writers worked to develop an objective style of writing. Since the source of bias in reports was people, they reasoned objectivity was best attained by emphasizing facts rather than the people involved in writing and reading reports. So they tried to take the human beings out of their reports. The result was impersonal writing, that is, writing in the third person—without *I*'s, *we*'s, or *you*'s.

■ Historically, objective writing has meant writing impersonally (no *I*'s, *we*'s, *you*'s).

In recent years, some writers have questioned impersonal report writing. They argue that personal writing is more forceful and direct than impersonal writing. They point out that writing is more conversational and therefore more interesting if it brings both the reader and the writer into the picture. They contend that objectivity is an attitude—not a matter of person—and that a report written in personal style can be just as objective as a report written in impersonal style. Frequently, these writers argue that impersonal writing leads to an overuse of the passive voice and a dull writing style. This last argument, however, lacks substance. The style of impersonal writing can and should be interesting. Any dullness that impersonal writing may have is the fault of the writer. As proof, one has only to look at the lively style of writers for newspapers, newsmagazines, and journals. Most of this writing is impersonal—but it is usually not dull.

■ Recently, some writers have argued that personal writing is more interesting than impersonal writing and just as objective.

As in most controversies, the arguments of both sides have merit. In some situations, personal writing is better. In other situations, impersonal writing is better. And in still other situations, either type of writing is good.

■ There is merit to both sides. You would be wise to do what is expected of you.

Your decision should be based on the facts of each report situation. First, you should consider the expectations of those for whom you are preparing the report. More than likely, you will find a preference for impersonal writing, for businesspeople have been slow to break tradition. Then you should consider the formality of the situation. You should use personal writing for informal situations and impersonal writing for formal situations.

■ Good advice is to use personal style for routine reports and impersonal style for more formal reports.

Perhaps the distinction between impersonal and personal writing is best made by illustration.

Personal

Having studied the advantages and disadvantages of using coupons, I conclude that your company should not adopt this practice. If you use the coupons, you would have to pay out money for them. You would also have to hire additional employees to take care of the increase in sales volume.

Impersonal

A study of the advantages and disadvantages of using coupons supports the conclusion that the Mills Company should not adopt this practice. The coupons themselves would cost extra money. Also, use of coupons would require additional personnel to take care of the increase in sales volume.

CONSISTENCY IN TIME VIEWPOINT

Presenting information in the right place in time is a major problem in keeping order in a report. Not doing so confuses the reader and creates barriers to communication. Thus, it is important that you maintain a proper time viewpoint.

■ Keep a consistent time viewpoint throughout the report.

You have two choices of time viewpoint—past and present. Although some authorities favor one or the other, either viewpoint can produce a good report. The important thing is to be consistent—to select one time viewpoint and stay with it. In other words, you should view all similar information in the report from the same position in time.

■ There are two time viewpoints—past and present. Select one, and do not change.

■ The past time viewpoint views the research and the findings as past, and prevailing concepts and proven conclusions as present.

If you adopt the past time viewpoint, you treat the research, the findings, and the writing of the report as past. Thus, you would report the results of a recent survey in past tense: "Twenty-two percent of the managers *favored* a change." You would write a reference to another part of the report this way: "In Part III, this conclusion *was reached.*" Your use of the past time viewpoint would have no effect on references to future happenings. It would be proper to write a sentence like this: "If the current trend continues, 30 percent *will favor* a change by 2003." Prevailing concepts and proven conclusions are also exceptions. You would present them in present tense. For examples, take the sentences: "Solar energy *is* a major potential source of energy" and "The findings *show* conclusively that managers are not adequately trained."

■ The present time viewpoint presents as current all information that can be assumed to be current at the time of writing.

Writing in the present time viewpoint presents as current all information that can logically be assumed to be current at the time of writing. All other information is presented in its proper place in the past or future. Thus, you would report the results of a recent survey in these words: "Twenty-two percent of the managers *favor* a change." You would refer to another part of the text like this: "In Part III, this conclusion *is reached.*" In referring to an old survey, you would write: "In 1997 only 12 percent *held* this opinion." And in making a future reference, you would write: "If this trend continues, 30 percent *will hold* this opinion by 2003."

NEED FOR TRANSITION

■ You should use transitions to connect the parts of the report.

A well-written report reads as one continuous story. The parts connect smoothly. Much of this smoothness is the result of good, logical organization. But more than logical order is needed in long reports. As you will see in Chapter 12, a coherence plan may be needed in such reports. In all reports, however, lesser transitional techniques are useful to connect information.

■ *Transition* means a "bridging across."

By *transition* we mean a "bridging across." Transitions are made by means of words or sentences that show the relationships of succeeding parts. They may appear at the beginning of a part as a way of relating this part to the preceding part. They may appear at the end of a part as a forward look. Or they may appear within a part as words or phrases that help move the flow of information.

■ Transitions should be used where there is a need to connect the parts of the report.

Whether you use transitional words or a transitional sentence in a particular place depends on need. If there is need to relate parts, you should use a transition. Because good, logical organization frequently makes clear the relationships of the parts in a short report, such reports may need only a few transitional words or sentences. Longer and more involved reports, on the other hand, usually require more.

■ They should be made naturally, not mechanically.

Before we comment more specifically on transitions, we should make one point clear. You should not use transitions mechanically. You should use them only when they are needed—when leaving them out would produce abruptness. Transitions should not appear to be stuck in. They should blend naturally with the surrounding writing. For example,

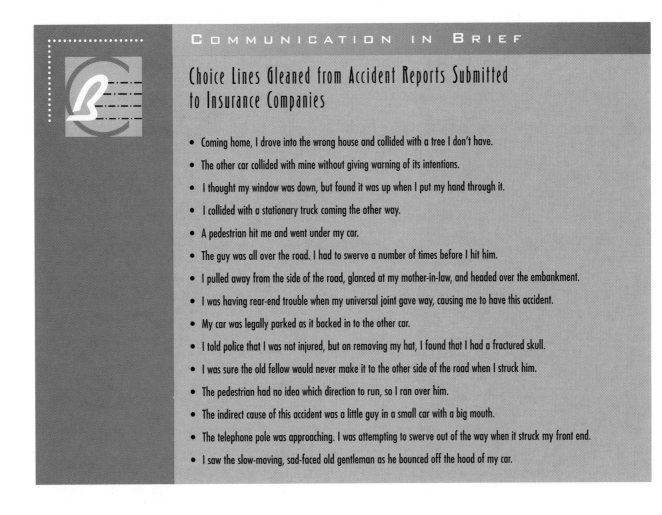

avoid transitions of this mechanical form: "The last section discussed Topic X. In the next section, Y will be analyzed."

SENTENCE TRANSITIONS. Throughout the report you can improve the connecting network of thought by the wise use of sentence transitions. You can use them especially to connect parts of the report. The following example shows how a sentence can explain the relationship between Sections A and B of a report. Note that the first words draw a conclusion for Section B. Then, with smooth tie-in, the next words introduce Section C and relate this part to the report plan. The words in brackets explain the pattern of the thought connections.

> ■ For connecting large parts, transition sentences may be used.

[Section B, concluded] . . . Thus, the data show only negligible differences in the cost for oil consumption [subject of Section B] for the three brands of cars.

[Section C] Even though the costs of gasoline [subject of Section A] and oil [subject of Section B] are the more consistent factors of operation expense, the picture is not complete until the costs of repairs and maintenance [subject of Section C] are considered.

In the following examples, succeeding parts are connected by sentences that make a forward-looking reference and thus set up the next subject. As a result, the shift of subject matter is smooth and logical.

These data show clearly that Edmond's machines are the most economical. Unquestionably, their operation by low-cost gas and their record for low-cost maintenance give them a decided edge over competing brands. *Before a definite conclusion about their merit is reached, however, one more vital comparison should be made.*

(The final sentence clearly introduces the subsequent discussion of an additional comparison.)

. . . At first glance the data appear convincing, but a closer observation reveals a number of discrepancies.

(Discussion of the discrepancies is logically set up by this sentence.)

Placing topic sentences at key points of emphasis is another way of using sentences to link the various parts of the report. Usually the topic sentence is best placed at the paragraph beginning. Note in the following example how topic sentences maintain the flow of thought by emphasizing key information.

Brand C accelerates faster than the other two brands, both on a level road and on a 9 percent grade. According to a test conducted by Consumption Research, Brand C reaches a speed of 60 miles per hour in 13.2 seconds. To reach the same speed, Brand A requires 13.6 seconds, and Brand B requires 14.4 seconds. On a 9 percent grade, Brand C reaches the 60-miles-per-hour speed in 29.4 seconds, and Brand A reaches it in 43.3 seconds. Brand B is unable to reach this speed.

Because it carries more weight on its rear wheels than the others, Brand C has the best traction of the three. Traction, which means a minimum of sliding on wet or icy roads, is important to safe driving, particularly during the cold, wet winter months. Since traction is directly related to the weight carried by the rear wheels, a comparison of these weights should give some measure of the safety of the three cars. According to data released by the Automobile Bureau of Standards, Brand C carries 47 percent of its weight on its rear wheels. Brands B and A carry 44 and 42 percent, respectively.

TRANSITIONAL WORDS.   Although the major transition problems concern connection between the major parts of the report, transitions are needed between the lesser parts. If the writing is to flow smoothly, you will need to connect clause to clause, sentence to sentence, and paragraph to paragraph. Transitional words and phrases generally serve to make such connections.

Numerous transitional words are available. The following list shows such words and how you can use them. With a little imagination to supply the context, you can easily see how these words relate ideas. For better understanding, the words are grouped by the relationships they show between what comes before and what follows.

Relationship	Word Examples
Listing or enumeration of subjects	In addition First, second, and so on Besides Moreover
Contrast	On the contrary In spite of On the other hand In contrast However
Likeness	In a like manner Likewise Similarly
Cause–result	Thus Because of Therefore Consequently For this reason
Explanation or elaboration	For example To illustrate For instance Also Too

■ Use of topic sentences also helps improve thought flow.

■ Transitional words show relationships between lesser parts.

■ This partial list shows how words explain relationships.

Like any other form of writing, report writing should be interesting. Actually, interest is as important as the facts of the report, for communication is not likely to occur without interest. Readers cannot help missing parts of the message if their interest is not held—if their minds are allowed to stray. Interest in the subject is not enough to ensure communication. The writing itself must be interesting. This should be evident to you if you have ever tried to read dull writing in studying for an examination. How desperately you wanted to learn the subject, but how often your mind strayed!

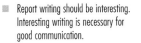

■ Report writing should be interesting. Interesting writing is necessary for good communication.

Perhaps writing interestingly is an art. But if so, it is an art in which you can develop ability by working at it. To develop this ability, you need to avoid the rubber-stamp jargon so often used in business and instead work to make your words build concrete pictures. You need to cultivate a feeling for the rhythmic flow of words and sentences. You need to remember that in back of every fact and figure there is life—people doing things, machines operating, a commodity being marketed. A technique of good report writing is to bring that life to the surface by using concrete words and active-voice verbs as much as possible. You should also work to achieve interest without using more words than are necessary.

■ Interesting writing is the result of careful word choice, rhythm, concreteness—in fact, all the good writing techniques.

Here a word of caution should be injected. You can overdo efforts to make report writing interesting. Such is the case whenever your reader's attention is attracted to how something has been said rather than to what has been said. Effective report writing simply presents information in a clear, concise, and interesting manner. Perhaps the purpose and definition of report-writing style are best summarized in this way: Report-writing style is at its best when the readers are prompted to say "Here are some interesting facts" rather than "Here is some beautiful writing."

■ But efforts to make writing interesting can be overdone. The writing style should never draw attention away from the information.

COLLABORATIVE REPORT WRITING

In your business career, you are likely to participate in collaborative writing projects. That is, you will work on a report with others. Group involvement in report preparation is becoming increasingly significant for a number of reasons. For one, the specialized knowledge of different people can improve the quality of the work. For another, the combined talents of the members are likely to produce a document better than could be done by any one of the members. A third reason is that dividing the work reduces the time needed for the project. And fourth, new software tools allow groups to collaborate from different places.

■ Collaborative report preparation is common for good reasons.

Some reports written in business are produced in collaboration with others. Although you will do some work individually, you can expect to plan, organize, and revise the report as a group.

DETERMINATION OF GROUP MAKEUP

■ Groups should have five or fewer members and include all pertinent specialization areas.

As a beginning step, the membership of the group should be determined. In this determination, the availability and competencies of the people in the work situation involved are likely to be the major considerations. As a minimum, the group will consist of two. The maximum will depend on the number actually needed to do the project. As a practical matter, however, a maximum of five is a good rule, for larger groups tend to lose efficiency. More important than size, however, is the need to include all major areas of specialization involved in the work to be done.

■ Preferably, the group has a leader, but there are exceptions.

In most business situations the highest ranking administrator in the group serves as leader. In groups made up of equals, a leader usually is appointed or elected. When no leader is so designated, the group works together informally. In such cases, however, an informal leader usually emerges.

TECHNIQUES OF PARTICIPATION

■ Leaders and participants have clear duties to make the procedure work.

The group's work should be conducted much the way a meeting should be conducted. As described in Chapter 14, leaders and members of meetings have clear roles and duties. Leaders must plan the sessions and follow the plan. They must move the work along. They must control the discussion, limiting those who talk too much and encouraging input from those who are reluctant to participate. Group members should actively participate, taking care not to monopolize. They should be both cooperative and courteous in their work with the group.

■ Groups often experience results that are less than ideal. Consult references on effective groups.

All too often, groups experience results that vary from these patterns. Although a discussion of group development and processes is beyond the scope of this book, you might want to consult one of the many references on the subject.[2] Group members should recognize that effective groups do not just happen. They have unique characteristics and processes that are planned for and managed explicitly.

PROCEDURE OF THE WORK

■ At least two meetings and a work period are needed.

As a general rule, groups working together on report projects need a minimum of two meetings with a work period between meetings. But the number of meetings required will vary with the needs of the project. For a project in which data gathering and other preliminary work must be done, additional meetings may be necessary. On the other hand, if only the writing of the report is needed, two meetings may be adequate.

ACTIVITIES INVOLVED

■ The following activities normally occur, usually in this sequence.

Whatever number of meetings are scheduled, the following activities typically occur, usually in the sequence shown. As you review them, it should be apparent that because of the differences in report projects, these activities vary in their implementation.

■ First, determine the report purpose.

DETERMINE THE PURPOSE.   As in all report projects, the participants must determine just what the report must do. Thus, the group should follow the preliminary steps of problem determination discussed previously.

■ Next, derive the factors involved.

DERIVE THE FACTORS.   The group next determines what is needed to achieve the purpose. This step involves determining the factors of the problem, as described earlier in the chapter. An advantage of collaboration is that several minds are available for the critical thinking that is so necessary for identifying the factors of the problem.

■ If necessary, make a plan for gathering the information needed.

GATHER THE INFORMATION NEEDED.   Before the group can begin work on the report, it must get the information needed. This activity could involve conducting any of the

---

[2] An especially good resource is Allan R. Cohen, Stephen L. Fink, Herman Gadon, and Robin D. Willits, *Effective Behavior in Organizations*, 6th ed. (Burr Ridge, IL: Irwin/McGraw-Hill, 1995). Note pages 94 and 157 for an excellent summary of group functioning.

Revision and Review Tools Help Track Others' Changes to Your Documents

The revision (review) tool found in most word processing software today helps when people work in groups. It allows you to track the number and the nature of changes group members contribute.

When others review, comment, and edit your document electronically, the revision tool will help you see what changes they suggest. In the example shown here, the reviewer simply clicks the Track Changes button on the revision toolbar. As changes are entered, the software tracks them by the person who made the change and by date. When the cursor is placed over the change, the name of the reviewer appears. You may also assign different colors to different reviewers.

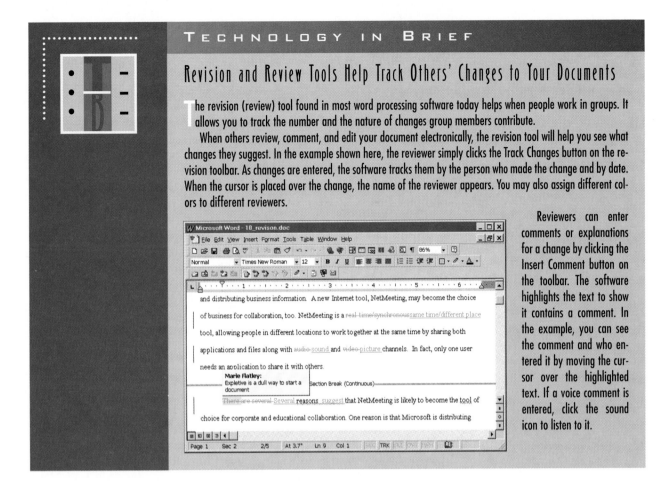

Reviewers can enter comments or explanations for a change by clicking the Insert Comment button on the toolbar. The software highlights the text to show it contains a comment. In the example, you can see the comment and who entered it by moving the cursor over the highlighted text. If a voice comment is entered, click the sound icon to listen to it.

---

research designs mentioned earlier in this chapter and in Chapter 19. In some cases, group work begins after the information has been assembled, thus eliminating this step.

INTERPRET THE INFORMATION.   Determining the meaning of the information gathered is the next logical step for the group. In this step, the participants apply the findings to the problem, thereby selecting the information to be used in the report. In applying the findings to the problem, they also give meaning to the facts collected. The facts do not speak for themselves. Rather, group participants must think through the facts, apply the facts to the problem, and derive logical meaning from the facts. Interpretations are no better than the thinking of the people in the group.

> ■ The members interpret the information, applying it to the problem.

ORGANIZE THE MATERIAL.   Just as in any other report-writing project, the group next organizes the material selected for presentation. They will apply time, place, quantity, factor (or combinations) relationships to the data collected in steps as shown in Figure 10.1.

> ■ They organize the information for presentation in the report.

PLAN THE WRITING.   A next logical step is that of planning the makeup of the report. In this step the formality of the situation and the audience involved determine the decision. In addition, matters of writing such as tone, style, and formality are addressed. Needs for coherence, time consistency, and interesting writing are usually reinforced.

> ■ They plan the writing of the report.

ASSIGN PARTS TO BE WRITTEN.   After the prewriting work has been done, the group next turns its attention to the work of writing. The usual practice is to assign each person a part of the report.

> ■ They assign themselves report parts to write.

- The members then write their parts.

WRITE PARTS ASSIGNED. Following comes a period of individual work. Each participant writes his or her part. Each will apply the ideas in Chapters 2 and 3 about word selection, sentence design, and paragraph construction to writing the assigned parts.

- The group members collaboratively review the writing.

REVISE COLLABORATIVELY. The group meets and reviews each person's contribution and the full report. This should be a give-and-take session with each person actively participating. It requires that every person gives keen attention to the work of each participant, making constructive suggestions wherever appropriate. It requires courteous but meaningful criticisms. It also requires that the participants be thick-skinned, keeping in mind that the goal is to construct the best possible document. In no case should the group merely give rubber-stamp approval to the work submitted. In cases of controversy, the majority views of the group should prevail.

- A selected member edits the final draft.

EDIT THE FINAL DRAFT. After the group has done its work, one member usually is assigned the task of editing the final draft. This gives the document consistency. In addition, the editor serves as a final proofreader. Probably the editor should be the most competent writer in the group.

If all the work has been done with care and diligence, this final draft should be a report better than anyone in the group could have prepared alone. Those who study groups use the word *synergistic* to refer to groups that function this way. The final report is better than the sum of the individual parts.

SUMMARY BY CHAPTER OBJECTIVES

1 State a problem clearly in writing.

1. Your work on a report begins with a problem (purpose, goal, objective).
   - Get the problem in mind by gathering all the information you need about it.
   - Then develop a problem statement from the information.
   - Phrase this statement as an infinitive phrase, a question, or a declarative statement.

2 List the factors involved in a problem.

2. From the problem statement, determine the factors involved.
   - These may be subtopics in information reports.
   - They may be hypotheses (possible explanations) in problems requiring a solution.
   - They may be bases of comparison in problems requiring evaluations.

3 Explain the common errors in interpreting and develop attitudes and practices conducive to good interpreting.

3. After you have gathered the information needed, interpret it as it applies to the problem.
   - Interpreting is mental and thus difficult to describe.
   - Heed this advice for avoiding human error:
     - Report the facts as they are.
     - Do not think that conclusions are always necessary.
     - Do not interpret a lack of evidence as proof to the contrary.
     - Do not compare noncomparable data.
     - Do not draw illogical cause-effect conclusions.
     - Beware of unreliable and unrepresentative data.
     - Do not oversimplify.
   - Adopt these attitudes and practices:
     - Maintain a judicial attitude.
     - Consult with others.
     - Test your interpretations by applying the test of experience (reason) and the negative test (question them).

4 Organize information in outline form, using time, place, quantity, factor, or a combination of these as bases for division.

4. Next, organize the information (construct an outline).
   - Probably you will use the conventional outline symbols (I, A, 1, a) or numeric symbols (1.0, 1.1, 1.11, 1.111) in structuring the outline.
   - Probably you will begin with an introduction and end with a summary, conclusion, or recommendation.

- Organize the report body (the part between the introduction and the ending section) by a process of division.
  - Look over the findings for ways of dividing on the basis of time, place, quantity, factor, or combinations.
  - Then divide, forming the major parts of the report (Roman numeral headings).
  - Next, look at these divisions for ways of dividing them (making the capital letter headings).
  - Continue to subdivide as far as necessary.
  - The end result is your outline.
5. Construct headings for each part in the outline.
   - Use the topic form (identifies topic).
   - Or use the talking form (identifies topic and says something about it).
   - Make the wording of comparable parts parallel grammatically.
   - Prune each caption for conciseness
   - Avoid excessive repetition of words.

5 Construct topic or talking headings that outline reports logically and meaningfully.

6. From the outline, write the report.
   - Follow the rules of clarity discussed previously in this book.
   - Maintain objectivity (no bias).
     - Impersonal writing style (third person) has long been associated with objectivity.
     - But some authorities question this style, saying personal style is more interesting.
     - The argument continues, although most formal reports are written in impersonal style.
   - Be consistent in time viewpoint—either past or present.
     - Past time viewpoint views the research and findings as past and prevailing concepts and conclusions as present.
     - Present time viewpoint presents as current all that is current at the time of writing.
   - Use transitions to make the report parts flow smoothly.
     - Between large parts, you may need to use full sentences to make connections.
     - Topic sentences also can help the flow of thought.
     - Use transitional words and phrases to connect the lesser parts.
   - Work to make the writing interesting.
     - Select words carefully for best effect.
     - Follow techniques of good writing (correctness, rhythmic flow of words, vigorous words, and such).
     - Do not overdo these efforts by drawing attention to how you write rather than what you say.

6 Write reports that are clear, objective, consistent in time viewpoint, smoothly connected, and interesting.

7. Expect that you will sometimes prepare reports collaboratively in groups.
   - Groups (two to five members) may produce better reports than individuals if all things go well.
   - Members of groups (leaders and participants) should have clear roles.
   - Groups should plan two or more meetings with a work period.
   - Groups should follow this procedure in writing reports collaboratively:
     - Determine report purpose.
     - Derive factors.
     - Collect facts for the report.
     - Interpret the facts.
     - Organize the facts.
     - Plan for writing.
     - Assign parts to members.
     - Write assigned parts.
     - Revise members' contributions collaboratively.
     - Edit the final draft.

7 Prepare reports collaboratively.

CRITICAL THINKING QUESTIONS

1. Explain the concept of outlining as a division process.

2. You are writing a report on the progress of your regional Bell Company's efforts to increase sales of five of its products through extensive advertising in print and online newspapers and magazines and on television and radio. Discuss the possibilities for major headings. Evaluate each possibility.

3. Not all business reports are written objectively. In fact, many are deliberately biased. Why, then, should we stress objectivity in a college course that includes report writing?

4. Explain how the question of personal and impersonal writing is related to objectivity.

5. Explain the differences between the present time viewpoint and the past time viewpoint.

6. Is it incorrect to have present, past, and future tense in the same report? In the same paragraph? In the same sentence? Discuss.

7. "Transitional sentences are unnecessary. They merely add length to a report and thus are contrary to the established rules of conciseness." Discuss.

8. "Reports are written for business executives who want them. Thus, you don't have to be concerned about holding your reader's interest." Discuss.

9. Collaborative reports are better than reports written by an individual because they use many minds rather than one. Discuss.

CRITICAL THINKING EXERCISES

1. For each of the following problem situations, write a clear statement of the problem and list the factors involved. When necessary, you may use your imagination logically to supply any additional information needed.

   a. A manufacturer of breakfast cereals wants to determine the characteristics of its consumers.

   b. The manufacturer of a toothpaste wants to learn what the buying public thinks of its product in relation to competing products.

   c. Southwestern Oil Company wants to give its stockholders a summary of its operations for the past calendar year.

   d. A building contractor engaged to build a new plant for Company X submits a report summarizing its monthly progress.

   e. The Able Wholesale Company must prepare a report on its credit relations with the Crystal City Hardware Company.

   f. The supervisor of Department X must prepare a report evaluating the performance of a secretary.

   g. Baker, Inc., wants a study made to determine why its employee turnover is high.

   h. An executive must rank three subordinates on the basis of their suitability for promotion to a particular job.

   i. The supervisor of production must compare three competing machines that are being considered for use in a particular production job.

   j. An investment consultant must advise a client on whether to invest in the development of a lake resort.

   k. A consultant seeks to learn how a restaurant can improve its profits.

2. Select a hypothetical problem with a time division possibility. What other division possibilities does it have? Compare the two possibilities as the main bases for organizing the report.

3. Assume that you are writing the results of a survey conducted to determine what styles of shoes are worn throughout the country on various occasions by women of all ages. What division possibilities exist here? Which would you recommend?

4. For the problem described in the preceding exercise, use your imagination to construct topic headings for the outline.

5. Point out any violations of grammatical parallelism in these headings:

   a. Region I sales lagging.

   b. Moderate increase seen for Region II.

   c. Region III sales remain strong.

6. Point out any error in grammatical parallelism in these headings:

   a. High cost of operation.

   b. Slight improvement in production efficiency.

   c. Maintenance cost is low.

7. Which of the following headings is logically inconsistent with the others?

   a. Agricultural production continues to increase.

   b. Slight increase is made by manufacturing.

   c. Salaries remain high.

   d. Service industries show no change.

8. Select an editorial, feature article, book chapter, or the like that has no headings. Write talking headings for it.

9. Assume that you are writing a report that summarizes a survey you have conducted. Write a paragraph of the report using the present time viewpoint; then write the paragraph using the past time viewpoint. The paragraph will be based on the following information:

   Answers to the question about how students view the proposed Aid to Education Bill in this survey and in a survey taken a year earlier (in parentheses).

   For, 39 percent (21); Against, 17 percent (43). No answer, undecided, etc., 44 percent (36).

11

Report Structure: The Shorter Forms

Upon completing this chapter, you will be able to write well-structured short reports. To reach this goal, you should be able to

1 Explain the structure of reports relative to length and formality.

2 Discuss the four major differences involved in writing short and long reports.

3 Write clear and well-organized short reports.

4 Write clear and well-organized letter and memorandum reports.

5 Adapt the procedures for writing short reports to such special reports as staff, audit, progress, and technical reports.

6 Write clear, well-organized, and effective proposals.

The Structure of Short Reports

Assume again the position of assistant to the president of Technicraft and the report-writing work necessary in this position. Most of the time, your assignments concern routine, everyday problems—human resource policies, administrative procedures, work flow, and the like. Following what appears to be established company practice, you write the reports on these problems in simple memorandum form.

Occasionally, however, you have a more involved assignment. Last week, for example, you investigated a union charge that favoritism was shown to the nonunion workers on certain production jobs. As your report on this very formal investigation was written for the benefit of ranking company administrators as well as union leaders, you dressed it up.

Then there was the report you had helped prepare for the board of directors last fall. That report summarized pressing needs for capital improvements. A number of plant administrators contributed to this project, but you were the coordinator. Because the report was important and was written for the board, you made it as formal as possible.

Clearly, reports vary widely in structure. How report structures vary is the first topic of this chapter. Because the shorter reports are more important to you, they are discussed next.

Before you can put your report in finished form, you will need to decide on its structure. Will it be a simple memorandum? Will it be a long, complex, and formal report? Or will it fall between these extremes?

AN OVERVIEW OF REPORT STRUCTURE

- Length and formality determine report structure.

- The following classification plan provides a general picture of report structure.

- It pictures report structure as a stairway (Figure 11.1). Long, formal reports are at the top. Prefatory pages dress up these reports.

- Prefatory pages consist of the title fly, title page, letter of transmittal, table of contents, and executive summary.

Your decision as to report structure will be based on the needs of your situation. Those needs are related to report length and the formality of the situation. The longer the problem and the more formal the situation, the more involved the report structure is likely to be. The shorter the problem and the more informal the situation, the less involved the report structure is likely to be. Such adjustments of report structure to length and formality help meet the etiquette needs of the situation.

So that you may understand the various report structures, we will review the possibilities. The following classification plan provides a very general picture of how reports are structured. This plan does not account for all the possible variations, but it does acquaint you with the general structure of reports. It should help you construct reports that fit your specific need.

The classification plan arranges all business reports as a stairway, as illustrated by the diagram in Figure 11.1. At the top of the stairway are the most formal, full-dress reports. Such reports have a number of pages that come before the text material, just as this book has pages that come before the first chapter. These pages serve useful purposes, but they also dress up the report. Typically, these *prefatory pages,* as they are called, are included when the problem situation is formal and the report is long. The exact makeup of the prefatory pages may vary, but the most common arrangement includes these parts: title fly, title page, letter of transmittal, table of contents, and executive summary. Flyleaves (blank pages at the beginning and end that protect the report) may also be included.

These parts are explained in Chapter 12, but a brief description of them at this point should help you understand their roles. The first two pages (title fly and title page) contain identification information. The *title fly* carries only the report title. The *title page* typically contains the title, identification of the writer and reader, and sometimes the date. As the words imply, the *letter of transmittal* is a letter that transmits the report. It is a personal message from the writer to the reader. The *table of contents,* of course, is a listing of the report contents. It is the report outline in finished form, with page numbers to indicate

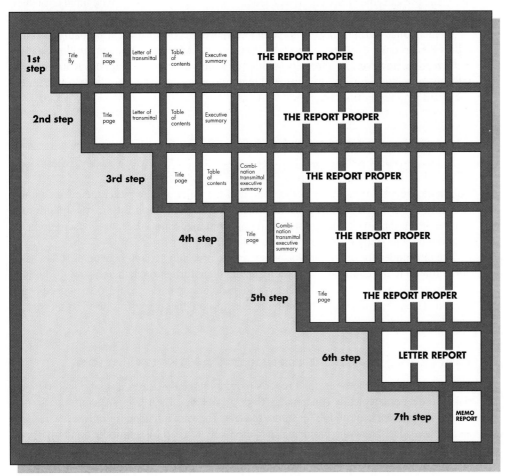

where the parts begin. It may also include a list of illustrations (tables, figures, diagrams), which may be a separate part. The *executive summary* summarizes whatever is important in the report—the major facts and analyses, conclusions, and recommendations.

As the need for formality decreases and the problem becomes smaller, the makeup of the report changes. The changes primarily occur in the prefatory pages. As we have noted, these pages give the report a formal appearance. So it is not surprising that they change as the report situation becomes less formal. Usually, such reports are shorter.

As reports become shorter and less formal, changes occur in this general order.

Although the changes that occur are far from standardized, they follow a general order. First, the title fly drops out. This page contains only the report title, which also appears on the next page. Obviously, the title fly is used primarily for reasons of formality.

The title fly drops out.

Next in the progression, the executive summary and the letter of transmittal are combined. When this stage is reached, the report problem is short enough to be summarized in a short space. As shown in Figure 11.1, the report at this stage has three prefatory parts: title page, table of contents, and combination transmittal letter and executive summary.

The executive summary and the letter of transmittal are combined.

A third step down, the table of contents drops out. The table of contents is a guide to the report text, and a guide has limited value in a short report. Certainly, a guide to a 100-page report is necessary. But a guide to a one-page report is not. Somewhere between these extremes a dividing point exists. You should follow the general guide of including a table of contents whenever it appears to be of some value to the reader.

Next, the table of contents is omitted.

Another step down, as formality and length requirements continue to decrease, the combined letter of transmittal and executive summary drops out. Thus, the report commonly called the *short report* now has only a title page and the report text. The title page remains

The combined letter of transmittal and executive summary drops out, and what is left forms the popular short report.

to the last because it serves as a very useful cover page. In addition, it contains the most important identifying information. The short report is a popular form in business.

Below the short-report form is a form that reinstates the letter of transmittal and summary and presents the entire report as a letter—thus, the *letter report*. And finally, for short problems of more informality, the *memorandum* form is used.

As mentioned earlier, this is a general analysis of report change; it probably oversimplifies the structure of reports. Few actual reports coincide with the steps in the diagram. Most reports, however, fit generally within the framework of the diagram. Knowledge of the general relationship of formality and length to report makeup should help you understand and plan reports.

■ The next step is the letter report, and the step after that is the memorandum report.

■ This progression of structure is general.

CHARACTERISTICS OF THE SHORTER REPORTS

The shorter report forms (those at the bottom of the stairway) are by far the most common in business. These are the everyday working reports—those used for the routine information reporting that is vital to an organization's communication. Because these reports are so common, our study of report types begins with them.

The techniques for organizing discussed in the preceding chapter cover all forms of reports. But there the emphasis was on organizing the information gathered—on the body of the report. As we noted, introductory and concluding parts would be attached when needed. Thus, the following discussion relates to how these parts are used in the shorter reports.

■ The shorter report forms are the most common in business.

■ Their need for introductions and conclusions varies.

LITTLE NEED FOR INTRODUCTORY INFORMATION

Most of the shorter, more informal reports require little (sometimes no) introductory material. These reports typically concern day-to-day problems. Their lives are short; that is, they are not likely to be kept on file for future readers. They are intended for only a few readers, and these readers know the problem. They are likely to need little introduction to it.

This is not to say that all shorter reports have no need for introductory material. Some do need it. In general, however, the need is likely to be small.

Determining what introductory material is needed is simply a matter of answering one question: What does my reader need to know before receiving this report? In very short reports, sufficient introductory material is provided by an incidental reference to the problem, authorization of the investigation, or the like. In extreme cases, however, you may need a detailed introduction comparable to that of the more formal reports.

Reports need no introductory material if their very nature explains their purpose. This holds true for personnel actions. It also holds true for weekly sales reports, inventory reports, and some progress reports.

■ Shorter reports have little need for introductory material.

■ Some shorter reports need introductory material. Include as much introductory material as is needed to prepare the reader for the report.

PREDOMINANCE OF THE DIRECT ORDER

Because the shorter reports usually solve routine problems, they are likely to be written in the direct order. By *direct order* we mean that the report begins with its most important information—usually the conclusion and perhaps a recommendation. Business writers use this order because they know that their readers' main concern is to get the information needed to make a decision. It is a way of practicing etiquette—of giving the readers what is most important to them. So they present this information right away.

As you will see in Chapter 12, the longer report forms may also use the direct order. Many longer reports do, but most do not. Most follow the traditional logical (introduction, body, conclusion) order. As one moves down the structural ladder toward the more informal and shorter reports, however, the need for the direct order increases. At the bottom of the ladder, the direct order is more the rule than the exception.

Deciding whether to use the direct order is best based on a consideration of your readers' likely use of the report. If your readers need the report conclusion or recommendation

■ The shorter reports usually begin directly—with conclusions and recommendations.

■ Sometimes, but not often, longer reports are written in the direct order.

■ Use the direct order when the conclusion or recommendation will serve as a basis for action.

Most short reports are personal, direct, and without formal introductions. Although exceptions exist, they provide everyday working information to organizations that is essential to survival.

as a basis for an action that they must take, directness will speed their effort by enabling them to quickly receive the most important information. If they have confidence in your work, they may choose not to read beyond this point and to quickly take the action that the report supports. Should they desire to question any part of the report, however, the material is there for their inspection.

On the other hand, if there is reason to believe that your readers will want to arrive at the conclusion or recommendation only after a logical review of the analysis, you should organize your report in the indirect (logical) order. This arrangement is especially preferable when your readers do not have reason to place their full confidence in your work. If you are a novice working on a new assignment, for example, you would be wise to lead them to your recommendation or conclusion by using the indirect order. As you can see, the indirect and direct orders are ways of relating to the information needs of the reader. As such, they are ways of practicing etiquette.

■ Use the indirect order when you need to take the readers through the analysis.

Because order is so vital a part of constructing the shorter reports, let us be certain that the difference between the direct arrangement and the indirect arrangement is clear. To make it clear, we will go through each, step by step.

The direct arrangement presents right away the most important part of the report. This is the answer—the achievement of the report's goal. Depending on the problem, the direct beginning could consist of a summary of facts, a conclusion, a recommendation, or some combination of summary, conclusion, and recommendation.

■ The direct order gives the main message first.

FRANK & ERNEST © (*United Feature Syndicate. Reprinted by permission.*)

A Point Well Made in a Memorandum Report

Mrs. Priddy telephoned the local utility company to complain that a line repairer has used "some mighty vulgar language" while working in front of her house. She wanted something done about it.

So the obliging supervisor called in the two men who had been on the job. "This is a serious charge," the supervisor explained. "So that I can get the facts straight, I want each of you to write a memo explaining what happened." One of the men submitted the following classic explanation:

Butch and I were splicing the cable in front of Mrs. Priddy's house. I was up on the pole, and Butch was down on the ground. Butch sent a pot of hot metal up to me. Just as it reached me, my foot slipped. The metal spilled down on Butch. It ran down his neck, through his overalls, and into his shoes. Butch leaped sideways, spun a couple of times, rolled on the ground, looked up at me, and said, "Cecil, you must be more careful hereafter."

■ Then it covers introductory material (if any), findings and analyses, conclusions, and recommendations.

Whatever introductory material is needed usually follows the direct opening. As noted previously, sometimes little or none is needed in the everyday, routine reports. Next come the report findings, organized in good order (as described in Chapter 10). From these facts and analyses comes the conclusion, and perhaps a recommendation.

Illustrating this arrangement is the following report of a short and simple personnel problem. For reasons of space economy, only the key parts of the report are shown here.

Clifford A. Knudson, administrative assistant in the accounting department, should be fired. This conclusion has been reached after a thorough investigation brought about by numerous incidents during the past two months . . . .

The recommended action is supported by this information from his work record for the past two months:
• He has been late to work seven times.
• He has been absent without acceptable excuse for seven days.
• Twice he reported to work in a drunken and disorderly condition.
• [And so on].

■ The indirect order has this sequence: introduction, facts and analyses, conclusions, and recommendations.

The indirect arrangement begins with whatever introductory material is needed to prepare the reader for the report. Then comes the presentation of facts, with analyses when needed. Next comes the part that accomplishes the goal of the report. If the goal is to present information, this part summarizes the information. If the goal is to reach a conclusion, this part reviews the analyses and draws a conclusion from them. And if the goal is to recommend an action, this part reviews the analyses, draws a conclusion, and, on the basis of the conclusion, makes a recommendation.

Using the simple personnel problem from the last example, the indirect arrangement would appear like this:

Numerous incidents during the past two months appear to justify an investigation of the work record of Clifford A. Knudson, administrative assistant in the accounting department.

The investigation of his work record for the past two months reveals these points:
• He has been late to work seven times.
• He has been absent without acceptable excuse for seven days.
• Twice he reported to work in a drunken and disorderly condition.
• [And so on to the conclusion that Knudson should be fired].

MORE PERSONAL WRITING STYLE

■ Personal writing is common in the shorter reports.

Although the writing for all reports is much the same, that in the shorter reports tends to be more personal. That is, the shorter reports are likely to use the personal pronouns *I, we,* and *you* rather than only the third person.

The reasons for this tendency toward personal writing in the shorter reports should be

Templates Help Writers Format Reports

Templates in full-feature word processors help report writers format reports easily and consistently. Once a template is selected, report writers can concentrate on the report message and let the software create a professional-looking image.

These templates contain margin settings, font type and size, headings and text, and graphic layout. While standard templates can be used, some companies design their own templates to give their reports consistent and distinct images.

Some word processors have templates that set up the report format and ask the user to click an area in which to enter specific information. Other programs use fill-in boxes and place information for you in the report. And some programs use both techniques. All of these features enhance the physical appearance of business reports.

---

obvious. In the first place, short-report situations usually involve personal relationships. Such reports tend to be from and to people who know each other and who normally address each other informally when they meet. In addition, the shorter reports are apt to involve personal investigations and to represent the observations, evaluations, and analyses of their writers. Finally, the shorter reports tend to deal with day-to-day, routine problems. These problems are by their very nature informal. It is logical to report them informally, and personal writing tends to produce this informal effect.

As explained in Chapter 10, your decision about whether to write a report in personal or impersonal style should be based on the situation. You should consider the expectations of those who will receive the report. If they expect formality, you should write impersonally. If they expect informality, you should write personally. If you do not know their preferences, you should consider the formality of the situation. Convention favors impersonal writing for the most formal situations. Like the direct and indirect order, the question of personal versus impersonal style involves the matter of etiquette—of relating to the reader in ways that he or she prefers.

From this analysis, it should be clear that either personal or impersonal writing can be appropriate for reports ranging from the shortest to the longest types. The point is, however, the short-report situations are most likely to justify personal writing.

■ The reasons are that the shorter reports usually (1) involve personal relationships, (2) concern a personal investigation, and (3) are routine.

■ Write impersonally (1) when your reader prefers it and (2) when the situation is formal.

Constructing short reports requires many of the same organization skills used to develop longer, more formal reports.

LESS NEED FOR A STRUCTURED COHERENCE PLAN

As you will see in Chapter 12, long and formal reports usually require a structured coherence plan. Short reports do not. This is not to say that coherence is not essential to short reports. It is. The point is that a *structured* plan is not needed. By structured coherence plan we mean an arrangement of summarizing, forward looking, and backward looking parts that tie together the report presentation. When you study this plan, you will understand why it has little use in the short reports. We mention it now primarily for the sake of completeness in covering differences between long and short reports.

FORMS OF SHORTER REPORTS

■ Following is a review of the more popular shorter reports.

As was noted earlier, the shorter report forms are by far the most numerous and important in business. In fact, the three forms represented by the bottom three steps of the stairway (Figure 11.1) make up the bulk of the reports written. Thus, a review of each of these three types is in order.

THE SHORT REPORT

■ The short report consists of a title page and the report text.

One of the more popular of the less formal report forms is the short report. Representing the fifth step in the diagram of report progression, this report consists of only a title page and text. Its popularity may be explained by the middle-ground impression of formality that it conveys. Including the most important prefatory part gives the report at least some appearance of formality. And it does this without the tedious work of preparing the other prefatory pages. The short report is ideally suited for the short but somewhat formal problem.

Like most of the less formal report forms, the short report may be organized in either the direct or indirect order. But the direct order is far more common. As illustrated by Figure 11.2, this plan begins with a quick summary of the report, including and emphasizing conclusions and recommendations. Such a beginning serves much the same function as the executive summary (described in Chapter 12) of a long, formal report.

■ It is usually in the direct order, beginning with the conclusion.

Following the summary come whatever introductory remarks are needed. (See Chapter 12 for a more detailed discussion of the introduction.) Sometimes this part is not needed. Usually, however, a single paragraph covers the facts of authorization and a brief statement of the problem and its scope. After the introductory words come the findings of the investigation. As in the longer report forms, the findings are presented, analyzed, and applied to the problem. From all this comes a conclusion and, if needed, a recommendation. These last two elements—conclusions and recommendations—may come at the end even though they also appear in the beginning summary. Omitting a summary or a conclusion would sometimes end the report abruptly. It would stop the flow of reasoning before reaching the logical goal.

■ The introduction comes next, then the findings and analyses, and finally the conclusions.

The mechanics of constructing the short report are much the same as the mechanics of constructing the more formal, longer types. The short report uses the same form of title page and page layout. Like the longer reports, it uses headings. But because of the short report's brevity, the headings rarely go beyond the two-division level. In fact, one level of division is most common. Like any other report, the short report uses graphics, an appendix, and a bibliography when these are needed.

■ See Figure 11.2 for this report form.

LETTER REPORTS

The second of the more common shorter report forms is the letter report, that is, a report in letter form. Letter reports are used primarily to present information to persons outside the organization, especially when the information is to be sent by mail or fax. For example, a company's written evaluation of a credit customer may be presented in letter form and sent to the person who requests it. An outside consultant may write a report of analyses and recommendations in letter form. Or the officer of an organization may report certain information to the membership in a letter.

■ Letter reports are reports in letter form.

Typically, the length of letter reports is three or four pages or less. But no hard-and-fast rule exists on this point. Long letter reports (10 pages and more) are not unusual.

■ They usually cover short problems.

As a general rule, letter reports are written personally, using *I, you,* and *we* references. (Exceptions exist, of course, such as letter reports for very important readers—for example, a company's board of directors.) Otherwise, the writing style recommended for letter reports is much the same as that recommended for any other reports. Certainly, clear and meaningful expression is a requirement for all reports (see Figure 11.3).

■ They are usually written in personal style.

Letter reports may be in either the direct order or the indirect order. If such a report is to be mailed, there is some justification for using the indirect order. Because such reports arrive unannounced, it is logical to begin with a reminder of what they are, how they originated, and the like. A letter report written to the membership of an organization, for example, might appropriately begin as follows:

■ Most of them begin indirectly.

As authorized by your board of directors last January 6, this report reviews member company expenditures for direct-mail selling.

If a letter report is begun in the direct order, a subject line is appropriate. The subject line consists of identifying words appearing at the top of the letter, usually right after the salutation. Another common practice is to omit the word *subject* and the colon and to type the entire subject description in capital letters. Although subject lines may be formed in many ways, one acceptable version begins with the word *subject* and follows it with words that identify the situation. As the following example illustrates, this identifying device helps overcome any confusion that the direct beginning might otherwise create.

■ Subject lines are appropriate to begin them.

Subject: Direct-mail Expenditures of Association Members, Authorized by Board of Directors, January 1999
Association members are spending 8 percent more on direct-mail advertising this year than they did the year before. Current plans call for a 10 percent increase for next year.

*5 Ws and
1 H produce
complete title*

RECOMMENDATIONS FOR DEPRECIATING DELIVERY TRUCKS

BASED ON AN ANALYSIS OF THREE PLANS

PROPOSED FOR THE BAGGET LAUNDRY COMPANY

Submitted to
Mr. Ralph P. Bagget, President
Bagget Laundry Company
312 Dauphine Street
New Orleans, Louisiana 70102-4162

*Use of three-
spot title page
gives good
emphasis to
writer-reader
relationship
and balances
page.*

Prepared by
Charles W. Brewington, C.P.A.
Brewington and Karnes, Certified Public Accountants
743 Beaux Avenue, New Orleans, Louisiana 70118-4913

April 16, 1999

FIGURE 11.2 (Continued)

<u>RECOMMENDATIONS FOR DEPRECIATING DELIVERY TRUCKS</u>

<u>BASED ON AN ANALYSIS OF THREE PLANS</u>

<u>PROPOSED FOR THE BAGGET LAUNDRY COMPANY</u>

Topic-sentence first paragraph designs and transition words give emphasis and forward movement to ideas.

<u>Recommendation of Reducing Charge Method</u>

Direct order accents report solution.

The Reducing Charge method appears to be the best method to depreciate Bagget Laundry Company delivery trucks. The relative equality of cost allocation for depreciation and maintenance over the useful life of the trucks is the prime advantage under this method. Computation of depreciation charges is relatively simple by the Reducing Charge plan but not quite so simple as computation under the second best method considered.

The second best method considered is the Straight-Line depreciation plan. It is the simplest to compute of the plans considered, and it results in yearly charges equal to those under the Reducing Charge method. The unequal cost allocation resulting from increasing maintenance costs in successive years, however, is a disadvantage that far outweighs the method's ease of computation.

Third among the plans considered is the Service Hours method. This plan is not satisfactory for depreciating delivery trucks primarily because it combines a number of undesirable features. Prime among these is the complexity and cost of computing yearly charges under the plan. Also significant is the likelihood of poor cost allocation under this plan. An additional drawback is the possibility of variations in the estimates of the service life of company trucks.

<u>The Whats and Whys of the Problem</u>

<u>Authorization by President Bagget</u>. This report on depreciation methods for delivery trucks of the Bagget Laundry Company is submitted on April 16, 1999, to Mr. Ralph P. Bagget, President of the Company. Mr. Bagget orally authorized Brewington and Karnes, Certified Public Accountants, to conduct the study on March 15, 1999.

<u>Problem of Selecting Best Depreciation Method</u>. Having decided to establish branch agencies, the Bagget Laundry Company has purchased delivery trucks to transport laundry back and forth from the central cleaning plant in downtown New Orleans. The Company's problem is to select from three alternatives the most advantageous method to depreciate the trucks. The three methods concerned are the Reducing Charge, Straight-Line, and Service-Hours. The trucks have an original cost of $15,000, a five-year life, and trade-in value of $3,000.

<u>Use of Company Records to Solve Problem</u>. In seeking an optimum solution to the Company's problem, we studied Company records and reviewed authoritative literature on the subject. We also applied our best judgment and our experience in analyzing the alternative methods. We based all conclusions on the generally accepted business principles in the field. Clearly, studies such as this involve subjective judgment, and this one is no exception.

1

FIGURE 11.2 (Continued)

2

Preview paragraph gives sequence of body divisions and justifies it.

Illustrations of Methods to Analyze Problem. In the following analysis, our evaluations of the three depreciation methods appear in the order in which we rank the methods. Since each method involves different factors, direct comparison by factors is meaningless. Thus our plan is that we evaluate each method in light of our best judgment.

Marked Advantages of the Reducing Charge Method

Sometimes called Sum-of-the-Digits, the Reducing Charge method consists of applying a series of decreasing fractions over the life of the property. To determine the fraction, first compute the sum of years of use for the property. This number becomes the denominator. Then determine the position number (first, second, etc.) of the year. This number is the numerator. Then apply the resulting fractions to the depreciable values for the life of the property. In the case of the trucks, the depreciable value is $12,000 ($15,000–$3,000).

Sub- ordinate reference to graphic aid allows main sentence to begin interpretation

As shown in Table I, this method results in large depreciation costs for the early years and decreasing costs in later years. But since maintenance and repair costs for trucks are higher in the later years, this method provides a relatively stable charge over the life of the property. In actual practice, however, the sums will not be as stable as illustrated, for maintenance and repair costs will vary from those used in the computation.

Graphic aids permit uncluttered analysis in report text

Table I

DEPRECIATION AND MAINTENANCE COSTS FOR DELIVERY TRUCKS OF BAGGET LAUNDRY FOR 1995–1999 USING REDUCING CHARGE DEPRECIATION

End of Year	Depreciation		Maintenance	Sum
1	5/15 ($12,000) =	$4,000	$ 200	$ 4,200
2	4/15 ($12,000) =	3,200	1,000	4,200
3	3/15 ($12,000) =	2,400	1,800	4,200
4	2/15 ($12,000) =	1,600	2,600	4,200
5	1/15 ($12,000) =	800	3,400	4,200
	Totals	$12,000	9,000	$21,000

In summary, the Reducing Charge method uses the most desirable combination of factors to depreciate trucks. It equalizes periodic charges, and it is easy to compute. It is our first choice for Bagget Laundry Company.

FIGURE 11.2 (Continued)

3

Incidental reference to graphic aid ties text and illustration together.

Runner-up Position of Straight-Line Method

The Straight-Line depreciation method is easiest of all to compute. It involves merely taking the depreciable value of the trucks ($12,000) and dividing it by the life of the trucks (5 years). The depreciation in this case is $2,400 for each year.

As shown in Table II, however, the increase in maintenance costs in later years results in much greater periodic charges in later years. The method is not usually recommended in cases such as this.

Table II

DEPRECIATION AND MAINTENANCE COSTS FOR DELIVERY TRUCKS OF BAGGET LAUNDRY FOR 1995–1999 USING STRAIGHT-LINE DEPRECIATION

End of	Depreciation		Maintenanc	Su
1	1/5 ($12,000) =	$2,400	$ 200	$2,600
2	1/5 ($12,000) =	2,400	1,000	3,400
3	1/5 ($12,000) =	2,400	1,600	4,200
4	1/5 ($12,000) =	2,400	2,600	5,000
5	1/5 ($12,000) =	2,400	3,400	5,800
	Totals	$12,000	$9,00	$21,00

In addition, the Straight-Line method generally is best when the properties involved are accumulated over a period of years. When this is done, the total of depreciation and maintenance costs will be about even. But Bagget Company has not purchased its trucks over a period of years. Nor is it likely to do so in the years ahead. Thus, Straight-Line depreciation will not result in equal periodic charges for maintenance and depreciation over the long run.

Summary statements at section endings provide reader with time to see solution unfold.

FIGURE 11.2 (Continued)

4

Poor Rank of Service-Hours Depreciation

The Service-Hours method of depreciation combines the major disadvantages of the other ways discussed. It is based on the principle that a truck is bought for the direct hours of service that it will give. The estimated number of hours that a delivery truck can be used efficiently according to automotive engineers is computed from a service total of 100,000 miles. The depreciable cost ($12,000) for each truck is allocated pro rata according to the number of service hours used.

The difficulty and expense of maintaining additional records of service hours is a major disadvantage of this method. The depreciation cost for the delivery trucks under this method will fluctuate widely between the first and last years. It is reasonable to assume that as the trucks get older more time will be spent on maintenance. Consequently, the larger depreciation costs will occur in the initial years. As can be seen by Table III, the periodic charges for depreciation and maintenance hover between the two previously discussed methods.

Table III

DEPRECIATION AND MAINTENANCE COSTS FOR DELIVERY TRUCKS OF BAGGET LAUNDRY FOR 1995–1999 USING SERVICE-HOURS DEPRECIATION

End of Year	Estimated Service-Miles	Depreciation	Maintenance	Sum
1	30,000	$3,600	$ 200	$3,800
2	25,000	3,000	1,000	4,000
3	20,000	2,400	1,800	4,200
4	15,000	1,800	2,600	4,400
5	10,000	1,200	3,400	4,600
	100,000	$12,000	$9,000	$21,000

The periodic charge for depreciation and maintenance increases in the later years of ownership. Another difficulty encountered is the possibility of a variance between estimated service hours and the actual service hours. The wide fluctuation possible makes it impractical to use this method for depreciating the delivery truck.

The difficulty of maintaining adequate records and increasing costs in the later years are the major disadvantages of this method. Since it combines the major disadvantages of both the Reducing Charge and Straight-Line methods, it is not satisfactory for depreciating the delivery trucks.

Completeness and detail in analysis give objectivity.

•••

FIGURE 11.3 Illustration of a Letter Report This direct-order letter report compares two hotels for a meeting site. Organized by the bases used in determining the choice, it evaluates the pertinent information and reaches a decision. The personal style is appropriate. Note the merge variables that form the inside address.

INTERNATIONAL COMMUNICATION ASSOCIATION

3141 Girard Street • Washington, D.C.

January 28, 1999

FIELD(Personal Title) FIELD(First Name) FIELD(Second Name) FIELD(Last Name)
Board of Directors
International Communication Association
FIELD(School or Company)
FIELD(Address)
FIELD(City), FIELD(State) FIELD(Zip)

Dear FIELD(Personal Title) FIELD(Last Name):

Subject: Recommendation of Convention Hotel for the 2000 Meeting

RECOMMENDATION OF THE MARRIOTT

Direct order emphasizes decision.

The Marriott Hotel is my recommendation for the International Communication Association meeting next January. My decision is based on the following summary of the evidence I collected. First, the Marriott has a definite downtown location advantage, and this is important to convention goers and their spouses. Second, accommodations, including meeting rooms, are adequate in both places, although the Hyatt's rooms are more modern. Third, Marriott room costs are approximately 15 percent lower than those at the Hyatt. The Marriott, however, would charge $500 for a room for the assembly meeting. Although both hotels are adequate, because of location and cost advantages the Marriott appears to be the better choice from the members' viewpoint.

Preview gives transition lead.

ORIGIN AND PLAN OF THE INVESTIGATION

In investigating these two hotels, as was my charge from you at our January 7th board meeting, I collected information on what I believed to be the three major factors of consideration in the problem. First is location. Second is adequacy of accommodations. And third is cost. The following findings and evaluations form the basis of my recommendation.

Bases of comparison (factors) permit hotels (units) to be compared logically.

THE MARRIOTT'S FAVORABLE DOWNTOWN LOCATION

The older of the two hotels, the Marriott is located in the heart of the downtown business district. Thus it is convenient to the area's two major department stores as well as the other downtown shops. The Hyatt, on the other hand, is approximately nine blocks from the major shopping area. Located in the periphery of the business and residential area, it provides little location advantage for those wanting to shop. It does, however, have shops within its walls which provide virtually all of the guest's normal needs. Because many members will bring spouses, however, the downtown location does give the Marriott an advantage.

Short sentences and transitional words increase readability and move ideas forward.

·FIGURE 11.3 (Concluded)

Alternate placement of topic sentences offers pattern variety.

Board of Directors   -2-   January 28, 1999

ADEQUATE ACCOMMODATIONS AT BOTH HOTELS

Talking captions (all noun phrases) help interpretation.

Both hotels can guarantee the 600 rooms we will require. Because the Hyatt is newer (since 1992), its rooms are more modern and therefore more appealing. The 9-year-old Marriott, however, is well preserved and comfortable. Its rooms are all in good repair, and the equipment is modern.

The Hyatt has 11 small meeting rooms and the Marriott has 13. All are adequate for our purposes. Both hotels can provide the 10 we need. For our general assembly meeting, the Marriott would make available its Capri Ballroom, which can easily seat our membership. It would also serve as the site of our inaugural dinner. The assembly facilities at the Hyatt appear to be somewhat crowded, although the management assures me that it can hold 600. Pillars in the room, however, would make some seats undesirable. In spite of the limitations mentioned, both hotels appear to have adequate facilities for our meeting.

Paragraph length shows good organization.

LOWER COSTS AT THE MARRIOTT

Text analysis relates facts to problem.

Both the Marriott and the Hyatt would provide nine rooms for meetings on a complimentary basis. Both would provide complimentary suites for our president and our secretary. The Marriott, however, would charge $500 for use of the room for the assembly meeting. The Hyatt would provide this room without charge.

Convention rates at the Marriott are $90–$100 for singles, $100–$110 for double-bedded rooms, and $99–$120 for twin-bedded rooms. Comparable rates of the Hyatt are $100–$110, $110–$120, and $110–$130. Thus, the savings at the Marriott would be approximately 15 percent per member.

Cost of the dinner selected would be $25 per person, including gratuities, at the Marriott. The Hyatt would meet this price if we would guarantee 600 plates. Otherwise, they would charge $27. Considering all of these figures, the total cost picture at the Marriott is the more favorable one.

Respectfully,

Willard K Mitchell

Willard K. Mitchell
Executive Secretary

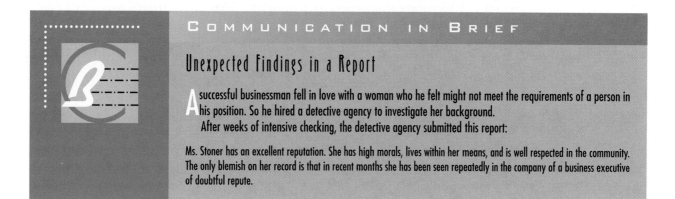
Regardless of which type of beginning is used, the organizational plans for letter reports correspond to those of the longer, more formal types. Thus, the indirect-order letter report follows its introduction with a logical presentation and analysis of the information gathered. From this presentation, it develops a conclusion or recommendation, or both, in the end. The direct-order letter report follows the initial summary-conclusion-recommendation section with whatever introduction is appropriate. For example, the direct beginning illustrated previously could be followed with these introductory sentences:

> These are the primary findings of a study authorized by your board of directors last January. Because they concern information vital to all of us in the Association, they are presented here for your confidential use.

Following such an introduction, the report would present the supporting facts and their analyses. The writer would systematically build up the case supporting the opening comment. With either the direct or indirect order, a letter report may close with whatever friendly, goodwill comment fits the occasion.

- The organizational plans of letter reports are much like those of longer reports.

- Supporting facts and analyses follow an appropriate introduction.

MEMORANDUM REPORTS

As we noted in Chapter 8, memorandums (commonly called *memos*) are the most widely used form of written communication in business. Although sometimes used for correspondence with outside parties, memorandums are primarily internal messages, especially with email. That is, they are written by and to people in an organization, as Figure 11.4 illustrates.

Because memorandums are primarily communications between people who know each other, they are usually informal. In fact, many are hurried, casual messages. Some memorandums, however, are formal, especially those directed to readers high in the administration of the organization.

As indicated in Chapter 8, some memorandums resemble letters. Others, however, are more appropriately classified as reports. Most report memorandums tend to be more formal and factual. In fact, some memorandum reports rival the longer forms in formality. Like the longer forms, they may use headings to display content and graphics to support the text. Memorandum reports tend to be problem related.

- Memorandums (internal written messages) are widely used.

- Most of them are written informally.

- Some resemble letters and follow letter form.

- Some are reports. Such memorandums tend to be formal, factual, and problem related.

SPECIAL REPORT FORMS

As noted previously, this review describes only generally the report forms used in business. Many variations exist, a few of which deserve emphasis.

- Some special report forms deserve review.

THE STAFF REPORT

One of the more popular forms of reports used in business is the staff report. Usually written in memorandum form, it can be adapted to any structural type, including the long, formal report.

- One is the staff report.

....

FIGURE 11.4 Illustration of a Progress Report in Memorandum Form This memorandum report summarizes a sales manager's progress in opening a new district. It begins with highlight information—all a busy reader may need to know. Organized by three categories of activity, the factual information follows. The writer-reader relationship justifies personal style.

MEMORANDUM

THE**M**URCHISON **C**O. **I**NC.

To: William T. Chysler
  Director of Sales

From: James C. Calvin, Manager *JCC* *Memorandum format gives introductory details.*
  Bloomington Sales District

Date: July 21, 1999

Subject Quarterly Report for Bloomington Sales District

Informational nature justifies topic captions. SUMMARY HIGHLIGHTS *Direct order provides overview.*

After three months of operation, I have secured office facilities, hired and developed three salespeople, and cultivated about half the customers available in the Bloomington Sales District. Although the district is not yet showing a profit, at the current rate of development it will do so this month. Prospects for the district are unusually bright.

OFFICE OPERATION

In April I opened the Bloomington Sales District as authorized by action of the Board of Directors last February 7. Initially I set up office in the Omni Suites, a hotel near the airport, and remained there three weeks while looking for permanent quarters. These I found in the Wingate Building, a downtown office structure. The office suite rents for $1,640 per month. It has four executive offices, each opening into a single secretarial office, which is large enough for two secretaries. Although this arrangement is adequate for the staff now anticipated, additional space is available in the building if needed.

PERSONNEL *Past-to-present paragraph sequence shows application of present time viewpoint.*

In the first week of operation, I hired an office secretary, Ms. Catherine Kruch. Ms. Kruch has good experience and has excellent credentials. She has proved to be very effective. In early April I hired two salespeople—Mr. Charles E. Clark and Ms. Alice E. Knapper. Both were experienced in sales, although neither had worked in apparel sales. Three weeks later I hired Mr. Otto Strelski, a proven salesperson whom I managed to attract from the Hammond Company. I still am searching for someone for the fourth subdistrict. Currently I am investigating two good prospects and plan to hire one of them within the next week.

FIGURE 11.4 (Concluded) 321

William T. Chysler
Page 2
July 21, 1999

PERFORMANCE

After brief training sessions, which I conducted personally, the salespeople were assigned the territories previously marked. They were instructed to call on the accounts listed on the sheets supplied by Mr. Henderson's office. During the first month, Knapper's sales totaled $20,431 and Clark's reached $16,490, for a total of $36,921. With three salespeople working the next month, total sales reached $130,605. Of the total, Knapper accounted for $40,345, Clark $34,690, and Strelski $55,570.

Although these monthly totals are below the $145,000 break-even point for the three subdistricts, current progress indicates that we will exceed this volume this month. Since we have made contact with only about one half of the prospects in the area, the potential for the district appears to be unusually good.

The staff report differs from other forms of reports primarily in the organization of its contents. It arranges contents in a fixed plan, similar to that used in technical writing. The plan remains the same for all problems. Because this arrangement leads systematically to conclusions and recommendations, it is especially useful for business problems.

Staff reports follow a fixed organization plan that leads to a conclusion.

Although the organization of staff reports varies by company, this plan used by a major metals manufacturer is typical:

A typical plan for staff reports has these parts:

Identifying information: Because the company's staff reports are processed with templates, the conventional identification information (*To, From, Date, Subject*) appears at the beginning.

Identifying information.

Summary: For the busy executive who wants the facts fast, the report begins with a summary. Some executives will read no further. Others will want to trace the report content in detail.

Summary.

The problem (or objective): As with all good problem-solving procedures, the report text logically begins with a clear description of the problem—what it is, what it is not, what its limitations are, and the like.

Problem (or objective).

Facts: Next comes the information gathered in the attempt to solve the problem.

Facts.

Discussion: This is followed by analyses of the facts and applications of the facts and the analyses to the problem. (The statement and discussion of the facts can often be combined.)

Discussion.

Conclusions: From the preceding discussion of the facts come the final meanings as they apply to the problem.

Conclusions.

Recommendation: If the problem's objective allows for it, a course of action may be recommended on the basis of the conclusions.

Recommendation.

One of the major users of staff reports are the branches of the Armed Forces, all of which use a standardized form. As shown in Figure 11.5, the military version of the staff report differs somewhat from the plan just described.

See Figure 11.5 for the military form of staff reports.

Anytime you use a standardized form, you will want to consider developing a template macro or merge document with your word processing software. A macro would fill in all the standard parts for you, pausing to let you enter the variable information. It would be most suitable for periodic reports, such as progress reports or quarterly sales reports. A template merge document would prompt you for the variables first, merging them with the primary document later. You'll find this feature most useful when you have to write several reports in short time intervals. For example, personnel evaluations for several potential employers illustrate good application of the merge.

THE PROGRESS REPORT

As its name implies, a progress report presents a review of progress made on an activity. For example, a fund-raising organization might prepare weekly summaries of its efforts to achieve its goal. Or a building contractor might prepare a report on progress toward completing a building for a customer. Typically, the contents of these reports concern progress made, but they may also include such related topics as problems encountered or anticipated and projections of future progress.

Progress reports review progress on an activity.

Progress reports follow no set form. They can be quite formal, as when a contractor building a large manufacturing plant reports to the company for whom the plant is being built. Or they can be very informal, as in the case of a worker reporting by email to his or her supervisor on the progress of a task being performed. Some progress reports are quite routine and structured, sometimes involving filling in blanks on forms devised for the purpose. Most, however, are informal, narrative reports, as illustrated by the example in Figure 11.4.

Most are informal and narrative; some are formal.

THE AUDIT REPORT

Short-form and long-form audit reports are well known in business. The short-form audit report is perhaps the most standardized of all reports—if, indeed, it can be classified as a report. Actually, it is a standardized statement verifying an accountant's inspection of a firm's financial records. Its wording seldom varies. Illustrations of this standard form are found in almost any corporate annual report.

Short- and long-form audit reports are well known in business.

FIGURE 11.5 Military Form of Staff Study Report

DEPARTMENT OF THE AIR FORCE
HEADQUARTERS UNITED STATES AIR FORCE
WASHINGTON, D.C. 20330

REPLY TO
ATTN OF   AFODC/Colonel Jones

SUBJECT   Staff Study Report

TO:

PROBLEM

1. ---
---.

FACTORS BEARING ON THE PROBLEM

2. Facts.

    a.---
--.
        b---.

3. Assumptions.

4. Criteria.

5. Definitions.

DISCUSSION

6. ---.

7. ---.

8. ---.

CONCLUSION

9. ---.

ACTION RECOMMENDED

10. ---.

11. ---.

JOHN J. JONES, Colonel, USAF   2 Atch
Deputy Chief of Staff, Operations   1. -----------------------
                                    2. -----------------------

Annotations:

Use only those portions of this format necessary for your particular report. If you omit certain paragraphs, renumber subsequent paragraphs accordingly.

Only long enough for identification.

Normally this caption is left blank on the staff study report.

Clear, but brief, statement of the problem.

Pertinent facts, assumptions (if necessary), criteria, and definitions (if necessary) used to solve the problem.

Briefly state background of problem.

List possible solutions that are most probable; test each possible solution, using criteria listed under FACTORS BEARING ON THE PROBLEM; compare all solutions; and select the best possible solution, giving reasons for choice. No set number of paragraphs is prescribed.

Restate the best possible solution to the problem, using only one paragraph.

Indicate clearly the action necessary to implement the solution.

Long-form audit reports vary greatly in their makeup. In fact, a national accounting association that studied the subject exhaustively found the makeup of these reports to be so varied that it concluded that no typical form existed.

> ■ Long-form audit reports vary in their makeup.

THE TECHNICAL REPORT

Although often treated as a highly specialized form, the technical report differs from other reports primarily in its subject matter. As you can see from Figure 11.6, a technical report can be much like the memorandum reports we have described. The longer technical reports, however, tend to follow a somewhat standardized arrangement.

> ■ Technical reports differ from other reports primarily in their subject matter.

This arrangement begins much like that of the traditional formal report. First come the title pages, although a routing or distribution form for intracompany use is frequently worked in. A letter of transmittal is likely to come next, followed by a table of contents and illustrations. From this point on, however, the technical report is different. Its differences lie mainly in two places: (1) beginning summary and (2) text organization.

Instead of having a standard summary, the long technical report often presents the summary information in a number of prefatory sections. There may be, for example, separate sections covering findings, conclusions, and recommendations. Parts of the conventional introduction, especially objectives and acknowledgments, sometimes appear as prefatory sections.

> ■ This arrangement of prefatory parts is typical: title pages, letter of transmittal, table of contents, summary parts (findings, conclusions, recommendations, objectives, acknowledgments).
>
> ■ The text of the long technical report is typically organized in a fixed order like this one: introduction, methodology, facts, discussion, conclusion, recommendation.

....

FIGURE 11.6 Illustration of a Technical Memorandum Report This memorandum report presents an investigation of a technical process the writer was asked to make. It begins with a brief introduction. Then comes a narrative summary of the investigation, organized by the major areas inspected. Note the use of graphic aids to help present somewhat difficult concepts.

MEMORANDUM

the **CROWELL COMPANY**, inc.

To: Charles E. Groom   May 3, 1999

From: Edmund S. Posner ESP

Subject: Graff Lining Company's Use of Kynar Pipe Lining

Following is the report you requested January 9 on the Graff Lining Company's process of using Kynar for lining pipe. My comments are based on my inspection of the facilities at the Graff plant and my conversations with their engineers.

Dimension Limitations

Graff's ability to line the smaller pipe sizes appears to be limited. To date, the smallest diameter pipe they have lined in 10-foot spool lengths is 2 inches. They believe they can handle 1 1/2-inch pipe in 10-foot spools, but they have not attempted this size. They question their ability to handle smaller pipe in 10-foot lengths.

This limitation, however, does not apply to fittings. They can line 1 1/2-inch and 1-inch fittings easily. Although they can handle smaller sizes than these, they prefer to limit minimum nipple size to 1 inch by 4 inches long.

Maximum spool dimensions for the coating process are best explained by illustration:

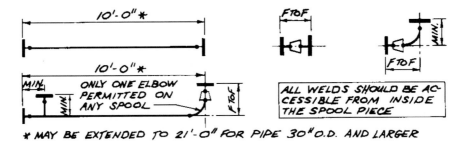

FIGURE 11.6 (Continued)

Charles E. Groom   2   May 3, 1999

Graff corrects defects found. If the defect is small, they correct by
retouching with sprayer or brush. If the defect is major, they remove all the
coating by turning and reline the pipe.

Recommendations for Piping

Should we be interested in using their services, Graff engineers made the
following recommendations. First, they recommend that we use forged
steel fittings rather than cast fittings. Cast fittings, they point out, have
excessive porosity. They noted, though, that cast fittings can be used and
are less expensive. For large jobs, this factor could be significant.

Second, they suggest that we make all small connections, such as those
required for instruments, in a prescribed manner. This manner is best
described by diagram:

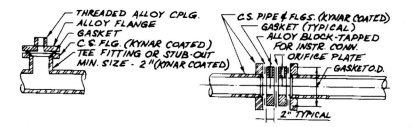

Graff engineers emphasized this point further by illustrating a common
form of small connections that will not work. Such connections are most
difficult to coat. Pinhole breaks are likely to occur on them, and a pinhole
break can cause the entire coating to disbond. A typical unacceptable
connection is the following:

FIGURE 11.6 (Continued)

Charles E. Groom   3   May 3, 1999

Preparation of Pipe for Lining

Graff requires that all pipe to be lined be ready for the coating process. Specifically, they require that all welds be ground smooth (to avoid pitting and assure penetration). Because welds are inaccessible in small pipe, they require forged tees in all piping smaller than 4 inches. In addition, they require that all attachments to the pipe (clips, base ells, etc.) be welded to the pipe prior to coating.

The Lining Procedure

The procedure Graff uses in lining the pipe begins with cleaning the pipe and inspecting it for cracked fittings, bad welds, etc. When necessary, they do minor retouching and grinding of welds. Then they apply the Kynar in three forms: primer, building, and sealer. They apply the building coat in as many layers as is necessary to obtain a finished thickness of 25 mils. They oven bake each coat at a temperature and for a time determined by the phase of the coating and the piping material.

Inspection Technique

Following the coating, Graff inspectors use a spark testing method to detect possible pinholes or other defects. This method is best explained by illustration:

FIGURE 11.6 (Concluded)

Charles E. Groom   4   May 3, 1999

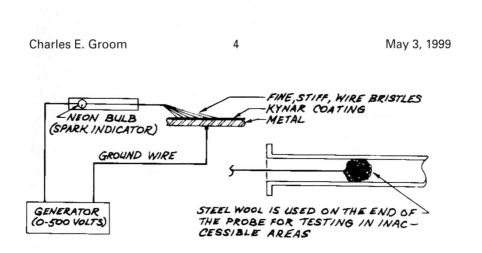

A third recommendation is that we establish handling procedures to protect the coated pipe. As the Kynar coating will chip, we would need to make certain that we protect all flange spaces. Also, we would need to be careful in shipping, handling, storing, and erecting the pipe.

Whether invited or prospecting, proposals must do an effective job of presenting a complete picture of what is being proposed. You must work hard to meet readers' needs so they can make decisions in your favor.

The long technical report usually follows a standard order similar to that of the staff report. The most common order is the following:

Introduction.

Methodology (or methods and materials).

Facts.

Discussion.

Conclusion.

Recommendation.

THE PROPOSAL

■ Proposals vary in length.

Whether proposals belong in a discussion of the shorter reports is debatable, for they are not always short. In fact, they range in length from just a few pages to several volumes. We discuss them here primarily as a matter of convenience.

■ A proposal is a presentation for consideration of something.

PROPOSALS DEFINED.   By definition, a *proposal* is a presentation for consideration of something. In actual practice, some proposals fit this definition well—for example, one company's proposal to merge with another company, an advertising agency's proposal to promote a product, or a city's proposal to induce a business to locate within its boundaries. But other proposals are more precisely described as appeals or bids for grants, donations, or sales of products or services. To illustrate, a college professor submits a request for research funds to a government agency, a community organization submits a request to a philanthropic foundation for help in establishing a drug rehabilitation facility, or a company submits a bid for the sale of its products or services.

■ Proposals are made by individuals or organizations to individuals or organizations.

Proposals are usually written, but they can be oral presentations or a combination of both. They may be made by individuals or organizations, including business organizations, and they may be made to any of a variety of individuals or organizations such as government agencies, foundations, businesses. They can even be made internally—by one part of a business to another part or to the management of the business. For example, a department might outline its needs for new equipment in a proposal to management.

■ They may be invited or prospecting.

INVITED OR PROSPECTING.   Proposals may be invited or prospecting. By *invited* we mean that the awarding organization announces to interested parties that it will make an award and that it is soliciting proposals. To illustrate, a government agency might have funds to award for research projects, a foundation might wish to make grants for educational innovations, or a business might want competing suppliers to bid on a product or service that it needs. In their announcements, the awarding organizations typically describe their needs and specify the unique requirements that the proposals should cover.

In business situations, invited proposals usually follow preliminary meetings between the parties involved. For example, if a business has a need for certain production equipment, its representatives might initiate meetings with likely suppliers of this equipment. At these meetings the representatives would discuss the need with suppliers. Each supplier would then be invited to submit a proposal for fulfilling the need with its equipment. In a sense, such a proposal is a bid supported by the documentation and explanation needed for conviction.

■ In business, invited proposals usually follow meetings.

Prospecting proposals are much like rational sales letters. They amount to descriptions of what the writer or the writer's organization could do if given an award by the reader's organization. For example, a university department that wishes to seek funding for the development of a new curriculum in international management might write proposals to philanthropic foundations describing the curriculum, outlining its financial needs for instituting the curriculum, and proposing that the foundation award the funds needed. Or a business supplying unique services might submit an unsolicited description of the services to a business that might use them. Such proposals differ from rational sales letters primarily in their physical form (they are in report form, not letter form). When products or services are being proposed, such proposals may also differ from rational sales letters by being specifically adapted to the reader's business.

■ Prospecting proposals are like sales letters.

FORMAT AND ORGANIZATION. The physical arrangement and organization of proposals vary widely. The simplest proposals resemble formal memorandums. Internal proposals (those written for and by people in the same organization) usually fall into this category, though exceptions exist. The more complex proposals may take the form of full-dress, long reports, including prefatory pages (title pages, letter of transmittal, table of contents, executive summary), text, and an assortment of appended parts. Most proposals have arrangements that fall somewhere between these extremes.

■ Their formats vary from memorandums to long-report forms.

Because of the wide variations in the makeup of proposals, you would be wise to investigate carefully before designing a particular proposal. In your investigation, try to determine what format is conventional among those who will read it. Look to see what others have done in similar situations. In the case of an invited proposal, review the request thoroughly, looking for clues concerning the preferences of the inviting organization. If you are unable to follow any of these courses, design a format based on your knowledge of report structure. Your design should be the one that you think is best for the one situation.

■ Select the format appropriate for your one case.

FORMALITY REQUIREMENTS. The formality requirements of proposals vary. In some cases (a university's proposal for a research grant, for example), strict formality is expected. In other cases (such as a manufacturing department's proposal that the plant manager change a production procedure), informality is in order. As with other reports, the decision should be based primarily on the relationship between the parties involved. If the parties are acquainted with each other, informality is appropriate. If they are not, a formal report is usually expected. An exception would be made in any case in which formality is expected regardless of the relationship of the parties.

■ The formality requirements of proposals vary. Do what is appropriate.

CONTENT. You should consider the needs of the individual case in determining the content of a proposal. In the case of an invited (solicited) proposal, review the proposal request (if the proposal is in writing). If the proposal results from a meeting, review your announcement of the meeting or the notes you took at the meeting. Such a review will usually tell you what is wanted. In fact, some written invitations even give a suggested plan for the proposal. It is highly important that you follow such guidelines, for in competitive situations the selection procedure frequently involves a checklist and rating for each point stated in the invitation.

■ Determine the content of a proposal by reviewing the needs of the case. If the proposal has been invited, review the invitation.

If you are submitting an uninvited proposal, you will have to determine what your readers need to know. Because each case will involve different needs, you will have to use your best judgment in making that determination.

Although the number of content possibilities is great, you should consider including the eight topics listed below. They are broad and general, and you can combine or subdivide them as needed to fit the facts of your case. (See Figure 11.7 for one logical application.)

1. Writer's purpose and the reader's need. An appropriate beginning is a statement of the writer's purpose (to present a proposal) and the reader's need (e.g., to reduce turnover of field representatives). If the report is in response to an invitation, that statement should tie in with the invitation (e.g., as described in the July 10 announcement). The problem should be stated clearly, in the way described in Chapter 10. This proposal beginning illustrates these recommendations:

> As requested at the July 10 meeting with Alice Burton, Thomas Cheny, and Victor Petrui in your Calgary office, the following pages present Murchison and Associates' proposal for reducing turnover of field representatives. Following guidelines established at the meeting, the proposal involves determining the job satisfaction of the current sales force, analyzing exit interview records, and comparing company compensation and human resource practices with industry norms.

If a proposal is submitted without invitation, its beginning has an additional requirement: it must gain attention. As noted previously, uninvited proposals are much like sales letters. Their intended readers are not likely to be eager to read them. Thus, their beginnings must overcome the readers' reluctance. An effective way of doing this is to begin by briefly summarizing the highlights of the proposal, with emphasis on its benefits. This technique is illustrated by the beginning of an unsolicited proposal that a restaurant consultant sent to prospective clients:

> The following pages present a proven plan for operations review that will (1) reduce food costs, (2) evaluate menu offerings for maximum profitability, (3) increase kitchen efficiency, (4) improve service, and (5) increase profits. Mattox and Associates proposes to achieve these results through its highly successful procedures, which involve analysis of guest checks and invoices and observational studies of kitchen and service work.

Your clear statement of the purpose and problem may be the most important aspect of the proposal. In order to win a contract, you must convince your reader that you have a clear understanding of what needs to be done.

2. Background. A review of background information promotes an understanding of the problem. Thus, a college's proposal for an educational grant might benefit from a review of the college's involvement in the area to which the grant would be applied. A company's proposal of a merger with another company might review industry developments that make the merger desirable. Or a chief executive officer's proposal to the board of directors that a company's administration be reorganized might present the background information that justifies the proposal.

3. Need. Closely related to the background information is the need for what is being proposed. In fact, background information may well be used to establish need. But because need can be presented without such support, we list it separately.

4. Description of plan. The heart of a proposal is the description of what the writer proposes to do. This is the primary message of the proposal. It should be concisely presented in a clear and orderly manner.

5. Particulars. Although the particulars of the proposal are a part of the plan description, they are discussed separately for reasons of emphasis. By *particulars* we mean the specifics—time schedules, costs, performance standards, means of appraising performance, equipment and supplies needed, guarantees, personnel requirements, and such. What is needed in a given case depends on its unique requirements. But in any event, the particulars should anticipate and answer the readers' questions.

6. Evidence of ability to deliver. The proposing organization must sometimes establish its ability to perform. This means presenting information on such matters as the qualifications of personnel, success in similar cases, the adequacy of equipment and facilities, op-

•••

FIGURE 11.7 Illustration of a Short Proposal This simple proposal seeks organization membership for its writer. It begins with a quick introduction that ties in with the reader's invitation for the proposal. Then it presents the case, logically proceeding from background information to advantages of membership, to costs. It concludes with the recommendation to sponsor membership.

MEMORANDUM

TO: Helen S. Hobson

DATE: May 19, 1998

FROM: Ross H. Jefferson *RHJ*

SUBJECT: Sponsored membership in the Association for
           Business Communication

Writer's purpose begins proposal. As you requested May 17, following is my proposal for Stoner to sponsor my membership in the Association for Business Communication (ABC).

Description of ABC

The primary professional organization in business communication, ABC is dedicated to keeping its members informed of the latest developments in business communication practice and theory. It informs its members through two quarterly publications: The Journal of Business Communication (research and theory) and Business Communication Quarterly (practice).

Descriptions give background details and establish credibility/need. In addition, the Association holds an annual meeting as well as regional meetings throughout the United States and Canada. The Southwest Region meets with the Southwestern Federation of Administrative Disciplines (SWFAD), the largest cross-discipline business meeting (13 divisions) in the nation. Papers presented at these meetings cover both the current theoretical and practical topics in business communication.

Recently, the Association added three international regions—Europe (including Africa and the Middle East); Caribbean, Central, and South America; and Asia and the Pacific. With representatives from these regions on the Board of Directors, ABC plans to hold regional meetings in each new geographical region soon. Such expansion in the organization should give ABC a truly global perspective. Moreover, ABC provides a listserv (BizCom) that serves as a discussion network for ABC members on current research and practice in the field.

Founded in 1936, ABC now has 2,213 members, including 829 institutions. Of the individual memberships, most (1,236) are academics from the United States and Canada. But 148 are business professionals. Companies represented include IBM, AT&T, Exxon, Imperial Oil, State Farm Insurance, McDonnell Douglas, and Aetna Insurance. ABC's diverse membership provides an effective exchange of experience and knowledge.

FIGURE 11.7

FIGURE 11.7 (Concluded)

Helen S. Hobson, May 19, 1998, page 2

Benefits of Membership

Membership in ABC would benefit Stoner as well as me personally. The meetings and the publications would enable me to bring the latest communication knowledge to my editorial work. ABC would be especially helpful in my assignments involving teaching communication to our employees, for much of its emphasis is on teaching techniques. Also, membership in ABC would enhance Stoner's image. ABC is a prestigious organization, and its members include the corporate elite. In addition, meeting with the members of other companies and exchanging ideas would help me do a better job of directing Stoner's communication activities.

Membership advantages to company and to individual add connection.

Costs of Membership

ABC annual dues are $60, which includes subscriptions to the Journal and the Quarterly. The costs of attending the meetings would vary with the meeting sites. For this year, the approximate costs for the international meeting in San Antonio would be $950 (registration, $120; transportation, $330; hotel, $320; meals, $140; miscellaneous, $40). For the regional meeting in Houston it would be $710 (registration, $70; transportation, $250; hotel, $240; meals, $120; miscellaneous, $30). The total cost for this year would be $1,660.

Particulars reinforce persuasive effort.

Recommended Action

Based on the preceding information, I believe that membership in ABC offers us benefits well worth the cost. Thus, I recommend that Stoner sponsor my membership on a one-year trial basis. At the end of this year, I would review actual benefits received and recommend whether to continue membership.

Specified action completes the plan.

erating procedures, and financial status. Whatever information will serve as evidence of the organization's ability to carry out what it proposes should be used.

7. Benefits of the proposal. The proposal might also describe good things that it would bring about, especially if a need exists to convince the readers. Reader benefits were what we stressed in sales writing, but as we have noted, proposals can be much like sales presentations. The greater the need to persuade, the more you should stress benefits. As noted in an earlier chapter, however, proposal writing is more objective and less flamboyant than sales writing.

■ 7. Benefits of the proposal (especially if selling is needed).

As an example of benefits logically covered in proposals, a college's request for funding to establish a program for employing the disabled could point to the bright futures that such funding would give these students. And a proposal offering a consulting service to restaurants could stress such benefits as improved work efficiency, reduced employee theft, savings in food costs, and increased profits.

8. Concluding comments. The proposal should end with words directed to the next step—acting on the proposal. One possibility is to present a summary review of the highlights. Another is to offer additional information that might be needed. Yet another is to urge (or suggest) action on the proposal.

■ 8. Concluding comments (words directed toward the next step).

SUMMARY BY CHAPTER OBJECTIVES

1. Length and formality determine the following general progression of report structure:
   - The very long ones have prefatory pages (title fly, title page, letter of transmittal, table of contents, executive summary).
   - As reports become shorter and less formal, the composition of the prefatory parts section changes, generally in this order:
     —First, the title fly drops out.
     —Then, in succession, the executive summary and letter of transmittal are combined,
     —The table of contents is omitted, and
     —The combined letter of transmittal and executive summary is dropped.
   - Below these steps are the letter report and the memorandum report.

1 Explain the structure of reports relative to length and formality.

2. The shorter and by far the most common reports are much like the longer ones except for these four differences:
   - They have less need for introductory material.
   - They are more likely to begin directly (conclusion and recommendation first).
   - They are more likely to use personal style.
   - They have less need for a formal coherence plan.

2 Discuss the four major differences involved in writing short and long reports.

3. One of the more popular forms of less formal reports is the short report.
   - It consists of a title page and report text.
   - Usually it begins with a summary or conclusion.
   - Then it presents findings and analyses.

3 Write clear and well-organized short reports.

4. Letter reports are another popular short form.
   - Usually they are written in the indirect order.
   - They are organized much like the longer reports.
   Memorandum reports are like letter reports.
   - They are usually written for and by people within an organization.
   - They are the most common report form.

4 Write clear and well-organized letter and memorandum reports.

5. Among the various special reports, four stand out.
   - The staff report follows a fixed organization plan (for example, identifying information, summary, problem, facts, discussion, conclusions, recommendation).
   - A progress report reviews the progress on an activity and follows no set form.
   - The audit report presents the results of an audit and follows a variety of forms.
   - The technical report differs primarily in its subject matter.
     —The longer ones may follow a specified order.

5 Adapt the procedures for writing short reports to such special reports as staff, audit, progress, and technical reports.

—One such order is introduction, methodology, facts, discussion, conclusion, recommendation.

6 Write clear, well-organized, and effective proposals.

6. A proposal is a presentation for the consideration of something—a merger, a bid for an account, a research grant, and so on.
   • Individuals and organizations make them to other individuals and organizations.
   • Some are made internally, from one department to another.
   • They may be invited or prospecting. They range from the very short to the very long.
   • They vary in form, from simple memorandums to full-dress reports.
   • They may be formal or informal.
   The contents of proposals vary with need, but one should consider these topics:
   • Writer's purpose and reader's need.
   • Background.
   • Need.
   • Plan description.
   • Particulars (time, schedule, costs, performance standards, and such).
   • Ability to deliver.
   • Benefits.
   • Concluding comments.

CRITICAL THINKING QUESTIONS

1. Discuss the effects of formality and problem length on the model of report makeup described in the chapter.
2. Which of the prefatory pages of reports appear to be related primarily to the length of the report? Which to the need for formality?
3. Explain why some routine report problems require little or no introduction.
4. Why is the direct order generally used in the shorter reports? When is the indirect order desirable for such reports?
5. Give examples of short report forms that are appropriately written in personal style. Do the same for impersonal style.
6. Describe the organization of the conventional short report.
7. What types of problems are written up as letter reports? As memorandum reports? Explain the differences.
8. Why is the order of the staff report said to be a problem-solving order?
9. Discuss the differences between technical reports and the other business reports.
10. "To be successful, a proposal must be persuasive. This quality makes the proposal different from most short reports (which stress objectivity)." Discuss.

CRITICAL THINKING EXERCISES

1. Review the following report situations and determine for each the makeup of the report you would recommend for it:
   a. A professional research organization has completed a survey of consumer attitudes toward the Alto Company. The survey results will be presented to the Alto president in a 28-page report, including seven charts and three tables.
   b. Eva Campbell was asked by her department head to inspect the work area and report on safety conditions. Her report is two pages long and written in personal style.
   c. Chad Benton has an idea for improving a work procedure in his department at Dorner Manufacturing Company. His department head suggested that Chad present his idea in a report to the production superintendent. The report is almost five pages long, including a full-page diagram. It is written in the personal style.
   d. Karen Canady, a worker in the supply room of Edmunds & Sons Plumbing Contractors, was asked by Doug Edmunds, its president, for current inventory information on a number of basic products. Her report is less than a full page and consists mostly of a list of items and numbers.
   e. Bryan Toups, a sales manager for the Batla Chemical Company, was asked by the vice president of marketing to prepare an analysis of the results of a promotional campaign conducted in Toups's district. The report is six pages long (including one chart) and is written in the personal style.

2. Following is a report that was written for the manager of a large furniture retail store by the manager's assistant. The manager was concerned about customer complaints of late deliveries of furniture purchased and wanted to know the cause of the delays. Critique this report.

   11-17-99

   TO: Martina Kalavoda

   FROM: Anthony Dudrow

   SUBJECT: Investigation requested 11-17-99

   This morning at staff meeting it was requested that an investigation be made of the status of home deliveries and of the causes of the delays that have occurred. The investigation has been made with findings as follows.

   Now that a new driver's helper, Morris Tunney, has been hired, there should be no more delays. This was the cause of the problem.

   Over the past two weeks (10 working days), a total of 143 deliveries were made; and of these, 107 were made on or before the date promised. But some of the deliveries were late because of the departure two weeks ago of the driver's helper, Sean Toulouse, who had to be fired because of dishonesty and could not be replaced quickly with a permanent, qualified helper. Now that a permanent, qualified helper has been hired, there should be no more delays in delivery as this was the cause of the problem.

   The driver was able to find a temporary helper, a man by name of Rusty Sellers, for some help in the unloading work, but he got behind and couldn't seem to catch up. He could have caught up by working overtime, in the opinion of the writer, but he refused to do so. Of the 36 deliveries that were late, all were completed within two days. The problem is over now that the driver has a helper, so there should be no additional delays.

CRITICAL THINKING PROBLEMS

SHORT LENGTH: MEMORANDUM AND LETTER REPORTS

1. *Solving a traffic problem on your campus.* Find some street, intersection, parking lot, or such on your campus where a traffic problem occurs. Study the situation carefully to determine causes. Then work out a solution. Present your analysis and recommendation to the appropriate person (chief of security, traffic control supervisor, or such). Write it in a memorandum report from you, chairman of the traffic control committee on your campus.

2. *Proposing a grade-review procedure for your school.* Assume that the administration at your university has concluded that some form of grade-review procedure should be set up for students who feel that they have not received a just grade. Although the administration believes that the vast majority of professors are conscientious and work hard to ensure fair grading, the current system does not guarantee students any rights. Thus, some change is needed to take care of the occasional instances when students are wronged, perhaps even unintentionally.

Now move over to a position on your faculty. The administration has asked faculty members to contribute their ideas on a grade-review plan. You have a definite one in mind. Submit it in a memorandum report directed to your president. Be sure that your ideas are sound, for you'll be graded on their quality as well as your organization and writing of them.

3. *Writing an evaluation report on Kim Henderson.* You are sales manager, Midwest Division, Megatech Electronics, Inc. It is time that you write your annual evaluation reports on your subordinates.

Megatech's evaluation reports are not the honey-worded types written at many places. They are honest. They praise when praise is deserved, and they criticize when criticism is in order. Their goal is to be constructive. These reports become a part of each person's personnel file, and the people evaluated receive copies of them.

At the moment you are working on the report for Ms. Kim Henderson, one of your newest salespersons. Your garbled notes on her are as follows:

A hard-working and vivacious performer. Outstanding personality—outgoing, good conversationalist, pleasant mannerisms. Have received three reports that she is too aggressive. More concerned with sales than service (reports investigated and appear valid). Sales volume for year was $1,988,000 ($238,000 above quota). Productive. Customer accounts increased from 59 to 83. Appears to go after the big orders and the big ticket items. Her calls on smaller accounts are not so regular as calls on large accounts. Late in submitting weekly reports 11 times. Contacts with her indicate that she knows products well—keeps up with innovations and improvements. A highly motivated individual with a good future with company.

Now you will organize this information into an orderly and meaningful report. You will use the company's standard memorandum form. Address it to Ms. Henderson. Identify the subject as "Annual Performance Evaluation." You may add additional specifics as long as they are consistent with the information given above.

4. *Recommending dismissal of a subordinate.* As regional sales manager for Macon-Boyd, Inc., publishers of college textbooks, you must write a very negative report on one of your representatives. Doyle O. Burr is the person, and following are the facts of the case.

Mr. Burr is just beginning his third year with the company. In his first year, sales dropped from $1,211,000 (his predecessor's volume) to $977,000. Last year Burr's sales dropped to $845,000. After hearing various reports from college professors in Burr's territory that they rarely see him, you made some personal checks.

At Northern State University you found that Burr worked on campus only three of the five days his reports indicated he was there. (You may supply the specific dates). You checked with three of the five professors he reported as luncheon guests on his expense account (total for the lunch, $72.80) and found they had not seen him.

You also checked at Baxter University. Here you found that Burr made a brief appearance one morning, saw two or three professors, and went fishing that afternoon with two graduate assistants. You could find no evidence that he worked the Baxter campus the next two days, even though his reports indicated that he worked the Baxter campus these days.

Just to be certain that your impressions were correct, yesterday you went to Milltown Community College, where Burr was scheduled to work. He didn't show up. Today he arrived on campus. When confronted with the evidence you had assembled, he admitted that your information was true. But he argued strongly that he was not neglecting his duties. He further argued that he was only doing what others were doing. He contended that he called on as many professors as the other representatives—that he just worked faster and more efficiently.

You do not buy his argument. You will report your findings to Helena Rodgers, vice president in charge of sales. And you will recommend that Burr be fired. Use Macon-Boyd's standard memorandum form for your report. Be sure to support your recommendations with a fair review of the facts.

5. *Improving personnel relations at Granite Mountain Insurance Company.* The good relations between the regional office personnel of Granite Mountain Insurance and the agents in the field are rapidly deteriorating. Agents frequently call in or send email messages "cussing out" the people who service their business in the regional office. In turn, the regional office personnel send equally venomous messages back to the agents.

Apparently, these conflicts are having a negative effect on sales. The agents spend more time grumbling and fighting with regional office personnel than they do in drumming up business—or so it would seem. A review of past skirmishes suggests that the trouble arises from three primary sources: (1) the agents' lack of understanding as to why the regional office personnel must turn down certain risky business; (2) the regional office personnel's impatience with the salespeople's distaste for "detail" work; and (3) the basic difference between regional office personnel and agents in terms of objectives. Probably other explanations may be added.

The regional office general manager, Naomi Smythe, has asked you, her assistant, to investigate the matter and to recommend a way (or ways) of alleviating the problem. Use your logic and imagination to supply you with the facts you would have if you actually were in this situation. Then think through the facts and arrive at a plan of action. Present your report in memorandum form. Write it in direct order—that is, with the most significant message right away.

6. *Interpreting public reactions to Capaccio's latest fashion designs.* A few weeks ago the House of Capaccio introduced its fashions for the coming season. To put it mildly, the new designs created interest. In short time, Capaccio's designs were widely discussed throughout the fashion world, in the press, and among the style-conscious public. Much of the comment was favorable; and this made Tony Capaccio happy. But much of it was not so favorable. In fact, the unfavorable comments appeared to be increasing. Soon Mr. Capaccio became alarmed, and he began to wonder whether he should cut production.

In his attempt to find the answer to his problem, Tony assigned you, his research assistant, to find out just what the public thinks. He wanted to know, in brief, which segments of the market were for his fashion line and which were against it.

For the next few weeks you busied yourself designing and conducting a survey of all economic and age segments of the female public. Although Capaccio's originals sell primarily to the affluent crowd, similar designs are mass-produced by subsidiaries and are sold to lower-income groups. Because your survey was short (one question relating to photographs of the Capaccio's designs), you and the college students you hired as interviewers were able to conduct 400 interviews in short time. Your sample was representative of the female adult population of New York City, which Tony considers to be a proper gauge of the style world.

Now the survey has been completed. The findings

TABLE 1 (PROBLEM 6) Percentage of Respondents Who Like, Dislike, or Have No Opinion about Capaccio's New Fashions

	Like	Dislike	No Opinion
All women	47	46	7
Women by ages			
20–29	25	73	2
30–39	41	58	1
40–49	55	38	7
50–59	59	28	13
60 and over	52	28	20
Women by economic groups:			
Upper	52	24	24
Upper middle	42	47	11
Middle	38	47	15
Lower	32	46	22

have been tabulated (Table 1) and are ready to be analyzed and written in report form. You will present it as a memorandum, using a direct beginning. In the report you will not need to describe your research methodology. Tony knows what you did, for he approved the money for your survey. He wants the facts. And he wants them right away.

7. *Should Finnerty Laboratories use a janitorial service?* As assistant to Diane Falkenstein, administrative director of Finnerty Laboratories, you have been asked to look into the possibility of using a janitorial service instead of the two full-time janitors now employed. In recent years this research branch of Finnerty Pharmaceuticals, Inc., has had difficulty keeping janitors. In fact, five people have filled the two $280-a-week positions within the past two years, the longest lasting 11 months. The two people now employed have been with Finnerty only three and seven weeks.

As you gather the facts, you learn that in addition to the two salaries, Finnerty must pay about $32 a week for janitorial supplies. Then, of course, there are the fringe benefits, which amount to an extra 22 percent. And once each year extra help costing about $1,800 has to be hired for major housecleaning. The Davenport Janitorial Service has offered to do all of Finnerty's janitorial work for $700 a week, including all additional expenses.

Your job is to analyze the facts and to reach a decision. You will give the cost factors heavy weight, but you must remember that there are other less obvious factors to be considered. Think through all the factors involved. Then write up your analysis and recommendation in a memorandum report. Address it to Ms. Falkenstein.

8. *Determining the advertising effectiveness of a cooking school.* Until recently the manufacturer of Master Chef, a quality line of cooking utensils, has depended almost totally on newspaper and magazine advertising to sell its products. Six months ago, however, the company decided to try a new form of advertising—a televised cooking school.

Before going into this form of advertising on a big scale, company management decided to experiment with the plan. Thus, they designed a before-and-after experiment, using Crescent City (population 191,000) as the test city and Willstown (population 179,000) as the control city. In each city, they selected five comparable stores for the study.

Sales of Master Chef units were recorded for all stores for one week. Then the cooking school was conducted over a Crescent City television station. Directed by a nationally prominent cooking authority, the school was held during a daytime hour that is popular for homemaker viewing. Although the school was primarily educational, Master Chef's utensils were subtly suggested in the instruction and strongly recommended in the commercials that were included in the 30-minute program. Weekly results of sales were kept for all of the stores in the experiment during and immediately after the program. Then, to determine long-run effects, additional records were

	Units Sold in Test City Stores	Units Sold in Control City Stores
Jan. 3–9, before school	95	84
Jan. 10–16, week of school	126	81
Jan. 17–23, week after school	119	82
Jan. 24–30, 2nd week after school	121	86
Apr. 4–10, 12th week after school	103	79
Jun 27—Jul 3, 24th week after school	105	86

collected 12 weeks and 24 weeks later. This information, which is summarized in Table 2, holds the key to the question of whether television cooking schools are effective means of advertising Master Chef's wares.

As research director for Master Chef, you have the task of analyzing the results of the experiment and of reporting your conclusions to management. Write your report in memorandum form, using the company standard memorandum format. Address the report to Mr. Amos M. Gardner, President.

9. *Assisting with the development of a drug-testing policy at Oxy Chemical.* The Oxy Chemical plant employs a large number of people—975 to be exact. It specializes in producing and distributing chemicals for industrial use. Indeed, the company's total quality orientation requires commitment and dedication from all Oxy team members to assure excellent and consistent products and services for its customers.

At the moment, drug use among employees seems to be a concern for Gay Mongan, president of Oxy, and her management team, all vice presidents of line-and-staff departments within the company. You are an administrative assistant to President Mongan. Although you attend all executive staff meetings, you are an ex-officio nonvoting member.

At the last weekly meeting, the executive committee discussed at length the problem of illegal drug use on the job. All members seemed firmly committed to the concept that company goals could not be met if employees used illegal substances (employees using prescription drugs were excluded). In addition, the committee noted that hiring and continuing to employ workers who used drugs would be contrary to the corporate citizen image the company had worked to attain. Therefore, the committee wants to move forward in its thinking to develop a drug testing policy for Oxy employees. But it does not want to alienate workers and thus attract union organizers. Oxy has been nonunionized for the 20 years of its existence, and the executive committee wants to keep it that way.

President Mongan assigned you the responsibility

When do you think it is justifiable to require current employees to take a drug test? (Mark as many as apply.)

	Percentage of Respondents	
	Production Workers	White-Collar Workers
Upon being hired (preemployment testing)	63%	82%
Anytime, as with random testing	16	42
Periodically, as upon returning to work or in regular physical exams	46	39
Whenever an employee has been involved in an accident	31	30
When an employee on the job appears to be under the influence of drugs	62	72
Never	12	4
No opinion	2	1
	($n = 315$)	($n = 96$)

of conducting an investigation and preparing a report for the committee. She said, "You can see the discomfort we all face with this drug testing issue. But for the good of everyone concerned, it must be done. It's a given that we will have a policy, but first we need to have a sample of our workers' opinions about the issue of testing. I suggest you do a short survey before the committee acts. They can use your findings to word the final policy. I will need your report next week."

Back in your office, you thought seriously about the assignment. You decided to ask a select group of production and white-collar employees one basic question with a number of possible responses.

After conducting the investigation, you now have the results neatly tabulated in Table 3. The next step will be to write up the meaning of these data in memo form for the executive committee. You will use the direct format and present and interpret (compare, contrast, etc.) the facts.

Prepare a well-thought-out memo that the executive committee can use in its policy-determining function.

10. *Determining the effectiveness of point-of-purchase advertising.* The grocery industry is competitive, especially for larger chain stores, which depend on high turnover to achieve acceptable profit margins. A good part of this turnover can be associated with product identity through advertising—specifically newspaper inserts and point-of-purchase displays.

At present, OK Grocers, Inc., a chain with 129 stores in the Midwest, wants to continue to compete with others as it has over its 15-year life span as a

Frozen Category	Change for Displayed Brands	Change for Nondisplayed Brands
Chicken	+189%	−54.8%
Dinners	+23	−23.4
Waffles	+22.8	−12.7
Potatoes	+16.3	N.A.
Pizza	+22.5	−5
Fish sticks/fillets	+9.8	−36.6
Pies	+8.5	−26.2
Dessert cakes	+7.7	−35.1
Coffee creamers	+6.8	−26.5
Orange juice	+4.5	+79.9
Family entrees	+0.2	−15.1
Prepared vegetables	−7.8	−11.4
Rice	−18.4	−4.4
Single-dish entrees	−19.5	−5.5
Average	**+21.4**	**−11**

corporation. It wants particularly to know about the effectiveness of its point-of-purchase advertising, the use of displays to feature products, and its overall convenience and value.

For the last six months, OK management has conducted an informal experiment to test the effectiveness of its point-of-purchase displays for its line of frozen foods. It has kept sales records of frozen-food items, some of which were featured in display advertising and some of which were not. Knowing that the true test of any promotional effort is at the checkout counter, OK management kept records of all frozen-food sales. Managers then aggregated the records for all stores, as shown in Table 4. As a research assistant in the central headquarters of OK Grocers, you now have the job of analyzing the facts to determine exactly where and to what extent the display promotion was effective. Thus, you will do more than a casual job of reporting. You will thoroughly interpret the facts for OK management.

Prepare your analysis in memo format. You will write it in third person to fit the formality of the situation.

11. *Comparing price differences for toys.* Play the role of a management trainee at the Royce City store of Burkharts, Inc., a major chain of department stores. This morning Patricia Rovela, manager of the Royce City store and your boss, asked you to make some price comparisons of toys at the two stores that give Burkharts the most competition.

"Select some of our best sellers," she instructed. "Then get the prices of these items at Supreme and at Best Dollar." (Supreme is the major discount store in the city; and Best Dollar is a chain variety store. "I

expect them to be lower than us because we offer services that they don't," she noted. "But they shouldn't beat us by more than 15 or 20 percent."

As instructed, you selected eight toy items that are predicted to be top sellers for this year's Christmas season. Then you visited the two competing stores and found out their prices on these toys. Now you have the following information:

Country Kid doll—Burkharts, $29.97; Supreme, $26.97; Best Dollar, $29.95.

Kuddly Bear—Burkharts, $26.00; Supreme, $16.84; Best Dollar, $18.99.

Space Barbie—Burkharts, $21.99; Supreme, $15.97; Best Dollar, $18.99.

Bill-Toys Construction Set (small)—Burkharts, $11.99; Supreme, $9.99; Best Dollar, $9.99.

Return of the Gazoo, computer game—Burkharts, $82.00; Supreme, $59.97; Best Dollar, $69.95.

Combat, handheld electronic game—Burkharts, $69.95; Supreme, $59.95; Best Dollar, $69.95.

Bonkers Boomerang—Burkharts, $12.95; Supreme, $9.50; Best Dollar, $10.99.

G.I. Jane figures—Burkharts, $8.00; Supreme, $6.87; Best Dollar, $7.99.

Your next task is to organize the information you have, and then you will interpret it. Your final task is to present your findings and your interpretations in a memorandum report to Ms. Rovela.

12. *A progress report on Augustine's new sales district.* One month ago, you were transferred by Augustine Insurance of Hartford, Connecticut, to Edge City to expand Augustine's sales coverage to this area. It is time now to make a progress report to the home office. Frankly, you do not have much to show in the way of real sales results, but you have put in a lot of work, and you think you have made good progress. As you recall, Charles Brownlee, district manager and recipient of your report, assured you that Augustine did not expect profits right off—that moving into a new territory requires time and patience.

In preparing your report, you first make random notes of the various things you have done during the month. Garbled as they are, your notes look like this:

Rented three-office suite, Staple Building, $9,110 per month.

Hired secretary (Ms. Dolores Chapa) at $1,100 per month. Picked from 10 applicants. Appears to be highly efficient—good work so far.

Visited two local newspapers. Bought space to announce Augustine's entry to area—cost $312 and $280 for four-column, eight-inch ads in *Daily Echo* and *Evening Chronicle*, respectively. Got free publicity in business sections of both papers. (You will attach clippings of ads and articles.)

Bought office furniture: 3 executive desks at $405 each; 3 swivel chairs at $85 each; 7 straight chairs at $46 each; 1 computer workstation at $245; 1 typist's chair at $58; 1 computer at $1,545; office supplies (stationery, stamps, paper clips, etc.), $87; 5 metal 3-drawer file cabinets at $217 each; 2 coat-trees at $33 each; 3 bookshelves at $84 each.

Visited Chamber of Commerce. Got names of 16 business leaders likely to help in finding agents. Visited all 16. Got names of 8 prospects. Interviewed all 8. Four not interested. Two ruled out—short on personality. Two were interested.

James Hickman: Took Augustine's aptitude test—made 96 (exceptional). Has 14 years' experience, but not in insurance. Sold business machines, securities, and industrial chemicals. Hired him. Have spent much time training him both in office and on sales calls. He is eager—a born salesperson. Good personality, high morals, intelligent. No sales yet, but several good prospects lined up. This man will go places.

Larry Chrisman: A proven insurance salesperson, with nine years of experience. Now with Northern Life, but is considering a change. Hasn't yet taken Augustine's aptitude test. Have discussed employment possibilities with him three times. Is definitely interested. Will continue discussion. Good chance of hiring him.

These are the major facts you have to report, although you may think of additional minor details as you write the report. You will use Augustine's conventional memorandum report form.

13. *Reporting a low-performing subordinate for good reason.* Even though you do not like to do so, today you must report Michael A. Finch for improper conduct and neglect of duty.

Mr. Finch joined your sales force about nine months ago after more than 19 years of sales experience with your rival company, Beard's Services, Inc. At first, Finch did a reasonably good job for you, making his quotas each of the first six months. Since that time, however, sales have dropped. In fact, last month he sold only 43 percent of quota, as compared with 67 percent the month earlier and 75 percent the preceding month.

About seven weeks ago, you learned from an old customer in Finch's territory that this customer had apparently been dropped from Finch's route without explanation. Further investigation revealed that at least six other customers were also dropped, apparently without cause.

You called Finch in, talked with him, and learned that marital trouble was to blame. Finch admitted not making many of his regular calls, and promised to do better, saying his troubles were behind him.

In following weeks, he showed no improvement. In fact, his work deteriorated more. Three additional talks with him produced only promises for improvement, but improvement never occurred. His sales continued to drop, and you continued to hear about lost and dissatisfied customers.

You really do not know just how many customers have been lost or the exact extent of the damage done. But you know that something has to be done soon. So you will recommend that Finch be relieved of his sales duties. Since basically he is a capable man with problems, you will recommend him in some other capacity—if he is willing.

Using standard memorandum form, write a report, stating your recommendation and backing it up with supportable reasoning. Use your imagination to supply details not given. Address the report to Ronald S. Joseph, sales manager.

14. *Reporting on switching to Styrofoam cups for the campus dining services.* As Larry Barrett, Director of Housing and Dining Services on your campus, you recognize that you have a continuing responsibility to focus on environmental issues. In fact, your department has a recycling program that has been recognized by many. While you know the ideal would be to eliminate all trash by using only reusable items, there are times when some of your customers need you to provide disposable products. For that reason, you need to determine whether the use of paper or Styrofoam cups is the most environmentally friendly choice.

You realize that there is new recognition that a complete life-cycle assessment is necessary to evaluate the impact of a product. Such an assessment would begin with the raw-material acquisition and continue through the various manufacturing processes, noting energy usage, waste products generated, recyclability, and ending with ultimate product disposal. The experts agree that analysis of the environmental merit of paper versus Styrofoam is a complex issue.

By keeping abreast of the latest information on the relative merits of disposable paper versus Styrofoam products, you've come across some surprising findings. Chlorofluorocarbons (CFCs) are no longer used in making Styrofoam. Paper starts with trees. Styrofoam starts with petroleum. Styrofoam needs no trees, but paper needs petroleum. In one source you've read, you learned that it takes four to six times the raw material for an uncoated paper cup as for a Styrofoam cup. Another source indicated that paper uses three times its final weight in raw wood. Additionally, it takes 10 times more steam and 14 to 20 times more electricity to produce a paper cup than to produce a Styrofoam cup. A *U.S. News and World Report* article credits the Director of Green Design Initiative at Carnegie Mellon University with the fact that it takes half the energy and 35 percent fewer toxic chemicals to make a Styrofoam than a paper cup.

And paper generates more waste. One source reported that a paper cup uses two times the cooling water and generates 300 times the waste water, 10 to 14 times the contaminants, and 1.3 to 1.8 times the emissions to air. Another source believes it uses six times the cooling water and 300 times the waste water as Styrofoam.

Costs favor Styrofoam, too. While one source reports paper costing 2.5 times the cost of Styrofoam, the actual bid quotations received for the products by the campus Dining Services were 2.1 times higher for paper, costing the campus more than $70,000 for paper cups than for Styrofoam cups.

And because paper weighs more than Styrofoam, it will cost more to transport. However, paper, unlike

Styrofoam, is biodegradable; but paper creates substantial quantities of methane gas in decomposing and uses over six times more space in landfills.

While neither product is friendly to the environment, Styrofoam may be the best choice. Therefore, you'll report to the vice president for operations that you recommend that the campus switch to Styrofoam cups. Use indirect organization and first-level headings in your report that you email to the vice president of operations (your instructor).

15. *Developing an email mentoring system with area schools.* As Mel Short, Director of Public Relations at Deere and Company in Moline, Illinois, you have been asked by the executive committee to investigate the possibility of supporting the area school children through an email mentoring program. The committee believes that this type of program has the potential to be a win-win investment. They believe Deere employees can help motivate students while providing the expertise a classroom teacher may not have. In turn, the company would improve its image in the community and eventually attract more good local residents to work for Deere.

In doing your research, you learned that Hewlett-Packard has been involved in a similar mentoring program. Their program is targeted to students in the 5th through 12th grades, and over 1,600 employees participate in 40 states. And while the periods of the mentoring range from 3 months to 12 months, some continue to keep in touch after the program is over. Employees who have participated report that it takes less than 45 minutes a week and can be done at their convenience. Students report feeling that their mentors are their friends. Topics discussed have varied from how to start looking for a college to how to deal with being the only girl in a computer class.

Teachers give numerous reasons on how this type of program helps their students. It improves attendance and increases students' interest in the subject matter. Mentors often help students find good web sites that help students with the subjects they are studying. One teacher mentioned that a student really got excited to learn about Egypt through exposure to various web sites her mentor found for her. It helped the teacher motivate other students to use the web to find good sources of information. Teachers also report that mentors help students think about career choices, which can lead to improved grades. And students definitely improve their writing skills as well as learn appropriate use of email.

Your research also revealed several web sites where ideas for such a program are posted, along with lesson plans for teachers to use to integrate the program into the curriculum. Additionally, you have found program evaluation forms used by the students, mentors, and teachers on the effectiveness of the program. Therefore, much of the groundbreaking efforts have already been made, helping Deere to get a program off the ground by the beginning of the next school term. Report your findings to the executive committee, recommending that Deere proceed with the program by selecting a coordinator to sign up and match students and mentors.

16. *Reporting on your company's efforts to retain customers.* As Linda Hittle, the finance manager of a small business that sells specialty printers, you have recently been asked to report the results of the business's efforts to retain current customers. When the owner learned that the cost of holding on to a customer is about one-fourth the cost of acquiring a new customer, you began a retention effort last month. You started a program that would survey customers on various aspects of satisfaction with the product, with its ability to meet their needs, with the training to use it, and with the sales and service support. The results are shown in Table 5.

Additionally, you have uncovered some other surprising findings. Through your sophisticated tracking and referral system, you have determined that dissatisfied customers who complain are more likely to be given referrals than those who don't complain. Just having the forum for complaining that you set up on your company web site has resulted in more referrals even if the complaints go unresolved.

By employing both your basic management skills and your basic statistical skills, you have analyzed the data you have on the lost accounts and developed a risk profile using regression analysis. For example, you have discovered that those customers who call for ink reorders more frequently are more likely to leave than those who seem to be able to manage their supply levels. You believe that using your computer system to identify or flag accounts with high numbers on some of the factors that your regression analysis has identified as key factors might help you retain some of these customers. For the customer with frequent reorders, you could have your salespeople call on them to develop improved reordering levels; or perhaps some automatic inventory level adjustment schedule can be set up.

In any case, you have been able to determine that even as small an improvement in customer retention

TABLE 5 (PROBLEM 16) **Customer Satisfaction Scores***

How Satisfied Are You with the Wiedenbach Printer's . . .	Average**
Reliability?	4.8
Type clarity?	4.8
Speed?	4.5
Meeting identified needs?	4.7
Training?	5.0
Sales support?	4.3
Service support?	4.4

*48 usable responses

**Scale of 1 to 5 with 5 as highest

as five percentage points can contribute as much as 20 percent improvement in net earnings. The program has definitely resulted in identifying factors that will contribute to improving the financial results of the company. Write up these findings in a report that you will send by email to the owner so that he can pick it up while on the road at a trade show.

INTERMEDIATE-LENGTH REPORTS

17. *Analyzing morale and employee problems at Excalibur Electronics, Inc.* At its executive committee meeting yesterday, the administrative officers of Excalibur discussed the possibility of morale problems at work. Some of the managers suspected that the problem might reside in various employee situations. Moreover, they wanted to know how the company thought its programs, supervisors, and activities could help.

As an administrative assistant to the director of the Human Resources Department, you have been asked to get information on the perceived problems and report it to the executive committee. To comply with this request, you conducted a survey. (Supply any details needed about methodology.) The results of your work are tallied in Tables 6 and 7. Now you must organize the data, relate them to Excalibur's problems, and determine whether significant problems really exist.

Write the report on employee morale and problems for the executive committee. You will use graphics

TABLE 6 (PROBLEM 17) Employee Satisfaction

Questions	Choices	Responses
1. Considering everything, how would you rate your overall satisfaction in the company at the present time?	Satisfied Dissatisfied Neither	58.3% 26.0 15.7
2. How do you feel about the amount of work you do?	Too much Right amount Too little	27.2% 62.3 10.5
3. How do you like your job—the kind of work you do?	Good Average Poor	61.8% 25.2 13.0
4. I feel my job makes the best use of my abilities.	Yes No	47.4% 52.6
5. How do you feel about the quality of supervision you get?	Good Average Poor	50.4% 29.6 20.0
6. Do you feel the company is concerned about your performance?	Yes No	75.2% 24.8

wherever they help to tell the report story. Select an appropriate format for this middle-length report.

18. *Preparing a report on consumer purchasing patterns.* The research department of the National Marketing Council conducts research designed to keep its membership informed on general marketing matters. You are a research associate with the NMC.

Your current assignment is to gather information

TABLE 7 (PROBLEM 17) Employee Perceptions of Problems

| Questions | Responses | | | | | |
	Alcohol Habit	Drug Habit	Marital	Over-weight	Psycho-logical	Smoking
1. Do you know of anyone in your unit who has missed work because of any of the following problems? Yes 26.1% No 73.9% Which problem?	8.7	1.7	14.8	6.1	12.2	2.6
2. In your opinion, has anyone in your organization hindered everyday business of the company because of a problem? Yes 27% No 73% Which problem?	10.4	3.5	12.2	3.5	13.9	3.5
3. Do you feel the company should provide private, personal assistance with a professional counselor in any of the following areas?	30.4	29.6	25.2	24.3	42.6	27.8
4. I think that programs such as these are a good idea and should be implemented. (Yes responses)	74.8	71.0	55.7	47.6	71.9	49.5
5. Would you seek information from one of these counselors if they were available on a confidential basis?	30.4	31.9	26.4	35.0	45.5	33.3
6. If you needed help in any of the above areas (alcohol, drug, etc.), would you feel free to speak to your supervisor about the problem? Yes 33.3% No 66.7%						
7. Should the supervisor be made aware if any of the employees in his or her unit has sought help in the following areas? (Yes responses)	43.6	40.9	21.7	19.8	33.3	19.4
8. The programs should take place inside the company. Inside 58.4% Outside 41.6%						
9. Should the company pay for the program? Company 46.8% Employee 12.6% Split 36.0%						

	Percentage Distribution of Expenditures of Consumption						
	Under 25	25–34	35–44	45–54	55–64	65–74	75 and Over
Food	21.6	23.2	24.8	24.0	24.9	25.7	26.7
Tobacco and liquor	3.3	3.5	3.6	3.7	3.3	2.9	1.7
Housing	30.7	31.3	28.5	27.2	28.8	32.6	35.9
Clothing	9.5	10.0	11.3	11.4	9.8	7.7	6.4
Personal care	2.8	2.8	2.9	2.9	2.9	2.8	2.7
Medical care	5.7	6.0	5.8	6.0	7.4	9.4*	12.0*
Recreation	4.6	4.5	4.4	4.1	3.5	2.7	1.7
Reading	0.8	0.9	0.9	0.9	1.0	1.1	1.2
Education	1.1	0.8	1.2	1.9	0.8	0.4	0.2
Transportation	18.8	15.6	14.4	15.1	14.6	12.5	8.7
Other expenditures	1.0	1.4	2.1	2.8	2.9	2.4	2.7

*In addition to Medicare.

on purchasing patterns of consumers across the nation. After conducting this research (you may supply any methodology details needed), you now have the data in tabular form (Table 8).

Your next task is to present the information in good report form. You will need to analyze the data for all meanings they might have for the membership. Often such data are useful in production planning and promoting goods and services. Perhaps there are other useful purposes.

Write the report in a good short-report form for the membership of the National Marketing Council. It will be duplicated and mailed to all members.

19. *Helping Mrs. Walzel with her investments.* (Requires research.) To the office of Dobbins Financial Planners, Inc., comes Mrs. E. I. Walzel, the widow of one of the area's more prominent business executives. Because she is not wise on matters of finance, she seeks the firm's advice.

Now that her husband's estate has been probated, it appears that Mrs. Walzel has an assortment of stocks. Those listed on the New York Stock Exchange are Micron Technology, 1,500 shares; Quaker State, 800 shares; Electronic Data Systems, 500 shares; Chevron Corporation, 600 shares; Sunstone Hotel Investments, 1,200 shares; and International Harvester, 500 shares. Mrs. Walzel explains that she isn't concerned about making a killing in the market. She wants security more than riches. But will these stocks serve her purpose? The answer to this question is her charge to you, an associate on the Dobbins staff.

Your task now is to study past and possible future movements of Mrs. Walzel's stocks. Then advise her about selling or holding. And if you advise selling any of the stocks, you should come up with some suggestions for investing the freed money. Write your analyses and recommendations in the form of a short report.

20. *Should Eifel-Varner, Inc., begin the practice of gift giving?* The management of Eifel-Varner, Inc., distributors of meats and fish to fine restaurants across the country, is considering giving presents to its customers. In fact, many of the company's competitors have been giving gifts for years, and company salespeople have been arguing that Eifel-Varner should do the same. The question has been discussed at great length at recent executive committee meetings, but to date no decision has been reached. As a result of these discussions, the committee has asked you, administrative assistant to the president, to get the information needed as the basis for an intelligent decision.

As you know, the practice of corporate gift-giving consists of giving presents to customers to show appreciation for their business. Usually, the gifts have nominal value, consisting of such goods as wines, liquors, golf balls, cheeses, fruits, and leather goods. Although some executives (including some at Eifel-Varner) look on the practice as a mild form of bribery, most consider it to be ethical as long as the gift values are kept low and gifts are uniformly given.

In getting information to guide you in making your recommendations, you used the facilities of your staff to conduct a small survey of other companies. Using various trade directories, you mailed questionnaires to 366 companies. You received 103 usable returns. Tabulations of your findings appear in Table 9.

Now you will analyze these findings and will present your analyses along with a recommendation in a report to Eifel-Varner management. Because the problem is not long and involved, you will present your report in short-report form (title page plus text). You will write the text in direct order, beginning with your recommendation and following it with supporting evidence.

TABLE 9 (PROBLEM 20) Answers to Survey
Questions in Percentages

1. Has your company ever given business gifts?
   yes 72%   no   38%
2. Does business gift-giving help build your business?
   yes   53%   no   47%
3. Did you send more gifts this year than last year?
   more 52%   fewer 48%
4. How much did they cost?
   a. under $5   38%
   b. $5–$9.99   33%
   c. $10–$14.99   17%
   d. $15–$19.99   5%
   e. $20–$25   6%
   f. more   1%
5. Did everyone receive the same gift or a different gift?
   same 58%   different 42%
6. Who received the business gifts?
   a. customers/clients   58%
   b. suppliers   22%
   c. other   20%
7. Why do you give business gifts?
   a. goodwill   46%
   b. appreciation   54%
8. Do you give business gifts on the same occasions every year?
   yes 78%   no   22%
9. If yes, on what occasions?
   a. Christmas   84%
   b. birthday   15%
   c. wedding   0
   d. other   11%
10. How does your company distribute business gifts?
    a. mail   49%
    b. in person   45%
    c. messenger   6%
11. What location are they sent to?
    home 45%   office 55%

21. *Recommending a purchase for Granite Mountain Insurance Company.* (Requires research.) The Granite Mountain Insurance Company needs to purchase a given quantity of _____ (personal computers, copy machines, fax machines, etc.—as determined by your instructor). You, assistant to the director of purchasing, have the assignment of helping to determine the model and brand to buy.

You begin your task by collecting all pertinent information (prices, features, maintenance records, dependability, etc.) on three competing brands or types of the product selected. You will compare the three by the appropriate factors to be considered in making a choice. Then you will reach your

conclusion. You will write your conclusion in short-report form. Address it to your boss, Cindy McDermott, director of purchasing.

22. *Determining whether to implement a no-show fee for all rentals.* Your company, Budget Rent-A-Car, recently conducted pilot tests of a new pricing plan in New York, Boston, and Seattle. The plan involved charging a no-show fee to customers who did not cancel at least 24 hours ahead. Though you and most other rental companies currently have such plans for specialty vehicles such as minivans, none have yet applied the no-show fee to all rentals. The amounts charged varied from $30 to $100, depending on the city and car model. The fee was charged to the credit card the customer used to guarantee the reservation. All customers who were charged a no-show fee were told of the no-show fee by the reservation agent handling the call and documenting the notification.

Currently, no-shows average 30 percent in the car-rental industry, causing companies to overbook to compensate. However, sometimes enough cars are not available for everyone with reservations. Budget hypothesized that the new plan would help customers by ensuring that a car would be available and help Budget by being able to manage its fleet maintenance more efficiently.

Some of the data collected are shown in Table 10. As assistant to the marketing director, you must analyze the results of the pilot test, interpret the data clearly, and recommend whether to implement the no-show policy companywide domestically (excluding Hawaii and Alaska). Present your findings to Don Zatyko, Director of Marketing, in a short-report format.

23 *Determining the basis for a nonsmoking policy at Le Triumph Restaurants.* You are an administrative assistant to Ms. Sandee Thomas, president of Le Triumph Restaurants (LTR), a national chain of quality restaurants located throughout the continental United States. The target market for LTR includes the upper-middle- and lower-upper-income strata. In food selections, dining atmosphere, and service quality, LTR seeks to attract and to satisfy the culinary appetites of people in the designated market segment. They have done so successfully for 15 years.

As with any marketing entity, the company must adjust to changing market preferences on a regular basis in terms of organizational policy. The problem that requires attention right now is that of smoking—not only by diners but by employees as well. The smoking problem has not been one of serious concern over the years even though federal law requires that nonsmoking areas be provided. But increasing requests by diners for nonsmoking areas and complaints by employees about fellow workers' smoking (plus above-average employee turnover) cause this problem to be more than routine.

Thus, President Thomas places the assignment squarely on your shoulders: "We have a problem here and I want you to investigate it thoroughly. Let me have your ideas in a report by Friday of next week. I

TABLE 10 (PROBLEM 22) Summary of No-Show Data

	Boston		New York		Seattle	
	90-day Test Period	Same 90-day Period Prior Year	90-day Test Period	Same 90-day Period Prior Year	90-day Test Period	Same 90-day Period Prior Year
Average daily car rental number	246	254	648	666	302	280
Average daily car rental rate	$56.95	$45.95	$69.95	$57.49	$54.95	$49.95
Total complaints	6	25	13	108	3	14
Car not available	0	16	1	46	0	8
Car ordered not available	1	6	1	30	0	3
No-show fee	2	0	3	0	2	0
All other complaints	3	3	8	32	1	3
Fleet maintenance fees per unit	$42.31	$38.51	$45.26	$41.78	$42.45	$44.58
Labor (regular and overtime)	$35.91	$32.11	$38.51	$35.03	$35.95	$38.08
Parts	$6.40	$6.40	$6.75	$6.75	$6.50	$6.50

can study the report over the weekend and share the results with the Operations Committee at our regular weekly meeting on Monday." When she leaves your office, you begin thinking about your objective. More specifically, your thoughts turn to how you will collect the facts that will be the basis of your report.

Using several search engines on the World Wide Web, you find repeated references to a study conducted by the National Restaurant Association (NRA) about preferences on smoking. You click on one reference and link to the home page of the NRA. Another click on their research and statistics division gives you the report, completed last year. Because the NRA is a prestigious industry association with many resources, you know the report was prepared by qualified research professionals. Thus, you consider it reliable and valid. You download the report to your computer.

You now must study, organize, and interpret the facts in light of the assignment President Thomas has given you. Ultimately, you will have to relate the facts to the smoking problem at LTR. At the moment, the figures in Table 11 provide the initial focus of your study.

Prepare the report in the conventional short form (title page and report text). You may select either the formal or informal tone (your instructor will decide). Also, you will need to use first-order talking captions and some graphics.

Now "get smoking" on the smoking report for President Thomas.

24. *Designing a training program for executives at Corpalice, Inc.* "Train, then trust!" has always been the motto at Corpalice, Inc. President Jack Duncan has gone on record officially numerous times saying that the company believes in giving the best resources to its managers so that they can meet the needs of

TABLE 11 (PROBLEM 23) Percentage of Adults Who Favor Designated Smoking Areas and Total Smoking Bans in Workplaces and Restaurants, by Selected Demographic Characteristics

	In Workplaces		In Restaurants	
	Designated Area	Total Ban	Designated Area	Total Ban
All adults	63%	32%	57%	38%
Age				
18 to 29	65%	30%	57%	39%
30 to 49	62	34	56	40%
50 to 64	65	33	57	41
65 and older	62	28	57	32
Region				
Northeast	65%	31%	54%	43%
Midwest	60	35	55	40
South	68	27	63	31
West	59	35	54	41
Education				
No college	69%	24%	64%	30%
Some college	67	29	54	43
College graduate	46	51	44	52
Postgraduate study	44	54	39	57
Income				
Less than $20,000	67%	26%	64%	31%
$20,000 to $29,999	66	30	56	37
$30,000 to $49,999	63	33	57	40
$50,000 or more	57	40	50	46

customers. One of those resources—management training—is your concern du jour. You are an assistant to Marilynn Glasscock, the training director at Corpalice.

Established 10 years ago, Corpalice provides real estate relocation services to companies and individuals seeking effective ways to reduce expenses related to geographic relocation. At its last meeting, the executive committee of the company indicated an existing need for training the three levels of company managers. But first they want to find out what preferences the managers have for training. Ms. Glasscock assigns you the task of surveying the managers and recommending a training plan for Mr. Duncan.

To collect the data, you design a questionnaire to be distributed and returned by the managers. It is relatively short and the interest in the topic is high, so you expect a high rate of return.

Specifically, you concentrate on educational attainment by management level, training needs by subject area, and training needs by management level. Individuals can denote their educational level simply by checking off the degrees they have attained. The other two areas could give results that could be less than meaningful. Thus, you decide to present 30 subject areas on the questionnaire and have respondents select and rank-order them. Then you will relate the top five rank-ordered subject areas to the three management levels.

Today, you have the results tallied as shown in Tables 12, 13, and 14. They represent an 80 percent return from the management workforce. Your assignment now is to analyze these figures and prepare the report, recommending a management training program to the president. Actually, the report will come from Director Glasscock's position. Because she's your boss and you do not want to

TABLE 12 (PROBLEM 24) Highest Educational Degree by Level of Management (%)*

Management Level	High School or Lower	Bachelor's Degree	Master's Degree	Doctoral Degree
Senior executives	7	41	46	6
Middle managers	14	59	24	4
Entry-level managers	26	56	17	1

*Percentages are rounded; therefore, totals by management level may not equal 100.

TABLE 13 (PROBLEM 24) Training Needs of Managers by Area

Area	Number of Managers Requesting	% of Total
Management of people	151	36.8%
English writing and oral presentation skills	129	31.5%
Finance and accounting	118	28.8%
Computer proficiency	47	11.5%
Economics	36	8.8%

TABLE 14 (PROBLEM 24) Training Needs by Level of Management

Area	Entry-Level Managers		Middle Managers		Senior Executives	
	Number	Percent	Number	Percent	Number	Percent
Management of people	34	31.5	95	34.7	22	32.8
English writing and oral presentation skills	36	33.3	79	28.8	14	20.9
Finance and accounting	26	24.1	63	23.3	29	43.3
Computer proficiency	22	20.4	23	8.4	2	3.0
Economics	10	9.3	16	5.9	10	15.0

TABLE 15 (PROBLEM 25) Summary of Answers to the Questions

Questions	Percent Agreeing by Professional Groups				
	MBAs	Lawyers	Engineers	Doctors	Combined
Existence of large corporations is essential to our economic growth.	78%	64%	72%	68%	73%
Many of the largest companies should be broken up for good of the country.	29	49	39	42	37
We can depend upon competition to keep prices at fair levels.	51	40	51	46	48
Some form of government regulation of wages and prices is needed to stem inflation.	35	50	45	49	42
Most large companies want to correct pollution problems they are causing.	39	28	35	24	34
Large corporations should be forced to fight pollution more aggressively.	68	76	72	89	73
Corporations fairly represent quality of their products and services.	57	38	48	40	49
Large companies are doing an adequate job of informing the public of their policy and activities.	22	22	20	20	22
Large corporations should be more active in politics by speaking out on public issues.	83	70	81	79	79
Large corporations should be more active in politics through lobbying.	33	24	23	23	28
Large corporations have a duty to better the quality of life through nonprofit expenditures.	68	67	70	78	69
Labor should take a more active role in corporate decision-making.	24	30	30	25	27

embarrass her, you plan to give your work the touch of professional class that only you can provide.

Prepare your work in short-report format—title page and text. Because of the situation, you will word it formally. There are opportunities for graphics, but you will remember that their function is to supplement words, not replace them.

Prepare the report on management training for Ms. Glasscock.

25. *Examining people's attitudes toward corporations.* For some time the members of the Strategic Alliance of Corporations have been concerned about the image held of corporations by the public. So great has been this concern that they have devoted much of their effort to public relations designed to improve the image.

To this point, much of SAC's effort has involved educational advertising—campaigns designed to educate the public on the role of corporations in the free enterprise system. But many of the members feel that these efforts have been futile. So now the organization is ready to take a new look at the question. And they have called you, a research associate on their payroll, to do the job.

Because SAC feels that the thinking of professional people is most meaningful and will help them best, they want you to survey this group. So they select for you four professional subgroups—MBAs, engineers, lawyers, and doctors. And they ask you to survey a representative number of them and to find out their thoughts about corporations.

From a random sample of 200 of each of the four subgroups, you have assembled the statistics in Table 15. Now you will analyze these data and present them in a report that will emphasize what they mean to SAC. Address the report to Bobby C. Vaught, president. You will use the short-report form. But you will write the report in the third person and use graphic aids.

26. *Analyzing grade inflation at Mitchell University.* In the position of assistant director of the office of institutional research, Mitchell University, write a report for the deans and directors of the school.

As explained to you by Dr. Jose Goris, dean of academic affairs, there is much concern among the deans and directors that grading has become softer in recent years. Those who feel this way present little factual support—only impressions. So Dean Goris wants you to look into the matter.

Specifically your charge is to gather grade data over the past 10 years. Then you will analyze the data and arrive at a conclusion as to the extent of grade inflation. You won't make any recommendations, for that area is the responsibility of the deans and directors.

In gathering the information, you conclude that grade point averages by class rank and distribution of A's, B's, C's, and so on will give you valuable insight into the problem. Then, because of the vital role grades have in weeding out entering freshmen, you feel that a summary of academic suspensions of freshmen will be helpful. You assembled these data in Tables 16, 17, and 18.

Now you are ready to write the report. Set it up in a form appropriate for the occasion. Address it to Dean Goris with copies to each of the deans and directors.

27. *How do off-campus stores' prices compare with other store prices?* (Requires research.) As a member of the student government at your school, you have been made chairman of a special committee to compare prices of off-campus stores with those in other parts of the city. Working with two other students, you work out a student's market basket list and do some objective comparison shopping. Of course, you ignore specials, promotions, or the like.

When you have finished your investigation, you organize your findings for effective presentation. Then you analyze them and present them in report form. As the information largely is statistical, you will present the major factors in graphic form. Your conclusion will determine whether there is truth to the often heard complaint that campus stores have higher prices. Address your report to your student body president.

TABLE 16 (PROBLEM 26) Grade-Point Averages* of Undergraduates by Student Level, Fall Semester, Past 10 Years

	10 years ago	9 years ago	8 years ago	7 years ago	6 years ago	5 years ago	4 years ago	3 years ago	2 years ago	Last year
GPA of all undergraduates	2.219	2.318	2.364	2.445	2.459	2.529	2.528	2.548	2.552	2.536
GPA of all freshmen	2.010	2.033	2.087	2.075	2.159	2.240	2.217	2.232	2.224	2.175
GPA of all sophomores	2.271	2.301	2.343	2.398	2.407	2.559	2.571	2.564	2.592	2.555
GPA of all juniors	2.462	2.486	2.509	2.586	2.608	2.716	2.709	2.734	2.736	2.745
GPA of all seniors	2.660	2.680	2.700	2.788	2.842	2.862	2.878	2.888	2.888	2.912

*Based on 4-point system (A = 4.0, B = 3.0, and so on).

TABLE 17 (PROBLEM 26) Number and Percent of Undergraduate Grades, Fall Semester, Past 10 Years

	A's	Percent	B's	Percent	C's	Percent	D's	Percent	F's	Percent	Satisfactory	Percent	Pass	Percent	Total	Percent
10 years ago	11,842	15.5	24,217	31.7	25,331	33.1	8,873	11.6	6,211	8.1	0	0	0	0	76,474	100.0
9 years ago	12,936	17.0	23,981	31.4	24,866	32.6	8,593	11.3	5,915	7.8	0	0	0	0	76,291	100.1
8 years ago	13,499	18.1	23,663	31.7	24,505	32.8	7,874	10.6	5,080	6.8	0	0	0	0	74,621	100.0
7 years ago	14,098	19.8	22,730	31.9	22,744	31.9	6,910	9.7	4,796	6.7	0	0	0	0	71,278	100.0
6 years ago	14,810	20.4	24,182	33.4	21,988	30.4	6,885	9.5	4,558	6.3	0	0	0	0	72,423	100.0
5 years ago	16,917	21.9	26,515	34.3	22,588	29.2	6,447	8.3	4,107	5.3	1	0	819	1.1	77,394	100.1
4 years ago	19,359	23.3	27,103	32.6	23,472	28.2	7,403	8.9	4,963	6.0	0	0	926	1.1	83,226	100.1
3 years ago	20,286	23.7	27,847	32.6	23,603	27.6	7,268	8.5	5,017	5.9	4	0	1,491	1.7	85,516	100.0
2 years ago	20,917	23.8	28,695	32.7	23,589	26.9	7,500	8.5	5,338	6.1	11	0	1,695	1.9	87,745	99.9
Last year	21,441	24.0	28,773	32.2	23,685	26.5	7,865	8.8	5,943	6.6	0	0	1,769	2.0	89,476	100.1

TABLE 18 (PROBLEM 26) Number and Percent of Freshmen Academic Suspensions, Fall Semester, Past 10 Years

10 years ago		9 years ago		8 years ago		7 years ago		6 years ago		5 years ago		4 years ago		3 years ago		2 years ago		Last year	
Number	Percent	Number	Percent	Number	Percent	Number	Percent	Number	Percent	Number	Percent	Number	Percent	Number	Percent	Number	Percent	Number	Percent
398	10.7	379	10.1	336	9.1	324	8.7	320	8.2	318	7.9	320	6.8	275	6.1	268	6.0	374	8.4

TOPICS FOR REPORT PROBLEMS

Following are topics that may be developed into reports of varying length and difficulty. In each case, the facts of the situation will need to be created through the student's (or the instructor's) imagination before a business-type problem exists. The information needed in most cases should be available in the library.

1. Recommend for X Company a city and hotel for holding its annual meeting of sales representatives.
2. Determine the problem areas and develop a set of rules for employees who work at home during business hours for X Company.
3. For an investment service, determine which mutual

funds do better: those that invest for the long run or those that emphasize market timing.

4. What can X Company (you choose the name and industry) do to improve the quality of its product or service?

5. Investigate the problem of worker theft and recommend ways to decrease it.

6. Evaluate the impact of the European Community on X Company (you choose the name and industry) profits.

7. Determine the problems of recycling and recommend ways to overcome them.

8. Investigate the advantages and disadvantages of requiring workers to wear uniforms and recommend whether X Company should require them.

9. Advise X Company on the advantages and disadvantages of hiring student interns from the local college.

10. Evaluate and compare the economic forecasts of three leading forecasters over the past five years.

11. Advise Company X on the desirability of establishing a child care center for the children of its employees.

12. Report to Company X management what other leading companies are doing to increase ethics consciousness among employees.

13. Report to a large chain of department stores on current means of reducing shoplifting.

14. Determine the effects of smoking on worker health and/or productivity.

15. Determine whether Company X should ban smoking in the workplace.

16. Evaluate the status of affirmative action in _____ (company, industry, country).

17. Report on the office design of the future for Company X.

18. What can Company X (you choose the type of company) do to improve productivity?

19. Determine how Company X should cope with the problem of an aging workforce.

20. Evaluate the advantages and disadvantages of flextime.

21. Determine the advantages and disadvantages of fixed-rate and variable-rate mortgages.

22. Study the benefits and problems of a two-career marriage, and draw conclusions on the matter.

23. Study and report on the more popular forms of creative financing being used in real estate today.

24. Review the literature to determine the nature and causes of executive burnout and remedies for it.

25. What should Company X do about employees who have been made obsolete by technological change?

26. Your company (to be specified by your instructor) is considering the purchase of _____ (number) laptop computers for its sales representatives. Evaluate three brands, and recommend one for purchase.

27. Evaluate _____ (city of your choice) as a site for the annual meeting of a large professional association (your choice), ending with a recommendation.

28. Advise Company X (a national grocery chain) on whether to use double coupons.

29. Investigate and report on the demand for college-trained people in the coming years.

30. Determine the status and progress of women's rights in business for _____ (association).

31. Determine the recent developments in, current status of, and outlook for _____ industry.

32. Investigate and report on the criminal liability of corporate executives.

33. Investigate whether hiring physically challenged workers is charity or good business for Company X.

34. Assess the status of pollution control in _____ industry for an association of firms in that industry.

35. Review the status of consumer protection laws, and recommend policies for Company X.

36. For the International Association of Secretaries, review current developments in word processing and determine whether we are truly moving toward the "paperless office."

37. Advise Company X (your choice of a specific manufacturer) on the problems and procedures involved in exporting its products to _____ (country or countries of your choice).

38. Report to Company X on the quality of life in your city. The company may open a factory there and would move some executives to it.

39. Report to Company X on the ethics and effectiveness of subliminal advertising.

40. Compare the costs, services, and other relevant factors of the major automobile rental firms, and recommend which of these firms Company X should use.

41. Survey the franchise possibilities for _____ (fast foods, automotive services, or such), and select one of these possibilities for a business client.

42. Advise Company X on developing a wellness (preventive health) program.

Additional topics are listed at the end of the long-length problem section following Chapter 12. Many of these topics are suitable for intermediate-length reports, just as some of the above topics are suitable for long reports.

Long, Formal Reports

12

CHAPTER OBJECTIVES

Upon completing this chapter, you will be able to construct long, formal reports for important projects. To reach this goal, you should be able to

1 Describe the roles and contents and construct the prefatory parts of a long, formal report.

2 Organize each introduction of a long report by considering the likely readers and selecting the appropriate contents.

3 Determine, based on the report's goal, the most effective way to end a report—a summary, a conclusion, a recommendation, or a combination of the three.

4 Describe the role and content of the appendix and bibliography of a report.

5 Prepare a structural coherence plan for a long, formal report.

INTRODUCTORY SITUATION

Long, Formal Reports

Assume the role of associate director of research, Midwestern Research, Inc. As your title indicates, research is your business. Perhaps it would be more accurate to say that research and reports are your business. Research is your primary activity, of course. But you must present your findings to your customers. The most efficient way of doing so is through reports.

Typical of your work is your current assignment with Armor Motors, a manufacturer of automobiles. The sales division of Armor wants information that will help improve the effectiveness of its salespeople. Specifically, it wants answers to the question of what its salespeople can do to improve their performance. The information gathered will be used in revising the curriculum of Armor's sales training program.

To find the answer to the basic question, you plan to investigate three areas of sales activities: how salespeople use their time, how they find prospects, and how they make sales presentations. You will get this information for two groups of Armor salespeople: the successful and the unsuccessful. Next, you will compare the information you get from these two groups. You will compare the groups on the three areas of sales activity (the bases of comparison). The differences you detect in these comparisons should identify the effective and the ineffective sales practices.

Your next task will be to determine what your findings mean. When you have done this, you will present your findings, analyses, conclusions, and recommendations in a report to Armor Motors. Because Armor executives will see the report as evidence of the work you did for the company, you will dress the report up. You know that what Armor sees will affect what it thinks of your work.

So you will use the formal arrangement that is traditional for reports of this importance. You will include the conventional prefatory pages. You will use headings to guide the readers through the text. And you will use graphics liberally to help tell the report story. If the situation calls for them, you may use appended parts. In other words, you will construct a report that matches the formality and importance of the situation. How to construct such reports is the subject of this chapter.

Although not numerous, long, formal reports are highly important in business. They usually concern major investigations, which explains their length. They are usually prepared for high-level executives, which explains their formality.

- Long, formal reports are important but not numerous in business.

ORGANIZATION AND CONTENT OF THE LONGER REPORTS

In determining the structure of the longer, more formal reports, you should view your work much as architects view theirs. You have a number of parts to work with. Your task is to design from those parts a report that meets your reader's needs. By meeting your reader's needs, you practice good etiquette.

- Needs should determine the structure of long, formal reports.

The first parts in your case are the prefatory pages. As noted in Chapter 11, the longest, most formal reports contain all of these. As the length of the report and the formality of the situation decrease, certain changes occur. As the report architect, you must decide which arrangement of prefatory parts meets the length and formality requirements of your situation.

- The need for the prefatory parts decreases as reports become shorter and less formal.

To make this decision, you need to know these parts. Thus, we will describe them in the following pages. In addition, we will describe the remaining structure of the longest, most formal report. As you proceed through these descriptions, it will be helpful to trace the parts through the illustration report at the end of this chapter. In addition, it will help to consult Appendix B for illustrations of page form.

- In determining which prefatory parts to include, you should know their roles and contents.

For convenience in the following discussion, the report parts are organized by groups. The first group comprises the prefatory parts, the parts that are most closely related to the formality and length of the report. Then comes the report proper, which, of course, is the meat of all reports. It is the report story. The final group comprises the appended parts. These parts contain supplementary materials, information that is not essential to the report but may be helpful to some readers. In summary, the presentation follows this pattern:

- Thus, they are reviewed in the following pages.

Introduction to long reports greets readers and prepares them for the facts and interpretations that will follow.

Prefatory parts: Title fly. Title page. Letter (memo) of authorization. Letter of transmittal, preface, or foreword. Table of contents and list of illustrations. Executive summary.

The report proper: Introduction. The report findings (presented in two or more divisions). Summary, conclusion, or recommendation.

Appended parts: Appendix. Bibliography.

THE PREFATORY PARTS

As you know from preceding discussion, there may be many variations in the prefatory parts of a formal report. Even so, the six parts covered in the following pages are generally included in the longer reports.

TITLE FLY

- The title fly contains only the report title.

- Construct titles to make them describe the report precisely.

- As a checklist, use who, what, where, when, why, and sometimes how.

The first of the possible prefatory report pages is the title fly (see page 365). It contains only the report title, and it is included solely for reasons of formality. Since the title appears again on the following page, the title fly is somewhat repetitive. But most books have one, and so do most formal reports.

Although constructing the title fly is simple, composing the title is not. In fact, on a per word basis, the title requires more time than any other part of the report. This is as it should be, for titles should be carefully worded. Their goal is to tell at a glance what the report does and does not cover. A good title fits the report like a glove. It covers all the report information snugly.

For completeness of coverage, you should build your titles around the five Ws: *who, what, where, when, why.* Sometimes *how* may be important. In some problems, you will not need to use all the Ws. Nevertheless, they serve as a good checklist for completeness. For example, you might construct a title for the report described at the chapter beginning as follows:

Who: Armor Motors
What: Sales training recommendations
Where: Implied (Armor dealerships)
When: 1999

Why: Understood (to improve sales training)

How: Based on a 1999 study of company sales activities

From this analysis comes this title: "Sales Training Recommendations for Armor Motors Based on a 1999 Study of Company Sales Activities."

For another example, take a report analyzing the Lane Company's 1999 advertising campaigns. This analysis would be appropriate:

Who: Lane Company

What: Analysis of advertising campaigns

Where: Not essential

When: 1999

Why: Implied

How: Not essential

Thus, this title emerges: "Analysis of Lane Company's 1999 Advertising Campaigns."

Obviously, you cannot write a completely descriptive title in a word or two. Extremely short titles tend to be broad and general. They cover everything; they touch nothing. Even so, your goal is to be concise as well as complete. So you must seek the most economical word pattern consistent with completeness. In your effort to be concise and complete, you may want to use subtitles. Here is an example: "A 1998 Measure of Employee Morale at Pfeifer's Mossback Plant: A Study Based on a Survey Using the Semantic Differential."

- One- or two-word titles are too broad. Subtitles can help conciseness.

TITLE PAGE

Like the title fly, the title page presents the report title. In addition, it displays information essential to identification of the report. In constructing your title page, you should include your complete identification and that of the authorizer or recipient of the report. You may also include the date of writing, particularly if the date is not in the title. An example of a three-spot title page appears in the report at the end of the chapter. You can see a four-spot arrangement (used when writer and reader are within the same organization) in Appendix B.

- The title page displays the title, identification of the writer and authorizer, and the date.

LETTER (MEMO) OF AUTHORIZATION

Although not illustrated in the diagram of report structure in Chapter 11 or in the report at the end of this chapter, a letter or memo of authorization can be a prefatory part. It was not shown in the diagram (Figure 11.1) because its presence in a report is not determined by formality or length but by whether the report was authorized in writing. A report authorized in writing should include a copy of the written authorization. This part usually follows the title page.

- Include the letter of authorization if the report was authorized in writing.

As the report writer, you would not write the letter (or memorandum) of authorization. But if you ever have to write one, handle it as you would a direct-order message. In the opening, authorize the research. Then cover the specific information that the reader needs to conduct it. This might include a clear description of the problem, time and money limitations, special instructions, and the due date. Close the letter or memo with appropriate goodwill comment.

- Write the letter of authorization in the direct order: authorization, information about the problem, goodwill close.

LETTER OF TRANSMITTAL, FOREWORD, PREFACE

Most formal reports contain a personal message of some kind from the writer to the reader. In most business reports, the letter of transmittal performs this function. In some cases, particularly where the report is written for a group of readers, a foreword or preface is used instead.

- The letter of transmittal is a personal message from the writer to the reader.

The letter of transmittal transmits the report to the reader. In less formal situations, the report is transmitted personally (orally). In more formal situations, a letter usually does the job. But keep in mind that the letter merely substitutes for a face-to-face meeting. What

- It substitutes for a face-to-face meeting.

you write in it is much like what you would say if you were face to face with the reader. Meeting your reader's needs enhances the communication effect of your report. It involves doing what is best for the reader, which of course is the practice of good business etiquette. You should use the occasion to display good etiquette.

Because the goal of transmitting the report is positive, you should begin the letter of transmittal directly, without explanation or other delaying information. Your opening words should say, in effect, "Here is the report." Tied to or following the transmittal of the report, you should briefly identify the report goal, and you can refer to the authorization (who assigned the report, when, why).

■ Its main goal is to transmit the report.

What else you include in the letter of transmittal depends on the situation. In general, you should include anything that would be appropriate in a face-to-face presentation. What would you say if you were handing the report to the reader? It would probably be something about the report—how to understand, use, or appreciate it. You might make suggestions about follow-up studies, warnings about limitations of the report, or comments about side issues. In fact, you might include anything that helps the reader understand and value the report—anything that enhances good etiquette. Typically, the letter of transmittal ends with appropriate goodwill comment. An expression of gratefulness for the assignment or an offer to do additional research if necessary makes good closing material.

■ In addition, it includes helpful comments about the report. The close is goodwill.

When you combine the letter of transmittal with the executive summary (an acceptable arrangement), you follow the opening transmittal statement with a summary of the report highlights. In general, you follow the procedure for summarizing described in the discussion of the executive summary. Following the summary, you include appropriate talk about the report. Then you end with a goodwill comment.

■ A summary follows the opening when the executive summary and the letter of transmittal are combined.

Because the letter of transmittal is a personal note to the reader, you may write in a personal style. In other words, you may use personal pronouns (*you, I, we*). In addition, you may write the letter in conversational language that reflects the warmth and vigor of your personality. You may not want to use the personal style in very formal cases. For example, if you were writing a report for a committee of senators or for other high-ranking dignitaries, you might elect to write the letter of transmittal impersonally. But such instances are rare. In whatever style, you should convey mannerly etiquette to give genuine warmth to the contact with another human being.

■ The letter of transmittal is usually in personal style.

As noted previously, you may transmit reports to broad audiences in a foreword or a preface. Minor distinctions are sometimes drawn between forewords and prefaces. But for all practical purposes, they are the same. Both are preliminary messages from the writer to the reader. Although forewords and prefaces usually do not formally transmit the report, they do many of the other things done by letters of transmittal. Like letters of transmittal, they seek to help the reader appreciate and understand the report. They may, for example, include helpful comments about the report—its use, interpretation, follow-up, and the like.

■ For broad audiences, a foreword (or preface) is used. Forewords do not transmit the report—they comment about it.

Playing possum doesn't work anymore, Stephmeyer! I want that report by 5 p.m. or else!
(*Reprinted by permission: Tribune Media Services.*)

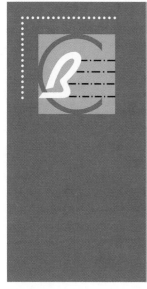

A Questionable Example of Effective Reporting

"How could I have hired this fellow Glutz?" the sales manager moaned as he read this first report from his new salesperson: "I have arrive in Detroit. Tomorry I will try to sell them companys here what ain't never bought nothing from us."

Before the sales manager could fire this stupid fellow, Glutz's second report arrived: "I done good here. Sold them bout haff a millun dollars wirth. Tomorry I try to sell to them there Smith Company folks what threw out that last feller what sold for us."

Imagine how the sales manager's viewpoint changed when he read Glutz's third report: "Today I seen them Smith folks and sole them bout a millun dollars wirth. Also after dinner I got too little sails mountin to bout half a millun dollars. Tomorry I going to do better."

The sales manager was so moved that he tacked Glutz's reports on the company bulletin board. Below them he posted his note to all the salespeople: "I want all you should reed these reports wrote by Glutz who are on the road doin a grate job. Then you should go out and do like he done."

In addition, they frequently contain expressions of indebtedness to those helpful in the research. Like letters of transmittal, they are usually written in the first person. But they are seldom as informal as some letters of transmittal. There is no established pattern for arranging the contents of forewords and prefaces.

TABLE OF CONTENTS, LIST OF ILLUSTRATIONS

If your report is long enough to need a guide to its contents, you should include a table of contents. This table is the report outline in finished form with page numbers. As noted in the discussion of outlining in Chapter 10, the outline headings appear in the text of the report as headings of the various parts. Thus, a listing showing the pages where the headings appear helps the reader find the parts of the report. A table of contents is especially helpful to the reader who wants to read only a few selected parts of the report.

■ Include a table of contents when the report is long enough to need a guide to its contents.

In addition to listing the text headings, the table of contents lists the parts of the report that appear before and after the report proper. Thus, it lists the prefatory parts, but usually only those that follow the table of contents. It also lists the appended parts (bibliography, appendix) and the figures and tables that illustrate the report. Typically, the figures and tables appear as separate listings following the listings reviewed above.

■ The table of contents lists text headings, prefatory parts, appended parts, and figures and tables. It gives page numbers.

EXECUTIVE SUMMARY

The executive summary (also called *synopsis, abstract, epitome, précis, digest*) is the report in miniature. It concisely summarizes whatever is important in the report. For some readers, the executive summary serves as a preview to the report. But it is written primarily for busy executives who may not have time to read the whole report. Perhaps they can get all they need to know by reading the executive summary. If they need to know more about any part, they can find that part through the table of contents. Thus, they can find out whatever they need to know quickly and easily.

■ The executive summary summarizes the report.

You construct the executive summary simply by reducing the parts of the report in order and in proportion. More specifically, you go through the report, selecting whatever is essential. You should include all the major items of information—the facts of the report. You should include all the major analyses of the information presented. And you should include all the conclusions and recommendations derived from these analyses. The finished product should be a miniature of the whole, with all the important ingredients. As a general rule, the executive summary is less than an eighth as long as the writing it summarizes.

■ It includes highlights of the facts, analyses, conclusions, and recommendations—in proportion.

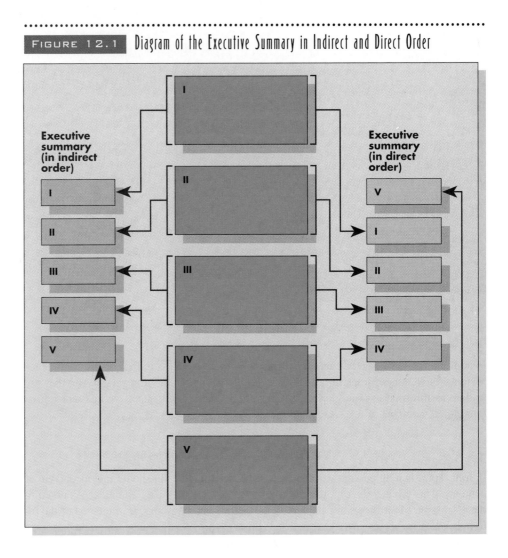

Because your goal is to cut the report to a fraction of its length, much of your success will depend on your skill in word economy. Loose writing is costly. But in your efforts to be concise, you are more likely to write in a dull style. You will need to avoid this tendency.

- Work on writing style in this part.

The traditional executive summary reviews the report in the indirect order (introduction, body, conclusion). In recent years, however, the direct order has gained in popularity. This order shifts the conclusions and/or recommendations (as the case may be) to the major position of emphasis at the beginning. Direct-order executive summaries resemble the short reports described in Chapter 11. From this direct beginning, the summary moves to the introductory parts and then through the major highlights of the report in normal order.

- Either direct or indirect order is appropriate.

Diagrams of both arrangements appear in Figure 12.1. Whichever arrangement you choose, you will write the executive summary after the report proper is complete.

THE REPORT PROPER

- Arrangements of the report proper may vary, but the following review of the indirect order should be helpful.

As noted in Chapter 11, most longer reports are written in the indirect order (introduction, body, conclusion). But there are exceptions. Some longer reports are in the direct order—with summaries, conclusions, or recommendations at the beginning. And some are in a prescribed order similar to that of the technical and staff reports described in Chapter 11. Even though the orders of longer reports may vary, the ingredients of all these reports are similar. Thus, the following review of the makeup of a report in the indirect order should help you in writing any report.

INTRODUCTION

The purpose of the introduction of a report is simply to prepare the readers to receive the report. Whatever will help achieve this goal is appropriate content. Giving your readers what they need makes a good first impression as well as displays your concern for good etiquette.

In determining what content is appropriate, consider all the likely readers of your report. As we noted earlier, the readers of many of the shorter reports are likely to know the problem well and have little or no need for an introduction. But such is not often the case for the longer reports. Many of these reports are prepared for a large number of readers, some of whom know little about the problem. These reports often have long lives and are kept on file to be read in future years. Clearly, they require some introductory explanation to prepare the readers.

Determining what should be included is a matter of judgment. You should ask yourself what you would need or want to know about the problem if you were in your readers' shoes. As the report's author, you know more about the report than anyone else. So you will work hard not to assume that readers have the same knowledge of the problem that you do. In selecting the appropriate information, you would do well to use the following checklist of likely introduction contents. Remember, though, that it is only a checklist. Only on rare occasions, such as in the longest, most complex reports, would you include all the items.

ORIGIN OF THE REPORT.   The first part of your introduction might well include a review of the facts of authorization. Some writers, however, leave this part out. If you decide to include it, you should present such facts as when, how, and by whom the report was authorized; who wrote the report; and when the report was submitted. Information of this kind is particularly useful in reports that have no letter of transmittal.

PROBLEM AND PURPOSE.   A vital part of almost every report is a statement of its problem. The *problem* is whatever the report seeks to do. It is the satisfaction of the need that prompted the investigation.

You may state the problem of your report in three ways, as shown in Chapter 10. One common way is to word it in the infinitive form: "To determine standards for corporate annual reports." Another common way is to word it as a question: "What retail advertising practices do Centerville consumers disapprove of?" Still another way is to word it as a declarative statement: "Company X wants to know the characteristics of the buyers of Y perfume as a guide to its advertising planning." Any of the three should give your reader a clear picture of what your report seeks to do. But the problem statement is not the only item you include. You will need to elaborate on what you are going to do.

Closely related to *what* you are doing is *why* you are doing it. The *purpose* (often called by other names such as *objective, aim, goal*) tells the reason of the report. For example, you might be determining standards for the corporate annual report *in order to streamline the production process*. You will need to weave the why and what of the report together for a smooth flow of thoughts.

SCOPE.   If the scope of the problem is not clearly covered in any of the other introductory parts, you may need to include it in a separate part. By *scope* we mean the boundaries of the problem. In this part of the introduction—in plain, clear language—you should describe what is included in the problem. You should also identify the delimitations—what you have not included.

LIMITATIONS.   In some reports, you will need to explain limitations. By *limitations* we mean things that impair the quality of your report. For example, you may not have been given enough time to do the work thoroughly. Or perhaps a short budget prevented you from doing everything that should have been done. And there are other limitations—unavoidable conditions, restrictions within the problem, absence of historical information. In general, this part of the introduction should include whatever you think might explain possible shortcomings in your report.

- The introduction should prepare the readers.

- In deciding what to include, consider all likely readers.

- Then determine what those readers need to know. Use the following checklist.

- 1. Origin—the facts of authorization.

- 2. Problem—what the report seeks to do.

- The problem is commonly stated in infinitive, question, or declarative form.

- The purpose is the reason for the report.

- 3. Scope—the boundaries of the problem.

- 4. Limitations—anything that impairs the quality of the report.

Using Styles to Format Documents

Corel WordPerfect - Document1

File Edit View Insert Format Tools Wind

Times New Roman 12 **B** *I* U

Table of Contents level: Mark 1 Mark 2

<< Table of Contents will generate here

Define Table of Contents

Number of levels (1-5): 5

Numbering format

Level	Style	Position	
1	TableofCont2	Text .....#	▼
2	TableofCont2	Text .....#	▼
3	TableofCont3	Text .....#	▼
4	TableofCont4	Text .....#	▼
5	TableofCont5	Text .....#	▼

OK   Cancel   Help

Styles...   Page Numbering...

American Literature .2
Late Nineteenth Century.
(1861-1914) .5
Humor: A Social
Critique .7
Samuel Clemens--
Mark Twain 7
How to tell a
Story .7

Display last level in wrapped format

Document1   AB Insert   Pg 1 Ln 1" Pos 3.88"

Styles help writers define how various parts of their documents will look. They can be applied to different parts of documents such as headings, lists, and text including characters, words, paragraphs. They free writers from having to worry about such formatting choices as font and size since these items are included in the style, which can be customized as needed.

Using styles in a report can be particularly helpful in generating the table of contents. Part of the default styles for headings includes a tag that will mark headings for inclusion in the table of contents. When writers use the styles feature of their word processor to mark headings by levels and apply a particular formatting treatment to those headings, they will be able at the completion of their document to command the word processor to generate the table of contents. With just a few keystrokes, the table of contents is produced and formatted along with leaders and page numbers. Writers save time and effort in both keying and trying to align and center the page. Also, the software determines the page numbers from the document as it generates the table of contents.

Styles provide consistency and are saved with the document for future use with that document. They can also provide consistency within an organization if writers all use the same defined style.

■ 5. History—how the problem developed and what is known about it.

HISTORICAL BACKGROUND.   Knowledge of the history of the problem is sometimes essential to understanding the report. Thus, you may need to cover that history in your introduction. You will need to do more than merely list and present facts. You will need to organize and interpret them for the readers. Your general aim in this part is to acquaint the readers with how the problem developed and what has been done about it. Your discussion here should bring out the main issues. It should review what past investigations have determined about the problem, and it should lead to what still needs to be done.

■ 6. Sources and methods—how you got the information.

SOURCES AND METHODS OF COLLECTING INFORMATION.   You usually need to tell the readers how you collected the information in the report. That is, you explain your research methodology and you justify it. You tell whether you used library research, surveys, experiments, or what not. And you describe the steps you followed. In general, you describe your work in enough detail to allow your readers to judge it. You tell them enough to convince them that your work was done competently.

■ Sometimes it is necessary to cite sources.

In a simple case in which you conducted library research, you need to say little. If most of your findings came from a few sources, you could name the sources. If you used a large number of sources, you would be wise to note that you used secondary research and refer to the bibliography in the report appendix.

■ More complex research requires thorough description.

More complex research usually requires a more detailed description. If you conducted a survey, for example, you would probably need to explain all parts of the investigation. You would cover sample determination, construction of the questionnaire, interview procedure, and checking techniques. In fact, you would include as much detail as is needed to gain the readers' confidence in your work.

DEFINITIONS, INITIALISMS, AND ACRONYMS. If you use words, initialisms, or acronyms that are likely to be unfamiliar to readers of the report, you should define these words and initials. You can do this in either of two ways: you can define each term in the text or as a footnote when it is first used in the report, or you can define all unfamiliar terms in a separate part of the introduction. This part begins with an introductory statement and then lists the terms with their definitions. If the list is long, you may choose to arrange the terms alphabetically.

■ 7. Definitions of unfamiliar words, acronyms, or initialisms used.

REPORT PREVIEW. In very long reports, a final part of the introduction should preview the report presentation. In this part you tell the readers how the report will be presented—what topics will be taken up first, second, third, and so on. Of even greater importance, you give your reasons for following this plan. That is, you explain the *strategy* of your report. In short, you give your readers a clear picture of the road ahead. As you will see later in the chapter, this part of the introduction is a basic ingredient of the coherence plan of the long report. Illustrations of report previews appear in the discussion of this plan (page 361) and in the report at the end of the chapter (page 372).

■ 8. Preview—a description of the route ahead.

THE REPORT BODY

In the report body, the information collected is presented and related to the problem. Normally, this part of the report comprises most of its content. In a sense, the report body is the report. With the exception of the conclusion or recommendation part, the other parts of the report are attached parts.

■ The report body presents and analyzes the information gathered.

Although the body makes up most of the report, practically all that we need to say about it has already been said. Its organization was discussed extensively in Chapter 10. It is written in accord with the instructions on clear writing presented in Chapters 2 and 3 and the writing techniques covered in Chapter 10. It uses good presentation form, with figures, tables, and caption display, discussed and illustrated at various places in this book. In fact, most of our discussion of report writing has concerned this major part of the report.

■ Writing this part involves instruction covered elsewhere in the book.

THE ENDING OF THE REPORT

You can end your report in any of a number of ways: with a summary, a conclusion, a recommendation, or a combination of the three. Your choice should depend on the goal of your report. You should choose the way that enables you to satisfy that goal.

■ Reports can end in various ways.

ENDING SUMMARY. When the goal of the report is to present information, the ending is logically a summary of the major findings. There is no attempt to interpret. Any interpretations of the information in the report occur on the reader's part, but not the writer's. Such reports usually have minor summaries at the end of the major sections. When this arrangement is followed, the ending summary recapitulates these summaries.

■ Informational reports usually end with a summary of the major findings.

You should not confuse the ending summary with the executive summary. The executive summary is a prefatory part of the report; the ending summary is a part of the report text. Also, the executive summary is more complete than the ending summary. The executive summary reviews the entire report, usually from the beginning to the end. The ending summary reviews only the highlights of the report.

■ The ending summary is not as complete as the executive summary.

CONCLUSIONS. Some reports must do more than just present information. They must analyze the information in light of the problem; and from this analysis, they must reach a conclusion. Such reports typically end with this conclusion.

■ Reports that seek an answer end with a conclusion.

The makeup of the conclusion section varies from case to case. In problems for which a single answer is sought, the conclusion section normally reviews the preceding information and analyses and, from this review, arrives at the answer. In problems with more than one goal, the report plan may treat each goal in a separate section and draw conclusions in each section. The conclusion section of such a report might well summarize the conclusions previously drawn. There are other arrangements. In fact, almost any plan that brings the analyses together to reach the goals of the report is appropriate.

■ The structure of the conclusion varies by problem.

Technical Writer's Report on Humpty Dumpty

A 72-gram brown Rhode Island Red country-fresh candled egg was secured and washed free of feathers, blood, dirt, and grit. Held between thumb and index finger, about 3 ft. or more from an electric fan (GE Model No. MC-2404, Serial No. JC23023, nonoscillating, rotating on "Hi" speed at approximately 1045.23 plus or minus 0.02 rpm), the egg was suspended on a pendulum (string) so that it arrived at the fan with essentially zero velocity normal to the fan rotation plane. The product adhered strongly to the walls and ceiling and was difficult to recover. However, using putty knives a total of 13 grams was obtained and put in a skillet with 11.2 grams of hickory-smoked Armour's old-style bacon and heated over a low Bunsen flame for 7 min. 32 sec. What there was of it was of excellent quality.

"The DP Report," Du Pont Explosives Department, Atomic Energy Division, Savannah River Laboratories, July 12, 1954.

■ Include recommendations when the readers want or expect them.

RECOMMENDATIONS.   When the goal of the report is not only to draw conclusions but also to present a course of action, a recommendation is in order. You may organize it as a separate section following the conclusion section. Or you may include it in the conclusion section. In some problems, the conclusion is the recommendation—or at least a logical interpretation of it. Whether you include a recommendation should be determined by whether the readers want or expect one.

APPENDED PARTS

■ Add an appendix or a bibliography when needed.

Sometimes you will need to include an appendix, a bibliography, or both at the end of the report. Whether you include these parts should be determined by need.

■ The appendix contains information that indirectly supports the report.

APPENDIX.   The appendix, as its name implies, is a tacked-on part. You use it for supplementary information that supports the body of the report but has no logical place within the body. Possible appendix contents are questionnaires, working papers, summary tables, additional references, and other reports.

■ Information that directly supports the report belongs in the text of the report.

As a rule, the appendix should not include the charts, graphs, and tables that directly support the report. These should be placed in the body of the report, where they support the findings. Reports should be designed for the convenience of the readers. Obviously, it is not convenient for readers to look to the appendix for illustrations of the facts they read in the report body. They would have to thumb back and forth in the report, thus losing their concentration. Such a practice would not help the reader. It would be bad business etiquette.

■ Include a bibliography if you make heavy use of published sources.

BIBLIOGRAPHY.   When your investigation makes heavy use of published sources, you normally include a bibliography (a list of the publications used). The construction of this list is described in Appendix E of this book.

STRUCTURAL COHERENCE HELPERS

■ Longer reports need structural coherence helpers.

As we have noted, the writing in the longer reports is much like the writing in the shorter ones. In general, the instructions given in earlier chapters apply to the longer reports. But the longer reports have one writing need that is not present in the shorter ones—the need for structural coherence helpers.

■ These are a network of explanations, introductions, summaries, and conclusions.

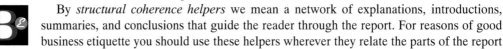

By *structural coherence helpers* we mean a network of explanations, introductions, summaries, and conclusions that guide the reader through the report. For reasons of good business etiquette you should use these helpers wherever they relate the parts of the report

FIGURE 12.2 Diagram of the Structural Coherence Plan of a Long, Formal Report

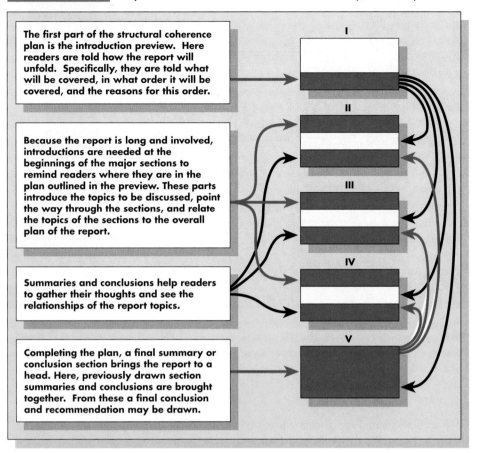

The first part of the structural coherence plan is the introduction preview. Here readers are told how the report will unfold. Specifically, they are told what will be covered, in what order it will be covered, and the reasons for this order.

Because the report is long and involved, introductions are needed at the beginnings of the major sections to remind readers where they are in the plan outlined in the preview. These parts introduce the topics to be discussed, point the way through the sections, and relate the topics of the sections to the overall plan of the report.

Summaries and conclusions help readers to gather their thoughts and see the relationships of the report topics.

Completing the plan, a final summary or conclusion section brings the report to a head. Here, previously drawn section summaries and conclusions are brought together. From these a final conclusion and recommendation may be drawn.

or move the message along. Although you should not use them mechanically, you will find that they are likely to follow the general plan described in Figure 12.2.

The coherence plan begins with the report preview in the introduction. As you will recall, the preview tells the readers what lies ahead. It covers three things: the topics to be discussed, their order, and the logic of that order. With this information in mind, the readers know how the parts of the report relate to one another. They know the overall strategy of the presentation. The following paragraphs do a good job of previewing a report comparing four automobiles to determine which is the best for a company's sales fleet.

> ■ The coherence plan begins with the preview, which describes the route ahead.

The decision as to which light car Allied Distributors should buy is reached by comparing the cars on the basis of three factors: cost, safety, and performance. Each of these factors is broken down into its component parts, which are applied to the specific makes being considered.

Because cost is the most tangible factor, it is examined in the first major section. In this section, the four makes are compared for initial and trade-in values. Then they are compared for operating costs, as determined by gasoline mileage, oil use, repair expense, and the like. In the second major section, the safety of the four makes is compared. Driver visibility, special safety features, brakes, steering quality, acceleration rate, and traction are the main considerations here. In the third major section, the dependability of the four makes is compared on the basis of repair records and salespersons' time lost because of automobile failure. In the final major section, weights are assigned to the foregoing comparisons, and the automobile brand that is best suited to the company's needs is recommended.

In addition to the preview in the introduction, the plan uses introductory and summary sections at convenient places throughout the report. Typically, these sections are at the beginning and end of major divisions, but you should use them wherever they are needed.

> ■ Introductions to and summaries of the report sections keep readers informed of where they are in the report.

Structural coherence helpers provide a network of explanations to guide readers through the report. Helpers are similar to freeway connections. Readers can see clearly where they have been, where they are, and where they will go next. By constructing paragraphs, sentences, and words at important positions throughout the report, readers can be guided skillfully to the report's ending.

Such sections remind the readers where they are in the report. They tell the readers where they have been, where they are going, and perhaps why they are going there. You will need to keep section introductions neutral; that is, you will not include facts, conclusions, references to graphic aids, and such in them. Other report elements (facts, conclusions, etc.) follow.

Illustrating this technique is the following paragraph, which introduces a major section of a report. Note how the paragraph ties in with the preceding discussion, which concerned industrial activity in three geographic areas. Note also how it justifies covering secondary areas.

Although the great bulk of industry is concentrated in three areas (Grand City, Milltown, and Port Starr), a thorough industrial survey needs to consider the secondary, but nevertheless important, areas of the state. In the rank of their current industrial potential, these areas are the Southeast, with Hartsburg as its center; the Central West, dominated by Parrington; and the North Central, where Pineview is the center of activities.

The following summary-conclusion paragraph is a good ending to a major section. The paragraph brings to a head the findings presented in the section and points the way to the subject of the next section.

These findings and those pointed out in preceding paragraphs all lead to one obvious conclusion. The small-business executives are concerned primarily with subject matter that will aid them directly in their work. That is, they favor a curriculum slanted in favor of the practical subjects. They insist, however, on some coverage of the liberal arts, and they are also convinced of the value of studying business administration. On all these points, they are clearly out of tune with the bulk of the big-business leaders who have voiced their positions on this question. Even the most dedicated business administration professors would find it difficult to support such an extremely practical concept. Nevertheless, these are the opinions of the small-business executives. Because they are the consumers of the business-education product, their opinions should at least be considered. Likewise, their specific recommendations on courses (the subject of the following section) deserve careful review.

Completing the coherence plan is the final major section of the report. In this section, you achieve the goal of the report. Here you recall from the preceding section summaries all the major findings and analyses. Then you apply them to the problem and present the conclusion. Sometimes you will make recommendations. Thus, you complete the strategy explained in the introduction preview and recalled at convenient places throughout the report.

Wise use of coherence helpers can form a network of connections throughout the report. You should keep in mind, however, that these helpers should be used only when they are needed. That is, you should use them when your readers need help in seeing relationships and in knowing where they are and where they are going. If you use them well, they will appear as natural parts of the report story. They should never appear to be mechanical additions. When paragraphs are combined with sentence and word transitions, as discussed in Chapter 10, the total plan should guide your readers smoothly and naturally through the report.

■ The final major section of the report brings together the preceding information and applies it to the goal.

■ Use coherence helpers naturally—when they are needed.

THE LONG ANALYTICAL REPORT ILLUSTRATED

Illustrating the long analytical report is the report presented at the end of this chapter (Figure 12.3). The report's structure parallels that of the formal type described in the preceding pages.

■ Figure 12.3 is an illustration of a long, formal report.

SUMMARY BY CHAPTER OBJECTIVES

1. The prefatory section of the long, formal report consists of these conventional parts:
   - Title fly—a page displaying only the title.
     —As a checklist for constructing the title, use the 5 Ws (*who, what, where, when, why*).
     —Sometimes *how* is important.
   - Title page—a page displaying the title, identification of writer and recipient, and date.
   - Letter of authorization—included only when a letter (or memorandum) authorized the report.
   - Letter of transmittal—a letter (or memorandum) transmitting the report (a *foreword* or *preface* in very long and highly formal papers).
     —This part takes the place of a face-to-face presentation.
     —Begin it with a presentation of the report.
     —Include comments about the report you would have made in a face-to-face presentation.
     —In some cases you may combine it with the executive summary.
     —Write the letter in personal style (first and second person).
   - Table of contents, list of illustrations—a listing of the report parts and illustrations with page numbers.
   - Executive summary—the report in miniature.
     —Include, in proportion, everything that is important—all the major facts, analyses, and conclusions.
     —Write it in either direct or indirect order.
2. The report introduction prepares the readers to receive the report.
   - Include whatever helps reach this goal.
   - Use these items as a checklist for content: purpose, scope, limitations, problem history, methodology, definitions, preview.
   - A preview telling the order and reasoning for the order is useful in longer, more involved reports.
3. The ending of the report achieves the report goal.
   - Use a summary if the goal is to review information.
   - Use a conclusion if the goal is to reach an answer.
   - Use a recommendation if the goal is to determine a desirable action.

1 Describe the roles and contents and construct the prefatory parts of a long, formal report.

2 Organize each introduction of a long report by considering all the likely readers and selecting the appropriate contents.

3 Determine, based on the report's goal, the most effective way to end a report—a summary, a conclusion, a recommendation, or a combination of the three.

Describe the role and content of the appendix and bibliography of a report.

5 Prepare a structural coherence plan for a long, formal report.

4. An appendix and/or bibliography can follow the report text.
   - The appendix contains items that support the text but have no specific place in the text (such as questionnaires, working papers, summary tables).
   - The bibliography is a descriptive list of the secondary sources that were used in the investigation.

5. The longer reports need various structural helpers to give them coherence.
   - These helpers consist of a network of explanations, introductions, summaries, and conclusions that guide the reader through the report.
   - Begin the coherence plan with the introduction preview, which tells the structure of the report.
   - Then use the introductions and summaries in following parts to tell readers where they are in this structure.
   - At the end, bring together the preceding information, analyses, and conclusions to reach the report goal.
   - Make these coherence helpers inconspicuous—that is, make them appear to be a natural part of the message.

Title fly

Checklist of 5Ws and 1H creates complete title.

What *Why* *Who*

SALES TRAINING RECOMMENDATIONS FOR ARMOR MOTORS

BASED ON A 1999 STUDY OF COMPANY SALES ACTIVITIES

When

How

FIGURE 12.3 (Continued)

Three-spot title page

<u>SALES TRAINING RECOMMENDATIONS FOR ARMOR MOTORS</u>

<u>BASED ON A 1999 STUDY OF COMPANY SALES ACTIVITIES</u>

Recipient of report receives prime position on page.

Prepared for
Mr. Peter R. Simpson, Vice President for Sales
Armor Motors, Inc.
72117 North Musselman Road
Dearborn, MI 48126-2351

Writer receives subordinate page position.

Prepared by
Ashlee P. Callahan
Callahan and Hebert Research Associates
Suite D, Brownfield Towers
212 North Bedford Avenue
Detroit, MI 48219-6708

November 17, 1999

FIGURE 12.3 (Continued)

Callahan and Herbert Research Associates
Suite D, Brownfield Towers
212 North Bedford Avenue
Detroit, MI 48219-6708

Letter of transmittal

November 17, 1999

Mr. Peter R. Simpson
Vice President for Sales
Armor Motors, Inc.
72117 North Musselman Road
Dearborn, MI 48126-2351

Dear Mr. Simpson:

Letter begins directly, with the transmittal.

Here is the report on the observational study of your salespeople you asked us to conduct last August 17.

Pertinent comments help the reader understand and appreciate the research.

As you will see, our observations pointed to some specific needs for sales training. Following the procedure we agreed to, we will prepare an outline of these needs in a revised curriculum plan that we will submit to your training director December 4. We are confident that this curriculum plan will aid in correcting the shortcomings in your sales force.

Goodwill comment ends letter.

We at Callahan and Hebert appreciate having this assignment. If you should need any assistance in interpreting this report or in implementing our recommendations, please call on us.

Sincerely yours,

Ashlee P. Callahan

Ashlee P. Callahan
Senior Research Associate

FIGURE 12.3 (Continued)

Table of contents

TABLE OF CONTENTS

Part	Page
Executive Summary	vi

Background details of the problem prepare the reader to receive the report.

THE PROBLEM AND THE PLAN 1

Incidentals of Authorization and Submittal 1

Objective of Sales Training Improvement 1

Use of Observational Techniques 1

Three areas of sales work investigated logically form main headings.

A Preview of the Presentation 2

ANALYSIS OF WORK TIME USE 2

Negative Effect of Idle Time 2

Divisions of main body parts by factors (and subdivisions) show good thought and logical solution to problem.

Subfactors of the work areas make logical second-level headings.

Correlation of Prospect Contacting and Success 3

Vital Role of Prospect Building 3

Necessity of Miscellaneous Activities 3

DIFFERENCES IN FINDING PROSPECTS 3

Near Equal Distribution of Walk-Ons 4

First- and second-level headings are parallel.

Value of Cultivating Old Customers 4

Limited Effectiveness of Using Bird Dogs 5

Talking captions avoid monotonous repetition in wording.

Scant Use of Other Techniques 5

OBSERVABLE DIFFERENCES IN 5

Conciseness in headings improve readability.

PRESENTATIONS 6

Positive Effect of Integrity 6

Apparent Value of Moderate Pressure 7

Necessity of Product Knowledge 8

FIGURE 12.3 (Continued)

*List of figures
(a continuation
of the table of
contents)*

LIST OF FIGURES

Page

*Titles use 5 Ws
and 1 H in their
construction.*

FIGURE 12.3 (Continued)

*Executive
summary*

*Following the direct-
order plan, this
executive summary
places the
recommendations
first. Highlights of
the supporting
findings follow.*

Executive Summary

The recommendations that result from this study are to add the following topics to Armor's sales training program:

1. Negative effects of idle time
2. Techniques of cultivating prospects
3. Development of bird dog networks
4. Cultivating repeat sales
5. Projection of integrity image
6. Use of moderate persuasion
7. Value of product knowledge

Supporting these recommendations are the following findings and conclusions drawn from an observational study comparing three types of sales activities of productive and marginal salespeople.

*Remaining
paragraphs
summarize the
major findings in
the order presented
in the report.*

The data show that the productive salespeople used their time more effectively than did the marginal salespeople. Compared with marginal salespeople, the productive salespeople spent less time in idleness (28% vs. 53%). They also spent more time in contact with prospects (31.3% vs. 19.8%) and more time developing prospects (10.4% vs. 4.4%).

Investigation of how the salespeople got their prospects showed that because floor assignments were about equal, both groups profited about the same from walk-ins. The productive group got 282; the marginal group got 274. The productive group used bird dogs more extensively, having 64 contacts derived from this source during the observation period. The marginal group had 8. Productive salespeople also were more successful in turning these contacts into sales.

*Significant
comparisons and
conclusions are
emphasized
throughout.*

Observations of sales presentations revealed that productive salespeople displayed higher integrity, used pressure more reasonably, and knew the product better than marginal salespeople. Of the 20 productive salespeople, 16 displayed images of moderately high integrity (Group II). Marginal group members ranged widely with 7 in Group III (questionable) and 5 each in Group II (moderately high integrity) and Group IV (deceitful). Most (15) of the productive salespeople used moderate pressure, whereas the marginal salespeople tended toward extremes (10 high pressure, 7 low pressure). On the product knowledge test, 17 of the productive salespeople scored excellent and 3 fair. Of the marginal members, 5 scored excellent, 6 fair, and 9 inadequate.

vi

FIGURE 12.3 (Continued)

<u>SALES TRAINING RECOMMENDATIONS FOR ARMOR MOTORS</u>

<u>BASED ON A 1999 STUDY OF COMPANY SALES ACTIVITIES</u>

THE PROBLEM AND THE PLAN

Incidentals of Authorization and Submittal

This study of Armor salespeople's sales activities is submitted to Mr. Peter R. Simpson, Vice President for Sales, on November 17, 1999. As authorized on August 28, the investigation was conducted under the direction of Ashlee P. Callahan of Callahan and Hebert Research Associates.

Objective of Sales Training Improvement

The objective of the study was to find means of improving the effectiveness of Armor salespeople. The plan for achieving this objective involved first determining the techniques and characteristics of effective selling. This information then will be used in improving Armor's sales training program.

Use of Observational Techniques

The methodology used in this investigation was an observational study of Armor salespeople. Specifically, the study employed the time-duty technique, which is a unique means of observing work performance under real conditions. A detailed description of this technique is a part of the proposal approved at the August meeting and is not repeated here. Specific items relative to the application of this method in this case are summarized below.

Two groups of 20 Armor salespeople were selected for the observation—a productive and a marginal group. The productive group was made up of the company's top producers for the past year; the marginal group comprised the lowest producers. Only salespeople with three years or more of experience were eligible.

A team of two highly trained observers observed each of the salespeople selected for a continuous period of five working days. Using specially designed forms, the observers recorded the work activities of the salespeople. At the end of the observation period, the observers conducted an exit interview, recording certain demographic data and administering a test of the salesperson's knowledge of Armor's automobiles.

1

FIGURE 12.3 (Continued)

2

A Preview of the Presentation

Preview prepares reader for what follows in body sections.

In the following pages, the findings and analysis appear in the arrangement discussed at the August meeting. First comes a comparison of how the productive and the marginal salespeople spend their work time. Second is an analysis of how the productive and the marginal salespeople find their prospects. Third is a comparative analysis of the observable differences in sales presentations of the two groups. Conclusions drawn from these comparisons form the bases for recommendations of content emphasis in Armor's sales training program.

Body sections contain facts, interpretations, and solutions to report problems.

ANALYSIS OF WORK TIME USE

The time-duty observation records were examined to determine whether differences exist between the productive and marginal salespeople in their use of work time. Activities were grouped into four general categories: (1) idleness, (2) contacting prospects, (3) finding prospects, and (4) miscellaneous activities. This examination revealed the following results.

Section introductions tell what follows in subdivisions.

Negative Effect of Idle Time

Subordinate reference to figure ties text and graphic together and allows interpretation to begin in main sentence.

As shown in Figure 1, the productive salespeople spent less work time in idleness (28%) than did the marginal salespeople (53%). Further

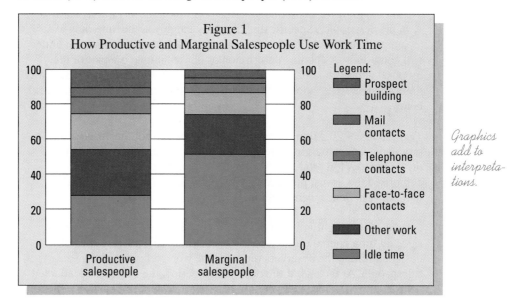

Figure 1
How Productive and Marginal Salespeople Use Work Time

Legend:
- Prospect building
- Mail contacts
- Telephone contacts
- Face-to-face contacts
- Other work
- Idle time

Graphics add to interpretations.

FIGURE 12.3 (Continued)

3

examination of the observations reveals that the top five of the 20 productive salespeople spent even less time in idleness (13%); and the bottom five of the marginal salespeople spent more time in idleness (67%). Clearly, these observations suggest the predictable conclusion that successful salespeople work more than their less productive counterparts.

Sentence conclusions complement formal coherence plan.

Correlation of Prospect Contacting and Success

Productive salespeople spent more time contacting prospects face to face, by telephone, and by mail (31.3%) than did marginal salespeople (19.8%). The specific means of making these contacts show similar differences. Productive and marginal salespeople spent their work time, respectively, 23.2% and 13.5% in face-to-face contacts, 4.8% and 2.0% in mail contacts, and 8.3% and 4.6% in telephone contacts. These data lend additional support to the conclusion that work explains sales success.

Report length and situation formality justify third-person writing.

Report text presents data thoroughly yet concisely — and with appropriate comparisons.

Vital Role of Prospect Building

During the observation period, productive salespeople spent more than twice as much time (10.5%) as marginal salespeople (4.4%) in building prospects. Activities observed in this category include contacting bird dogs (people who give sales leads) and other lead sources and mailing literature to established and prospective customers.

Report length and situation formality justify third-person writing.

Necessity of Miscellaneous Activities

Both productive and marginal salespeople spent about a fourth of their work time in miscellaneous activities (tending to personal affairs, studying sales literature, attending sales meetings, and such). The productive group averaged 25.2%; the marginal group averaged 22.5%. As some of this time is related to automobile sales, productive salespeople would be expected to spend more time in this category.

Section summary helps the reader identify and remember the major findings.

The preceding data reveal that the way salespeople spend their time affects their productivity. Productive salespeople <u>work</u> at selling. In sharp contrast with the marginal salespeople, they <u>spend</u> little time in idleness. They work hard to contact prospects and to build prospect lists. Like all automobile salespeople, they spend some time in performing miscellaneous duties.

Tense consistency places concepts in appropriate time frames and gives a present time viewpoint.

DIFFERENCES IN FINDING PROSPECTS

Section introduction continues formal coherence plan.

A comparison of how productive and marginal salespeople find prospects and measurement of the productivity of these methods was a <u>second</u> area of investigation. For this study, the observations were classified by the four primary sources of prospects: (1) walk-ins, (2) bird dogs and other referrals, (3) repeat customers, and (4) other. Only prospects that were contacted

Key transitional words used in emphasis positions keep ideas moving.

FIGURE 12.3 (Continued)

4

in person or by telephone during the observation period were included. Prospects were counted only once, even though some were contacted more than once.

Near Equal Distribution of Walk-Ins

As expected, most of the contacts of both productive and marginal salespeople were walk-ins. Because both groups had about equal floor assignments, they got about the same number of prospects from this source. As illustrated in Figure 2, productive members got 282 (an average of 14.1 each), and marginal members got 274 (an average of 13.7 each).

Color adds interest and helps reader visualize comparisons in graphics.

Use of graphics allows only important details to be emphasized in report text.

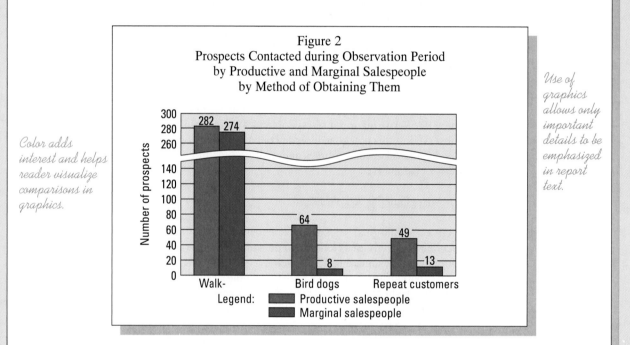

Figure 2
Prospects Contacted during Observation Period
by Productive and Marginal Salespeople
by Method of Obtaining Them

Variety in sentence design helps maintain reader interest.

Although both groups got about the same number of prospects from walk-ins, productive salespeople got better results. A review of sales records shows that productive salespeople averaged 2.6 sales per week from walk-ins; marginal salespeople averaged 2.2. The difference, although appearing slight, represents roughly 16 automobiles per year.

Value of Cultivating Long-Standing Customers

Returning long-standing customers and friends referred by them constitute the second most productive source of prospects. During the observation period,

FIGURE 12.3 (Continued)

5

productive salespeople had contacts with 49 such prospects; marginal salespeople had 13. Productive salespeople also had better sales success with these prospects, turning 40 of them into sales—an average of two per week. Marginal group members made sales to seven of these prospects—an average of 0.35 per person. These differences appear to be a direct result of effort (or lack of it) in maintaining contacts with customers after the sale.

Predominance of active voice verbs provide flow and concreteness in text.

Limited Effectiveness of Using Bird Dogs

Contacts from bird dogs comprise the third largest group, producing 64 total contacts for the productive and 8 for the marginal salespeople. Sales from this source totaled 9 for productive salespeople and 2 for marginal salespeople—an average of 0.45 and 0.1 sales per person, respectively. Although not large in terms of volume, these data explain much of the difference between the two groups. The use of bird dogs involves work, and the willingness to work varies sharply between the two groups.

Interweaving facts and interpretations gives good emphasis.

Talking headings help emphasize the major findings.

Scant Use of Other Techniques

Other prospect gaining techniques were little used among the salespeople observed. Techniques long discussed in industry sales literature such as cold-spearing, placing written messages on automobile windshields, and random telephoning produced no prospects for either group during the observation period. All of the salespeople observed noted that they had used these techniques in the past, but with little success. The lack of evidence in this study leaves unanswered the question of the effectiveness of these techniques.

Word choice and sentence length contribute to readability.

Sectional summary draw ideas together before report moves to next section.

The obvious conclusion drawn from the preceding review of how prospects are found is that the productive salespeople work harder to get them. Although both groups get about the same number of walk-ins, the successful ones work harder at maintaining contacts with past customers and at getting contacts from a network of bird dogs and friends.

OBSERVABLE VARIATIONS IN PRESENTATIONS

Differences in the sales presentations used constituted the third area of study. Criteria used in this investigation were (1) integrity, (2) pressure, and (3) product knowledge. Obviously, the first two of these criteria had to be evaluated subjectively. Even so, the evaluations were made by highly trained observers who used comprehensive guidelines. These guidelines are described in detail in the approved observation plan.

Formal coherence pattern continues with sectional introduction.

FIGURE 12.3 (Continued)

6

Positive Effect of Integrity

Evaluations of the salespeople's integrity primarily measured the apparent degree of truthfulness of the sales presentations. The observers classified the images of integrity they perceived during the sales presentations into four groups: Group I—Impeccable (displayed the highest degree of truthfulness), Group II—Moderately High (generally truthful, some exaggeration), Group III—Questionable (mildly deceitful and tricky); and Group IV—Deceitful (untruthful and tricky).

Of the 20 productive salespeople observed, 16 were classified in Group II as shown in Figure 3. Of the remaining four, 2 were in Group I and 2 in Group III.

Pattern of subordinate reference to graphic and interpretation of facts shows effective report structure throughout.

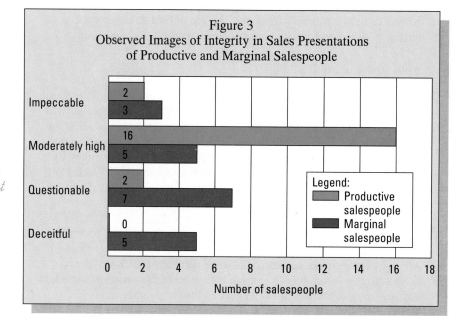

Figure 3
Observed Images of Integrity in Sales Presentations
of Productive and Marginal Salespeople

Distribution of the marginal salespeople was markedly different: 3 in Group I, 5 in Group II, 7 in Group III, and 5 in Group IV. Clearly, integrity was more apparent among the productive salespeople.

Apparent Value of Moderate Pressure

Measurements (by observation) of pressure used in the sales presentations were made in order to determine the relationship of pressure to sales success. Using the guidelines approved at the August meeting, the observers classified

Figure 12.3 **(Continued)**

7

Page layout shows good balance and symmetry.

each salesperson's presentations into three categories: (1) high pressure, (2) moderate pressure, and (3) low pressure. Observers reported difficulties in making some borderline decisions, but they felt that most of the presentations were easily classified.

Interpretation of significant report facts follow subordinate reference to graphic.

Of the 20 productive salespeople, 15 used moderate pressure, 3 used low pressure, and 2 used high pressure, as depicted in Figure 4. The 20 marginal

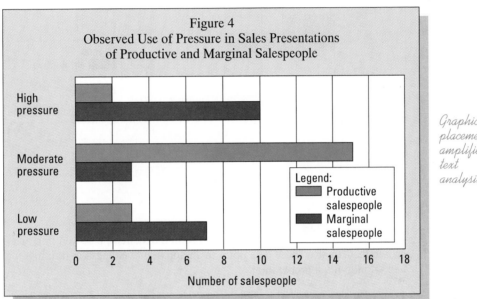

Figure 4
Observed Use of Pressure in Sales Presentations
of Productive and Marginal Salespeople

Graphic placement amplifies text analysis.

The facts are not just presented. They are compared and conclusions are drawn from them.

salespeople presented a different picture. Only 3 of them used moderate pressure. Of the remainder, 10 used high pressure and 7 used low pressure. The evidence suggests that moderate pressure is most effective.

Balanced, short paragraphs indicate good organization of thought and improve readability.

Necessity of Product Knowledge

Central idea and factual support demonstrate paragraph unity.

Product knowledge, a generally accepted requirement for successful selling, was determined during the exit interview. Using the 30 basic questions developed by Armor management from sales literature, observers measured the salespeople's product knowledge. Correct responses to 27 or more of the questions was determined to be excellent, 24 through 26 was fair, and below 24 was classified as inadequate.

Productive salespeople displayed superior knowledge of the product with 17 of the 20 scoring excellent. As shown in Figure 5, the remaining 3 scored fair.

FIGURE 12.3 (Continued)

8

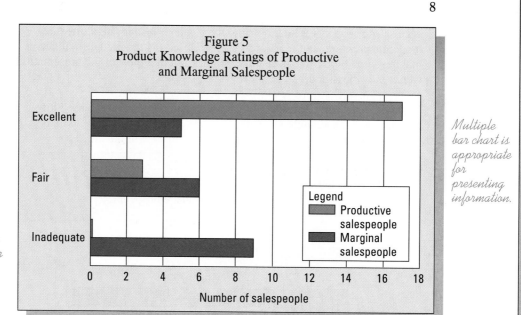

Figure 5
Product Knowledge Ratings of Productive
and Marginal Salespeople

Multiple bar chart is appropriate for presenting information.

Text and graphics work closely together to present the information.

Scores for product knowledge were sharply different in the marginal salesperson group. Although 5 of them scored excellent, 6 scored fair, and 9 scored inadequate. These data point to an apparent weakness in training or a lack of individual preparation.

Another summary-conclusion brings section to a close.

The preceding presentation reveals some basic differences in the sales presentations of the productive and marginal salespeople. The productive salespeople displayed higher integrity (though not the highest). They used moderate pressure, whereas the marginal people tended toward high or low extremes. Also, the productive people knew their products better.

RECOMMENDATIONS FOR TRAINING

From the summary-conclusions of the preceding three sections the recommendations are derived.

The conclusions reached in preceding sections suggest certain actions that Armor Motors should take in training its sales force. Specifically, the instruction should be altered to include the following topics:

1. Importance of minimizing idle time.

2. Sales rewards from productive work (mailing literature, telephoning, cultivating prospects, etc.).

FIGURE 12.3 (Concluded)

9

3. Significance of creating a network of bird dogs and friends in building prospects.

4. Value of maintaining contacts with past customers.

Numbering makes the recommendations stand out.

5. Need for integrity, within reasonable limits.

6. Use of moderate pressure, avoiding extremes in either direction.

7. Need for a thorough knowledge of the product.

FIGURE 12.3 (Concluded)

379

CRITICAL THINKING QUESTIONS

1. Long, formal reports are not often written in business. So why should you know how to write them?

2. A good title should be complete and concise. Are not these requirements contradictory? Explain.

3. Discuss the relative importance of the title fly and the title page in a report.

4. Distinguish among the letter of transmittal, the foreword, and the preface.

5. Describe the role and content of a letter of transmittal.

6. Why is personal style typically used in the letter of transmittal?

7. What is the basis for determining whether a report should have a table of contents?

8. Discuss the construction of the executive summary.

9. Why does the executive summary include the facts and figures in addition to the analyses and conclusions drawn from them?

10. Some reports need little or no introduction; others need a very long introduction. Why is this so?

11. Give examples of report problems that require introductory coverage of methods of collecting data, historical background, and limitations.

12. Give examples of report problems that require, respectively, (a) an ending summary, (b) an ending conclusion, and (c) an ending recommendation.

13. Using as a guide the diagram in Figure 12.2, summarize the coherence plan of the long, formal report.

CRITICAL THINKING EXERCISES

1. Making any assumptions needed, construct complete yet concise titles for the reports described below:

   a. A report writer reviewed records of exit interviews of employees at Marvel-Floyd Manufacturing Company who quit their jobs voluntarily. The objective of the investigation was to determine the reasons for leaving.

   b. A researcher studied data from employee personnel records at Magna-Tech, Inc., to determine whether permanent (long-term) employees differ from short-term employees. Any differences found would be used in hiring employees in the future. The data studied included age, education, experience, sex, marital status, test scores, and such.

   c. A report writer compared historical financial records (1935 to the present) of Super Saver Foods to determine whether this grocery chain should own or rent store buildings. In the past it did both.

2. Criticize the following beginning sentences of letters of transmittal:

   a. "In your hands is the report you requested January 7 concerning . . ."

   b. "As you will recall, last January 7 you requested a report on . . ."

   c. "That we should open a new outlet in Bragg City is the conclusion of this report, which you authorized January 7."

3. In a report comparing four automobiles (Alpha, Beta, Gamma, and Delta) to determine which one is the best buy for a company, section II of the report body covered these cost data: (a) initial costs; (b) trade-in values; and (c) operating expenses. Section III presented a comparison of these safety features of the automobiles: (a) standard safety features; (b) acceleration data; (c) weight distribution; and (d) braking quality.

   a. Criticize this introductory paragraph at the beginning of section III:

   In the preceding section was presented a thorough analysis of the cost data. Now safety of the cars will be compared. Although costs are important, Warren-Burke also is concerned about the safety of its salespeople, who spend almost half their work time driving.

   b. Write a more appropriate introductory paragraph.

4. The next section of the report (section IV) covered these topics: (a) handling; (b) quality of ride; and (c) durability.

   a. Criticize this introductory paragraph for the section:

   This section of the report presents a comparison of the overall construction of the four automobiles. These considerations also are important because they affect how a car rides, and this is important. Thus, we will take up in this order: handling, general riding quality, and construction qualities.

   b. Write a more appropriate introductory paragraph.

5. Criticize this final paragraph (a preview) of the introduction of the report described above:

   This report compares the automobiles by three factors. These are costs, safety, and comfort and construction, in that order. Costs include initial expenditure, trade-in value, and operating expense. Safety covers safety devices, acceleration, weight distribution, and braking. Comfort and construction includes handling, ride quality, and durability. A ranking is derived from this comparison.

CRITICAL THINKING PROBLEMS

REPORT PROBLEMS: LONG

1. *Evaluating the competitiveness and innovation in manufacturing between Japan and the United States.* For quite some time, many people have assumed that Japan's innovation and technology are superior to those of the United States. To be sure, the consequences of these assumptions give one country a competitive advantage over the other in the marketplace. The heart of the matter rests in the speed (time) that each country takes to translate innovation into commercial products and processes. The country that has the lowest translation time is the more successful. There are many implications, such as balance of payments and global competition.

Today's assignment places you in the role of research assistant to the director of competitiveness and innovation for the National Association for Manufacturing (NAM). As the representative for American manufacturing, the NAM keeps a close finger on the pulse of the competitiveness of American industry in general and manufacturing in particular.

Your boss, Mr. Richard Menchaca, maintains a healthy skepticism about the recent reports of Japan's superiority in manufacturing. He comments to you one day as follows: "I question the studies that are presently available for several reasons. First, I'd like

to see the specifics of the Japan/U.S. comparisons. Everything I see and read is conceptual, not concrete. More specifically, I'd like to know how much of an advantage, if any, Japan has. And I'd like also to find out what facts determine the advantage, if indeed there is one. Second, most of the data I see about Japan's industries and firms are reported by Japanese. I wonder if we are all on the same page. Look into this area and write me a report of your findings. I'm giving a speech in several weeks and I'd like to use your findings in it. Please submit a report to me in two weeks."

This is my big chance to "walk the talk," you think as you return to your office. A well-written report would catch the eye of many people who are key players in your professional future. As a plus, you too are quite interested in the topic.

As you begin your research, you scan the bibliographic material available to you on the web. This search leads to foundation studies and even committee reports in Congress. As you continue your search, you locate several studies cited in the literature that provide insight into the concerns of Mr. Menchaca.

You assemble the data as shown in Tables 1, 2, and 3. Now that the facts are arranged in an orderly fashion, you can begin your analysis of them in detail. You will need to be thorough in this stage, because

TABLE 1 (Problem 1) Percentage Distribution of Innovation Costs for 100 Firms, Japan and the United States, 1998

Industry and Nationality*	Percent of Innovation Cost Going For					
	Applied Research	Preparation of Product Specifications	Tooling and Prototype or Pilot Plant	Manufacturing Equipment and Facilities	Manufacturing Startup	Marketing Startup
All industries combined						
Japan	14	7	16	44	10	8
United States	18	8	17	23	17	17
Chemicals						
Japan	18	9	13	42	6	11
United States	29	7	13	22	13	17
Electrical and instruments						
Japan	21	7	18	26	18	10
United States	16	8	11	26	18	21
Machinery						
Japan	6	5	20	58	5	6
United States	6	11	23	20	21	18
Rubber and metals						
Japan	9	8	6	66	6	5
United States	15	4	15	45	15	6

*The sample sizes are as follows: all industries combined, 100; chemicals, 36; electrical and instruments, 20; machinery, 30; and rubber and metals, 14.

Industry	Japan (1998)	United States (1998)
Food	0.8	0.4
Textiles	1.2	0.5
Paper	0.7	1.3
Chemicals	3.8	4.7
Petroleum	0.4	0.7
Rubber	2.9	2.2
Ferrous metals	1.9	0.5
Nonferrous metals	1.9	1.4
Fabricated metal products	1.6	1.3
Machinery	2.7	5.8
Electrical equipment	5.1	4.8
Motor vehicles	3.0	3.2
Other transportation equipment	2.6	1.2
Instruments	4.5	9.0
Total manufacturing	2.7	2.8

your final report will be no better than the thinking you do throughout the entire report-writing process.

Now it is time for you to begin constructing the report. Because of the formality of the situation, you decide that a title page, table of contents, and executive summary are needed as prefatory parts. In addition, you will write the report in the impersonal tone, using first- and second-degree captions and the indirect order. And graphics will find good use in

telling the specifics of your analysis. You will write a conclusion but not recommend actions for NAM.

Write the report for Mr. Menchaca, as he requested.

2. *Evaluating the effectiveness of Starr's sales force.* For the past five years, Starr Electronics, Inc., has failed to keep pace with its competition in the television market. Naturally, Starr executives have become alarmed; and they have been searching for remedies to the problem. In their efforts to find the information they need, they have engaged the marketing consulting services of Patterson-Petri Management Consultants. You, a senior research associate with Patterson-Petri, have been given the assignment.

About a month ago you began the task. Your first efforts consisted of gathering background facts about Starr's operations. Among other things, you learned that Starr is one of five leading manufacturers in the field. The other four are the Disch Company, Honshu Manufacturing, Erath Industries, and Tojo Manufacturing Company. Until recently Starr ranked first in volume of sales. Now it is third. Like its competitors, Starr sells to exclusive distributors; and the distributors sell to dealers in their territories. Obviously, Starr is highly dependent on its distributors' salespeople.

Because Starr is so dependent on its distributors, its executives suspect that much of the blame for the sales decline should be placed on these distributors. But they can't be certain without evidence. So they want you to check out their hypothesis. In addition, they want you to find any additional information that will give them an overall picture of the operations of dealers at the retail level.

After collecting the necessary background data,

Industry and Nationality*	Percentage of R&D Expenditures Devoted To					
	Basic Research	Applied Research	Products (Rather Than Processes)	New Products and Processes	Projects with Less Than 0.5 Chance of Success	Projects That Will Last Longer Than 5 Years
All industries combined						
Japan	10	27	36	32	26	38
United States	8	23	68	47	28	38
Chemicals (including drugs)						
Japan	11	42	48	42	24	39
United States	11	39	74	43	39	41
Machinery (including electrical equipment and computers), instruments, metals, and rubber						
Japan	9	23	32	28	26	37
United States	4	9	62	51	16	36

*The sample sizes are as follows: all industries combined, 100; chemicals, 36; electrical and instruments, 20; machinery, 30; and rubber and metals, 14.

you designed and conducted a survey of television dealers. You made interviews in three major retail areas (Chicago, Toronto, and Dallas). In each area you and your assistants interviewed a proportionate number of randomly selected dealers of all five leading brands. Then you tabulated the responses.

Now you have the findings logically arranged in two tables. In one (Table 4), you have tabulated the answers to the questions asked about the dealers' experiences with distributors' sales representatives. In the other (Table 5), you have assembled the summary percentages of the factors that tell about the overall operations of dealers.

Your next step is to interpret your findings as they apply to Starr's problem. Then you will organize the material for the best possible communication effect; and you will write the report. You hope that you will be able to draw a clear conclusion on the major

TABLE 4 (Problem 2) Tabulation of Replies to TV Dealer–Distributor Questionnaire

	Starr		Disch		Honshu		Erath		Tojo	
	No.	%	No.	%	No.	%	No.	%	No.	%
Total dealers	199	100.0	120	100.0	125	100.0	110	100.0	133	100.0
1. Salespeople called										
Weekly	76	38.2	40	33.3	44	35.2	31	28.2	44	33.1
Every two weeks	67	33.7	44	36.7	38	30.4	37	33.6	41	30.8
Every three weeks	25	12.6	15	12.5	18	14.4	27	24.5	15	11.3
Every four weeks	10	5.0	9	7.5	11	8.8	5	4.6	13	9.8
Over a month ago	15	7.5	8	6.7	11	8.8	3	2.7	14	10.5
Don't know	3	1.5	3	2.5	1	0.8	1	0.9	2	1.5
Never	3	1.5	1	0.8	2	1.6	5	4.6	4	3.0
No answer	—	—	—	—	—	—	1	0.9	—	—
2. Asked for window										
Yes	39	19.6	25	20.8	31	24.8	19	17.3	28	21.0
No	155	77.9	95	79.2	88	70.4	88	80.0	102	76.7
D.K. and N.A.	5	2.5	—	—	6	4.8	3	2.7	3	2.3
3. Installed window										
Yes	10	5.0	5	4.2	4	3.2	1	0.9	—	—
No	185	93.0	115	95.8	119	95.2	105	95.5	130	97.7
D.K. and N.A.	4	2.0	—	—	2	1.6	4	3.6	3	2.3
4. Brought displays										
Yes	40	20.1	35	29.2	23	18.4	8	7.3	17	12.8
No	138	69.3	73	60.8	86	68.8	84	76.4	97	72.9
D.K. and N.A.	21	10.6	12	10.0	16	12.8	18	16.3	19	14.3
5. Explained line's features										
Yes	67	33.7	65	54.2	45	36.0	22	20.0	48	36.0
No	131	65.8	55	45.8	78	62.4	85	77.3	83	62.5
D.K. and N.A.	1	0.5	—	—	2	1.6	3	2.7	2	1.5
6. Dealer has folders										
Yes	134	67.3	87	72.5	89	71.2	66	60.0	91	68.3
No	65	32.7	33	27.5	36	28.8	43	39.1	42	31.5
D.K. and N.A.	—	—	—	—	—	—	1	0.9	—	—
7. Salespeople sold on floor										
Yes	8	4.0	10	8.3	4	3.2	2	1.8	6	4.5
No	190	95.5	110	91.7	120	96.0	106	96.4	126	94.7
D.K. and N.A.	1	0.5	—	—	1	0.8	2	1.8	1	0.8
8. Helped plan advertising										
Yes	29	14.6	17	14.2	18	14.4	6	5.5	19	14.3
No	169	84.9	103	85.8	106	84.8	102	92.7	113	84.9
D.K. and N.A.	1	0.5	—	—	1	0.8	2	1.8	1	0.8

TABLE 4 (Concluded)

	Starr		Disch		Honshu		Erath		Tojo	
	No.	%	No.	%	No.	%	No.	%	No.	%
9. Understands problems										
Thoroughly	37	18.6	28	23.3	19	15.2	11	10.0	20	15.0
To some extent	85	42.8	54	45.0	53	42.4	43	39.1	55	41.4
Not at all	55	27.6	32	26.7	40	32.0	41	37.3	46	34.6
D.K. and N.A.	22	11.0	6	5.0	13	10.4	15	13.6	12	9.0
10. Helped with financial arrangements										
Yes	6	3.0	2	1.7	2	1.6	—	—	7	5.3
No—no need	181	91.0	116	96.7	118	94.4	103	93.7	117	87.9
No—needed help	5	2.5	1	0.8	2	1.6	3	2.7	5	3.8
D.K. and N.A.	7	3.5	1	0.8	3	2.4	4	3.6	4	3.0
11. Interested in window service										
Yes	87	43.7	36	30.0	45	36.0	39	35.5	62	46.6
No	108	54.3	82	68.3	78	62.4	70	63.6	69	51.9
D.K. and N.A.	4	2.0	2	1.7	2	1.6	1	0.9	2	1.5
12. Prominence of display										
Best	30	15.1	54	45.0	44	35.2	11	10.0	23	17.3
Second best	46	23.1	34	28.3	39	31.2	22	20.0	41	30.8
Third best	43	21.6	13	10.8	27	21.6	42	38.2	34	25.6
Fourth best	42	21.1	7	5.8	6	4.8	16	14.5	24	18.0
No answer	8	4.0	8	6.7	8	6.4	8	7.3	8	6.0
13. Attractiveness of displays										
Excellent	53	26.6	54	45.0	48	38.4	9	8.2	21	15.8
Good	43	21.6	34	28.3	26	20.8	41	37.3	39	29.4
Fair	44	22.1	16	13.3	27	21.6	28	25.4	36	27.0
Poor	51	25.7	11	9.2	19	15.2	25	22.7	29	21.8
No answer	8	4.0	5	4.2	5	4.0	7	6.4	8	6.0

Key to Questions in Table 4

No.	Question

1. Which of the following comments best explains how often the distributor's salesperson calls on you?

2. On the last call, did the salesperson ask to set up a window display?

3. On the last call, did the salesperson set up a window display?

4. On the last call, did the salesperson bring displays with him or her?

5. On the last call, did the salesperson present his or her line's selling points to your personnel?

6. Do you now have a supply of booklets, brochures, envelope stuffers, and so on, left by distributor's salesperson?

7. Did the salesperson actually work with your sales personnel selling the product in the last 30 days?

8. Has the salesperson helped you plan any advertising, promotions, and so on, in the past six months?

9. How well do you think this salesperson understands your problems in handling his or her products?

10. Has the salesperson given you any assistance in working out financial arrangements within the past year?

11. Would you be interested in window-trimming services provided by the distributor?

12. How would you rank the quality of the displays you have seen for each of the five brands?

13. How would you rank the attractiveness of the displays of the five brands?

TABLE 5 (Problem 2) Comparative Data Regarding Inventories and Dealer Attitudes

1. Number of leading brands stocked by Starr dealers (in percent)

Only Starr	14.1%
Starr and one other brand	12.6
Starr and two other brands	30.1
Starr and three other brands	17.3
Starr and all four leaders	24.7

2. Percent of Starr dealers who also handle:

Disch	60.3%
Honshu	62.8
Erath	55.3
Tojo	66.8

3. Average share of sets by make per store

Starr	7.5%
Disch	14.2
Honshu	11.1
Erath	6.6
Tojo	8.4
All other makes	25.2

4. Percent of Starr dealers with each type of Starr set in stock

Portable (miniature)	90.2%
Portable (regular)	55.6
Table model	58.2
Console	28.1

5. Percent of dealers with Starr sets in windows, by type of set

Portable (miniature)	22.2%
Portable (regular)	51.0
Table model	20.1
Console	10.8

6. Percent of dealers who suggested that manufacturers:

a. Stop tie-in sales and overloading	36.5%
b. Provide better salespeople	27.4
c. Restrain price-cutters	23.6
d. Provide better margins	18.9
e. Improve service	13.8

hypothesis; and in the process you will try to give Starr an overall picture of the current market. Should you need additional background information, problem facts, survey methodology, and so on, use your imagination logically to supply it. And consider using graphics wherever they can help tell the report story. Use the formal report structure that this situation requires. Address the report to Madeline B. Valentine, Vice President for Marketing.

3. *What small-business leaders think education for business should be.* Three months ago the State Association of Small Business Executives hired your private research organization to conduct a study on business education. It seems that a number of the ranking members of the organization are serving on advisory committees for some of the business schools in the state. The advice they give has been their own,

but they wonder whether they truly represent the total business leader population. It would be good, they feel, if they could know the opinions and experiences of other business leaders on the subject. So this year they persuaded the association's board of directors to conduct a survey on this subject as the association's special project for the year. And this is where you come in.

In general, the objective of the study is to learn whatever can be learned that will help in determining the ideal curriculum for educating future leaders of small business. As you see the problem, it concerns learning what business leaders do. With this information, one can better determine what should be taught in preparing students for the job. It involves learning what businesspeople feel young people should study in order to perform well in business. It means learning how businesspeople feel about the adequacy of their own education for business and about education in general.

In planning the survey you worked out a two-phase questionnaire. First, you sought to find what small-business executives do on the job. Here you asked each respondent to describe her or his performance of each of the major functions of a business executive. And you asked each respondent to keep a record of his or her activities for a working day. Second, you asked specific questions about the executive's experiences with and opinions on education for business. Specifically, you asked for evaluations of the executives on their experiences with each of the subjects traditionally offered in business colleges. In addition, you asked for opinions on the general nature of education for business.

Next, using your membership rolls, you constructed a random sample of 200 leaders of small business in the state (only 161 proved to be usable). So that all segments of business would be covered, you classified them by general types (manufacturing, wholesaling, retailing, service). And so that you could have some insight into their own preparation, you classified all respondents by their educational background (business degree, nonbusiness degree, or no degree). With your sample selected, you and two assistants traveled throughout the state conducting exhaustive interviews. Your findings, arranged for you in summary form, appear in Tables 6–11.

The task facing you now is that of writing up your results. You will, of course, organize your findings so that they most appropriately meet the requirements of your objective. Primarily, you will write for the association leadership, although it is likely that copies may be sent to educators in the state. Because the formality and length requirement of the situation justify it, you will give the report all the appropriate prefatory parts.

In writing the introductory part, you decide to include only a brief description of your research methodology. (For purposes of this exercise, you may use your logical imagination as needed.) A more complete description will appear in the appendix of your report (you may assume this part). As defined by

TABLE 6 (Problem 3) Size and Type Distribution of Companies of the Executives Comprising the Sample

Company Size in Number of Employees	Type of Company				
	Manufacturing	Wholesaling	Retailing	Service	Total
1–15	6	7	20	14	47
16–50	5	17	14	16	52
51–100	4	9	3	8	24
101+	7	4	14	13	38
Total	22	37	51	51	161

your association, *small business* refers to any organization employing fewer than 500 people.

4. *Interpreting survey findings for State Mutual Insurance.* For the past month Business Research, Incorporated, has been actively working on a survey for the State Mutual Insurance Company. In a nutshell, the objective of the survey was to find out why people buy automobile insurance and how they buy it. In all, they conducted 1,600 interviews from a scientifically designed sample of policyholders over the geographic area served by the company.

The research has been completed, and the findings have been tabulated. Now, as an analyst for Business Research, you have the assignment of interpreting, organizing, and presenting the findings in report form. In interpreting the findings you will keep in mind that State Mutual intends to use them to good advantage in forming its marketing strategy. Especially does it hope to find information useful in improving sales techniques. The organization plan you use will give appropriate emphasis to the highlights of your presentation. And the report format you choose will be one befitting the formality of this one situation. (For class purposes, you will need to use your logic and imagination to supply the facts you would know if you really were in this situation—research methodology, current company practices, etc.) You will address the report to Mr. Conrad A. Dunbar, Vice President in Charge of Marketing.

Tabulations of the findings by question are as follows:

Question: How did you first get in touch with your present company—that is, how did you hear about it?
46%—Through a friend, neighbor, or relative.
23%—Know the agent (good friend, neighbor, relative).
8%—Don't remember.
4%—Through car dealer or person who sold respondent the car.
4%—Saw or heard company's advertising and called company.

TABLE 7 (Problem 3) Activities Contributed To or Carried On by Executives Participating in the Study

Activity	Percentage of Executives Involved in the Activity
Determining policy	90
Supervising personnel	87
Handling adjustments	81
Evaluating personnel	79
Handling grievances	79
Motivating personnel	77
Pricing	73
Forecasting	73
Financing operations	71
Product improvement	69
Purchasing	67
Hiring-firing	66
Advertising	65
Training	64
Checking production performance	64
Credits and collections	63
Establishing production standards	57
Budgeting	54
Inventory control	51
Accounting	50
Production planning	49
Research	47
Work methods	46
Display	35
Transportation and delivery	30
Conducting labor relations	26
Manufacturing	15
Other controls	12

TABLE 8 (Problem 3) Percentage Distribution of Opinions of Small-Business Executives on Liberal-Practical Balance in Business Education (by Educational Backgrounds of the Executives)

| | Educational Background of Executives | | | |
Opinion of Proper Balance	College Degree in Business*	College Degree Other Than in Business†	No College Degree‡	All Executives
Entirely liberal	0	8.8	2.7	4.3
Mostly liberal, some practical	9.0	14.7	10.8	11.8
About half liberal and half practical	37.5	23.5	21.6	28.0
Mostly practical, some liberal	44.5	47.1	56.8	48.4
Entirely practical	9.0	5.9	8.1	7.5
Total	100.0	100.0	100.0	100.0

*Total of 56.
†Total of 68.
‡Total of 37.

TABLE 9 (Problem 3) Percentage Distribution of Opinions of Small-Business Executives on Adequate of Their Educations for Their Careers

| | Form of Education | | | |
Opinion of Adequacy	College Degree in Business*	College Degree in Liberal Arts†	College Degree in Other Nonbusiness Areas‡	No College Degrees§
Adequate	91.1	30.6	56.2	16.7
Not adequate	8.9	69.4	43.8	83.3
Total	100.0	100.0	100.0	100.0

*Total of 56.
†Total of 36.
‡Total of 32.
§Total of 37.

Problem 4 (continued)

3%—Agent called on respondent.
3%—Other agent recommended it.
2%—Friend or relative worked for the company.
2%—Carried other kinds of insurance with company.
1%—Through bank or loan company where car was financed.
7%—Other sources.

Question: The last time you bought auto insurance did you "shop around"—that is, did you get prices from different companies? (Yes or No)

18%—Did shop.
82%—Did not shop.

Question: (If "yes" to previous question) How did you go about finding the names of companies to contact?

8%—Friends, relatives, neighbors.
2%—Phone book.
2%—Advertising.
3%—Went to different insurance offices.
2%—Other.
3%—Don't remember.

Question: What reasons were most important to you in choosing the company you did? . . . Any others? (Probe)

24%—Save money, cheaper.
18%—Good company, reputable, reliable, good service.
17%—Agent is a friend, relative, neighbor, etc.
17%—Heard about company through friends, relatives.
12%—Better coverage, different types.
12%—No reason given.

TABLE 10 (Problem 3) Ranking of the Traditional Business Courses on Basis of Combined Classification* of Essential and Desirable

Rank	Course	Percentage Classifying as Essential	Percentage Classifying as Desirable	Total† Essential and Desirable
1	Accounting (basic)	84.9	13.2	98.1
2	Business Communication	73.0	22.6	95.6
3	Economics (basic)	50.9	42.8	93.8
4	Business Law	53.5	36.4	89.9
5	Management (Human Resources)	60.4	28.9	89.3
6	Information Systems	70.4	18.2	88.7
7	Basic Management	47.8	38.4	86.2
8	Advertising	45.3	38.4	83.6
9	Corporation Finance	40.9	39.6	80.5
10	Sales Management	56.6	23.3	79.9
11	Money and Banking	44.7	34.6	79.2
12	Basic Marketing	44.7	34.0	78.6
13	Small Business Management	47.8	30.8	78.6
14	Office Management	32.1	41.5	73.6
15	Statistics	31.4	37.7	69.2
16	Retailing	39.0	28.9	67.9
17	Accounting (advanced)	30.8	32.7	63.5
18	Insurance	28.3	34.0	62.3
19	Wholesaling	30.2	31.4	61.6
20	Investments	17.6	40.9	58.5
21	Marketing Research	21.4	32.7	54.1
22	Economics (advanced)	10.1	41.5	51.6
23	Labor (collective bargaining)	22.0	28.9	50.9
24	Management (industrial)	12.6	27.0	39.6
25	Real Estate	15.7	20.8	36.5

*Total of 161 interviews.

†Difference between this figure and 100 is percentage classifying course as "not desirable."

Problem 4 (continued)

9%—Settle claims promptly, fairly.
2%—Insured through finance company—no choice.
2%—Conveniently located.
2%—Heard about agent through friends.
1%—Insurance in connection with job.
1%—Offered payment plan.
1%—Wanted all insurance with one company.
6%—Other reasons.

Question: Do you think there is a big difference in what different companies would charge you for the same kind and amount of auto insurance, or a small difference, or do you think that they all charge about the same?
38%—Insurance charges are about the same.

24%—There is a big difference in insurance charges.
21%—There is a small difference in insurance charges.
17%—Don't know.

Question: (If difference between companies indicated) Do you think that the cost of your present car insurance is higher than most companies', lower than most other companies', or about the same?
73%—Lower than most companies'.
21%—Don't know.
5%—Higher than most companies'.
1%—About the same as most companies'.

Question: When you bought your present policy, did you contact the agent, or did the agent contact you?

Rank	Course	Percentage Classifying as Essential	Percentage Classifying as Desirable	Total† Essential Plus Desirable
1	Speech	75.8	13.0	88.8
2	English Composition	62.1	20.5	82.6
3	Psychology	49.1	32.9	82.0
4	Government	49.1	22.9	72.0
5	Foreign Language	25.5	39.7	65.2
6	History	34.8	29.2	64.0
7	Science	24.2	39.8	64.0
8	English Literature	41.0	20.5	61.5
9	Mathematics	42.2	18.0	60.2
10	Sociology	23.0	36.6	59.6
11	Philosophy	19.3	39.1	58.4

*Total of 161 interviews.

†Difference between this percentage and 100 is percentage classifying courses as "not desirable."

Problem 4 (continued)

25%—The agent contacted me.

72%—I contacted the agent.

3%—Don't remember or question not appropriate.

Question: (If respondent contacted agent, ask:) How did you first get the agent's name?

31%—Through friends, relatives, neighbors.

19%—Knew agent.

6%—Saw advertising.

6%—Don't remember.

All other reasons accounted for 3% or less each.

Question: What were the main sales points the agent made about your present insurance?

39%—Don't remember.

18%—Trusted agent, didn't have to give sales talk.

14%—Costs less.

12%—Trusted person who recommended agent.

10%—Better coverage, more protection.

6%—Company has good reputation.

4%—Fair handling of claims.

1%—Insured through finance company or bank.

5%—Other reasons.

Question: People give different reasons for taking out auto insurance. Which one of these do you think is *most* important to most people?

89%—Cover responsibility for damage to other person.

5%—Required by law.

3%—Cover against damage to own car.

3%—Other and none.

Question: Here are some of the things about auto insurance companies that some people feel are important. (Show set of 7 yellow cards.) Now can you tell me which one of these is most important to you personally? (Record "1" below and ask.) And of these left, which one is the most important? (Record "2" and proceed until all cards have been ranked.)

Percent ranking feature as number 1:

23%—Quick settlement of claims.

18%—Fair treatment by company.

17%—Well-known company.

15%—Low cost of insurance.

13%—Good service from local agent.

7%—Claim adjusters in all parts of the United States.

2%—Installment plan for payments.

Question: (For each company bought from previously, but not now carried) Why do you no longer carry (each company) insurance on your car?

Of those switching from State Mutual, the following reasons were given:

50%—No reason given.

18%—State Mutual rates too high; present company cheaper.

16%—Agent is personal friend. (State Mutual agent died, got sick, left the town, switched companies, etc.)

10%—Poor claims handling.

9%—Poor service—did not bill promptly.

9%—Other company had better coverage.

6%—Let insurance expire.

5%—Insured through finance company, loan company, insurance payments made with car payments.

24%—Other reasons.

Of those switching to State Mutual, the following reasons were given:

47%—No reason given.

21%—Rates too high, State Mutual cheaper.

7%—State Mutual has better coverage.

6%—State Mutual agent is personal friend.

3%—Let insurance expire.

3%—Insured through finance company, loan company, bank company selected, included with car payments, etc.

3%—Poor claims handling by other company.

2%—Poor service from other company.

11%—Other reasons.

5. *Determining whether to voice-enable your company's email system.* (Requires research.) Last year your company decided to give all salespeople as well as other key personnel cell phones. Not only have cell phones become small and lightweight, but also the average local monthly bill for their use dropped dramatically from around $100 in 1987 to just under $50 in 1997. Your salespeople and your company have benefited tremendously from this decision. The salespeople said it has allowed them to manage their time better and to contact key customers with up-to-date information quickly. It has also given them added personal security while on the road. However, most use this media exclusively, even for communication that could be done more efficiently by email.

So when you recently learned of a new technology called PureVoice for voice-enabling email, you decided to determine whether it, too, would leverage the productivity of these key people. PureVoice is a standard in wireless CDMA cellular technology that is being added to email. This technology was developed by Qualcomm for use with their digital cellular telephones.

PureVoice with Smart Rate compresses incoming speech in digital format with a high compression factor without significant loss of voice quality. In fact, when used on the Internet with personal computers, it can reduce both file size and transmission time. Compared to common formats such as .wav or Macintosh .snd format, PureVoice improves the time and size performance by more than a factor of 10. A one-minute voice mail using .wav format would take seven minutes to transmit with a 28.8 modem and use about 1 megabyte of disk space. That same one-minute message with PureVoice would take just 45 seconds to transmit and require only 60-K of disk

space. And these measures are conservative, representing typical conversational speech.

Since the average person speaks between 140 and 160 words per minute, leaving a voice email rather than a typed one would save considerable input time. This communication medium could be used when immediate response to a message is not necessary. While not providing the same kind of record a printed message would, a voice file could still provide a record that can replayed as needed. And its use would reduce the cell phone costs as well.

Before you decide to implement it, you want to anticipate your key potential users' reaction to it. Since everyone in your company has an email account, you will survey by email all those who are also using cell phones for company business. You want to learn their resistance levels and factors that might reduce that resistance. For example, you might ask about the type and length of training they prefer. Also, you might ask in what specific ways they expect to use voice-enabled email as well as to how they expect it might change their use of cell phones. You might want to ask about acceptable message time and length as well other features they want. Of course, you will ask for standard demographic information, too. However, you will let them know their responses are confidential.

From the information you gather, draw conclusions and report the results along with your recommendation on whether or not to implement voice-enabled email at this time. Include at least one graphic in the report proper and a copy of the survey you use in the report's appendix along with any other nice-to-know information you collect. You will make sure your survey conforms to good sampling techniques and questionnaire design discussed in Chapter 19.

6. *Investigating the outlook for investments.* (Requires research.) Assume you are employed in the Investments Research Department of the Whitmore Foundation, a philanthropic trust with over $300 million of invested funds. You have been assigned the task of determining the general outlook for investments in the _____ industry (your choice).

Specifically, you will review past and present status of the industry's profits, sales, production, and the like. From these reviews you may be able to detect trends that may continue into the immediate future. Too, you will gather all facts and authoritative opinion relating to future growth. From all of this you hope to be able to make a somewhat specific recommendation about investments in the industry in general.

Although your report will concern the industry rather than a specific company (or companies), you are likely to refer frequently to the major firms in the industry. And your recommendation might point out the industry leaders. Write your report in a form appropriate for the formality of this situation. Submit it to the Investment Board, Whitmore Building, 317 Berry Avenue, Cleveland, OH.

7. *Determining what business will be like in the months ahead.* (Requires research.) Roland A. Anderson, president of _____ (company of your choice), has

assigned you, his assistant, to write a consensus business forecast for presentation at next Wednesday's meeting of the board of directors. The company does not employ an economist; Anderson does not believe in such frills. "Why should we pay for one," he says, "when the current business periodicals give us free forecasts by all the leading economists?"

Since Anderson's instructions were—as usual—quite vague, much of what you do will depend on your good judgment. All Anderson said was that he wanted you to survey the predictions of the leading economic forecasters for the months ahead and to present your findings in a clear and meaningful report to the board. And he wanted the forecasts consolidated—that is, he did not want a mere succession of individual forecasts. Your report, covering the entire economy, will, of course, be largely general in nature. But you will give special emphasis to forecasts pertaining to your industry.

The report will be in a form appropriate for the board. Because the board members will want to get at the most important material quickly, be sure to include a fast-moving executive summary. Address the report to President Anderson, who also chairs the board.

8. *What will your team be like next year?* (Requires research.) Assume that you are doing a bit of advance research for a rival school (you name it). Your assignment is to collect, analyze, and report the information available on each of the teams (football, baseball, or whatever your instructor specifies) on the schedule. One, or course, is your own school's team; and that's the one you'll work on first.

You will begin your work by collecting all the available information on who the players will be—who is returning, who is coming up from the freshman squad, and the like. Then you'll collect all the available information on abilities and performance records. Next you will systematically analyze this information. Your analysis will lead to a conclusion on the team's overall strength.

Of course, you will present the report in an appropriate form.

9. *Getting the facts about living in your area for DeVillier Instruments.* (Requires research.) DeVillier Instruments, Inc., a major international manufacturer of electronic equipment, is considering a move of its corporate headquarters to _____ (your city or a city selected by your instructor). If the move is made, as many of the 1,800 employees at DeVillier's current headquarters as choose to will come to the _____ area. Before DeVillier decides to make the move, it will need additional information.

DeVillier already has the economic data needed for the decision, and these data are generally favorable. What it needs now is information about the quality of life that its employees would have in the _____ area. Quality of life includes just about everything that employees consider important to their well-being. It includes all levels of the private and public educational system. It includes the availability of recreational opportunities—parks, athletic facilities,

theaters, restaurants, clubs, and cultural activities. It includes the availability and quality of housing. It includes the job market (many of the employees' spouses will seek employment). And it includes natural endowments—the weather, geography, and proximity to lakes, woodlands, streams, and other geographic points of interest. DeVillier needs information on these and other factors that might affect the quality of life of its employees if the move were made.

As a management trainee serving as a special assistant to Leo T. Romanowski, the president of DeVillier, you have been given the task of gathering the needed information. In Mr. Romanowski's words, "I want you to go to the _____ area, look it over, and gather information on all the things that will affect the lives of the people who move there. Be as objective as you can. Don't be influenced by the fact that you're likely to be living there yourself if we select the place."

With Mr. Romanowski's instructions in mind, you begin your plan for the assignment. You will look the area over. You will gather information about living there from all the likely sources—chamber of commerce, local libraries, community leaders, public offices, and so on. Then you will review and analyze the information you have collected. You will organize it in an order that conveys your message quickly and easily, and you will present it in a report appropriate for the somewhat formal situation. That is, the report will contain the prefatory parts that show formality. Although the board of directors will in all probability see the report, you will address it to Mr. Romanowski.

10. *Presenting the pros and cons of gun control to an arms manufacturer.* (Requires research.) Assume the position of a research associate employed by the Jones and Easton Company, manufacturer of a full line of rifles, shotguns, and handguns. In recent years, advocates of gun control have exerted increasing pressure on the company. Until now, the management of Jones and Easton has ignored them. But now it believes that their position must be given due consideration. As a result, you were called into a long executive staff meeting, in which President Samuel A. Simon's final words summarized your instructions:

"As you can see, we're disturbed. We think we should know more about this matter. So we're asking you to give us the principal arguments for and against gun control and the supporting evidence for those arguments. This should lead to recommendations concerning what our stand should be, what messages we should communicate, what actions we should take, and so on. Of course, we're biased—guns are our bread and butter. But we want your report to look at this question objectively. Please have your research in our hands for the board meeting one month from today."

You view this as your most important assignment at Jones and Easton. A good job here could mean much for your future success and for that of the company. So you will do your very best.

You will begin your work in the company library with a thorough search of the literature on gun control. Newspapers and other periodicals have covered the question for years. And organizations have prepared a great deal of material that either supports or opposes gun control. Obviously, you must be alert to the possibility of bias in the sources you consult. You will rely only on reasonable and factual accounts.

When you have selected the material that you will report, you will consider how to organize it. You might organize it by pros and cons or by arguments under which pros and cons are cited. And there are probably other possibilities. You will select the one that arranges the material best and leads to the recommended arguments, positions, and actions that the final section of your report will comprise.

Because this report is extensive and the situation is somewhat formal, you will provide the appropriate prefatory parts. If some of your supporting data are quantitative, you will use graphics. Address the report to Mr. Simon with copies to all vice presidents.

11. *Solving a problem on your campus.* (Requires research.) Certain problems exist on many college campuses. At least, they exist in the minds of many of the faculty, students, and staff. From the following list of such problems, select one that you think needs attention at your college:

Library operation
Campus security
Policies on sales of tickets to athletic events
Regulation of social activities
Student government
Registration procedure

Faculty–student relations
Orientation program for freshmen
Curriculum improvement
Increasing enrollments
Scholastic honesty
Campus crime
Improving cultural atmosphere on campus
Class attendance policies
Scholastic-probation policies
Parking, traffic control
Grade inflation
Student government
Emphasis on athletics
Campus beautification
Fire prevention

You will first gather all the significant facts regarding the problem you select. When you are thoroughly acquainted with them, you will gather authoritative opinions concerning the solution.

Obtaining such information may involve looking through bibliographic sources to find out what has been done on other campuses. It may involve interviewing people on campus who are attempting to deal with the problem. Next you will carefully analyze your problem in light of all you have learned about it. Then you will develop a solution to the problem.

To make the situation appear realistic, place yourself in the proper role at your school. Write a formal report, with all the conventional prefatory parts. Address the report to the appropriate administrator.

TOPIC SUGGESTIONS FOR INTERMEDIATE-LENGTH AND LONG REPORTS

Following are suggestions for additional report problems ranging from the simple to the highly complex. You can convert them into realistic business problems by supplying details and/or adapting them to real-life business situations. For most of these problems, you can obtain the needed information through secondary research. The topics are arranged by business field, although many of them cross fields.

ACCOUNTING

1. Report on current depreciation accounting practices, and recommend depreciation accounting procedures for Company X.

2. Design an inventory control system for X Company.

3. Report to Company X executives on how tax court decisions handed down over the past six months will affect their firm.

4. What security measures should Company X take with access to its accounting data?

5. Advise the managers of X Company on the accounting problems that they can anticipate when the company begins overseas operations.

6. Analyze break-even analysis as a decision-making tool for X Company.

7. Explain to potential investors which sections in Company X's most recent annual report they should review most carefully.

8. Analyze the relative effects on income of the first in, first out (FIFO) and last in, first out (LIFO) methods of inventory valuation during a prolonged period of inflation.

9. Write a report for the American Accounting Association on the demand for accountants with computer systems training.

10. Develop for accounting students at your college

information that will help them choose between careers in public accounting and careers in private accounting.

11. Advise the management of X Company on the validity of return on investment as a measure of performance.

12. Report on operations research as a decision-making tool for accountants and managers.

13. Report to the management of X Company on trends in the content and design of corporate annual reports.

14. Report to an association of accountants the status of professional ethics in accounting.

15. Report to management of X Company on the communication skills important to accounting.

16. Investigate the matching principle and its effects on financial statements for Company X.

17. Report to the board of directors at X Company whether the balance sheet fails to recognize important intangible assets.

18. Explain the extent to which accounting reflects the intent of Company X's business decisions.

19. Review for Company X whether disclosure could be an effective substitute for recognition in financial statements.

20. Report to the management of Company X whether intangible assets have finite or infinite lives.

21. Advise the founders of new Company X on income tax considerations in the selection of a form of business organization.

22. Review for Company X the pros and cons of installing a computerized accounting system.

GENERAL BUSINESS

23. Evaluate the adequacy of current college programs for developing business leadership.

24. Which business skills should schools and colleges teach, and which should companies teach?

25. What should be the role of business leaders in developing courses and curricula for business schools?

26. Report on ways to build and use good teams in the workplace.

27. Identify the criteria Company X should use in selecting a public relations firm.

28. Report on the advisability of including business internships in a business degree program.

29. What images of business and businesspersons do current business textbooks convey?

30. How does today's business community regard the master of business administration (MBA) degree?

31. Evaluate the contribution that campus business and professional clubs make to business education.

32. How effective is computer-based training in education for business?

33. Should education for business be specialized, or should it provide a generalized, well-rounded education?

34. Determine how to get and use permissions for music added to business presentations.

35. Determine which of three franchises (your instructor will select) offer the best opportunity for investment.

36. Determine guidelines for avoiding sexual harassment for Company X.

37. Determine cultural problems likely to be encountered by employees going to work in _____ (a foreign country).

38. What have been the effects of the North American Free Trade Agreement (NAFTA) on the auto parts (or another) industry?

39. Should Company X use the U.S. Postal Service or a private courier (Federal Express, United Parcel Service)?

40. For an energy company, answer the question of whether fears about global warming are legitimate.

41. Advise a client on whether to invest in a company producing renewable energy (wind, solar, etc.).

LABOR

42. For the executives of the National Association of Manufacturers (or some such group), report on the outlook for labor-management relations in the next 12 months.

43. For the officers of a major labor union, research and report progress toward decreasing job discrimination against minorities.

44. For X Union, project the effects that technology will have on traditionally unionized industries by the year 20XX.

45. Advise the management of X Company on how to deal with Y Union, which is attempting to organize the employees of X Company.

46. Interpret the change in the number of union members over the past _____ years.

47. Report on the successes and failures of employee-run businesses.

48. Report on the status and effects of "right to work" laws.

49. Evaluate the effects of a particular strike (your choice) on the union, the company, the stockholders, and the public. Write the report for a government investigating committee.

50. For Union X, prepare an objective report on union leadership in the nation during the past decade.

51. Layoffs based on seniority are causing a disproportionate reduction in the number of women and minority workers at Company X. Investigate alternatives that the company can present to the union.

52. Investigate recent trends relative to the older worker and the stands that unions have taken in this area.

53. Review the appropriateness of unionizing government workers, and recommend to a body of government leaders the stand they should take on this issue.

54. Report on the role of unions (or managements) in politics, and recommend a course for them to follow.

55. Reevaluate _____ (unions or employment relations—your instructor will specify) for the management of X Company.

56. Analyze the changing nature of work for the leaders of _____ union (your instructor will designate).

57. Report on the blending of work and family issues for X Union.

FINANCE

58. As a financial consultant, evaluate a specific form of tax shelter for a client.

59. Review the customer-relations practices of banks, and recommend customer relations procedures for Bank X.

60. Review current employee loan practices and recommend whether Company X should make employee loans.

61. Report on what Company X needs to know about financial matters in doing business with _____ (foreign country).

62. Give estate planning advice to a client with a unique personal situation.

63. Advise X Company on whether it should lease capital equipment or buy it.

64. Advise Company X on whether it should engage in a joint venture with a company overseas or establish a wholly owned foreign subsidiary.

65. Compare the costs for X Company of offering its workers child care or elder care benefits.

66. Should Company X accept national credit cards or set up its own credit card system?

67. Advise Company X on how to avoid a hostile takeover.

68. Which will be the better investment in the next three years, stocks or bonds?

69. Advise Company X on whether it should list its stock on a major stock exchange.

70. Advise Company X, which is having problems with liquidity, on the pros and cons of factoring accounts receivable.

71. Recommend the most feasible way to finance newly formed X Company.

MANAGEMENT

72. Develop for Company X a guide to ethics in its highly competitive business situation.

73. After reviewing pertinent literature and experiences of other companies, develop a plan for selecting and training administrators for an overseas operation on Company X.

74. Survey the current literature and advise Company X on whether its management should become politically active.

75. After reviewing the pros and cons, advise X Company on whether it should begin a program of hiring the handicapped or disadvantaged.

76. Report on the behavioral and psychological effects of introducing wellness programs to Company X.

77. The executives of X Company (a manufacturer of automobile and truck tires) want a report on recent court decisions relating to warranties. Include any recommendations that your report justifies.

78. Report on the problems involved in moving Company X headquarters from _____ (city) to _____ (city).

79. After reviewing current practices with regard to worker participation in management, advise Company X on whether it should permit such participation.

80. Should Company X contract for _____ (service) or establish its own department?

81. Review the advantages and disadvantages of rotating executive jobs at Company X, and then make a recommendation.

82. What should be Company X's policy on office romances?

83. Develop an energy conservation or recycling plan for X Company.

84. Evaluate internal communications in X Company and make specific suggestions for improvement.

85. Design a security system for preventing computer espionage at Company X, a leader in the highly competitive _____ industry.

86. Evaluate the various methods for determining corporate performance and select the one most appropriate for Company X.

87. Advise X Company on the procedures for incorporating in _____ (state or province).

88. Survey the literature to find meaningful criteria for selecting executives for foreign service for X Company.

89. Report to Company X on the civil and criminal liabilities of its corporate executives.

90. Report on the quality awards being given to businesses.

91. Determine for a legislative committee the extent of minority recruiting, hiring, and training in the _____ industry.

92. As a consultant for an association of farmers, evaluate the recent past and project the future of growing or raising _____ (your choice—cattle, poultry, wheat, soybeans, or the like).

93. Develop a plan for reducing employee turnover for Company X.

94. Report to a labor union on recent evidence of sexual

harassment, and recommend steps that the union should take to correct any problems you find.

95. Investigate the feasibility of hiring older workers for part-time work for X Company.

PERSONNEL/HUMAN RESOURCE ADMINISTRATION

96. Report on and interpret for X Company the effects of recent court decisions on the testing and hiring of employees.

97. Survey company retirement practices and recommend retirement policies for Company X.

98. Report on practices in compensating key personnel in overseas assignments and recommend for X Company polices for the compensation of such personnel.

99. Report on what human resource executives look for in application letters and résumés.

100. Report on the advantages and disadvantages of Company X's providing on-site day care for children of employees.

101. After reviewing the legal and ethical questions involved, make a recommendation concerning the use of honesty tests in employee hiring.

102. Review what other companies are doing about employees suffering from drug or alcohol abuse, and recommend a policy on the matter for Company X.

103. Report on effective interviewing techniques used to identify the best people to hire.

104. Investigate the impact of the Americans with Disabilities Act on X Company.

105. Compare the pros and cons of alternative methods of dispute resolution.

106. Report on ways Company X can link performance improvement plans to discipline and pay.

107. Investigate the impact of the legal aspects of human resource management (EEO, ADA, wrongful termination, harassment, family care and medical leave, workplace violence—your instructor will select one or several) on Company X.

108. Analyze the impact of changing work priorities in a culturally diverse workplace for Company X.

109. Report on recent issues in employee communication for Company X.

MARKETING

110. Review the available literature and advise Company X on whether it should franchise its _____ business.

111. Select a recent national marketing program and analyze why it succeeded or failed.

112. Advise the advertising vice president of Company X on whether the company should respond to or ignore a competitor's direct attack on the quality of its product.

113. Review the ethical considerations involved in advertising to children and advise X Company on the matter.

114. Determine for Company X the social and ethical aspects of pricing for the market.

115. Explore the possibilities of trade with _____ (a foreign country) for X Company.

116. Determine for a national department store chain changing trends in the services that customers expect.

117. Prepare a report to help a contingent of your legislature decide whether current regulation of advertising should be reduced.

118. Determine the problems X Company will encounter in introducing a new product to its line.

119. Report on the success of rebates as a sales stimulator and advise Company X on whether it should use rebates.

120. Should Company X rent or lease trucks for distributing its products?

121. Determine the trends in packaging in the _____ industry.

122. Should X Company establish its own sales force, use manufacturer's agents, or use selling agents?

123. How should Company X evaluate the performance of its salespeople?

124. Determine for X Company how it can evaluate the effectiveness of its advertising.

125. Select the best channel of distribution for new product Y and justify your choice.

126. Should X Company establish its own advertising department or use an advertising agency?

127. Make a market study of _____ (city) to determine whether it is a suitable location for ____ (a type of business).

128. Report to X Company on telemarketing and recommend whether it should use telemarketing to increase sales.

129. Investigate the factors to consider when marketing online through the Internet to children.

130. Explore segmentation schemes of _____ (cities, countries, regions, e.g., East Africa; trade agreements, e.g., NAFTA; income/nonincome variables, e.g., literate, having telephone; or cultural groups, e.g., ethnic, linguistic, religious—your instructor will assign one or more) for Company X.

COMPUTER APPLICATIONS

131. Determine whether any of the products of Company X are good candidates for infomercials.

132. Recommend a laptop computer for use by the salespeople of Company X when they are traveling.

133. Advise Company X about the steps it can take to protect its computerized files from sabotage.

134. Determine whether Company X should purchase or lease its computer equipment.

135. Report to the president of Company X the copyright and contract laws that apply to the use of computer programs.

136. What are the potential applications of artificial intelligence in the ____ industry?

137. Determine which positions Company X should designate as possible telecommuting candidates.

138. Report to the International Organization of Business Communications on the impact of electronic technology on business communication.

139. Report on the future developments of robotics in the _____ industry.

140. Review and rank for possible adoption three software packages that Company X might use for its _____ work (name the field of operations).

141. Determine for Company X the factors it should consider in selecting computer insurance.

142. Report on the types of training available to X Company for its staff when upgrading its current word processing software.

143. Report on building a responsive information technology infrastructure for Company X.

144. Explore the procedures and methods for measuring information system effectiveness and productivity for Company X.

145. Investigate how to improve information security and control for Company X.

146. Compare the ways to manage and facilitate decision and executive support systems for Company X.

147. Should _____ (a small company) use the Internet as a marketing tool?

BUSINESS EDUCATION

148. Evaluate the effect of remodeling your new office site with both ergonomic and feng shui principles applied.

149. Report on ways companies now use and plan to use desktop videoconferencing.

150. Analyze the possibility of instituting companywide training on etiquette, covering everything from handling telephone calls, to sexual harassment, to dining out.

151. Advise management on the importance of the air quality in its offices.

152. Investigate ways to complete and submit company forms on the web or company intranet.

153. Evaluate the reprographic services and practices at your school from an environmental perspective.

154. Report on ways to hire and keep the best employees in the computer support center.

155. Report on ways to improve literacy in the workplace.

156. Report on the availability and quality of online training programs.

157. Report on ways to improve the communication of cross-cultural work groups.

158. Analyze the possibility of using voice-recognition software with the products available today.

Graphics

Upon completing this chapter, you will be able to use graphics effectively in business reports. To reach this goal, you should be able to

1 Determine which parts of your report should be communicated by graphics and where in the report the graphics should appear.

2 Know the general mechanics of constructing graphics—size, layout, type, rules and borders, color and cross-hatching, clip art, numbering, titles, title placement, and footnotes and acknowledgments.

3 Construct textual graphics such as tables, in-text displays, flowcharts, and process charts.

4 Construct and use visual graphics such as bar charts, pie charts, line charts, pictograms, and combination charts.

5 Explain computer graphics as they relate to visual communication in a report.

Graphics

In your job in the Cory, Inc., word processing section, your assignment today is to proofread reports prepared by your co-workers. Because Cory manufactures electronic equipment, many of the reports are highly technical and complex. Many others, especially those coming from finance and sales, are filled with facts and figures. In your judgment, most of the reports you have proofread are hard to understand.

The one you are looking at now is packed with page after page of sales statistics. Your mind quickly gets lost in the mass of details. Why didn't the writer take the time to summarize the more important figures in a chart? And why didn't the writer put some of the details in tables? Many of the other reports you have been reading, especially the technical ones, are in equal need of graphics. Bar charts, pie charts, and maps would certainly help explain some of the concepts discussed. If only report writers would understand that words alone sometimes cannot communicate clearly—that words sometimes need to be supplemented with visual communication techniques. If the writers of your reports studied the following review of graphics, your job would be easier and more enjoyable. So would the jobs of the readers of those reports.

▪ A graphic is any form of illustration.

In many of your reports you will need to use graphics to help convey information quickly and accurately. By *graphics* we mean any form of illustration: charts, pictures, diagrams, maps. Although tables and bulleted lists are not truly graphic, they are included in this definition. In fact, most computer presentation software includes them.

PLANNING THE GRAPHICS

▪ You should plan the use of graphics.

You should plan the graphics for a report soon after you organize your findings. Your planning of graphics should be based on the need to communicate. Graphics serve one purpose—to communicate—and you should use them primarily for that purpose. Graphics can clarify complex or difficult information, emphasize facts, add coherence, summarize data, and provide interest. Of course, well-constructed graphics also enhance the appearance of a report.

▪ In planning their use, look for parts that they should communicate.

In selecting graphics, you should review the information that your report will contain, looking for any possibility of improving communication of the report through the use of graphics. Specifically, you should look for complex information that visual presentation can make clear, for information too detailed to be covered in words, and for information that deserves special emphasis.

▪ Plan graphics with your reader in mind.

Of course, you will want to plan with your reader in mind. You will choose graphics appropriate to both the content and context where they are presented. The time and money you spend on gathering information or creating a graphic should be balanced in terms of the importance of the message you want to convey. Thus, you construct graphics to help the reader understand the report quicker, easier, and more completely. As such, graphics assist with business etiquette.

▪ But remember that graphics supplement and do not replace the writing.

As you plan the graphics, remember that, as a general rule, they should supplement the writing or speaking—not take its place. They should help the wording by covering the more difficult parts, emphasizing the important points and presenting details. But the words should carry the main message—all of it.

PLACING THE GRAPHICS
IN THE REPORT

▪ Place the graphics near the first place in the text in which you refer to them.

For the best communication effect, you should place each graphic near the place where it is covered in writing. Exactly where on the page you should place it, however, should be determined by its size. If the graphic is small, you should place it within the text that covers it. If it is a full page, you should place it on the page following the first reference to the information it covers.

Some writers like to place all graphics at the end of the report, usually in the appendix. This arrangement may save time in preparing the report, but it does not help the readers. They have to flip through pages every time they want to see a graphic. Business etiquette requires that you place graphics in such a way as to help readers understand the report.

Sometimes you may need to include graphics that do not fit a specific part of the report. For example, you may have a graphic that is necessary for completeness but is not discussed in the report. Or you may have summary charts or tables that apply to the entire report but to no specific place in it. When such graphics are appropriate, you should place them in the appendix. And you should refer to the appendix somewhere in the report.

Graphics communicate most effectively when the readers see them at the right place in the report. Thus, you should refer the readers to them at the right place. That is, you should tell the readers when to look at a graphic and what to see. You can do this best through an incidental reference to the information in the graphic. Of the many wordings used for this purpose, these are the most common:

..., as shown in Figure 4, ...

..., indicated in Figure 4, ...

..., as a glance at Figure 4 reveals, ...

... (see Figure 4) ....

When you refer to graphics subordinately, the main parts of your sentences can interpret the meaning of the graphics for your reader.

DETERMINING THE GENERAL MECHANICS OF CONSTRUCTION

In constructing graphics, you will be concerned with various mechanical matters. The most common are summarized in the following paragraphs.

SIZE DETERMINATION

One of the first decisions you must make in constructing a graphic is determining its size. This decision should not be arbitrary, and it should not be based on convenience. You should give the graphic the size its contents justify. If a graphic is simple (with only two or three quantities), a quarter page might be more than enough and a full page would be too much. But if a graphic must display complex or detailed information, a full page might be justified.

With extremely complex, involved information, you may need to use more than a full

"He still grunts in an annoying monotone, but excellent use of visual aids."

(© Chris Wildt)

page. When you do, make certain that this large page is inserted and folded so that the readers can open it easily. The fold you select will be determined by the size of the page. You simply have to experiment until you find a convenient fold.

LAYOUT ARRANGEMENT

■ Size and contents determine the shape of graphics.

You should determine the layout (shape) of the graphic by size and content requirements. Sometimes a tall, narrow rectangle (portrait) is the answer; sometimes the answer is a short, wide rectangle or a full-page rectangle (landscape). You simply consider the logical possibilities and select the one that appears best.

TYPE

■ Choose a type to help convey the message clearly.

Type used in graphics throughout a report is generally consistent in both style and font. Style refers to the look of the type such as bold or italics; font refers to the look of the letters such as with or without feet (i.e., *serif* or *sans serif*). Occasionally you may want to vary the type, but do so by design for some special reason. Be aware that even the design of the font you choose will convey a message, a message that should work with the text content and design.

■ Choose a type size that is readable.

Size is another variable to watch. Major headings will be larger than subheads. Subheads will be larger than text in labels and legends. The size you choose should look appropriate in the context you use it. Your top priority in choosing type style, font, and size should be readability.

RULES AND BORDERS

■ Use rules and borders when they help appearance.

You should use rules and borders when they help the appearance of the graphic. Rules help distinguish one section or graphic from another, while borders help separate graphics from the text. In general, you should place borders around graphics that occupy less than a full page. You can also place borders around full-page graphics, but such borders serve little practical value. Except in cases in which graphics simply will not fit into the normal page layout, you should not extend the borders of graphics beyond the normal page margins.

COLOR AND CROSS-HATCHING

■ Color and cross-hatching can improve graphics.

Color and cross-hatching, appropriately used, help readers see comparisons and distinctions. In fact, research has found that color in graphics improves the comprehension, retention, and ease of extracting information.[1] Also, both color and cross-hatching add to the attractiveness of the report. Because color is especially effective for this purpose, you should use it whenever practical.

CLIP ART

■ Use clip art to help your reader understand your message.

Today you can get good-looking clip art easily—so easily in fact that some writers often overuse it. While clip art can add interest and bring the reader into a graphic effectively, it can also overpower and distract the reader. The general rule is to keep in mind the purpose your clip art is serving—to help the reader understand the content. It should be appropriate in both its nature and size. It should also be appropriate in its representation of gender. A recent study revealed that much of the clip art bundled with today's software programs is biased.[2] Be sure to select your clip art to avoid the gender, race, and age bias. Also, if it is copyrighted, you need permission to use it.

---

[1] Ellen D. Hoadley, "Investigating the Effects of Color," *Communications of the ACM* 33, no. 2 (February 1990), p. 121.

[2] Marilyn A. Dyrud, "An Exploration of Gender Bias in Computer Clip Art, *Business Communication Quarterly* 60, no. 4 (December 1997), pp. 30–51.

Clear Evidence of the Value of Accurate Charts

"To what do you attribute your company's success?" asked the interviewer.

"A line chart," replied the executive. "In the early years of our company, we had some real problems. Productivity was low, and we were losing money. So to impress our problem on our workers, I had a line chart painted on the wall of our main building. Every day, when the workers arrived, they saw our profit picture. Well, the profit line kept going down. It went from the third floor, to the second, to the first, to ground level. Then we had to bring in digging equipment to keep the line going. But keep it going we did—until the line dramatically reversed direction."

"The workers finally got the message?" asked the interviewer.

"No," replied the executive, "the digger struck oil."

NUMBERING

Except for minor tabular displays that are actually a part of the text, you should number all the graphics in the report. Many schemes of numbering are available to you, depending on the makeup of the graphics.

> ■ Number graphics consecutively by type.

If you have many graphics that fall into two or more categories, you may number each of the categories consecutively. For example, if your report is illustrated by six tables, five charts, and six maps, you may number these graphics Table 1, Table 2, . . . Table 6; Chart 1, Chart 2, . . . Chart 5; and Map 1, Map 2, . . . Map 6.

But if your graphics comprise a wide mixture of types, you may number them in two groups: tables and figures. Figures, a miscellaneous grouping, may include all types other than tables. To illustrate, consider a report containing three tables, two maps, three charts, one diagram, and one photograph. You could number these graphics Table 1, Table 2, and Table 3 and Figure 1, Figure 2, . . . Figure 7. By convention, tables are not grouped with other types of graphics. But it would not be wrong to group and number as figures all graphics other than tables even if the group contained sufficient subgroups (charts, maps, and the like) to permit separate numbering of each of them.

> ■ Figures are a miscellaneous grouping of types. Number tables separately.

CONSTRUCTION OF TITLES

Every graphic should have a title that adequately describes its contents. Like the headings used in other parts of the report, the title of the graphic has the objective of concisely covering the contents. As a check of content coverage, you might well use the journalist's five Ws—*who, what, where, when, why,* and sometimes you might also use *how* (the classification principle). But because conciseness is also desired, it is not always necessary to include all the Ws in the title. A title of a chart comparing the annual sales volume of the Texas and California branches of the Brill Company for the years 1997–98 might be constructed as follows:

> ■ The titles should describe content clearly (consider the five Ws—who, what, where, when, why).

Who: Brill Company

What: Annual sales

Where: Texas and California branches

When: 1997–98

Why: For comparison

The title might read, "Comparative Annual Sales of Texas and California Branches of the Brill Company, 1997–98." For even more conciseness, you could use a major title and subtitle. The major title might read, "A Texas and California Sales Comparison"; the subtitle might read, "Brill Company 1997–98."

PLACEMENT OF TITLES

- The conventional placement of titles is at the top for tables and at the bottom for charts. But many place all titles at the top.

Titles of tables conventionally appear above the tabular display; titles of all other types of graphics conventionally appear below it. It is also conventional to use a larger type for table titles than for the titles of other graphics. There has been a trend toward the use of lowercase type for all illustration titles and to place the titles of both tables and figures at the top. In fact, most presentation software defaults to the top. These practices are simple and logical; yet you should follow the conventional practices for the more formal reports.

FOOTNOTES AND ACKNOWLEDGMENTS

- Use footnotes to explain or elaborate.

Parts of a graphic sometimes require special explanation or elaboration. When this happens, as when similar situations arise in connection with the text of the report, you should use footnotes. Such footnotes are concise explanations placed below the illustration and keyed to the part explained by means of a superscript (raised) number or symbol (asterisk, dagger, double dagger, and so on). Footnotes for tables are best placed immediately below the graphic presentation. Footnotes for other graphic forms follow the illustration when the title is placed at the bottom of the page.

- Acknowledge source of data with note below.

Usually, a source acknowledgment is the bottom entry made in the graphic context. By *source acknowledgment* we mean a reference to the body or authority that deserves the credit for gathering the data used in the illustration. The entry consists simply of the word *Source* followed by a colon and the source name. A source note for data based on information gathered by the U.S. Department of Commerce might read like this:

Source: U.S. Department of Commerce

- "Source: Primary" is the proper note for data you gathered.

If you or your staff collected the data, you may either omit the source note or give the source as "Primary," in which case the note would read like this:

Source: Primary

CONSTRUCTING TEXTUAL GRAPHICS

- Graphics fall into two general categories: (1) textual (words and numerals) and (2) visual (pictures).

Graphics for communicating report information fall into two general categories: those that communicate primarily by their textual content (words and numerals) and those that communicate primarily by some form of picture. Included in the textual group are tables, in-text displays, and a variety of flow and process charts (Gantt, flow, organization, and such).

TABLES

- A table is an orderly arrangement of information.

A *table* is an orderly arrangement of information in rows and columns. As we have noted, tables are not truly graphic (not really pictures). But they communicate like graphics, and they have many of the characteristics of graphics.

- You may use general-purpose tables (those containing broad information),

Two basic types of tables are available to you—the general-purpose table and the special-purpose table. General-purpose tables cover a broad area of information. For example, a table reviewing the answers to all the questions in a survey is a general-purpose table. Such tables usually belong in the appendix.

- or you may use special-purpose tables (those covering a specific area of information).

Special-purpose tables are prepared for one special purpose—to illustrate a particular part of the report. They contain information that could be included with related information in a general-purpose table. For example, a table presenting the answer to one of the questions in a survey is a special-purpose table. Such tables belong in the report text near the discussion of their contents.

- See Figure 13.1 for details of table arrangement.

Aside from the title, footnotes, and source designation previously discussed, a table contains stubs, heads, and columns and rows of data, as shown in Figure 13.1. Stubs are the titles of the rows of data, and heads are the titles of the columns. The heads, however, may be divided into subheads—or column heads, as they are sometimes called.

TABLE 6.1 Good Arrangement of the Parts of a Typical Table

Stub Head	TABLE NO. Table Title*			
	Spanner Head			
	Column Head	Column Head	Column Head	Column Head
Stub	XXX	XXX	XXX	XXX
Stub	XXX	XXX	XXX	XXX
Stub	XXX	XXX	XXX	XXX
Stub	XXX	XXX	XXX	XXX
"	"	"	"	"
"	"	"	"	"
"	"	"	"	"
"	"	"	"	"
"	"	"	"	"
"	"	"	"	"
Total	XXX	XXX	XXX	XXX

*Footnotes
Source:

The construction of text tables is largely influenced by their purpose. Nevertheless, a few general construction rules may be listed:

- If rows are long, the stubs may be repeated at the right.

- The em dash (—) or the abbreviation *n.a.* (or *N.A.* or *NA*), but not the zero, is used to indicate data not available.

- Footnote references to numbers in the table should be keyed with asterisks, daggers, double daggers, and such. Numbers followed by footnote reference numbers may cause confusion. Small letters of the alphabet can be used when many references are made.

- Totals and subtotals should appear whenever they help the purpose of the table. The totals may be for each column and sometimes for each row. Row totals are usually placed at the right; but when they need emphasis, they may be placed at the left. Likewise, column totals are generally placed at the bottom of the column, but they may be placed at the top when the writer wants to emphasize them. A ruled line (usually a double one) separates the totals from their components.

- The units in which the data are recorded must be clear. Unit descriptions (bushels, acres, pounds, and the like) appropriately appear above the columns, as part of the headings or subheadings. If the data are in dollars, however, placing the dollar mark ($) before the first entry in each column is sufficient.

IN-TEXT DISPLAYS

Tabular information need not always be presented in formal tables. In fact, short arrangements of data may be presented more effectively as parts of the text. Such arrangements are generally made as either leaderwork or text tabulations.

- Tabular information can also be presented as (1) leaderwork (as illustrated here),

Leaderwork is the presentation of tabular material in the text without titles or rules. (*Leaders* are the repeated dots with intervening spaces.) Typically, a colon precedes the tabulation, as in this illustration:

The August sales of the representatives in the Western Region were as follows:

Charles B. Brown $13,517
Thelma Capp 19,703
Bill E. Knauth 18,198

Text tabulations are simple tables, usually with column heads and some rules. But they are not numbered, and they have no titles. They are made to read with the text, as in this example:

■ (2) text tabulations (as illustrated here), and

In August the sales of the representatives in the Western Region increased sharply from those for the preceding month, as these figures show:

Representative	July Sales	August Sales	Increase
Charles B. Brown	$12,819	$13,517	$ 698
Thelma Capp	17,225	19,703	2,478
Bill E. Knauth	16,838	18,198	1,360

■ (3) bullet lists.

Bulleted lists are listings of points arranged with bullets (•) to set them off. These lists can have a title that covers all the points, or they can appear without titles, as they appear at various places in this book. When you use this arrangement, make the points grammatically parallel. If the points have subparts, use sub-bullets for them. Make the sub-bullets different by color, size, shape, or weight. Darts, check marks, squares, or triangles can be used for the secondary bullets.

FLOWCHARTS AND PROCESS CHARTS

■ Various specialized management charts are useful in reports—for example, organization charts, Gantt charts, and flowcharts.

If you have studied business management, you know that administrators use a variety of specialized charts in their work. Often these charts are a part of the information presented in reports. Perhaps the most common of these is the *organization chart* (see Figure 13.2). These charts show hierarchy of positions, divisions, departments, and such in an organization. *Gantt charts* are graphic presentations that show planning and scheduling activities. As the word implies, a *flowchart* (see Figure 13.3) shows the sequence of activities in a process. Traditionally, flowcharts use specific designs and symbols to show process variations. A variation of the flowchart is the *decision tree*. This chart helps one follow a path

FIGURE 13.2 An Organization Chart with Employee Names

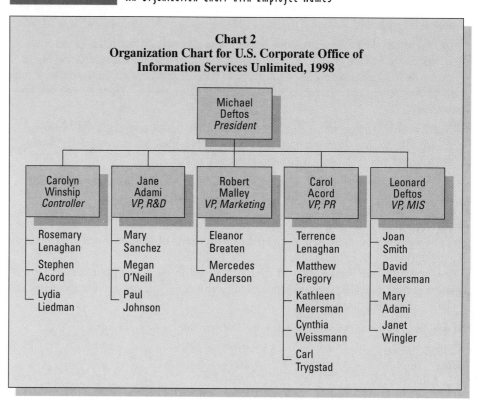

FIGURE 13.3 A Flowchart

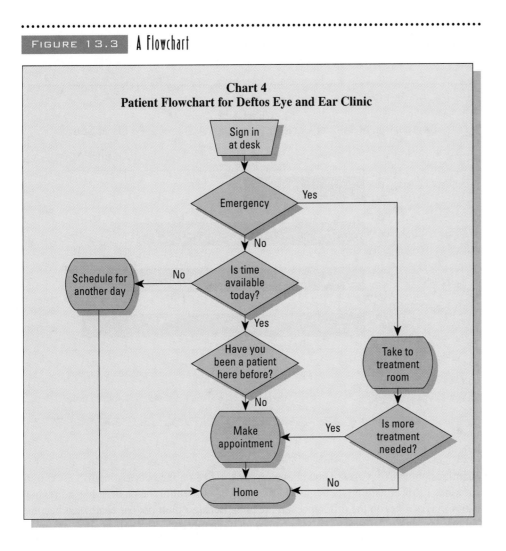

**Chart 4
Patient Flowchart for Deftos Eye and Ear Clinic**

to an appropriate decision. You can easily construct these charts with presentation and drawing software.

CONSTRUCTING VISUAL GRAPHICS

The truly visual types of graphics include a variety of forms—data-generated charts as well as artwork and photographs. Data-generated charts are ones built with raw data and include bar, pie, and line charts and all their variations and combinations. Artwork includes maps, diagrams, drawings, cartoons, and such.

> ■ Visual graphics include data-generated charts, photographs, and artwork.

BAR CHARTS

Simple bar charts compare differences in quantities by differences in the lengths of the bars representing those quantities. You should use them primarily to show comparisons of quantity changes over time or over geographic distances.

> ■ Simple bar charts compare differences in quantities by varying bar lengths.

As shown in Figure 13.4, the main parts of the bar chart are the bars and the grid (the field on which the bars are placed). The bars, which may be arranged horizontally or vertically, should be of equal width. You should identify each bar, usually with a caption at the left or bottom. The grid (field) on which the bars are placed is usually needed to show the magnitudes of the bars, and the units (dollars, pounds, miles, and such) are identified by the scale caption below.

When you need to compare two or three different kinds of quantities in one chart, you can use a *multiple* (or *clustered*) *bar chart*. In such a chart, bars show the values of the

> ■ Multiple bar charts are useful in comparing two or three kinds of quantities.

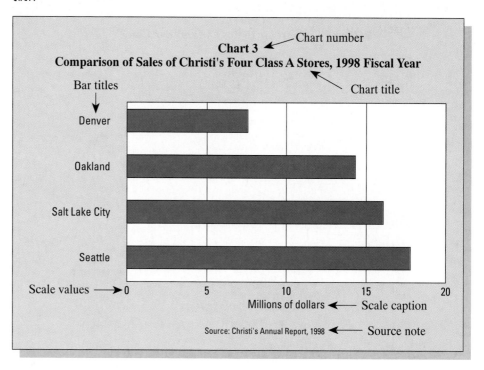

quantities compared. Cross-hatching, colors, or the like on the bars distinguish the different kinds of information (see Figure 13.5). Somewhere within the chart, a legend (explanation) gives a key to the differences in the bars. Because multiple bar charts can become cluttered, usually you should not compare more than three kinds of information on one of them.

When you need to show plus and minus differences, bilateral bar charts are useful.

When you need to show plus and minus differences, you can use *bilateral bar charts.* The bars of these charts begin at a central point of reference and may go either up or down, as illustrated in Figure 13.6. Bar titles appear either within, above, or below the bars, depending on which placement fits best. Bilateral bar charts are especially good for showing percentage changes, but you may use them for any series in which plus and minus quantities are present.

To compare subdivisions of bars, use a subdivided bar chart.

If you need to compare subdivisions of bars, you can use a *subdivided (stacked) bar chart.* As shown in Figure 13.7, such a chart divides each bar into its parts. It distinguishes these parts by color, cross-hatching, or the like; and it explains these differences in a legend. This subdivided bar may be difficult for your reader to interpret since both the beginning and ending points need to be found. Then the reader has to subtract to find the size of the bar component. Multiple bar charts or pie charts do not introduce such errors.

Two-dimensional bars on two-dimensional axes are easiest for readers to use.

Another feature that can lead to reader error in interpreting bar chart data is the use of three dimensions. A recent study evaluated the speed and accuracy of readers' interpretation of two-dimensional bars on two-dimensional axes with three-dimensional bars on two-dimensional axes and three-dimensional bars on three-dimensional axes. The results showed that readers were able to extract information from the bar chart fastest and most accurately when it was presented in the simple two-dimensional bar on the two-dimensional axis.[3]

You can also use such a chart for comparing subdivisions of percentages.

A special form of subdivided (stacked) bar chart is used to compare the subdivisions of

---

[3] Theophilus B. A. Addo, "The Effects of Dimensionality in Computer Graphics," *The Journal of Business Communication* 31, no. 4 (1994), p. 253.

FIGURE 13.5 Illustration of a Multiple Bar Chart

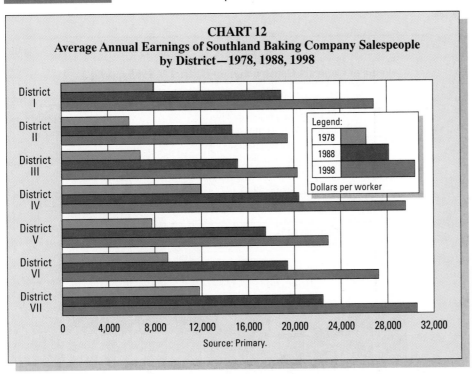

CHART 12
Average Annual Earnings of Southland Baking Company Salespeople by District—1978, 1988, 1998

Legend:
1978
1988
1998
Dollars per worker

Source: Primary.

FIGURE 13.6 Illustration of a Bilateral Bar Chart

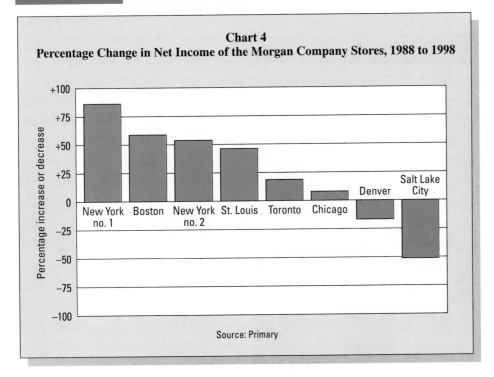

Chart 4
Percentage Change in Net Income of the Morgan Company Stores, 1988 to 1998

Source: Primary

percentages. In this form, all the bars are equal in length, for each represents 100 percent. Only the subdivisions within the bars vary. The objective of this form is to compare differences in how wholes are divided. The component parts may be labeled, as shown in Figure 13.8, but they may also be explained in a legend.

FIGURE 13.7 Illustration of a Subdivided (Stacked) Bar Chart with Bars of Unequal Lengths

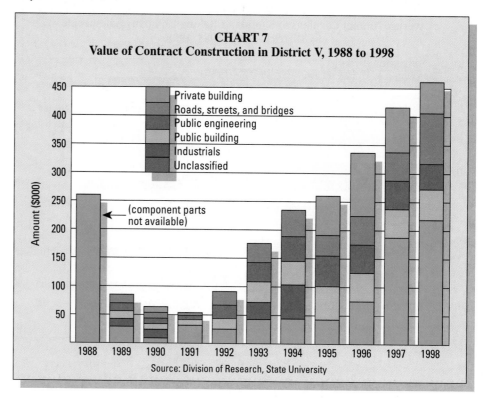

CHART 7
Value of Contract Construction in District V, 1988 to 1998

Source: Division of Research, State University

FIGURE 13.8 Illustration of a Subdivided Bar Chart with Bars of Equal Lengths

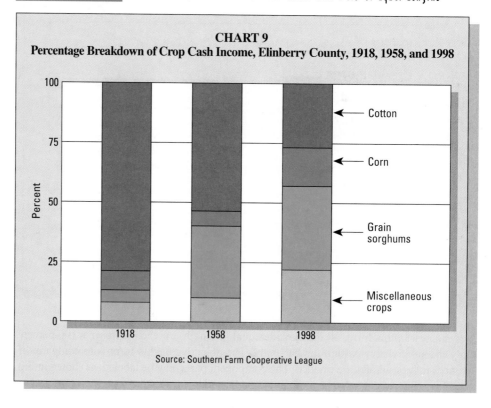

CHART 9
Percentage Breakdown of Crop Cash Income, Elinberry County, 1918, 1958, and 1998

Source: Southern Farm Cooperative League

PIE CHARTS

Also important in comparing the subdivisions of wholes is the *pie chart* (see Figure 13.9). As the name implies, pie charts show the whole of the information being studied as a pie (circle), and the parts of this whole as slices of the pie. The slices may be distinguished by labeling and color or cross-hatching. A single slice can be emphasized by exploding—pulling out—a piece. Because it is hard to judge the values of the slices with the naked eye, it is good to include the percentage values within or near each slice. A good rule to follow is to begin slicing the pie at the 12 o'clock position and then to move around clockwise. It is also good to arrange the slices in descending order from largest to smallest.

In using pie charts to compare two or more wholes, you should never vary the sizes of the pies. Such comparisons are almost meaningless. The human eye simply cannot judge circle sizes accurately.

■ Pie charts show subdivisions of a whole.

■ But do not vary sizes of the pies.

LINE CHARTS

Line charts are useful in showing changes of information over time. For example, changes in prices, sales totals, employment, or production over a period of years can be shown well in a line chart.

In constructing a line chart, you draw the information to be illustrated as a continuous line on a grid (see Figure 13.10). The grid is the area in which the line is displayed. It is scaled to show time changes from left to right across the chart (X-axis) and quantity changes from bottom to top (Y-axis). You should mark clearly the scale values and the time periods. They should be in equal increments.

You may also compare two or more series on the same line chart (see Figure 13.11). In such a comparison, you should clearly distinguish the lines by color or form (dots, dashes, dots and dashes, and the like). You should clearly label them by a legend somewhere in the chart. But the number of series that you may compare on one line chart is limited. As a practical rule, the maximum number is four or five.

■ Line charts show changes over time.

■ The line appears on a grid (a scaled area) and is continuous.

■ Two or more lines may appear on one chart.

FIGURE 13.9 Illustration of a Pie Chart

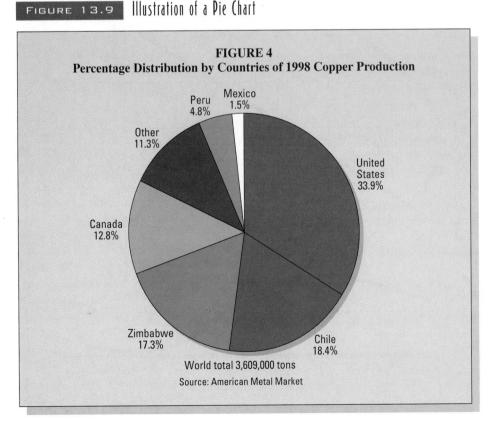

FIGURE 4
Percentage Distribution by Countries of 1998 Copper Production

Mexico 1.5%
Peru 4.8%
Other 11.3%
United States 33.9%
Canada 12.8%
Zimbabwe 17.3%
Chile 18.4%

World total 3,609,000 tons
Source: American Metal Market

FIGURE 13.10   A Line Chart with One Series

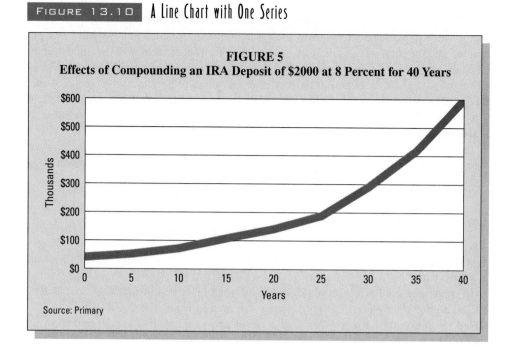

FIGURE 5
Effects of Compounding an IRA Deposit of $2000 at 8 Percent for 40 Years

Source: Primary

FIGURE 13.11   A Line Chart Comparing More than One Series

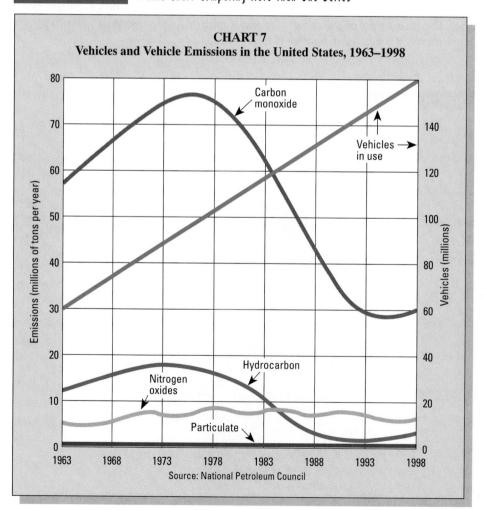

CHART 7
Vehicles and Vehicle Emissions in the United States, 1963–1998

Source: National Petroleum Council

It is also possible to show parts of a series by use of an *area* chart—sometimes called a *surface* chart. Such a chart, however, can show only one series. You should construct this type of chart, as shown in Figure 13.12, with a top line representing the total of the series. Then, starting from the base, you should cumulate the parts, beginning with the largest and ending with the smallest. You may use cross-hatching or coloring to distinguish the parts.

■ Area charts show the makeup of a series.

Line charts that show a range of data for particular times are called *variance* or *hi-lo* charts (see Figure 13.13). Some variance charts show high and low points as well as the mean, median, or mode. When used to chart daily stock prices, they typically include closing price in addition to the high and low. When you use points other than high and low, be sure to make it clear what these points are.

■ Variance charts show high and low points—sometimes more.

Line charts are simple to construct, but you should guard against three common errors in their construction. The first is the error of violating the zero beginning of the series. For accuracy, you should begin the scale at zero. But when all the information shown in the chart has high values, it is awkward to show the entire scale from zero to the highest value. For example, if the quantities compared range from 1,320 to 1,350 and the chart shows the entire area from zero to 1,350, the line showing these quantities would be almost straight and very high on the chart. Your solution in this case is not to begin the scale at a high number (say, 1,300), for this would distort the information, but to begin at zero and show a scale break. Realize, however, that while this makes the differences easier to see, it does exaggerate the differences. The following two ways of showing scale breaks are recommended:

■ But avoid these errors: (1) failure to start at zero (you can show scale breaks),

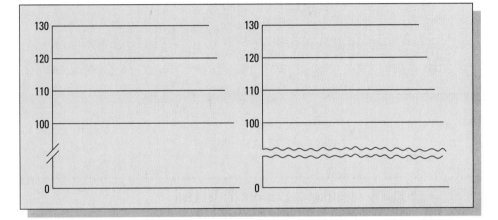

A second error in constructing line charts is failing to keep the chart scales uniform. All the dimensions from left to right (X-axis) should be equal; and the dimensions from bottom to top (Y-axis) should be equal. Otherwise, an incorrect picture would be shown.

■ (2) failure to keep scales uniform,

A third error is using grid distances that do not give a true picture of the information. Expanding a scale can change the appearance of the line. For example, if the values on a chart are plotted ½ inch apart instead of ¹⁄₁₆ inch apart, changes appear much more suddenly. Determining the distances that present the most accurate picture is a matter of judgment.

■ (3) use of distances on the grid that do not show the true picture.

STATISTICAL MAPS

You may also use *statistical maps* to communicate quantitative as well as geographic information. They are useful primarily when quantitative information is to be compared by geographic areas. On such maps, the geographic areas are clearly outlined; and some graphic technique is used to show the differences between areas. Of the numerous techniques available to you, these are the most common:

■ You can show quantitative information for geographic areas in a statistical map.

■ Showing quantitative differences of areas by color, shading, or cross-hatching is perhaps the most popular technique (see Figure 13.14). Of course, maps using this technique must have a legend to explain the quantitative meanings of the various colors, cross-hatchings, and so forth.

■ Here are some specific instructions for statistical maps.

FIGURE 13.12 Illustration of an Area Line Chart

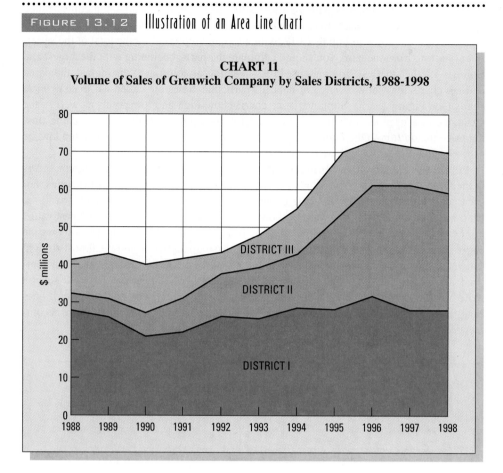

CHART 11
Volume of Sales of Grenwich Company by Sales Districts, 1988-1998

FIGURE 13.13 Illustration of a Variance (Hi-Lo) Chart

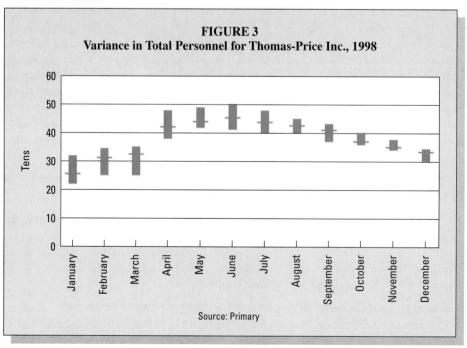

FIGURE 3
Variance in Total Personnel for Thomas-Price Inc., 1998

Source: Primary

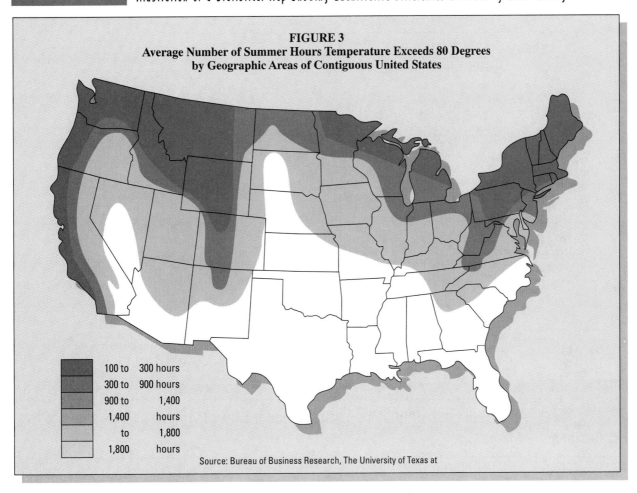

FIGURE 3
Average Number of Summer Hours Temperature Exceeds 80 Degrees
by Geographic Areas of Contiguous United States

	100 to 300 hours
	300 to 900 hours
	900 to 1,400
	1,400 hours
	to 1,800
	1,800 hours

Source: Bureau of Business Research, The University of Texas at

- Some form of chart may be placed within each geographic area to depict the quantity for that area, as illustrated in Figure 13.15. Bar charts and pie charts are commonly used in such statistical maps.

- Placing the quantities in numerical form within each geographic area, as shown in Figure 13.16, is another widely used technique.

- Dots, each representing a definite quantity (see Figure 13.17), may be placed within the geographic areas in proportion to the quantities for those areas.

PICTOGRAMS

A *pictogram* is a bar chart that uses bars made of pictures. The pictures are typically drawings of the items being compared. For example, a company's profits over a period of years, instead of being shown by ordinary bars (formed by straight lines), could be shown by bar drawings of stacks of coins. This type of bar chart is a pictogram (see Figure 13.18).

In constructing a pictogram, you should follow the procedures you used in constructing bar charts and two special rules. First, you must make all the picture units equal in size. That is, you must base the comparisons wholly on the number of picture units used and never on variation in the areas of the units. The reason for this rule is obvious. The human eye is grossly inadequate in comparing geometric designs that vary in more than one dimension. Second, you should select pictures or symbols that fit the information to be illustrated. In comparing the cruise lines of the world, for example, you might use ships. In comparing computers used in the world's major countries, you might use computers. The meaning of the drawings you use must be immediately clear to the readers.

■ Pictograms are bar charts made with pictures.

■ In constructing pictograms, follow the procedure for making bar charts.

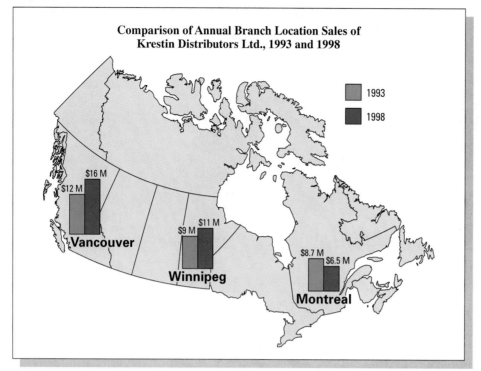

Comparison of Annual Branch Location Sales of
Krestin Distributors Ltd., 1993 and 1998

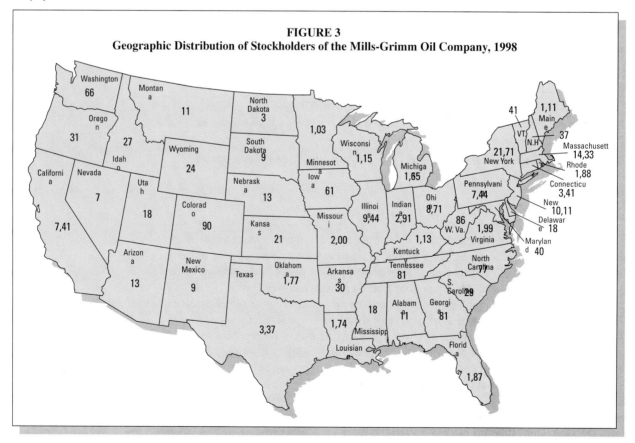

FIGURE 3
Geographic Distribution of Stockholders of the Mills-Grimm Oil Company, 1998

· ·

FIGURE 13.17   Illustration of a Statistical Map Using Dots to Show Quantitative Differences by Geographic Areas

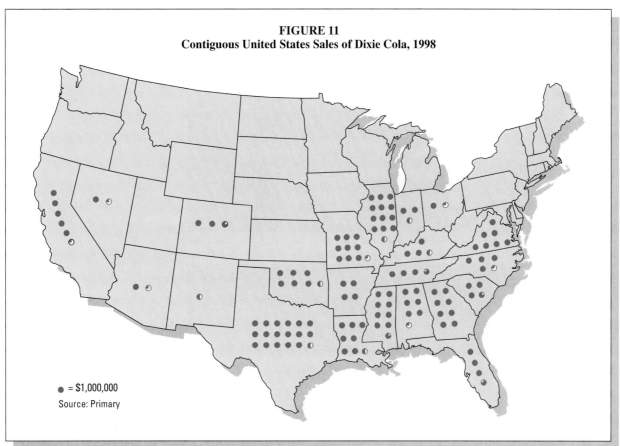

FIGURE 11
Contiguous United States Sales of Dixie Cola, 1998

● = $1,000,000
Source: Primary

· ·

FIGURE 13.18   Illustration of the Pictogram

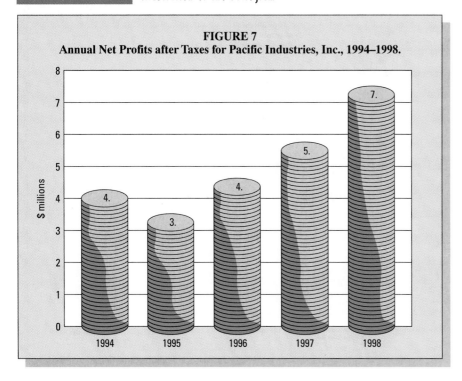

FIGURE 7
Annual Net Profits after Taxes for Pacific Industries, Inc., 1994–1998.

FIGURE 13.19 Illustration of a Combination Chart (Variance, Bar)

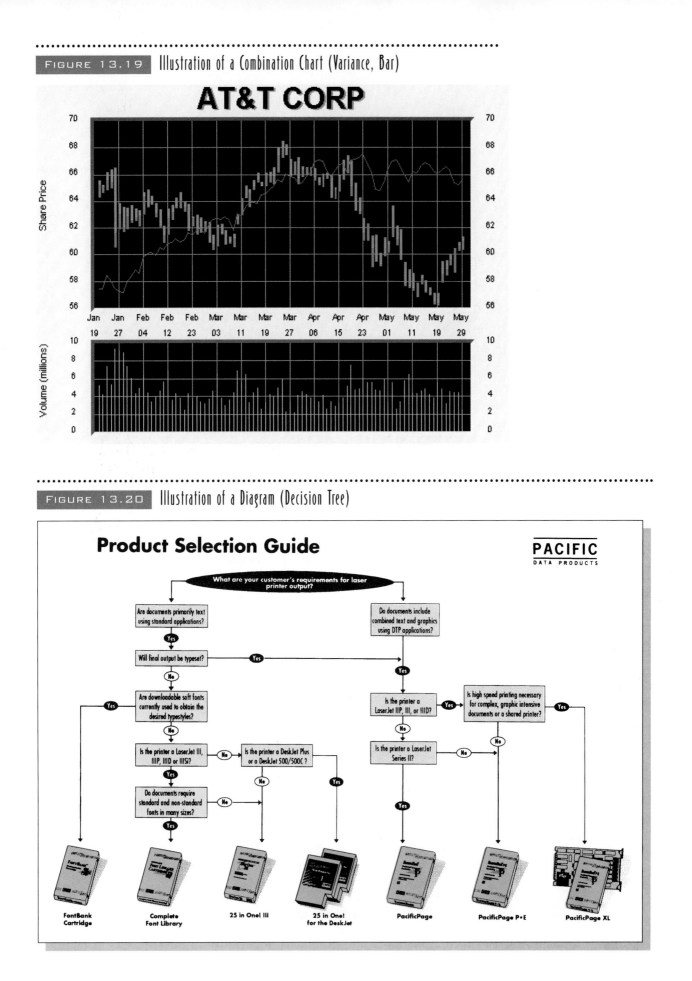

FIGURE 13.20 Illustration of a Diagram (Decision Tree)

FIGURE 13.21 Illustration of a Drawing

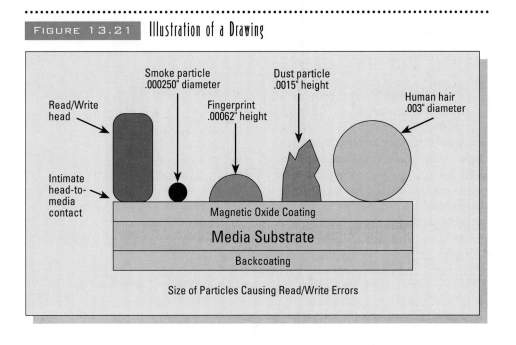

Size of Particles Causing Read/Write Errors

COMBINATION CHARTS

Combination charts often serve readers extremely well by allowing them to see relationships of different kinds of data. The example in Figure 13.19 shows the reader the price of stock over time (the trend) as well as the volume of sales over time (comparisons). It allows the reader to detect whether the change in volume affects the price of the stock. This kind of information would be difficult to get from raw data.

■ Sometimes a combination of chart types is effective.

OTHER GRAPHICS

The types of graphics discussed thus far are the ones most commonly used. Other types also may be helpful. *Photographs* may serve a useful communication purpose. *Diagrams* (see Figure 13.20), and drawings (see Figure 13.21) may help simplify a complicated explanation or description. *Icons* are another useful type of graphic. You can create new icons and use them consistently, or you can draw from an existing body of icons with easily recognized meanings, such as ⬡ . Even carefully selected *cartoons* can be used effectively. *Video clips* and *animation* are now used in electronic documents. For all practical purposes, any graphic is acceptable as long as it helps communicate the true story. The possibilities are almost unlimited.

■ Other graphics available to you are diagrams, drawings, and photographs—even cartoons.

USING COMPUTER GRAPHICS

If you have access to the appropriate computer, printer, and software, you can use them to prepare graphics quickly and easily. Unlike the earlier versions, today's computer graphics software programs are simple and easy to use. With some of them, you need only choose the form of graphic you want and then, using simple English instructions, supply the information the program requests. For example, when using one popular program to construct a bar chart, you simply respond "Bar" to the initial request for chart type. Then you supply plain English answers to a series of questions covering number, names, and values of bars, and the like. As you supply the answers, the results appear on the screen. After producing the bar chart on the screen, you can manipulate its design until it meets your requirements. When you are satisfied with the design you see on the screen, you print the chart in black and white or in color, depending on your equipment.

■ Easy-to-use computer graphics are available.

Because computer graphics are easy to make and can be exciting and colorful, you may be tempted to overuse them. Keep in mind that the one requirement for including a graphic

■ But do not overuse them.

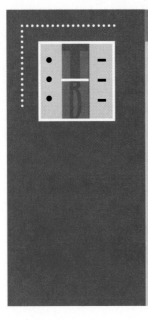

Practicing Visual Ethics

As you have learned in this chapter, graphics can serve several useful purposes for the business writer. However, the writer needs to be accountable in using graphics to present graphics that in the eye and mind of the reader communicate accurately and completely. To do this, the careful writer pays attention to both the design and content of the graphic. These are particularly important, for readers often skim text but see the graphics. Research shows that people remember images much better and longer than text.

The following guides will help you in evaluating the graphics you use:

- Does the document's design create accurate expectations?
- Does the story told match the data?
- Is the implied message congruent with the actual message?
- Will the impact of the visual on your audience be appropriate?
- Does the visual convey all critical information free of distortion?
- Are the data depicted accurately?

Adapted from Donna S. Kienzler, "Visual Ethics," *The Journal of Business Communication*, April 1997, pp. 171–87.

in a report is usefulness in communicating the report message. Too many graphics can clutter the report and cause confusion.

Also keep in mind that clarity is a major requirement of graphics and that even computer-generated graphics can be unclear. The possibilities for changing and enhancing graphics can lead to interesting, beautiful, and exciting—but confusing—results. Thus, the purpose of graphics—to communicate instantly clear messages—is defeated. Even though the software package will do much of the preparation for you, you should take care to follow the guidelines presented in this chapter as you construct graphics by computer.

> ■ Make sure the graphics you use help to communicate.

Currently available software packages are capable of producing all the common forms of graphics, and more.

SUMMARY BY CHAPTER OBJECTIVES

1 Determine which parts of your report should be communicated by graphics and where in the report the graphics should appear.

1. Because graphics are a part of the communication in a report, you should plan for them.
   - But remember that they supplement the writing; they do not replace it.
   - Use them wherever they help communicate the report information.
   - Place them near the text part they illustrate.

- Invite the readers to look at them at the appropriate place.
- Place in the appendix those that you do not discuss in the text.

2. Construct each graphic carefully, following these general instructions:
   - Give each the size and arrangement its contents justify.
   - Choose a readable type.
   - Use rules, borders, and color when they help.
   - Use clip art appropriately.
   - Number the graphics consecutively by type.
   - Construct titles for them using the five Ws (*who, what, where, when, why*) and 1 H (*how*) as a checklist.
   - Use footnotes and acknowledgments when needed, placing them below the graphic.

3. Construct tables to display the larger groups of data.
   - Use general-purpose tables for information that is broad in scope.
   - Use special-purpose tables for information that is specific in scope.
   - See Figure 13.1 for the details of table construction.
   - Use in-text displays for less formal presentations.
     — You can do this as leaderwork.
     — You can do it as text tabulations or bulleted lists.
   - Use flowcharts and process charts to show activity sequences.

4. In selecting a graphic, consider these primary uses of each:
   - *Simple bar chart*—shows quantity comparisons over time or over geographic distances.
   - *Multiple bar chart*—shows two or three kinds of quantities on one chart.
   - *Bilateral bar chart*—shows plus and minus differences and is especially good for showing percentage changes.
   - *Stacked (subdivided) bar chart*—used to compare differences in the division of wholes.
   - *Pie chart*—used to show how wholes are divided.
   - *Line chart*—useful in showing changes over time. Variations include belt charts, surface charts, and variance charts.
   - *Statistical map*—shows quantitative differences by geographic areas.
   - *Pictogram*—shows quantitative differences in picture form.

   For instructions on preparing each, review the text illustrations.

   Apply other graphics to serve special needs:
   - Photographs.
   - Diagrams and drawings.
   - Icons.
   - Cartoons.
   - Video clips and animation.

5. When you have the equipment and software, prepare graphics on your computer.
   - They are easy to construct with modern software.
   - But do not overuse them.
   - Make sure you follow the chapter guidelines when you prepare computer graphics.

2 Know the general mechanics of constructing graphics—size, layout, type, rules and borders, color and cross-hatching, clip art, numbering, titles, title placement, and footnotes and acknowledgments.

3 Construct textual graphics such as tables, in-text displays, and flowcharts and process charts.

4 Construct and use visual graphics such as bar charts, pie charts, line charts, pictograms, and combination charts.

5 Explain computer graphics as they relate to visual communication in a report.

CRITICAL THINKING QUESTIONS

1. For the past 20 years, Professor Kupenheimer has required that his students include five graphics in the long, formal report he assigns them to prepare. Evaluate this requirement.

2. Because it was easier to do, a report writer prepared each of the graphics on a full page. Some of these graphics were extremely complex; some were very simple. Comment on this policy.

3. "I have placed every graphic near the place I write about it. The reader can see the graphic without any *additional* help from me. It just doesn't make sense to direct the reader's attention to the graphics with words." Evaluate this comment.

4. A report has five maps, four tables, one chart, one diagram, and one photograph. How would you number these graphics?

5. How would you number these graphics in a report: seven tables, six charts, nine maps?

6. Discuss the logic of showing scale breaks in a line chart grid.

7. Discuss the dangers of using illogical proportions in constructing a chart grid.

8. Discuss the techniques that may be used to show quantitative differences by area on a statistical map.

9. Select data that are ideally suited for presentation in a pictogram. Explain why use of a pictogram is good for this case.

10. Discuss the dangers of using pictograms.

CRITICAL THINKING EXERCISES

1. Construct a complete, concise title for a bar chart showing annual attendance at home football (or basketball, or hockey) games at your school from 1988 to the present.

2. The table prepared in Question 1 requires an explanation for the years 1990 to the present. In each of those years, one extra home game was played. Explain how you would provide the necessary explanation.

3. For each of the areas of information described below, which form of graphic would you use? Explain your decision.
   a. Record of annual sales for the Kenyon Company for the past 20 years.
   b. Comparison of Kenyon Company sales, by product, for this year and last year.
   c. Monthly production of the automobile industry in units.
   d. Breakdown of how the average middle-income family in your state (or province) disposes of its income dollar.
   e. How middle-income families spend their income dollar as compared with how low-income families spend their income dollar.
   f. Comparison of sales for the past two years for each of the B&B Company's 14 sales districts. The districts cover all 50 states, Canada, and Puerto Rico.
   g. National production of automobiles from 1930 to present, broken down by manufacturer.

4. For each of the following sets of facts, (*a*) determine the graphic (or graphics) that would be best, (*b*) defend your choice, and (*c*) construct the graphic.

   a. Average (mean) amount of life insurance owned by Fidelity Life Insurance Company policyholders. Classification is by annual income.

Income	Average Life Insurance
Under $30,000	$15,245
$30,000–34,999	24,460
$35,000–39,999	36,680
$40,000–44,999	49,875
$45,000–49,999	61,440
$50,000 and over	86,390

   b. Profits and losses for D and H Food Stores, by store, 1994–98, in dollars.

Year	Able City	Baker	Charleston	Total
1994	23,421	13,241	9,766	46,428
1995	22,911	−1,173	21,847	43,585
1996	23,843	−2,241	21,606	43,208
1997	22,673	6,865	23,551	53,089
1998	23,008	9,145	25,482	57,635

   c. Share of real estate tax payments by ward for Bigg City, 1993 and 1998, in thousands of dollars.

	1993	1998
Ward 1	17.1	21.3
Ward 2	10.2	31.8
Ward 3	19.5	21.1
Ward 4	7.8	18.2
City total	54.6	92.4

d. Percentage change in sales by employee, 1997–1998, District IV, Abbott, Inc.

Employee	Percentage Change
Joan Abraham	+ 7.3
Helen Calmes	+ 2.1
Edward Sanchez	– 7.5
Clifton Nevers	+41.6
Wilson Platt	+ 7.4
Clara Ruiz	+11.5
David Schlimmer	– 4.8
Phil Wirks	– 3.6

5. The basic blood types are O, A, B, and AB. These can be either positive or negative. With some basic research, determine what percentage of each type people in the United States have. Choose an appropriate graph type and create it to convey the data.

6. Through your research, find the approximate milligrams of caffeine in the following items and create an appropriate graphic for Affiliated Food Products, Inc. to illustrate your findings.
   5-oz. cup of coffee (drip brewed)
   7-oz. glass of iced tea
   6-oz. glass of soda with caffeine
   1-oz. dark chocolate, semisweet

7. Choose five or six outdoor summer sport activities. In a graphic identify the activity and whether it affects cardiovascular, arms, legs, back, or abdominals. You can assume these activities can affect more than one fitness zone. You work for the Parks and Recreation Department of a city of your choosing.

Other Forms of Business Communication

Informal Oral Communication

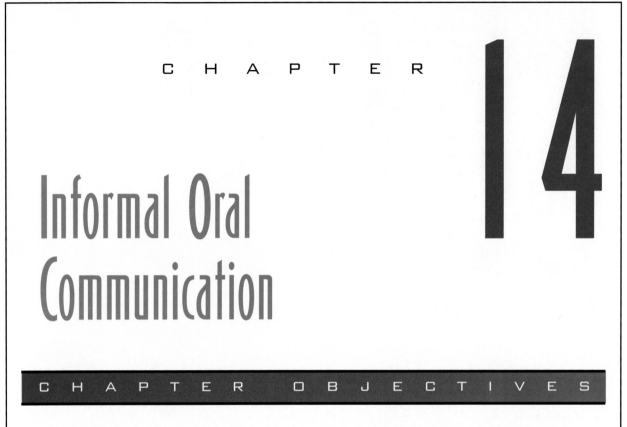

Upon completing this chapter, you will be able to understand and use good speaking and listening techniques, conduct interviews, lead and participate in meetings, communicate by telephone, and dictate messages. To reach this goal, you should be able to

1 Discuss talking and its key elements.

2 Explain the listening problem and how to solve it.

3 Describe the nature and role of nonverbal communication.

4 Practice good interviewing and listening techniques.

5 Discuss the techniques for conducting and participating in meetings.

6 Describe good telephone and voice-mail techniques.

7 Dictate messages and reports in an organized and effective manner.

Informal Oral Communication on the Job

Your job as assistant director in the Public Relations Department at Mastadon Chemicals, Inc., seems somewhat different from what you expected. It makes full use of your specialized college training, as you expected; but it also involves duties for which you did not train because you did not expect them. Most of these duties seem to involve some form of oral communication. In fact, you probably spend more of your work time in talking and listening than in any other activity.

To illustrate, take today's activities. Early this morning, your boss asked you to interview a prospective employee. After that, you conducted a meeting of the special committee to plan the department's annual picnic. As chairperson, you ran the meeting. It was a disaster, you felt—everybody talking at once, interrupting, arguing. It was a wonder that the committee made any progress. It seemed that everybody wanted to talk but nobody wanted to listen.

In the afternoon, you had other job duties involving oral communication. After you returned from lunch, you must have had a telephone conversation every 20 minutes or so. You felt comfortable with most of these calls, but you thought some of the callers needed a lesson or two in telephone etiquette. Also, you dictated a few letters and emails (using voice recognition on your computer) between telephone calls.

You most certainly do a lot of talking (and listening) on your job, as do most of the people at Mastadon (and just about everywhere else). Oral communication is a vital part of your work. Perhaps you can become better at it by studying the following review of oral communication techniques.

As you know, your work will involve oral as well as written communication. The written communication will probably give you more problems, but the oral communication will take up more of your time. In fact, you are likely to spend more time in oral communication than in any other work activity.

■ You will spend more time talking than writing in business.

Much of the oral communication that goes on in business is the informal, person-to-person communication that occurs whenever people get together. Obviously, we all have experience with this form of communication, and most of us do it reasonably well. But all of us can improve our informal speaking and listening with practice.

■ Most of your oral communication will be informal.

In addition to informal talking and listening, various kinds of other more formal oral communication take place in business. Sometimes businesspeople interview job applicants, departing workers, and workers being evaluated. Sometimes they conduct and participate in committee meetings, conferences, and group discussions. Often they call one another on the telephone. Even their letters and reports are usually begun orally as spoken dictation. And frequently, they are called upon to make formal presentations—speeches, lectures, oral reports, and the like. All of these kinds of oral communication are a part of the work that businesspeople do.

■ But some of it will be formal, as in interviews, meetings, telephone calls, dictation, speeches, and oral reports.

This and the following chapter cover these kinds of oral communication. This chapter reviews the somewhat less formal kinds: informal talking, listening, conducting interviews, participating in meetings, talking by telephone, and dictating. The following chapter presents the two most formal kinds: public speaking and oral reporting. Together, the two chapters should give you an understanding of the types of oral communication situations you will encounter in business.

■ This and the following chapter cover these types of oral communication.

INFORMAL TALKING

As indicated previously, most of us do a reasonably good job of informal talking. In fact, we do such a good job that we often take talking for granted, and we overlook the possibility for improving our talking ability. To improve our talking, we need to be aware of its nature and qualities. As we become aware of these features, we can then improve our informal talking efforts. And when we improve them, other types of talking (interviewing, telephoning, and such) will improve as well. The following paragraphs review the basics of talking.

■ Most people talk reasonably well. But all of us can improve if we know the nature of talking and its qualities.

Voice Input for Creating Business Documents

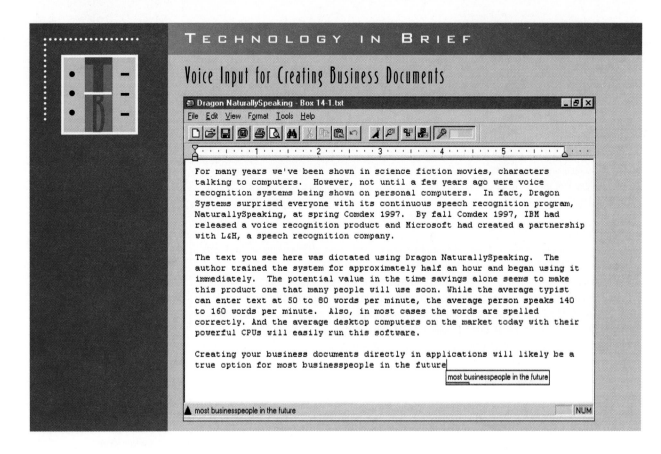

Dragon NaturallySpeaking - Box 14-1.txt

File Edit View Format Tools Help

For many years we've been shown in science fiction movies, characters talking to computers. However, not until a few years ago were voice recognition systems being shown on personal computers. In fact, Dragon Systems surprised everyone with its continuous speech recognition program, NaturallySpeaking, at spring Comdex 1997. By fall Comdex 1997, IBM had released a voice recognition product and Microsoft had created a partnership with L&H, a speech recognition company.

The text you see here was dictated using Dragon NaturallySpeaking. The author trained the system for approximately half an hour and began using it immediately. The potential value in the time savings alone seems to make this product one that many people will use soon. While the average typist can enter text at 50 to 80 words per minute, the average person speaks 140 to 160 words per minute. Also, in most cases the words are spelled correctly. And the average desktop computers on the market today with their powerful CPUs will easily run this software.

Creating your business documents directly in applications will likely be a true option for most businesspeople in the future

most businesspeople in the future

NUM

DEFINITION OF TALKING

- Think about having no words to speak. If you try to express yourself, you probably become frustrated.

Imagine for a few moments what it would be like to have no words to express your ideas. Trying as hard as you can, you have no words to utter to express the meanings in your mind. All that you have to express your thoughts are grunts, groans, and other such utterances. Of course, you have various nonverbal symbols such as pointing your fingers, nodding your head, and the like. As you find yourself increasingly in need of expressing yourself, you probably become more and more emotional and frustrated—to the point of exaggerating the nonverbal symbols and experiencing many physical symptoms such as redness of the face, heavy breathing, and an increased heartbeat.

- Thus, we learn words to control ourselves and the world about us.

More than likely, the foregoing analogy describes the way you learned to talk. As a dependent child, you expressed yourself with screams, cries, and nonverbal symbols. But as you matured, you learned words, and the words greatly reduced the frustrations of the past. They enabled you to communicate with others more exactly. They enabled you to relate better to the world about you and to some extent to control it.

- Talking, then, is the oral expression of knowledge, viewpoints, and emotions through words.

The foregoing review of how you learned to talk gives us the basis for defining talking. From it we can derive this definition: *talking* is the oral expression of knowledge, viewpoints, and emotions through words. Also, from this review we can see that talking replaces many of the body movements we made before we were able to talk. And as we will see, it is supplemented by various body movements we have acquired as we learned to talk—gestures, facial expressions, body positions, and such.

- Think about the best and worst speakers you can imagine. This contrast should give you the qualities of good talking—voice quality, speaking style, word choice, adaptation.

As a first step in improving your talking ability, think for a moment about the qualities you like in a good talker—one whom you would enjoy talking with in ordinary conversation. Then think about the opposite—the worst conversationalist you can imagine. If you will get these two images in mind, you will have a good picture of the characteristics of good talking. Probably this mental picture includes good voice quality, excellence in talking style, accuracy of word choice, and adaptation. As these elements control the overall quality of oral expression, we will now review them.

▌Good talking is the foundation for other types of discourse—interviewing, conducting meetings, telephoning, etc. You should develop good voice quality, perfect effective style, and select words that fit the mind of a listener.

ELEMENTS OF GOOD TALKING

Although the four qualities of good talking are important individually, you should remember that it is their purpose—to communicate better—that is of primary significance. Put differently, you want each of the following four qualities to help you deliver your message better to your listener. It is with that point in mind that we examine them.

■ Qualities of good talking help you communicate your message better.

VOICE QUALITY.   It should be obvious that a good voice is central to good talking. But this obvious point needs underscoring as we concentrate on developing qualities of effective talking. Good voice quality means vocal expressions that vary in pitch, change in delivery speed, and alternate in volume. Because we will say more about these three qualities in our discussion of formal speeches in Chapter 15, we need only to recognize their importance to effective informal talking at this point.

■ (1) Good voice quality means varying the pitch, changing delivery speed, and alternating volume.

To illustrate their importance, imagine meeting someone who has an unpleasant voice. Probably, this person talks in a monotone, a quality of voice that needs pitch variety. Moreover, the person delivers words at the same rate of speed. And the volume of speaking remains constant throughout. After several minutes of hearing such a voice, you probably will conclude that the person is unenthusiastic or disinterested.

■ Imagine an unpleasant voice. It probably is monotone, spoken at the same speed, constant in volume.

To correct such unpleasant qualities, we must first be aware of them. We must remember that all of us need to improve our voice quality from time to time. After we become aware of the need to change, we can then practice, which is the second step to correcting unpleasant voice quality. The story is told about a visitor to New York City who wanted to attend a concert at Carnegie Hall. Not knowing the local subway system, she asked a street-corner musician, "How do I get to Carnegie Hall?" The musician's response: "Practice, lady, practice!"

■ To correct unpleasant voice quality, do two things: (a) be aware of the unpleasantness and (b) practice.

That advice is also sound for those wanting to improve voice quality. Concentrate on words and their pronunciation. Note the range of your voice in speaking. And vary the volume from loud to soft. If you will practice these and other variations, you will find that you can indeed improve your voice quality. Like good actors, good speakers can select from a number of alternatives in their attempts to express orally their thoughts and feelings to others.

■ Especially practice word pronunciation, voice range, and volume.

TALKING STYLE.   Talking style refers to how the three parts of voice quality—pitch, speed, and volume—blend together. But it also means more. It means how well talkers

■ (2) Talking style means pitch, speed, and volume—plus personality.

project their personalities through their oral expression. As such, style refers to a set of behaviors of an individual that give uniqueness to that person.

When we refer to a talker as one who has a sharp, smooth, or polished style, we usually mean one whose pitch, volume, and speed are consistent with certain attitudes we infer—attitudes such as sincerity, kindness, understanding, and courtesy. When these attitudes produce certain behaviors and blend with voice quality, we can say that a talker has a style. While it is beyond our purpose to analyze style in detail, we must note that it does exist; and it is a vital part of talking. But remember that as we noted about writing style, *what* you speak is more important than *how* you speak it. The best that a listener can say after hearing you speak is "These are interesting ideas" rather than "You have a beautiful voice."

WORD CHOICE AND VOCABULARY. Still another quality of effective talking is word choice. By selecting the right word or words that create clear pictures in a listener's mind, good talkers are able to communicate better and more quickly. They do so because they have more choices available to them. Thus, vocabulary is a critical factor for good talking. The larger the vocabulary, the more selections that are available for creating pictures in the listener's mind.

As discussed in Chapter 2, there are a number of suggestions to use in choosing words that do a good job of communicating. These suggestions are just as important to talking as they are to writing. Because we have already covered them, we will not repeat them here. Nonetheless, they are important. In fact, using them in speaking requires quicker judgment because of the shorter time involved in selecting words. This shorter time cycle should underscore again the need to practice in selecting different words for different effects.

CENTRAL ROLE OF ADAPTATION. Adaptation, a fourth quality of good talking, in effect sums up the previous three qualities of voice quality, style, and word choice. As discussed in Chapter 2, adaptation means fitting a message to a specific receiver. In our speaking efforts, all that we do is for adaptation. That is, we select the right words and use the right voice pitch, speed, volume, and style for the one intended listener. By positioning the listener as the central focus of our talking effort we practice good business etiquette.

To illustrate, assume that you must report to your boss about a specific project you are working on. Your boss has a master's degree and 15 years of experience with your organization. In speaking to her, you choose certain words to fit her education and experience; and you deliver them with a style and quality to accomplish the purpose you seek. But contrast that situation with another: that of instructing your subordinates. These subordinates have a high school education and less than one year on the job. The words, style, and voice quality of your oral direction probably would be quite different. Yet both messages would fit the minds of the listeners. And both messages would contain all the aspects of professional respect and etiquette.

LISTENING

Up to this point, our review of oral communication has been about sending information (talking). Certainly, this is an area in which businesspeople need help. But evidence shows that the receiving side (listening) causes more problems.

THE IMPORTANCE OF LISTENING

Listening is important to us in our study of communication for at least three reasons. Foremost is the fact that listening is the first verbal skill we acquire as we develop the ability to use language, followed in sequence by speaking, reading, and writing. Second, listening accounts for about 45 percent of our verbal communication time—more than any other skill area—according to most authorities. Third, listening is an important area to business. When workers are asked what they like about supervisors, "They listen to me!" ranks at or near the top of the responses.

But listening well requires clear thinking, patience, high motivation, and hard work, as we will see. To listen well, people need to be open-minded and receptive to improvement.

Good style implies that voice quality is consistent with positive attitudes.

(3) Word choice allows speakers to communicate better and more quickly by giving more selections.

The suggestions for word choice in Chapter 2 apply to speaking as well. Use them, and practice.

(4) Adaptation is fitting a message to a specific listener.

For example, your message would differ for people with great differences in education and experience.

Poor listening is a major cause of miscommunication.

Listening is important—in language skill development, in time spent communicating, and in business relations.

Most of us assume others cause communication problems.

Often we do not want to improve. That is, we smugly assume that our communication efforts are better than those of other people. And those other people—not us—are the ones who cause all the communication problems.

Studies of listening effectiveness show similar results: That we are much less effective in listening than we think we are. These studies indicate also that people often overestimate their actual listening ability—frequently by two or three times what it truly is. Unless we develop more humility and see the need to change our listening habits, we will not improve.

■ We assume, too, that we listen better than we do.

CONTRASTING ILLUSTRATIONS OF LISTENING

Listening is a decoding skill. To listen well, you must receive a message and take it apart to get meaning from it. The model of communication presented in Chapter 1 emphasized speaking. If we look back at the model (Figure 1.2) from a listening perspective, we can grasp what is involved on the receiving side of the communication equation. To do that, let us assume that Marci receives these words from Kevin: "Marci, I got your email about the graphics. I can't do them right now. I'm not Superman, you know!"

■ Effective listening requires that we know what is involved in the entire listening process. We can describe listening by looking again at Figure 1.2.

The message that Kevin sends for Marci to hear consists of a series of spoken words. Along with those words are facial expressions, gestures, and voice inflections to supplement the words. All are symbols, for they stand for something. In reality, all are merely vibrations of air and light waves sent to possibly stimulate Marci's sensory receptors.

■ Marci receives a message from Kevin. It consists of symbols—words, gestures, voice inflections, facial expressions.

When Kevin sends his message to Marci, his symbols enter Marci's sensory world. This sensory world consists of more than Kevin's message. It includes all stimuli that are capable of detection by Marci's sensory receptors—her ears, eyes, nose, skin, and mouth. For sure, Kevin's message has much competition in this multisensory world.

■ Marci's sensory world includes many stimuli, part of which is Kevin's message.

If Kevin is lucky, his vibrations and light waves will register on Marci's ears and eyes. But Marci cannot detect all the stimuli in her sensory world, for several reasons. One is that Marci's senses are limited when compared to reality. Her ears and eyes only pick up part of what truly exists in light and sound. Another reason is that Marci's degree of mental alertness can vary—from being preoccupied to alert. Moreover, Marci's background and viewpoints condition her to be more sensitive to some stimuli than others.

■ Marci detects stimuli selectively because of sensory limitations, varying degrees of alertness, and conditioning.

When Marci's ears and eyes detect Kevin's message, the stimuli flow through her nervous system to her brain, where the stimuli are given meaning. In the process of giving the stimuli meaning, Marci's brain filters Kevin's message. That is, Marci's experience, viewpoints, and emotions associate with the stimuli, sift them, and provide meaning for them in her mind. As you can imagine, this meaning is unique to Marci's filter because her filter is different from all others. Also, Marci's filter changes constantly as she receives a continuous stream of stimuli from her sensory apparatus.

■ As Marci picks up Kevin's message, her nervous system sends impulses to the brain, which filters the message and gives it meaning.

After Marci's mind gives meaning to Kevin's message, it begins to search for ways to express the meaning she has received. In some cases, she will elect not to respond—at least outwardly. In others, she will begin to select symbols for a return message to Kevin. In this selection process, her vocabulary and intellect will affect the type of message she sends. In general, her message will project the state of her filter at the time she receives and constructs her message.

■ Marci's filter then searches for ways to respond to the meaning. Her intellect and vocabulary affect the message she constructs.

When the message is completed, it is sent through symbols (words, body language, and voice tones) into Kevin's sensory environment, where it vies for attention with his sensory receptors. And Kevin goes through the same stages when he receives Marci's message. This cycle of sending and receiving can continue, as long as the need to communicate exists between these two people.

■ When completed, she sends the message to Kevin. The cycle can continue.

With this description of the listening process in mind, consider the following dialog between Marci and Kevin. As each response is sent, preceding it is the cycle of listening just described—sensory detection, flow to the brain, meaning, message construction, and response. Try to predict the internal states of both Marci and Kevin as you proceed through each verbal exchange.

■ Consider two applications of the listening process. Analyze the exchanges and the results in the first one.

Kevin: Marci, I got your email about the graphics. I can't do them right now. I'm not Superman, you know.

Marci: That's an order from the big boss, not me! He told me to make sure everything was on time for his report. Our little part of his action is the graphics because that's what this department does. So I'd appreciate your getting to them right away. We've got more than his work around here to do this week. There are also the illustrations for marketing and the diagrams for the production manual.

Kevin: Doesn't he know we're stacked knee-deep in work already? Since Mary Lynn was out last week with the flu, we just can't seem to catch up.

Marci: I'm just doing what the boss told me to. I don't set his deadlines. If he wants the graphics by noon on Friday, then that's what I have to get for him.

Kevin: I sure don't like it. And I won't forget it, either.

Marci: That's your problem. Think anything you like as long as you get me those graphics on time.

■ It has misunderstandings throughout and leads to disagreement.

As you read through the exchanges, you probably noted that the situation worsens. At the end of the dialogue, the participants are less understanding and more disagreeable than they were before they started the exchange. Each one's verbal messages are virtually ignored by the other and quickly replaced by responses that echo the needs of the speaker and not the listener. Certainly, listening as we envision it should not result in such opposite and opposing dialogue—or behavioral disposition. If Marci is to perform her job as department head effectively, she must think and listen differently if she wishes to get the information she needs for her work.

■ Now analyze the second example.

Let's consider a second example. In this one, note how Marci listens and responds to Kevin. As you did for the first example, try to predict the internal states of Marci and Kevin as the dialogue develops.

Kevin: Marci, I got your e-mail about the graphics. I can't do them right now. I'm not Superman, you know.

Marci: Sounds like you're overloaded with work, Kevin.

Kevin: Yes, I am. We were trying to get back on schedule after Mary Lynn's bout with the flu. And we were making good progress with everybody back at 100 percent. Then you start ragging me about those graphics and deadlines.

Marci: My reminder was just the final straw, right?

Kevin: Right! I never seem to get caught up—always one step behind.

Marci: I guess you feel it's not quite right to ask you to do anything else.

Kevin: Well, sometimes it's like that for everyone, I assume. But we're al survivors here. We've made deadlines before. Better get back to work!

■ This one ends with more understanding and agreement.

Compared to the first example, this second one ends with better rapport between Marci and Kevin and, more important, with an emphasis on work. Rather than angering Kevin, Marci responds with words showing that she understands Kevin's state of mind from his point of view. Thus, Marci does more than receive stimuli and respond with symbols that reflect her first reactions. In effect, she delays, assesses the message, and considers other types of responses—ones that relate to Kevin's situation. In other words, Marci sees the situation as Kevin experiences it. She listens with her whole mind and empathizes.

■ Marci used principles of *effect* from Chapter 4 in her listening. She practiced professional etiquette.

In her listening role, Marci practiced the you-viewpoint, as discussed in Chapter 4. She listened to Kevin's needs as she filtered his incoming message and not her own. Then she selected words that focused on those needs. Thus, Marci used professional etiquette to alleviate Kevin's anxieties and to communicate the internal operational message necessary in her job. She also used indirect strategy and other principles of effect such as conversational tone, sincerity, avoiding anger, positive emphasis, and such. Can you point out where she used them in her listening? Can you identify other techniques she used?

■ The contrasting examples illustrate two extremes—nonlistening and active listening.

These two examples show opposite extremes in listening behavior. Some refer to the first example as *nonlistening.* By whatever name, the results are ineffective. At the other extreme, the second example illustrates *active listening,* a form of listening in which a participant in a dialogue searches for total meaning in a spoken message (both verbal and nonverbal).

■ Active listening does more than sense sounds. It attempts to get the true meaning from a message.

Active listening can be likened to a slow-motion video showing outside events in your mind. You are attentive and thoughtful in your efforts to capture the total meaning of another's spoken message. You sense words, gestures, facial expressions, and the like as symbols that stand for something going on within the speaker. As you filter the message and get meaning from it, you consider the alternative meanings the symbols elicit. Because you can listen faster than you can speak, you have time to consider differences in meaning that a speaker may intend with symbols sent. Put differently, you infer the meanings of the message. Then you test the probability of correctness of your inferences and form a response based on the various meanings that you have considered.

For example, you hear "I'm not Superman, you know!" spoken with more volume, a higher pitch, and more speed than the preceding words in the message. You may also see a slight grin but with a wrinkled forehead, narrowed eyes, and no eye contact. Is the speaker happy? Sad? Sarcastic? Angry? Tense? Relaxed? As these thoughts pass through your filter, you determine that something with deep emotion and feeling is going on within the speaker—enough so that part of it is reflected in what symbols are chosen and how those symbols are arranged. If you responded with words such as "That's an order from the boss, not me!" delivered in an equally forceful and direct manner, you would likely get an angry response, as illustrated in the first example. And each successive exchange would open the argument umbrella wider until both parties were locked into opposite positions.

In contrast, if the words, nonverbals, and forcefulness of the message were interpreted differently, a more indirect approach with gentle probing such as "Sounds like you are overloaded with work, Kevin!" would invite a more honest reply. As each message is evaluated in deliberate and similar fashion, the two parties become more united. Thus, active listening becomes a catalyst for bringing people together and refocusing on work. It results in the practice of good business etiquette.

Not all situations can be resolved as easily as the one presented here appears to be. Nor is active listening a panacea for all human-relations ills. But the principles for practicing active listening are the same. The keys are to listen for total meaning, practice mental delay while evaluating different meanings, and choose carefully the symbols in constructing the return message to the speaker. To be sure, there are varying degrees of effectiveness between the two extremes in the examples; but the two anchor points provide positions from which to assess the degree of listening effectiveness.

NATURE OF LISTENING

Quite often, we think of listening as primarily the act of sensing sounds. But our previous illustrations have shown that listening is more than sound detection. In human communication, the sounds are mainly spoken words; and they are detected by our ears. From a communication standpoint, the listening process involves the additional activities of filtering and remembering.

SENSING.   How well we sense the words spoken around us is determined by two factors. One factor is our ability to sense sounds—how well our ears can pick them up. As you know, we do not all hear equally well, although mechanical devices (hearing aids) can reduce our differences in this respect.

The other factor is our attentiveness to listening. More specifically, this is our mental concentration—our will to listen. As was noted in Chapter 1, our mental concentration on the communication symbols that our senses can detect varies from moment to moment. It can range from almost totally blocking out those symbols to concentrating on them very intensely. From your own experience, you can recall moments when you were oblivious to the words spoken around you and moments when you listened with all the intensity you could muster. Most of the time, your listening fell somewhere between these extremes.

FILTERING.   From our illustrations between Kevin and Marci and the model of the communication process in Chapter 1, you know that the filtering process enables you to give meaning to the symbols you sense. In the filtering process, the contents of the mind serve as a sort of filter through which you give meaning to incoming messages.

The filtering process in listening can vary in terms of quality and accuracy as the examples have demonstrated. And you sometimes give messages meanings that are different from meanings others give them. An awareness of these differences and variations should help you focus the intensity of your thinking on the total meaning intended, thereby using your filter actively in the listening process.

Listening Error in a Chain of Communication

Colonel to the executive officer: "Because the general feels the soldiers are unaware of the danger of drinking impure water, he wishes to explain the matter to them. Have all personnel fall out in fatigues at 1400 hours in the battalion area, where the general will address them. In the event of rain, assemble them in the theater."

Executive officer to company commander: "By order of the colonel, tomorrow at 1400 hours all personnel will fall out in fatigues in the battalion area if it rains to march to the theater. There the general will talk about their unawareness of the dangers of drinking."

Company commander to lieutenant: "By order of the colonel, in fatigues the personnel will assemble at the theater at 1400 hours. The general will appear if it rains to talk about the dangers of the unawareness of drinking."

Lieutenant to sergeant: "Tomorrow at 1400 hours the troops will assemble at the theater to hear the general talk about unawareness of drinking dangerously."

Sergeant to the enlisted personnel: "Tomorrow at 1400 hours the drunken general will be at the theater in his underwear talking dangerously. We have to go and hear him."

■ Remembering what we hear is a part of listening.

REMEMBERING.   Remembering what we hear is the third activity involved in listening. Unfortunately, we retain little of what we hear. We remember many of the comments we hear in casual conversation for only a short time—perhaps for only a few minutes or hours. Some we forget almost as we hear them. According to authorities, we even quickly forget most of the message in formal oral communications (such as speeches), remembering only about one-fourth after two days.

IMPROVING YOUR LISTENING ABILITY

■ You must prepare your mind if you want to improve your listening.

Improving your listening does not involve memorizing and practicing a list of techniques in a mechanical way. Rather it includes being aware of certain guidelines in your mental preparation for listening. After you have prepared your mind for listening, you can practice more commonly accepted techniques.

■ You must want to improve.

COMMIT TO IMPROVE.   As we have emphasized, mental conditioning is central to listening improvement. You must concentrate on the activities of sensing by being more perceptive to your speaker's message.

■ Be alert. Force yourself to pay attention.

FOCUS ATTENTION.   After you have decided that you want to listen better, you must make an effort to pay attention. How you do this will depend on your mental makeup, for the effort requires disciplining the mind. You must force yourself to be alert, to pay attention to words spoken.

■ Concentrate on improving your mental filtering.

IMPROVE ACCURACY OF FILTERING.   In addition to working on the improvement of your sensing, you should work on the accuracy of your filtering. To do this, you will need to think in terms of what words mean to the speakers who use them rather than what the dictionary says they mean or what they mean in your mind. You must try to think like the speaker thinks—judging the speaker's words by the speaker's knowledge, experiences, viewpoints, and such. Like improving your sensing, improving your filtering requires conscious effort.

■ Use your faster filtering time in listening to determine the total meaning the speaker is sending.

One way to be conscious and deliberate in your filtering effort is to realize that you can think (filter) much faster than you can talk—about three to four times as fast. Thus, you should caution yourself about jumping to quick conclusions, interrupting, rehearsing what you are going to say when the other person quits talking, and other nonproductive activity. Instead, you should use the extra mental time to determine the true meaning that the speaker intends.

Some Sound Advice on Listening

Living in a competitive culture, most of us are most of the time chiefly concerned with getting our own views across, and we tend to find other people's speeches a tedious interruption of the flow of our own ideas. Hence, it is necessary to emphasize that listening does not mean simply maintaining a polite silence while you are re-hearsing in your mind the speech you are going to make the next time you can grab a conversational opening. Nor does listening mean waiting alertly for the flaws in the other fellow's arguments so that later you can mow him down. Listening means trying to see the problem the way the speaker sees it—which means not sympathy, which is *feeling* for him, but empathy, which is *experiencing* with him. Listening requires entering actively and imaginatively into the other fellow's situation and trying to understand a frame of reference different from your own. This is not always an easy task.

S. I. Hayakawa

For example, you should realize that 90 percent or more of the meaning we receive from a speaker comes from nonword symbols—gestures, the speed/pitch/volume of the voice, facial expressions, and such. As you sense the words of a speaker, you should sense the nonword symbols also. You should be aware that what speakers communicate mirrors the meaning in their minds. So you need to sense and observe the word and nonword symbols being sent. If you focus on the total meaning the speaker conveys, you are practicing active listening; that is, you are mentally active in attempting to determine the meaning conveyed in a message.

■ Listen actively by focusing on word and nonword symbols.

CONCENTRATE ON REMEMBERING. Remembering what you hear also requires conscious effort. Certainly, there are limits to what the mind can retain; but authorities agree that few of us come close to them. By taking care to hear what is said and by working to make your filtering process give you more accurate meanings to the word and nonword symbols you perceive, you add strength to the messages you receive. The result should be improved retention.

■ Consciously try to remember.

APPLY TECHNIQUES. In addition to the foregoing advice, various practical steps may prove helpful. Assembled in a classic document titled "The Ten Commandments of Listening,"[1] the following list summarizes the most useful of them:

■ And follow these practical guidelines (summarized in italics).

1. *Stop talking.* Unfortunately, most of us prefer talking to listening. Even when we are not talking, we are inclined to concentrate on what to say next rather than on listening to others. So you must stop talking before you can listen.

2. *Put the talker at ease.* If you make the talker feel at ease, he or she will do a better job of talking. Then you will have better input to work with.

3. *Show the talker you want to listen.* If you can convince the talker that you are listening to understand rather than oppose, you will help create a climate for information exchange. You should look and act interested. Doing things like reading, looking at your watch, and looking away distracts the talker.

4. *Remove distractions.* The things you do can also distract the talker. So don't doodle, tap with your pencil, shuffle papers, or the like.

5. *Empathize with the talker.* If you place yourself in the talker's position and look at things from the talker's point of view, you will help create a climate of understanding that can result in a true exchange of information.

6. *Be patient.* You will need to allow the talker plenty of time. Remember that not everyone can get to the point as quickly and clearly as you. And do not interrupt. Interruptions are barriers to the exchange of information.

7. *Hold your temper.* From our knowledge of the workings of our minds, we know that anger impedes communication.

---

[1] To some anonymous author goes a debt of gratitude for these classic and often-quoted comments about listening.

Angry people build walls between each other. They harden their positions and block their minds to the words of others.

8. *Go easy on argument and criticism.* Argument and criticism tend to put the talker on the defensive. He or she then tends to "clam up" or get angry. Thus, even if you win the argument, you lose. Rarely does either party benefit from argument and criticism.

9. *Ask questions.* By frequently asking questions, you display an open mind and show that you are listening. And you assist the talker in developing his or her message and in improving the correctness of meaning.

10. *Stop talking!* The last commandment is to stop talking. It was also the first. All the other commandments depend on it.

From the preceding review it should be clear that to improve your listening ability, you must set your mind to the task. Poor listening habits are ingrained in our makeup. We can alter these habits only through conscious effort.

THE REINFORCING ROLE OF NONVERBAL COMMUNICATION

- Nonverbal communication accounts for more of a total message than words do.

In either your role of speaker or listener in oral communication, you will need to be aware of the nonverbal—nonword—part of your communication. In both roles, nonverbal communication accounts for a larger part of the total message than do the words you send or receive. Usually, we use nonverbal communication to supplement and reinforce our words. Sometimes, nonverbal communication communicates by itself. Because it is so important to both sides of the oral communication equation, we will look at the nature of nonverbal communication and some types of it.

NATURE OF NONVERBAL COMMUNICATION

- Nonverbal (nonword) communication means all communication without words. It is broad and imprecise.

Nonverbal or nonword communication means all communication that occurs without words. As you can see, the subject is a broad one. And because it is so broad, nonverbal communication is quite vague and imprecise. For instance, a frown on someone's forehead is sometimes interpreted to mean worry. But could it be that the person has a headache? Or is the person in deep thought? No doubt, there could be numerous meanings given to the facial expression.

- Cross-cultural aspects give many meanings to nonverbal communication.

The number of possible meanings is multiplied even more when we consider the cross-cultural side of communication. As noted in Chapter 17, culture teaches us about body positions, movements, and various factors that affect human relationships (intimacy, space, time, and such). Thus, the meanings we give to nonverbal symbols will vary depending on how our culture has conditioned us.

Farcus
by David Waisglass
Gordon Coulthart

"My name is Joe, and I can't stop attending meetings."

Because of these numerous meanings, you need to be sensitive to what others intend with nonverbal communication. And you need to make some allowance for error in the meanings you receive from nonverbal symbols. As a listener, you need to go beyond the obvious to determine what nonword symbols mean. As we have said about word symbols, you need to see what people intend with their nonverbal symbols as well. Perhaps one good way to grasp the intent of this suggestion is to look at the intended meanings you have for the nonverbal symbols you use.

- Be sensitive to intended nonverbal meanings. Go beyond the obvious.

Think for a few moments about the smile on your face, a gesture, or such. What do you mean by it? What could it mean to others? Is it exactly as you intend? Could it be interpreted differently? Could someone from a different culture give a different meaning to it? Only if you look at nonverbal symbols through the prism of self-analysis and realize their multiple meaning potential can you get some idea of how they might be interpreted differently. And when you become aware of the many differences, you then can become sensitive to the meaning intended by the nonverbal communication.

- Realize that nonverbal symbols can have many meanings.

In order to become sensitive to the myriad of nonverbal symbols, we will look at some types of nonverbal communication. Specifically, we will study three types of communication that occur without words.

TYPES OF NONVERBAL COMMUNICATION

Although there are many ways to classify nonverbal communication, we will examine four of the more common types—body language, space, time, and paralanguage. These three types are especially important to our discussion of speaking and listening.

- We will look at three common types of nonverbal communication: (1) body language, (2) space, (3) time.

BODY LANGUAGE.   Much of what we send to others without using words is sent through the physical movements of our bodies. When we wave our arms and fingers, wrinkle our foreheads, stand erect, smile, gaze at another, wear a coat and tie, and so on, we convey certain meanings; and others convey meanings to us in return. In particular, the face and eyes, gestures, posture, and physical appearance reflect the inner workings of emotions in our bodies.

- Our bodies send nonword messages—through arms, fingers, expressions, posture, and so on.

The face and eyes are by far the most important features of body language. We look to the face and eyes to determine much of the meaning behind body language and nonverbal communication. For example, happiness, surprise, fear, anger, and sadness usually require definite facial expressions and eye patterns. Thus, you should be aware of these two aspects of body language as you speak and listen to others.

- The face and eyes are the most important.

In addition, gestures are another way we send nonword messages through our body parts. *Gestures* are physical movements of our arms, legs, hands, torsos, and heads. Through the movement of each of these body parts, we can accent and reinforce our verbal messages. And we can observe how others punctuate their verbal efforts with gestures. For example, observe the hand movements of another person while he or she is talking. Consider whether this person is fluid or sporadic with such hand movements. As you observe these gestures, you will get a good picture of the internal emotional state of the person. Moreover, speaking and gestures appear to be linked. In general, the louder someone speaks, the more emphatic the gestures used, and vice versa.

- Gestures (physical movements of the arms, legs, torso, and head) send nonword messages.

Another area of body language is physical appearance—our clothing, hair, and adornments (jewelry, cosmetics, and such). The appearance of our bodies indicates how our body movements are seen. Consider, for example, how you might perceive a speaker at a formal banquet dressed in faded blue jeans. No doubt, the speaker's gestures, facial features, posture, and such would be perceived in relation to attire. Accordingly, you want to make sure that your appearance fits the situation. And you want to make sure that you know that appearance is an important part of the body messages that are sent and received in oral communication.

- Physical appearance—clothing, hair, jewelry, cosmetics, and so on—also communicates.

SPACE.   Another type of nonverbal communication involves space and how it communicates meaning in speaking and listening. How we use space and what we do in certain spaces we create tell much about us. Thus, each of us has a space language just as we do a body language. And this space language is crafted by our culture.

- Space is another type of nonverbal language.

- Four types of space exist: (1) intimate, (2) personal, (3) social, and (4) public. Communication behavior differs in each.

Authorities tell us that we create four different types of space: intimate (physical contact to 18 inches); personal (18 inches to 4 feet); social (4 to 12 feet); and public (12 feet to range of seeing and hearing). In each of these spaces, our communication behaviors differ and convey different meanings. For example, consider the volume of your voice when someone is 18 inches from you. Do you shout? Whisper? Now contrast the tone of your voice when someone is 12 feet away. Unquestionably, there is a difference, just because of the distance involved.

- Communication behaviors are learned from cultures.

Also, our behaviors in each type of space are learned from our cultures. Thus, you will need to be sensitive to the spaces of others—especially those from different cultures. As noted in Chapter 17, when people's attitudes toward space are different, their actions are likely to be misinterpreted.

- Time is a third type of nonverbal communication.

TIME.   A third type of nonverbal communication involves time. Just as there is a body and space language, there is also a time language. That is, how we give meaning to time communicates to others. To illustrate, think about how you manage your daily schedule. Do you arrive early for most appointments? Do you prioritize telephone calls? Do you prepare agendas for meetings? How you respond to time communicates to others. And, of course, others' use of time communicates to you. In terms of nonverbal communication, you should recognize that time orientations are not always the same—especially in the cross-cultural arena—but they do communicate. As such, they become parts of the messages we send to and receive from one another.

- Paralanguage involves *how* we say something.

PARALANGUAGE.   *Paralanguage,* meaning "like language," is a fourth type of nonverbal communication. Of all the types, it is the closest to communication with word symbols. It has to do with the sound of a speaker's voice, the "how" of it—those hints and signals in the way words are delivered.

To illustrate, read the following series of statements, emphasizing the *italicized* word in each.

I am a good communicator.

I *am* a good communicator.

I am *a* good communicator.

I am a *good* communicator.

I am a good *communicator.*

- You can change the meaning of spoken sentences by accenting different words in each.

By emphasizing the underscored word in each statement, you change the meaning of that statement from the others even though you used the same words. You do so by the way in which the word sequence sounds. As another example, try counting from 1 to 10 a number of times, each time expressing a different emotional state—say anxiety, anger, or happiness. The way you state each sequence of numbers will show what you intend quite accurately.

- Paralanguage creates meanings because of speed, pitch, volume, and connection of words.

Paralanguage is the communication effect of the speed, pitch, volume, and connectivity of spoken words. Are they fast or slow? Are they high pitched or deep? Are they loud and forceful or barely audible? Are they smooth or disjointed? These questions are examples of the types you would ask to analyze the nonverbal symbols of paralanguage. The symbols become a part of the meaning that is filtered from a spoken message.

- Degrees of consistency between what and how someone says something convey meaning.

Paralanguage meanings are also conveyed by consistencies and inconsistencies in what is said and how it is said. Depending on the circumstance, a person's voice may or may not be consistent with the intended word meanings. But you should make every effort to avoid inconsistencies that will send a confusing message. Consistency among the words you choose and how you deliver them to create clear meaning should be your goal.

- Expectancies about background, appearance, and personality are part of paralanguage.

Senders and receivers have certain expectancies about how a message should sound. Whether real or imagined, people infer background factors (race, occupation, etc.); physical appearance (age, height, gender); and personality (introversion, social orientation, etc.) when they receive and filter voice patterns. When you speak, you should do whatever you can to influence these expectancies positively. Many of the suggestions in this chapter and the following one should help you deliver a consistent and effective message. Active listeners, too, will want to listen between the lines of a spoken message to determine the true meaning sent by a speaker.

OTHER TYPES OF NONVERBAL COMMUNICATION.   Other types of nonverbal communication exist. But the preceding four types are the primary forms. For example, color communicates different meanings to us. Artists, interior decorators, and "image consultants" believe that different colors project different meanings. What meanings do you get from red, yellow, black, blue? That you can answer at all should prove that colors produce meanings in our minds. Applications of the idea to speaking and listening include visual-aid construction, wardrobe, office decor, and the like. Thus, you should give more than casual attention to color as a type of nonverbal communication. You indeed will want to create a specific and intended meaning with it.

■ Two other nonverbal types exist, but they are minor. One is color.

Still another type of nonverbal communication involves the structure of our physical context—its layout and design. In an office, the physical arrangements—furniture, carpeting, size, location, and decorations—all communicate meaning to us and to others. These elements provide the context for many of our speaking and listening activities. As such, we should consider them as part of the messages we send and receive.

■ Another is physical context—office, carpeting, decorations, and such.

INTERVIEWING PEOPLE

In your work in business, you may need to participate in a variety of types of interviews. Perhaps the best-known type is the employment interview discussed in Chapter 9. But there are others. Interviews are often involved in the periodic evaluations that some companies make of their workers. These interviews are primarily a means of communicating the evaluations. When workers leave a company, they may be interviewed to determine their reasons for leaving. Interviews are sometimes conducted to gather information on such matters as worker attitudes, working conditions, managerial effectiveness, and worker plans.

■ Interviews are conducted in business for employment purposes, to get information, and to give information.

Because interviewing is a form of personal communication, usually between two people, it is not a precise activity—that is, no hard-and-fast rules exist. Rather, interviewing is a flexible activity that requires the good judgment of the people involved. Nevertheless, well-established guidelines exist, and you should follow them. In the following pages they are presented from the side of both the interviewer and the interviewee.

■ Although interviewing is not a precise activity, the following guidelines will help you.

GUIDELINES FOR THE INTERVIEWER

Because the interviewer is in charge, the success of the interview is in his or her hands. Thus, it is especially important that the interviewer know and follow these general guidelines.

■ Here are some guidelines for the interviewer:

PLAN THE INTERVIEW.   You conduct most interviews because you need information. So as a starting point you should determine your information needs. You can usually express these needs in a list of specific questions. You should make such a list and use it as the outline for the interview.

■ (1) plan (determine what information is needed),

PUT THE INTERVIEWEE AT EASE.   The chances are that the interviewee will be nervous. Since nervous people are not good subjects for interviewing, you should try to put the interviewee at ease. How you should do this varies with the person involved and with your social skills. You could, for example, begin with some friendly talk on a point of common interest. Or you could begin with comments or questions about the interviewee—hometown, sports interests, hobbies, and the like.

■ (2) put the interviewee at ease (using your social skills),

MAKE THE PURPOSE CLEAR.   The interviewee should know the purpose of the interview from the beginning. Of course, the interviewee sometimes knows the purpose from the nature of the interview, as in an employment interview. But if she or he does not know the purpose, you should explain it clearly and honestly.

■ (3) explain the purpose when it is not apparent,

Employment interviews are the most widely recognized type. There are others—performance appraisals, exit interviews, and research situations. For interviews to be successful, both parties must plan for them.

• (4) allow the interviewee to do the talking.

LET THE INTERVIEWEE DO MOST OF THE TALKING. You can get the information you seek only when the interviewee talks. Thus, you should let the interviewee do most of the talking. Such a strategy is not only good for communication; it shows good etiquette as well. You should talk only to guide the course of the interview—to carry the discussion through the specific questions you want to cover. If the interviewees are reluctant to talk, you will need to work to get them to talk. But you should never put words in their mouths.

• (5) guide the interview through the plan (ask questions and end answers),

GUIDE THE INTERVIEW. Even though the interviewee does most of the talking, your task is to guide the interview so as to obtain the needed information. That is, you follow the plan you set up in the beginning. You ask specific questions, and you end answers when you have the information you need. In guiding the interview, you will need to handle moments of silence. Brief periods of silence are all right, for additional information sometimes comes after them. But too much silence can be awkward for both parties.

• (6) listen and make it apparent that you are listening,

LISTEN. You should listen carefully to all that the interviewee says. The purpose of an interview is to get certain information—by listening. You will need to practice the techniques of good listening presented previously in this chapter. And you will need to be aware of the reinforcing role of nonverbal communication, too.

In addition to listening, you should give the appearance of listening. Your interviewees will be more relaxed and will talk more if they believe they have your undivided attention. Business etiquette would demand nothing less.

• (7) record information either during the interview or soon after, and

KEEP A RECORD. Because you conduct interviews to get information, you will need to make a record of the information. How you record the information may vary with the situation. When you need much detailed information, you may have to take notes during the interview. Because your writing may be disturbing to the interviewee, you should explain at the beginning of the interview why you must take notes. Even after explaining, you should write as quickly and briefly as possible.

When you can remember the information you seek, you need not write during the interview. But you should record that information soon after the interview is over. As you know, not many of us can remember such information for very long.

END THE INTERVIEW. You are in charge of the interview, and therefore you should end it. If the situation justifies it, some friendly talk can follow the questioning. But you should avoid letting the conversation trail off to meaningless talk. One good way of ending interviews is to ask a finalizing question—one that tells the interviewee that the interview is over. This one does the job well: "Is there anything else you would like to tell me? If not, thanks for giving me your time."

■ (8) end the interview, perhaps with a finalizing question.

GUIDELINES FOR THE INTERVIEWEE

When you are the person being interviewed, you may have little control over the situation. Nevertheless, you can help make the interview successful. The following guidelines tell you how.

■ Here are some guidelines for the interviewee:

PREPARE FOR THE INTERVIEW. When you know the nature of the interview, prepare for it. Your preparation should consist mainly of thinking about the questions you are likely to be asked and formulating answers to them. It may also include gathering additional information. In a job interview, for example, you would be wise to learn what you can about the company—its history, its current activities, its plans. By showing your knowledge of the company during the interview, you can impress the interviewer with your interest in it. Even if you prepare diligently, you are not likely to cover all that will be asked. So be prepared for the unexpected.

■ (1) prepare (anticipate questions and form answers),

MAKE AN APPROPRIATE APPEARANCE. What the interviewer sees is a part of the message that he or she receives. So you should do what you can to make an appropriate appearance. As what is appropriate varies with the situation, you should consider the situation. You will find that the conventional standards of neatness and dress are desirable in most cases. In addition, you will usually want your posture, facial expressions, and physical movements to give favorable impressions. You will especially want to avoid the appearance of nervousness.

■ (2) make an appropriate appearance,

SHOW INTEREST. You can improve the impression you make in most interview situations by showing interest. How you should show interest varies with the occasion. But you always help your case by looking at the interviewer and by giving her or him your undivided attention. You approach each situation with your best professional etiquette.

■ (3) show interest (look at the interviewer and pay attention),

ANSWER CORRECTLY AND COMPLETELY. If the interview serves a good purpose, it deserves correct and complete answers. You should give them. Dishonest answers benefit no one.

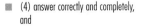

■ (4) answer correctly and completely, and

PRACTICE COURTESY. You probably know very well the value of courtesy and etiquette in business. You know that they are major parts of the impression you make in every human contact. The interview is no exception.

■ (5) be courteous.

CONDUCTING AND PARTICIPATING IN MEETINGS

From time to time, you will participate in business meetings. They will range from extreme formality to extreme informality. On the formal end will be conferences and committee meetings. On the informal end will be discussions with groups of fellow workers. Whether formal or informal, the meetings will involve communication. In fact, the quality of the communication will determine their success. As noted in Chapter 10, collaborative report-writing groups should use the suggestions for conducting effective meetings.

■ Meetings involve oral communication.

Your role in a meeting will be that of either leader or participant. Of course, the leader's role is the primary one, but good participation is also vital. The following paragraphs review the techniques of performing well in either role.

■ In a meeting you will be either a leader or a participant.

Collaborative Tools for Virtual Meetings

Virtual meetings are becoming common occurrences in many of today's business settings. No longer do businesses need sophisticated teleconferencing equipment to work together from different locations; a typical

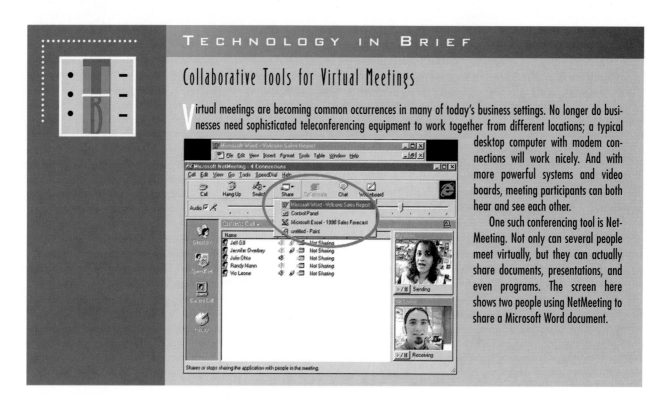

desktop computer with modem connections will work nicely. And with more powerful systems and video boards, meeting participants can both hear and see each other.

One such conferencing tool is Net-Meeting. Not only can several people meet virtually, but they can actually share documents, presentations, and even programs. The screen here shows two people using NetMeeting to share a Microsoft Word document.

TECHNIQUES OF CONDUCTING MEETINGS

- To lead some formal meetings, you should know parliamentary procedure. So study the subject.

How you conduct a meeting depends on the formality of the occasion. Meetings of such groups as formal committees, boards of directors, and professional organizations usually follow generally accepted rules of conduct called *parliamentary procedure*. These very specific rules are too detailed for review here. When you are involved in a formal meeting, you would do well to study one of the many books covering parliamentary procedure before the meeting. In addition, you should know and practice the following techniques. For less formal meetings, you can depart somewhat from parliamentary procedure and those techniques. But you should keep in mind that every meeting has goals and that such departures should never hinder you from reaching them.

- In addition, you should do the following: (1) plan the items to be covered (the agenda),

PLAN THE MEETING. A key to conducting a successful meeting is to plan it thoroughly. That is, you develop an agenda (a list of topics to be covered) by selecting the items that need to be covered to achieve the goals of the meeting. Then arrange these items in the most logical order. Items that explain or lead to other items should come before the items that they explain or lead to. After preparing the agenda, if the meeting is formal, make it available to those who will attend. For informal meetings, you may find keeping the agenda in mind satisfactory.

- (2) follow the plan item by item,

FOLLOW THE PLAN. You should follow the plan for the meeting item by item. In most meetings the discussion tends to stray and new items tend to come up. As leader, you should keep the discussion on track. If new items come up during the meeting, you can take them up at the end—or perhaps postpone them to a future meeting.

- (3) move the discussion along,

MOVE THE DISCUSSION ALONG. As leader, you should control the agenda. When one item has been covered, bring up the next item. When the discussion moves off subject, move it back on subject. In general, do what is needed to proceed through the items efficiently. But you should not cut off discussion before all the important points have been made. Thus, you will have to use your good judgment. Your goal is to permit complete discussion on the one hand and to avoid repetition, excessive details, and useless comments on the other.

CONTROL THOSE WHO TALK TOO MUCH. Keeping certain people from talking too much is likely to be one of your harder tasks. A few people usually tend to dominate the discussion. Your task as leader is to control them. Of course, you want the meeting to be democratic, so you will need to let these people talk as long as they are contributing to the goals of the meeting. However, when they begin to stray, duplicate, or bring in useless matter, you should step in. You can do this tactfully and with all the decorum of business etiquette by asking for other viewpoints or by summarizing the discussion and moving on to the next topic.

■ (4) allow no one to talk too much,

ENCOURAGE PARTICIPATION FROM THOSE WHO TALK TOO LITTLE. Just as some people talk too much, some talk too little. In business groups, those who say little are often in positions lower than those of other group members. Your job as leader is to encourage these people to participate by asking them for their viewpoints and by showing respect for the comments they make, even though the comments may be illogical.

■ (5) encourage everybody to take part,

CONTROL TIME. When your meeting time is limited, you need to determine in advance how much time will be needed to cover each item. Then, at the appropriate times, you should end discussion of the items. You may find it helpful to announce the time goals at the beginning of the meeting and to remind the group members of the time status during the meeting.

■ (6) control time when time is limited, and

SUMMARIZE AT APPROPRIATE PLACES. After a key item has been discussed, you should summarize what the group has covered and concluded. If a group decision is needed, the group's vote will be the conclusion. In any event, you should formally conclude each point and then move on to the next one. At the end of the meeting, you can summarize the progress made. You should also summarize whenever a review will help the group members understand their accomplishments. For some formal meetings, minutes kept by a secretary provide this summary.

■ (7) at appropriate places, summarize what the group has covered and concluded.

TECHNIQUES FOR PARTICIPATING IN A MEETING

From the preceding discussion of the techniques that a leader should use, you know something about the things that a participant should do. The following review emphasizes them for you.

■ As a participant in a meeting you should

FOLLOW THE AGENDA. When an agenda exists, you should follow it. Specifically, you should not bring up items not on the agenda or comment on such items if others bring them up. When there is no agenda, you should stay within the general limits of the goal for the meeting.

■ (1) follow the agenda,

PARTICIPATE. The purpose of meetings is to get the input of everybody concerned. Thus, you should participate. Your participation, however, should be meaningful. You should talk only when you have something to contribute, and you should talk whenever you have something to contribute. Practice your professional etiquette skills as you work courteously and cooperatively with others in the group.

■ (2) participate in the meeting,

DO NOT TALK TOO MUCH. As you participate in the meeting, be aware that other people are attending. You should speak up whenever you have something to say, but do not get carried away. As in all matters of etiquette, always respect the rights of others. As you speak, ask yourself whether what you are saying really contributes to the discussion.

■ (3) avoid talking too much,

COOPERATE. A meeting by its very nature requires cooperation from all the participants. So keep this in mind as you participate. Respect the leader and her or his efforts to make progress. Respect the other participants, and work with them in every practical way.

■ (4) cooperate with all concerned, and

■ (5) practice courtesy.

BE COURTEOUS. Perhaps being courteous is a part of being cooperative. In any event, you should be courteous to the other group members. Specifically, you should respect their rights and opinions, and you should permit them to speak.

USING THE TELEPHONE

■ Many businesspeople are discourteous and inefficient in telephone communication.

A discussion of business telephone techniques may appear trivial at first thought. After all, most of us have had long experience in using the telephone and may feel that we have little to learn about it. No doubt, some of us have excellent telephone skills. But you have only to call a few randomly selected businesses to learn that not everyone who talks on the telephone is proficient in its use. You will get some gruff, cold greetings, and you will be subjected to a variety of discourtesies—those that break standards of business etiquette. And you will find instances of inefficient use of time (which, of course, is costly). This is not to say that the problem is major, for most progressive businesses are aware of the need for good telephone habits and do something about it. But poor telephone techniques are found often enough to justify reviewing the subject of telephone use in a business communication textbook.

NEED FOR FAVORABLE VOICE QUALITY

■ Because only sound is involved, friendly voices are important.

In reviewing good telephone techniques, keep in mind that a telephone conversation is a unique form of oral communication. Only voices are heard; the speakers are not seen. Impressions are received only from the words and the quality of the voices. Thus, when speaking by telephone, it is extremely important that you work to make your voice sound cheerful and friendly.

■ So talk as if you were in a face-to-face conversation.

One often-suggested way of improving your telephone voice is to talk as if you were face to face with the other person—even smiling and gesturing as you talk, if this helps you be more natural. In addition, you would do well to put into practice the suggestions given earlier in this chapter concerning the use of the voice in speaking (voice quality, variation in pitch, and speed). Perhaps the best instructional device for this problem is to record one of your telephone conversations. Then judge for yourself how you come across and what you need to do to improve.

TECHNIQUES OF COURTESY

■ Be courteous.

■ When calling, immediately introduce yourself and ask for the person you want (or explain your purpose).

If you have worked in business for any length of time, you have probably experienced most of the common telephone discourtesies. You probably know that most of them are not intended as discourtesies but result from ignorance or unconcern. The following review should help you avoid them and incorporate the qualities of business etiquette into your telephone conversations.

The recommended procedure when you are calling is to introduce yourself immediately and then to ask for the person with whom you want to talk:

"This is Wanda Tidwell of Tioga Milling Company. May I speak with Mr. José Martinez?"

If you are not certain with whom you should talk, explain the purpose of your call:

"This is Wanda Tidwell of Tioga Milling Company. We have a question about your service warranty. May I talk with the proper executive about it?"

■ When receiving a call, identify your company or office; then offer assistance.

When a secretary or someone else who is screening calls answers the telephone, the recommended procedure is to first identify the company or office and then to make a cheerful offer of assistance:

"Rowan Insurance Company. How may I help you?"

"Ms. Santo's office. May I help you?"

When a call goes directly into the office of the executive, the procedure is much the same, except that the executive identifies herself or himself:

"Bartosh Realty. Toby Bartosh speaking. May I help you?"

Cellular telephones allow people to communicate throughout the world instantly. To use telephones effectively, you need good voice quality, courtesy, effective procedures, and sound techniques.

When a secretary answers for an executive (the usual case), special care should be taken not to offend the caller. Following a question like "Who is calling?" by "I am sorry, but Mr. Gordon is not in" leaves the impression that Gordon may be in but does not want to talk with this particular caller. A better procedure would be to state directly "Mr. Gordon is not in right now. May I ask him to return your call?" Or perhaps "May I tell him who called?" or "Can someone else help you?" could be substituted for the latter sentence.

- Secretaries should avoid offending callers by asking misleading questions, by making misleading comments, or

Especially irritating to callers is being put on hold for unreasonable periods of time. If the person being called is on another line or involved in some other activity, it may be desirable to place the caller on hold. But good business etiquette dictates that the choice should be the caller's. If the hold continues for a period longer than anticipated, the secretary should check back with the caller periodically showing concern and offering assistance. Equally irritating is the practice of having a secretary place a call for an executive and then put the person called on hold until the executive is free to talk. While it may be efficient to use secretaries for such work, as a matter of courtesy and etiquette the executive should be ready to talk the moment the call goes through.

- by being inconsiderate in placing callers on hold. Let the callers choose, and check on the hold status continually.

Secretaries to busy executives often screen incoming calls. In doing so, they should courteously ask the purpose of the calls. The response might prompt the secretary to refer the caller to a more appropriate person in the company. It might also reveal that the executive has no interest in the subject of the call, in which case the secretary should courteously yet clearly explain this to the caller. If the executive is busy at the moment, the secretary should explain this and either suggest a more appropriate time for a call or promise a callback by the executive. But in no case should the secretary promise a callback that will not be made. Such a breach of etiquette would likely destroy any goodwill between the caller and the company.

- Secretaries often screen calls. They should do this courteously and honestly.

EFFECTIVE TELEPHONE PROCEDURES

At the beginning of a telephone conversation that you have initiated, it is good practice to state the purpose of the call. Then you should cover systematically all the points involved. For really important calls, you should plan your call, even to the point of making notes of the points to cover. Then you should follow your notes to make certain you cover them all.

- When calling, state your purpose early. Then cover your points systematically. Plan important calls.

Courteous procedure is much the same in a telephone conversation as in a face-to-face conversation. You listen when the other person is talking. You refrain from interrupting.

- Be considerate, listen, and do not dominate. Use time efficiently.

Voice Annotations: An Important Part of Multimedia/Hypermedia Documents

As more and more desktop computers with multimedia capacity arrive in the workplace, we are bound to see more business writers use sound in their documents. Some will use it as an integral part of a document, serving as an introduction or as part of the dialogue. Others will use it for glitter or for supplementing the information they are presenting in the message. For example, for glitter one might add a sound clip of honking horns to a report of a conference held in New York City. For supplemental purposes, one might add a sound annotation that reads the text in English or perhaps even in another language. A hypermedia use of a sound annotation might be a link to the pronunciation of a proper name. In this age of digital convergence, it's likely that adding a sound annotation to your documents will be as easy as clicking on a button and speaking into a microphone. Planning its most effective use will be the challenge the technology presents.

You avoid dominating the conversation. And perhaps most important of all, you cover your message quickly, saving time (and money) for all concerned.

EFFECTIVE VOICE MAIL TECHNIQUES

- Voice mail is becoming common in business.

Sometimes when the person you are calling is not available, you will be able to leave a voice message in an electronic voice mailbox. Not only does this save you the time involved in calling back the person you are trying to reach, but it also allows you to leave a more detailed message than you might leave with a secretary. However, you need to be prepared for this to be sure your message is both complete and concise.

- Use it much as you would any other telephone call,

You begin the message nearly the same way you would a telephone call. Be as courteous as you would on the telephone and speak as clearly and distinctly as you can. Tell the listener in a natural way your name and affiliation. Begin with an overview of the message and continue with details. If you want the listener to take action, call for it at the end. If you want the listener to return your call, state that precisely, including when you can be reached. Slowly give the number where your call can be returned. Close with a brief goodwill message. For example, as a program coordinator for a professional training organization, you might leave this message in the voice mailbox of one of your participants:

- as in this example.

This is Ron Ivy from Metroplex Development Institute. I'm calling to remind Ms. Melanie Wilson about the Chief Executive Round Table (CERT) meeting next week (Wednesday, July 20) at the Crescent Hotel in Dallas. Dr. Ken Cooper of the Dallas Aerobics Center will present the program on Executive Health in the 21st century. We will begin with breakfast at 7:30 AM and conclude with lunch at noon. Some of the CERT members will play golf in the afternoon at Dallas Country Club. If Ms. Wilson would like to join them, I will be glad to make a tee time for her. She can contact me at 940-240-1003. We look forward to our Chief Executive Round Table meeting next Wednesday.

DICTATING MESSAGES AND REPORTS

- You will probably dictate most letters and some reports.

The odds are that you will dictate many of the letters you write in business. You may even dictate reports—especially the shorter, more informal ones. Developing good dictation skills offers many advantages. First, it is much faster than handwriting at around 15 words per minute or even keying at 80 words per minute. The average person speaks at approximately 160 words per minute. Second, if you use dictation equipment, you can dictate when you are ready. In some companies, you can even call in your dictation from remote locations and often at any time of the day or night. Finally, activated systems are currently available for personal computers. Also, some word processing packages already handle voice input. No doubt, these features will continue to increase quickly in the future. Thus, the following summary of the techniques of dictating should be useful to you.

TECHNIQUES OF DICTATING

GATHER THE FACTS.   Your first logical step in dictating is to get all the information you need for the message. This step involves such activities as getting past correspondence from the files, consulting with other employees, and ascertaining company policy. Unless you get all the information you need, you will be unable to work without interruption.

▦ You should (1) get all the information you need, to avoid interruptions later;

PLAN THE MESSAGE.   With the facts of the case before you, you next plan the message. You may prefer to do this step in your mind or to jot down a few notes or an outline. Whatever your preference, your goal in this step is to decide what your message will be and how you will present it. In this step you apply the procedures covered in our earlier review of letter and report writing.

▦ (2) plan the message (following procedures described in preceding chapters);

GIVE PRELIMINARY INFORMATION AND INSTRUCTIONS.   Your first step in the actual process of dictating is to give the transcriptionist specific instructions. These include instructions about special handling, enclosures, form, and page layout. They also include all the necessary additional information about the message—such information as the mailing address, subject line, attention line, and salutation. When this information is easily available, you need only refer to the source (for example, "Get their address from their letter").

▦ (3) dictate instructions, such as form, enclosures, inside address, and subject line;

MAKE THE WORDS FLOW.   Your next step is to talk through the message. Simple as this step appears, you are likely to have problems with it. Thinking out loud to a secretary or to dictation equipment frightens most of us at first. The result is likely to be slow and awkward dictation.

▦ (4) talk through the message,

Overcoming this problem requires self-discipline and practice. You should force yourself to concentrate and to make the words flow. Your goal should be to get the words out— to talk through the message. You need not be concerned with producing polished work on the first effort. You will probably need to revise, perhaps many times. After you have forced your way through enough messages, your need to revise will decrease and the speed and quality of your dictation will improve.

▦ forcing the words to flow if necessary (you can revise later);

SPEAK IN A STRONG, CLEAR VOICE.   Because your dictation must be heard, you should dictate in a strong, clear voice. Speak at a speed slow enough to clearly separate the words. Words that do not stand out clearly can cause delays in work as well as errors in the message. Be especially careful when using dictation equipment, for it sometimes does not reproduce voices well.

▦ (5) speak so that the transcriptionist can understand each word;

GIVE PARAGRAPHING, PUNCTUATION, AND OTHER MECHANICS AS NEEDED.   How much of the paragraphing, spelling, punctuation, and other mechanics you should include in your dictation depends on your transcriptionist's ability. You may leave these matters to a transcriptionist who is competent in writing correctness and form. On most occasions, however, it would be wise to dictate most such information. Your dictation might well sound like this: "Dear Ms. Mott *colon paragraph* On Friday *comma* November 12 *comma* your order for 18 cases Bug-Nix *comma* 12 *hyphen* ounce packages *comma* should reach your loading docks *period*." (The instructions are indicated by italics.) It is also a good idea to spell out difficult, confusing, and unusual words and names such as *cyberpunk, suite* instead of *sweet,* and *Browne* instead of *Brown.*

▦ (6) give as much instruction on paragraphing, punctuation, and mechanics as is needed; and

AVOID ASIDES.   Asides (side comments not intended to be a part of the message) should be avoided. They tend to confuse the transcriptionist, who must determine which words are part of the message and which are not. As proof, imagine the transcriptionist's difficulty in handling the following dictation (asides in italics):

▦ (7) avoid asides (side comments).

Dear Mr. Dobbs: Well, *let's see. How about this?* The attached check for $19.45 . . . *Is that the right figure?* . . . is our way of showing you that your good faith in us is appreciated. *That should make him happy.* Our satisfaction-or-money-back policy means much to us.

■ Read back when this helps you.

READ BACK INTELLIGENTLY. Although you should try to talk through the message without interruption, you will sometimes need to stop and get a read-back of what you have dictated. But do this only when necessary. More than likely, the need for a read-back results from confused thinking. When you are learning to dictate, however, some confused thinking is normal. Until you gain experience, you may profit from read-backs. You will find a read-back especially helpful at the end of the message to give you a check on the overall effect of your words.

MESSAGE DICTATION ILLUSTRATED

■ Here is an illustration of the dictation of a letter.

Many of the foregoing techniques are illustrated in the following example of the dictation of a routine letter. This example shows all the dictator's words, with instructions and asides in italics. Note that the dictator does not give some of the more obvious punctuation (such as a colon after the salutation). Also note that the dictation gives unusual spelling.

Let's acknowledge the Key Grocery Company order next. Get the address from the order. It's No. 9. Dear Mr. Key: Three crates of orchard *hyphen* fresh Texacates should be in your store sometime Wednesday morning as they were shipped today by Greene *that's G-R-E-E-N-E* Motor Freight *period.* As you requested in your August 29 order *comma* the $61.60 *parenthesis* Invoice 14721 *parenthesis* was credited to your account *period.* *Paragraph* Your customers will go for these large, tasty avocados *comma* I am sure *period.* They are the best we have handled in months *period.* *Paragraph* Thanks *comma* Mr. Key *comma* for another opportunity to serve you *period.* Sincerely *Type it for my signature.*

VOICE RECOGNITION WITH COMPUTERS

■ Dictating to your computer is now possible.

Voice activation technology now permits you to dictate to your computer. Some software programs possess a potential of 150 words per minute with 95 percent accuracy as well as a vocabulary of up to 64,000 words, with even more capability as a backup. Such voice recognition technology benefits those with limited keyboarding skills, repetitive-stress-related hand injuries, and disabilities that affect hand-eye coordination.

■ Voice recognition software creates digital signals from spoken sounds.

Voice recognition software translates spoken information into digital signals that can be recognized by computers. To be able to make such translations, you must have a high-end computer system. And you will need to spend three or four hours training your computer to receive your messages by reading passages to it.

■ Continuous software (which allows you to speak naturally) is replacing discrete software (which requires you to pause after words).

In addition, continuous voice recognition software is rapidly replacing discrete software. Continuous systems permit you to speak at your own natural rhythm, while discrete software requires you to pause after each word, thus slowing the speaking process and interfering with creative thought. With continuous speech, the only interruptions are the user's pauses and corrections of unrecognizable words.

■ Voice recognition has many business applications—and the potential for even more.

You can use voice recognition software for letters, memos, reports, computerized forms, data entry, spreadsheet, and database maintenance. Because voice recognition is a continually evolving technology, you can expect more developments of it in the immediate future.

Your ability to communicate aloud is one of the most important factors contributing to your success on the job. Your attention to the skills discussed in this chapter and your continual efforts to get a bit better at each one will be worth the effort.

SUMMARY BY CHAPTER OBJECTIVES

1 Discuss talking and its key elements.

1. Talking is the oral expression of our knowledge, viewpoints, and emotions. It depends on four critical factors:

- Voice quality—talking that varies in pitch, delivery, and volume.
- Speaking style—blending voice quality and personality.
- Word choice—finding the right word or words for the listener.
- Adaptation—fitting a message to the mind of a unique listener.

2. Listening is just as important as talking in oral communication; but it causes more problems.

2 Explain the listening problem and how to solve it.

- Most of us think we listen better than we do.
- Active listening—a focus on the total meaning of an incoming message—is better than nonlistening. It includes:
  —evaluating meaning and delaying responses.
  —selecting symbols carefully.
- Listening involves how we sense, filter, and retain incoming messages.
- To improve our listening, we need to:
  —commit to improve.
  —focus attention.
  —improve the accuracy of our filtering.
  —concentrate on remembering.
  —follow "The Ten Commandments of Listening."

3 Describe the nature and role of nonverbal communication.

3. Nonverbal (nonword) communication is the communication that occurs without words.
- One major type is body language—the movements of our arms, fingers, facial muscles, and such.
  —Our face and eyes are the most expressive parts of body language.
  —Gestures also send messages.
  —Our physical appearance (clothing, cosmetics, jewelry, hairstyle) communicates about us.
- Space is a second major type of nonverbal communication.
  —We create four unique types of spaces: (1) intimate, (2) physical, (3) social, and (4) public.
  —We communicate differently in each space, as determined by our culture.
- How we give meaning to time is a third type of nonverbal communication.
- Meanings the sounds of our voices convey (paralanguage) is a fourth type.
- Color and physical context are minor nonverbal forms.
- In our speaking, we should use nonverbal communication to accent our words.
- In listening, we need to "hear" the nonverbal communication of others.

4 Practice good interviewing and listening techniques.

4. In conducting the various types of interviews in business (employment, evaluation, and job exit), follow these guidelines:
- Plan the interview to get the information you need.
- Begin by putting the interviewee at ease.
- Make certain the interviewee knows the purpose.
- Let the interviewee do most of the talking.
- Guide the interview, making sure you get what you need.
- Listen carefully and give the appearance of listening.
- Keep a record (take notes).
- End the interview, perhaps with a finalizing question.

5 Discuss the techniques for conducting and participating in meetings.

5. In business, you are likely to participate in meetings, some formal and some informal.
- If you are in charge of a meeting, follow these guidelines.
  —Know parliamentary procedure for formal meetings.
  —Plan the meeting; develop an agenda and circulate it in advance.
  —Follow the plan.
  —Keep the discussion moving.
  —Control those who talk too much.
  —Encourage participation from those who talk too little.
  —Control time, making sure the agenda is covered.
  —Summarize at appropriate times.
- If you are a participant at a meeting, follow these guidelines:

—Stay with the agenda; do not stray.
—Participate fully.
—But do not talk too much.
—Cooperate.
—Be courteous.

6 Describe good telephone and voice-mail techniques.

6. To improve your telephone and voice-mail techniques, consider the following:
   • Cultivate a pleasant voice.
   • Talk as if in a face-to-face conversation.
   • Follow courteous procedures.
     —When calling, introduce yourself and ask for the person you want.
     —State your purpose early.
     —Cover points systematically.
     —When receiving, identify your company or office and offer assistance.
     —When answering for the boss, do not offend by asking questions or making comments that might give a wrong impression; and do not neglect callers placed on hold.
     —When screening calls for the boss, be courteous and honest.
     —Listen when the other person is talking.
     —Do not interrupt or dominate.
     —Plan long conversations; and follow the plan.
   • For good communication using voice mail, follow these suggestions:
     —Identify yourself by name and affiliation.
     —Deliver a complete and accurate message.
     —Speak naturally and clearly.
     —Give important information slowly.
     —Close with a brief goodwill message.

7 Dictate letters and reports in an organized and effective manner.

7. In dictating messages and reports, follow these suggestions.
   • First, gather all the information you will need so you will not have to interrupt your dictating to get it.
   • Next, plan (think through) the message.
   • Begin the dictation by giving the transcriptionist any special information or instructions needed (enclosures, forms, address, and the like).
   • Then talk through the message.
   • Until you are experienced, force the words—then revise.
   • Remember, also, to speak in a strong, clear voice.
   • And give punctuation and paragraphing in the dictation.
   • Avoid asides (side comments not intended to be a part of the message).
   • Read back only when necessary.

CRITICAL THINKING QUESTIONS

1. Talking is a natural occurrence, so we should give it little attention. Discuss.

2. How do the elements of talking help us communicate better?

3. Explain how each type of nonverbal communication relates to speaking and to listening.

4. Discuss why we have difficulty in listening.

5. What can you do to improve your listening?

6. Assume that you are being interviewed for the job of _____ (your choice) with _____ (company of your choice). What questions would you anticipate? How would you answer them?

7. Assume that you are the interviewer for the interview in Question 6 (above). Discuss specific ways in which you would put the interviewee at ease.

8. The people attending a meeting—not the leader—should determine the agenda. Discuss.

9. As meetings should be democratic, everyone present should be permitted to talk as much as he or she wants without interference from the leader. Discuss.

10. Describe an annoying telephone practice that you have experienced or know about (other than the ones discussed in the chapter). Explain and/or demonstrate how it should be corrected.

11. Describe the strengths and weaknesses of voice-mail systems with which you are familiar.

12. Justify each of the dictating techniques suggested in the chapter.

13. Use the Internet to gather information and present a report on recent developments in voice recognition.

CRITICAL THINKING EXERCISES

LISTENING

After the class has been divided into two (or more) teams, the instructor reads some factual information (newspaper article, short story, or the like) to only one member of each team. Each of these team members tells what he or she has heard to a second team member, who in turn tells it to a third team member—and so on until the last member of each team has heard the information. The last person receiving the information reports what she or he has heard to the instructor, who checks it against the original message. The team able to report the information with the greatest accuracy wins.

INTERVIEWING

Working with a classmate, assume that you are an interviewer visiting your campus. Interview your classmate for a job in his or her field of specialization. Before beginning, explain any significant facts of the situation (nature of company, job requirements, applicant's limitations, and such). After finishing the interview, exchange your roles.

MEETINGS

Because group meetings are meaningful only when they concern problems that the participants know about and understand, the following topics for meetings involve campus situations. For one of these topics, develop a specific problem that would warrant a group meeting. (Example: For student government, the problem might be "To determine the weaknesses of student government on this campus and what should be done to correct them.") Then lead the class (or participate) in a meeting on the topic. Class discussion following the meeting should reinforce the text material and bring out the good and bad of the meeting.
   a. Student discipline
   b. Scholastic dishonesty

   c. Housing regulations
   d. Student-faculty relations
   e. Student government
   f. Library
   g. Grading standards
   h. Attendance policies
   i. Varsity athletics
   j. Intramural athletics
   k. Degree requirements
   l. Parking
   m. Examination scheduling
   n. Administrative policies
   o. University calendar
   p. Homework requirements
   q. Tuition and fees
   r. Student evaluation of faculty
   s. Community-college relations
   t. Maintenance of files of old examinations for students
   u. Computer availability

TELEPHONING

Make a list of bad telephone practices that you have experienced or heard about. With a classmate, first demonstrate the bad practice and then demonstrate how you would handle it. Some possibilities: putting a caller on hold tactlessly, harsh greeting, unfriendly voice quality, insulting comments (unintended), attitude of unconcern, cold and formal treatment.

DICTATING

Working with a classmate, select a letter problem from the problems following the letters chapters. Then dictate the letter to your classmate. Because your classmate will probably take your dictation in longhand, you may need to dictate slowly. After you have finished your dictation, exchange roles with your classmate.

15

Public Speaking and Oral Reporting

Upon completing this chapter, you will be able to use good speaking and oral-reporting techniques. To reach this goal, you should be able to

1 Select and organize a subject for effective formal presentation to a specific audience.

2 Describe how personal aspects and audience analysis contribute to formal presentations.

3 Explain the use of voice quality and physical aspects such as posture, walking, facial expression, and gestures in effective oral communication.

4 Plan for visuals (graphics) to support speeches and oral reports.

5 Work effectively with a group in preparing and making a team presentation.

6 Define oral reports and differentiate between them and written reports on the basis of their advantages, disadvantages, and organization.

Formal Speaking

I n addition to your informal speaking and listening activities at Mastadon Chemicals, you have more formal ones involving oral communication.

Take last week, for example. Malra Cody (your boss) asked you to do something very special for the company. It seems that each year Mastadon Chemicals awards a $5,000 scholarship to a deserving business student at State University. The award is presented at the business school's annual Honors Day Convocation, usually by Ms. Cody. To show the business school's appreciation for the award, its administration requested that Ms. Cody be the speaker at this year's convocation. But Ms. Cody has a conflicting engagement, so you got the assignment. You responded to the challenge as well as you could, but you were not pleased with the results.

Then, at last month's meeting, Mastadon's executive committee asked you for a special oral report from your department for about the fifth time. This time the report concerned the results of a survey that your department conducted to determine local opinions about a dispute between Mastadon and its union. You did your best, but you felt uneasy about what you were doing.

Such assignments are becoming more and more a part of your work as you move up the administrative ladder at Mastadon. You must try to do them better, for your future promotions are involved. The following review of formal oral presentations (speeches and reports) should help you in this effort.

MAKING FORMAL SPEECHES

The most difficult kind of oral communication for many people is a formal speech. Most of us do not feel comfortable speaking before others, and we generally do a poor job of it. But it need not be this way. With effort, we can improve our speaking. We can do this by learning what good speaking techniques are and then putting those techniques into practice.

- Speeches are difficult for most of us. The following techniques should help you.

SELECTION OF THE TOPIC

Your first step in formal speechmaking is to determine the topic of your presentation. In some cases, you will be assigned a topic, usually one within your area of specialization. In fact, when you are asked to make a speech on a specified topic, it is likely to be because of your knowledge of the topic. In some cases, your choice of topic will be determined by the purpose of your assignment, as when you are asked to welcome a group or introduce a speaker.

- Your topic may be assigned.

If you are not assigned a topic, then you must find one on your own. In your search for a suitable topic, you should be guided by three basic factors. The first is your background and knowledge. Any topic you select should be one with which you are comfortable—one within your areas of proficiency. The second basic factor is the interests of your audience. Selecting a topic that your audience can appreciate and understand is vital to the success of your speech. The third basic factor is the occasion of the speech. Is the occasion a meeting commemorating a historic event? A monthly meeting of an executives' club? An annual meeting of a hairstylists' association? Whatever topic you select should fit the occasion. A speech about Japanese management practices might be quite appropriate for the members of the executives' club, but not for the hairstylists. Your selection should be justified by all three factors.

- If you must select a topic, consider (1) your knowledge, (2) your audience, and (3) the occasion.

PREPARATION OF THE PRESENTATION

After you have decided what to talk about, you should gather the information you need for your speech. This step may involve searching through your mind for experiences or ideas, conducting research in a library or in company files, gathering information online, or con-

- Conduct research to get the information you need.

The 5th Wave   By Rich Tennant

(© The 5th Wave by Rich Tennant, Rockport, MA. Email: the5wave@tiac.net)

sulting people in your own company or other companies. In short, you do whatever is necessary to get the information you need.

Then organize the information.

When you have that information, you are ready to begin organizing your speech. Although variations are sometimes appropriate, you should usually follow the time-honored order of a speech: *introduction, body, conclusion.* This is the order described in the following paragraphs.

The greeting usually comes first.

Although not really a part of the speech, the first words usually spoken are the greeting. Your greeting, of course, should fit the audience. "Ladies and gentlemen" is appropriate for a mixed audience; "gentlemen" fits an all-male audience; and "my fellow Rotarians" fits an audience of Rotary Club members. Some speakers eliminate the greeting and begin with the speech, especially in more informal and technical presentations.

Gain attention in the opening.

INTRODUCTION.   The introduction of a speech has much the same goal as the introduction of a written report: to prepare the listeners (or readers) to receive the message. But it usually has the additional goal of arousing interest. Unless you can arouse interest at the beginning, your presentation is likely to fail. The situation is somewhat like that of the sales letter. At least some of the people with whom you want to communicate are not likely to be interested in receiving your message. As you will recall from your study of listening, it is easy for a speaker to lose the audience's attention. To prove the point, ask yourself how many times your mind has drifted away from the speaker's words when you have been part of an audience. There is no question about it: you, the speaker, will have to work to gain and hold the attention of your audience.

There are many opening possibilities—human interest,

The techniques of arousing interest are limited only by the imagination. One possibility is a human-interest story, for storytelling has strong appeal. For example, a speaker presenting a message about the opportunities available to people with original ideas might open this way: "Nearly 150 years ago, an immigrant boy of 17 walked the streets of our town. He had no food, no money, no belongings except the shabby clothes he wore. He had only a strong will to work—and an idea."

humor,

Humor, another possibility, is probably the most widely used technique. To illustrate, an investment broker might begin a speech on investment strategy as follows: "What you want me to give you today is some 'tried and trusted' advice on how to make money in the stock market. This reminds me of the proverbial 'tried and trusted' bank teller. He was trusted; and when they caught him, he was tried." Humor works best and is safest when it is closely related to the subject of your presentation.

quotations, questions, and so on.

Other effective ways for gaining attention at the opening are by using quotations and questions. By quoting someone the audience would know and view as credible, you build interest in your topic. You can also ask questions. One kind of question is the rhetorical question—the one everyone answers the same, such as "Who wants to be freed of burdensome financial responsibilities?" Another kind of question gives you background information on how much to talk about different aspects of your subject. With this kind of question, you must follow through your presentation based on the response. If you had asked "How many of you have IRAs?" and nearly everyone put a hand up, you wouldn't want to talk about the importance of IRAs. You could skip that part of your presentation, spending more time on another aspect, such as managing your IRA effectively.

Yet another possibility is the startling statement, which presents facts and ideas that awaken the mind. Illustrating this possibility is the beginning of a speech to an audience of merchants on a plan to reduce shoplifting: "Last year, right here in our city, in your stores, shoplifters stole over $3.5 million of your merchandise! And most of you did nothing about it."

In addition to arousing interest, your opening should lead into the theme of your speech. In other words, it should set up your message as the above examples do.

The opening should set up your subject.

Tell the subject of your speech . . .

Following the attention-gaining opening, it is appropriate to tell your audience the subject (theme) for your speech. In fact, in cases where your audience already has an interest in what you have to say, you can begin here and skip the attention-gaining opening. Presentations of technical topics to technical audiences typically begin this way. Whether you lead into a statement of your topic or begin with it, that statement should be clear and complete.

Because of the nature of your subject, you may find it undesirable to reveal a position early. In such cases, you may prefer to move into your subject indirectly—to build up your case before revealing your position. This inductive pattern may be especially desirable when your goal is to persuade—when you need to move the views of your audience from one position to another. But in most business-related presentations you should make a direct statement of your theme early in the speech.

unless you have reason not to, as when you must persuade.

BODY.   Organizing the body of your speech is much like organizing the body of a report (see Chapter 10). You take the whole and divide it into comparable parts. Then you take those parts and divide them. And you continue to divide as far as it is practical to do so. In speeches, however, you are more likely to use factors rather than time, place, or quantity as the basis of division because in most speeches your presentation is likely to be built around issues and questions that are subtopics of the subject. Even so, time, place, and quantity subdivisions are possibilities.

Organize most speeches by factors, as you would a report.

You need to emphasize the transitions between the divisions because, unlike the reader who can see them, the listener may miss them if they are not stressed adequately. Without clear transitions, you may be talking about one point and your listener may be relating those ideas to your previous point.

Emphasize transitions between parts.

CONCLUSION.   Like most reports, the speech usually ends by drawing a conclusion. Here you bring all that you have presented to a head and achieve whatever goal the speech has. You should consider including these three elements in your close: (1) a restatement of the subject, (2) a summary of the key points developed in the presentation, and (3) a statement of the conclusion (or main message). Bringing the speech to a climactic close— that is, making the conclusion the high point of the speech—is usually effective. Present the concluding message in strong language—in words that gain attention and will be remembered. In addition to concluding with a summary, you can give an appropriate quote, use humor, and call for action. The following close of a speech comparing Japanese and American management techniques illustrates this point: "These facts make my conclusion crystal clear. We are not Japanese. We do not have the Japanese culture. Most Japanese management methods have not worked—cannot work—will not work in our society."

The ending usually (1) restates the subject, (2) summarizes key points, and (3) draws a conclusion.

DETERMINATION OF THE PRESENTATION METHOD

With the speech organized, you are ready to prepare its presentation. At this time, you need to decide on your method of presentation—that is, whether to present the speech extemporaneously, to memorize it, or to read it.

Choose one of these presentation methods.

■ (1) extemporaneous presentation (thorough preparation, uses notes, rehearsed),

PRESENTING EXTEMPORANEOUSLY.   Extemporaneous presentation is by far the most popular and effective method. With this method, you first thoroughly prepare your speech, as outlined above. Then you prepare notes and present the speech from them. You usually rehearse, making sure you have all the parts clearly in mind, but you make no attempt to memorize. Extemporaneous presentations generally sound natural to the listeners, yet they are (or should be) the product of careful planning and practice.

■ (2) memorizing, or

MEMORIZING.   The most difficult method is memorizing. If you are like most people, you find it hard to memorize a long succession of words. And when you do memorize, you are likely to memorize words rather than meanings. Thus, when you make the speech, if you miss a word or two, you become confused—and so does your speech. You may even become panic-stricken.

Probably few of the speakers who use this method memorize the entire speech. Instead, they memorize key passages and use notes to help them through the speech. A delivery of this kind is a cross between an extemporaneous presentation and a memorized presentation.

■ (3) reading.

READING.   The third presentation method is reading. Unfortunately, most of us tend to read aloud in a dull monotone. We also miss punctuation marks, fumble over words, lose our place, and so on. Of course, many speakers overcome these problems, and with effort you can too. One effective way is to practice with a recorder and listen to yourself. Then you can be your own judge of what you must do to improve your delivery. You would be wise not to read speeches until you have mastered this presentation method. In most settings, it is a breach of etiquette to read. Your audience is likely to be insulted, and reading is unlikely to be as well received as an extemporaneous delivery. However, when you are in a position where you will be quoted widely, such as president of the United States or the CEO of a major company, reading from a carefully prepared speech is recommended.

CONSIDERATION OF PERSONAL ASPECTS

■ A logical preliminary to speechmaking is to analyze yourself as a speaker. You are a part of the message.

A preliminary to good speechmaking is to analyze yourself as a speaker. In oral presentations you, the speaker, are a very real part of the message. The members of your audience take in not only the words you communicate but also what they see in you. And what they see in you can significantly affect the meanings that develop in their minds. Thus, you should carefully evaluate your personal effect on your message. You should do whatever you can to detect and overcome your shortcomings and to sharpen your strengths. And you should follow the conventions and practices of good business etiquette in meeting the expectations of your listeners.

■ You should seek the following four characteristics:

The following summary of characteristics that should help you as a speaker may prove useful, but you probably already know what they are. To some extent, the problem is recognizing whether you lack these characteristics. To a greater extent, it is doing something

| Good speakers project their personal qualities—confidence, sincerity, friendliness, enthusiasm, and interest.

about acquiring them. The following review should help you pinpoint and deal with your problem areas.

CONFIDENCE.   A primary characteristic of effective oral reporting is confidence—your confidence in yourself and the confidence of your audience in you. The two are complementary, for your confidence in yourself tends to produce an image that gives your audience confidence in you; and your audience's confidence in you can give you a sense of security that increases your confidence in yourself.

(1) Having confidence in yourself is important. So is having the confidence of your audience.

Typically, you earn your audience's confidence over periods of association. But there are things you can do to project an image that builds confidence. For example, preparing your presentation diligently and practicing it thoroughly gives you confidence in yourself. That confidence leads to more effective communication, which increases your listeners' confidence in you. Another confidence-building technique is an appropriate physical appearance. Unfair and illogical as it may seem, certain types of dress and hairstyles create strong images in people's minds, ranging from highly favorable to highly unfavorable. Thus, if you want to communicate effectively, you should analyze the audience you seek to reach. And you should work to develop the physical appearance that projects an image in which that audience can have confidence. Yet another confidence-building technique is simply to talk in strong, clear tones. Such tones do much to project an image of confidence. Although most people can do little to change their natural voice, they can use sufficient volume.

You must earn the confidence of your audience, project the right image, and talk in a strong, clear voice.

SINCERITY.   Your listeners are quick to detect insincerity. And if they detect it in you, they are likely to give little weight to what you say. On the other hand, sincerity is valuable to conviction, especially if the audience has confidence in your ability. The way to project an image of sincerity is clear and simple: You must *be* sincere. Pretense of sincerity is rarely successful.

(2) Sincerity is vital. You convey an image of sincerity by being sincere.

THOROUGHNESS.   Generally, a thorough presentation is better received than a scanty or hurried presentation. Thorough coverage gives the impression that time and care have been taken, and this tends to make the presentation believable. But thoroughness can be overdone. Too much detail can drown your listeners in a sea of information. The secret is to leave out unimportant information. This, of course, requires good judgment. You must

(3) Thoroughness—giving your listeners all they need—helps your image.

Presentation Delivery Tools

While you must prepare and deliver oral presentations, delivery tools can help you do a better job. One tool within PowerPoint, Stage Manager, helps you plan, practice, and deliver good presentations. Several of its major tools are shown in the screen shot here. However, you can select as many or as few tools as needed. In planning a presentation, you could set timings for each slide. The timer tool would show you both in practice and delivery how close to your plan you were. Stage Manager shows you the slide currently being projected as well as the next one coming up. And your notes can be shown in a separate window as well. Special navigation buttons give you flexibility in delivering presentations. For example, to draw attention away from the visual and back to yourself, you would simply click the blank screen button. Or you may want to emphasize an item on the screen with a drawing tool. Furthermore, if you needed to skip slides or find new ones to help in a question and answer session, the tool allows you to navigate easily through a set of slides. This tool is clearly one that can give a professional polish to your presentations.

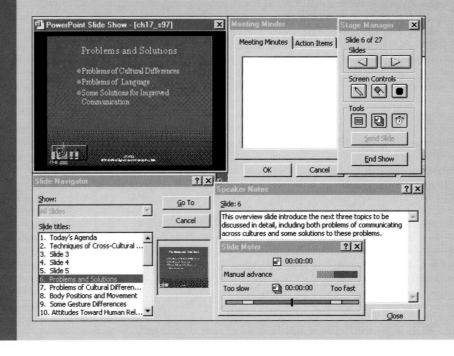

ask yourself just what your listeners need to know and what they do not need to know. Striking such a balance is the secret to achieving good etiquette in your presentation.

■ (4) Projecting an image of friendliness helps your communication effort.

FRIENDLINESS.   A speaker who projects an image of friendliness has a significant advantage in communicating. People simply like friendly people, and they are generally receptive to what such people say. Like sincerity, friendliness is hard to feign and must be honest to be effective. Both are parts of the conventions of business etiquette. Most people are genuinely friendly. Some, however, are just not able to project a genuinely friendly image. With a little self-analysis and a little mirror watching as you practice speaking, you can find ways of improving your projection of your friendliness.

These are but a few of the characteristics that should assist you as a speaker. There are others—*interest, enthusiasm, originality, flexibility,* and so on. But the ones discussed are the most significant and the ones that most speakers need to work on. Through self-analysis and dedicated effort, you can improve your speaking ability.

▌ Oral presentations to large audiences usually require formality and thorough preparation.

AUDIENCE ANALYSIS

One requirement of good speechmaking is to know your audience. You should study your audience both before and during the presentation.

■ You should know your audience.

PRELIMINARY ANALYSIS.   Analyzing your audience before the presentation requires that you size it up—that you search for audience characteristics that could affect how you should present your speech.

For example, the size of your audience is likely to influence how formal or informal your speech should be. As a rule, large audiences require more formality. Personal characteristics of your audience, such as age, sex, education, experience, and knowledge of subject matter, should also influence how you make your speech. They should affect the words, illustrations, and level of detail you use. Like writing, speeches should be adapted to the audience with every consideration given to good business etiquette. And the more you know about the audience, the better you will adapt your presentation to them.

■ Size up the audience in advance. Look for audience characteristics that will affect your speech—things like the size, sex, age, education, and knowledge of the audience.

ANALYSIS DURING PRESENTATION.   Your audience analysis should continue as you make the speech. *Feedback* is information about how your listeners are receiving your words. Armed with this information, you can adjust your presentation to improve the communication result.

Your eyes and ears will give you feedback information. For example, facial expressions will tell you how your listeners are reacting to your message. Smiles, blank stares, and movements will give you an indication of whether they understand, agree with, or accept it. You can detect from sounds coming (or not coming) from them whether they are listening. If questions are in order, you can learn directly how your message is coming across. In general, you can learn much from your audience by being alert; and what you learn can help you make a better speech.

■ Analyze audience reactions during the speech (called feedback). Facial expressions, movements, and noises give you feedback information that helps you adapt to the audience.

APPEARANCE AND PHYSICAL ACTIONS

As your listeners hear your words, they are looking at you. What they see is a part of the message and can affect the success of your speech. What they see, of course, is

■ Your audience forms impressions from these six factors:

you and what surrounds you. In your efforts to improve the effects of your oral presentations, you should understand the communication effects of what your listeners see. Some of the effects that were mentioned in Chapter 14 are expanded on here because they are particularly important to speeches and oral reports. Good etiquette requires that you use your appearance, physical actions, and physical context to meet the communication needs of your audience.

■ (1) all that surrounds you (stage, lighting, and the like),

THE COMMUNICATION ENVIRONMENT.   Much of what your audience sees is the physical things that surround you as you speak—the stage, lighting, background, and so on. These things tend to create a general impression. Although not visual, outside noises have a related influence. For the best communication results, the factors in your communication environment should contribute to your message, not detract from it. Your own experience as a listener will tell you what factors are important.

■ (2) your personal appearance,

PERSONAL APPEARANCE.   Your personal appearance is a part of the message your audience receives. Of course, you have to accept the physical traits you have, but most of us do not need to be at a disadvantage in appearance. All that is necessary is to use what you have appropriately. Specifically, you should dress in a manner appropriate for the audience and the occasion. Be clean and well groomed. Use facial expressions and physical movements to your advantage. Just how you should use facial expressions and physical movements is described in the following paragraphs.

■ (3) your posture,

POSTURE.   Posture is likely to be the most obvious of the things that your audience sees in you. Even listeners not close enough to detect such things as facial expressions and eye movements can see the general form of the body.

You probably think that no one needs to tell you about good posture. You know it when you see it. The trouble is that you are not likely to see it in yourself. One solution is to have others tell you whether your posture needs improvement. Another is to practice speaking before a mirror or watch yourself on videotape.

In your efforts to improve your posture, keep in mind what must go on within your body to form a good posture. Your body weight must be distributed in a way consistent with the impression you want to make. You should keep your body erect without appearing stiff and comfortable without appearing limp. You should maintain a poised, alert, and communicative bearing. And you should do all this naturally. The great danger with posture is an appearance of artificiality.

■ (4) your manner of walking,

WALKING.   Your audience also forms an impression from the way you walk before it. A strong, sure walk to the speaker's position conveys an impression of confidence. Hesitant, awkward steps convey the opposite impression. Walking during the presentation can be good or bad, depending on how you do it. Some speakers use steps forward and to the side to emphasize points. Too much walking, however, attracts attention and detracts from the message. You would be wise to walk only when you are reasonably sure that this will have the effect you want. You would not want to walk away from a microphone.

■ (5) facial expressions (smiles, frowns), and

FACIAL EXPRESSION.   As noted in Chapter 14, probably the most apparent and communicative physical movements are facial expressions. The problem, however, is that you may unconsciously use facial expressions that convey unintended meanings. For example, if a frightened speaker tightens the jaw unconsciously and begins to grin, the effect may be an ambiguous image that detracts from the entire communication effort. A smile, a grimace, and a puzzled frown all convey clear messages. Without question, you should use these effective communication devices.

Eye contact is important. The eyes, which have long been considered "mirrors of the soul," provide most listeners with information about the speaker's sincerity, goodwill, and flexibility. Some listeners tend to shun speakers who do not look at them. On the other hand, discriminate eye contact tends to show that you have a genuine interest in your audience.

GESTURES. Like posture, gestures contribute to the message you communicate. Just what they contribute, however, is hard to say, for they have no definite or clear-cut meanings. A clenched fist, for example, certainly adds emphasis to a strong point. But it can also be used to show defiance, make a threat, or signify respect for a cause. And so it is with other gestures. They register vague meanings, as discussed in Chapter 14.

■ (6) gestures.

Even though gestures have vague meanings, they are strong, natural helps to speaking. It appears natural, for example, to emphasize a plea with palms up and to show disagreement with palms down. Raising first one hand and then the other reinforces a division of points. Slicing the air with the hand shows several divisions. Although such gestures are generally clear, we do not all use them in exactly the same way.

■ Gestures have vague meanings, but they communicate.

In summary, it should be clear that physical movements can help your speaking. Just which physical movements you should use, however, is hard to say. The appropriateness of physical movements is related to personality, physical makeup, and the size and nature of the audience. A speaker appearing before a formal group should generally use relatively few physical movements. A speaker appearing before an informal group should use more. Which physical movements you should use on a given occasion is a matter for your best judgment.

■ In summary, your physical movements help your speaking.

USE OF VOICE

Good voice is an obvious requirement of good speaking. Like physical movements, the voice should not hinder the listener's concentration on the message. More specifically, it should not detract attention from the message. Voices that cause such difficulties generally fall into these areas of fault: (1) lack of pitch variation, (2) lack of variation in speed, (3) lack of vocal emphasis, and (4) unpleasant voice quality. Although these areas are mentioned in Chapter 14, we will examine them here because of their key significance to formal oral communication.

■ Good voice is a requirement of good speaking. Four faults affect voice:

LACK OF PITCH VARIATION. Speakers who talk in monotones are not likely to hold the interest of their listeners for long. Since most voices are capable of wide variations in pitch, the problem can usually be corrected. The failure to vary pitch generally is a matter of habit—of voice patterns developed over years of talking without being aware of their effect.

■ (1) lack of variation in pitch (usually a matter of habit),

LACK OF VARIATION IN SPEAKING SPEED. Determining how fast to talk is a major problem. As a general rule, you should present the easy parts of your message at a fairly fast rate and the hard parts and the parts you want to emphasize at a slower rate. The reason for varying the speed of presentation should be apparent; it is more interesting. A slow presentation of easy information is irritating; hard information presented fast may be difficult to understand.

■ (2) lack of variation in speed (cover the simple quickly, the hard slowly),

A problem related to the pace of speaking is the incorrect use of pauses. Properly used, pauses emphasize upcoming subject matter and are effective means of gaining attention. But frequent pauses for no reason are irritating and break the listeners' concentration. Pauses become even more irritating when the speaker fills them in with distracting nonwords such as *uh, you know,* and *OK.*

LACK OF VOCAL EMPHASIS. A secret of good speaking is to give words their proper emphasis by varying the manner of speaking. You can do this by (1) varying the pitch of your voice, (2) varying the pace of your presentation, and (3) varying the volume of your voice. As the first two techniques have already been discussed, only the use of voice volume requires comment here.

■ (3) lack of vocal emphasis (gain emphasis by varying pitch, pace, and volume), and

You must talk loudly enough for your entire audience to hear you, but not too loudly. Thus, the loudness—voice volume—for a large audience should be greater than that for a small audience. Regardless of audience size, however, variety in voice volume is good for interest and emphasis. It produces contrast, which is one way of emphasizing the subject matter. Some speakers incorrectly believe that the only way to show emphasis is to get louder and louder. But you can also show emphasis by going from loud to soft. The contrast with what has gone on earlier provides the emphasis. Again, variety is the key to making the voice more effective.

■ (4) unpleasant voice (improvement is often possible).

UNPLEASANT VOICE QUALITY. It is a hard fact of communication that some voices are more pleasant than others. Fortunately, most voices are reasonably pleasant. But some are raspy, nasal, or unpleasant in another way. Although therapy can often improve such voices, some speakers must live with them. But concentrating on variations in pitch, speed of delivery, and volume can make even the most unpleasant voice acceptable.

■ You can correct the foregoing faults through self-analysis and work.

IMPROVEMENT THROUGH SELF-ANALYSIS AND IMITATION. You can overcome any of the foregoing voice faults through self-analysis. In this day of tape recorders, it is easy to hear yourself talk. Since you know good speaking when you hear it, you should be able to improve your vocal presentation. One of the best ways to improve your presentation skills is through watching others. Watch your instructors, your peers, television personnel, professional speakers, and anyone else who gives you an opportunity. Analyze these speakers to determine what works for them and what does not. Imitate those good techniques that you think would help you and avoid the bad ones. Take advantage of any opportunity you have to practice speaking.

USE OF VISUALS (GRAPHICS)

■ Visuals (graphics) can sometimes help overcome the limitations of spoken words.

The spoken word is severely limited in communicating. Sound is here briefly and then gone. A listener who misses the vocal message may not have a chance to hear it again. Because of this limitation, speeches often need strong visual support—charts, tables, boards, film, and the like. Visuals (graphics) may be as vital to the success of a speech as the words themselves.

■ Use visuals for the hard parts of the message.

PROPER USE OF DESIGN. Effective visuals are drawn from the message. They fit the one speech and the one audience.

In selecting visuals you should search through your presentation for topics that appear vague or confusing. Whenever a visual of some kind will help eliminate vagueness or confusion, you should use it. You should use visuals to simplify complex information and improve cohesiveness, as well as to emphasize or add interest. Visuals are truly a part of your message, and you should look at them as such.

■ Use the type of visual (chart, diagram, picture) that communicates the information best.

After deciding that a topic deserves visual help, you determine what form that help should take. That is, should the visual be a chart, a diagram, a picture, or what? You should select your visuals primarily on the basis of their ability to communicate. Simple and obvious as this injunction may appear, people violate it all too often. They select visuals more for appearance and dramatic effect than for communication effect.

■ Select from the various available types of visuals.

TYPES TO CONSIDER. Because no one type of visual is best for all occasions, you should have a flexible attitude toward visuals. You should know the strengths and weaknesses of each type, and you should know how to use each type effectively.

In selecting visuals, you should keep in mind the available types. You will mainly consider the various types of graphics—the charts, line graphs, tables, diagrams, and pictures discussed in Chapter 13. Each of these types has its strengths and weaknesses and can be displayed in various ways—for example, by LCD screen and computer; by flip chart; by easel display; on a presentation board; or on a felt board. And each of these display methods has its strengths and weaknesses. In addition to using graphics to support your speech, you can support it with videotapes, photographs, models, samples, demonstrations, and the like.

AUDIENCE SIZE, COST, AND EASE OF PREPARATION CONSIDERATIONS. Your choice of visuals should also be influenced by the audience size and formality, the cost of preparing and using the media (visuals), and the ease and time of preparation. The table below illustrates how the different media fare on these dimensions.

Mark Twain on "Knowing When to Stop Talking"

These words by Mark Twain carry a vital message for windy speakers:

"Some years ago in Hartford, we all went to church one hot sweltering night to hear the annual report of Mr. Hawley, a city missionary who went around finding people who needed help and didn't want to ask for it. He told of the life in cellars, where poverty resided; he gave instances of the heroism and devotion of the poor. 'When a man with millions gives,' he said, 'we make a great deal of noise. It's noise in the wrong place, for it's the widow's mite that counts.' Well, Hawley worked me up to a great pitch. I could hardly wait for him to get through. I had $400 in my pocket. I wanted to give that and borrow more to give. You could see greenbacks in every eye. But instead of passing the plate then, he kept on talking and talking, and as he talked it grew hotter and hotter, and we grew sleepier and sleepier. My enthusiasm went down, down, down, down—$100 at a clip—until finally, when the plate did come around, I stole ten cents out of it. It all goes to show how a little thing like this can lead to crime."

· ·

Presentation Media Comparison

Media	Image Quality	Audience Size	Cost	Ease of Preparation
Photos	Good–very good	2–20	Low	Easy
Slides	Very good	20–200	Low	Very easy
Overhead transparency	Good–very good	2–200	Low	Very easy
Video monitors	Good	2–50	Medium	Easy–fair
HiRes television	Very good	2–100	High	Fair
LCD screens	Poor	2–20	Medium	Easy
Video projection	Good	20–200	High	Fair
Film	Very good	2–200	High	Difficult
Computer graphics	Very good	2–200	High	Easy–fair

Source: Adapted from G. A. Marken, "Visual Aids Strengthen In-House Presentations," *Office Systems,* February 1990, p. 34.

TECHNIQUES IN USING VISUALS.   Visuals usually carry key parts of the message. Thus, they are points of emphasis in your presentation. You blend them in with your words to communicate the message. How you do this is to some extent an individual matter, for techniques vary. They vary so much, in fact, that it would be hard to present a meaningful summary of them. It is more meaningful to present a list of dos and don'ts. Such a list follows:

■ Make the visuals points of interest in your presentation.

■ Make certain that everyone in the audience can see the visuals. Too many or too-light lines on a chart, for example, can be hard to see. An illustration that is too small can be meaningless to people far from the speaker.

■ Explain the visual if there is any likelihood that it will be misunderstood.

■ Organize the visuals as a part of the presentation. Fit them into the presentation plan.

■ Emphasize the visuals. Point to them with physical action and words.

■ Talk to the audience—not to the visuals. Look at the visuals only when the audience should look at them.

■ Avoid blocking the listeners' view of the visuals. Make certain that the listeners' views are not blocked by lecterns, pillars, chairs, and such. Take care not to stand in anyone's line of vision.

■ Here are specific suggestions for using visuals.

A SUMMARY LIST OF SPEAKING PRACTICES

The foregoing review of business speaking has been selective, for the subject is broad. In fact, entire books have been devoted to it. But this review has covered the high points, es-

■ This review has covered the high points of speaking.

pecially those that you can easily transfer into practice. Perhaps even more practical is the following list of what to do and not to do in speaking.

■ This summary checklist of good and bad speaking practices should prove helpful.

- Organize the speech so that it leads the listeners' thoughts logically to the conclusion.
- Move surely and quickly to the conclusion. Do not leave a conclusion dangling, repeat unnecessarily, or appear unable to close.
- Use language specifically adapted to the audience.
- Articulate clearly, pleasantly, and with proper emphasis. Avoid mumbling and the use of nonwords such as *ah, er, uh,* and *OK.*
- Speak correctly, using accepted grammar and pronunciation.
- Maintain an attitude of alertness, displaying appropriate enthusiasm and confidence.
- Employ body language to best advantage. Use it to emphasize points and to assist in communicating concepts and ideas.
- Be relaxed and natural. Avoid stiffness or rigidity of physical action.
- Look the listeners in the eye and talk directly to them.
- Keep still. Avoid excessive movements, fidgeting, and other signs of nervousness.
- Punctuate the presentation with reference to visuals. Make them a part of the speech text.
- Even when faced with hostile questions or remarks, keep your temper. To lose your temper is to lose control of the presentation.

TEAM (COLLABORATIVE) PRESENTATIONS

■ Group presentations require individual speaking skills plus planning for collaboration. Adapt the ideas on collaborative writing in Chapter 10 to team presentations.

Another type of presentation you may be asked to give is a group or team presentation. To give this type of presentation, you will need to use all you have learned about giving individual speeches. Also, you will need to use many of the topics discussed in Chapter 10 on collaborative writing groups. But you will need to adapt the ideas to an oral presentation setting. Some of the adaptations should be obvious. We will mention others that you should give special thought to in your team presentation.

■ Plan for the order of the presentation and each member's part.

First, you will need to take special care to plan the presentation—to determine the sequence of the presentation as well as the content of each team member's part. You will also need to select carefully supporting examples to build continuity from one part of the presentation to the next.

■ Plan for the physical factors.

Groups should plan for the physical aspects of the presentation, too. You should coordinate the type of delivery, use of notes, graphics, and styles and colors of attire to present a good image of competence and professionalism. And you should plan transitions so that the team will look coordinated.

■ Plan for the physical staging.

Another presentation aspect—physical staging—is important as well. Team members should know where to sit or stand, how visuals will be handled, and how to change or adjust microphones and how to enter and leave the speaking area.

■ Plan for the close.

Attention to the close of the presentation is especially strategic. Teams need to decide who will present the close and what will be said. If a summary is used, the member who presents it should attribute key points to appropriate team members. If there is to be a question-and-answer session, the team should plan how to conduct it. For example, will one member take the questions and direct them to a specific team member? Or will the audience be permitted to ask questions to specific members? Some type of final note of appreciation or thanks needs to be planned with all the team nodding in agreement or acknowledging the final comment in some way.

■ Plan to rehearse the presentation.

In all of their extra planning activities, teams should not overlook the need to plan for rehearsal time. Teams should consider practicing the presentation in its entirety several times as a group before the actual presentation. During these rehearsals, individual members should critique thoroughly each other's contributions, offering specific ways to improve. After first rehearsal sessions, outsiders (nonteam members) might be asked to view the team's presentation and critique the group. Moreover, the team might consider video-

In oral reports as well as formal speeches, visuals are effective in communicating important parts of the message.

taping the presentation so that all members can evaluate it. In addition to a more effective presentation, the team can enjoy the by-products of group cohesion and *esprit de corps* by rehearsing the presentation. Successful teams know the value of rehearsing and will build such activity into their presentation planning schedules.

These points may appear minor. But careful attention to them will result in a polished, coordinated team presentation.

REPORTING ORALLY

A special form of speech is the oral report. You are more likely to make oral reports than speeches in business, and the oral reports you make are likely to be important to you. Unfortunately, most of us have had little experience and even less instruction in oral reporting. Thus, the following review should be valuable to you.

■ The oral report is a form of speech.

A DEFINITION OF ORAL REPORTS

In its broadest sense, an oral report is any presentation of factual information and its interpretation using the spoken word. A business oral report would logically limit coverage to factual business information. By this definition, oral business reports cover much of the information and analysis exchanged daily in the conduct of business. They vary widely in formality. At one extreme, they cover the most routine and informal reporting situations. At the other, they include highly formal and proper presentations. Because the more informal oral exchanges are little more than routine conversations, the emphasis in the following pages is on the more formal ones. Clearly, these are the oral reports that require the most care and skill and are the most deserving of study.

■ An *oral report* is defined as an oral presentation of factual information.

DIFFERENCES BETWEEN ORAL AND WRITTEN REPORTS

Oral reports are much like written reports, so there is little need to repeat much of the previously presented material on reports. Instead, we will focus on the most significant differences between oral and written reports. Three in particular stand out.

■ Oral reports differ from written reports in these ways:

VISUAL ADVANTAGES OF THE WRITTEN WORD. The first significant difference between oral and written reports is that writing permits greater use of visuals to communication than does speaking. With writing, you can use paragraphing to show readers the structure of the message and to make the thought units stand out. In addition, you can use punctuation to show relationships, subordination, and qualification. These techniques improve the communication effect of the entire message.

On the other hand, when you make an oral presentation, you cannot use any of these techniques. However, you can use techniques peculiar to oral communication. For example, you can use inflection, pauses, volume emphasis, and changes in the rate of delivery. Depending on the situation, the techniques used in both oral and written reports are effective in assisting communication. But the point is that the techniques are different.

READER CONTROL OF WRITTEN PRESENTATION. A second significant difference between oral and written reports is that the readers of a written report, unlike the listeners to an oral report, control the pace of the communication. They can pause, reread, change their rate of reading, or stop as they choose. Since the readers set the pace, writing can be complex and still communicate. However, since the listeners to an oral report cannot control the pace of the presentation, they must grasp the intended meaning as the speaker presents the words. Because of this limiting factor, good oral reporting must be relatively simple.

EMPHASIS ON CORRECTNESS IN WRITING. A third significant difference between oral and written reports is the different degrees of correctness that they require. Because written reports are likely to be inspected carefully, you are likely to work for a high degree of correctness when you prepare them. That is, you are likely to follow carefully the recognized rules of grammar, punctuation, sentence structure, and so on. When you present oral reports, on the other hand, you may be more lax about following these rules. One reason is that usually oral reports are not recorded for others to inspect at their leisure. Another is that oral communication standards of correctness are less rigid than written communication standards. This statement does not imply that you should avoid good language in oral communication, however.

The differences between writing and speaking—visual aspects, reader control, and correctness—can become planning parts to improve your oral report. You will need to identify these advantages of written reports as barriers to your oral report. You will then need to think of ways to overcome them. Such a process is an essential preliminary step to the actual planning of oral reports.

PLANNING THE ORAL REPORT

As with written reports, planning is the logical first step in your work on oral reports. For short, informal oral reports, planning may be minimal. But for the more formal oral reports, particularly those involving audiences of more than one, proper planning is likely to be as involved as that for a comparable written report.

DETERMINATION OF REPORT OBJECTIVE. Logically, your first task in planning an oral report is to determine your objective. Just as was described for the written report in Chapter 10, you should state the report objective in clear, concise language. Then you should clearly state the factors involved in achieving this objective. Doing these things gives you a guide to the information you must gather and to the framework around which you will build your presentation.

In determining your report objective, you must be aware of your general objective. That is, you must decide on your general purpose in making the presentation. Is it to persuade? To inform? To recommend? This decision will have a major influence on your development of material for presentation and perhaps even on the presentation itself.

Margin notes:

- (1) writing and speaking each have special advantages and disadvantages;

- (2) the speaker controls the pace of an oral report, and the reader controls the pace of a written report; and

- (3) written reports place more stress on correctness.

- Planning is the first step in preparing oral reports.

- First determine the objective and what must be done to reach it.

ORGANIZATION OF CONTENT. The procedure for organizing oral reports is similar to that for organizing written reports. You have the choice of using either the direct or indirect order. Even so, the same information is not necessarily presented in the same way orally and in writing. Time pressure, for example, might justify direct presentation for an oral report on a problem that, presented in writing, might be better arranged in the indirect order. Readers in a hurry can always skip to the conclusion or ending of the report. Listeners do not have this choice.

■ Next organize content. Either the indirect or direct order is all right,

Although oral reports may use either the direct or indirect order, the indirect is the most logical order and by far the most widely used order. Because your audience is not likely to know the problem well, introductory remarks are needed to prepare it to receive your message. In addition, you may need such remarks to arouse interest, stimulate curiosity, or impress the audience with the importance of the subject. The main goal of the introductory remarks is to state the purpose, define unfamiliar terms, explain limitations, describe scope, and generally cover all the necessary introductory subjects (see discussion of introduction, Chapter 11).

■ but the indirect order is more common.

In the body of the oral report, you should work toward the objective you have set. Here, too, the oral report closely resembles the written report. Division of subject matter into comparable parts, logical order, introductory paragraphs, concluding paragraphs, and the like are equally important to both forms.

■ The organization of oral and written reports is much the same, except that oral reports usually have a closing summary.

The major difference in the organization of the written and the oral report is in the ending. Both forms may end with a conclusion, a recommendation, a summary, or a combination of the three. But the oral report is likely to have a final summary, whether or not it has a conclusion or a recommendation. In a sense, this final summary serves the purpose of an executive summary by bringing together all the really important information, analyses, conclusions, and recommendations in the report. It also assists the memory by emphasizing the points that should stand out. Oral and nonverbal emphasis techniques should help memory as well.

SUMMARY BY CHAPTER OBJECTIVES

1. Consider the following suggestions in selecting and organizing a speech.
   • Begin by selecting an appropriate topic—perhaps one in your area of specialization and of interest to your audience.
   • Organize the message (probably by introduction, body, conclusion).
   • Consider an appropriate greeting ("Ladies and Gentlemen," "Friends").
   • Design the introduction to meet these goals:
     —Arouse interest with a story, humor, or such.
     —Introduce the subject (theme).
     —Prepare the reader to receive the message.
   • Use indirect order presentation to persuade and direct order for other cases.
   • Organize like a report—divide and subdivide, usually by factors.
   • Select the most appropriate ending, usually restating the subject and summarizing.
   • Consider using a climactic close.
   • Choose the best manner of presentation.
     —Extemporaneous is usually best.
     —Memorizing is risky.
     —Reading is difficult unless you are skilled.
2. To improve your speaking, take these steps:
   • Work on these characteristics of a good speaker:
     —Confidence.
     —Sincerity.
     —Thoroughness.
     —Friendliness.

1 Select and organize a subject for effective formal presentation to a specific audience.

2 Describe how personal aspects and audience analysis contribute to formal presentations.

- Know your audience.
  - —Before the presentation, size them up—looking for characteristics that affect your presentation (sex, age, education).
  - —During the presentation, continue to analyze them, looking at facial expressions, listening to noises, and such—and adapt to them.

3 Explain the use of voice quality and physical aspects such as posture, walking, facial expression, and gestures in effective oral communication.

3. What the listeners see and hear affects the communication.
   - They see the physical environment (stage, lighting, background), personal appearance, posture, walking, facial expressions, gestures, and such.
   - They hear your voice.
     - —For best effect, vary the pitch and speed.
     - —Give appropriate vocal emphasis.
     - —Cultivate a pleasant quality.

4 Plan for visuals (graphics) to support oral reports and speeches.

4. Use visuals (graphics) whenever they help communicate.
   - Select the types that do the best job.
   - Blend the visuals into your speech, making certain that the audience sees and understands them.
   - Organize your visuals as a part of your message.
   - Emphasize the visuals by pointing to them.
   - Talk to the audience, not the visuals.
   - Do not block your audience's view of the visuals.

5 Work effectively with a group in preparing and making a team presentation.

5. Group presentations have special problems.
   - They require all the skills of individual presentation.
   - In addition, they require extra planning
     - —To reduce overlap and provide continuity.
     - —To improve transition between presentations.
     - —To coordinate questions and answers.

6 Define oral reports and differentiate between them and written reports on the basis of their advantages, disadvantages, and organization.

6. Business oral reports are spoken communications of factual business information and its interpretation.
   - Written and oral reports differ in three significant ways.
     - —Written reports permit more use of visual helps to communication (paragraphing, punctuation, and such); oral reports allow voice inflection, pauses, and the like.
     - —Oral reports permit the speaker to exercise greater control over the pace of the presentation; readers of a written report control the pace.
     - —Written reports place more emphasis on writing correctness (grammar, punctuation, etc.).
   - Plan oral reports just as you do written ones.
     - —First, determine your objective and state its factors.
     - —Next, organize the report, using either indirect or direct order.
     - —Divide the body based on your purpose, keeping the divisions comparable and using introductory/concluding paragraphs, logical order, and the like.
     - —End the report with a final summary—a sort of ending executive summary.

CRITICAL THINKING QUESTIONS

1. Assume that you must prepare a speech on the importance of making good grades for an audience of college students. Develop some attention-gaining ideas for the introduction of this speech. Do the same for a climactic close for the speech.

2. When is an extemporaneous presentation desirable? When should a speech be read? Discuss.

3. Explain how a speaker's personal characteristics influence the meanings of his or her spoken words.

4. An employee presented an oral report to an audience of 27 middle- and upper-level administrators. Then she presented the same information to three top executives. Note some of the probable differences between the two presentations.

5. Explain how feedback can be used in making a speech.

6. One's manner of dress, choice of hairstyle, physical characteristics, and the like are personal. They should have no influence on any form of oral communication. Discuss.

7. By description (or perhaps by example), identify good and bad postures and walking practices for speaking.

8. Explain how facial expressions can miscommunicate.

9. Give some illustrations of gestures that can be used to communicate more than one meaning. Demonstrate them.

10. "We are born with voices—some good, some bad, and some in between. We have no choice but to accept what we have been given." Comment.

11. What should be the determining factors in the use of visuals (graphics)?

12. Discuss (or demonstrate) some good and bad techniques of using visuals.

13. In presenting an oral report to a group composed of fellow workers as well as some bosses, a worker is harassed by the questions of a fellow worker who is trying to embarrass him. What advice would you give the worker? Would your advice be different if the critic were one of the bosses? What if the speaker were a boss and the critic a worker? Discuss.

14. Give examples of ways a team could provide continuity between members through the use of supporting examples. Be specific.

15. Explain the principal differences between written and oral reports.

16. Compare the typical organization plans of oral and written reports. Note the major differences between the two kinds of plans.

CRITICAL THINKING EXERCISES

SPEECHES

Since a speech can be made on almost any topic, it is not practical to list topics for speeches. You or your instructor can generate any number of interesting and timely topics in a short time. Whatever topic you select, you will need to determine the goals clearly, to work out the facts of the situation, and to set a time limit.

ORAL REPORTS

Most of the written report problems presented in the problem section following Chapter 11 can also serve as oral report problems. The following problems, however, are especially suitable for oral presentation.

1. Survey the major business publications for information about the outlook for the national (or world) economy for the coming year. Then present a summary report to the directors of Allied Department Stores, Inc.

2. As a student leader on your campus, you have been asked by the faculty senate (or a comparable faculty group) to report to its members on the status of faculty–student relations. You will include recommendations on what can be done to improve those relations.

3. Report to a meeting of a wildlife-protection organization on the status of an endangered species in your area. You will need to gather the facts through research, probably in wildlife publications.

4. A national chain of _____ (your choice) is opening an outlet in your city. You have been assigned the task of reviewing site possibilities. Gather the pertinent information and make an oral recommendation to the board of directors.

5. The Future Business Leaders Club at your old high school has asked you to report to it on the nature and quality of business study at your college. You will cover all the factors that you think high school students need to know. Include visuals in your presentation.

6. As representative of a travel agency, present a travel package on _____ (place or places of your choice) to the members of the Adventurer Travel Club. You will describe places to be visited, and you will cover all the essential details—dates, hotels, guide service, meals, costs, manner of travel, and so on.

7. Report to a meeting of Consumers' Alliance (a consumer-protection organization) on the economics of renting telephones from the telephone company versus buying telephones. You will need to gather facts through research.

8. Look through current newspapers, magazines, the web, and so on, and get the best available information on the job outlook for this year's college graduates. You will want to look at each major field separately. You may also want to show variations by geographic area, degree, and schools. Present your findings in a well-organized and illustrated oral report.

9. Present a plan for improving some phase of operation on your campus (registration, scholastic honesty, housing, grade appeals, library, cafeteria, traffic, curricula, athletics, computer labs, or the like).

10. Present an objective report on some legislation of importance to business (right-to-work laws, environmental controls, taxes, or the like). Take care to present evidence and reasoning from all the major viewpoints. Support your presentation with facts, figures, and so on whenever they will help. Prepare visual supports.

11. Assume that you are being considered by a company of your choice for a job of your choice. Your prospective employer has asked you to make a _____-minute report (your instructor will specify) on your qualifications. You may project your education to the date you will be in the job market, making assumptions that are consistent with your record to date.

12. Prepare and present a report on how individuals may reduce their federal or state income tax payments. You will probably want to emphasize the most likely sources of tax savings, such as tax sheltering and avoiding common errors.

13. Make a presentation to a hypothetical group of investors that will get you the investment money you need for a purpose of your choice. Your purpose could be to begin a new business, to construct a building, to develop land—whatever interests you. Make your presentation as real (or realistic) as you can. And support your appeal with visuals.

14. As chairperson of the site-selection committee of the National Federation of Business Executives, present a report on your committee's recommendation. The committee has selected a city and a convention hotel (you may choose each). Your report will give your recommendation and the reasons that support it. For class purposes, you may make up whatever facts you may need about the organization and its convention requirements and about the hotel. But use real facts about the city.

15. As a buyer of men's (or women's) clothing, report to the sales personnel of your store on the fashions for the coming season. You may get the necessary information from publications in the field.

16. The top administrators of your company have asked you to look into the matter of whether the company should own automobiles, lease automobiles, or pay mileage costs on employee-owned automobiles. (Automobiles are used by sales personnel.) Gather the best available information on the matter and report it to the top administrators. You may make up any company facts you need; but make them realistic.

17. In a group designated or approved by your instructor, present a persuasive presentation proposing that your school make more computing equipment available for student use. Be sure to cover all aspects of such a decision including cost, access, security, and so on.

18. Choose a graphics package most of your classmates could use to prepare visuals for oral reports. Report on the features, documentation, and cost. Feel free to use visuals to support your report.

CHAPTER

16

Technology–Enabled Communication

CHAPTER OBJECTIVES

Upon completing this chapter, you will be able to describe the role of technology in business communication. To reach this goal, you should be able to

1 Explain how technology helps in constructing messages.

2 Identify appropriate software tools for different stages in the writing process.

3 Discuss how technology helps in the presentation of messages.

4 Explain basic concepts of document layout and design.

5 Discuss various ways to transmit messages and the hardware currently used.

6 Describe how technology assists in collaboration.

7 Discuss what impact future developments in technology might have on business communication.

Business Communication *Is* Technology . . . *Is Lesikar*

In today's competitive work environment, technology and business communication go hand-in-hand. That's why the chapter you are about to read in **Lesikar's Basic Business Communication** is also featured as a complete, online, and interactive chapter on the web. This hands-on chapter will be regularly updated by the authors to en-sure the inclusion of the latest developments in technology and how they impact the world of business com-munication.

So visit our website often at **www. mhhe. com/lesikar** to get the most up-to-date information about the technological changes that affect the way we communicate in business. We look forward to your feedback.

Using Technology in Communication Tasks

The company that hired you after your recent graduation is looking into ways the management information system (MIS) department can empower its employees with technological support. Your new boss has asked you to be on the team that is to propose new ideas. The boss has told you that this team, composed of employees from a variety of divisions, will discuss both hardware and software. One of the main focuses will be on identifying ways to help employees improve their day-to-day communication.

This chapter is designed to help you—to give you a picture of where we are now and where we may be going. It provides a structure for continuing to build your understanding of how future technology will assist you in communication tasks.

The rapid advances in computer technologies that support the communication process make this chapter an appropriate one to view on the Web. In addition to allowing you to always have an up-to-date chapter, the Web enables you to get links, presentations, and interactive material that enhance this chapter.

The figure you see here from *The Future of IT,* published by the Gartner Group, predicts a time line for some of these technologies.

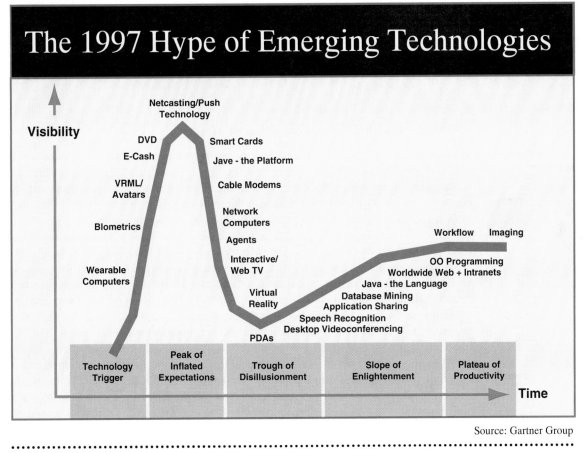

Source: Gartner Group

The 1997 Hype Cycle of Emerging Technologies

Technological tools can enhance the uniquely human ability to communicate. But as with any set of tools, how one uses them determines their degree of effectiveness. By using your mind both to create messages and to focus the technology appropriately, you can improve the quality of your communication.

Appropriately used, technology can assist individuals and groups with both the routine work related to writing as well as the creative, thinking aspects. William Zinsser, author of *On Writing Well,* compares one tool—the word processor—to a dishwasher. He describes it as liberating one from a chore that's not creative and that saps one's energy. As you'll learn, several technological tools assist you in this fashion. George Gilder, publisher of the $600 per year *Gilder Technology Report,* believes the new technologies affirm our intellectual power and creativity. And Bill Gates, CEO of Microsoft, predicts that technology will bring us voice recognition as well as enhanced sharing or collaboration. Gilder concurs with Gates, predicting that within five years everyone in the United States will be able to have a video teleconference anywhere in the world. Technology assists the communicator in many ways.

When you think of enhancing the communication process with technology, you probably first think of using word processing software on a personal computer. While that is one important tool, there are numerous hardware and software tools that can help improve your messages. These tools help with the construction, presentation, and transmission of messages as well as with collaboration.

TOOLS FOR CONSTRUCTING MESSAGES

Computer tools for constructing written messages can be associated with the different stages of the writing process—planning, gathering and collecting information, analyzing and organizing information, and writing and rewriting. In the past, many of these tools were discrete tools. But today, as we move toward greater integration, they often work seamlessly with each other. And, of course, many of the formerly discrete tools have become integral parts of today's word processors. The more skilled you become with each of these tools, the better they serve you.

COMPUTER TOOLS FOR PLANNING

Whether you are writing a short letter or long report, you can use a computer to help you plan both the document and the writing project. In planning the content of the document, *outlining* or *brainstorming* tools are useful. You can brainstorm, listing your ideas as they occur to you. Later you tag related ideas, asking the computer to group them. Outlining tools are included in most word processors. One way to use an outliner is with a split screen, as shown in Figure 16.1. In one part of the screen you'll see your outline and in another part the document you are writing. Today's large-screen monitors make this an effective use. Another way you can use an outliner is as a separate document. In this case your outline is held in memory; you can toggle back and forth to view it and store it when you are finished. An excellent discrete or specialty tool for planning is a concept-mapping/idea-generation program called Inspiration. As you see in Figure 16.2, on page 476, the program provides both a visual and an outlining mode, which allows users to toggle back and forth or work primarily in the mode that suits their particular tasks.

When you are working on a long writing project, several projects, or one carried over a long time, *project management software* is excellent for planning the project. It allows you to identify all the tasks needed to complete the project, to determine how much time each task might take, and to generate a time-and-task chart (commonly called a Gantt chart). Also, it helps you keep track of your progress and determine how to reallocate your resources to complete the project on time or within budget. You can see a Gantt chart in Figure 16.3 on page 477.

Finding time for writing, of course, is one of the major challenges for businesspeople. By using *personal information management (PIM) software,* you can plan time for completing writing projects. These time-management tools are merely annotated electronic calendars. However, they are excellent planning tools for scheduling your writing tasks. They will remind you of tasks to complete and days remaining before a document needs to be completed. Electronic calendar software is readily available. One simple but widely

FIGURE 16.1

Illustration of an Outlining Tool for Planning

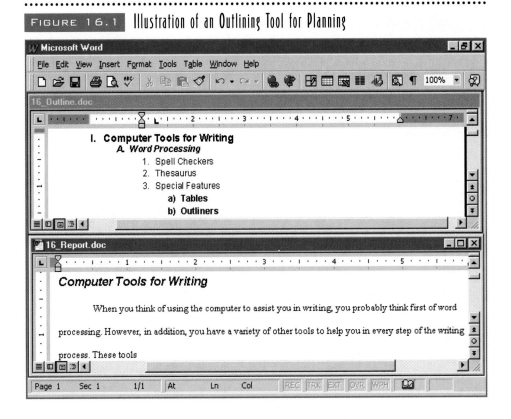

available calendar is a desktop accessory tool that is part of Windows. You can choose from a slew of other time-management tools. These offer a variety of ways to help you plan time for writing tasks from the day-to-day scheduling to longer-term planning. Figure 16.4 on page 477 shows the way one tool looks. The bell icon in front of the time shows that this writer set an alarm to let the computer remind him or her when it was time to write. The alarm sounds and the window opens at the designated time with a precise message of what needs to be done.

Some research identifies planning as the primary step that separates good writers from others. However, few writers have discovered the power of electronic planning tools. Using the powerful features that both project management and PIM tools provide will give you the potential to produce high-quality work in a timely fashion.

COMPUTER TOOLS FOR GATHERING AND COLLECTING INFORMATION

Before you can write, you have to have something to say. Sometimes you may be writing about your own ideas, but often you will supplement them with facts. Gathering facts or data is one of the most important jobs of the writer. Today you will want to combine your manual search for facts with electronic searches. The computer can help you find a variety of information quickly and accurately because today much of our printed information is available electronically. In fact, some kinds of information are only available electronically.

■ When you need information for a writing task, consider conducting an electronic search.

From the numerous headlines about the World Wide Web, you are probably well aware that computers can connect with other computers all over the world. While the way physical connections are made is interesting to some, as a writer you only need to know that it can be done so you can take advantage of it.

What you are looking for are facts. These facts can be stored in databases, which can either be internal or external. Your report due today at 1:00 PM might be on the current inventory of your on-site manufacturing product line. You could simply connect to your company's intranet at noon and download (copy to your computer system) the most recent data before completing your report. However, if you need to project the number of com-

■ Data can be gathered from internal or external computers.

FIGURE 16.2 Illustration of an Idea Generation Tool for Planning

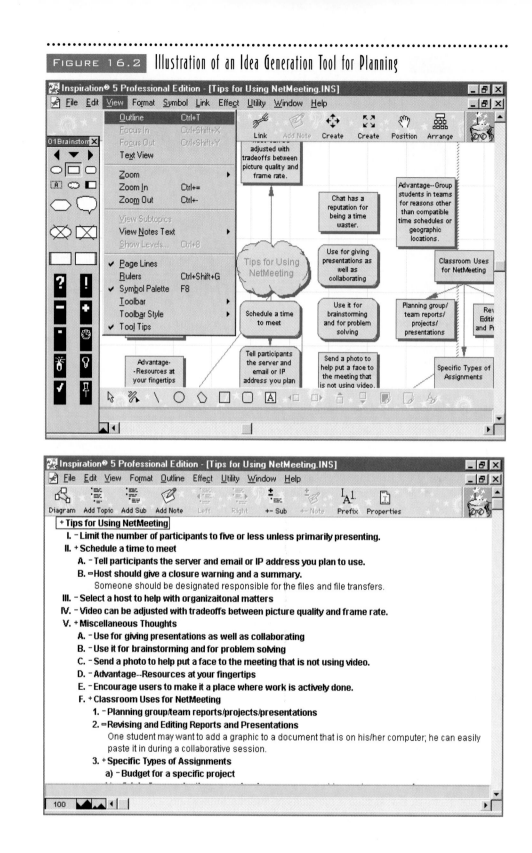

pleted units by the end of the month, you may also need to connect to your supplier's extranet to check the inventory of the parts you will need to complete your units. In this case, you will be using your computer to find facts both internally (from within your company) and externally (from your suppliers).

Most libraries are now allowing their online catalogs and databases to be accessed both internally and externally. This means you can use the on-line catalog from terminals within

Communications software connects over the telephone lines to external computers.

FIGURE 16.3 Illustration of a Planning Tool

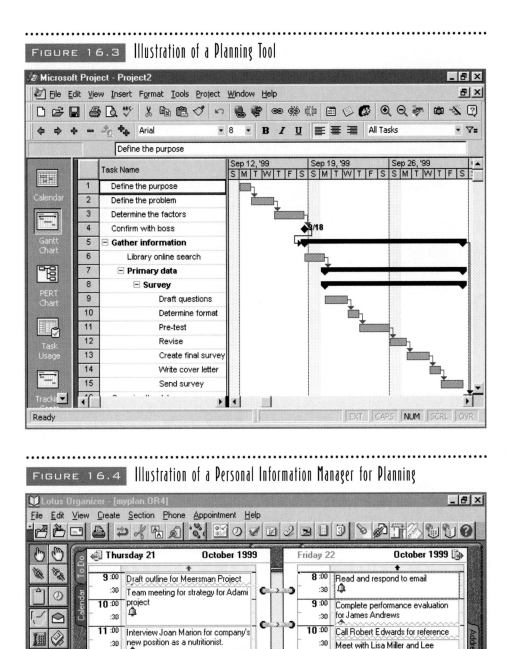

FIGURE 16.4 Illustration of a Personal Information Manager for Planning

the library or with a computer with *communications ability* (and with a modem or network connection) from anywhere outside the library. Many college networks also allow you to connect to the library resources from campus computer labs, dormitories, and remote and satellite offices.

▌ While technology makes constructing documents with graphics easy, writers still need to carefully review the messages they send.

With communications ability, you can also gather facts through the Internet. This expands your resources immensely beyond your local library. Not only can you reach the Library of Congress, but you also can search libraries in other countries. You can gather information from sources not available in any library anywhere. While you do need to be especially critical of the sources of your facts, using the Internet effectively to gather information can give you a tremendous competitive advantage.

Currently you can use technology to push the information you want to your desktop. By personalizing the channel selection and specifying the type of content you want to see from that channel, you will be setting up filters to work for you. You can also use software agents to monitor sources and notify you when information you specify is available. And, of course, you can re-run the results page that you have saved from a search using a well-designed search strategy. The new results page will be updated to reflect the information available at the moment.

Once you have gathered the facts, you will want to store them in some organized fashion so you can retrieve them readily when needed. *Database software* will help you immensely here. If your company is interested in developing a new product for a newly defined market niche, you may want to collect information about the targeted market, potential suppliers of components of your new product, sites for producing the product, projected labor costs, and so on. You could do this simply by entering the facts of publication and abstracted information in your individually designed form created with database software. The source information you have collected will be available whenever you need it. You can search and sort it on any of the categories (called fields) you set up on your data entry screen.

Variations of the generic database are the specialty tools such as ProCite, Reference Manager, Endnote, and others. These specialty programs allow you to collect information and enter it manually as you do with database software; and they allow you to enter it automatically as you download from a wide variety of online catalogs and services as well as CD-ROM and diskette-based services. Figure 16.5 gives you an example of this type of data manager.

In Chapter 19, which discusses business research methods, you will learn about other online information providers for business information. The major point to remember is that in business it is not necessarily what you know that really counts, but what you can find out. No one can know all there is to know about a subject, but those who are skilled at using a computer to gather information will find it a real asset.

▨ Database software provides a convenient way to collect information.

▨ Specialty tools help you collect facts, too.

FIGURE 16.5 Illustration of a Specialty Tool for Collecting Data

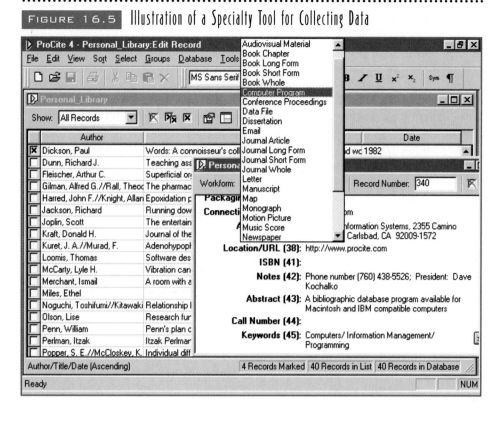

COMPUTER TOOLS FOR ANALYZING AND ORGANIZING

Three tools that writers find useful in analyzing data are statistics, graphics, and spreadsheet software. Since sometimes you cannot say very much about raw numbers, combining them or viewing them in different ways gives you a clearer picture of their meaning. Today, some very sophisticated *statistical software* has been made user-friendly, allowing those with little computer expertise to use it easily. Some programs will even query you about the nature of your data and recommend which statistical tests to use. Also, most *spreadsheet software* will compute a broad range of statistics to help writers give meaningful interpretations to data.

Graphics software helps writers in several ways. First, graphics reveal trends and relationships in data that are often hard to picture from raw data. This helps writers interpret clearly the meaning of their data. Second, graphics software helps writers explain more clearly to readers what the data mean. For example, you can direct the reader to look at the red and blue lines for the last five years on a line chart, noting the trend of increasing rate of profits. You can create graphics easily with all three tools. Also, most of these tools have features that allow you to annotate the graphic, directing the reader's attention to some particular aspect of the graph. You no longer have to be a graphic artist to create clear, good-looking graphics.

Outlining or *brainstorming software* is an organizing tool for the writer as well as a planning tool. Once you have captured your ideas and grouped related ideas, you can re-arrange items into a meaningful order, organizing with the reader in mind. You can also collapse or expand the outline to view as few or as many levels as you want. This lets you see a macro view or big picture of your document as well as a micro or detailed view, so you can check for consistency at all levels.

COMPUTER TOOLS FOR WRITING

Word processing software is clearly the dominant writing tool of most writers. Today's word processors are becoming more and more document-centric, allowing you to use other writing tools from within the word processor or that integrate seamlessly with it. Other

- Computer software helps you analyze and interpret data with statistics and graphics.

- Graphics software helps you understand the data and create graphics.

- Outlining and brainstorming software helps you organize your information.

computer writing tools that help writers include *spelling checkers, electronic thesauruses, grammar and style checkers, electronic references, graphics, drawing packages,* and *voice recognition tools.* The following discussion of these computer writing tools will point out how they can be used as well as caution you about any limitations.

WORD PROCESSING SOFTWARE.   By liberating you from tiresome chores, word processing gives you time to spend on revising, editing, and other document-polishing efforts. Some of the most common features of word processing software for revising and editing include insert/delete, move and copy, and search and replace.

Insert allows the writer to add characters at any point, while *delete* lets the writer delete characters. Major word processing programs also allow you to change your mind and undo the most recent insert and delete changes. Some writers rarely delete text, moving the text to the end of the file or to another file for possible future use. The search and replace feature can be used several ways. One way might be to search for the name in a file of someone who got married, retired, or was promoted and replace that name with the new name. Usually the writer decides whether to replace automatically every occurrence of the item or to check each occurrence. The search feature is usually used to find a particular word, name, or place. However, sometimes writers add asterisks or other symbols to mark copy or to add remarks or reminders—similar to the way one would use the bookmark feature. Later they search for those symbols to find the points in the document that need attention. You will find that these common features will be useful over and over.

Two other useful features of word processing are basic math and simple sorting. The basic math feature lets the writer enter columns or rows of numbers, leaving the calculation job for the software. The sorting feature lets the writer enter columns or rows of words, leaving the alphabetic sorting for the software. While these are useful features of word processing software, the writer has to be careful to enter or mark the copy exactly the way the software needs it to do the proper calculating or sorting.

The tables feature is another tool that enables you to do simple math and sort. It works similarly to a spreadsheet by allowing you to enter formulas in table cells, freeing you from the math. You can also link a table to a spreadsheet. When numbers change in the linked spreadsheet, they are automatically changed in the table with which they are linked. The tables feature allows formatting of individual cells, rows, and columns. It is useful for presenting data as well as textual material in rows and columns.

Another nice feature of many word processing programs is the hidden text or remark feature. If you insert the proper symbol, the comments that follow will be recorded in the file but not printed unless you tell the software to print them. Teachers can use this feature to put test answers in files but not on the test; later they can print a second copy and direct the software to print the comments. This feature can be used for reminders, detailed information, and such. For example, one might note that the vice president directed that an exception to company policy be granted under some special circumstances. Or one might leave a reminder to verify the statistics presented at a particular point in a document. In Figure 16.6, on page 482, you can see both the display of a comment and the printed document without the comment.

Two additional editing features involve the physical presentation of documents. These features are hyphenation and format change. Both help you change how the physical output looks. Hyphenation, for example, is a feature that helps the right margin appear less ragged than when it is not used. A ragged margin does not usually bother most people on a full page with full-length lines; however, when one is using a short line without hyphenating, the right margin can be distracting if it appears ragged. The example of column text in Figure 16.7 on page 483, with and without hyphenation illustrates how hyphenation can smooth out a ragged right margin. Format change also helps you change margins, tabs, spacing, and so on. Formatting is particularly useful when you are changing letterheads, paper sizes, type styles, or binding. It allows you to experiment easily to find the most appropriate form to present the document to the reader.

Since revising and editing are extremely important to turning out well-written business documents, these are tools you will use often.

Some other word processing features that make the writing job easier are footnoting,

---

■ Word processing helps you capture, manipulate, edit, and revise your messages.

■ Insert, delete, move and copy, and search and replace enable you to do what the terms suggest.

■ Basic math calculates columns and sorting arranges information in an order.

■ The tables feature also allows you to do simple math with data and to sort them.

■ The hidden text feature permits inserting information that is not printed until you choose to print it.

■ Hyphenation and format change enable you to control evenness of right margin.

■ Footnoting, table of contents generating, and index building are features that make writing easier.

Technology in Brief

Backing Up Frequently Is the Writer's Responsibility

Some programs will create an automatic backup file, but it is the writer's responsibility to be sure it is set up appropriately and working properly. Some writers back up their work every 15 minutes or so, while others back up every page. Most writers know how difficult it is to create a document, much less re-create it, so they are willing to spend a few seconds regularly to protect their investment. To further protect your documents, alternate the backup media you use. If one is damaged or becomes infected with a computer virus, you will still have another copy. Using different-colored disks or labels for different days and using odd-numbered disk on an odd-dated day and an even-numbered one on an even-dated day are techniques some writers use to make their backup procedures safer. Some even store their most important documents on other computers. One way to do this is to e-mail the document to yourself. It will sit on your e-mail server until you download it. Other writers also grandfather their files by giving each revision a new name in order to help re-create the document from earlier drafts should the current file become unusable for any reason. Some software will even create versions for you without your having to rename the file each time if it is set up that way. Backing up is the writer's insurance on the product.

---

table of contents generating, and index building. Most high-end word processors include the footnoting feature. It allows the writer to mark the place where the footnote occurs, entering the footnote at that point. The software then keeps track of the line count, placing each footnote at the bottom of the page on which it occurs, as well as numbering the footnotes consecutively. Also, the software will move a footnote if the text associated with it is moved. Another chore word processing software assists with is table of contents generation. Using the particular tagging system your software requires, you simply tell the software to generate the table of contents. In some cases you get to select from a variety of formats, and in other cases you can define the format. Closely related to the table of contents generator is the index builder. The writer simply tags the words to be indexed, including cross-references, or creates a list of words and the software builds an alphabetic index with associated page numbers. This procedure is particularly helpful with long, frequently referenced documents.

Word processing also has four other features that save the writer from having to re-enter the same information: merge, macros, Quick and Auto, and headers and footers. The merge feature permits you to combine one form document with a document containing variable data. Merge is particularly useful in early- and late-stage collection letters, where names and amounts are variable but the message is the same. Another feature, called *macros,* allows you to enter any characters you want to call up at the command of a few keystrokes. This feature is useful for calling up form paragraphs for answering commonly occurring questions as well as bringing up repeatedly used memo headings or letter closings. Quick and Auto features in WordPerfect and Word allow users to define shortcuts, which can be used for frequently entered, long, or difficult terms and phrases. You simply enter the shortcut and the software automatically substitutes the term, name, or phrase. You can also use these features for formatting and font attributes. Headers and footers also let the software enter repeated information at the top and bottom of pages as well as count and print the page numbers.

■ Using advanced word processing features saves time.

There are also special features of word processing software for using columns, fonts, importing graphics and spreadsheet files, and so on. Knowing how to exploit the features of the word processing software you use will definitely make writing and revising easier for you.

■ Learn to exploit the features of your word processor.

SPELLING CHECKERS. Along with AutoCorrect and QuickCorrect, spelling checkers are relied on daily by business writers. However, they are effective only if the writer uses them. And they are only effective at identifying words not in their dictionary. Therefore, spellers could miss some of your mistakes. Mistakes you will want to watch out for

■ Spelling checkers supplement proofreading but do not replace it.

FIGURE 16.6 Illustration of the Comment Tool for Writing

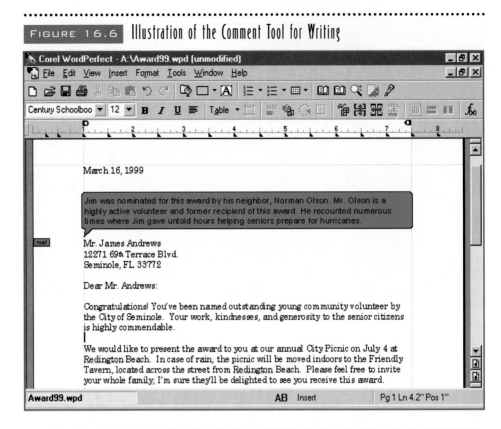

include wrong word errors such as "compliment" for "complement" or "imply" for "infer." A spell checker will also miss errors such as "desert" for "dessert" or misused words such as "good" for "well." Also, if any misspelled words have inadvertently been added to its dictionary, the speller will skip those words too. Therefore, careful proofreading is still in order after a document has been checked with a spelling program. Taking care to proofread carefully is a simple courtesy your reader will appreciate.

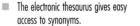
The electronic thesaurus gives easy access to synonyms.

THESAURUS SOFTWARE.   While some serious writers have a bound thesaurus on hand, many use an electronic thesaurus with great ease and efficiency. The ease of popping up a window with suggested synonyms is hard to beat. Most word processors include a thesaurus; however, several good independent programs are available. One thesaurus in-

Computers, Human Intellect, and Organizational Nervous Systems

An executive provides vision and direction, makes decisions, diagnoses and solves problems, negotiates, convinces, and selects and coaches people. All these actions depend on the excutive's ability to think creatively and communicate clearly; clear communication and creative thinking can be enhanced by the use of computers.

Unfortunately, most people don't realize this. The computer's role as a valuable thinking tool seems to be a secret. Instead, many intelligent people, even today, believe that computers are best suited to clerical and administrative tasks. They see the computer as only a convenience or an operational necessity. I see the computer as an extension of the human brain.

An understanding of the connection between the evolution of the human mind and computers takes us back in time.

Note the ragged margin before the hyphenation feature is turned on.

Computers, Human Intellect, and Organizational Nervous Systems

An executive provides vision and direction, makes decisions, di-agnoses and solves problems, nego-tiates, convinces, and selects and coaches people. All these actions depend on the excutive's ability to think creatively and communicate clearly; clear communication and creative thinking can be enhanced by the use of computers.

Unfortunately, most people don't realize this. The computer's role as a valuable thinking tool seems to be a secret. Instead, many intelligent people, even to-day, believe that computers are best suited to clerical and adminis-trative tasks. They see the comput-er as only a convenience or an op-erational necessity. I see the com-puter as an extension of the hu-man brain.

An understanding of the con-nection between the evolution of the human mind and computers takes us back in time.

Note that after the hyphenation feature is used, the right margin is smoothed out.

cluded with a popular word processor gives the part of speech and meaning along with the synonyms. You can page through different uses of the word, selecting the synonym from a new list for each different use. The thesaurus is a powerful tool, and the computer has made it faster to use and easier to access.

GRAMMAR AND STYLE CHECKERS. The value of grammar and style checkers is often debated. Unlike spelling programs, which are easily able to identify "wrong" words (words that are not in their dictionaries), grammar and style checkers identify "possible problems" with "suggestions" for revision. It is then your responsibility to decide whether the "possible problem" is a problem and whether the "suggestion" is the best solution. Making this decision requires that you have a good understanding of basic grammar. One recent study of accounting students' writing identified their most common writing errors. When a grammar checker was run on these common errors, less than half had been detected. Microsoft Word '97 found only 3 of the 13 errors and suggested 3 correct revisions; WordPerfect 8 found 6 of the 13 errors, but only 5 of the 6 revisions were appropriate.[1] However, these programs are improving rapidly, adding expert system techniques to identify "possible problems" in context more accurately.

■ Grammar and style checkers are only suggestion systems.

---

[1] G. E. Whittenburg and Marie E. Flatley, "The Most Common Writing Errors Made by Accounting Students," *Proceedings of the Western Decision Sciences Institute,* Reno, Nevada, April 1998.

In addition to checking grammar, style, word usage, and punctuation, these programs now report readability, strength, descriptive, and jargon indexes. They also perform sentence structure analysis, suggesting that you use simpler sentences, vary the sentence beginnings, use more or fewer prepositional phrases, and make various other changes. Grammar and style checkers also identify "possible problems" with specific words that might be slang, jargon, misspelled, misused, negative, or difficult for readers to understand. These programs also give word counts such as average length of sentences, longest sentence, shortest sentence, number of words in a document, and number of times each word is used. An example of the interactive use of one grammar checker is shown in Figure 16.8.

While the debate goes on, the tool is getting better. Recent versions address some of the issues concerning writers. For example, recent versions of grammar and style checkers are much more flexible than older versions. If you are writing in an informal environment where your boss finds beginning sentences with "And" and "But" acceptable, you can turn off the rule that would identify those beginnings as problems. Also, you can choose the level of writing your intended audience wants. These are just a few examples of the flexibility in the newest versions of grammar and style checkers.

Grammar and style checkers are definitely important for the business writer. But, like all tools, the more appropriately you use them the better job they do for you.

REFERENCE SOFTWARE.   Reference software is just what its name suggests—software that presents reference books such as dictionaries, style manuals, zip code directories, and so on. While a few of these reference programs are on floppy disks, the larger ones containing dictionaries, thesauruses, books of quotations, zip code directories, the world almanac, and several other references are on compact discs (CDs). CD references include such things as pronunciation of words in audio form and pictures, including video and animation.

GRAPHICS AND DRAW TOOLS.   Graphics and draw tools are becoming more important for the writer every day. Not only are these programs becoming easier to use, but you also can now launch them from within your word processor. In most cases, your draw-

FIGURE 16.8   Illustration of a Grammar Style Checker for Writing

Corel WordPerfect - C:\Data\PROFESS\JEB_Paper.wpd (unmodified)

File   Edit   View   Insert   Format   Tools   Window   Help

Times New Roman   12   B   I   U   Table

developed to provide students with access to computing resources that simulated

work environments.

As computing power, mobility, and software improved, pioneering faculty

Spell Checker | Grammatik | Thesaurus

Replacements: give students
send students

New sentence: As a result, computer labs were developed to give students access to computing resources that

Wordy: Consider revising.

Replace   Auto Replace
Skip Once   Undo
Skip All   Options
Turn Off
Check: Document

Close   Help

JEB_Paper.wpd   AB   Insert   Pg 3 Ln 7.55" Pos 2.4" ing is pasted in your document at the point you left it. The introduction of ready-made graphs and pictures (called clip art), low-cost scanners, and digital cameras, and photo libraries have made it easier to supplement text with professional-looking graphics. Also, the cost of color output is dropping, making it more desirable to use colored graphics and drawings. You learned how to use graphics effectively in Chapter 13. The important point to remember here is that the computer enables you to enhance textual communication with graphics.

VOICE RECOGNITION TOOLS.   Recently several companies have introduced some good tools for continuous voice input. Although they are priced favorably, they have not yet gained wide acceptance in most businesses. However, as businesspeople begin to realize how easily they can compose their messages by talking to their computer systems and even editing through voice commands, their acceptance is likely to grow.

> Voice input is new technology that will free the writer from keying messages.

As you have learned, technology is certainly an important tool for the writer in constructing messages. While word processing is the writer's primary tool in constructing a message, a wide variety of other tools will help in the planning, gathering and collecting, analyzing and organizing, and writing stages.

TOOLS FOR PRESENTING
MESSAGES

After you have completed the document, you need to consider how to present it. This decision involves both software and hardware choices.

SOFTWARE

Today you can publish your document in print or electronic form. For print publication, you can use desktop publishing software or word processing software. Desktop publishing software is particularly good for layout of long documents that combine text, graphics, and design elements such as long reports, newsletters, manuals, and proposals. This software enables you to present professional-looking documents. Word processors are also capable of combining these elements. Most are capable of doing nearly 80 percent of the tasks full-featured desktop publishing software can do if you take advantage of their features.

> Today's software gives the writer many options for presenting messages.

For electronic publication, you can also use these programs to generate files in hypertext markup language (html) or portable document file (pdf) format. In addition to the text, graphics, and design elements, electronic documents can contain links, audio, and video elements. At the moment, authoring software is more fully featured for creating html documents (web documents). Web documents allow the writer to have some control over the presentation of the document, but today's browsers allow the reader to override the web documents and present them in a format the reader prefers. Also, browsers often display these html documents differently; therefore, it is the writer's responsibility to test the documents (at least in the default mode) on the most commonly used browsers to assure that the visual look of their documents does not distract from or interfere with the message content. Some writers prefer to keep this control and create electronic documents in pdf, a format that gives the writer control over both the content and look.

Ironically, professionals engaged in designing documents for publication have the same major objective as writers—to communicate effectively. Professionals aim for designs that attract the reader but do not distract. Also, they understand that the most successful publications are those in which the design enhances or complements the meaning of the writer.

With publishing software, you can break out of the traditional-looking page with its roots in the typewriter era to give the reader the best looking, most readable document possible. However, to do this, you need to know about some basic design principles. These principles cover three areas: layout, typography, and art.

BASIC LAYOUT PRINCIPLES.   Roger Parker, a nationally recognized expert on design, defines layout as simply "the arrangement of text and graphics on a page." Suzanne West, another expert, goes further with, "A layout is a composition of interrelated

> Writers can control the look of their messages through effective layout.

elements on a page." While similar, the latter implies that the writer has some control over the results through careful composition of the elements. These elements include *white space, text, visuals,* and *graphic design elements* such as circles, lines, and bullets.

White space adds emphasis and affects readability.

You might find surprising that today a commonly accepted ratio of white space to text is 1:1. That means half of your page is devoted to text and half to white space. This ratio provides optimum readability. Readability is also improved by using lines 35 to 40 characters long. Therefore, with these two factors in mind, you can clearly see in Figure 16.9 that instead of using a full page of long, double-spaced lines it is better to use short lines with less spacing between them. This deliberate shifting of the white space to the margins keeps the 1:1 ratio but improves the readability.

Use white space consistently.

In planning the placement of white space in documents with facing pages, you will want to be sure your elements line up at the top and at the left. The example in Figure 16.10 shows a facing page layout with consistent use of white space in margins and between the lines.

Use it to give emphasis.

White space can also be used for emphasis. As you have already learned, space denotes importance. When you are writing about a topic, the more space you give it the more emphasis it gets. The same principle applies to white space. If you leave more white space around certain text or graphics, you will be giving that text or graphic more emphasis.

Type size and style also affect readability.

Another way to get emphasis in the text is through type size and style. Of course, you want headings to stand out, but they should be balanced with the rest of the text. The size

FIGURE 16.9 Illustration of Before and After Layout for Presenting

Before
Double-spaced with long lines

After
Short lines with white space moved to margins

FIGURE 16.10 Illustration of a Facing-Page Layout for Presenting

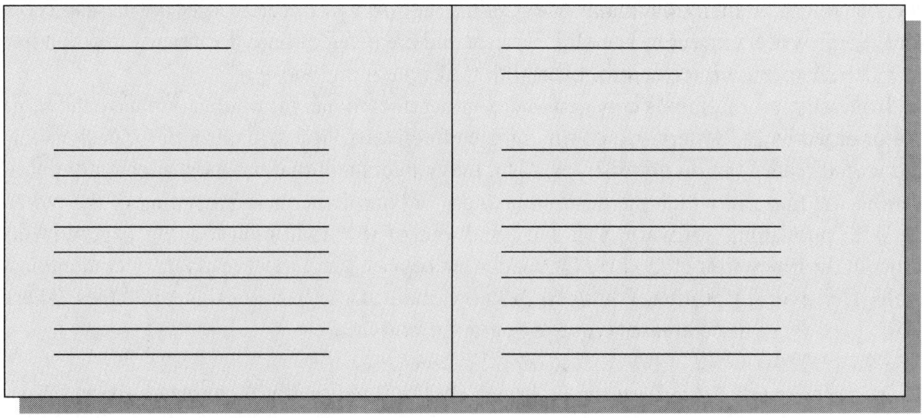

This facing, double-page spread illustrates copy aligned at top and left, the way our eye has been trained to read pages.

of your main heading will also be governed by the number of levels of subheadings you plan to use. And you will want to use a type size smaller than your text type size for captions and footnotes so they do not distract the reader from the text. Type style elements such as bold, italic, or bold italic can also be added to headings, subheadings, text, captions, and footnotes for more emphasis.

One means of emphasis that should be used sparingly is all uppercase. Using both uppercase and lowercase in headings makes the headings easier to read. However, all uppercase in short phrases will work effectively.

Good layout always includes careful planning of visuals—graphics and drawings. In planning them, give attention to placement and size as well as content. Also, be sure you plan space for the captions in your layout.

A final element of layout is the graphic device. Lines or rules around text or separating text from visuals or white space can be very effective for directing the eye to where you want it to go. The thickness of a line can be varied to give differing degrees of emphasis to the material it is highlighting. Tints or shading are other graphic devices that attract attention. Usually these are used to separate related copy in the same text. *Business Week* often uses this device. For example, it may run a story on General Motors Corporation, including a brief profile of a GM executive in a shaded box accompanying the article. Or it may be reporting on a specific industry in general, detailing explicit facts on specific companies in a table in a shaded box.

■ Graphic devices can direct the eye, giving attention to particular parts of the message.

Graphic devices should enhance the text, not distract from it. If your reader just reads the shaded boxes and overlooks the primary content of the report, your layout is not successful. Careful planning for effective use of graphic devices is a prerequisite to effective layout, as discussed in Chapter 13.

■ Plan them to enhance the text.

When the layout is good, it works well with the typography and art. Now that we have touched on the importance of type size and style in planning the textual component of layout, let us look at some basic principles of typography.

TYPOGRAPHY BASICS.   Although you may not be doing much yourself with the technical aspect of type in the majority of documents you produce, knowing the concepts and basic vocabulary is important. Not only will you be able to communicate more effectively with those who work on your documents, but you also will help them to produce better layouts for you.

■ Understanding type and its terminology helps you communicate with publishing professionals.

Some word processing terms for measuring, such as pitch and space, are carryovers from the typewriter era. However, the publishing and typesetting world measures in *points* and *picas*. A point is about 1/72 of an inch, and a pica is 12 points, or about 1/6 of an inch. When you are specifying type size, generally 14-point type and smaller is considered appropriate for text, while type larger than 14 points is usually used for headings. Some software gives you the choice of specifying in inches, centimeters, or picas. If you are working closely with people in the publishing world, you would be wise to work with the terminology they understand.

■ A *point* is 1/72 inch; a *pica* is 12 points.

Another term from this area is *kerning*. Kerning refers to the spacing between characters. While standard typewriters, dot matrix printers, and fixed fonts generally use equal spacing for each character, in publishing this space is variable. For example, in the word "The" a publishing system would allow the *T* to overhang, moving the *h* in for an even-appearing spacing. A fixed-pitch printer, on the other hand, would place the *h* after the overhang, appearing to leave more space between the *T* and *h* than between the *h* and *e*. Also, if copy doesn't quite fit the page, you can squeeze it or stretch it by tightening or loosening the kerning or spacing between characters.

■ *Kerning* is the spacing between characters.

Leading (pronounced *leding*) is similar to kerning except that it refers to vertical spacing rather than horizontal. When your lines are too close together, you can increase the leading to add more white space between lines. As with kerning, you can adjust the leading to fit copy to the space available.

■ *Leading* is the spacing between lines.

One other term commonly used in the publishing industry is *typeface*. Typeface refers to the design of the entire uppercase and lowercase set of letters. While there are hundreds of typefaces available today, two common typefaces in use are Times Roman and Helvetica (see Figure 16.11). Times Roman is a serif type, having feet (cross-lines) at the end

FIGURE 16.11 Illustration of Serif and Sans Serif Fonts

Times Roman (Serif)

Helvetica (Sans Serif)

of the main strokes. Helvetica is a sans serif type, having no feet at the ends of its main strokes.

When you are talking to computer-oriented people about publishing, you may hear the term *font* used for typeface. However, a font is one typeface in one size and style. Therefore, if you wanted to use a Helvetica type with standard, bold, and italics in four sizes, you would need 12 fonts—one for each size and one for each style. Today we often use scalable fonts, fonts that can be changed in size within a range. The most commonly used fonts today for the Mac and Windows-based systems are Postscript and TrueType. Numerous font libraries are available for purchase, allowing you to prepare a custom document.

Since type is a key element in most business documents, you'll want to pay special attention to it. Usually, it will account for more than 90 percent of your document. Your care in selecting and using type will have a big impact on the effectiveness of your design.

ART FUNDAMENTALS. *Art* as used here in its broadest sense refers to drawings, graphs, photos, and other illustrations. As a writer you primarily need to remember that art should always serve a message's purpose; it must never serve its own. Whenever you are about to place an art element on a page, ask yourself what purpose it serves. As noted in Chapter 13, need is the sole criterion for including a graphic in a document. Graphics help the reader understand. They are essential to good business etiquette.

One purpose of art is to break up large blocks of text. While we often try to conjure up an idea for drawings, graphs, or photos, we can also use the space to emphasize a key idea. By quoting from within the document and setting it off in larger type with ruling lines, we use a technique called a *pull quote.*

Whatever the reason we have for our art, we should also strive to use the best art possible. Look for interesting photos, not merely mug shots. Crop photos, cutting out any material that does not work to enhance the text. Choose your art with the reader in mind. In some cases these suggestions might mean using cartoons or illustrations you scan or import from various clip art software, and in other cases it might mean using high-quality color photos or significant pull quotes. Of course, you need to be sure you do not violate copyrights.

Good design expertly integrates layout, typography, and art elements. You will probably want to begin with either some very basic applications or the prepared templates or style sheets bundled with the publishing software. You will get better with practice. Also, you will get better if you read books and magazines on design, pay attention to the designs of others (noting what seems to work), and keep a file of ideas. By always keeping the reader in mind as you design your documents, you will be effective in communicating your message. You will use good etiquette in your message design.

HARDWARE

Software is just one component of presenting a message; hardware is another. If the software has features your printer or other output device cannot print, the features are useless. On the other hand, if your hardware has features your software cannot produce, they, too, are useless. Both must work together to produce your message.

The most common output device is still the printer. Depending on the formality of your communication, you may find yourself using ink-jet printers for one type of message and

- Computer people use the term *font* for typeface.

- Art should serve the message's purpose.

- Use it to break up blocks of text.

- Choose art for the best communication effect.

- Effective design integrates layout, type, and art.

- Your choice of output hardware is critical to the appearance of your message.

- Print and some electronic documents give the writer control of appearance.

laser printers for others. In circumstances where you must have the best-looking documents, you may even use typeset output. Appearance does convey a message, and the hardware you choose to complete the presentation of your document is an important consideration.

Electronic documents have different hardware considerations. Portable document publishers such as Envoy and Acrobat prepare documents to be used across platforms. Readers will read them on screens, not paper. And because of hypertext links within the document, reading an electronic document may vary substantially from reading the same document in print form. Keeping readers apprised of where they are at all times within a document is important. Also, it is important to always give a reader ways to move around the document; including both buttons and keystroke alternatives is essential.

TOOLS FOR TRANSMITTING MESSAGES

Transmitting means to send the message. The medium in which you choose to transmit a message communicates to the receiver the importance you attach to the message. Usually a written message gets more attention than an oral message, and a special delivery or urgent message gets more attention than an ordinary message. Even the method of special delivery chosen conveys a message. The client who electronically sends you the document you requested is perceived differently from the client who sends it on paper through Federal Express. Knowing what technologies are available to transmit the message will help you decide which is the most appropriate medium to use.

■ The medium in which you choose to send your message is important.

Technologies for sending a variety of oral and visual messages are widely used in business. One booming technology for oral communication is the cellular phone. Once predominantly used in cars, cell phones can be used in any area of the country equipped for them. With a phone that fits in the palm of the hand, businesspeople can now be reached for important calls as well as conduct business from otherwise inaccessible places. While you are delayed in a traffic jam on your way to the airport, you can call your office, your important client, or your company's computer. Cellular phones enable businesspeople to make more productive use of their time. However, the courteous user will be discreet about the time and place of use. Most people do not want to overhear your business calls; therefore, it is best to make them where using your cellular phone will not disturb others. And when in doubt, ask before you make that intrusive call.

■ Cellular technology expands the physical environment of the message sender.

As was mentioned in Chapter 14, another widely used oral communication technology is the voice messaging system. Not only do these systems answer phones, direct calls, and take messages, but they also act as voice storage systems. For example, you can ask the

■ Voice messaging systems are gaining business use.

"Thank you for calling. Please leave a message. In case I forget to check my messages, please send your message as an audio file to my e-mail, then send me a fax to remind me to check my e-mail, then call back to remind me to check my fax."

Source: © Randy Glasbergen, 1997.

| Transmitting messages by cellular allows you and your receiver the freedom to move around.

system to retrieve messages for a particular date or from a particular person. You can also take a message you receive, annotate it with your voice message, and pass it along to another person's voice mailbox. You can even record a message for the system to deliver to several people's voice mailboxes at a specified time. By eliminating telephone tag and interruptions, this technology, too, improves the productivity of those using it.

One technology that combines oral and video communication effectively is videoconferencing. While it has been around for a while, new developments in optical fibers, satellite transmission, and software and chip technology will push videoconferencing into even more favor. New developments are making the systems better and lowering the costs. Videoconferencing systems save travel time and expense, and they help eliminate many scheduling problems. Even small and medium-sized companies with not enough use to justify setting them up are using them through providers such as Kinko's. And as desktop monitors are added to computer systems, desktop conferencing use will grow.

Technology also gives us the option of adding audio and video to our written messages. The sounds can be words dictated and attached to a document, or they can be sounds from other sources such as sound clip libraries. Sounds can be used to add interest, emphasis, and clarity to a document. Video can also be added to email. In fact, many current video email systems simply attach video files to email messages. As more offices get computer systems equipped with these capabilities, we will see a growth in the use of the compound document.

Written communication, on the other hand, can be transmitted effectively with two proven technologies—email and facsimile. Email transmissions work with computer systems, sending documents to an electronic mailbox. These electronic mailboxes can be set up on a company's computer, on a service provider's computer, or on a private subscriber information service's computer. In any case, you need to know the electronic address of the receiver in order to send the message. Also, the receiver needs to check the electronic mailbox to receive the message. However, most of today's email systems will notify you when a message has arrived for you. Furthermore, pager systems can both notify you and send you email.

Facsimile transmission (fax) uses telephone lines to send a copy of the document. Faxing is much like photocopying or printing, but the copy is delivered elsewhere. As with email, you need to know the telephone number of the receiving fax in order to send the message, and someone on the receiving end needs to check the fax and deliver the message. Currently, you can also use the web to send or retrieve a fax. Many companies are setting up these systems on their intranets so users can send and retrieve faxes from their desktops.

Videoconferencing combines oral and video media.

Technology enables us to add audio and video to our written documents.

E-mail and facsimile transmission are gaining use for transmitting written messages.

Both email and fax are being effectively used for transmitting written messages. However, while both have the advantage of immediacy, they are both less formal than sending a printed document. To use good etiquette you need to evaluate carefully the need for formality in choosing your transmission medium.

Knowing that you have a choice of media for transmitting the message and knowing how to use each one are both important in order to choose the most appropriate medium. Because this technology is developing rapidly, you need to make it a priority to keep up-to-date on the latest developments.

■ Although they communicate in writing, email and fax are viewed as informal.

■ So use them appropriately.

TOOLS FOR COLLABORATION

As discussed in Chapter 10, collaborative writing or group writing tasks occur regularly in business, and they vary widely in the form and nature of the work. However, there is a wide range of computer tools to support various aspects of the process. These tools for computer-supported collaborative work group writing can be divided into two classifications: asynchronous and synchronous. Asynchronous tools are used for different-time/different-place collaboration; synchronous tools, on the other hand, are used for same-time/any-place collaboration.

■ Computer tools assist groups on a wide variety of tasks.

ASYNCHRONOUS COMPUTER TOOLS

Asynchronous tools include word processing, conferencing systems, electronic mail systems, portable document publishers, and group authoring systems. Word processing features useful in group writing include commenting and reviewing. Commenting allows you to insert comments in a document written by someone else. Reviewing allows others to edit your documents, which will appear as strikeouts (for deletions) or redlining (for insertions). Different colors can be assigned to different reviewers so you know which reviewer made the suggestions. The writer can view the document and decide whether to accept or reject each suggestion. As shown in Figure 16.12, the writer can see the reviewer's suggestions as an insert when viewing a document.

■ Several computer tools assist the traditional group.

FIGURE 16.12 Illustration of a Reviewing Tool for Collaboration

Group-centered Computer Classroom Design for Business

At many universities ~~there is a~~ rush to create computer classrooms ~~that is~~

~~often driven~~ [Marie Flatley: Perhaps we should just say administrators.] ~~d in~~ day-to-day classroom teaching ~~on a~~

~~day to day basis~~. Sometimes these classrooms designs are driven by the hottest,

latest technology rather than its appropriate use. These designers often assume

that using the best tools results in the best learning. However, with careful

planning by design teams combining both faculty and other experts, classrooms

can be created where form follows function. In these classrooms, students will use

tools in the most appropriate settings for enhancing their learning.

- Computer conferencing is useful when distance or time make getting together difficult.

Another group writing tool is computer conferencing. As noted in Chapter 14, this tool is useful when groups have a difficult time meeting due to distance and time. To begin, the lead writer would enter some text. Others would access the system, review the comments, and enter their own comments. All comments can be reviewed by all members of the group. In some systems, group members have anonymity, but others maintain audit trails so comments can be attributed to specific group members.

- Electronic mail permits communicating to intended receivers only.

Electronic mail (e-mail) systems or listservs provide a means for one writer to send a message to others. Unlike conferencing, in these systems access to others' mailboxes is restricted. While you can distribute messages to a whole group, you do not have access to messages one member sends to someone else.

- Collaborative writing is helped by group authoring software.

Group authoring systems are software programs designed specifically for group work. While different products have varied features, most are designed to allow document versions to be compared, to allow comments and suggestions to be entered at appropriate places, and to allow the use of common editing tools such as insert, delete, paragraph, and stet.

All these tools are designed to work the way groups have traditionally worked. The planning, writing, and revising occur much the way they occur in traditional groups. However, the tools contribute to improvements in both speed and the quality of the final documents.

SYNCHRONOUS COMPUTER TOOLS

- Collaborative tools change the group process and improve its output quality.

Synchronous computer tools are used by all group members at the same time. However, they can be used either at the same place or at different places. Same-place tools are generally referred to as electronic meeting systems (EMS). Different-place tools are sometimes called whiteboard or collaborative tools.

With the same-place EMS tools, a facilitator conducts the meeting and operates the software that runs on a network. The facilitator may start the group with a question or statement. The group members will comment on the statement through their computers simultaneously and anonymously. For example, members may brainstorm new company policy statements and comment on them. The group under the direction of the facilitator might use other EMS tools to group related comments, rank-order them, and vote for the final policy statement. This kind of EMS collaborative tool has been shown to produce significantly higher quality output than non-computer-supported meetings.

With the different-place collaborative tools, one member of the group initiates the process either on a network or through modem connections. This tool often provides both a chat box or audio connection where users can talk to each other, a video connection where members can see each other, and a place where a shared document can be viewed and manipulated. The software can be set for different levels and types of control. As the hardware comes into greater use in business, we are likely to see much more use of distributed teams working together on projects.

A LOOK TO THE FUTURE

- Computer tools will continue to enhance the communication process . . .

In addition to the technological developments discussed thus far, you can anticipate further rapid development. Bill Gates, CEO of Microsoft, believes these systems will be friendlier and seamlessly blended. He predicted that exponential improvements will continue, empowering people with rich sets of communication tools. Digital convergence, where all information is in digital form, will provide the vehicle for on-demand transactions of all types. In early 1998, digital television products were first introduced, paving the way for further convergence. We can also expect to see improvements in display technology, especially the growth in flat screen monitors. Future advances may bring us displays such as the glasses envisioned by Hitachi in Figure 16.13. You are likely to see more voice and handwriting input, too. Systems are currently being marketed that get better at voice and handwriting recognition as you use them. You must make it a priority to keep abreast of these developments in order to identify tools that will make your job easier.

- . . . but the human mind still controls it.

However, whatever form these developments take, human minds will continue to con-

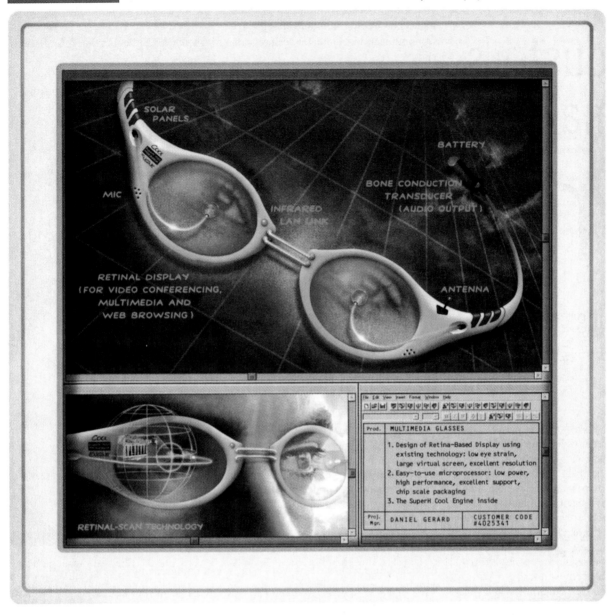

trol message formulation. In fact, there is no evidence whatsoever that the need for messages communicated in writing and speaking will decrease. Even more important, there is absolutely no evidence that these messages can be handled in a way that does not require basic writing and speaking skills. Business communication is here to stay. In fact, the increasing advancement of the technology of the future is likely to require more—not less—of it.

SUMMARY BY CHAPTER OBJECTIVES

1. Technology helps a writer construct messages through every step of the writing process including:
   • Planning,
   • Gathering and collecting information,
   • Analyzing and organizing information, and
   • Writing and rewriting.

1 Explain how technology helps in constructing messages.

2 Identify appropriate software tools for different stages in the writing process.

2. Each stage of the writing process has a set of software tools most appropriate for the tasks in that stage. These include the following:
   - Outlining or brainstorming, project management, and personal information management programs for planning;
   - Communications and database programs for gathering and collecting information; and
   - Statistical, spreadsheet, graphics, and outlining or brainstorming software for analyzing and organizing information, and word processing, spelling, thesaurus, grammar and style checking, reference, graphics, draw, and voice recognition programs for writing.

3 Discuss how technology helps in the presentation of messages.

3. Technology helps in the presentation of documents with both sophisticated hardware and software.
   - Hardware contributes in the printing of documents.
   - Software contributes with publishing features that combine text, graphics, links, audio, and video and that promote good layout and design.

4 Explain basic concepts of document layout and design.

4. Layout and design refers to the arrangement of text and graphics on a page. Layout involves the careful composition of these basic elements:
   - White space for manipulating emphasis and readability,
   - Text for emphasis and balance as well as for visual clues of organization,
   - Visuals such as graphics and drawings, and
   - Graphic design elements to direct the eye.

   Layout and design are also affected by typography. Aspects writers need to know about include:
   - Points and picas, which represent height,
   - Kerning, which determines the spacing between letters,
   - Leading, which determines the spacing between lines, and
   - Typeface, which refers to the design of an entire set of letters.

   Art is a final aspect of layout and design. Its main purpose is always to serve a message's purpose.

5 Discuss various ways to transmit messages and the hardware currently used.

5. Communicators have a variety of choices of media for transmitting their messages.
   - Oral messages can be sent by cellular phone, voice messaging systems, and sound clips.
   - Videoconferencing technology combines oral and visual messages.
   - Written messages can be transmitted by email or fax.

6 Describe how technology assists in collaboration.

6. A range of software tools assists groups of writers in asynchronous and synchronous writing environments.
   - Asynchronous tools such as word processing, conferencing systems, e-mail, portable document publishers, and group authoring systems are used for different-time/different-place collaboration.
   - Synchronous tools allow writers to work on a document at the same time. Electronic meeting system tools are used for same-time/same-place writing, and collaboration tools are used for same-time/different-place writing.

7 Discuss what impact the future developments might have on business communication.

7. Future developments expect to integrate present technologies more smoothly, making them easier to use. Digital convergence will provide the vehicle for bringing us on-demand transactions. Future developments will likely mean more need for good basic communication skills.

CRITICAL THINKING QUESTIONS

1. Explain how technology can help the writer with both creative and tedious writing tasks.
2. Identify specific software tools that assist with constructing written messages. Explain what each does.
3. Word processing software is the writer's primary tool. Identify five basic features and two advanced features useful to business writers.
4. Discuss the advantages and disadvantages of spelling checkers and grammar and style checkers.
5. Describe ways graphics software helps writers.
6. Explain what a writer should know about layout and design and why it is important.
7. Identify various ways business writers can transmit oral and written messages.
8. How can technology assist in collaboration?
9. What can we expect to see in future technological developments that will affect business communication?

CRITICAL THINKING EXERCISES

1. Investigate the school and/or local libraries to determine what current (or future) computer systems will help one find information for business. Report your findings to the class.
2. Compile an annotated list of at least six web sites with good links to business sources. Two of these links should be for local business information.
3. Locate six examples of electronic clip art and sound clips you might use in a business document. Print the examples along with a brief explanation of a good use in a business document.
4. Identify where computers, printing equipment, and faxes are available at or around your college. Prepare a table with this information, listing times available as well as any costs. Also, be sure to include computer configurations and software available.
5. Choose a feature from your word processor (such as index, table of contents, templates, or macros) that you have not used much. Learn how to use it and create an example of its use in a business document. Write a brief description of its application.
6. Select a dozen idioms from a reference book (found in your library or bookstore) that seem common to you. Type these into your word processor and run the file through a grammar and style checker. Print a copy of the results and bring it to class for discussion.
7. From a current computer magazine, find an article that relates to communication in business. Write a one-paragraph reaction to it and send your paragraph electronically (email) to someone selected by your instructor.

17

Techniques of Cross-Cultural Communication

Upon completing this chapter, you will be able to describe the major barriers to cross-cultural communication and how to overcome them. To reach this goal, you should be able to

1 Explain why communicating clearly across cultures is important to business.

2 Define culture and explain its effects on cross-cultural communication.

3 Describe cultural differences in body positions and movements and use this knowledge effectively in communicating.

4 Describe cultural differences in attitudes toward time, space, odors, and such and use this knowledge effectively in communicating.

5 Explain the language equivalency problem as a cause of miscommunication.

6 Describe what one can do to overcome the language equivalency problem.

Cross-Cultural Communication

To introduce yourself to this chapter, assume the position of assistant to the president of Thatcher-Stone and Company, a small manufacturer of computer components. Your boss, gregarious old Vernon Thatcher, invited you to join him at a luncheon meeting with a group of Asian business executives in which negotiations for the sale of Thatcher-Stone products would be opened. Because Thatcher-Stone's domestic sales have been lagging, the company badly needs these customers.

The Asian guests entered the room, bowing as introductions were made. Mr. Thatcher attempted to put them at ease. "No need to do that," he said. "I'm just plain Vernon Thatcher. Just relax and make yourself at home." You noticed that the Asians appeared bewildered. They appeared even more bewildered when early in the meeting Mr. Thatcher made this statement: "We've only got the lunch hour, gents. I know you'll appreciate getting right down to business."

Throughout the meeting Mr. Thatcher was in his best conversational mood—laughing, backslapping, telling jokes. But none of this seemed to make an impression on the guests. They seemed confused to you. They smiled and were extremely polite, but they seemed to understand little of what Mr. Thatcher was saying. Although he tried again and again to move to business talk, they did not respond. The meeting ended pleasantly, but without a sale.

"They're a strange people," Mr. Thatcher commented when he got back to his office. "They have a lot to learn about doing business. It doesn't look like they're going to deal with us, does it?" Mr. Thatcher was right in his last comment. They did not.

As you review the meeting, you cannot help but feel that Mr. Thatcher spoiled the deal, for he failed miserably in communicating with the Asians. The fact is that there is much to know about communicating in cross-cultural settings. The goal of this chapter is to introduce this issue to you.

Technological advances in communication, travel, and transportation have made business increasingly global. This trend is expected to continue in the foreseeable future. Thus, the chances are good that you will have to communicate with people from other cultures.

■ Business has become more global.

Both large and small businesses want you to be able to communicate clearly with those from other cultures for several reasons. A primary reason is that businesses sell their products and services both domestically and internationally. Being able to communicate with others helps you be more successful in understanding customers' needs, communicating how your company can meet these needs, and winning their business. Another reason is that in addition to being a more effective worker, you will be more efficient both within and outside your company. You will be able to work harmoniously with those from other cultures, creating a more comfortable and productive workplace. Furthermore, with cultural barriers broken down, you will be able to hire good people despite their differences. Also, you will avoid problems stemming solely from misinterpretations. A final reason is that your attention to communicating clearly with those from other cultures will enrich your business and personal life.

■ Communicating across cultures effectively improves your productivity and efficiency and promotes harmonious work environments.

In preparing to communicate with people from other cultures, you might well begin by reviewing the instructions given in this book. Most of them fit all people. But many do not, especially those involving letter writing. To determine which do not, you must study the differences among cultures, for cultural differences are at the root of the exceptions. In addition, you must look at the special problems that our language presents to those who use it as a second language. It is around these two problem areas that this review of cross-cultural communication is organized.

■ Cross-cultural communication involves understanding cultural differences and overcoming language problems.

PROBLEMS OF CULTURAL DIFFERENCES

A study of the role of culture in international communication properly begins with two qualifying statements. First, culture is often improperly assumed to be the cause of miscommunication. Often it is confused with the other human elements involved. We must re-

■ Two qualifying statements begin this study of culture: (1) It is improperly blamed for some miscommunication.

member that communication between people of different cultures involves the same problems of human behavior that are involved when people of the same culture communicate. In either case, people can be belligerent, arrogant, prejudiced, insensitive, or biased. The miscommunication these types of behavior cause is not a product of culture.

- (2) It is easy to overgeneralize cultural practices.

Second, one must take care not to overgeneralize the practices within a culture. We say this even though some of the statements we make in the following paragraphs are overgeneralized. But we have little choice. In covering the subject, it is necessary to make generalizations such as "Latin Americans do this" or "Arabs do that" in order to emphasize a point. But the truth of the matter is that in all cultures, subcultures are present; and what may be the practice in one segment of a culture may be unheard of by other segments. Within a culture townspeople differ from country dwellers, the rich differ from the poor, and the educated differ from the uneducated. Clearly, the subject of culture is highly complex and should not be reduced to simple generalizations.

- Culture is the shared ways groups of people view the world.

Culture has been defined in many ways. The classic definition most useful in this discussion is one derived from anthropology: *Culture* is "a way of life of a group of people . . . the stereotyped patterns of learning behavior, which are handed down from one generation to the next through means of language and imitation."[1] Similarly, a modern definition is that culture is "the shared ways in which groups of people understand and interpret the world."[2]

While we can all talk on cellular phones and drink Coca-Cola at McDonald's, these activities can be interpreted very differently in different cultures. A Coke at McDonald's in America and a conversation on a cell phone in Israel may be common occurrences, but in Moscow a trip to McDonald's is a status symbol, as is a cell phone in some parts of the United States. In other words, people living in different countries have developed not only different ways to interpret events. They have different habits, different values, and different ways of relating to one another.

- Two major kinds of cultural differences affect communication.

These differences are a major source of problems when people of different cultures try to communicate. Unfortunately, people tend to view the ways of their culture as normal and the ways of other cultures as bad, wrong, peculiar, or such. Because of this view they do not practice good etiquette. Specifically, these problems are related to two kinds of cultural differences: (1) differences in body positions and movements and (2) differences in attitudes toward various factors of human relationships (time, space, intimacy, and so on).

BODY POSITIONS AND MOVEMENTS

- Body positions and movements differ among cultures. For example, in some cultures, people sit; in other cultures, they hunker.

One might think that the positions and movements of the body are much the same for all people. But such is not the case. These positions and movements differ by culture, and the differences can affect communication. For example, in our culture most people sit when they wish to remain in one place for some time, but in much of the world people squat. Because we do not squat, we tend to view squatting as primitive. This view obviously affects our communication with people who squat, for what we see when we communicate is a part of the message. But how correct is this view? Actually, squatting is a very normal body position. Our children squat quite naturally—until their elders teach them to sit. Who is to say that sitting is more advanced or better?

- Manners of walking differ among cultures.

For another example, people from our culture who visit certain Asian countries are likely to view the fast, short steps taken by the inhabitants as peculiar or funny and to view our longer strides as normal. And when people from our culture see the inhabitants of these countries bow on meeting and leaving each other, they are likely to interpret the bowing as a sign of subservience or weakness. Similarly, people from our culture see standing up as the appropriate thing to do on certain occasions (as when someone enters the room), whereas people from some other cultures do not.

---

[1] V. Barnouw, *Culture and Personality* (Chicago: Dorrsey Press, 1963), p. 4.

[2] Fons Trompenaars, *Riding the Waves of Culture: Understanding Diversity in Global Business* (Burr Ridge, IL; Irwin Professional Publishing, 1994), pp. 3–4.

This body position is quite natural for this Vietnamese woman as she shops in Ho Chi Minh City.

As you know, movements of certain body parts (especially the hands) are a vital form of human communication. Some of these movements have no definite meaning even within a culture. But some have clear meanings, and these meanings may differ by culture. To us an up-and-down movement of the head means yes and a side-to-side movement of the head means no. These movements may mean nothing at all or something quite different to people from cultures in which thrusting the head forward, raising the eyebrows, jerking the head to one side, or lifting the chin are used to convey similar meanings.

In addition, the two-fingered "victory" sign is as clear to us as any of our hand gestures. To an Australian, whose culture is not vastly different from ours, the sign has a most vulgar meaning. The "OK" sign is terribly rude and insulting in such diverse places as Russia, Germany, and Brazil.[3] In Japan, a similar sign represents money. If a businessperson completing a contract gave this sign, the Japanese might think they needed to give more money, perhaps even a bribe. Even the widely used "thumbs up" sign for "things are going well" could get you into trouble in countries from Nigeria to Australia. And so it is with many of our other body movements. They differ widely, even within cultures.

The meanings that movements of our eyes convey also vary by culture. In North America, we are taught not to look over the heads of our audience but to maintain eye contact in giving formal speeches. In informal talking, we are encouraged to look at others but not to stare. In Indonesia, looking directly at people, especially those in higher positions and older, is considered to be disrespectful. On the other hand, our practices of eye contact are less rigorous than the British and Germans. Unless one understands these cultural differences, how one uses eye movement can be interpreted as being impolite on the one hand or being shy on the other.

Touching and particularly handshaking differences are important to understand in cross-cultural communication. This is made difficult by other cultures adopting Western greetings. However, some cultures, like the Chinese, do not like much touching. They will give a handshake you might perceive as weak. Other cultures that like touching will give

- Communication with body parts (hands, arms, head, etc.) varies by culture.

- Hand gestures differ by culture.

- So do eye movements,

- touching, and handshaking.

---

[3] Roger E. Axtell, *Gestures: The Dos and Taboos of Body Language Around the World* (New York: John Wiley & Sons, Inc., 1993), p. 41.

Carefully Present and Receive a Business Card in Japan

In Japan, it is considered bad manners to go to a business meeting without a business card, or meishi. While there are a number of ways to present the card, receiving it is an art, too. If you want to make a good impression on the presenter, receive it in both hands, especially when the other party is senior in age or status or a potential customer. Be careful not to fiddle with the card or put it in your rear pocket—that is considered crude. Put it in some distinctive case. Those who do business in both countries often have their business cards translated on the back, as the examples here show.

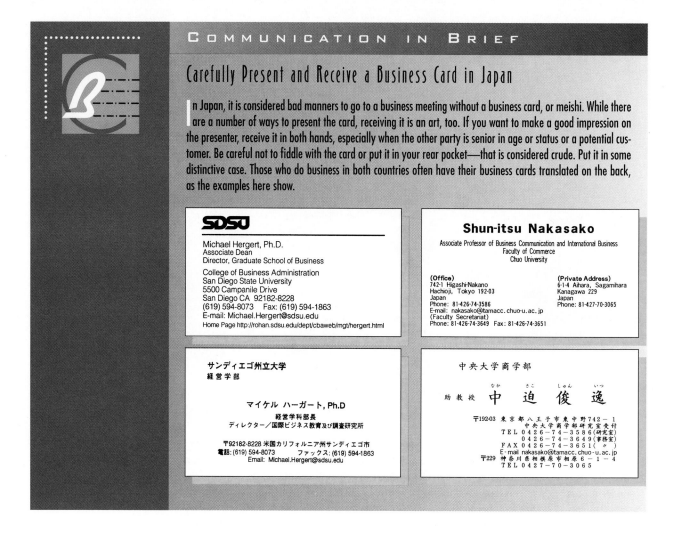

you greetings ranging from full embraces and kisses to nose rubbing. If you can avoid judging others from different cultures on their greeting based on your standards for others like you, you can seize the opportunity to access the cultural style of another. Here are some types of handshakes by culture.

Culture	Handshakes
Americans	Firm
Germans	Brusque, firm, repeated upon arrival and departure
French	Light, quick, not offered to superiors, repeated upon arrival and departure
British	Soft
Hispanics	Moderate grasp, repeated frequently
Latin Americans	Firm, long-lasting
Middle Easterners	Gentle, repeated frequently
Asians	Gentle; for some, shaking hands is unfamiliar and uncomfortable (an exception to this is the Korean, who generally has a firm handshake)

■ A smile can be a sign of weakness, and the left hand may be taboo.

In our culture, smiles are viewed positively in most situations. But in some other cultures (notably African cultures), a smile is regarded as a sign of weakness in certain situations (such as bargaining). Receiving a gift or touching with the left hand is a serious breach of etiquette among Muslims, for they view the left hand as unclean. We attach no such meaning to the left hand. And so it is with other body movements—arching the eyebrows, positioning the fingers, raising the arms, and many more. All cultures use body movements in communicating, but in different ways.

A Classic Defense of Cultural Difference

The classic "ugly American" was traveling in a faraway land. He had been critical of much of what he experienced—the food, the hotels, the customs in general. One day he came upon a funeral. He observed that the mourners placed food on the grave—and left it there.

"What a stupid practice!" he exclaimed to his native host. "Do your people actually think that the dead person will eat the food?"

At this point, the host had taken all the insults he could handle for one day. So he replied, "Our dead will eat the food as soon as your dead smell the flowers you place on their graves."

ATTITUDES TOWARD FACTORS OF HUMAN RELATIONSHIPS

Probably causing even more miscommunication than differences in body positions and movements are the different attitudes of different cultures toward various factors of human relationships. For illustrative purposes, we will review seven major factors: time, space, odors, frankness, intimacy of relationships, values, and expression of emotions.

■ Differing attitudes toward various factors of human relationships cause communication problems.

TIME. In our culture, people tend to regard time as something that must be planned for the most efficient use. They strive to meet deadlines, to be punctual, to conduct business quickly, and to work on a schedule.

■ Views about time differ widely. Some cultures stress punctuality; some do not.

In some other cultures (especially those of the Middle East and some parts of Asia), people view time in a more relaxed way. They see planning as unwise and unnecessary. Being late to a meeting, a social function, or such is of little consequence to them. In fact, some of them hold the view that important people should be late to show that they are busy. In business negotiations, the people in these cultures move at a deliberately slow pace, engaging in casual talk before getting to the main issue. It is easy to see how such different views of time can cause people from different cultures to have serious miscommunication problems.

SPACE. People from different cultures often vary in their attitudes toward space. Even people from the same culture may have different space preferences, as noted in Chapter 14. North Americans tend to prefer about two feet or so of distance between themselves and those with whom they speak. But in some cultures (some Arabian and South American cultures), people stand closer to each other; not following this practice is considered impolite and bad etiquette. For another example, North Americans view personal space as a right and tend to respect this right of others; thus, they stand in line and wait their turn. People from some other cultures view space as belonging to all. Thus, they jostle for space when boarding trains, standing at ticket counters, shopping in stores, and such. In encounters between people whose cultures have such different attitudes toward space, actions are likely to be misinterpreted.

■ Space is viewed differently by different cultures. In some cultures, people want to be far apart; in other cultures, they want to be close.

ODORS. People from different cultures may have different attitudes toward body odors. To illustrate, Americans work hard to neutralize body odors or cover them up and view those with body odors as dirty and unsanitary. On the other hand, in some Asian cultures people view body odors not as something to be hidden but as something that friends should experience. Some of the people from these cultures feel that it is an act of friendship to "breathe the breath" of the person with whom they converse and to feel their presence by smelling. Clearly, encounters between people with such widely differing attitudes could lead to serious miscommunication.

■ Some cultures view body odors as bad; others view them as normal.

FRANKNESS. North Americans tend to be relatively frank or explicit in their relationships with others, quickly getting to the point and perhaps being blunt and sharp in doing

■ High-context cultures are more frank and explicit than low-context cultures.

Greetings vary among cultures.

so. Asians tend to be far more reticent or implicit and sometimes go to great lengths to save face or not to offend. Americans belong to a high-context culture, a culture which explicitly shares all relevant background information in our communication. Asians, on the other hand, belong to a low-context culture, extracting limited background information and thus communicating more implicitly.[4] Thus, Asians may appear evasive, roundabout, and indecisive to North Americans; and North Americans may appear harsh, impolite, and aggressive to Asians. Telephone customs may be an exception, especially among the Chinese, who tend to end telephone calls abruptly after their purpose has been accomplished. North Americans, on the other hand, tend to move on to friendly talk and clearly prepare the listener for the end of the call.

- Intimacy among people varies in different cultures.

INTIMACY OF RELATIONSHIPS. In many cultures, strict social classes exist, and class status determines how intimately people are addressed and treated in communication. For this reason, a person from such a culture might quiz a person from another culture to determine that person's class status. Questions concerning occupation, income, title, and such might be asked.[5] People from cultures that stress human equality are apt to take offense at such questioning about the notion of class status. This difference in attitude toward class status is also illustrated by differences in the familiarity of address. Some Americans are quick to establish a first-name basis. This practice is offensive to people from some other cultures, notably the English and the Germans, who expect such intimate address only from long-standing acquaintances.

- How people view superior–subordinate relations also differs.

Similarly, how people view superior–subordinate relations can vary by culture. The dominant view in Latin America, for example, is a strong boss with weak subordinates doing as the boss directs. In sharp contrast is the somewhat democratic work arrangement of the Japanese in which much of the decision making is by consensus. Most in our culture view as appropriate an order between these extremes. These widely differing practices have led to major communication problems in joint business ventures involving people from these cultures.

- So does the role of women.

The role of women varies widely by culture. In North America, we continue to move toward a generally recognized goal of equality. In many Islamic cultures, the role of women is quite different. To many in our culture, the practices of the people of these other

---

[4] Christopher Englholm and Diana Rowland, *International Excellence: Seven Breakthrough Strategies for Personal and Professional Success* (New York: Kodansha International, Inc.), 1996, p. 75.

[5] Jeanette W. Gilsdorf, "Metacommunication Effects on International Business Negotiating in China," *Business Communication Quarterly,* June 1997, pp. 29–32.

cultures suggest severe restriction of human rights. In the view of the people of these cultures, their practices are in accord with their religious convictions. They see us as being the ones out of step.

VALUES. Also differing by culture are our values—how we evaluate the critical matters in life. Americans, for example, have been indoctrinated with the Protestant work ethic. It is the belief that if one puts hard work ahead of pleasure, success will follow. The product of this thinking is an emphasis on planning, working efficiently, and maximizing production. Of course, not all of us subscribe to this ethic, but it is a strong force in the thinking of many in our culture. The prevailing view in some other cultures is quite different. In some, the major concern is for spiritual and human well-being. The view of work is relaxed, and productivity is, at best, a secondary concern.

■ Each culture has different values—concerning such matters as attitude toward work,

Views about the relationships of employers and employees also may differ by culture. North American workers expect to change companies in their career a number of times; and they expect companies to fire them from time to time. Employees expect to move freely from job to job, and they expect employers to hire and fire as their needs change. Expectations are quite different in some other cultures. In Japan, for example, employment tends to be for a lifetime. The workplace is viewed much like a family, with loyalty expected from employees and employer. Such differences have caused misunderstandings in American–Japanese joint ventures.

■ employee–employer relations,

How employees view authority is yet another question that cultures view differently. We North Americans generally accept authority, yet we fiercely maintain the rights of the individual. In many Third World cultures, workers accept a subservient role passively. Autocratic rule is expected—even wanted.

■ and authority.

EXPRESSION OF EMOTIONS. From culture to culture, differences in social behavior develop. To illustrate, in some Asian cultures public displays of affection are strongly frowned upon—in fact, considered crude and offensive. Westerners, on the other hand, accept at least a moderate display of affection. To Westerners, laughter is a spontaneous display of pleasure, but in some cultures (Japanese, for one), laughter can also be a controlled behavior—to be used in certain social situations. Even such emotional displays as sorrow are influenced by culture. In some Middle Eastern cultures, sorrow is expressed with loud, seemingly uncontrolled wailing. In similar situations, Westerners typically respond with subdued and controlled emotions.

■ Social behavior varies by culture, such as practices concerning affection, laughter, and emotion.

We all have observed the emotion and animation people of the Mediterranean cultures display as they communicate. And we have seen the more subdued communication of others—notably northern Europeans. The first group tends to see the second as disinterested and lacking in friendliness. The second sees the first as excitable, emotional, perhaps even unstable.

■ Included is the degree of animation displayed.

Many more such practices exist. Some cultures combine business and social pleasure; others do not. Some expect to engage in aggressive bargaining in business transactions; others prefer straightforward dealings. Some talk loudly and with emotion; others communicate orally in a subdued manner. Some communicate with emphasis on economy of expression; others communicate with an abundance of verbiage.

■ Many more such practices exist.

The comparisons could go on and on, for there are countless differences in cultures. But it is not necessary to review them all. What is important is that we recognize their existence, that we look for them, and that we understand them. We should guard against ethnocentrism, the use of cultural practices as standards for determining meaning in cross-cultural communication.

■ We must recognize them, look for them, and understand them.

EFFECTS ON BUSINESS COMMUNICATION TECHNIQUES

The foregoing examples illustrate only a few of the numerous differences that exist among cultures. Books have been written on the subject. Our objective here is only to establish the point that the differences among cultures affect communication between people of different cultures.

■ Cultural differences affect communication.

The communication techniques presented in this book should be modified in light of

■ Our communication techniques are not universally acceptable.

Web Tools for Cross-Cultural Communication

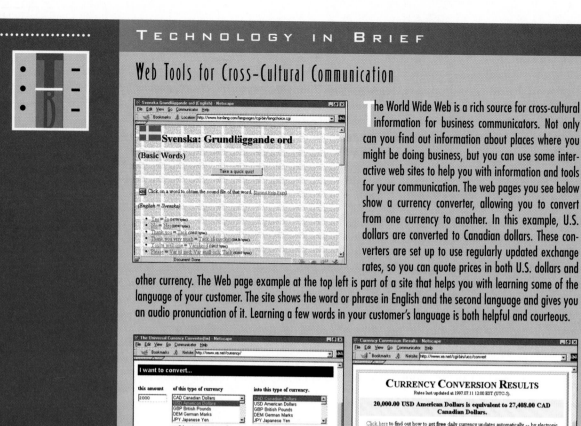

The World Wide Web is a rich source for cross-cultural information for business communicators. Not only can you find out information about places where you might be doing business, but you can use some interactive web sites to help you with information and tools for your communication. The web pages you see below show a currency converter, allowing you to convert from one currency to another. In this example, U.S. dollars are converted to Canadian dollars. These converters are set up to use regularly updated exchange rates, so you can quote prices in both U.S. dollars and other currency. The Web page example at the top left is part of a site that helps you with learning some of the language of your customer. The site shows the word or phrase in English and the second language and gives you an audio pronunciation of it. Learning a few words in your customer's language is both helpful and courteous.

cultural differences, but it is difficult to say how this should be done. You simply have to apply your knowledge of the culture involved to each of these techniques. For example, the Japanese have difficulty saying no emphatically. They often see it as a personal attack, so they give a *tatemae* response. This response is what they think should be said, not necessarily the whole truth. They believe this will help save face for all involved. A major cultural phenomenon that is important to understand when doing business with Mexicans is the *mañana* syndrome. While it is often used derogatorily to imply that Mexicans are lazy, understanding how and when it is used will help you communicate deadlines clearly. As you can see, much that is acceptable in our business communication must be modified for readers from other cultures.

- These techniques do not work even with all English-speaking people.

Cultural differences even cause communication problems among people using the same language. For example, even though the United States and other countries have a common language, communication problems occur between them. Such small differences as calling an elevator a *lift* or the hood of a car a *bonnet* can be very confusing. Just telling time with a 24-hour clock can be very confusing. The Canadian who told you he fell asleep at *22:00* on the *chesterfield* can be easily misunderstood.

- Overcome communication problems stemming from cultural differences by learning about cultures.

Without question, cultural differences can cause communication problems. But there is a way to overcome those problems. You can become a student of cultures—that is, you can learn about the cultures of the people with whom you communicate. In doing so, you must take care not to overgeneralize or oversimplify, for cultural differences are highly complex. You must also take care not to exaggerate the effects of cultural differences. Not all miscommunication between people of different cultures results from cultural differences. While there are many variations and exceptions within and between cultures, there are similarities, too. As a student of cultures, you understand that finding those similarities will help you communicate clearly. This effort is not easy, and it will never be completely successful; but it is the only strategy to follow in cross-cultural communication.

PROBLEMS OF LANGUAGE

The people on earth use more than 3,000 languages. Because few of us can learn more than one or two other languages well, problems of miscommunication are bound to occur in international communication.

■ Communication problems are caused by the existence of many languages.

LACK OF LANGUAGE EQUIVALENCY

Unfortunately, wide differences among languages make precisely equivalent translations difficult. One reason for such differences is that languages are based on the concepts, experiences, views, and such of the cultures that developed them. And different cultures have different concepts, experiences, views, and such. For example, we think of a florist as someone who sells flowers and related items in a store. In some cultures, however, flowers are sold by street vendors, mainly women and children. Obviously, our *florist* does not have a precise equivalent in the language of such cultures.

■ Differences among languages make equivalent translations difficult.

Similarly, our *supermarket* has no equivalent in some languages. The French have no word to distinguish between *house* and *home, mind* and *brain,* and *man* and *gentleman.* The Spanish have no word to distinguish between a *chairman* and a *president* while Italians have no word for *wishful thinking.* And Russians have no words for *efficiency, challenge,* and *having fun.* However, Italians have nearly 500 words for types of pasta, and the Eskimo have over 100 words for types of snow. And so it is with words for many other objects, actions, concepts, and such (for example, *roundup, interview, strike, tough, monopoly, domestic, feminine, responsible, aloof*).

■ Examples prove the point.

Another explanation for the lack of language equivalency is the grammatical and syntactic differences among languages. Some languages (Urdu, for example) have no gerunds, and some have no adverbs and/or adjectives. Not all languages deal with verb mood, voice, and tense in the same way. The obvious result is that even the best translators often cannot find literal equivalents between languages.

■ Grammar and syntax differences add to the difficulty.

Adding to these equivalency problems is the problem of multiple word meanings. Like English, other languages have more than one meaning for many words. Think, for example, of our numerous meanings for the simple word *run* (to move fast, to compete for office, a score in baseball, a break in a stocking, a fading of colors, and many more). Or consider the multiple meanings of such words as *fast, cat, trip, gross, ring,* and *make.* The Oxford English Dictionary uses over 15,000 words to define *what.* Unless one knows a language well, it is difficult to know which of the meanings is intended.

■ So do the multiple meanings of words.

Overcoming such language problems is difficult. The best way, of course, is to know more than one language well; but the competence required is beyond the reach of most of us. Thus, your best course is first to be aware that translation problems exist and then to ask questions—to probe—to determine what the other person understands. For very important oral messages, documents, or such, you might consider using a procedure called *back translating.* This procedure involves using two translators, one with first-language skills in one of the languages involved and one with first-language skills in the other language. The first translator translates the message into his or her language, and the second translator then translates the message back into the original. If the translations are good, the second translation matches the original.

■ Overcome such language problems by knowing languages well and by questioning.

■ Use back translating for important communications.

DIFFICULTIES IN USING ENGLISH

Fortunately for us, English is the primary language of international business. This is not to say that other languages are not used in international business, for they are. When business executives from different countries have a common language, whatever it may be, they are likely to use it. For example, an executive from Iraq and an executive from Saudi Arabia would communicate with each other in Arabic, for Arabic is their common language. For

■ English is the primary language of international business.

the same reason, an executive from Venezuela would use Spanish in dealing with an executive from Mexico. However, when executives have no common language, they are likely to use English. The members of the European Free Trade Association conduct all their business in English even though not one of them is a native English speaker. And when a Swiss company and a Swedish company merged, they decided to make English the official company language.[6]

■ But many foreigners have problems using English.

Although we can take comfort from knowing that ours is the primary language of international business, we must keep in mind that it is not the primary language of many of those who use it. Since many of these users have had to learn English as a second language, they are likely to use it less fluently than we and to experience problems in understanding us. Some of their more troublesome problems are reviewed in the following pages.

■ Two-word verbs are hard for foreigners to understand,

TWO-WORD VERBS. One of the most difficult problems to nonnative speakers of English involves the use of two-word verbs. By *two-word verbs* we mean a wording consisting of (1) a verb and (2) a second element that, combined with the verb, produces a meaning that the verb alone does not have. For example, take the verb *break* and the word *up*. When combined, they have a meaning quite different from the meanings the words have alone. And look how the meaning changes when the same verb is combined with other words: *break away, break out, break in, break down*. Dictionaries are of little help to nonnatives who are seeking the meanings of these word combinations.

■ as in these combinations.

There are many two-word verbs—so many, in fact, that a special dictionary of them has been compiled.[7] Following are a few of them arranged by the more common words that combine with the verbs:

Verb Plus "Away"

give away

keep away

lay away

pass away

put away

throw away

Verb Plus "Back"

cut back

feed back

keep back

play back

read back

take back

turn back

win back

Verb Plus "Down"

calm down

die down

hand down

keep down

let down

lie down

Verb Plus "Down"

mark down

pin down

play down

put down

run down

shut down

sit down

wear down

Verb Plus "In"

cash in

cave in

close in

dig in

give in

run in

take in

throw in

Verb Plus "Off"

break off

brush off

buy off

check off

---

[6] Bill Bryson, *The Mother Tongue: English and How It Got That Way* (New York: William Morrow and Company, Inc., 1990), p. 12.

[7] George A. Meyer, *The Two-Word Verb* (The Hague, Netherlands: Mouton, 1975).

Verb Plus "Off"

clear off

cool off

cut off

finish off

let off

mark off

pay off

run off

send off

show off

shut off

sound off

start off

take off

write off

Verb Plus "Out"

blow out

clean out

clear out

crowd out

cut out

die out

dry out

even out

figure out

fill out

find out

give out

hold out

lose out

pull out

rule out

tire out

wear out

work out

Verb Plus "Over"

check over

do over

hold over

pass over

Verb Plus "Over"

put over

run over

stop over

take over

talk over

think over

win over

Verb Plus "Up"

blow up

build up

call up

catch up

cover up

dig up

end up

fill up

get up

hang up

hold up

keep up

look up

mix up

pick up

save up

shake up

shut up

slow up

split up

wrap up

Verb Plus Miscellaneous Words

bring about

catch on

get across

pass on

put across

put forth

roll over

set forth

stop over

Of course, nonnatives studying English learn some of these word combinations, for they are part of the English language. But many of them are not covered in language textbooks or listed in dictionaries. It is apparent that we should use these word combinations sparingly when communicating with nonnative speakers of English. Whenever possible,

■ Use two-word verbs sparingly. Find substitutes, as shown here.

we should substitute for them words that appear in standard dictionaries. Following are some two-word verbs and suggested substitutes:

Two-Word Verbs	Suggested Substitutes
give up	surrender
speed up, hurry up	accelerate
go on, keep on	continue
put off	defer
take off	depart, remove
come down	descend
go in, come in, get in	enter
go out, come out, get out	exit, leave
blow up	explode
think up	imagine
figure out	solve
take out, take away	remove
go back, get back, be back	return

■ Some two-word verbs have noun and adjective forms. Use these sparingly.

Additional problems result from the fact that some two-word verbs have noun and adjective forms. These also tend to confuse nonnatives using English. Examples of such nouns are *breakthrough, cover-up, drive-in, hookup, show-off,* and *sit-in.* Examples of such adjectives are *going away* (a going-away gift), *cover-up* (cover-up tactics), *cleanup* (cleanup work), and *turning-off* (turning-off place). Fortunately, some nouns and adjectives of this kind are commonly used and appear in standard dictionaries (words such as *hookup, feedback, breakthrough, lookout,* and *takeover*). In writing to nonnative readers, you will need to use sparingly those that do not appear in standard dictionaries.

■ Culturally derived words, especially slang, cause problems.

CULTURALLY DERIVED WORDS. Words derived from our culture also present problems. The most apparent are the slang expressions that continually come into and go out of use. Some slang expressions catch on and find a place in our dictionaries *(brunch, hobo, blurb, bogus).* But most are with us for a little while and then are gone. Examples of such short-lived slang expressions are the "twenty-three skiddoo" and "oh you kid" of the 1920s and the *ritzy, scram, natch, lousy, soused, all wet, hep, in the groove,* and *tops* of following decades. More recent ones that are probably destined for the same fate include *nerd, wimp, earth pig, pig out, waldo, squid, grimbo,* and *dexter.*

■ So avoid slang.

Most slang words are not in dictionaries or on the word lists that non-English speaking people study to learn English. The obvious conclusion is that you should not use slang in cross-cultural communication.

■ Words derived from sports, social activities, and so on cause problems.

Similar to and in fact overlapping slang are the words and expressions that we derive from our various activities—sports, social affairs, work, and the like. Sports especially have contributed such words, many of which are so widely used that they are part of our everyday vocabulary. From football we have *kickoff, goal-line stand,* and *over the top.* Baseball has given us *out in left field, strike out, touch base, off base, right off the bat, a steal, squeeze play, balk,* and *go to bat for.* From boxing we have *knockout, down for the count, below the belt, answer the bell,* and *on the ropes.* From other sports and from sports in general we have *jock, ace, par, stymie, from scratch, ballpark figure,* and *get the ball rolling.*

■ Colloquialisms also cause problems.

Similar to these words and expressions are words and expressions developed within our culture (colloquialisms). Some of these have similar meanings in other cultures, but most are difficult for nonnatives to understand. Following are some examples:

head for home	in the groove
have an itching palm	nuts (crazy)
grasp at straws	grand (thousand)

flat-footed

on the beam

out to pasture

sitting duck

crying in his beer

in orbit

a honey

a flop

dope (crazy)

hood (gangster)

up the creek without a paddle

a fish out of water

a chicken with its head cut off

circle the wagons

shoot from the hip

tuckered out

gumption

tote (carry)

in a rut

pump priming

make heads or tails of it

tearjerker

countdown

shortcut

educated guess

If you are like most of us, many of these words and expressions are a part of your vocabulary. You use them in your everyday communicating, which is all right. They are colorful, and they can communicate clearly to those who understand them. Nonnative English speakers are not likely to understand them, however, so you will need to eliminate such words and expressions in communicating with them. You will need to use words that are clearly defined in the dictionaries that these people are likely to use in translating your message. Following are some examples:

■ We use such words in everyday communication. But avoid them in cross-cultural correspondence.

Not This

We were caught flat-footed.

He frequently shoots from the hip.

We would be up the creek without a paddle.

They couldn't make heads or tails of the report.

The sales campaign was a flop.

I'll touch base with you on this problem in August.

Take an educated guess on this question.

Your sales report put us in orbit.

We will wind down manufacturing operations in November.

Your prediction was right on the beam.

But This

We were surprised.

He frequently acts before he thinks.

We would be in a helpless situation.

They couldn't understand the report.

The sales campaign was a failure.

I'll talk with you about this problem in August.

Answer this question to the best of your knowledge.

Your sales report pleased us very much.

We will end manufacturing operations in November.

Your prediction was correct.

A General Suggestion for Communicating across Cultures

In addition to the specific suggestions for improving your communication in English with nonnative English speakers, you should follow one general suggestion: write (or talk) simply and clearly. Talk slowly and enunciate each word. Remember that because most nonnative speakers learned English in school, they are acquainted mainly with primary dictionary meanings and are not likely to understand slang words or shades of difference in the meanings we give words. Thus, they will understand you better if you use simple, basic English. It is good etiquette to do so.

You will also communicate better if you carefully word your questions. Be sure your questions are not double questions. Avoid "Do you want to go to dinner now or wait until after the rush hour is over?" Also, avoid the yes/no question that some cultures may have difficulty answering directly. Use more open-ended questions such as "When would you like to go to dinner?" Also, avoid negative questions such as "Aren't you going to dinner?" In some cultures a yes response confirms whether the questioner is correct; in other cultures the response is directed toward the question being asked.

Finally, try to check and clarify your communication through continuous confirmation.

■ Use simple, basic English.

■ Word questions carefully to elicit the response intended.

■ Continually check the accuracy of the communication.

Summarizing in writing also is a good idea, and today's technology enables parties to do this on the spot. It allows you to be certain you've conveyed your message and received theirs accurately. Even in Britain, a culture similar to ours, similar words can have vastly different meanings. For example, we use a billion to mean 1,000,000,000 whereas the British use it to mean 1,000,000,000,000. Continually checking for meaning and using written summaries can help ensure the accuracy of the communication process.

SUMMARY BY CHAPTER OBJECTIVES

1 Explain why communicating clearly across cultures is important to business.

1. Businesses are becoming increasingly global in their operations.
   • Being able to communicate across cultures is necessary in these operations.
   • Specifically, it helps in gaining additional business, in hiring good people, and generally in understanding and satisfying the needs of customers.

2 Define culture and explain its effects on cross-cultural communication.

2. *Culture* may be defined as "the way of life of a group of people."
   • Cultures differ.
   • People tend to view the practices of their culture as right and those of other cultures as peculiar or wrong.
   • These views cause miscommunication.

3 Describe cultural differences in body positions and movements and use this knowledge effectively in communicating.

3. Variations in how people of different cultures use body positions and body movements is a cause of miscommunication.
   • How people walk, gesture, smile, and such varies from culture to culture.
   • When people from different cultures attempt to communicate, each may not understand the other's body movements.

4 Describe cultural differences in attitudes toward time, space, odors, and such and use this knowledge effectively in communicating.

4. People in different cultures differ in their ways of relating to people.
   • Specifically, they differ in their practices and thinking concerning time, space, odors, frankness, relationships, values, and social behavior.
   • We should not use our culture's practices as standards for determining meaning.
   • Instead, we should try to understand the other culture.

5 Explain the language equivalency problem as a cause of miscommunication.

5. Language equivalency problems are another major cause of miscommunication in cross-cultural communication.
   • About 3,000 languages are used on earth.
   • They differ greatly in grammar and syntax.
   • Like English, most have words with multiple meanings.
   • As a result, equivalency in translation is difficult.

6 Describe what one can do to overcome the language equivalency problem.

6. Overcoming the language equivalency problems involves hard and tedious work.
   • The best advice is to master the language of the nonnative English speakers with whom you communicate.
   • Also, you should be aware of the problems caused by language differences.
   • Ask questions carefully to make sure you are understood.
   • For important communications, consider back translation—the technique of using two translators, the first to translate from one language to the other and the second to translate back to the original.
   • Check the accuracy of the communication with written summaries.

▌DILBERT © United Feature Syndicate. Reprinted by permission.

CRITICAL THINKING QUESTIONS

1. "Just as our culture has advanced in its technological sophistication, it has advanced in the sophistication of its body signals, gestures, and attitudes toward time, space, and such. Thus, the ways of our culture are superior to those of most other cultures." Discuss this view.

2. What are the prevailing attitudes in our culture toward the following, and how can those attitudes affect our communication with nonnatives? Discuss.
   a. Negotiation methods
   b. Truth in advertising
   c. Company–worker loyalty
   d. Women's place in society

3. Some of our letter-writing techniques are said to be unacceptable to people from such cultures as those of Japan and England.

a. Which techniques in particular do you think would be most inappropriate in these cultures?

b. Why?

4. Think of English words (other than text examples) that probably do not have a precise equivalent in some other culture. Tell how you would attempt to explain each of these words to a person from that culture.

5. Select a word with at least five meanings. List those meanings and tell how you would communicate each of them to a nonnative.

6. From newspapers or magazines, find and bring to class 10 sentences containing words and expressions that a nonnative English speaker would not be likely to understand. Rewrite the sentences for this reader.

7. Is conversational style appropriate in writing to nonnative readers? Discuss.

8. Interview a nonnative speaker of English about communication differences between cultures he or she has experienced. Report your findings to the class in a 10-minute presentation.

9. Research a non-English-speaking country on the Internet or in your library. Look for ways in which business communication can vary by culture. Report your work to the class in a short presentation.

CRITICAL THINKING EXERCISES

Instructions: Rewrite the following sentences for a nonnative English speaker.

1. Last year our laboratory made a breakthrough in design that really put sales in orbit.

2. You will need to pin down Mr. Wang to put across the need to tighten up expenses.

3. Recent losses have us on the ropes now, but we expect to get out of the hole by the end of the year.

4. We will kick off the advertising campaign in February, and in April we will bring out the new products.

5. Maryellen gave us a ballpark figure on the project, but I think she is ready to back down from her estimate.

6. We will back up any of our products that are not up to par.

7. Mr. Maghrabi managed to straighten out and become our star salesperson.

8. Now that we have cut back on our advertising, we will have to build up our personal selling.

9. If you want to improve sales, you should stay with your prospects until they see the light.

10. We should be able to bring about a savings of 8 or 10 grand.

Correctness of Communication

18

Upon completing this chapter, you will be able to use the accepted standards of English grammar and punctuation in written business communications. To reach this goal, you should be able to

1 Punctuate messages correctly.

2 Write complete, grammatically correct sentences, avoiding such problems as awkward construction, dangling modifiers, and misuse of words.

3 Determine when to spell out numbers and when to express them in numeral form according to standards of correctness.

4 Spell words correctly by applying spelling rules and using a dictionary or spell checker.

5 Use capital letters for all proper names, first words of sentences, and first words of complimentary closes.

The Effects of Correctness on Communication

Play the role of Mike Rook, a purchasing agent for Hewlett-Packard, and read through today's mail. The first letter comes from Joe Spivey, sales manager, B and B Manufacturing Company. You have not met the writer, though you talked to him on the telephone a few days ago. At that time, you were favorably impressed with Spivey's enthusiasm and ability, and with B and B. In fact, you assumed that after he gave you the information you needed about B and B's products and services, you would begin buying from it.

As you read Spivey's letter, however, you are startled. "Could this be the same person I talked with?" you ask yourself. There in the first paragraph is an *it don't*, a clear error of subject–verb agreement. Farther down, an *it's* is used to show possession rather than *it is*. Spivey apparently uses the sprinkle system for placing commas—that is, he sprinkles them wherever his whims direct. His commas often fall in strange places. For example, he writes, "Our salespeople, say the Rabb Company engineers, will verify the durability of Ironskin protective coating," but you think he means "Our salespeople say the Rabb Company engineers will verify the durability of Ironskin protective coating." The two sentences, which differ only in their punctuation, have distinctly different meanings. Spivey's letter is filled with such errors.

In general, you now have a lower opinion of Spivey and his company. Perhaps you'll have to take a long look at B and B's products and services. After all, the products and services that a company provides are closely related to the quality of its people.

The problem just described is a very real one in business. Image does influence the success of both companies and people. And correctness in writing influences image. Thus, you will want to make certain that your writing is correct, so that it helps form a favorable image both of you and of your company. The material presented in the pages that follow should help you in that effort.

The correctness of your communication will be important to you and your company. It will be important to you because people will judge you by it, and how they judge you will help determine your success in life. It will be important to your company because it will help convey the image of competence that companies like. People judge a company by how its employees act, think, talk, and write. Company executives want such judgments to be favorable.

> ■ People judge you and your company by the correctness of your communication.

THE NATURE OF CORRECTNESS

Not all people agree that there are standards for correct communication. In fact, some people think there should be no general standards of this kind, that whatever communicates in a given case is all right. Businesspeople, however, generally accept the standards for correct usage that educated people have developed over the years. These are the standards that you have studied in your English composition classes and that appear in textbooks. Businesspeople expect you to follow them.

> ■ Businesspeople expect you to follow the generally accepted standards of English.

These standards of correctness have one basic purpose: to assist in communicating. To some people the standards of correctness appear arbitrary or unnecessary. But such is not the case. They are designed to reduce misunderstanding—to make communication more precise. When you communicate precisely, you practice good etiquette by meeting your reader's needs for understandable messages. It is only in this light that we can justify studying them.

> ■ These standards of correctness assist in communicating.

The practical value of these standards is easily illustrated. Take, for example, the following two sentences. Their words are the same; only their punctuation differs. But what a difference the punctuation makes!

"The teacher," said the student, "is stupid."

The teacher said, "The student is stupid."

Or what about the following pair of sentences? Who is speaking, the Democrats or the Republicans? The commas make a difference.

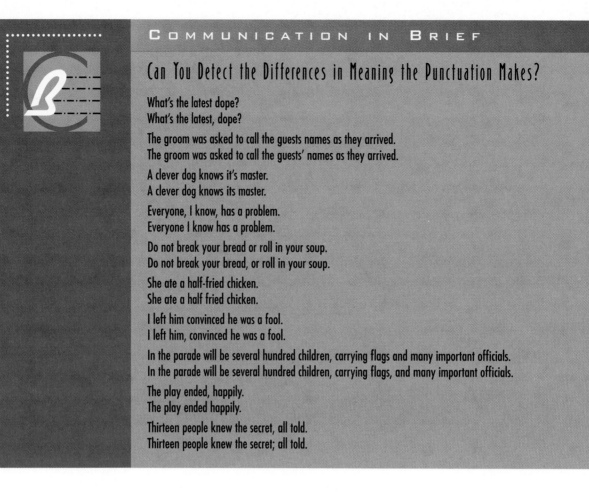

Can You Detect the Differences in Meaning the Punctuation Makes?

What's the latest dope?
What's the latest, dope?

The groom was asked to call the guests names as they arrived.
The groom was asked to call the guests' names as they arrived.

A clever dog knows it's master.
A clever dog knows its master.

Everyone, I know, has a problem.
Everyone I know has a problem.

Do not break your bread or roll in your soup.
Do not break your bread, or roll in your soup.

She ate a half-fried chicken.
She ate a half fried chicken.

I left him convinced he was a fool.
I left him, convinced he was a fool.

In the parade will be several hundred children, carrying flags and many important officials.
In the parade will be several hundred children, carrying flags, and many important officials.

The play ended, happily.
The play ended happily.

Thirteen people knew the secret, all told.
Thirteen people knew the secret; all told.

The Democrats, say the Republicans, will win.
The Democrats say the Republicans will win.

Here are two more sentences. The difference here needs no explanation.

He looked at her stern.
He looked at her sternly.

> The following review covers the major standards. They are coded for your convenience.

Because the standards of correctness are important to your communication in business, this chapter will review them. The review is not complete, for much more space would be needed for complete coverage. But the major standards are covered, those that most often present problems in your writing. For your convenience, the standards are coded with symbols (letters and numbers). You should find these symbols useful in identifying the standards. Your instructor should find them useful as grading marks to identify errors in your writing.

> Take the self-analysis test to determine your present knowledge of the standards.

You probably already know many of the standards of correctness, so the following information will not all be new to you. To help you determine how much you know and do not know, you should take the self-analysis test at the end of the chapter. This will enable you to study the standards selectively. Because the self-analysis test covers only the more frequently used standards, however, you would be wise to review the entire chapter.

STANDARDS FOR PUNCTUATION

The following explanations cover the most important standards for correctness in punctuation. For reasons of accuracy, the explanations use some technical words. Even so, the illustrations should make the standards clear.

Apostrophe: Apos 1

Use the apostrophe to show the possessive case of nouns and indefinite pronouns. If the word does not end in *s*, add an apostrophe and an *s*. If the word ends in *s*, add only an apostrophe.

■ Use the apostrophe to show possession.

Nominative Form	**Possessive Form**
company	company's
employee	employee's
companies	companies'
employees	employees'

Proper names and singular nouns ending in *s* sounds are exceptions. To such words you may add either an apostrophe and an *s* or just an apostrophe. Add only an apostrophe to the nominative plural.

Nominative Form	**Possessive Form**
Texas (singular)	Texas's, Texas'
Jones (singular)	Jones's, Jones'
Joneses (plural)	Joneses'
countess (singular)	countess's, countess'

Apos 2

Use an apostrophe to mark the place in a contraction where letters are omitted.

■ Mark omissions in contractions with the apostrophe.

it is = it's

has not = hasn't

cannot = can't

Brackets: Bkts

Set off in brackets words that you wish to insert in a quotation.

■ Use brackets to set off words that you insert in a quotation.

"The use of this type of supervisor [the communications expert] may still be increasing."

"Direct supervision has diminished in importance during the past decade [the report was written in 1989], when 43 percent of the reporting business firms that started programs used teams."

Colon: Cln 1

Use the colon to introduce a statement of explanation, an enumeration, or a formal quotation.

■ Use the colon to introduce formal statements.

Enumeration: Working in this department are three classes of support: clerical support, computer support, and customer support.

Formal quotation: President Hartung had this to say about the proposal: "Any such movement that fails to get the support of the workers in this plant fails to get my support."

Explanation: At this time the company was pioneering a new marketing idea: It was attempting to sell its products directly to consumers by means of vending machines.

Cln 2

Do not use the colon when the thought of the sentence should continue without interruption. If introducing a list by a colon, the colon should be preceded by a word that explains or identifies the list.

■ Do not use the colon when it breaks the thought flow.

Not this: Cities in which new sales offices are in operation are: Fort Smith, Texarkana, Lake Charles, Jackson, and Biloxi.

But this: Cities in which new sales offices are in operation are Fort Smith, Texarkana, Lake Charles, Jackson, and Biloxi.

Or this: Cities with new sales offices are as follows: Fort Smith, Texarkana, Lake Charles, Jackson, and Biloxi.

COMMA: CMA 1

- Use the comma to separate clauses connected by *and, but, or, nor, for.*

Use the comma to separate principal clauses connected by a coordinating conjunction. The coordinating conjunctions are *and, but, or, nor,* and *for.* (A principal clause has a subject and a verb and stands by itself. A coordinating conjunction connects clauses, words, or phrases of equal rank.)

Only two components of the index declined, and these two account for only 12 percent of the total weight of the index.

New automobiles are moving at record volumes, but used-car sales are lagging behind the record pace set two years ago.

Make exceptions to this rule, however, in the case of compound sentences consisting of short and closely connected clauses.

We sold and the price dropped.

Sometimes we win and sometimes we lose.

CMA 2.1

- Use the comma to separate (1) items in a series and

Separate the items listed in a series by commas. In order to avoid misinterpretation of the rare instances in which some of the items listed have compound constructions, it is always good to place the comma between the last two items (before the final conjunction).

Good copy must cover facts with accuracy, sincerity, honesty, and conviction.

Direct advertising can be used to introduce salespeople, fill in between salespeople's calls, cover territory where salespeople cannot be maintained, and keep pertinent reference material in the hands of prospects.

A survey conducted at the 1999 automobile show indicated that green, white, blue, and black cars were favored by the public.

CMA 2.2

- (2) adjectives in a series.

Separate coordinate adjectives in a series by commas if they modify the same noun and if no *and* connects them. A good test to determine whether adjectives are coordinate is to insert an *and* between them. If the *and* does not change the meaning, the adjectives are coordinate.

Miss Pratt has been a reliable, faithful, efficient employee for 20 years.

We guarantee that this is a good, clean car.

Blue office furniture is Mr. Orr's recommendation for the new conference room. (Office furniture is practically a compound noun; blue modifies both words.)

A big crescent wrench proved to be best for the task. (The *and* won't fit between *big* and *crescent.*)

CMA 3

Set off nonrestrictive modifiers by commas. By a *nonrestrictive modifier* we mean a modifier that could be omitted from the sentence without changing its meaning. Restrictive modifiers (those that restrict the words they modify to one particular object) are not set off by commas. A restrictive modifier cannot be left out of the sentence without changing its meaning.

■ Use commas to set off nonrestrictive modifiers (those that could be left out without changing the meaning of the sentence).

Restrictive: The salesperson who sells the most will get a bonus. (*Who sells the most* restricts the meaning to a particular salesperson.)

Nonrestrictive: James Smithers, who was the company's top salesperson for the year, was awarded a bonus. (If the clause *who was the company's top salesperson for the year* is omitted, the meaning of the sentence is not changed.)

Restrictive: J. Ward & Company is the firm that employs most of the physically disabled in this area.

Nonrestrictive: J. Ward & Company, the firm that employs most of the physically disabled in this area, has gained the admiration of the community.

Notice that some modifiers can be either restrictive or nonrestrictive, depending on the writer's intended meaning.

Restrictive: All the suits that were damaged in the fire were sold at a discount. (Implies that some of the suits were not damaged.)

Nonrestrictive: All the suits, which were damaged by the fire, were sold at a discount. (Implies that the entire stock of suits was damaged.)

CMA 4.1

Use commas to set off parenthetic expressions. A parenthetic expression consists of words that interrupt the normal flow of the sentence. In a sense, they appear to be "stuck in." In many instances, they are simply words out of normal order. For example, the sentence "A full-page, black-and-white advertisement was run in the *Daily Bulletin*" contains a parenthetic expression when the word order is altered: "An advertisement, full-page and in black and white, was run in the *Daily Bulletin.*"

■ Use commas to set off (1) parenthetic expressions (comments "stuck in"),

This practice, it is believed, will lead to ruin.

The Johnston Oil Company, so the rumor goes, has sharply reduced its exploration activity.

Although in such cases you may use dashes or the parentheses in place of commas, the three marks differ in the degree to which they separate the enclosed words from the rest of the sentence. The comma is the weakest of the three, and it is best used when the material set off is closely related to the surrounding words. Dashes are stronger marks than commas and are used when the material set off tends to be long or contains internal punctuation marks. Parentheses, the strongest of the three, are primarily used to enclose material that helps explain or supplement the main words of the sentence.

CMA 4.2

Use commas to set off an appositive (a noun or a noun and its modifiers inserted to explain another noun) from the rest of the sentence. In a sense, appositives are parenthetic expressions, for they interrupt the normal flow of the sentence.

■ (2) apposition words (words explaining another word),

The Baron Corporation, our machine-parts supplier, is negotiating a new contract.

St. Louis, home office of our Midwest district, will be the permanent site of our annual sales meeting.

President Cartwright, a self-educated woman, is the leading advocate of our night school for employees.

But appositives that identify very closely are not set off by commas.

The word *liabilities* is not understood by most people.

Our next shipment will come on the ship *Alberta*.

CMA 4.3

■ (3) certain parenthetic words (*in fact, however*), and

Set off parenthetic words such as *however, in fact, of course, for example,* and *consequently* with commas.

It is apparent, therefore, that the buyers' resistance has been brought about by an overvigorous sales campaign.

After the first experiment, for example, the traffic flow increased 10 percent.

The company will, however, be forced to abandon the old pricing system.

Included in this group of parenthetic words may be introductory interjections (*oh, alas*) and responsive expressions (*yes, no, surely, indeed, well,* and *so on*). But if the words are strongly exclamatory or are not closely connected with the rest of the sentence, they may be punctuated as a sentence. (*No. Yes. Indeed.*)

Yes, the decision to increase production has been made.

Oh, contribute whatever you think is appropriate.

CMA 4.4

■ (4) units in a date or address.

When more than one unit appears in a date or an address, set off the units by commas.

One unit: December 30 is the date of our annual inventory.

One unit: The company has one outlet in Ohio.

More than one unit: December 30, 1906, is the date the Johnston Company first opened its doors.

More than one unit: Richmond, Virginia, is the headquarters of the new sales district.

CMA 5.1

■ Use the comma after (1) introductory subordinate clauses and

Use the comma after a subordinate clause that precedes the main clause.

Although it is durable, this package does not have eye appeal.

Since there was little store traffic on Aisle 13, the area was converted into office space.

CMA 5.2

■ (2) introductory verbal phrases.

Place a comma after an introductory verbal phrase. A verbal phrase is one that contains some verb derivative—a gerund, a participle, or an infinitive.

Gerund phrase: After gaining the advantage, we failed to press on to victory.

Participle phrase: Realizing his mistake, the foreman instructed his workers to keep a record of all salvaged equipment.

Infinitive phrase: To increase our turnover of automobile accessories, we must first improve our display area.

Cma 6.1

Use the comma only for good reason. It is not a mark to be inserted indiscriminately at the writer's whim. As a rule, the use of commas should be justified by one of the standard practices previously noted.

■ Do not use the comma without good reason,

Cma 6.1.1

Do not be tricked into putting a comma between the subject and the verb.

The thought that he could not afford to fail spurred him on. (No comma after *fail.*)

■ such as between the subject and the verb.

Cma 6.2

Take exception to the preceding standards wherever the insertion of a comma will help clarity of expression.

Not this: From the beginning inventory methods of Hill Company have been haphazard.
But this: From the beginning, inventory methods of Hill Company have been haphazard.

Not this: Ever since she has been a model worker.
But this: Ever since, she has been a model worker.

■ Use the comma wherever it helps clarity.

Dash: Dsh

Use the dash to set off an element for emphasis or to show interrupted thought. In particular, use it with long parenthetic expressions or parenthetic expressions containing internal punctuation (see Cma 4.1). Most word processing software will usually allow you to insert a dash with a special character code. Depending on the software, you either insert the code through a combination of keystrokes or by selecting the character from a character map. With some word processing software, make the dash by striking the hyphen twice, without spacing before or after.

■ Use the dash to show interruption or emphasis.

Budgets for some past years—1997, for example—were prepared without consulting the department heads.

The test proved that the new process is simple, effective, accurate—and more expensive.

Only one person—the supervisor in charge—has authority to issue such an order.

If you want a voice in the government—vote.

Exclamation Mark: Ex

Use the exclamation mark at the end of a sentence or an exclamatory fragment to show strong emotion. But use it sparingly; never use it with trivial ideas.

■ Use exclamation marks to show strong feeling.

We've done it again!

Congratulations! Your biographical listing will appear in Marquis's 15th edition of *Who's Who in the World.*

Hyphen: Hpn 1

Use the hyphen to indicate the division of a word at the end of the line. You must divide between syllables. It is generally impractical to leave a one-letter syllable at the end of a line (*a-bove*) or to carry over a two-letter syllable to the next line (*expens-es*).

■ Mark word divisions with hyphens.

If you turn on the hyphenation feature of your word processing software, you can let it automatically take care of hyphenating words. Several programs permit you to set a hyphenation range. The wider the range the fewer words that will be hyphenated and the more ragged your margin; the narrower the range the more words that will be hyphenated and the smoother your right margin. Some have the option of allowing you to control the hyphenation you desire. You can accept what the program recommends, suggest a different place to hyphenate, or tell it not to hyphenate. Most programs will use their internal dictionaries for determining where to hyphenate words; some programs allow you to use an external dictionary for hyphenating words. These external dictionaries usually can be modified to suit your needs and preferences.

Hpn 2

■ Place hyphens between the parts of compound words.

Place hyphens between the parts of some compound words. Generally, the hyphen is used whenever its absence would confuse the meaning of the words.

Compound nouns: brother-in-law, cure-all, city-state.

Compound numbers twenty-one through ninety-nine: fifty-five, seventy-seven.

Compound adjectives (two or more words used before a noun as a single adjective): *long-term* contract, *50-gallon* drum, *door-to-door* selling, *end-of-month* clearance.

Prefixes (most have been absorbed into the word): co-organizer, ex-chairperson, anti-inflation.

Hpn 2.1

■ Do not place hyphens between (1) proper names and

A proper name used as a compound adjective needs no hyphen or hyphens to hold it together as a visual unit for the reader. The capitals perform that function.

Correct: A Lamar High School student.

Correct: A United Airlines pilot.

Hpn 2.2

■ (2) words that only follow each other.

Two or more modifiers in normal grammatical form and order need no hyphens. Particularly, a phrase consisting of an unmistakable adverb (one ending in *ly*) modifying an adjective or participle that in turn modifies a noun shows normal grammatical order and is readily grasped by the reader without the benefit of the hyphen. But an adverb not ending in *ly* is joined to its adjective or participle by the hyphen.

No hyphen needed: A poorly drawn chart.

Use the hyphen: A well-prepared chart.

Italics: Ital 1

■ Use italics for (1) publication titles,

For the use of italics for book titles, see QM 4. Note that italics are also used for titles of periodicals, works of art, long musical compositions, and names of naval vessels and aircraft.

Ital 2

■ (2) foreign words and abbreviations, and

Italicize rarely used foreign words—if you must use them (*ad vivum, bonne bouche, ma chère, ich dien*). After a foreign word is widely accepted, however, it does not need to be italicized (bon voyage, pizza, rancho). A current dictionary is a good source for information on which foreign words are italicized.

Ital 3

■ (3) a word used as its own name.

Italicize a word, letter, or figure used as its own name. Without this device, we could not write this set of rules. Note the use of italics throughout to label name words.

The little word *sell* is still in the dictionary.

The pronoun *which* should always have a noun as a clear antecedent. (Without the italics, this one becomes a fragment ending in midair.)

Reference Software Tools

Reference software, like reference books, allows writers to look up facts when they need them. All kinds of reference materials are available electronically, from dictionaries to grammar and style guides, encyclopedias, ZIP code directories, quotation databases, maps, and much, much more. These programs vary widely in their similarities to and differences from traditional reference books.

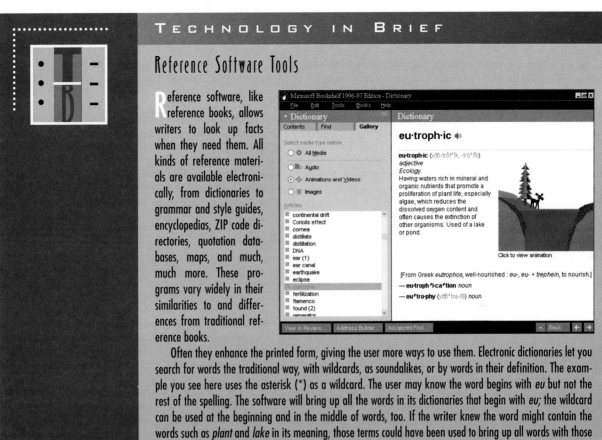

Often they enhance the printed form, giving the user more ways to use them. Electronic dictionaries let you search for words the traditional way, with wildcards, as soundalikes, or by words in their definition. The example you see here uses the asterisk (*) as a wildcard. The user may know the word begins with *eu* but not the rest of the spelling. The software will bring up all the words in its dictionaries that begin with *eu;* the wildcard can be used at the beginning and in the middle of words, too. If the writer knew the word might contain the words such as *plant* and *lake* in its meaning, those terms could have been used to bring up all words with those terms in their definition.

Electronic dictionaries go beyond the printed dictionary by providing animation, video, and audio. The user here, looking up the word *eutrophic*, would simply click on the sound icon to hear the word pronounced or click on the image to view an animation of eutrophication. Additionally, electronic dictionaries often use links to other definitions to help users. Such dictionaries, as well as all reference software, require writers to think clearly and take time to provide correctness in their writing.

PARENTHESES: PARENS

Use the parenthesis to set off words that are parenthetic or are inserted to explain or supplement the principal message (see Cma 4.1).

Peter Drucker's phenomenal predictions (*Forbes,* March 10, 1997) have made some business executives revise their plans.

As soon as Smith was elected chairperson (the vote was almost 2 to 1), he introduced his plan for reorganization.

■ Set off parenthetic words with parentheses.

PERIOD: PD 1

Use the period to indicate the end of a declarative sentence, an imperative statement, or a courteous request.

Declarative sentence: The survey will be completed and returned by October 26.

Imperative statement: Complete and return the survey by October 26.

Courteous request: Will you please complete and return the survey by October 26.

■ End a declarative sentence, an imperative statement, or a courteous request with a period.

Pd 2

■ Use periods in abbreviations.

Use periods after abbreviations or initials.

Ph.D., Co., Inc., A.D., etc.

But omit the periods and use all capitals in the initials or acronyms of agencies, networks, associations, and such: IRS, NBC, OPEC.

Pd 3

■ Use a series of periods to show omissions.

Use ellipses (a series of periods) to indicate the omission of words from a quoted passage. If the omitted part consists of something less than a sentence, three periods are customarily placed at the point of omission (a fourth period is added if the omission is a sentence or more). If the omitted part is a paragraph or more, however, a full line of periods is used. In all cases, the periods are separated by spaces.

Logical explanations, however, have been given by authorities in the field. Some attribute the decline . . . to recent changes in the state's economy. . . .

. . . .

Added to the labor factor is the high cost of raw material, which has tended to eliminate many marginal producers. Moreover, the rising cost of electric power in recent years may have shifted the attention of many industry leaders to other forms of production.

Question Mark: Q

■ End direct questions with the question mark.

Place a question mark at the end of sentences that are direct questions.

What are the latest quotations on Disney common stock?

Will this campaign help sell Microsoft products?

But do not use the question mark with indirect questions.

The president was asked whether this campaign would help sell Microsoft products.

He asked me what the latest quotations on Disney common stock were.

Quotation Marks: QM 1

■ Use quotation marks to enclose a speaker's or writer's exact words.

Use quotation marks to enclose the exact words of a speaker or, if the quotation is short, the exact words of a writer.

Short written quotations are quotations of four lines or less, although authorities do not agree on this point. Some suggest three lines—others up to eight. Longer written quotations are best displayed without quotation marks and with indented right and left margins.

Short written quotation: H. G. McVoy sums up his presentation with this statement: "All signs indicate that change will be evolutionary, not revolutionary."

Oral quotation: "This really should bring on a production slowdown," said Ms. Kuntz.

If a quotation is broken by explanation or reference words, each part of the quotation is enclosed in quotation marks.

"Will you be specific," he asked, "in recommending a course of action?"

QM 2

■ Use single quotation marks for a quotation within a quotation.

Enclose a quotation within a quotation with single quotation marks.

President Carver said, "It has been a long time since I have heard an employee say, 'Boss, I'm going to beat my quota today.'"

QM 3

Always place periods and commas inside quotation marks. Place semicolons and colons outside the quotation marks. Place question marks and exclamation points inside if they apply to the quoted passage only and outside if they apply to the whole sentence.

"If we are patient," he said, "prosperity will arrive someday." (The comma and the period are within the quotation marks.)

"Is there a quorum?" he asked. (The question mark belongs to the quoted passage.)

Which of you said, "I know where the error lies"? (The question mark applies to the entire sentence.

I conclude only this from the union's promise to "force the hand of management": A strike will be its trump card.

■ Periods and commas go inside quotation marks; semicolons and colons go outside; question marks and exclamation points go inside when they apply to the quoted part and outside when they apply to the entire sentence.

QM 4

Enclose in quotation marks the titles of parts of publications (articles in a magazine, chapters in a book). But italicize the titles of whole publications. If your software or printer will not italicize, use underscoring.

The third chapter of the book *Elementary Statistical Procedure* is titled "Concepts of Sampling."

Ann Fisher's most recent article, "Will a Career Switch Mean Less Pay?" appears in the current issue of *Fortune*.

■ Use quotation marks to enclose titles of parts of a publication.

SEMICOLON: SC 1

Use the semicolon to separate independent clauses that are not connected by a conjunction.

Cork or asbestos sheeting must be hand-cut; polyurethane may be poured into a mold.

The new contract provides wage increases; the original contract emphasized shorter hours.

Covered by this standard are independent clauses connected by conjunctive adverbs such as *however, nevertheless, therefore, then, moreover,* and *besides.*

The survey findings indicated a need to revise the policy; nevertheless, the president vetoed the amendment.

Small-town buyers favor the old model; therefore, the board concluded that both models should be marketed.

■ Use the semicolon to separate independent clauses not connected by a conjunction.

SC 2

You may use the semicolon to separate independent clauses joined by *and, but, or, for, or nor* (coordinating conjunctions) if the clauses are long or if they have other punctuation in them. In such situations, you may also use the semicolon for special emphasis.

The OCAW and the NUPNG, rivals from the beginning of the new industry, have shared almost equally in the growth of membership; but the OCAW predominates among workers in the petroleum-products crafts, including pipeline construction and operation, and the NUPNG leads in memberships of chemical workers.

The market price was $6; but we paid $10.

■ You may choose to separate with a semicolon independent clauses joined by a conjunction.

SC 3

Separate by semicolons the items in a list when the items have commas in them.

The following gains were made in the February year-to-year comparison: Fort Worth, 7,300; Dallas, 4,705; Lubbock, 2,610; San Antonio, 2,350; Waco, 2,240; Port Arthur, 2,170; and Corpus Christi, 1,420.

■ Use the semicolon to separate items in a list when the items contain commas.

Get It Wright!

Don't use no double negative.
Make each pronoun agree with their antecedent.
Join clauses good, like a conjunction should.
About them sentence fragments.
When dangling, watch your participles.
Verbs has to agree with their subjects.
Just between you and I, the case is important too.
Don't write run-on sentences they are hard to read.
Don't use commas, which aren't necessary.
Its important to use your apostrophe's correctly.
Proofread your writing to see if you any words out.
Correct spelling is esential.

Elected for the new term were Anna T. Zelnak, attorney from Cincinnati; Wilbur T. Hoffmeister, stockbroker and president of Hoffmeister Associates of Baltimore; and William P. Peabody, a member of the faculty of the University of Georgia.

SC 4

■ Use the semicolon only between equal units.

Use the semicolon between equal (coordinate) units only. Do not use it to attach a dependent clause or phrase to an independent clause.

Not this: The flood damaged much of the equipment in Building 113; making it necessary for management to stop production and lay off all production workers.

But this: The flood damaged much of the equipment in Building 113, making it necessary for management to stop production and lay off all production workers.

Or this: The flood damaged much of the equipment in Building 113; thus, it was necessary for management to stop production and lay off all production workers.

STANDARDS FOR GRAMMAR

Like the review of punctuation standards, the following summary of grammatical standards is not intended as a complete handbook on the subject. Rather, it is a summary of the major trouble spots encountered by business writers. If you learn these grammatical principles, you should be able to write with the correctness expected in business.

ADJECTIVE–ADVERB CONFUSION: AA

■ Do not use adjectives for adverbs.

Do not use adjectives for adverbs or adverbs for adjectives. Adjectives modify only nouns and pronouns; and adverbs modify verbs, adjectives, or other adverbs.

Possibly the chief source of this confusion occurs in statements in which the modifier follows the verb. If the modifier refers to the subject, an adjective should be used. If it refers to the verb, an adverb is needed.

Not this: She filed the records *quick.*
But this: She filed the records *quickly.* (Refers to the verb.)

Not this: John doesn't feel *badly.*
But this: John doesn't feel *bad.* (Refers to the noun.)

Not this: The new cars look *beautifully.*
But this: The new cars look *beautiful.* (Refers to the noun.)

It should be noted that many words are both adjective and adverb (*little, well, fast, much*). And some adverbs have two forms, of which one is the same as the adjective and the other adds *ly* (*slow* and *slowly, cheap* and *cheaply, quick* and *quickly*).

Acceptable: All our drivers are instructed to drive slow.

Acceptable: All our drivers are instructed to drive slowly.

SUBJECT–VERB AGREEMENT: AGMT SV

Nouns and their verbs must agree in number. A plural noun must have a plural verb form; a singular noun must have a singular verb form.

> ■ Verbs must agree in number with their subjects.

Not this: Expenditures for miscellaneous equipment *was* expected to decline. (*Expenditures* is plural, so its verb must be plural.)
But this: Expenditures for miscellaneous equipment *were* expected to decline.

Not this: The *president,* as well as his staff, *were* not able to attend. (*President* is the subject, and the number is not changed by the modifying phrase.)
But this: The *president,* as well as his staff, *was* not able to attend.

Compound subjects (two or more nouns joined by *and*) require plural verbs.

> ■ Compound subjects require plural verbs.

Not this: The *salespeople* and their *manager is* in favor of the proposal. (*Salespeople* and *manager* are compound subjects of the verb, but *is* is singular.)
But this: The *salespeople* and their *manager are* in favor of the proposal.

Not this: Received in the morning delivery *was* a *word processing program* and two *reams* of letterhead paper. (*Word processing program* and *reams* are the subjects; the verb must be plural.)
But this: Received in the morning delivery *were* a *word processor* and *two reams* of letterhead paper.

Collective nouns may be either singular or plural, depending on the meaning intended.

> ■ Collective nouns may be singular or plural.

The *committee have* carefully *studied* the proposal. (*Committee* is thought of as separate individuals.)

The *committee has* carefully *studied* the proposal. (The *committee* is thought of as a unit.)

As a rule, the pronouns *anybody, anyone, each, either, everyone, everybody, neither, nobody, somebody,* and *someone* take a singular verb. The word *none* may be either singular or plural, depending on whether it is used to refer to one unit or to more than one unit.

> ■ The pronouns listed here are singular.

Either of the advertising campaigns *is* costly.

Nobody who watches the clock *is* successful.

None of the workers *understands* his assignment.

None of the workers *understand* their assignments.

ADVERBIAL NOUN CLAUSE: AN

Do not use an adverbial clause as a noun clause. Clauses beginning with *because, when, where, if,* and similar adverbial connections are not properly used as subjects, objects, or complements of verbs.

> ■ Do not use an adverbial clause as a noun clause.

Not this: The reason was *because* he did not submit a report.
But this: The reason was *that* he did not submit a report.

Not this: A time-series graph is *where* (or *when*) changes in an index such as wholesale prices are indicated.
But this: A time-series graph is the picturing of . . .

AWKWARD: AWK

■ Avoid awkward writing.

Avoid awkward writing. By *awkward writing* we mean word arrangements that are unconventional, uneconomical, or simply not the best for quick understanding.

DANGLING MODIFIERS: DNG

■ Avoid dangling modifiers (those that do not clearly modify a specific word).

Avoid the use of modifiers that do not logically modify a word in the sentence. Such modifiers are said to dangle. They are both illogical and confusing. You can usually correct sentences containing dangling constructions by inserting the noun or pronoun that the modifier describes, or by changing the dangling part to a complete clause.

Not this: Believing that credit customers should have advance notice of the sale, special letters were mailed to them.

But this: Believing that credit customers should have advance notice of the sale, we mailed special letters to them. (Improvement is made by inserting the pronoun modified.)

Or this: Because we believed that credit customers should have advance notice of the sale, we mailed special letters to them. (Improvement is made by changing the dangling element to a complete clause.)

Dangling modifiers are of four principal types: participial phrases, elliptical clauses, gerund phrases, and infinitive phrases.

Not this: Believing that District 7 was not being thoroughly covered, an additional salesperson was assigned to the area. (Dangling participial phrase.)
But this: Believing that District 7 was not being thoroughly covered, the sales manager assigned an additional salesperson to the area.

Not this: By working hard, your goal can be reached. (Dangling gerund phrase.)
But this: By working hard, you can reach your goal.

Not this: To succeed at this job, long hours and hard work must not be shunned. (Dangling infinitive phrase.)
But this: To succeed at this job, one must not shun long hours and hard work.

Not this: While waiting on a customer, the watch was stolen. (Dangling elliptical clause—a clause without a noun or verb.)
But this: While the salesperson was waiting on a customer, the watch was stolen.

■ Some introductory phrases are permitted to dangle.

However, several generally accepted introductory phrases are permitted to dangle. Included in this group are *generally speaking, confidentially speaking, taking all things into consideration,* and such expressions as *in boxing, in welding,* and *in farming.*

Generally speaking, business activity is at an all-time high.

In farming, the land must be prepared long before planting time.

Taking all things into consideration, this applicant is the best for the job.

SENTENCE FRAGMENT: FRAG

■ Avoid sentence fragments (words used as a sentence that are not a sentence).

Avoid the sentence fragment. Although the sentence fragment may sometimes be used to good effect, as in sales writing, it is best avoided by all but the most skilled writers. The sentence fragment consists of any group of words that are used as if they were a sentence but are not a sentence. Probably the most frequent cause of sentence fragments is the use of a subordinate clause as a sentence.

Not this: Believing that you will want an analysis of sales for November. We have sent you the figures.
But this: Believing that you will want an analysis of sales for November, we have sent you the figures.

Not this: He declared that such a procedure would not be practical. And that it would be too expensive in the long run.

But this: He declared that such a procedure would not be practical and that it would be too expensive in the long run.

PRONOUNS: PN 1

Make certain that the word each pronoun refers to (its antecedent) is clear. Failure to conform to this standard causes confusion, particularly in sentences in which two or more nouns are possible antecedents or the antecedent is far away from the pronoun.

■ A pronoun should refer clearly to a preceding word.

Not this: When the president objected to Mr. Carter, he told him to mind his own business. (Who told whom?)
But this: When the president objected to Mr. Carter, Mr. Carter told him to mind his own business.

Not this: The mixture should not be allowed to boil; so when you do it, watch the temperature gauge. (*It* doesn't have an antecedent.)
But this: The mixture should not be allowed to boil; so when conducting the experiment, watch the temperature gauge.

Not this: The Model V is being introduced this year. Ads in *Time, The Wall Street Journal,* and big-city newspapers over the country are designed to get sales off to a good start. It is especially designed for the novice boater who is not willing to pay a big price.
But this: The Model V is being introduced this year. Ads in *Time, The Wall Street Journal,* and big-city newspapers over the country are designed to get sales off to a good start. The new model is especially designed for the novice boater who is not willing to pay a big price.

Confusion may sometimes result from using a pronoun with an implied antecedent.

Not this: Because of the disastrous freeze in the citrus belt, it is necessary that most of them be replanted.

But this: Because of the disastrous freeze in the citrus belt, most of the citrus orchards must be replanted.

Except when the reference of *which, that,* and *this* is perfectly clear, it is wise to avoid using these pronouns to refer to the whole idea of a preceding clause. Many times you can make the sentence clear by using a clarifying noun following the pronoun.

■ Usually avoid using *which, that,* and *this* to refer to broad ideas.

Not this (following a detailed presentation of the writer's suggestion for improving the company suggestion-box plan): This should be put into effect without delay.

But this: This suggestion-box plan should be put into effect right away.

PN 2

The number of the pronoun should agree with the number of its antecedent (the word it stands for). If the antecedent is singular, its pronoun must be singular. If the antecedent is plural, its pronoun must be plural.

■ The number of a pronoun should be the same as that of the word to which the pronoun refers.

Not this: Taxes and insurance are necessary evils in any business, and it must be considered carefully in anticipating profits.
But this: Taxes and insurance are necessary evils in any business, and they must be considered carefully in anticipating profits.

Not this: Everybody should plan for their retirement. (Such words as *everyone, everybody,* and *anybody* are singular.)
But this: Everybody should plan for his or her retirement.

PN 3

Take care to use the correct case of the pronoun. If the pronoun serves as the subject of the verb, or if it follows a form of the infinitive *to be,* use a pronoun in the nominative case. (The nominative personal pronouns are *I, you, he, she, it, we,* and *they*).

■ Use the correct case of pronoun.

He will record the minutes of the meeting.

I think it will be he.

If the pronoun is the object of a preposition or a verb, or if it is the subject of an infinitive, use the objective case. (The objective personal pronouns are *me, you, him, her, it, us, them.*)

Not this: This transaction is between you and *he.* (*He* is nominative and cannot be the object of the preposition *between.*)
But this: This transaction is between you and *him.*

Not this: Because the investigator praised Ms. Smith and *I,* we were promoted.
But this: Because the investigator praised Ms. Smith and *me,* we were promoted.

The case of a relative pronoun (*who, whom*) is determined by the pronoun's use in the clause it introduces. One good way of determining which case to use is to substitute the personal pronoun for the relative pronoun. If the case of the personal pronoun that fits is nominative, use *who.* If it is objective, use *whom.*

George Cutler is the salesperson *who* won the award. (*He,* nominative, could be substituted for the relative pronoun; therefore, nominative *who* should be used.)

George Cutler is the salesperson *whom* you recommended. (Objective *him* could be substituted; thus, objective *whom* is used.)

The possessive case is used for pronouns that immediately precede a gerund (a verbal noun ending in *ing*).

Our selling of the stock frightened some of the conservative members of the board.

Her accepting the money ended her legal claim to the property.

PARALLELISM: PRL

Express equal thoughts in parallel (equal) grammatical form.

Parts of a sentence that express equal thoughts should be parallel (the same) in grammatical form. Parallel constructions are logically connected by the coordinating conjunctions *and, but,* and *or.* Care should be taken to see that the sentence elements connected by these conjunctions are of the same grammatical type. That is, if one of the parts is a noun, the other parts should also be nouns. If one of the parts is an infinitive phrase, the other parts should also be infinitive phrases.

Not this: The company objectives for the coming year are to match last year's production, higher sales, and improving customer relations.
But this: The company objectives for the coming year are to match last year's production, to increase sales, and to improve customer relations.

Not this: Writing copy may be more valuable experience than to make layouts.
But this: Writing copy may be more valuable experience than making layouts.

Not this: The questionnaire asks for this information: number of employees, what is our union status, and how much do we pay.
But this: The questionnaire asks for this information: number of employees, union affiliation, and pay rate.

TENSE: TNS

■ The tense of each verb should show the logical time of happening.

The tense of each verb, infinitive, and participle should reflect the logical time of happening of the statement: Every statement has its place in time. To communicate that place exactly, you must select your tenses carefully.

TNS 1

■ Use present tense for current happenings.

Use present tense for statements of fact that are true at the time of writing.

Not this: Boston was not selected as a site for the headquarters because it *was* too near the coast. (Boston is still near the coast, isn't it?)

But this: Boston was not selected as a site for the headquarters because it *is* too near the coast.

TNS 2

Use past tense in statements covering a definite past event or action.

Not this: Mr. Burns *says* to me, "Bill, you'll never become an auditor."

But this: Mr. Burns *said* to me, "Bill, you'll never become an auditor."

■ Use past tense for past happenings.

TNS 3

The time period reflected by the past participle (*having been . . .*) is earlier than that of its governing verb. The present participle (*being . . .*) reflects the same time period as that of its governing verb.

Not this: These debentures are among the oldest on record, *being* issued in early 1937.
But this: These debentures are among the oldest on record, *having been* issued in early 1937.

Not this: Ms. Sloan, *having been* the top salesperson on the force, was made sales manager. (Possible but illogical.)
But this: Ms. Sloan, *being* the top salesperson on the force, was made sales manager.

■ The past participle (*having been . . .*) indicates a time earlier than that of the governing verb, and the present participle (*being . . .*) indicates the same period as that of the governing verb.

TNS 4

Verbs in subordinate clauses are governed by the verb in the principal clause. When the main verb is in the past tense, you should usually also place the subordinate verb in a past tense (past, past perfect, or present perfect).

I *noticed* [past tense] the discrepancy, and then I *remembered* [same time as main verb] the incidents that had caused it.

If the time of the subordinate clause is earlier than that of the main verb in past tense, use past perfect tense for the subordinate verb.

Not this: In early July, we *noticed* [past] that he *exceeded* [logically should be previous to main verb] his quota three times.

But this: In early July, we *noticed* that he *had exceeded* his quota three times.

The present perfect tense is used for the subordinate clause when the time of this clause is subsequent to the time of the main verb.

Not this: Before the war we *contributed* [past] generously, but lately we *forget* [should be a time subsequent to the time of the main verb] our duties.

But this: Before the war we *contributed* generously, but lately we *have forgotten* our duties.

■ Verbs in the principal clause govern those in subordinate clauses.

■ Present perfect tense (*have . . .*) refers to the indefinite past.

TNS 5

The present perfect tense does not logically refer to a definite time in the past. Instead, it indicates time somewhere in the indefinite past.

Not this: We *have audited* your records on July 31 of 1997 and 1998.

But this: We *audited* your records on July 31 of 1997 and 1998.

Or this: We *have audited* your records twice in the past.

■ Use of present perfect tense indicates time somewhere in the indefinite past.

WORD USE: WU

Misused words call attention to themselves and detract from the writing. The possibilities of error in word use are infinite; the following list contains only a few of the common errors of this kind.

■ Use words correctly.

Don't Use	Use
a long ways	a long way
and etc.	etc.
anywheres	anywhere
continue on	continue
different than	different from
have got to	must
in back of	behind
in hopes of	in hope of
in regards to	in regard to
inside of	within
kind of satisfied	somewhat satisfied
nowhere near	not nearly
nowheres	nowhere
over with	over
seldom ever	seldom
try and come	try to come

WRONG WORD: WW

■ Check the spelling and meanings of words carefully.

Wrong words refer to meaning one word and using another. Sometimes these words are confused by their spelling and sometimes by their meanings. Here are a few examples:

affect	effect
among	between
bow	bough
capital	capitol
cite	sight
collision	collusion
complement	compliment
cooperation	corporation
deferential	differential
desert	dessert
except	accept
implicit	explicit
imply	infer
plane	plain
principal	principle
stationary	stationery

STANDARDS FOR THE USE OF NUMBERS: NO

Quantities may be spelled out or expressed as numerals. Whether to use one form or the other is often a perplexing question. It is especially perplexing to business writers, for much of their work deals with quantitative subjects. Because the proper expression of quantities is vital to business writers, the following notes on the use of numbers are presented.

No 1

Although authorities do not agree on number usage, business writers would do well to follow the rule of nine. By this rule, you spell out numbers nine and below. You use figures for numbers above nine.

The auditor found 13 discrepancies in the stock records.
The auditor found nine discrepancies in the stock records.

Apply the rule to both ordinal and cardinal numbers:

She was the seventh applicant.
She was the 31st applicant.

■ Spell out numbers nine and under, and use figures for higher numbers, except as follows:

No 2

Make an exception to the rule of nine when a number begins a sentence. Spell out all numbers in this position.

Seventy-three bonds and six debentures were destroyed.
Eighty-nine strikers picketed the north entrance.

■ Spell out numbers that begin a sentence.

No 3

In comparisons, keep all numbers in the same form. If any number requires numeral form, use numerals for all the numbers.

We managed to salvage 3 lathes, 1 drill, and 13 welding machines.

■ Keep in the same form all numbers in comparisons.

No 4

Use numerals for all percentages.

Sales increases over last year were 9 percent on automotive parts, 14 percent on hardware, and 23 percent on appliances.

On whether to use the percent sign (%) or the word, authorities differ. One good rule to follow is to use the sign in papers that are scientific or technical and the word in all others. Also, it is conventional to use the sign following numbers in graphics. The trend in business appears to be toward using the sign. Consistent use of either is correct.

■ Use numerals for percentages.

No 5

Present days of the month in figure form when the month precedes the day.

July 3, 1998.

When days of the month appear alone or precede the month, they may be either spelled out or expressed in numeral form according to the rule of nine.

I will be there on the 13th.
The union scheduled the strike vote for the eighth.
Ms. Millican signed the contract on the seventh of July.
Sales have declined since the 14th of August.

■ Use figures for days of the month when the month precedes the day.

No 6

Use either of the two orders for date information. One, preferred by the *Chicago Manual of Style,* is day, month, and year:

On 29 June 1998 we introduced a new product line.

The other is the conventional sequence of month, day, and year. This order requires that the year be set off by commas:

On June 29, 1998, we introduced a new product line.

■ For dates, use either day, month, year or month, day, year sequence, the latter with year set off by commas.

No 7

■ Present amounts like other numbers, spelling units when numbers are spelled and using appropriate symbols or abbreviations when in figures.

Present money amounts as you would other numbers. If you spell out the number, also spell out the unit of currency.

Twenty-seven dollars

If you present the number as a figure, use the $ symbol with Canadian and U.S. currency and the appropriate abbreviation or symbol with other currencies.

U.S. and Canada	$27.33
France	Fr 743.21
Germany	DM 45.72
Great Britain	£231.91

No 8

■ Usually spell indefinite numbers and amounts.

Usually spell out indefinite numbers and amounts.

Over a million people live there.
The current population is about four hundred thousand.
Bill Gates's net worth is in the billions.

No 9

■ Spell out fractions that stand alone or begin a sentence. Use numerics with whole numbers and in technical contexts.

Spell out a fraction such as one-half that stands alone (without a whole number) or begins a sentence. However, if this results in long and awkward wording or if it is technical, use the numeric form.

Jobs in the information industry account for two-thirds of all jobs in the US.
The share price of IBM rose by 3⅞ today.

No 10

■ Only use both words and figures for legal reasons.

Except in legal documents, do not express amounts in both figures and words.

For legal purposes: 25 (twenty-five)
For business use: either the figure or the word, depending on circumstance

SPELLING: SP

■ Spell words correctly. Use the dictionary.

Misspelling is probably the most frequently made error in writing. And it is the least excusable. It is inexcusable because all one needs to do to virtually eliminate the error is to use a dictionary or a spell checker. Unfortunately, spell checkers cannot detect a correctly spelled, but misused, word.

■ See Figure 18.1 for the 80 most commonly misspelled words.

We must memorize to spell. Thus, becoming a good speller involves long, hard work. Even so, you can improve your spelling significantly with relatively little effort. Studies show that fewer than 100 words account for most spelling errors. So if you will learn to spell these most troublesome words, you will go a long way toward solving your spelling problems. Eighty of these words appear in Figure 18.1. Although English spelling follows little rhyme or reason, a few helpful rules exist. You would do well to learn and use them.

RULES FOR WORD PLURALS

■ These three rules cover plurals for most words.

1. To form the plurals of most words, add *s*.

cat, cats

dog, dogs

2. To form the plurals of words ending in *s, sh, ch,* and *x,* usually add *es* to the singular.

| glass, glasses | bunch, bunches |
| dish, dishes | ax, axes |

FIGURE 18.1 Eighty of the Most Frequently Misspelled Words

absence	desirable	irritable	pursue
accessible	despair	leisure	questionnaire
accommodate	development	license	receive
achieve	disappear	misspelling	recommend
analyze	disappoint	necessary	repetition
argument	discriminate	ninety	ridiculous
assistant	drunkenness	noticeable	seize
balloon	embarrassment	occasionally	separate
benefited	equivalent	occurrence	sergeant
category	exceed	panicky	sheriff
cede	existence	parallel	succeed
changeable	forty	paralyze	suddenness
committee	grammar	pastime	superintendent
comparative	grievous	persistent	supersede
conscience	holiday	possesses	surprise
conscious	incidentally	predictable	truly
deductible	indispensable	privilege	until
definitely	insistent	proceed	vacuum
dependent	irrelevant	professor	vicious
description	irresistible	pronunciation	weird

3. To form the plural of words ending in *y*, if a consonant precedes the *y*, drop the *y* and add *ies*. But if the *y* is preceded by a vowel, add *s*.

pony, ponies

chimney, chimneys

OTHER SPELLING RULES

1. Words ending in *ce* or *ge* do not drop the *e* when adding *ous* or *able*.

charge, chargeable

change, changeable

notice, noticeable

service, serviceable

■ These rules cover four other trouble areas of spelling.

2. Words ending in *l* do not drop the *l* when adding *ly*.

final, finally

principal, principally

3. Words ending in silent *e* usually drop the *e* when adding a suffix beginning with a vowel.

have, having

believe, believable

dive, diving

time, timing

4. Place *i* before *e* except after *c*.

relieve conceive

believe receive

Exception: when the word is sounded as long *a*.

neighbor   weigh

Exceptions:

either	Fahrenheit	height
seize	surfeit	efficient
sufficient	neither	foreign
leisure	ancient	seizure
weird	financier	codeine
forfeit	seismograph	sovereign
deficient	science	counterfeit

CAPITALIZATION: CAP

■ Capitalize all proper names and the beginning words of sentences.

Use capitals for the first letters of all proper names. Common examples are these:

Streets: 317 East Boyd Avenue

Geographic places: Chicago, Indiana, Finland

Companies: Berkowitz Manufacturing Company, Inc.

Title preceding names: President Watkins

Titles of books, articles, poems: Lesikar's Basic Business Communication

First words of sentences and complimentary closes

*The word **number** (or its abbreviation) when used with a figure to identify something:* Number 1, Oak Circle

As noted earlier, other standards are useful in clear communication. But those covered in the preceding pages will help you through most of your writing problems. By using them, you can give your writing the precision that good communication requires.

CRITICAL THINKING EXERCISES

Correct any punctuation or grammar errors you can find in the following sentences. Explain your corrections.

1. Charles E. Baskin the new member of the advisory committee has been an employee for seven years.

2. The auditor asked us, "If all members of the work group had access to the petty cash fund?"

3. Our January order consisted of the following items; two dozen Norwood desk calendars, note size, one dozen desk blotters, 20 by 32 inches, and one dozen bottles of ink, permanent black.

4. The truth of the matter is, that the union representative had not informed the workers of the decision.

5. Sales for the first quarter were the highest in history, profits declined for the period.

6. We suggest that you use a mild soap for best results but detergents will not harm the product.

7. Employment for October totaled 12,741 an increase of 3.1 percent over September.

8. It would not be fair however to consider only this point.

9. It is the only wrinkle-resistant snagproof and inexpensive material available.

10. Todd Thatcher a supervisor in our company is accused of the crime.

11. Mr. Goodman made this statement, "Contrary to our expectations, Smith and Company will lose money this year."

12. I bought and he sold.

13. Soon we saw George Sweeney who is the auditor for the company.

14. Sold in light medium and heavy weight this paper has been widely accepted.

15. Because of a common belief that profits are too high we will have to cut our prices on most items.

16. Such has been the growth of the cities most prestigious firm, H.E. Klauss and Company.

17. In 1997 we were advised in fact we were instructed to accept this five year contract.

18. Henrys goofing off has got him into trouble.

19. Cyrus B. Henshaw who was our leading salesperson last month is the leading candidate for the position.

20. The sales representative who secures the most new accounts will receive a bonus.

21. The word phone which is short for telephone should be avoided in formal writing.

22. In last weeks issue of Fortune appeared Johnson's latest article Tiger! The Sky's the Limit for Golf.

23. Yes he replied this is exactly what we mean.

24. Why did he say John it's too late?

25. Place your order today, it is not too late.

26. We make our plans on a day to day basis.

27. There is little accuracy in the 60 day forecast.

28. The pre Christmas sale will extend over twenty six days.

29. We cannot tolerate any worker's failure to do their duty.

30. An assortment of guns, bombs, burglar tools, and ammunition were found in the cellar.

31. If we can be certain that we have the facts we can make our decision soon.

32. This one is easy to make. If one reads the instructions carefully.

33. This is the gift he received from you and I.

34. A collection of short articles on the subject were printed.

35. If we can detect only a tenth of the errors it will make us realize the truth.

36. She takes criticism good.

37. There was plenty of surprises at the meeting.

38. It don't appear that we have made much progress.

39. The surface of these products are smooth.

40. Everybody is expected to do their best.

41. The brochures were delivered to John and I early Sunday morning.

42. Who did he recommend for the job.

43. We were given considerable money for the study.

44. He seen what could happen when administration breaks down.

45. One of his conclusions is that the climate of the region was not desirable for our purposes.

46. Smith and Rogers plans to buy the Moline plant.

47. The committee feels that no action should be taken.

48. Neither of the workers found their money.

49. While observing the employees, the work flow was operating at peak perfection.

50. The new building is three stories high, fifteen years old, solid brick construction, and occupies a corner lot.

51. They had promised to have completed the job by noon.

52. Jones has been employed by Kimberly Clark for twenty years.

53. Wilson and myself will handle the job.

54. Each man and woman are expected to abide by this rule.

55. The boiler has been inspected on April 1 and May 3.

56. To find problems and correcting them takes up most of my work time.

57. The case of canned goods were distributed to the employees.

58. The motor ran uneven.

59. All are expected except John and she.

60. Everyone here has more ability than him.

A SELF-ADMINISTERED DIAGNOSTIC TEST OF CORRECTNESS

The following test is designed to give you a quick measure of your ability to handle some of the most troublesome punctuation and grammar situations. First, correct all the errors in each sentence. Then turn to Appendix A for the recommended corrections and the symbols for the punctuation and grammar standards involved. Next, study the standards that you violate.

1. An important fact about this keyboard is, that it has the patented "ergonomic design".

2. Goods received on Invoice 2741 are as follows; 3 dozen white shirts, size 15–33, 4 mens felt hats, brown, size 7, and 5 dozen assorted ties.

3. James Silver President of the new union had the priviledge of introducing the speaker.

4. We do not expect to act on this matter however until we hear from you.

5. Shipments through September 20, 1998 totaled 69,485 pounds an increase of 17 percent over the year ago total.

6. Brick is recommended as the building material but the board is giving serious consideration to a substitute.

7. Markdowns for the sale total $34,000, never before has the company done anything like this.

8. After long experimentation a wear resistant high grade and beautiful stocking has been perfected.

9. Available in white green and blue this paint is sold by dealers all over the country.

10. Julie Jahn who won the trip is our most energetic salesperson.

11. Good he replied, sales are sure to increase.

12. Hogan's article Retirement? Never!, printed in the current issue of Management Review, is really a part of his book A Report on Worker Security.

13. Formal announcement of our Labor Day sale will be made in thirty-two days.

14. Each day we encounter new problems. Although they are solved easily.

15. A list of models, sizes, and prices of both competing lines are being sent to you.

16. The manager could not tolerate any employee's failing to do their best.

17. A series of tests were completed only yesterday.

18. There should be no misunderstanding between you and I.

19. He run the accounting department for five years.

20. This report is considerable long.

21. Who did you interview for the position?

22. The report concluded that the natural resources of the Southwest was ideal for the chemical industry.

23. This applicant is six feet in height, 28 years old, weighs 165 pounds, and has had eight years' experience.

24. While reading the report, a gust of wind came through the window, blowing papers all over the room.

25. The sprinkler system has been checked on July 1 and September 3.

C H A P T E R

19

Business Research Methods

Upon completing this chapter, you will be able to design and implement a plan for conducting the research needed for a business report. To reach this goal, you should be able to

1 Explain the difference between primary and secondary research.

2 Use appropriate procedures for direct and indirect library research.

3 Describe the procedures for searching through company records.

4 Conduct an experiment for a business problem.

5 Design an observational study for a business problem.

6 Use sampling to conduct a survey.

7 Select a sample, construct a questionnaire, develop a working plan, and conduct a pilot test for a survey.

8 Analyze and interpret information clearly and completely for your reader.

Business Research Methods

Introduce yourself to this chapter by assuming the position of administrative assistant to Carmen Bergeron, the vice president for human resources for Mammoth Industries. Today at a meeting of administrators, someone commented about the low morale among sales representatives since the merger. The marketing vice president immediately came to the defense of his area, claiming that there is no proof of the statement—that in fact the opposite is true. Others joined in with their views, and in time a heated discussion developed. In an effort to ease tensions, Ms. Bergeron suggested that her office conduct a survey of plant personnel "to learn the truth of the matter." The administrators liked the idea.

After the meeting, Ms. Bergeron called you in to tell you that you would be the one to do the research. And she wants the findings in report form in time for next month's meeting. She didn't say much more. No doubt she thinks your college training equipped you to handle the assignment.

Now you must do the research. This means you will have to work out a plan for a survey. Specifically, you will have to select a sample, construct a questionnaire, devise an interview procedure, conduct interviews, record findings—and more. All these activities require much more than a casual understanding of research. There are right ways and wrong ways of going about them. How to do them right is the subject of this chapter.

- The two basic forms of research are secondary research (getting information from published sources) and primary research (getting information firsthand).

You can collect the information needed for your report by using the two basic forms of research—secondary research and primary research. Secondary research is research utilizing material that someone else has published—through periodicals, brochures, books, electronic publication, and such. Commonly called *library research,* secondary research may be the first form of research that you use in some problems (see The Preliminary Investigation in Chapter 10). Primary research is research that uncovers information firsthand. It is research that produces new findings.

To be effective as a report writer, you should be familiar with the techniques of both secondary and primary research. A brief summary of each appears in the following pages.

SECONDARY RESEARCH

- Secondary research can be a rich source of information if you know what to look for and where to look.

Secondary research materials are potentially the least costly, the most accessible, and the most complete source of information. However, to take full advantage of the available materials, you must know what you are looking for and where and how to find it.

The task can be complex and challenging. You can meet the challenge if you become familiar with the general arrangement of a library or other repositories of secondary materials and if you learn the techniques of finding those materials. Also, research must be orderly if it is to be reliable and complete.

- Keep track of the sources you gather in an orderly way.

In the past, researchers used a card system to help them keep track of the sources they identified. This card system can be combined with and adapted to a computer system quite easily. The manual system of organization required that the researcher complete two sets of cards. One set was simply a bibliography card set, containing complete information about sources. A researcher numbered these cards consecutively as the sources were identified. A second set of cards contained the notes from each source. Each of these cards was linked to its source through the number of the source in the bibliography card set.

Since the computer systems in today's libraries often allow users to print or download the citations they find from the indexes and databases, it makes sense to number the source on the printout rather than recopy the source to a card. Not only is the printout usually more legible than one's handwriting, but it is also complete. Some researchers cut their printouts apart and tape them to a master sheet. Others will enter these items in databases they build. And still others will download items directly into specialty databases, letting the software organize and number them. With the widespread use of notebook and laptop computers, many researchers are taking notes on computers rather than cards. These notes can be linked to the original source by number as in the manual system.

No matter whether you use a manual, combined, or computer system, using an orderly system is essential.

FINDING PUBLICATION COLLECTIONS

The first step in an orderly search for printed information is to determine where to begin. The natural place, of course, is a library. However, since different types of libraries offer different kinds of collections, it is helpful to know what types of libraries are available and to be familiar with their contents.

General libraries are the best known and the most accessible. General libraries, which include college, university, and most public libraries, are called *general* to the extent that they contain all kinds of materials. Many general libraries, however, have substantial collections in certain specialized areas.

Libraries that limit their collections to one type or just a few types of material are considered *special libraries.* Many such libraries are private and do not invite routine public use of their materials. Still, they will frequently cooperate on research projects that they consider relevant and worthwhile.

Among the special libraries are the libraries of private businesses. As a rule, such libraries are designed to serve the sponsoring company and provide excellent information in the specialized areas of its operations. Company libraries are less accessible than other specialized libraries, but a letter of inquiry explaining the nature and purpose of a project or a letter of introduction from someone known to the company can help you gain access to them.

Special libraries are also maintained by various types of associations—for example, trade organizations, professional and technical groups, chambers of commerce, and labor unions. Like company libraries, association libraries may provide excellent coverage of highly specialized areas. Although such libraries develop collections principally for members or a research staff, they frequently make resources available to others engaged in reputable research.

A number of public and private research organizations also maintain specialized libraries. The research divisions of big-city chambers of commerce and the bureaus of research of major universities, for example, keep extensive collections of material containing statistical and general information on a local area. State agencies collect similar data. Again, though these materials are developed for a limited audience, they are often made available upon request.

Several guides are available in the reference department of most general libraries to help you determine what these research centers and special libraries offer and whom to contact for permission to use their collections. The *American Library Directory* is a geographic listing of libraries in the United States and Canada. It gives detailed information on libraries, including special interests and collections. It covers all public libraries as well as many corporate and association libraries. Also, the Special Libraries Association has chapters in many large cities that publish directories for their chapter areas. Particularly helpful in identifying the information available in research centers is *The Research Centers Directory.* Published by Gale Research Company, it lists the research activities, publications, and services of 7,500 university-related and other nonprofit organizations. It is supplemented between editions by a related publication, *New Research Centers.*

Gale Research also publishes three comprehensive guides to special library collections. *The Directory of Special Libraries and Information Centers* describes the contents and services of 16,500 information centers, archives, and special and research libraries. Each entry includes the address and telephone number of the facility and the name and title of the individual in charge. A companion guide, *Subject Directory of Special Libraries and Information Centers,* organizes the same information by subject. The third guide, *New Special Libraries,* is a periodic supplement of the first.

- ■ A library is the natural place to begin secondary research.

- ■ General libraries offer the public a wide variety of information sources.

- ■ Special libraries have limited collections and circulation, such as

- ■ private business,

- ■ associations, and

- ■ research organizations.

- ■ Consult a directory to determine what special libraries offer.

Taking the Direct Approach

When you have found the appropriate library for your research, you are ready for the next challenge. With the volume of material available, how will you find what you need? Many cost-conscious businesses are hiring professionals to find information for them. These professionals' charges range from $40 to $80 per hour in addition to any online charges incurred. Other companies like to keep their information gathering more confidential; some employ company librarians, and others expect their employees to gather the information. If you know little about how material is arranged in a library, you will waste valuable time on a probably fruitless search. However, if you are familiar with certain basic reference materials, you may be able to proceed directly to the information you seek. And if the direct approach does not work, there are several effective indirect methods of finding the material you need.

Taking the direct approach is advisable when you seek quantitative or factual information. The reference section of your library is where you should start. There, either on your own or with the assistance of a research librarian, you can discover any number of timely and comprehensive sources of facts and figures. Although you cannot know all these sources, as a business researcher you should be familiar with certain basic ones. These sources are available in either print or electronic forms. You should be able to use both.

ENCYCLOPEDIAS.   Encyclopedias are the best-known sources of direct information and are particularly valuable when you are just beginning a search. They offer background material and other general information that give you a helpful introduction to the area under study. Individual articles or sections of articles are written by experts in the field and frequently include a short bibliography.

Of the general encyclopedias, two worthy of special mention are *The Encyclopedia Americana* and the *Encyclopaedia Britannica.* Others gaining wide use and acceptance are Grolier's *Academic American Encyclopedia* and Microsoft's *Encarta.* These are available either on several information services and updated every three months, for sale in software outlets, or even bundled with multimedia computer systems. Also helpful are such specialized encyclopedias as the *Encyclopaedia of the Social Sciences,* the *Encyclopedia of Accounting Systems,* the *Encyclopedia of Banking and Finance,* and the *Encyclopedia of Management.*

BIOGRAPHICAL DIRECTORIES.   A direct source of biographical information about leading figures of today or of the past is a biographical directory. The best-known biographical directories are *Who's Who in America* and *Who's Who in the World,* annual publications that summarize the lives of living people who have achieved prominence. Similar publications provide coverage by geographic area: *Who's Who in the East* and *Who's Who in the South and Southwest,* for example. For biographical information about prominent Americans of the past, the *Dictionary of American Biography* is useful.

Specialized publications will help you find information on people in particular professions. Among the most important of these are *Who's Who in Finance and Industry; Standard & Poor's Register of Corporations, Directors, and Executives; Dun & Bradstreet's Reference Book of Corporate Management; Who's Who in Labor; Who's Who in Economics; The Rand McNally International Bankers Directory; Who's Who in Insurance;* and *Who's Who in Computer Education and Research.* Nearly all business and professional areas are covered by some form of directory.

ALMANACS.   Almanacs are handy guides to factual and statistical information. Simple, concise, and selective in their presentation of data, they should not be underestimated as references. *The World Almanac and Book of Facts,* published by Funk & Wagnalls is an excellent general source of facts and statistics. The *Information Please Almanac* is another excellent source for a broad range of statistical data. One of its strongest areas is information on the labor force. The *Universal Almanac* presents much of its data in charts and graphs. It has excellent coverage of business and the economy. If you need business and investment data, the *Irwin Business & Investment Almanac* provides comprehensive cov-

---

Marginal notes:

■ You can begin your research using the direct approach, but you must be familiar with basic references.

■ The direct approach is especially effective with quantitative information.

■ Encyclopedias offer both general and detailed information.

■ Biographical directories offer information about influential people.

■ Almanacs provide factual and statistical information.

▌ Much secondary research can be done through the use of computers.

erage of timely information. Some of the information you will find in it is a chronological presentation of business events during the past year; industry surveys; financial general business, and economic indicators; stock market data; a glossary; and more.

TRADE DIRECTORIES.   For information about individual businesses or the products they make, buy, or sell, directories are the references to consult. Directories compile details in specific areas of interest and are variously referred to as *catalogs, listings, registers,* or *source books.* Some of the more comprehensive directories indispensable in general business research are the following: *The Million Dollar Directory* (a listing of U.S. companies compiled by Dun & Bradstreet), *Thomas Register of American Manufacturers,* and *The Datapro Directory.* Some directories that will help you determine linkages between parent entities and their subsidiaries include *America's Corporate Families* and *Who Owns Whom* (both compiled by Dun & Bradstreet) as well as the *Directory of Corporate Affiliations.* Thousands of directories exist—so many, in fact, that there is a directory called *Directories in Print.*

■ Trade directories publish information about individual businesses and products.

GOVERNMENT PUBLICATIONS.   Governments (national, state, local, etc.) publish hundreds of thousands of titles each year. In fact, the U.S. government is the world's largest publisher. Surveys, catalogs, pamphlets, periodicals—there seems to be no limit to the information that various bureaus, departments, and agencies collect and make available to the public. The challenge of working with government publications, therefore, is finding your way through this wealth of material to the specifics you need. That task can sometimes be so complex as to require indirect research methods. However, if you are familiar with a few key sources, the direct approach will often produce good results.

■ Governments (national, state, provincial, etc.) publish extensive research materials.

In the United States, it may be helpful to consult the *Monthly Catalog of U.S. Government Publications.* Issued by the Superintendent of Documents, it includes a comprehensive listing of annual and monthly publications and an alphabetical index of the issuing agencies. It can be searched online. The Superintendent of Documents also issues *Selected United States Government Publications,* a monthly list of general-interest publications that are sold to the public.

■ The U.S. government publishes guides to its publications.

Routinely available are a number of specialized publications that are invaluable in business research. These include *Census of Population, Census of Housing, Annual Housing Survey, Consumer Income and Population Characteristics, Census of Governments, Census of Retail Trade, Census of Manufacturers, Census of Agriculture, Census of Construction Industries, Census of Transportation, Census of Service Industries, Census of Whole-*

■ These government publications are invaluable in business research.

sale Trade, and *Census of Mineral Industries.* The *Statistical Abstract of the United States* is another invaluable publication, as are the *Survey of Current Business,* the *Monthly Labor Review,* the *Occupational Outlook Quarterly,* and the *Federal Reserve Bulletin.* To say the least, government sources are extensive.

DICTIONARIES. Dictionaries are helpful for looking up meanings, spellings, and pronunciations of words or phrases. Electronic dictionaries add another option; they let you find words when you know the meaning. Dictionaries are available in both general and specialized versions. While it might be nice to own an unabridged dictionary, an abridged collegiate or desk dictionary will answer most of your questions. You should be aware that the name *Webster* can be legally used by any dictionary publisher. Also, dictionaries often include added features such as style manuals, signs, symbols, and weights and measures. Because dictionaries reflect usage, you want to be sure the one you use is current. Not only are new words being added but spellings and meanings change, too. Several good dictionaries are the *American Heritage Dictionary,* the *Funk & Wagnalls Standard Dictionary,* the *Random House Webster's College Dictionary,* and *Webster's New Collegiate Dictionary.*

Specialized dictionaries concentrate on one functional area. Some business dictionaries are the *Dictionary of Management,* the *MBA's Dictionary, The Dictionary of Business and Management,* the *McGraw-Hill Dictionary of Modern Economics,* and the *Computer Glossary.* There are also dictionaries of acronyms, initialisms, and abbreviations. Two of these are the *Acronyms, Initialisms, and Abbreviations Dictionary* and the *Abbreviations Dictionary.*

ADDITIONAL STATISTICAL SOURCES. Today's businesses rely heavily on statistical information. Not only is this information helpful in the day-to-day business operations, but it also is helpful in planning future products, expansions, and strategies. Some of this information can be found in the publications previously mentioned, especially the government publications. More is available online and can be seen long before it is printed. Even more is available from the various public and private sources described below.

In order to facilitate the collection and retrieval of statistical data for industry, the US government developed a classification system, called the Standard Industrial Classification (SIC) code. In the 1930s, this system used a four-digit code for all manufacturing and nonmanufacturing industries.

In 1997, the U.S. government introduced a new industrial classification system—the North American Industry Classification System (NAICS) to replace the SIC code. The new system is more flexible than the old one and accounts for changes in the global economy by allowing the United States, Mexico, and Canada to compare economic and financial statistics better. It is also expanded to include new sectors such as the information sector; the health care and social assistance sector; and the professional, scientific, and technical services sector. The United States and Canada began using this system in 1997, and Mexico in 1998. The first NAICS-based statistics will be issued in 1999.

Some of the basic comprehensive publications include the *Handbook of Basic Economic Statistics,* the *Statistical Abstract of the United States,* the *Predicasts Basebook,* and *Standard & Poor's Statistical Service.* These sources are a starting point when you are not familiar with more specialized sources. They include historical data on American industry, commerce, labor, and agriculture; industry data by NAICS codes; numerous indexes such as producer price indexes, housing indexes, and stock price indexes. Additionally, the *Statistical Abstract of the United States* contains an extremely useful guide to sources of statistics.

If you are not certain where to find statistics, you may find various guides useful. The *American Statistics Index* is an index to statistics published by all government agencies. It identifies the agency, describes the statistics, and provides access by category. The *Encyclopedia of Business Information Sources* provides a list of information sources along with names of basic statistical sources. The *Statistical Reference Index* publishes statistical sources other than the government, such as trade and professional associations. Useful for current forecasting of statistical sources, *Predicasts Forecasts* documents the source of the data and has a source directory arranged by title, geographic index, and NAICS codes. These four directories will help direct you to specialized statistics when you need them.

Sidenotes (left margin):

■ Dictionaries provide meanings, spellings, and pronunciations for both general and specialized words and phrases.

■ Statistical information is available both online and in printed form.

■ A new classification system will enable users to compare economic and financial statistics better.

■ Basic publications provide broad coverage and source listings for more detailed statistics.

■ Guides help locate sources.

BUSINESS INFORMATION SERVICES.   Business services are private organizations that supply a variety of information to business practitioners, especially investors. Libraries also subscribe to their publications, giving business researchers ready access to yet another source of valuable, timely data.

Private business services collect and publish data. Many such reports are available in public and university libraries.

Moody's Investors' Service, one of the best known of such organizations, publishes a weekly *Manual* in each of six business areas: transportation, industrials, over-the-counter (OTC) industrials, public utilities, banks and finance, and municipals and governments. These reports summarize financial data and operating facts on all major American companies, providing information that an investor needs to evaluate the investment potential of individual securities or of fields as a whole. *Corporation Records,* published by Standard & Poor's Corporation, presents similar information in loose-leaf form. Both Moody's and Standard & Poor's provide a variety of related services, including *Moody's Investors' Advisory Service* and Standard & Poor's *Value Line Investment Service.*

Two other organizations whose publications are especially helpful to business researchers are Predicasts, Inc., and Gale Research Company. Predicasts, Inc., provides seven business services, although it is best known for publications featuring forecasts and market data by country, product, and company (*Predicasts, World-Regional-Casts, World-Product-Casts,* and *Expansion and Capacity Digest*). Similarly, Gale Research Company provides numerous services to business researchers.

Another type of business service provides loose-leaf services and audiotapes. For keeping up-to-date on particular topics, services offer excellent loose-leaf publications with weekly and biweekly supplements that report on topics such as human resources and labor, legal rules, and other areas.

Some provide loose-leaf and audiotape services.

Technology has brought us another kind of business service—document delivery services. These services will fax, email, or mail copies of articles to you. They are particularly helpful both for getting information quickly and getting information your local library does not have on hand. They charge for their services and for any copyright fees the publisher charges.

Document delivery services provide information for a fee.

INTERNATIONAL SOURCES.   In today's global business environment, we often need information outside our borders. Many of the sources we have discussed have counterparts with international information. *Principal International Businesses* lists basic information on major companies located around the world. *Major Companies of Europe* and *Japan Company Handbook* are two sources providing facts on companies in their respective areas. The *International Encyclopedia of the Social Sciences* covers all important areas of social science, including biographies of acclaimed persons in these areas. General and specialized dictionaries are available, too. *The Multilingual Commercial Dictionary* and the *International Business Dictionary in Nine Languages* include commonly used business terms in several languages. You will even be able to find trade names in the *International Trade Names Dictionary* published by Gale Research. For bibliographies and abstracts, available sources include *International Business Reference Sources, Business International Index,* the *Foreign Commerce Handbook,* and several more. Even statistical information is available in sources such as the *Index to International Statistics, Statistical Yearbook,* and *Worldcasts.* In addition, libraries usually contain many references for information on international marketing, exporting, tax, and trade.

Statistical information for the international business environment is available in a wide range of documents.

USING INDIRECT METHODS

If you cannot move directly to the information you need, you must use indirect methods to find it. The first step in this approach is preparing a bibliography or a list of prospective sources. The next two steps are gathering the publications in your bibliography and systematically checking them for the information you need.

When you cannot find secondary materials directly, try the indirect approach. Start by preparing a bibliography of needed sources.

These two steps are elementary but nonetheless important. Your acquisition of secondary materials must be thorough. You should not depend solely on the material you find on the shelves of your library. Rather, you should use interlibrary loan services and database and Internet searches. And you should write for company or government documents. All checking of the sources you gather must be equally thorough. For each source, review the

Gather all available publications. Check each systematically for the information you need.

pages cited in your bibliographic reference. Then take time to learn about the publication by reviewing its table of contents, its index, and the endnotes or footnotes related to the pages you are researching. You should be familiar with both the source and the context of all the information you plan to report; they are as significant as the information itself.

However, the first step, preparing the bibliography, is still the most demanding and challenging task in indirect research. It is therefore helpful to review what this task involves.

PREPARED BIBLIOGRAPHIES.   You should begin the preparation of your own bibliography by looking for one that has already been prepared. Lists of published materials are available through a number of sources, and finding such a list may save you the time and trouble of developing a bibliography from scratch.

■ Try to find a prepared bibliography. It will save you time and trouble.

Start your search in the reference section of your library. Prepared bibliographies are sometimes published as reference books, and individual entries in these books often include a description of sources. In the reference section you may also find bibliographies that have been compiled by associations or government agencies. Encyclopedias are also a helpful source of published materials; most articles in them conclude with a bibliography.

■ Begin searching in the reference section of the library.

Another way to discover prepared bibliographies is to consult texts, articles, and master's and doctor's theses that deal with your subject. If books include bibliographies, it is noted in the online catalog. Academic papers routinely include complete bibliographies. Articles present the most challenging task, for not all of them list their sources. Since articles that do are likely to include very timely and selective listings, it is worth the effort to check them individually.

■ Consult texts, articles, theses, and so on.

THE ONLINE CATALOG.   If you are not able to locate a prepared bibliography, or if the bibliographies you have identified are inadequate, you must develop your own list of prospective sources. Here the library's on-line catalog is very helpful.

■ The library's on-line catalog is another resource for developing a bibliography.

If the catalog you are using is composed of cards, it offers three distinct ways of identifying and locating desired references: by author, by title, and by subject. However, today many libraries use electronic catalogs, giving you numerous ways to locate sources. As you can see from the main menu screen of one system in Figure 19.1, in some ways electronic catalogs are similar to card catalogs. You can still locate sources by author, title, and subject. In addition, the electronic catalogs give you more main options and more options within each choice. The options you have will depend on the system installed and the way your librarians designed it.

■ It lists the holdings of each library.

Two options you need to understand clearly are WORDS in the TITLE and SUBJECT. When the WORDS in the TITLE option is selected, the system will ask you for the keywords and then search only the title entries for those keywords. This means the items it finds will likely relate to the subject you need. However, it misses all those entries whose titles do not contain the words you keyed in. For example, if you wanted to know more about cross-cultural communication, using these words in the title would find only those entries containing those exact words in the title. It would miss titles with the words *intercultural communication, international communication,* and *global communication.* If you did multiple searches using similar terms, the search would still miss those titles without the keywords, such as Robert Axtell's *Dos and Taboos Around the World.*

■ Electronic catalogs give many search options.

The subject search, on the other hand, is broader. Using the subject *intercultural communication,* you will find items on the subject, whether or not the exact words appear in the title. For example, you might find a management book with a chapter on *intercultural* communication; however, the book's emphasis might be on something else, such as crisis management or conflict resolution.

The electronic catalog never gets tired. If you key in the words accurately, it will always produce a complete and accurate list of sources. Let us look at a few results from a subject search on *intercultural* communication. Notice in Figure 19.2 that the system found 211 sources. Assume that is more than you really want; so you decide to select the Limit/Sort shown at the bottom of the screen to limit your search. This system then gives you options for limiting your search (see Figure 19.3). You decide to limit the search by material type and year, telling it you want it to find all sources that are Books after 1995 (see Figure 19.4). As you can see in Figure 19.5, 26 entries were found. When you ask the system to

A Menu for an Online Catalog

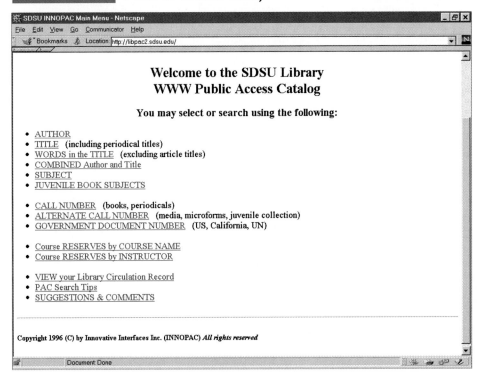

Illustration of Online Search Results

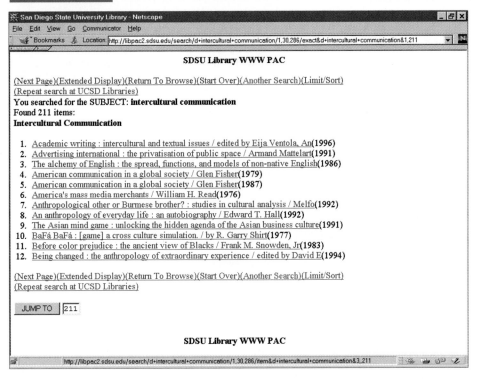

display the record, it brings up the screen shown in Figure 19.6. Not only will you find the title and author, but you will also find complete bibliographic information, the call number, and the status along with subjects this book fits. Furthermore, the system gives you the option of browsing through other books nearby on the shelf.

FIGURE 19.3 Examples of Material-Type Search Options

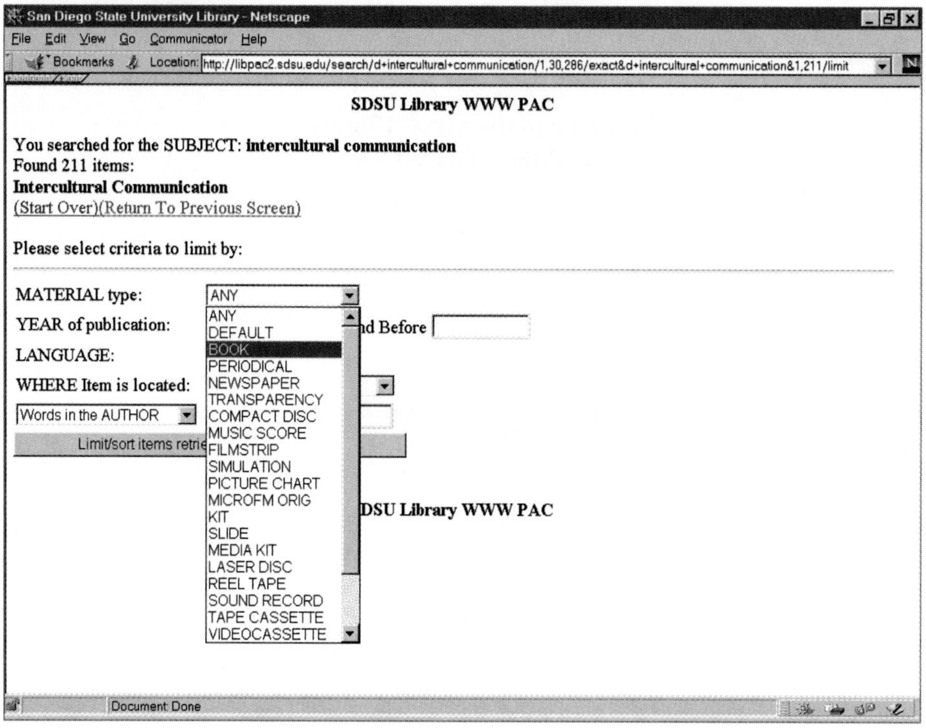

FIGURE 19.4 Search Options for Books Published after 1995

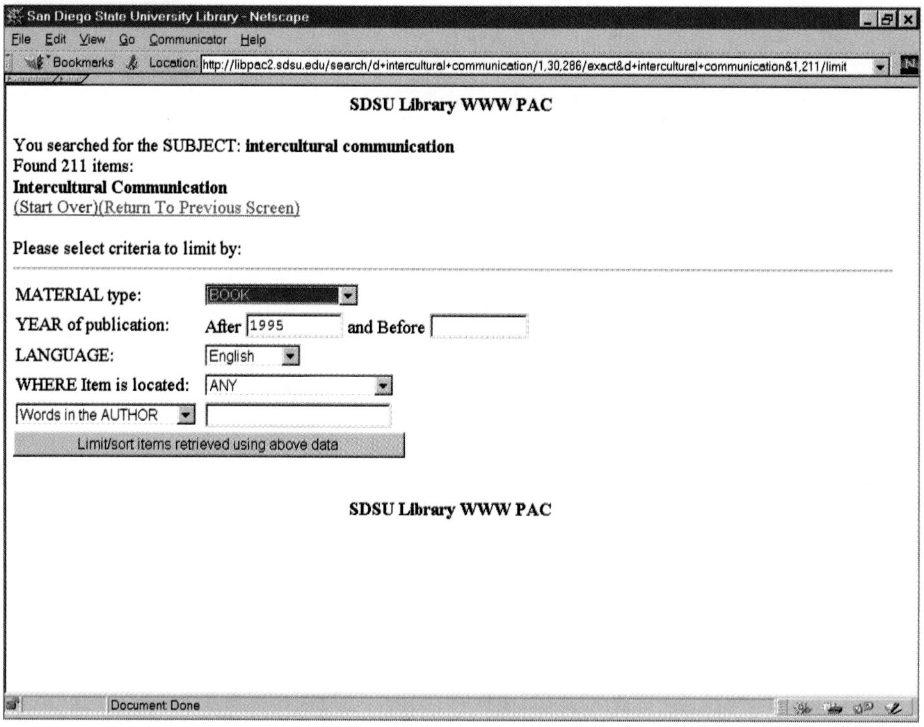

The online catalog is a useful source of information for your library's holdings. Learning how to use it effectively will save you time and will help your searches be fast and accurate.

FIGURE 19.5 Search Results for Books Published after 1995

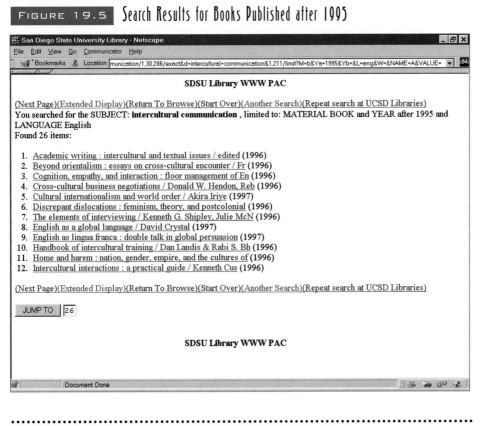

FIGURE 19.6 Illustration of a Retrieved Record

PERIODICAL INDEXES. The on-line catalog helps you identify books for your bibliography. To identify articles published in newspapers, magazines, or journals, you will need to consult an index, either a general one or one that specializes in the field you are

■ To identify articles for your list of prospective sources, consult a periodical index.

researching. Regularly updated indexes are available in the reference section of most libraries.

If you are like most business researchers, you will start your search for periodical literature with the *Business Periodicals Index.* Issued monthly and cumulated yearly, this index covers articles in 300 major business periodicals and indexes, by subject headings and company references. Another index that you may find useful is the *United States Predicasts F & S Index,* which covers over 700 business-oriented periodicals, newspapers, and special reports. A third index that may be helpful is the *Public Affairs Information Service Bulletin.* It lists by subject information relating to economics and public affairs. In addition, you may find useful such specialized indexes as *Findex: the Directory of Market Research; Reports, Studies, and Surveys; Marketing Information Guides;* and the *Accountant's Index.*

Some business indexes are available on CD-ROMs.

Infotrak, Wilsonline, and University Microfilms are providers of CD-ROM products on business information. The CD-ROMs give the researcher a simple citation, an abstract, or even full text. For business information, the *Academic Index* and the *Business Index* from Infotrak are particularly useful. *Wilson Business Abstracts* from Wilsonline is an excellent source for general business information. *ABI/INFORM* and *Business Dateline* are good business CD-ROM indexes from University Microfilms.

Computers organize and store vast amounts of data.

ONLINE DATABASES. The capacity of computers to collect and retrieve information continues to expand phenomenally with business research a primary beneficiary. Much of the information routinely recorded in printed form and accessed through directories, encyclopedias, bibliographies, indexes, and the like is now collected and stored in computer files as well. When these files of related information, known collectively as *databases,* are accessed by computer, the result is a set of facts that can be more extensive, complete, and accurate than any compiled manually.

Private services offer many databases.

Databases, many of which are produced by private information services, offer a variety of materials essential to business research. For example, Knight-Ridder Information Services, Inc., includes in its selection of 450 databases the *American Statistics Index;* the *Encyclopedia of Associations;* a number of Predicasts services (*PTS F&S Indexes, International Forecasts,* and *Promt*); and *Standard & Poor's News.* Two other private information services, Bibliographic Retrieval System (BRS) and LEXIS/NEXIS, offer many of the same information files. In addition, prominent business resources, including Dow Jones & Company, the *Harvard Business Review,* the *New York Times,* and Standard & Poor's, now offer computer access to their data and files.

Many libraries offer facilities for computer-searching of databases.

Most public, college, and university libraries offer database searching services, usually for a fee that reflects the computer time employed and the number of items identified. They also usually require you to work closely with trained staff to design a strategy that will use computer time effectively to retrieve the most relevant information. However, considering the potential advantages of computer-assisted searching, the cost of the service and the initial inconvenience of designing a computer search strategy are a small price to pay. Many of these information providers, such as Knight-Ridder and Dow Jones News Retrieval Services, offer special price packages. You can search their databases during off-peak times at reduced rates, or you can subscribe to some services for a flat fee. Developing your own searching skills will also help to keep costs down.

Developing good search strategies will help you keep costs down when using online systems.

Several other ways may reduce costs. One way is to plan carefully before you go online to shorten the amount of time you need to be connected to the database. Another way is to choose the correct database the first time. Some database providers have a selection utility you can use. You request the subject you need; then the utility recommends appropriate databases to use. Using these kinds of "assistants" will pay off by eliminating trial-and-error charges. A third way to cut costs is to know what to do when your search contains too many or two few citations.

Know what to do when your results include too many or too few citations.

If your search gives you more citations than you can handle, limit the search. Know beforehand how you might do this. Most systems let you restrict your search by language and year. Sometimes you can add a NOT term, which eliminates citations with a particular word from your search. If your search comes up short, you need to check for spelling errors and limitations. If you have a difficulty adding terms to broaden your search, look at the keywords or descriptors of the items that have already been identified. Often these will give you ideas of terms to broaden the search. In addition, be sure to keep track of the strategies that work so you can use them in future searches. Learning how to extract information efficiently from databases will pay off immensely, putting just the right information at your fingertips.

THE INTERNET.   The Internet is a network of networks. It operates in a structure originally funded by the National Science Foundation. However, no one organization owns or runs this globally connected network. Its users work together to develop standards, which are still emerging. The network provides a wide variety of resources, including many useful to business. Since no one is officially in charge, finding information on the Internet can be difficult. Nevertheless, this network of loosely organized computer systems does provide some search tools.

■ A wide variety of business sources are available through the Internet.

These tools can search for files as well as text on various topics. They can search titles as well as the documents themselves. Since the World Wide Web is a rapidly growing medium for publishing, the browsers that allow users to view the electronic pages incorporate links to search tools. Most of the links currently are to individual search engines such as Alta Vista, Lycos, Infoseek, WebCrawler, Excite, and Yahoo. Some of these engines compile their indexes using human input, some use software robots, and some use a combination. WebCrawler, whose simple, clean screens you see in Figures 19.7 and 19.8, uses a combination. A user can easily enter a term, as shown in Figure 19.7, to search a robotically compiled index or select a subject channel organized by topics through human and robotic collaboration as shown in Figure 19.8.

■ Using online individual search tools will help find files and text.

As search engines evolve to meet the changing needs of the Internet's content and its users, new forms of these tools are emerging as well. Currently, several web sites sport multi- and metasearch tools. Multisearch tools are simply web sites where users can select from a variety of individual tools and directories. Metasearch tools, on the other hand, let searchers enter the search once, running it simultaneously with several individual search engines and compiling a combined results page. Examples of these include Search.com, All-in-One, Beaucoup, Savvy Search, and Metacrawler. Metacrawler, shown in Figures

■ Multi- and metasearch tools help one use several individual tools more easily.

··

FIGURE 19.7   Illustration of an Individual Web Search Engine—WebCrawler

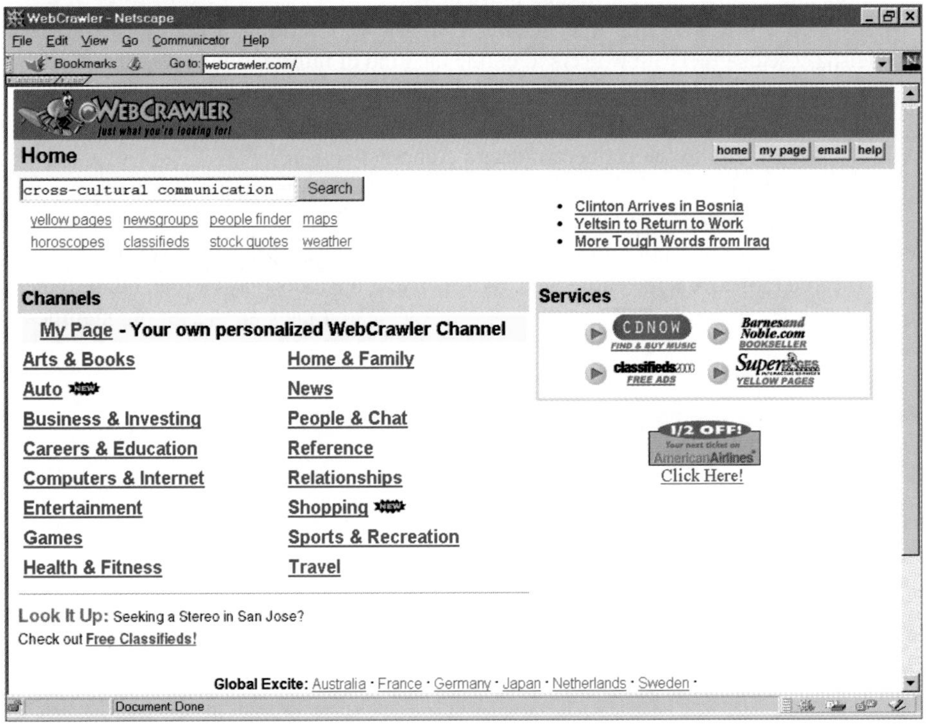

FIGURE 19.8 Topics in the Business WebCrawler Channel

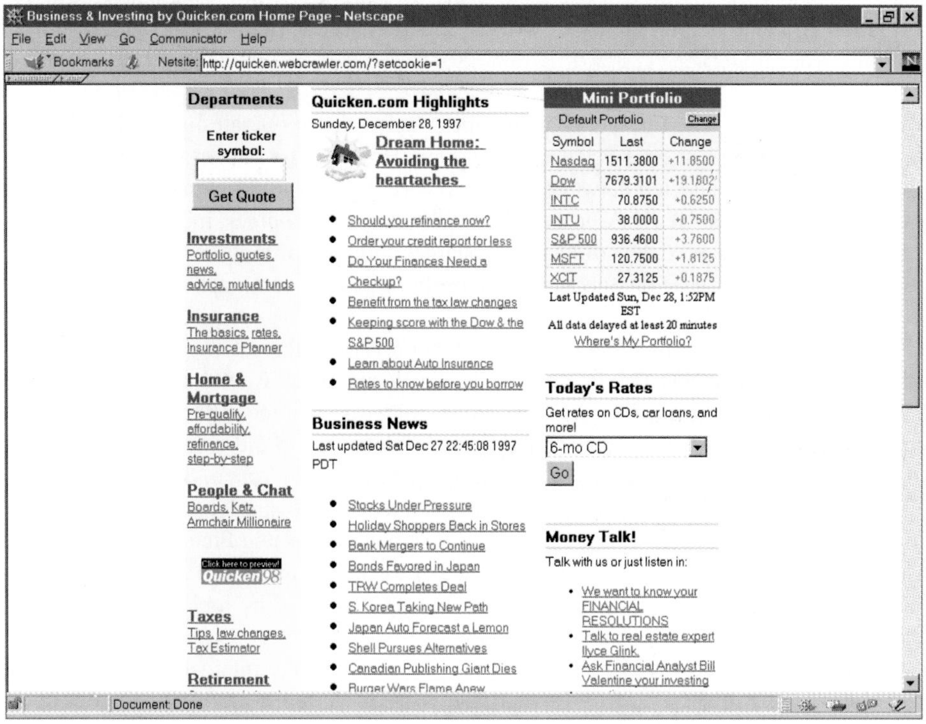

19.9 and 19.10, illustrates how the phrase *cross-cultural communication* is searched once and then the results are combined and reported along with a confidence rating and the identity of the search tool used to find it.

■ Specialized search engines run efficient searches on clearly identified subject-related sites.

Another new type of search tool that is emerging is the specialized search engine. Examples of some of these tools are Four11 for finding people, DejaNews for searching newsgroups, Edgar for finding government information, FindLaw for gathering legal information, and Mediafinder for finding news items.

■ User defined channels help personalize information needs.

A newer form of gathering information from the web is through use of personalized channels. These channels allow users to define the kind of information they want to gather. They can be ready and waiting when users access their personalized channels, such as at My Excite Channel. Or they can be in the form of "push technology" such as Pointcast and are broadcast directly to the connected user's computer screen.

■ Users must evaluate the results carefully for both accuracy and completeness.

While these tools assist users in finding helpful web documents, it is crucial to remember the tools are limited. You must evaluate the source of the information critically. Also, you must recognize that not all of the documents published on the Web are indexed and that no search tool covers the entire web. Skill in using the tools plays a role, but judgment in evaluating the accuracy and completeness of the search pays an even more significant role.

PRIMARY RESEARCH

■ Primary research employs four basic methods.

When you cannot find the information you need in secondary sources, you must get it firsthand. That is, you must use primary research, which employs four basic methods:

1. Search through company records
2. Experimentation
3. Observation
4. Survey

FIGURE 19.9 Example of a Metasearch Engine—Metacrawler

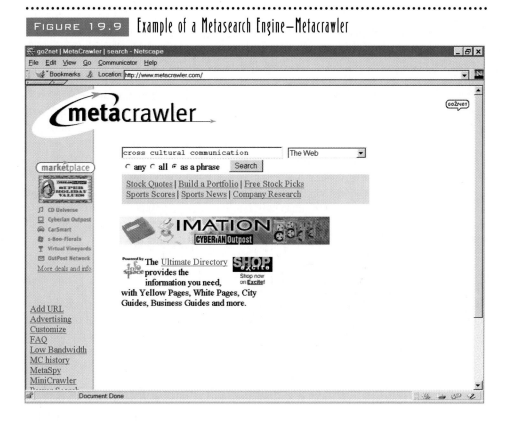

FIGURE 19.10 Search Results of a Combined Metasearch Report

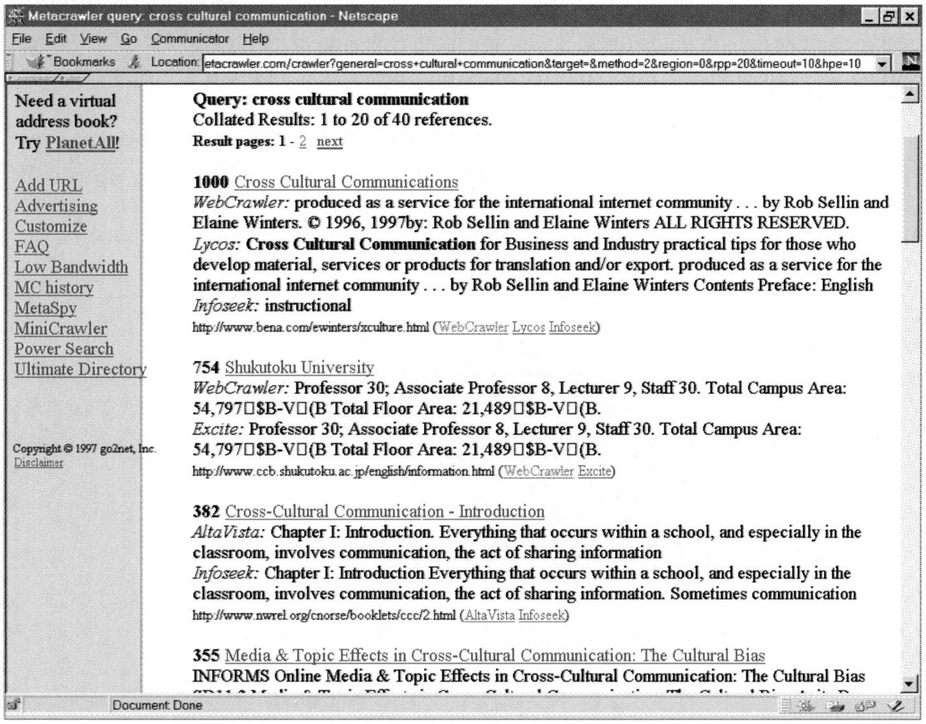

- Company records are an excellent source of firsthand information.

Since many of today's business problems involve various phases of company operations, a company's internal records—production data, sales records, merchandising information, accounting records, and the like—are frequently an excellent source of firsthand information.

- Make sure you (1) have a clear idea of the information you need, (2) understand the terms of access and confidentially, and (3) cooperate with company personnel.

There are no set rules on how to find and gather information through company records. Record-keeping systems vary widely from company to company. However, you are well advised to keep the following standards in mind as you conduct your investigation. First, as in any other type of research, you must have a clear idea of the information you need. Undefined, open-ended investigations are not appreciated—nor are they particularly productive. Second, you must clearly understand the ground rules under which you are allowed to review materials. Matters of confidentiality and access should be resolved before you start. And third, if you are not intimately familiar with a company's records or how to access them, you must cooperate with someone who is. The complexity and sensitivity of such materials require that they be reviewed in their proper context.

CONDUCTING THE EXPERIMENT

- Experimentation manipulates one factor and holds others constant.

The experiment is a very useful technique in business research. Originally perfected in the sciences, the experiment is an orderly form of testing. In general, it is a form of research in which you systematically manipulate one variable factor of a problem while holding all the others constant. You measure quantitatively or qualitatively any changes resulting from your manipulations. Then you apply your findings to the problem.

For example, suppose you are conducting research to determine whether a new package design will lead to more sales. You might start by selecting two test cities, taking care that they are as alike as possible on all the characteristics that might affect the problem. Then you would secure information on sales in the two cities for a specified time period before the experiment. Next, for a second specified time period, you would use the new package design in one of the cities and continue to use the old package in the other. During that period, you would keep careful sales records and check to make sure that advertising, economic conditions, competition, and other factors that might have some effect on the experiment remain unchanged. Thus, when the experimentation period is over, you can attribute any differences you found between the sales of the two cities to the change in package design.

- Design each experiment to fit the problem.

Each experiment should be designed to fit the individual requirements of the problem. Nonetheless, a few basic designs underlie most experiments. Becoming familiar with two of the most common designs—the before–after and the controlled before–after—will give you a framework for understanding and applying this primary research technique.

FIGURE 19.11 The Before–After Experimental Design

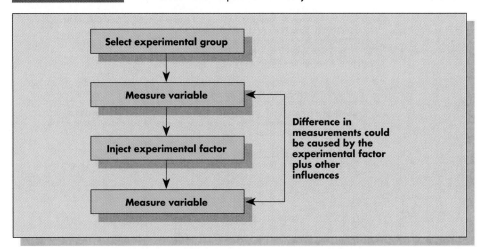

THE BEFORE–AFTER DESIGN.   The simplest experimental design is the before–after design. In this design, illustrated in Figure 19.11, you select a test group of subjects, measure the variable in which you are interested, and then introduce the experimental factor. After a specified time period, during which the experimental factor has presumably had its effect, you again measure the variable in which you are interested. If there are any differences between the first and second measurements, you may assume that the experimental factor is the cause plus any uncontrollable factors.

■ The before–after design is the simplest. You use just one test group.

Consider the following application. Assume you are conducting research for a retail store to determine the effect of point-of-sale advertising. Your first step is to select a product for the experiment, Gillette razor blades. Second, you record sales of Gillette blades for one week, using no point-of-sale advertising. Then you introduce the experimental variable—the Gillette point-of-sale display. For the next week you again record sales of Gillette blades; and at the end of that week, you compare the results for the two weeks. Any increase in sales would presumably be explained by the introduction of the display. Thus, if 500 packages of Gillette blades were sold in the first week and 600 were sold in the second week, you would conclude that the 100 additional sales can be attributed to point-of-sale advertising.

You can probably recognize the major shortcoming of the design. It is simply not logical to assume that the experimental factor explains the entire difference in sales between the first week and the second. The sales of Gillette razor blades could have changed for a number of other reasons—changes in the weather, holiday or other seasonal influences on business activity, other advertising, and so on. At best, you have determined only that point-of-sale advertising *could* influence sales.

■ The changes recorded in a before–after experiment may not be attributable to the experimental factor alone.

THE CONTROLLED BEFORE–AFTER DESIGN.   To account for influences other than the experimental factors, you may use designs more complex than the before–after design. These designs attempt to measure the other influences by including some means of control. The simplest of these designs is the controlled before–after design.

■ In the controlled before–after experiment, you use two identical test groups. You introduce the experimental factor into one group, then compare the two groups. You can attribute any difference between the two to the experimental factor.

In the controlled before–after design, you select not one group, but two—the experimental group and the control group. Before introducing the experimental factor, you measure in each group the variable to be tested. Then you introduce the experimental factor into the experimental group only.

When the period allotted for the experiment is over, you again measure in each group the variable being tested. Any difference between the first and second measurements in the experimental group can be explained by two causes—the experimental factor and other influences. But the difference between the first and second measurements in the control group can be explained only by other influences, for this group was not subjected to the experimental factor. Thus, comparing the "afters" of the two groups will give you a measure of the influence of the experimental factor, as diagrammed in Figure 19.12.

FIGURE 19.12 The Controlled Before-After Experimental Design

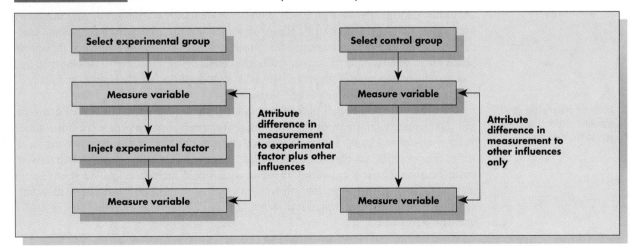

In a controlled before–after experiment designed to test point-of-sale advertising, you might select Gillette razor blades and Shick razor blades and record the sales of both brands for one week. Next you introduce point-of-sale displays for Gillette only and you record sales for both Gillette and Shick for a second week. At the end of the second week, you compare the results for the two brands. Whatever difference you find in Gillette sales and Shick sales will be a fair measure of the experimental factor, independent of the changes that other influences may have brought about.

For example, without point-of-sales displays in the control group if 400 packages of Shick blades are sold the first week, and 450 packages are sold the second week, the increase of 50 packages (12.5 percent) can be attributed to influences other than the experimental factor, the point-of-sale display. If 500 packages of Gillette blades are sold the first week, and 600 are sold the second week, the increase of 100 can be attributed to both the point-of-sale display and other influences. To distinguish between the two, you note that other influences accounted for the 12.5 percent increase in the sales of Shick blades. Because of the experimental control, you attribute 12.5 percent of the increase in Gillette sales to other influences as well. An increase of 12.5 percent on a base of 500 sales is 63 sales, indicating that 63 of the 100 additional Gillette sales are the result of other influences. However, the sale of 37 additional packages of Gillette blades can be attributed to point-of-sale advertising.

USING THE OBSERVATION TECHNIQUE

- Research by observation involves watching phenomena and recording what is seen.

Like the experiment, observation is a technique perfected in the sciences that is also useful in business research. Simply stated, observation is seeing with a purpose. It consists of watching the events involved in a problem and systematically recording what is seen. In observation, you do not manipulate the details of what you observe; you take note of situations exactly as you find them.

- This form of observation does not involve experimentation.

Note that observation as an independent research technique is different from the observation you use in recording the effects of variables introduced into a test situation. In the latter case, observation is a step in the experiment, not an end in itself. The two methods, therefore, should not be confused.

To see how observation works as a business technique, consider this situation. You work for a fast-food chain, such as McDonald's, that wants to check the quality and consistency of some menu items throughout the chain. By hiring observers, sometimes called mystery shoppers, you can gather information on the temperature, freshness, and speed of delivery of various menu items. This method may reveal important information that other data collection methods cannot.

- Observation requires a systematic procedure for observing and recording.

Like all primary research techniques, observation must be designed to fit the requirements of the problem being considered. However, the planning stage generally requires two steps. First, you construct a recording form; second, you design a systematic procedure for observing and recording the information of interest.

- The recording form should enable you to record details quickly and accurately.

The recording form may be any tabular arrangement that permits quick and easy recording of that information. Though observation forms are hardly standardized, one commonly used arrangement (see Figure 19.13) provides a separate line for each observation. Headings at the top of the page mark the columns in which the observer will place the appropriate mark. The recording form identifies the characteristics that are to be observed and requires the recording of such potentially important details as the date, time, and place of the observation and the name of the observer.

- An effective observation procedure ensures the collection of complete and representative information.

The observation procedure may be any system that ensures the collection of complete and representative information. But every effective observation procedure includes a clear focus, well-defined steps, and provisions for ensuring the quality of the information collected. For example, an observation procedure for determining the courtesy of employees toward customers when answering the telephone would include a detailed schedule for making calls, detailed instructions on what to ask, and provisions for dealing with different responses the observer might encounter. In short, the procedure would leave no major question unanswered.

FIGURE 19.13 Excerpt of a Common Type of Observation Recording Form

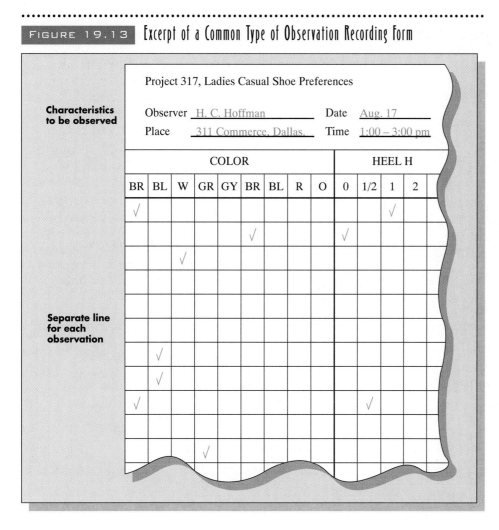

COLLECTING INFORMATION BY SURVEY

The premise of the survey as a method of primary research is simple: You can best determine certain types of information by asking questions. Such information includes personal data, opinions, evaluations, and other important material. It also includes information necessary to plan for an experiment or an observation or to supplement or interpret the data that result.

Once you have decided to use the survey for your research, you have to make decisions about a number of matters. The first is the matter of format. The questions can range from spontaneous inquiries to carefully structured interrogations. The next is the matter of delivery. The questions can be posed in a personal interview, asked over the telephone, or presented in printed or electronic form.

But the most important is the matter of whom to survey. Except for situations in which a small number of people are involved in the problem under study, you cannot reach all the people involved. Thus, you have to select a sample of respondents who represent the group as a whole as accurately as possible. There are several ways to select that sample, as you will see.

SAMPLING AS A BASIS. Sampling theory forms the basis for most research by survey, though it has any number of other applications as well. Buyers of grain, for example, judge the quality of a multi-ton shipment by examining a few pounds. Quality-control supervisors spot-check a small percentage of products ready for distribution to determine

- You can best determine certain information by asking questions.

- Decide which survey format and delivery will be most effective in developing the information you need.

- Also decide whom to interview. If the subject group is large, select a sample.

- Survey research is based on sampling.

Survey Software Helps Writers Lay Out, Analyze, and Report Results of Questionnaires

Survey software, such as Survey Pro illustrated here, helps design professional looking questionnaires as well as compile and analyze the data collected. Additionally, Survey Pro and others allow you to convert the questionnaires to HTML format for easy publishing on the web.

Special data entry screens assist in selecting the types of questions and desired layout. They then arrange the questionnaire automatically while giving the freedom to drag and drop questions to change the ordering and arrangement if desired. They also let you create open-ended questions. All

of these questions can be saved in a library for reuse.

As shown, the program creates a variety of graphics, helping you to report the results clearly and accurately.

This software can be used by businesses in a variety of applications, including training program evaluations, employee feedback on policies and procedures, longitudinal studies of ongoing practices such as network advertising revenues, opinion surveys of customers and potential customers, and feedback on customer satisfaction.

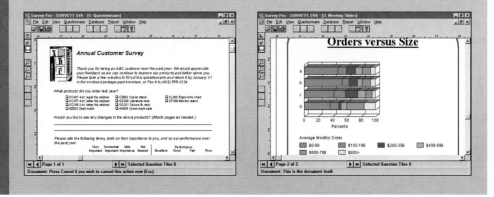

▪ Good samples are reliable, valid, and controlled for sampling error.

whether production standards are being met. Auditors for large corporations sample transactions when examining the books. Sampling is generally used for economy and practicality. However, for a sample to be representative of the whole group, it must be designed properly.

Two important aspects to consider in sample design are controlling for sampling error and bias. Sampling error results when the sample is not representative of the whole group. While all samples have some degree of sampling error, you can reduce the error through techniques used to construct representative samples. These techniques fall into two groups—probability and nonprobability sampling.

PROBABILITY SAMPLING TECHNIQUES.   Probability samples are based on chance selection procedures. Every element in the population has a known nonzero probability of selection.[1] These techniques include simple random sampling, stratified random sampling, systematic sampling, and cluster or area sampling.

▪ In random sampling, every item in the subject group has an equal chance of being selected.

Random Sampling.   Random sampling is the technique assumed in the general law of sampling. By definition, it is the sampling technique that gives every member of the group under study an equal chance of being included. To assure equal chances, you must first identify every member of the group and then, using a list or some other convenient format, record all the identifications. Next, through some chance method, you select the members of your sample.

---

[1] William G. Zikmund, *Business Research Methods,* 5th ed. (Fort Worth, TX: The Dryden Press, 1997), p. 430.

The interview is a widely used form of primary research in business. It is especially useful for gathering marketing information.

For example, if you are studying the job attitudes of 200 production workers and determine that 25 interviews will give you the information you need, you might put the names of each worker in a container, mix them thoroughly, and draw out 25. Since each of the 200 workers has an equal chance of being selected, your sample will be random and can be presumed to be representative.

Stratified Random Sampling. Stratified random sampling subdivides the group under study and makes random selections within each subgroup. The size of each subgroup is usually proportionate to that subgroup's percentage of the whole. If a subgroup is too small to yield meaningful findings, however, you may have to select a disproportionately large sample. (Of course, when the study calls for statistics on the group as a whole, the actual proportion of such a subgroup must be restored.)

> ■ In stratified random sampling, the group is divided into subgroups and the sample is randomly selected from each subgroup.

Assume, for example, that you are attempting to determine the curriculum needs of 5,000 undergraduates at a certain college and that you have decided to survey 20 percent of the enrollment, or 1,000 students. To construct a sample for this problem, first divide the enrollment list by academic concentration: business, liberal arts, nursing, engineering, and so forth. Then draw a random sample from each of these groups, making sure that the number you select is proportionate to that group's percentage of the total undergraduate enrollment. Thus, if 30 percent of the students are majoring in business, you will randomly select 300 business majors for your sample; if 40 percent of the students are liberal arts majors, you will randomly select 400 liberal arts majors for your sample; and so on.

Systematic Sampling. Systematic sampling, though not random in the strictest sense, is random for all practical purposes. It is the technique of taking selections at constant intervals (every nth unit) from a list of the items under study. The interval used is based, as you might expect, on the size of the list and the size of the desired sample. For example, if you want a 10 percent sample of a list of 10,000, you might select every 10th item on the list.

> ■ In systematic sampling, the items are selected from the subject group at constant intervals.

However, your sample would not really be random. By virtue of their designated place on the original list, items do not have an equal chance of being selected. To correct that problem, you might use an equal-chance method to determine what *n* to use. Thus, if you selected the number 7 randomly, you would draw the numbers 7, 17, 27, and so on to 9,997 to make up your sample. Or, if you wanted to draw every 10th item, you might first scramble the list and then select from the revised list numbers 10, 20, 30, and so on up to 10,000 and make up your sample that way.

Area or Cluster Sampling.

In area sampling, the items for a sample are drawn in stages. This sampling technique is appropriate when the area to be studied is large and can be broken down into progressively smaller components. For example, if you want to draw an area sample for a certain city, you may use census data to divide the city into homogeneous districts. Using an equal-chance method, you then select a given number of districts to include in the next stage of your sample. Next you divide each of the selected districts into subdistricts—city blocks, for example. Continuing the process, you randomly select a given number of these blocks and subdivide each of them into households. Finally, using random sampling once more, you select the households that will constitute the sample you will use in your research.

Area or cluster sampling is not limited to geographic division, however. It is adaptable to any number of applications. For example, it is an appropriate technique to use in a survey of the workers in a given industry. An approach that you may take in this situation is to randomly select a given number of companies from a list of all the companies in the industry. Then, using organization units and selecting randomly at each level, you break down each of these companies into divisions, departments, sections, and so on until you finally identify the workers you will survey.

NONPROBABILITY SAMPLING TECHNIQUES. Nonprobability samples are based on an unknown probability of any one of a population being chosen. These techniques include convenience sampling, quota sampling, and referral sampling.[2]

Convenience Sampling.

A convenience sample is one whose members are convenient and economical to reach. When professors use their students as subjects for their research, they are using a convenience sample. Researchers generally use this sample to reach a large number quickly and economically. This kind of sampling is best used for exploratory research.

A form of convenience sampling is *judgment* or *expert* sampling. This technique relies on the judgment of the researcher to identify appropriate members of the sample. Illustrating this technique is the common practice of predicting the outcome of an election, based on the results in a bellwether district.

Quota Sampling.

Quota sampling is another nonrandom technique. Also known as *controlled sampling,* it is used whenever the proportionate makeup of the universe under study is available. The technique requires that you refer to the composition of the universe in designing your sample, selecting items so that your sample has the same characteristics in the same proportion as that universe. Specifically, it requires that you set quotas for each characteristic that you want to consider in your research problem. Within those quotas, however, you will select individual items randomly.

Let us say that you want to survey a college student body of 4,000 using a 10 percent sample. As Figure 19.14 illustrates, you have a number of alternatives for determining the makeup of your sample, depending on the focus of your research. Keep in mind, though, that no matter what characteristic you select, the quotas the individual segments represent must total 100 percent and the number of items in the sample must total 400. Keep in mind also that within these quotas you will use an equal-chance method to select the individual members of your sample.

---

[2] *Ibid.,* p. 428.

FIGURE 19.14 Example of Quota Sample

	Number in Universe	Percent of Total	Number to Be Interviewed
Total student enrollment	4,000	100	400
Sex			
Men students	2,400	60	240
Women students	1,600	40	160
Fraternity, sorority membership			
Members	1,000	25	100
Nonmembers	3,000	75	300
Marital status			
Married students	400	10	40
Single students	3,600	90	360
Class rank			
Freshman	1,600	40	160
Sophomores	1,000	25	100
Juniors	800	20	80
Seniors	400	10	40
Graduates	200	5	20

Referral Sampling.   Referral samples are those whose members are identified by others from a random sample. This technique is used to locate members when the population is small or hard to reach. For example, you might want to survey rolle bolle players. To get a sample large enough to make the study worthwhile, you could ask those from your town to give you the names of other players. Perhaps you are trying to survey the users of project management software. You could survey a user's group and ask those members for names of other users. You might even post your announcement on a newsgroup or listserv; users of the system would send you the names for your sample.

■ Referral samples are used for small or hard-to-reach groups.

CONSTRUCTING THE QUESTIONNAIRE.   Most orderly interrogation follows a definite plan of inquiry. This plan is usually worked out in a published (print or electronic) form, called the *questionnaire.* The questionnaire is simply an orderly arrangement of the questions, with appropriate spaces provided for the answers. But simple as the finished questionnaire may appear to be, it is the subject of careful planning. You should plan carefully so that the results are *reliable;* a test of a questionnaire's reliability is its repeatability with similar results. You also want your questionnaire to be *valid,* measuring what it is supposed to measure. It is, in a sense, the outline of the analysis of the problem. In addition, it must observe certain rules. These rules sometimes vary with the problem. The more general and by far the more important ones follow.

■ Construct a questionnaire carefully so that the results it provides are both reliable and valid.

Avoid Leading Questions.   A leading question is one that in some way influences the answer. For example, the question "Is Dove your favorite bath soap?" leads the respondent to favor Dove. Some people who would say yes would name another brand if they were asked, "What is your favorite brand of bath soap?"

■ Avoid leading questions (questions that influence the answer).

Make the Questions Easy to Understand.   Questions not clearly understood by all respondents lead to error. Unfortunately, it is difficult to determine in advance just what respondents will not understand. As will be mentioned later, the best means of detecting such questions in advance is to test the questions before using them. But you can be on the alert for a few general sources of confusion.

■ Word the questions so that all the respondents understand them.

Vagueness of expression, difficult
words, and two questions in one cause
misunderstanding.

One source of confusion is vagueness of expression, which is illustrated by the ridiculous question "How do you bank?" Who other than its author knows what the question means? Another source is using words not understood by the respondents, as in the question "Do you read your house organ regularly?" The words *house organ* have a specialized, not widely known meaning, and *regularly* means different things to different people. Combining two questions in one is yet another source of confusion. For example, "Why did you buy a Ford?" actually asks two questions: "What do you like about Fords?" and "What don't you like about the other automobiles?"

Avoid Questions That Touch on Personal Prejudices or Pride.

For reasons of pride or prejudices, people cannot be expected to answer accurately questions about certain areas of information. These areas include age, income status, morals, and personal habits. How many people, for example, would answer no to the question "Do you brush your teeth daily?" How many people would give their ages correctly? How many solid citizens would admit to fudging a bit on their tax returns? The answers are obvious.

But one may ask, "What if such information is essential to the solution of the problem?" The answer is to use less direct means of inquiry. To ascertain age, for example, investigators could ask for dates of high school graduation, marriage, or the like. From this information, they could approximate age. Or they could approximate age through observation, although this procedure is acceptable only if broad age approximations would be satisfactory. They could ask for such harmless information as occupation, residential area, and standard of living and then use that information as a basis for approximating income. Another possibility is to ask range questions such as "Are you between 18 and 24, 25 and 40, or over 40?" This technique works well with income questions, too. People are generally more willing to answer questions worded by ranges rather than specifics. Admittedly, such techniques are sometimes awkward and difficult. But they can improve on the biased results that direct questioning would obtain.

Seek Facts as Much as Possible.

Although some studies require opinions, it is far safer to seek facts whenever possible. Human beings simply are not accurate reporters of their opinions. They are often limited in their ability to express themselves. Frequently, they report their opinions erroneously simply because they have never before been conscious of having them.

When opinions are needed, it is usually safer to record facts and then to judge the thoughts behind them. This technique, however, is only as good as the investigators' judgment. But a logical analysis of fact made by trained investigators is preferable to a spur-of-the-moment opinion.

A frequent violation of this rule results from the use of generalizations. Respondents are sometimes asked to generalize an answer from a large number of experiences over time. The question "Which magazines do you read regularly?" is a good illustration. Aside from the confusion caused by the word *regularly* and the fact that the question may tap the respondent's memory, the question forces the respondent to generalize. Would it not be better to phrase it in this way: "What magazines have you read this month?" The question could then be followed by an article-by-article check of the magazines to determine the extent of readership.

Ask Only for Information That Can Be Remembered.

Since the memory of all human beings is limited, the questionnaire should ask only for information that the respondents can be expected to remember. To make sure that this is done, a knowledge of certain fundamentals of memory is necessary.

Recency is the foremost fundamental. People remember insignificant events that occurred within the past few hours. By the next day, they will forget some. A month later they may not remember any. One might well remember, for example, what one ate for lunch on the day of the inquiry, and perhaps one might remember what one ate for lunch a day, or two days, or three days earlier. But one would be unlikely to remember what one ate for lunch a year earlier.

The second fundamental of memory is that significant events may be remembered over long periods. One may long remember the first day of school, the day of one's wedding, an automobile accident, a Christmas Day, and the like. In each of these examples there was an intense stimulus—a requisite for retention in memory.

A third fundamental of memory is that fairly insignificant facts may be remembered over long time periods through association with something significant. Although one would not normally remember what one ate for lunch a year earlier, for example, one might remember if the date happened to be one's wedding day, Christmas Day, or one's first day at college. Obviously, the memory is stimulated, not by the meal itself, but by the association of the meal with something more significant.

■ (3) association.

Plan the Physical Layout with Foresight.
The overall design of the questionnaire should be planned to facilitate recording, analyzing, and tabulating the answers. Three major considerations are involved in such planning.

■ Design the form for each recording.

First, answers should be allowed sufficient space for recording. When practical, a system for checking answers may be set up. Such a system must always provide for all possible answers, including conditional answers. For example, a direct question may provide for three possible answers: Yes _____, No _____, and Don't know _____.

■ Provide sufficient space.

Second, adequate space for identifying and describing the respondent should be provided. In some instances, such information as the age, sex, and income bracket of the respondent is vital to the analysis of the problem and should be recorded. In other instances, little or no identification is necessary.

■ Provide adequate identification space.

Third, the best possible sequence of questions should be used. In some instances, starting with a question of high interest value may have psychological advantages. In other instances, it may be best to follow some definite order of progression. Frequently, some questions must precede others because they help explain the others. Whatever the requirements of the individual case may be, however, careful and logical analysis should be used in determining the sequence of questions.

■ Arrange the questions in logical order.

Use Scaling When Appropriate.
It is sometimes desirable to measure the intensity of the respondents' feelings about something (an idea, a product, a company, and so on). In such cases, some form of scaling is generally useful.

■ Provide for scaling when appropriate.

Of the various techniques of scaling, ranking and rating deserve special mention. These are the simpler techniques and, some believe, the more practical. They are less sophisticated than some others,[3] but the more sophisticated techniques are beyond the scope of this book.

The ranking technique consists simply of asking the respondent to rank a number of alternative answers to a question in order of preference (1, 2, 3, and so on). For example, in a survey to determine consumer preferences for toothpaste, the respondent might be asked to rank toothpastes A, B, C, D, and E in order of preference. In this example, the alternatives could be compared on the number of preferences stated for each. This method of ranking and summarizing results is reliable despite its simplicity. There are various more complicated ranking methods (such as the use of paired comparison) and methods of recording results.

■ Ranking of responses is one form.

The rating technique graphically sets up a scale showing the complete range of possible attitudes on a matter and assigns number values to the positions on the scale. The respondent must then indicate the position on the scale that indicates his or her attitude on that matter. Typically, the numeral positions are described by words, as the example in Figure 19.15 illustrates.

■ Rating is another.

Because the rating technique deals with the subjective rather than the factual, it is sometimes desirable to use more than one question to cover the attitude being measured. Logically, the average of a person's answers to such questions gives a more reliable answer than does any single answer.

---

[3] Equivalent interval techniques (developed by L. L. Thurstone), scalogram analysis (developed by Louis Guttman), and the semantic differential (developed by C. E. Osgood, G. J. Suci, and P. H. Tannenbaum) are more complex techniques.

FIGURE 19.15 Illustration of a Rating Question

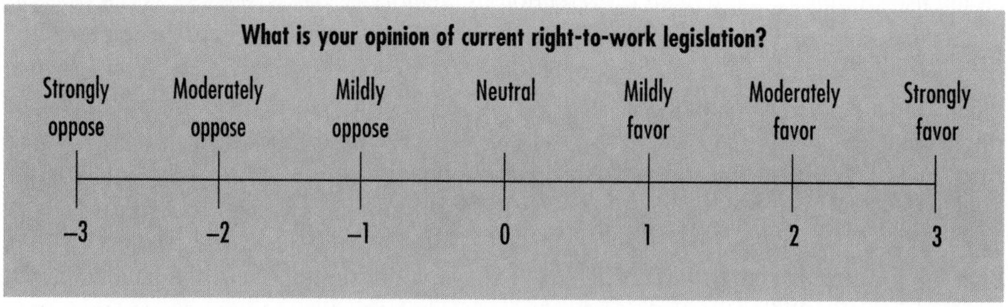

What is your opinion of current right-to-work legislation?

Strongly oppose	Moderately oppose	Mildly oppose	Neutral	Mildly favor	Moderately favor	Strongly favor
−3	−2	−1	0	1	2	3

SELECTING THE MANNER OF QUESTIONING. You can get responses to the questions you need answered in three primary ways: by personal (face-to-face) contact, by telephone, or by mail (print or electronic). You should select the way that in your unique case gives the best sample, the lowest cost, and the best results. By *best sample* we mean respondents who best represent the group concerned. And *results* are the information you need. As you can see in Figure 19.16, other factors will influence your choice.

- Select the way of asking the questions (by personal contact, telephone, or mail) that gives the best sample, the lowest cost, and the best results.

DEVELOPING A WORKING PLAN. After selecting the manner of questioning, you should carefully develop a working plan for the survey. As well as you can, you should anticipate and determine how to handle every possible problem. If you are conducting a mail survey, for example, you need to develop an explanatory message that moves the subjects to respond, tells them what to do, and answers all the questions they are likely to ask. If you are conducting a personal or telephone survey, you need to cover this information in instructions to the interviewers. You should develop your working plan before conducting the pilot study discussed in the following section. You should test that plan in the pilot study and revise it based on the knowledge you gain from the pilot study.

- Develop a working plan that covers all the steps and all the problems.

CONDUCTING A PILOT STUDY. Before doing the survey, it is advisable to conduct a pilot study on your questionnaire and working plan. A pilot study is a small-scale version of the actual survey. Its purpose is to test what you have planned. Based on your experience in the pilot study, you modify your questionnaire and working plan for use in the full-scale survey that follows.

- Test the questionnaire and the working plan. Make any changes needed.

EVALUATING AND REPORTING DATA

Gathering information from secondary sources is one step in processing facts for your report. You also need to evaluate it. Ask yourself questions about the writer's credibility, including methods of collecting facts and ability to draw inferences from the facts presented. Does the author draw conclusions that can be supported by the data presented? Are the sources reliable? Are the data or interpretations biased in any way? Are there any gaps or holes in the data or interpretation? You need to be a good judge of the material and feel free to discard it if it does not meet your standard for quality.

- Carefully evaluate the secondary information you find.

In this chapter, you have also learned how to plan and carry out primary data collection properly. Now that you have good data to work with, you must interpret it accurately and clearly for your reader (see Chapter 10 for interpreting procedure). If you are unsure of your reader's level of expertise in understanding descriptive statistics such as measures of central tendency and cross-tabulations, present the statistic and tell the reader what it means. In general, you can expect to explain the statistics from univariate, bivariate, and multivariate analyses. In many cases, graphics help tremendously because they show trends and relationships, ably. Statistical programs such as SPSS, which is illustrated in Figure 19.17, help you analyze, report, and graph your data. Finally, you have an ethical

- Report statistics from primary research clearly and completely.

FIGURE 19.16 Comparison of Data Collection Methods

	Personal	Telephone	Mail
Data collection costs	High	Medium	Low
Data collection time required	Medium	Low	High
Sample size for a given budget	Small	Medium	Large
Data quantity per respondent	High	Medium	Low
Reaches widely dispersed sample	No	Maybe	Yes
Reaches special locations	Yes	Maybe	No
Interaction with respondents	Yes	Yes	No
Degree of interviewer bias	High	Medium	None
Severity of non-response bias	Low	Low	High
Presentation of visual stimuli	Yes	No	Maybe
Field worker training required	Yes	Yes	No

Source: Pamela L. Alreck and Robert B. Settle, *The Survey Research Handbook* (Burr Ridge, IL: Richard D. Irwin, 1995), p. 32.

FIGURE 19.17 Illustration of Some of the Statistics That SPSS Will Calculate

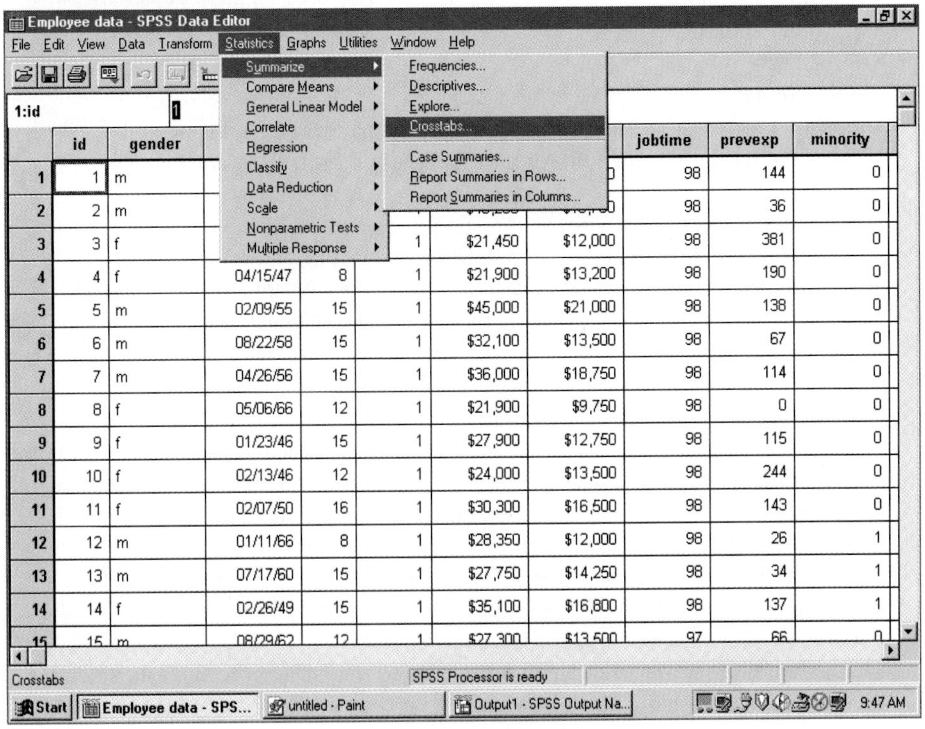

responsibility to present your data honestly and completely. Omitting an error or limitation of the data collection is often viewed as seriously as hiding errors or variations from accepted practices. Of course, any deliberate distortion of the data is unethical. It is your responsibility to communicate the findings of the report accurately and clearly.

1 Explain the difference between primary and secondary research.

1. Primary research is firsthand research. You can conduct primary research in four major ways:
   - Looking through company records
   - Conducting an experiment
   - Recording observations
   - Conducting a survey

   Secondary research is secondhand research or library research. You conduct secondary research in either a general library (usually public), a special library (usually private, or by computer).

2 Use appropriate procedures for direct and indirect library research.

2. If you need quantitative or factual information, you may be able to go directly to it, using such sources as the following:
   - Encyclopedias
   - Biographical directories
   - Almanacs
   - Trade directories
   - Government publications
   - Dictionaries
   - Statistical sources
   - Business information services

   When you cannot go directly to the source, you use indirect methods. You may begin by searching the following sources:
   - Prepared bibliographies in books, theses, research periodicals, or such
   - The on-line catalog
   - Periodical indexes
   - Databases
   - The Internet

3 Describe the procedures for searching through company records.

3. Company records are usually confidential. You must either ask the person responsible for the information for it or gather it yourself from company databases.

4 Conduct an experiment for a business problem.

4. An experiment is an orderly form of testing. It can be designed using the before–after design or the controlled before–after design.
   - The simplest is the before–after design. It involves selecting a group of subjects, measuring the variable, introducing the experimental factor, and measuring the variable again. The difference between the two measurements is assumed to be the result of the experimental factor.
   - The controlled before–after design involves selecting two groups, measuring the variable in both groups, introducing the experimental factor in one group, and then measuring the variable again in both groups. The second measurement enables you to determine the effect of the experimental factor and of other factors that might have influenced the variable between the two measurements.

5 Design an observational study for a business problem.

5. The observation method may be defined as seeing with a purpose. It consists of watching the events involved in a problem and systematically recording what is seen. The events observed are not manipulated.

6 Use sampling to conduct a survey.

6. A sample is a group representative of the whole group. The procedure for selecting the group is called sampling. A good sample is controlled for sampling error. You may use any of a variety of sample designs. Those discussed in this chapter include probability and nonprobability sampling.
   - Probability sampling is based on chance selection procedures. Every element in the population has a known nonzero probability of selection. Some of the techniques are described below.
     —Simple random sampling involves chance selection, giving every member of the group under study an equal chance of being selected.
     —Stratified random sampling involves proportionate and random selection from each major subgroup of the group under study.

—Systematic sampling involves taking selections at constant intervals (every fifth one, for example) from a complete list of the group under study.

—Cluster or area sampling involves dividing into parts the area that contains the sample, selecting from these parts randomly, and continuing to subdivide and select until you have your desired sample size.

- Nonprobability sampling is based on an unknown probability of any one of a group being studied. Some of the techniques are described below.

—Convenience sampling involves selecting members that are convenient, easy to reach, and appropriate as judged by the researcher.

—Quota sampling requires that you know the proportions of certain characteristics (sex, age, education, etc.) in the group under study. You then select respondents in the same proportions.

—Referral sampling involves building your sample from other participants' referrals.

7. The questions you ask should follow a definite plan, usually in the form of a questionnaire. You should construct the questionnaire carefully, ensuring that it is valid and reliable, and the questionnaire should follow these general rules.

- Avoid leading questions.
- Make the questions easy to understand (avoid vagueness, difficult words, technical words).
- Avoid questions that touch on personal prejudices or pride.
- Seek facts as much as possible.
- Ask only for what can be remembered (consider the laws of memory, recency, intensity, and association).
- Plan the layout with foresight (enough space for answers and identifying information, proper sequence of questions).
- Use scaling when appropriate.

You develop a working plan for conducting the questioning—one that covers all the possible problems and clearly explains what to do. It is usually advisable to test the questionnaire and working plan through a pilot study. This enables you to make changes in the questionnaire and improve the working plan before conducting the survey.

8. You need to evaluate the facts you gather from secondary research carefully before you include them in your report. Check to make sure they meet the following tests.

- Can the author draw the conclusions from the data presented?
- Are the sources reliable?
- Has the author avoided biased interpretation?
- Are there any gaps in the facts?

You must present the primary information you collect clearly and completely. It is your responsibility to explain statistics the reader may not understand.

7 Construct a questionnaire, develop a working plan, and conduct a pilot test for a survey.

8 Analyze and interpret information clearly and completely for your reader.

THE WIZARD OF ID   Brant parker and Johnny hart

By permission of Johnny Hart and Creators Syndicate, Inc.

CRITICAL THINKING QUESTIONS

1. Suggest a hypothetical research problem that would make good use of a specialized library. Justify your selection.

2. What specialized libraries are there in your community? What general libraries?

3. Under what general condition are investigators likely to be able to proceed directly to the published source of the information sought?

4. Which index is most likely to contain information on each of the following subjects?
   a. Labor–management relations
   b. Innovation in sales promotion
   c. Accident proneness among employees
   d. Recent advances in computer technology
   e. Trends in responsibility accounting
   f. Labor unrest in the 1800s
   g. Events leading to enactment of a certain tax measure in 1936
   h. Textbook treatment of business writing in the 1930s
   i. Viewpoints on the effect of deficit financing by governments
   j. New techniques in interviewing

5. What advice would you give an investigator who has been assigned a task involving analysis of internal records of several company departments?

6. Define *experimentation*. What does the technique of experimentation involve?

7. Explain the significance of keeping constant all factors other than the experimental variable of an experiment.

8. Give an example of (*a*) a problem that can best be solved through a before–after design, and (*b*) a problem that can best be solved through a controlled before–after design. Explain your choices.

9. Define *observation* as a research technique.

10. Select an example of a business problem that can be solved best by observation. Explain your choice.

11. Point out violations of the rules of good questionnaire construction in the following questions. The questions do not come from the same questionnaire.
    a. How many days on the average do you wear a pair of socks before changing?
    b. (The first question in a survey conducted by Coca-Cola.) Have you ever drunk a Diet Coke?
    c. Do you consider the ideal pay plan to be one based on straight commission or straight salary?
    d. What kind of gasoline did you purchase last time?
    e. How much did you pay for clothing in the past 12 months?
    f. Check the word below that best describes how often you eat dessert with your noon meal.
       Always
       Usually
       Sometimes
       Never

12. Explain the difference between random sampling and convenience sampling.

13. Discuss the writer's responsibility in explaining and reporting data.

CRITICAL THINKING EXERCISES

1. Using your imagination to supply any missing facts you may need, develop a plan for the experiment you would use in the following situations.
   a. The Golden Glow Baking Company has for many years manufactured and sold cookies packaged in attractive boxes. It is considering packaging the cookies in recyclable bags and wants to conduct an experiment to determine consumer response to this change.
   b. The Miller Brush Company, manufacturers of a line of household goods, has for years sold its products through conventional retail outlets. It now wants to conduct an experiment to test the possibility of selling through catalogs (or home shopping networks or the web).
   c. A national chain of drugstores wants to know whether it would profit by doubling the face value of coupons. It is willing to pay the cost of an experiment in its research for an answer.
   d. The True Time Watch Company is considering the use of automated sales displays ($49.50 each) instead of stationary displays ($24.50 each) in the 2,500 retail outlets that sell True Time watches.

   The company will conduct an experiment to determine the relative effects on sales of the two displays.
   e. The Marvel Soap Company has developed a new cleaning agent that is unlike current soaps and detergents. The product is well protected by patent. The company wants to determine the optimum price for the new product through experimentation.
   f. National Cereals, Inc., wants to determine the effectiveness of advertising to children. Until now, it has been aiming its appeal at parents. The company will support an experiment to learn the answer.

2. Using your imagination to supply any missing facts you may need, develop a plan for research by observation for these problems.
   a. A chain of department stores wants to know what causes differences in sales by departments within stores and by stores. Some of this information it hopes to get through research by observation.
   b. Your university wants to know the nature and extent of its parking problem.

c. The management of an insurance company wants to determine the efficiency and productivity of its data-entry department.

d. Owners of a shopping center want a study to determine shopping patterns of their customers. Specifically they want to know such things as what parts of town the customers come from, how they travel, how many stores they visit, and so on.

e. The director of your library wants a detailed study of library use (what facilities are used, when, by whom, and so on).

f. The management of a restaurant wants a study of its workers' efficiency in the kitchen.

3. Using your imagination to supply any missing facts you may need, develop a plan for research by survey for these problems.

a. The American Restaurant Association wants information that will give its members a picture of its customers. The information will serve as a guide for a promotion campaign designed to increase restaurant eating. Specifically it will seek such information as who eats out, how often, where they go, how much they spend. Likewise, it will seek to determine who does not eat out and why.

b. The editor of your local daily paper wants a readership study to learn just who reads what.

c. The National Beef Producers Association wants to determine the current trends in meat consumption. The association wants such information as the amount of meat people consume, whether people have reduced their meat consumption, and so on.

d. The International Association of Publishers wants a survey of the reading habits of adults in the United States and Canada. It wants such information as who reads what, how much, when, where, and so on.

e. Your boss wants to hire an experienced computer programmer for your company. Because you have not hired anyone in this category for a long time, you were asked to survey experienced programmers using the web or Usenet groups to gather salary figures.

Corrections for the Self-Administered Diagnostic Test of Correctness

Following are the corrected sentences for the diagnostic test at the end of Chapter 18. The corrections are underscored, and the symbols for the standards explaining the correction follow the sentences.

1. An important fact about this keyboard is‗ that it has the patented "ergonomic design"‗.
An important fact about this keyboard is that it has the patented "ergonomic design." *Cma 6.1, QM 3*

2. Goods received on invoice 2741 are as follows‗ 3 dozen white shirts, size 15–33‗ 4 mens‗felt hats, brown, size 7‗ and 5 dozen assorted ties.
Goods received on Invoice 2741 are as follows: three dozen white shirts, size 15–33; four men's felt hats, brown, size 7; and five dozen assorted ties. *Cln 1, Apos 1, SC 3, No 1*

3. James Silver‗President of the new union‗had the <u>priviledge</u> of introducing the speaker.
James Silver, president of the new union, had the privilege of introducing the speaker. *Cma 4.2, Cap, SP*

4. We do not expect to act on this matter‗however‗until we hear from you.
We do not expect to act on this matter, however, until we hear from you. *Cma 4.3*

5. Shipments through September 20, 1998‗totaled 69,485 pounds‗an increase of 17 percent over the year‗ago total.
Shipments through September 20, 1998, totaled 69,485 pounds, an increase of 17 percent over the year-ago total. *Cma 4.4, Cma 4.1, Hpn 2*

6. Brick is recommended as the building material‗but the board is giving serious consideration to a substitute.
Brick is recommended as the building material, but the board is giving serious consideration to a substitute. *Cma 1*

7. Markdowns for the sale total $34,000‗ never before has the company done anything like this.
Markdowns for the sale total $34,000; never before has the company done anything like this. *SC 1*

8. After long experimentation a wear‗resistant‗high‗grade‗and beautiful stocking has been perfected.
After long experimentation a wear-resistant, high-grade, and beautiful stocking has been perfected. *Hpn 2, Cma 2.2*

9. Available in white_green_and blue_this paint is sold by dealers all over the country.
    Available in white, green, and blue, this paint is sold by dealers all over the country. *Cma 2.1, Cma 3*

10. Julie Jahn_who won the trip_is our most energetic salesperson.
    Julie Jahn, who won the trip, is our most energetic salesperson. *Cma 3*

11. _Good_he replied_sales are sure to increase.
    "Good," he replied. "Sales are sure to increase." QM 1, Pd 1, *Cap*

12. Hogan's article_Retirement? Never!,_printed in the current issue of <u>Management Review</u>, is really a part of his book <u>A Report</u>
    <u>on Worker Security</u>.
    Hogan's article, "Retirement? Never!," printed in the current issue of *Management Review,* is really a part of his book, *A Report on Worker Security. Cma 4.2, QM 4, Ital 1*

13. Formal announcement of our Labor Day sale will be made in <u>thirty-two</u> days.
    Formal announcement of our Labor Day sale will be made in <u>32</u> days. *No 1*

14. Each day we encounter new problems._Although they are solved easily.
    Each day we encounter new problems, although they are solved easily. *Cma 5.1, Frag*

15. A list of models, sizes, and prices of both competing lines <u>are</u> being sent you.
    A list of models, sizes, and prices of both competing lines <u>is</u> being sent you. *Agmt SV*

16. The manager could not tolerate any employee's failing to do <u>their</u> best.
    The manager could not tolerate any employee's failing to do <u>his</u> or her best. *Pn 2*

17. A series of tests <u>were</u> completed only yesterday.
    A series of tests was completed only yesterday. *Agmt SV*

18. There should be no misunderstanding between you and <u>I</u>.
    There should be no misunderstanding between you and <u>me</u>. *Pn 3*

19. He <u>run</u> the accounting department for five years.
    He <u>ran</u> the accounting department for five years. *Tns 2*

20. This report is <u>considerable</u> long.
    This report is considerably long. *AA*

21. <u>Who</u> did you interview for the position?
    <u>Whom</u> did you interview for the position? *Pn 3*

22. The report concluded that the natural resources of the Southwest <u>was</u> ideal for the chemical industry.
    The report concluded that the natural resources of the Southwest <u>are</u> ideal for the chemical industry. *Agmt SV, Tns 1*

23. This applicant is six feet in height, _28 years old, weighs 165 pounds, and has had eight years' experience.
    This applicant is six feet in height, <u>is</u> 28 years old, weighs 165 pounds, and has had eight years' experience. *Prl*

24. While _ reading the report, a gust of wind came through the window, blowing papers all over the room.
    While <u>she</u> was reading the report, a gust of wind came through the window, blowing papers all over the room. *Dng*

25. The sprinkler system <u>has been</u> checked on July 1 and September 3.
    The sprinkler system <u>was</u> checked on July 1 and September 3. *Tns 5*

APPENDIX

Physical Presentation of Letters, Memos, and Reports

The appearance of a letter, memo, or report plays a significant role in communicating the message. Attractively presented messages reflect favorably on the writer and the writer's company. They give an impression of competence and care; and they build credibility for the writer. Their attractiveness tells the readers that the writer thinks they are important and deserving of a good-looking document. It reflects the good business etiquette of the writer. On the other hand, sloppy work reflects unfavorably on the writer, the company, and the message itself. Thus, you should want your messages to be attractively displayed.

Currently, the writer has better control over the display in print and portable document format (pdf) than in email and hypertext markup language (html). However, as applications migrate to html output and as more browsers and email programs display standardized html similarly, the writer will gain better control over these electronic displays, too. The material presented here will help you present your documents attractively and appropriately in whichever medium you choose.

Advances in word processing have finally relieved us of much of the tedious, repetitive tasks involved in presenting documents. Yesterday's hot feature in word processing software was a feature called styles. Styles allowed writers to define and apply a set of commands or keystrokes to a single style just once and then reuse the style. Writers could format a level-one heading once and reuse its style each time they needed to format a level-one heading. Also, if a writer decided to change the level-one formatting, only the style needed to be changed, for the software automatically changed all occurrences linked to the styles. While styles let writers create formatting for use anywhere within a document, today's automated formatting with interactive assistants help you create a variety of documents.

In addition to creating a professional image consistently, companies that use automated formatting usually are more productive. Not only will the company save time formatting documents, but the assistants also can act as prompts to the writer. This can help ensure that all components are included. Most major word processors include automated formatting for a full range of documents and formats can be customized to serve the precise needs of a business. The formats can include text, graphics, macros, styles, keyboard assignments, and custom toolbars.

Several word processors help users create custom formats from existing documents. The user simply identifies the document and the software will build the format, a process similar to reverse engineering that's long been part of manufacturing.

Furthermore, automated formatting is easy to use. Both Word and WordPerfect use *wizards* or *experts* to lead one through the creation of most kinds of business documents. This is especially helpful for the first time one creates a document and for those documents that one creates infrequently. Figures B.1 and B.2 illustrate the process of creating a letter using the *wizard* and the *expert* tools. Notice that the writer simply fills in text, clicks buttons, or checks boxes or radio buttons.

BASICS FOR ALL DOCUMENT PREPARATION

To understand formats most effectively, you should know the basic components and how they are used for the documents you create. These basic components are presented here after a discussion of elements that are common to all documents—layout, type, and media.

LAYOUT. Common layout decisions involve grids, spacing, and margins. Grids are the non-printed horizontal and vertical lines that determine placement of your document on the page. They allow you to plan the placement of your text and graphics on the page for consistency. The examples shown in Figure B.3 illustrate the placement of text on two-, three-, and six-column grids. You can readily see how important it is to plan for this element.

To make your document look its best, you must consider both external and internal spacing. External spacing is the white space—the space some never think about carefully. Just as volume denotes importance in writing, white space denotes importance. Surrounding text or a graphic with white spaces sets it apart, emphasizing it to the reader. Used effectively, white space has also been shown to increase the readability of your documents, giving your readers' eyes a rest. Ideally, white space should be a careful part of the design of your document.

As discussed in Chapter 16, internal spacing refers to both vertical and horizontal spacing. The spacing between letters on a line is called kerning. With word processing software, you can adjust how close the letters are to each other. This software also allows you to adjust how close the lines

FIGURE B.1 These Steps Are Followed in Creating a Basic Business Letter Using Microsoft Word's Letter Wizard   Step 1

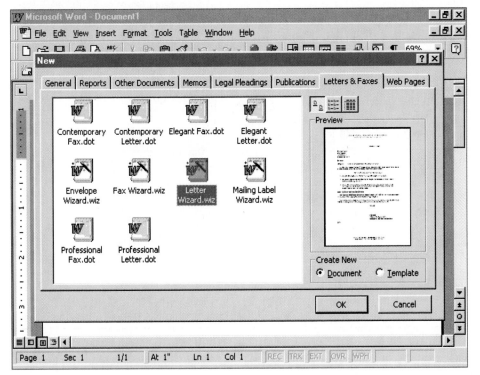

are to each other vertically, called leading. Currently, many still refer to spacing in business documents as single or double spacing. However, this is a carryover from the typewriter era when a vertical line space was always ⅙ inch or when six lines equaled an inch. Today's software and hardware allow you to control this aspect of your document as well. Deciding on the best spacing to use de-

Letter Wizard - Step 2 of 4

Letter Format | Recipient Info | Other Elements | Sender Info

Information about the person you are sending a letter to.

Click here to use Address Book:

Recipient's name: Ms. Cheri Orwig

Delivery address: 3137 Calle Suenos NE
Rio Rancho, NM 87124-2417

Recipient Info

Enter the name, address and salutation for the person you're sending the letter to.

HINT: You can also choose a name from Address Book to automatically enter information.

Salutation

Example: Dear Mr. Jones:

Dear Ms. Orwig:

○ Informal
○ Formal
● Business
○ Other

Cancel | <Back | Next> | Finish

Letter Wizard - Step 3 of 4

Letter Format | Recipient Info | Other Elements | Sender Info

Include

☐ Reference line: RE:

☑ Mailing instructions: PERSONAL

☐ Attention: Attention:

☑ Subject: Subject: Georgia O'Keefe Museum Visit

Other Elements

Select other elements to include in your letter.

HINT: Click the arrow next to each item for a list of frequently used text.

Courtesy copies (cc)

Click here to use Address Book:

Cc: Brynn Orwig
Rosemary Lenaghan

Cancel | <Back | Next> | Finish

pends on the typeface you decide to use. In any case, you need to make a conscious decision about the spacing aspect of the layout of your documents.

Another aspect of layout is your margin settings. Ideally, you should want your document to look like a framed picture. This arrangement calls for all margins to be equal. However, some businesses

FIGURE B.1 Step 6

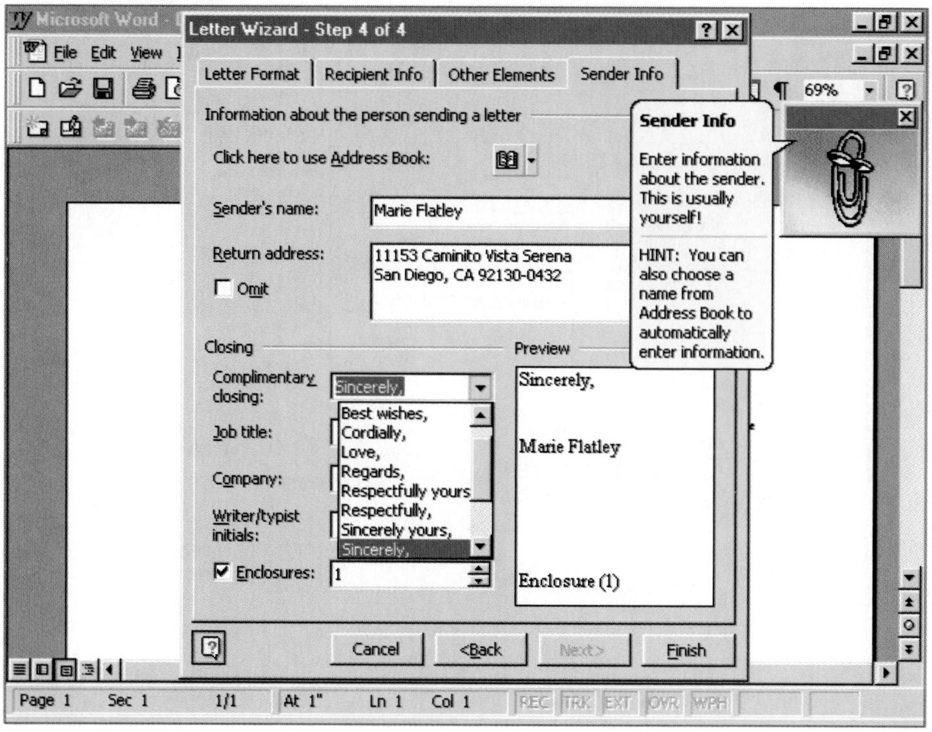

FIGURE B.1 Step 7

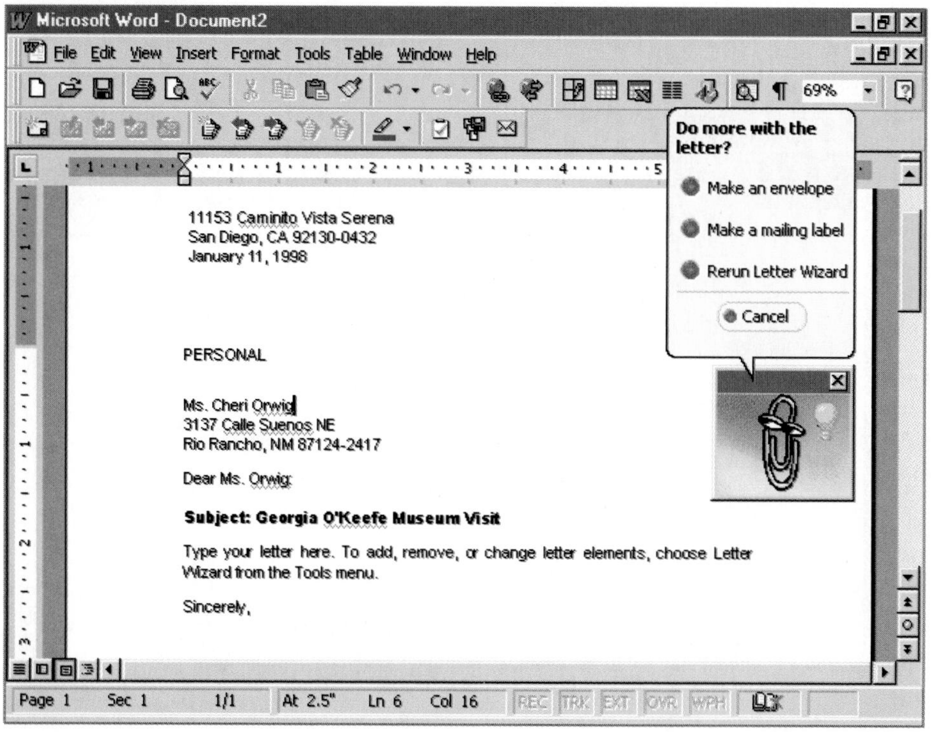

use a fixed margin on all documents regardless of their length. Some do this to line up with design features on their letterhead; others believe it increases productivity. In either case, the side margins will be equal. And with today's software you easily make your top and bottom margins equal by telling the software to center the document vertically on the page. Although all margins will not be exactly equal,

FIGURE B.1 (Concluded) Step 8

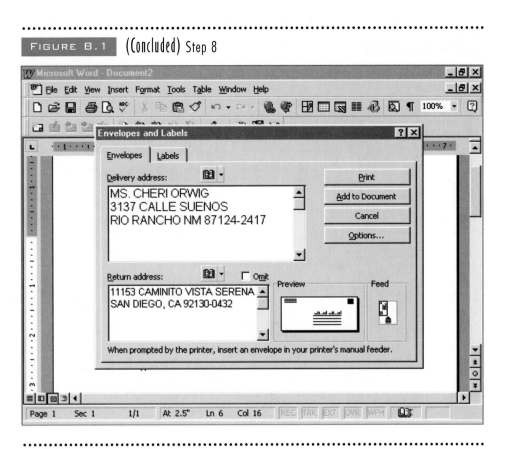

FIGURE B.2 Steps Involved in Creating a Basic Business Letter Using Corel
WordPerfect's Letter Expert   Step 1

the page will still have horizontal and vertical balance. And some word processors are adding "make it fit" experts. With this feature, the writer tells the software the number of pages, allowing the software to select such aspects as margins, font size, and spacing to fit the message to the desired space.

Today's software also has the capability to align your type at the margins or in the center. This is called *justification*. Left justification aligns every line at the left, right justification aligns every line at the right, and full justification aligns every line at both the left and the right (see Figure B.4). Unless you are using a proportional font, full justification takes the extra spaces between the last word and the right margin and distributes them across the line. This adds extra white spaces across the line,

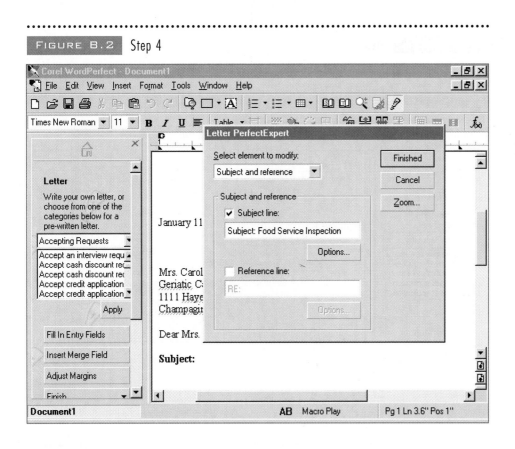

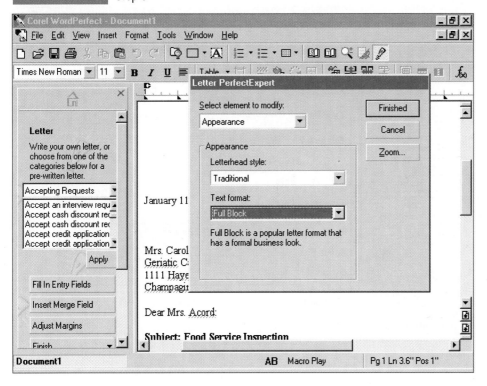

stopping most readers' eyes a bit. Therefore, it is usually best to set a left-justified margin and ignore the resulting ragged right margin. However, if your document's right margin is distracting, you may want to turn on the hyphenation feature. Your software will then hyphenate words at the end of lines, smoothing the raggedness of the right margin.

TYPE. Type is purported to influence the appearance of your document more than any other aspect. You need to make decisions on the typeface, the type style, and the type size. Typeface refers to the font or shape of the characters. Although thousands of fonts are available, they are generally classified as *serif* or *sans serif*. Serif typefaces have feet; sans serif do not. You can see this clearly in the examples that follow.

FIGURE B.2 (Concluded) Step 8

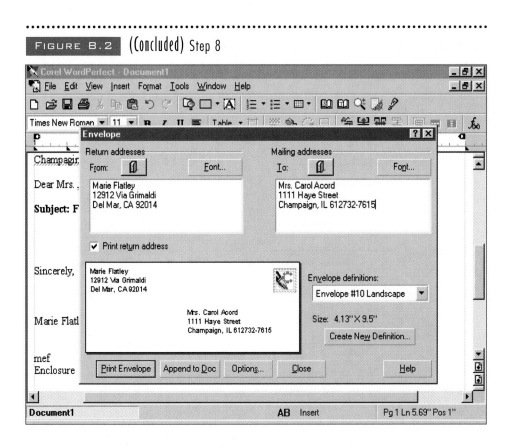

. . . .

FIGURE B.3 Layout Illustrations on Different Grids

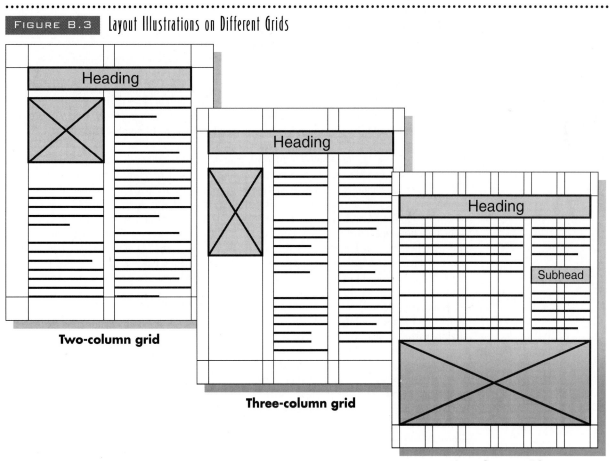

Two-column grid

Three-column grid

Six-column grid

FIGURE B.4 Different Forms of Justification

Left-justified　　　**Right-justified**　　　**Fully justified**

New Century Schoolbook and Times Roman are serif typefaces.

Helvetica and Futura are sans serif typefaces.

Since readers use the visual cues they get from the feet to form the words in their minds, they find the text of documents easier to read if a serif typeface is used. Sans serif typefaces are particularly good for headings where clear, distinct letters are important.

Type style refers to the way the typeface can be modified. The most basic styles include normal, **bold,** *italic,* and ***bold italic.*** Depending on your software and printer, you may have other options such as outline or shadow. You will usually decide to use modifications for specific reasons. For example, you may want all actions you want the reader to take to appear in boldface type. Or you may decide to apply different styles to different levels of headings. In any case, use of type styles should be planned.

Finally, you will need to decide on size of type. Type is measured in points. Characters one inch high are 72 points. While this is a standard measure, different typefaces in the same size often appear to be a different size. You need to consider your typeface in choosing size for your documents. Generally, body text is between 9 and 14 points, and headings are 15 points and larger.

MEDIA.　　The media you choose to transmit your documents also communicate. Most electronic mailboxes today are perceived as an informal medium. But using this medium tells the reader that you are a user of computer technology and may imply that you are also up to date in your business. Choosing to send your message by fax, especially a webfax gateway, may also imply your currency with the technology. Also, sending a formatted document, an html file, or a pdf document as an attached file both illustrates your currency and gives you some control over your document's display. However, because you cannot be assured of the quality of the output at the other end, your faxed or attached document may suffer in appearance due to either print quality or paper quality. By choosing paper as your medium, you will have control over appearance while relinquishing control over delivery to company and mail-delivery systems.

Today, paper is still a common choice of media. In the United States, standard business paper size is 8½ by 11 inches; in international business its measurements are metric, resulting in paper sized slightly narrower than 8½ inches and slightly longer than 11 inches. Occasionally, half-size (5½ × 8½) or executive size (7¼ × 10½) is used for short messages. Other than these standards, you have a variety of choices to make for color, weight, texture, and such.

The most conservative color choice is white. Of course, you will find that there are numerous variations of white. In addition, there are all the colors of the palette and many tints of these colors. You want your paper to represent you and your business but not to distract your reader from the message. The color you choose for the first page of your document should also be the color you use for the second and continuing pages. This is the color you would usually use for envelopes, too.

Some businesses even match the color of the paper with the color of their printer ink and the color of their postage meter ink. This, of course, communicates to the reader that the writer or company is detail conscious. Such an image would be desirable for accountants or architects where attention to detail is perceived as a positive trait.

The weight and texture of your paper also communicate. While "cheap" paper may denote control of expenses to one reader, it may denote cost cutting to another. Usually businesses use paper with a weight of 16 to 20 pounds and a rag or cotton content of 25 to 100 percent. The higher the numbers, the higher the quality. And, of course, many readers often associate a high-quality paper with a high-quality product or service.

The choice of medium to use for your documents is important because it, too, sends a message. By being aware of these subtle messages, you will be able to choose the most appropriate medium for your situation.

With the basics taken care of, now we can move on to the specifics for the letter, memo, or report.

FORM OF BUSINESS LETTERS

The layout of a letter (its shape on the page) accounts for a major part of the impression made by the appearance of the letter. A layout that is too wide, too narrow, too high, too low, or off-center may impress the reader unfavorably. The ideal letter layout is one that has the same shape as the space in which it is formed. It fits that space much as a picture fits a frame. That is, a rectangle drawn around the processed letter has the same shape as the space under the letterhead. The top border of the rectangle is the dateline, the left border is the line beginnings, the right border is the average line length, and the bottom border is the last line of the notations.

As to the format of the layout, any generally recognized one is acceptable. Some people prefer one format or another, and some people even think the format they prefer is the best. Automated formatting allows you to choose your own format preferences. Generally, the most popular formats are block, modified block, and AMS simplified. These are illustrated in Figure B.5. In all formats, single-spacing is the general rule. The standard formats included with word processors give users a choice of layout. Figure B.6 shows the standard choices available in WordPerfect.

Agreement has not been reached on all the practices for setting up the parts of the letter. The suggestions below, however, follow the bulk of authoritative opinion.

Dateline.   You should use the conventional date form, with month, day, and year (December 19, 1999). When you are using a word processor's date feature, be sure to select the appropriate one. If you insert a date code, the date will be updated each time you retrieve the letter. If you use the date text feature, you insert the date the letter was created, and it does not change when you retrieve the letter in the future. Thus, when it is important that you have a record of the date you created the letter, this is the date feature you should use. Abbreviated date forms such as 12-19-99 or Dec. 9, '99 are informal and leave unfavorable impressions on some people. Most word processors allow you to set up your preference and will use that preference when you use the date feature.

Return Address.   In most cases, your return address is printed on the letterhead or filled in on it during automated formatting.

Inside Address.   The mailing address, complete with the title of the person being addressed, makes up the inside address. Preferably, form it without abbreviations, except for commonly abbreviated words (*Dr., Mr., Mrs., Ms.*).

Attention Line. Some executives prefer to emphasize the company address rather than the individual offices. Thus, they address the letter to the company in the inside address and then use an attention line to direct the letter to a specific officer or department. The attention line is placed a double space after the inside address and a double space before the salutation. When used, the typical form of attention line is

Attention: Mr. William O'Brien, Vice President

Salutation.   The salutation you choose should be based on your familiarity with the reader and on the formality of the situation. As a general rule, remember that if the writer and the reader know each other well, the salutation may be by first name (*Dear Joan*). A salutation by last name (*Dear Mr. Baskin*) is appropriate in most cases.

If you do not know and cannot find out the name of the person to whom you are sending the letter, use a position title. By directing your letter to Director of Human Resources or Public Relations Manager, you are helping your letter reach the appropriate person.

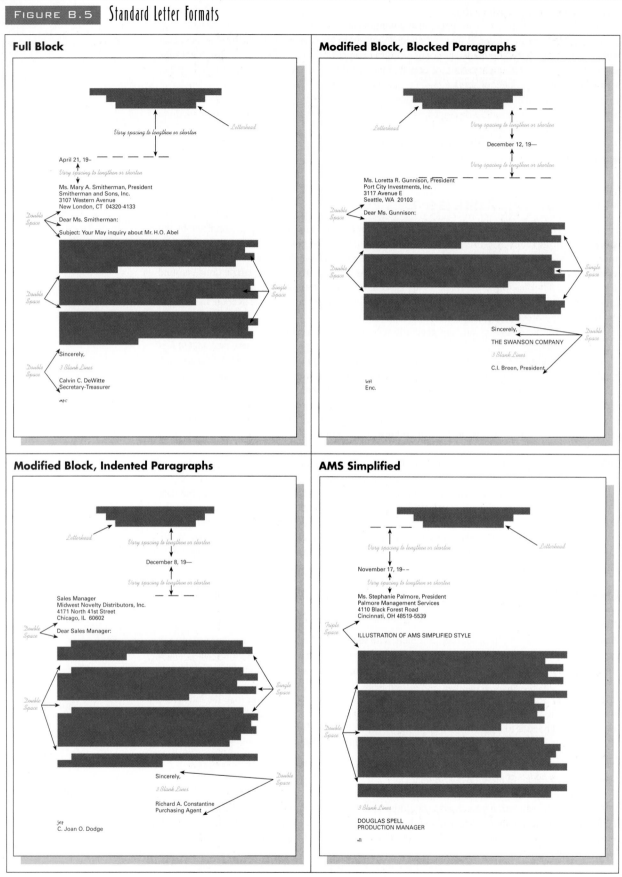

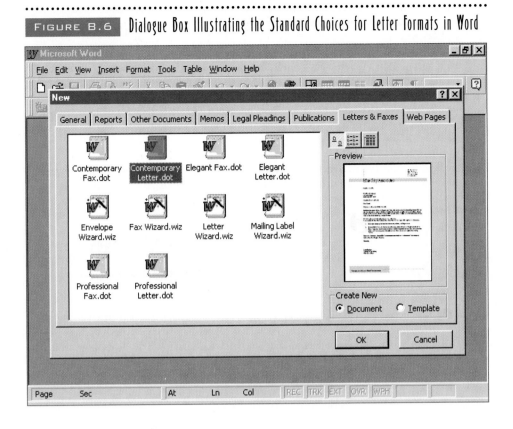

Women's preferences have sharply reduced the use of *Mrs.* and *Miss.* The question many women ask is, Why distinguish between married and single women, when we make no such distinction between married and single men? The logical solution advanced is to use *Ms.* for all women, just as *Mr.* is used for all men. If you know that the woman you are writing has another preference, however, you should adhere to that preference.

Mixed or Open Punctuation. The punctuation following the salutation and the closing is either mixed or open. Mixed punctuation employs a colon after the salutation and a comma after the complimentary close. Open punctuation, on the other hand, uses no punctuation after the salutation and none after the complimentary close. These two forms are used in domestic communication. In international communication, you may see letters with closed punctuation—punctuation distinguished by commas after the lines in the return and inside addresses and a period at the end of the complimentary close.

Subject Line. So that both the sender and the receiver may quickly identify the subject of the correspondence, many offices use the subject line in their letters. The subject line tells what the letter is about. In addition, it contains any specific identifying material that may be helpful—date of previous correspondence, invoice number, order number, and the like. It is usually placed a double space below the salutation, though some companies prefer to place it higher—often in the upper right corner of the letter layout. The block may be headed in a number of ways, of which the following are representative:

Subject: Your July 2nd inquiry about . . .
RE: Please refer to File H-320.

Second Page Heading. When the length of a letter must exceed one page, you should set up the following page or pages for quick identification. Always print such pages on plain paper (no letterhead). These two forms are the most common:

Ms. Helen E. Mann   2   May 7, 1999

Ms. Helen E. Mann
May 7, 1999
Page 2

Most standard templates automatically insert this information—name of addressee, date, and page number—on the second and following pages of your letter.

Closing.   By far the most commonly used complimentary close is *Sincerely. Sincerely yours* is also used, but in recent years the *yours* has been fading away. *Truly* (with and without the *yours*) is also used, but it has also lost popularity. Such closes as *Cordially* and *Respectfully* are appropriate when their meanings fit the writer–reader relationship. A long-standing friendship, for example, would justify *Cordially;* the writer's respect for the position, prestige, or accomplishments of the reader would justify *Respectfully.* WordPerfect's letter template has an insert feature that allows the writer to select the letter's closing (see Figure B.7).

Signature Block.   The printed signature conventionally appears on the fourth line below the closing, beginning directly under the first letter for the block form. Most templates will insert the closing. A short name and title may appear on the same line, separated by a comma. If either the name or title is long, the title appears on the following line, blocked under the name. The writer's signature appears in the space between the closing and the printed signature.

Some people prefer to have the firm name appear in the signature block. The conventional form for this arrangement places the firm name in solid capitals and blocked on the second line below the closing phrase. The typed name of the person signing the letter is on the fourth line below the firm name.

Information Notations.   In the lower left corner of the letter may appear abbreviated notations for enclosures (*Enc., Enc.*—3, and so on) and for the initials of the writer and the typist (*WEH:ga*). However, many businesses are dropping these initials since the reader does not need this information and since most word processors allow businesses to put this information in the document summary. Also, businesses are no longer including filename notations on the letters, since readers do not need them and today's word processors can find files by searching for specific content. Indications of copies prepared for other readers may also be included (*cc. William E. Sutton, Copy to William E. Sutton*). (See Figure B.2, Step 6.)

Postscripts.   Postscripts, commonly referred to as the *PS,* are placed after any notations. While rarely used in most business letters because they look like afterthoughts, they can be very effective as added punch in sales letters.

FIGURE B.7   An Illustration of the Choices for Complimentary Closings in Word

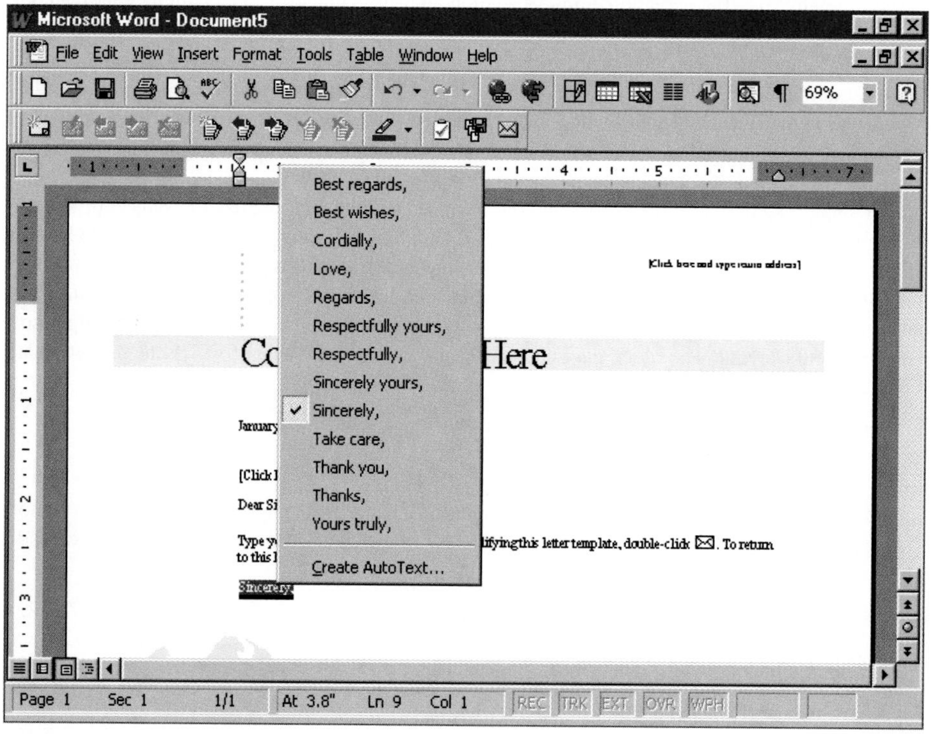

Folding.   The carelessly folded letter is off to a bad start with the reader. Neat folding will complete the planned effect by (1) making the letter fit snugly in its cover, (2) making the letter easy for the reader to remove, and (3) making the letter appear neat when opened.

The two-fold pattern is the easiest. It fits the standard sheet for the long (Number 10) envelope as well as some other envelope sizes. As shown in Figure B.8, the first fold of the two-fold pattern is from the bottom up, taking a little less than a third of the sheet. The second fold goes from the top down, taking exactly the same panel as the bottom segment. (This measurement will leave the recipient a quarter-inch thumbhold for easy unfolding of the letter.) Thus folded, the letter should be slipped into its envelope with the second crease toward the bottom and the center panel at the front of the envelope.

The three-fold pattern is necessary to fit the standard sheet into the commonly used small (Number 6¾) envelope. Its first fold is from the bottom up, with the bottom edge of the sheet riding about a quarter inch under the top edge to allow the thumbhold. (If the edges are exactly even, they are harder to separate.) The second fold is from the right side of the sheet toward the left, taking a little less than a third of the width. The third fold matches the second: from the left side toward the right, with a panel of exactly the same width. (This fold will leave a quarter-inch thumbhold at the right, for the user's convenience.) So that the letter will appear neat when unfolded, the creases should be neatly parallel with the top and sides, not at angles that produce "dog-ears" and irregular shapes. In the three-fold form, it is especially important for the side panels produced by the second and third folds to be exactly the same width; otherwise, the vertical creases are off-center and tend to throw the whole carefully planned layout off-center.

The three-fold letter is inserted into its cover with the third crease toward the bottom of the envelope and the loose edges toward the stamp end of the envelope. From habit, most recipients of business letters slit envelopes at the top and turn them facedown to extract the letter. The three-fold letter inserted as described thus gives its reader an easy thumbhold at the top of the envelope to pull it out by and a second one at the top of the sheet for easy unfolding of the whole.

Envelope Address.   So that optical character recognition (OCR) equipment may be used in sorting mail, the U.S. Postal Service requests that all envelopes be typed as follows (see Figure B.9):

· ·

FIGURE B.8 Two Ways of Folding and Inserting Letters (See Text Descriptions for Dimensions)

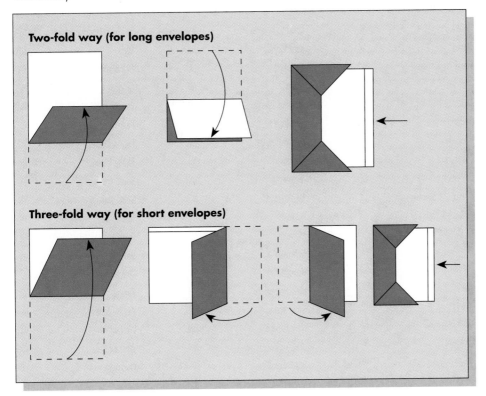

Form for Addressing Envelopes Recommended by the U.S. Postal Service

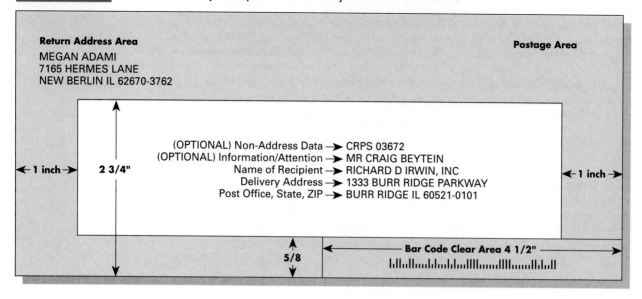

1. Place the address in the scannable area as shown in the white box in Figure B.9. Best to use a sans serif font in 10 to 12 points.
2. Use a block address format.
3. Single-space.
4. Use all uppercase letters (capitals). While today's OCR equipment can read lowercase, the post office prefers uppercase.
5. Do not use punctuation, except for the hyphen in the nine-digit zip code.
6. Use the two-letter abbreviations for the U.S. states and territories and the Canadian provinces.

   Use other address abbreviations as shown in the most recent edition of the Post Office Directory (see www.usps.com). When sending to a foreign country, include only the country name in uppercase on the bottom line.

States and Possessions of the United States

Alabama	AL	Kansas	KS	Northern Mariana Islands	MP
Alaska	AK	Kentucky	KY	Ohio	OH
American Samoa	AS	Louisiana	LA	Oklahoma	OK
Arizona	AZ	Maine	ME	Oregon	OR
Arkansas	AR	Marshall Islands	MH	Palau	PW
California	CA	Maryland	MD	Pennsylvania	PA
Colorado	CO	Massachusetts	MA	Puerto Rico	PR
Connecticut	CT	Michigan	MI	Rhode Island	RI
Delaware	DE	Minnesota	MN	South Carolina	SC
District of Columbia	DC	Mississippi	MS	South Dakota	SD
Federated States of Micronesia	FM	Missouri	MO	Tennessee	TN
		Montana	MT	Texas	TX
Florida	FL	Nebraska	NE	Utah	UT
Georgia	GA	Nevada	NV	Vermont	VT
Guam	GU	New Hampshire	NH	Virginia	VA
Hawaii	HI	New Jersey	NJ	Virgin Islands	VI
Idaho	ID	New Mexico	NM	Washington	WA
Illinois	IL	New York	NY	West Virginia	WV
Indiana	IN	North Carolina	NC	Wyoming	WY
Iowa	IA	North Dakota	ND		

Canadian Provinces and Territories

Alberta	AB	Newfoundland	NF	Prince Edward Island	PE
British Columbia	BC	Northwest Territories	NT	Quebec	PQ
Manitoba	MB	Nova Scotia	NS	Saskatchewan	SK
New Brunswick	NB	Ontario	ON	Yukon Territory	YT

7. The last line of the mailing address should contain no more than 28 characters. The city should be 13 or fewer characters. Also, there should be one space between city and state; two spaces for the state or province abbreviation; two spaces between the state and zip code; and 10 characters for the zip + 4 code.

8. When the return address must be typed (it is usually printed), block it in the left corner, beginning on the second line from the top of the envelope and three spaces from the left edge of the envelope.

9. Print any on-arrival instructions ("Confidential," "Personal") four lines below the return address.

10. Place all notations for the post office ("Special Delivery") below the stamp and at least three lines above the mailing address.

FORM OF MEMORANDUMS

Memorandums (memos) have basic components in common, but their form varies widely from organization to organization. The basic components are the heading and body. The heading has four elements: *To, From, Date,* and *Subject.* These elements are arranged in various placements, but all are present.

The body of the memo is usually single-spaced with double-spacing between paragraphs. First-level headings are frequently used in memos. And notations for typist and enclosures are included just as they are in letters. An example of typical template format choices is shown in Figure B.10.

FORM OF LETTER AND MEMORANDUM REPORTS

Because letter reports are actually letters, the review of letter form presented earlier in this appendix applies to them. Memorandum reports, however, are somewhat different. The conventional memorandum form uses the introductory information: *To, From, Date, Subject.* Many large companies have stationery on which this information is printed or use standard macros, templates, or styles. The report text follows the introductory information.

FIGURE B.10 Illustration of Memo Formats in WordPerfect

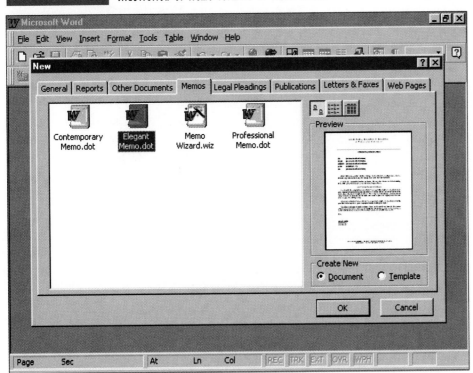

Both letter and memorandum reports may use headings (captions) to display the topics covered. The headings are usually displayed in the margins, on separate lines, and in a different style. Memorandum and letter reports may also differ from ordinary letters by having illustrations (charts, tables), an appendix, and/or a bibliography.

FORM OF FORMAL REPORTS

Like letters, formal reports should be pleasing to the eye. Well-arranged reports give an impression of competence—of work professionally done. Because such an impression can affect the success of a report, you should make good use of the following review of report form.

GENERAL INFORMATION ON REPORT PRESENTATION. Your formal reports are likely to be prepared with word processing software. You will not need to know the general mechanics of manuscript preparation if you use automated formatting such as those shown in Figure B.11. However, even if you do not have to format your own reports, you should know enough about report presentation to be sure your work is done right. You cannot be certain that your report is in good form unless you know good form.

Conventional Page Layout. For the typical text page in a report, a conventional layout appears to fit the page as a picture fits a frame (see Figure B.12). This eye-pleasing layout, however, is arranged to fit the page space not covered by the binding of the report. Thus, you must allow an extra half inch or so on the left margins of the pages of a left-bound report and at the top of the pages of a top-bound report.

Special Page Layouts. Certain text pages may have individual layouts. Pages displaying major titles (first pages of chapters, tables of contents, executive summaries, and the like) conventionally have an extra half inch or so of space at the top. Figure B.13 illustrates that some special pages can be created with templates.

Letters of transmittal and authorization may also have individual layouts. They are arranged in any conventional letter form. In the more formal reports, they may be carefully arranged to have the same general shape as the space in which they appear using the "make-it-fit" feature.

Choice of Form. It is conventional to double-space reports. This procedure stems from the old practice of double-spacing to make typed manuscripts more readable to the proofreader and printer. The

FIGURE B.11 Illustration of Report Formats in WordPerfect

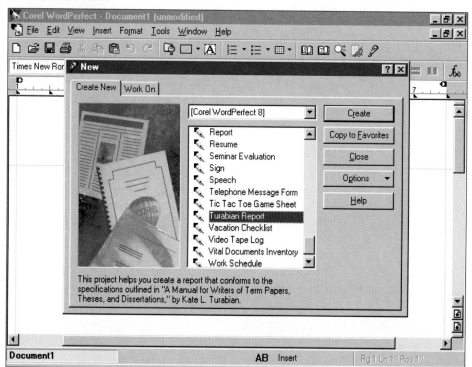

• •

FIGURE B.12   Recommended Page Layouts

Double-spaced Page

Single-spaced Page

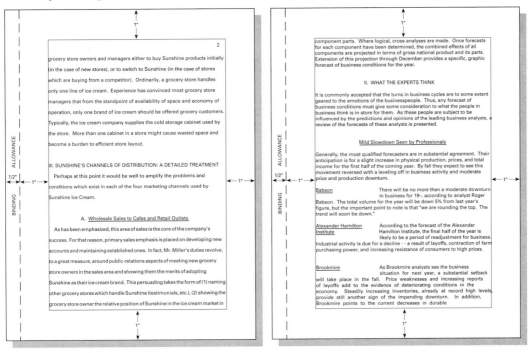

FIGURE B.13   Illustration of the Report Title Page in WordPerfect

practice has been carried over into work that is not to be reproduced. Advocates of double-spacing claim that it is easier to read than single-spacing, as the reader is less likely to lose line place.

In recent years, single-spacing has gained in popularity. The general practice is to single-space within paragraphs, double-space between paragraphs, and triple-space above all centered heads.

Supporters of single-spacing contend that it saves space and facilitates reading, as it is like the printing that most people are accustomed to reading.

Patterns of Indentation.   You should indent the paragraph beginnings of double-spaced typing. On the other hand, you should block single-spaced typing, because its paragraph headings are clearly marked by extra line spacing.

No generally accepted distance of indentation exists. Some sources suggest 4 spaces, some prefer 5, some like 8, and others like 10 and more. Any decision as to the best distance to use is up to you, though you would do well to follow the practice established in the office, group, or school for which you write the report. Whatever your selection, you should be consistent.

Numbering of Pages.   Two systems of numbers are used in numbering the pages of the written report. Arabic numerals are conventional for the text portion, normally beginning with the first page of the introduction and continuing through the appendix. Small Roman numerals are standard for the pages preceding the text. Although these prefatory pages are all counted in the numbering sequence, the numbers generally do not appear on the pages before the table of contents.

Placement of the numbers on the page varies with the binding used for the report. In reports bound at the top of the page, you should center all page numbers at the bottom of the page, a double or triple space below the layout used in the body.

For left-sided binding, you should place the numbers in the upper right corner, a double or triple space above the top line and in line with the right margin. Exception to this placement is customarily made for special-layout pages that have major titles and an additional amount of space displayed at the top. Such pages may include the first page of the report text; the executive summary; the table of contents; and, in very long and formal works, the first page of each major division or chapter. Numbers for these pages are centered a double or triple space below the imaginary line marking the bottom of the layout.

In documents printed back-to-back, page numbers are usually placed at the top of the page even with the outside margin. Today's word processing programs are capable of automatically placing page numbers this way if directed.

Display of Headings.   Headings (captions) are the titles of the parts of the report. Designed to lead the readers through the report, they must show at a glance the importance of the information they cover.

In showing heading importance by position, you have many choices. If your software and printer make available a variety of typefaces, you can select various progressions of font sizes and styles to fit your needs. Your goal, of course, should be to select forms that show differences in importance at first glance—much as is done in the printing of this book.

You can use any combination of form and position that clearly shows the relative importance of the headings. The one governing rule to follow in considering form and positions of headings is that no heading may have a higher-ranking form or position than any of the headings of a higher level. But you can use the same form for two successive levels of headings as long as the positions vary. And you can use the same position for two successive levels as long as the forms vary. You can also skip over any of the steps in the progression of form or position. If you had selected the *Chicago Manual of Style* format, the headings would be set up for you (see Figure B.14).

MECHANICS AND FORMAT OF THE REPORT PARTS.   The foregoing notes on physical appearance apply generally to all parts of the report. But special notes are needed for the individual construction of the specific report pages. So that you may be able to get and follow these notes, a part-by-part review of the physical construction of the formal report follows.

Title Fly.   The title fly contains only the report title. Print the title in the highest-ranking form used in the report, and double-space it if you need more than one line. If your report cover has a window for the title to show through, make sure you place the title in the window.

Title Page.   The title page normally contains three main areas of identification, although some forms present this information in four or five spots on the page. In the typical three-spot title page, the first area of identification covers the report title. Preferably, use the highest-ranking form used in the report.

The second area of identification names the individual (or group) for whom the report has been prepared. Precede it with an identifying phrase indicating that individual's role in the report, such as "Prepared for" or "Submitted to." In addition to the recipient's name, include the identification of the

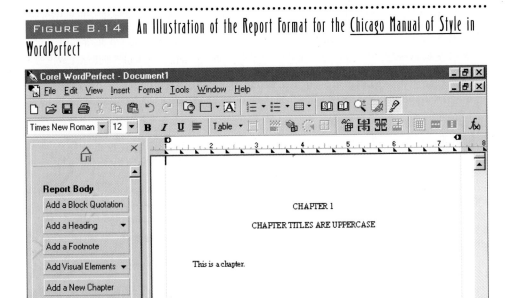

recipient by title or role, company, and address, particularly if you and the recipient are from different companies.

The third area of identification names you, the writer of the report. It is also preceded by an identifying phrase—"Prepared by," "Written by," or similar wording describing your role in the report—and it may also identify title or role, company, and address. As a final part of this area of information, you may include the date of publication. Placement of the three areas of identification on the page should make for an eye-pleasing arrangement. Most word processing software will help you place this page vertically.

Letters of Transmittal and Authorization.   As their names imply, the letters of transmittal and authorization are actual letters. You should print them in any acceptable letter form. If the report is important, you should give the letter an ideal layout. An ideal layout is one that fits the letter into a rectangle of the same shape as the space within which it is printed.

Acknowledgments.   When you are indebted to the assistance of others, it is fitting that you acknowledge the indebtedness somewhere in the report. If this number is small, you may acknowledge them in the introduction of the report or in the letter of transmittal. In the rare event that you need to make numerous acknowledgments, you may construct a special section for this purpose. This section, bearing the simple title "Acknowledgments," has the same layout as any other text page in which a title is displayed.

Table of Contents.   The table of contents is the report outline in its polished, finished form. It lists the major report headings with the page numbers on which those headings appear. Although not all reports require a table of contents, one should be a part of any report long enough to make such a guide helpful to the readers. Most word processors are capable of generating a table of contents—complete with page numbers.

The table of contents is appropriately titled "Contents" or "Table of Contents." The layout of the table of contents is the same as that used for any other report page with a title display. Below the title, set up two columns. One contains the outline headings, generally beginning with the first report part following the table of contents. You have the option of including or leaving out the outline letters and numbers.

In the table of contents, as in the body of the report, you may vary the form to distinguish different heading levels. But the form variations of the table of contents need not be the same as those used in the text of the report. The highest level of headings is usually distinguished from the other levels, and sometimes typeface differences are used to distinguish second-level headings from lower-level headings. It is acceptable to show no distinction by using plain capitals and lowercase for all levels of headings.

Table of Illustrations.   The table (list) of illustrations may be either a continuation of the table of contents or a separate table. Such a table lists the graphics presented in the report in much the same way as the table of contents lists the report parts.

In constructing this table, head it with an appropriately descriptive title, such as "Table of Charts and Illustrations," or "List of Tables and Charts," or "Table of Figures." If you place the table of illustrations on a separate page, layout for this page is the same as that for any other text page with a displayed title. And if you place it as a continued part of the table of contents, you should begin it after the last contents entry.

The table consists of two columns—the first for the graphics titles and the second for the pages on which the graphics appear. Head the second column "Page." And connect the two columns by leader lines of spaced periods. The periods should be aligned vertically. Line spacing in the table of illustrations is optional, again depending on the line lengths of the entries. Preceding the title of each entry, place that entry's number; and should these numbers be Roman or otherwise require more than one digit, align the digits at the right. If your report contains two or more illustration types (tables, charts, maps, and the like) and you have given each type its own numbering sequence, you should list each type separately.

References (or Bibliography).   Anytime you use another's idea, you need to give credit to the source. Sometimes business writers interweave this credit into the narrative of their text. But often these sources are listed in a reference or bibliography section at the end of the report. Typically, these sections are organized alphabetically, but they can also be organized by date, subject, or type of source.

The format and content of citations vary by style used as described in Appendix E. Among the widely used formats are *The Chicago Manual of Style, The MLA Style Sheet,* and the *Publication Manual of the American Psychological Association.* The content for most items on the list of references is similar to the footnote. This format can be set up by the report format.

Need to Improvise.   The foregoing review covers most of the problems of form you will encounter in preparing reports. But there will be others. When you encounter other problems, you simply improvise an arrangement that appears right to the eye. After all, what appears right to the eye is the basis of conventional report form.

C

A Grading Checklist for Letters

THE OPENING

O Ind *Indirectness needed.*   This opening gets to the goal too fast.

O Dir *Directness needed.*   This opening is too slow in getting to the goal.

O Qual *Quality.*   This opening could be improved by making it more (1) on subject, (2) logical, or (3) interesting.

COVERAGE

C Inc *Incomplete.*   You have not covered all the important information.

C Ex *Excess information.*   You have included more information than is needed.

C Exp *Explanation.*   More or better explanation is needed here.

C Id *Identification.*   Completely identify the situation, either in the letter or in a subject line.

ENDING

E AC *Action close.*   A drive for action is appropriate in this situation.

E AC S *Action strong.*   This action drive is too strong.

E AC W *Action weak.*   This action drive is too weak.

E IT *Individually tailored.*   Make your close fit the one case.

E OS *Off subject.*   An off-subject close is best for this case. These words recall unpleasant things in the reader's mind.

TECHNIQUE

Adp *Adaptation.*   Your words should be adapted to the one reader. Here yours are (1) above or (2) below your reader.

Awk *Awkward word arrangement.*

Bky *Bulky arrangement.*   Make your paragraphs more inviting by breaking them into shorter units of thought.

Chop *Choppy writing.*   A succession of short sentences produces an irritating effect.

DL *Dull writing.*   Bring your writing back to life with vivid, concrete words.

Emp + *Emphasis, too much.*

Emp − *Emphasis, too little.*   Here you have given too much or too little (as marked) emphasis by (1) placement, (2) volume, or (3) words or mechanical means.

Intp *Interpretation.*   Do more than just present facts. In this situation, something more is needed. Make the data meaningful in terms of the reader's situation.

Los *Loose writing.*   Use words more economically. Write concisely.

Ord *Order of presentation.*   This information does not fall into a logical order. The information is mixed up and confusing.

RS *Rubber-stamp expression.*   Timeworn words from the past have no place in modern business writing.

Trans *Transition.*   Abrupt shift of thought here.

EFFECT

Conv *Conviction.*   This is less convincing than it should be. More fact or a more skillful use of words is needed.

GW *Goodwill.*   The letter needs more goodwill. Try to make your words convey friendliness. Here you tend to be too dull and matter-of-fact.

Hur *Hurried treatment.*   Your coverage of the problem appears to be hurried. Thus, it tends to leave an effect of routine or brusque treatment. Conciseness is wanted, of course, but you must not sacrifice your letter's objectives for it.

Log *Logic.*   Is this really logical? Would you do it this way in business?

Neg *Negative effect.*   By word or implication, this part is more negative than it should be.

Pers + *Too persuasive.*   Your words are too high-pressure for this situation.

Pers − *Not persuasive enough.*   More persuasion, by either words or facts, would help your letter.

Ton *Tone of the words.*   Your words create a bad impression on the reader. Words work against the success of your letter if they talk down, lecture, argue, accuse, and the like.

YVP *You-viewpoint.*   More you-viewpoint wording and adaptation would help the overall effect of your letter.

D

A Grading Checklist for Reports

The following checklist should serve both as a guide for preparing reports and as a tool for grading reports. (Your instructor can use the symbols to mark errors.) The checklist covers all types of reports—from simple memorandums to long analytical reports. For each report type, you need only use the items that apply.

TITLE (T)

T 1 Complete? The title should tell what the report contains. Use the five Ws and 1 H as a check for completeness (*who, what, where, when, why*—sometimes *how*).

T 2 Too long. This title is longer than it needs to be. Check it for uneconomical wording or unnecessary information.

LETTER OF TRANSMITTAL (LT)

LT 1 More directness is needed in the opening. The letter should present the report right away.

LT 2 Content of the letter needs improvement. Comments that help the readers understand or appreciate the report are appropriate.

LT 3 Do not include findings unless the report has no executive summary.

LT 4 A warm statement of your attitude toward the assignment is appropriate—often expected. You either do not make one, or the one you make is weak.

LT 5 A friendlier, more conversational style would improve the letter.

EXECUTIVE SUMMARY (ES)

ES 1 (*If the direct order is assigned*) Begin directly—with a statement of findings, conclusion, or recommendation.

ES 2 (*If the indirect order is assigned*) Begin with a brief review of introductory information.

ES 3 The summary of highlights should be in proportion and should include major findings, analyses, and conclusions. Your coverage here is (*a*) scant or (*b*) too detailed.

ES 4 Work for a more interesting and concise summary.

ORGANIZATION—OUTLINE (O)

O 1 This organization plan is not the best for this problem. The main sections should form a logical solution to the problem.

O 2 The order of the parts of this outline is not logical. The parts should form a step-by-step route to the goal.

O 3 Do not let one major section account for the entire body of the report.

O 4 One-item subdivisions are illogical. You cannot divide an area without coming up with at least two parts.

O 5 These parts overlap. Each part should be independent of the other parts. Although some repetition and relating of parts may be desirable, outright overlap is a sign of bad organization.

O 6 More subparts are needed here. The subparts should cover all the information in the major part.

O 7 This subpart does not fit logically under this major part.

O 8 These parts are not equal in importance. Do not give them equal status in the outline.

O 9 (*If talking headings are assigned.*) These headings do not talk well.

O 10 Coordinate headings should be parallel in grammatical structure.

O 11 This (these) heading(s) is (are) too long.

O 12 Vary the wording of the headings to avoid monotonous repetition.

INTRODUCTION (I)

I 1 This introduction does not cover exactly what the readers need to know. Although the readers' needs vary by problem, these topics are usually important: (*a*) origin of the problem, (*b*) statement of the problem, (*c*) methods used in researching the problem, and (*d*) preview of the presentation.

I 2 Coverage of this part is (*a*) scant or (*b*) too detailed.

I 3 Important information has been left out.

I 4 Findings, conclusions, and other items of information are not a part of the introduction.

COVERAGE (C)

C 1 The coverage here is (*a*) scant or (*b*) too detailed.

C 2 More analysis is needed here.

C 3 Here you rely too heavily on a graphic. The text should cover the important information.

C 4 Do not lose sight of the goal of the report. Relate the information to the problem.

C 5 Clearly distinguish between fact and opinion. Label opinion as opinion.

C 6 Your analyses and conclusions need the support of more fact and authoritative opinion.

WRITING (W)

W 1 This writing should be better adapted to your readers. It appears to be (*a*) too heavy or (*b*) too light for your readers.

W 2 Avoid the overuse of passive voice.

W 3   Work for more conciseness. Try to cut down on words without sacrificing meaning.

W 4   For this report, more formal writing is appropriate. You should write consistently in impersonal (third-person) style.

W 5   A more personal style is appropriate for this report. That is, you should use more personal pronouns (*I*'s, *we*'s, *you*'s).

W 6   The change in thought is abrupt here.

(*a*)   Between major parts, use introductions, summaries, and conclusions to guide the readers' thinking.

(*b*)   Use transitional words, phrases, or sentences to relate minor parts.

W 7   Your paragraphing is questionable. Check the paragraphs for unity. Look for topic sentences.

GRAPHICS (GA)

GA 1   You have (*a*) not used enough graphics or (*b*) used too many graphics.

GA 2   For the information presented, this graphic is (*a*) too large or (*b*) too small.

GA 3   This type of graphic is not the best for presenting the information.

GA 4   Place the graphic near the place where its contents are discussed.

GA 5   The text must tell the story; so don't just refer the reader to a figure or table and let it go at that.

GA 6   The appearance of this graphic needs improvement. This may be your best work, but it does not make a good impression on the readers.

GA 7   Refer the readers to the graphics at the times that the readers should look at them.

GA 8   Interpret the patterns in the graphic. Note central tendencies, exceptions, ranges, trends, and such.

GA 9   Refer to the graphics incidentally, in subordinate parts of sentences that comment on their content (for example, ". . . as shown in Figure 5" or "see Figure 5").

LAYOUT AND MECHANICS (LM)

LM 1   The layout of this page is (*a*) too fat, (*b*) too skinny, or (*c*) too low, high, or off-center (as marked).

LM 2   Neat? Smudges and light type detract from the message.

LM 3   Make the margins straighter. The raggedness here offends the eye.

LM 4   The spacing here needs improvement. (*a*) Too much space here. (*b*) Not enough space here.

LM 5   Your page numbering is not the best. See the text for specific instructions.

LM 6   This page appears (*a*) choppy or (*b*) heavy.

LM 7   Your selection of type placement and style for the headings is not the best.

LM 8   This item or form is not generally acceptable.

A P P E N D I X E

Documentation and the Bibliography

In writing reports, you will frequently use information from other sources. Because this material is not your own, you may need to acknowledge it. Whether and how you should acknowledge it are the subject of this brief review.

WHEN TO ACKNOWLEDGE

Your decision to acknowledge or not acknowledge a source should be determined mainly on the basis of giving credit where credit is due. If you are quoting the words of another, you must give credit. If you are paraphrasing (using someone else's ideas in your own words), you should give credit unless the material covered is general knowledge.

HOW TO ACKNOWLEDGE

Acknowledge sources by citing them in the text, using one of a number of reference systems. Three of the most commonly used systems are the Chicago (*The Chicago Manual of Style*), MLA (Modern Language Association), and APA (American Psychological Association). Although all are similar, they differ somewhat in format, as you will see in the following pages. Because the Chicago system is the most widely used in business books and journals, we will review it first. Then we will illustrate the MLA and APA systems to note primary differences.

After you have selected a system, you must choose a method of acknowledgment. Two methods are commonly used in business: (1) parenthetic author–date references within the text, and (2) footnote references. A third method, endnote references, is sometimes used, although it appears to be losing favor. Only the first two are discussed here.

THE PARENTHETIC AUTHOR–DATE METHOD. In recent years, the author–date method has become the most popular reference method in business. It involves placing the author's last name and year of publication in parentheses immediately following the material cited:

(Calahan 1998)

The reference is keyed to a list of all the publications cited (a bibliography), which appears at the end of the report (see discussion of the bibliography in a following section). If specific page numbers are needed, they follow the date:

(Calahan 1998, 117–18)

The last names are listed of works with two or three authors:

(Smith, Corley, and Doran 1997, 31)

For works with more than three authors, et al. is used:

(Clovis et al. 1995)

When no author is listed, as in unsigned publications issued by a company, government agency, labor union, or such, the author's name is the organization name:

(U.S. Department of Labor 1996)

(American Federation of Labor 1995, 31)

As noted earlier, these references are keyed to a bibliography that appears at the end of the report. To find the details of a reference, the reader turns to the bibliography and traces the reference through the alphabetical listing. For the reference (Sanders 1996), for example, the reader would find Sanders in its alphabetical place. If more than one publication by Sanders is listed, the reader would refer to the one written in 1996.

THE FOOTNOTE METHOD. The traditional method of acknowledging sources (preferred in the humanities) is by footnotes; that is, the references are placed at the bottom of the page and are keyed to the text material by superscripts (raised Arabic numbers). The numbering sequence of the superscripts is consecutive—by page, by chapter, or by the whole work. The footnotes are placed inside the page layout, single-spaced, and indented or blocked just as the text is typed.

Although footnote form varies from one source to another, one generally accepted procedure is presented here. It permits two structures: an abbreviated structure that is used with a bibliography in the report and a structure that is used when the report has no bibliography.

In the abbreviated structure (not accepted by everyone), the footnote reference needs to contain only these parts: (1) author's surname; (2) title of the article, bulletin, or book; and (3) page number.

[3] Wilson, *The Report Writer's Guide,* 44 (book reference).
[4] Allison, "Making Routine Reports Talk," 71 (periodical reference).

For the complete reference (usually preferred), the descriptive points are listed in the order mentioned below. Capitals are used only with proper nouns, and abbreviations are acceptable if used consistently.

In the following lists, all the items that could be placed in each type of entry are named in the order of arrangement. Items that are unavailable or unimportant should be passed over. In other words, the following lists give, in order, all the possible items in an entry. The items listed should be used as needed.

Book Entry

1. *Superscript.* Arabic numeral keyed to the text reference and placed before the first part of the entry without spacing.

2. *Name of the author, in normal order.* If a source has two or three authors, all are named. If a source has more than three authors, the name of the first author followed by the Latin et al. or its English equivalent "and others" may be used.

3. *Capacity of the author.* Needed only when the person named is actually not the author of the book but an editor, compiler, or the like.

4. *Chapter name.* Necessary only in the rare instances in which the chapter title helps the reader find the source.

5. *Book title.* Book titles are placed in italics. In typewritten work, italics are indicated by underscoring.

6. *Edition.*

7. *Location of publisher.* If more than one city is listed on the title page, the one listed first should be used. If the population exceeds half a million, the name of the city is sufficient; otherwise, the city and state (or province) are best given.

8. *Publishing company.*

9. *Date.* Year of publication. If revised, year of latest revision.

10. *Page or pages.* Specific page or inclusive pages on which the cited material is found.

The following are examples of book entries:

A TYPICAL BOOK:

[1] Cindy Burford, Aline Culberson, and Peter Dykus, *Writing for Results,* 4th ed., New York: Charles Storm Publishing Company, 1995, 17–18.

A BOOK WRITTEN BY A STAFF OF WRITERS UNDER THE DIRECTION OF AN EDITOR (chapter title is considered helpful):

[2] W. C. Butte and Ann Buchanan, eds., "Direct Mail Advertising," *An Encyclopedia of Advertising,* New York: Binton Publishing Company, 1996, 99.

A BOOK WRITTEN BY A NUMBER OF COAUTHORS:

[3] E. Butler Cannais et al., *Anthology of Public Relations,* New York: Warner-Bragg, Inc., 1998, 137.

Periodical Entry

1. *Superscript.*

2. *Author's name.* Frequently, no author is given. In such cases, the entry may be skipped, or if it is definitely known to be anonymous, the word *anonymous* may be placed in the entry.

3. *Article title.* Typed within quotation marks.

4. *Periodical title.* Set in italics, which are indicated by underscoring.

5. *Publication identification.* Volume number in Arabic numerals followed by date of publication (month and year or season and year). Volume number is not needed if complete (day, month, year) date is given. See examples below for punctuation differences with and without complete date.

6. *Page or pages.*

Examples of periodical entries are shown below:

[1] Mildred C. Kinnig, "A New Look at Retirement," *Modern Business,* July 31, 1997, 31–32.
[2] William O. Schultz, "How One Company Improved Morale," *Business Leader,* August 31, 1995, 17.
[3] Mary Mitchell, "Report Writing Aids," *ABC Bulletin* 46 (October 1991): 13.

Newspaper Article

1. *Superscript.*

2. *Source description.* If article is signed, give author's name. Otherwise, give description of article, such as "Associated Press dispatch" or "Editorial."

3. *Main head of article.* Subheads not needed.

4. *Newspaper title.* City and state (or province) names inserted in brackets if place names do not appear in newspaper title. State (or province) names not needed in case of very large cities, such as New York, Toronto, and Los Angeles.

5. *Date of publication.*

6. *Page* (p.) *and column* (col.). May be used—optional.

The following are typical newspaper article entries:

[1] Associated Press dispatch, "Rival Unions Sign Pact," *Morning Advocate* [Baton Route, Louisiana], September 3, 1997.

[2] Editorial, "The North Moves South," *Austin* [Texas] *American,* February 3, 1996, p. 2-A, col. 3.

Letters or Documents

1. *Nature of communication.*

2. *Name of writer.* ⎡*With identification by title and*⎤
3. *Name of recipient.* ⎣*organization where helpful.*⎦

4. *Date of writing.*

5. *Where filed.*

An example of an entry citing a letter is given below:

[1] Letter from J. W. Wells, president, Wells Equipment Co., to James Mattoch, secretary-treasurer, Southern Industrialists, Inc., June 10, 1990, filed among Mr. Mattoch's personal records.

■ You could use both format methods to cite electronic sources. The parenthetic author–date method is more practical.

ELECTRONIC DOCUMENTATION. Theoretically, you could use both of the previous two methods to document facts from electronic sources of information within the text of business reports. In all likelihood, however, you will find the parenthetic author–date method more practical as you acknowledge electronic sources. To cite an entry, you would follow the format given earlier: (Jones

1997). If you should need to cite a specific part of an electronic source and no page numbers are given, you should refer to the paragraph(s) in the citation: (Jones 1997, paragraph 10). The bibliography entry would tie to these in-text citations with more elaborate identifying information.

Because research using electronic media is recent, standards for referencing electronic sources are in the development stage. At present, these emerging standards are often inconsistent. Thus, universal formats for referencing electronic media do not exist.

Despite these inconsistencies, two printed sources are the most authoritative on the subject: (1) Li and Cranes's 1996 *Electronic Style: A Guide to Citing Electronic Information Sources* and (2) the 1994 *Publication Manual of the American Psychological Association.* Drawing from Li and Crane, the APA style guide, and several web sites, the following suggestions for referencing electronic sources are given. They are presented by category and by example first. Then guidelines for documenting electronic sources are offered.

- Electronic documentation is new. Standards are not consistent.

- Examples illustrate how to acknowledge electronic sources. Guidelines will follow examples.

Traditional Sources

Individual Works

Smith, A. (1776). *An inquiry into the nature and causes of the wealth of nations* [Online]. Available: http://www.bibliomania.com/NonFiction/Smith/Wealth/index.html [1997, September 15].

Parts of Works

Smith, A. (1776). Book 3—Progress of opulence of different nations. In *An inquiry into the nature and causes of the wealth of nations* [Online]. Available: http://www.bibliomania.com/NonFiction/Smith/Wealth/Bk3Chap01.html [1997, April 25].

Industrial Revolution. (1995). In *Britannica Online: Macropaedia* [Online]. Available: http://www.eb.com:282/cgibin/g?keywords=industrial+revolution+&hits=10 [1997, April 24].

Journal Articles

Pettit, J., Goris, J., Vaught, B. (1997). An Examination of organizational communication as a moderator of the relationship between job performance and job satisfaction. *Journal of Business Communication* [CD-ROM], *34* (1), 81–98. Available: telnet: http://db.texshare.edu/ovidweb/ovidweb.cgi?T=selCit&F=all&A=display&ST=2&R=7&totalCit=8&D= info97&S=1048311 [1997, April 20].

Mabry, E. A. (1997). Framing flames: The structure of argumentative messages on the net. *Journal of Computer-Mediated Communication* [Online], *2*, (4) 55 paragraphs. Available: http://207.201.161.120/jcmc/vol2/issue4/mabry.html [1997, April 28].

Magazine Articles

Schwartz, N. (1997, May 12). 6 ways to win. *Fortune Text Edition* [Online], 43 paragraphs. Available: http://www.pathfinder.com/@@G1fRdQcAs7JnroqH/fortune/1997/970512/inv.html [1997, April 27].

Flannery, T.P., Hofrichter, D.A., Platten, P.E. (1996). People, Performance, and Pay. *Sternbusiness Magazine* [Online], *3*, (3), 28 paragraphs. Available: http://equity.stern.nyu.edu/Webzine/Sternbusiness/Fall96/ppp.html [1997, April 24].

Newspaper Articles

McMorris, F. (1997, February 20). Legal beat: Age-bias suits may become harder to prove. *The Wall Street Journal* [CD-ROM], Sec B, p.1 (953 words). Available: Proquest Wall Street Journal Ondisc January 1995–February 1997/Accession Number 970220000159 [1997, April 26].

Hamilton, M. (1997, October 1). Can BP stack up on global warming? Oil company will try trading system to cut harmful emissions. *Washington Post* [Online]. 20 paragraphs. Available: http://www.washingtonpost.com/wp-srv/WPlate/1997-10/01/0631-100197-idx.html [1997, October 1]

Informal Sources

Personal Communication

Lesikar, R. V. (lesikar@tstar.net). (1997, April 20). *Progress on Lesikar's Basic Business Communication.* Email to J. D. Pettit (jdp0009@jove.acs.unt.edu) and M. E. Flatley (marie.flatley@sdsu.edu).

Discussion List Messages

O'Flahavan, O. (1997, May 5). Research for article on business writing. *Bizcom* [Online]. Available Email: bizcom@ebbs. english.vt.edu [1997, May 5].

Other Sources

Abstracts

Stevens, J. C. (1985). *Auditing organizational communication: The Development of an instrument for measuring information gathering processes of managers* [CD-ROM]. Available: ProQuest File: Dissertion Abstracts Item: 45/09 [1997, May 5].

Databases

Research and Development Database (1996) [Online]. Washington D.C.: U.S. Census Bureau. Available: http://www.census.gov/pub/econ/www/mu1300.html [1997, April 23].

As you can see, numerous sources of information are available electronically. Like printed sources, the quality or degree of credibility can vary from one source to the next. Thus, you will need to assess the quality of any reference source before you use it in a business report. All too often, novice report writers think that an electronic source is valid and credible because it is available by computer. Such is not the case; any source of information must be assessed for quality and validity.

From the foregoing examples, we can derive some guidelines to follow for electronic documentation. Because of their evolving nature, these guidelines are general and will likely change as more thought is given to electronic information sources.

1. Use *Type of Medium* and *Available* in reference formats to describe electronic sources. The *Available* part replaces place of publication and publishers in print formats.

2. Give enough identifying information to locate the source. If you must choose between more or less information, choose more.

3. Select *Online, CD-ROM, Disk,* or *Tape* as the *Type of Medium.*

4. Select *http, ftp, gopher,* and *telnet* as the computer protocol in the *Available* part of the entry. Gopher is used presently, but it will be quickly replaced by *http.* A protocol is the set of agreed-on rules that computers use to communicate with one another.

5. Give the date you accessed the source as the last item in the reference.

6. Use the capitals-and-lowercase style for titles of magazines, journals, and newspapers. Capitalize the first letters of adjectives, adverbs, nouns, verbs, any beginning words, and any word with four or more characters.

7. Capitalize the first word; the first important word after an indirect and direct article (a, an, the); a proper noun; and the first word after a colon in titles of books and in journal, magazine, newspaper articles.

8. Italicize titles of books, journals, magazines, and newspapers.

9. Place a long electronic address on a line by itself or break it at a logical place, such as after a slash (/) or period. Do not add other punctuation marks.

10. Consult with your instructor, organization, or institution for preferences for documenting electronic sources. Often, these preferences are available electronically and will override other formats.

Because they relate directly to business reports, only APA format standards are covered here. Some, however, may prefer to use the MLA (Modern Language Association) format. Both are illustrated in the web site of Li and Crane: http://www.uvm.edu/~ncrane/estyles/.

In addition, you may want to conduct a search of the World Wide Web using one of the search engines available—Yahoo, WebCrawler, Lycos, Excite, Alta Vista, and such. You would likely want to search using the term *electronic style.*

Still another way to find current information on electronic documentation is to ask business librarians—professionals who deal with the topic regularly. You may contact them through BUSLIB-L, a free subscription service consisting of business librarians throughout the nation. By posting a question you have about electronic documentation (or other library matters), you would receive comments from a large group of library specialists. You can subscribe to BUSLIB-L by sending an email message to LISTSERV@IDBSU.IDBSU.EDU, leaving the subject line blank and typing SUBSCRIBE BUSLIB-L as the message text.

In the future, we can expect librarians to be a part of the planning and design sources of Internet information. At present, computer engineers and scientists design such sources. Thus, electronic sources do not fit established categories of human knowledge. As librarians and other user-friendly professionals become more involved in the process, we can expect information to be more accessible and identifiable. And ways to document these sources will be more consistent.

Margin notes:

- Quality varies in all information sources. Assess sources for quality before using them.

- 10 guidelines should help you in documenting electronic sources.

- APA and MLA guidelines are available online.

- You may also use search engines.

- Or you can consult business librarians.

- They can design documents for ease of use. When this happens, referencing will become more consistent.

The types of entries discussed in the preceding paragraphs are those most likely to be used. Yet many unusual types of publications (not books or periodicals) are likely to come up. When they do, you should classify the source by the form it most closely resembles—a book or a periodical. Then you should construct the entry that describes the source most correctly. Frequently, you will need to improvise—to use your best judgment in determining the source description.

STANDARD REFERENCE FORMS.   Certain forms are conventionally used in handling repeated references in footnotes. The more common of these are the following.

Ibid., literally means "in the same place." It is used to refer the reader to the preceding footnote. The entry consists of the superscript, *ibid.*, and the page number if the page number is different as shown in these entries:

[1] Janice Smith, *How to Write the Annual Report,* Chicago: Small-Boch, Inc., 1997, 173.
[2] *Ibid.,* 143 (refers to Smith's book).

Op. cit. ("in the work cited") and *loc. cit.* ("in the place cited") also can refer to references cited earlier in the paper. But they are rarely used today. It is better to use in their place a short reference form (author's last name, title of work, date).

Other abbreviations used in footnote entries are as follows:

Abbreviation	Meaning
cf.	Compare (directs reader's attention to another passage)
cf. ante	Compare above
cf. post	Compare below
ed.	Edition
e.g.	For example
et al.	And others
et passim	And at intervals throughout the work
et seq.	And the following
f, ff.	Following page, following pages
i.e.	That is
infra	Below
l., ll.	Line, lines
MS, MSS	Manuscript, manuscripts
n.d.	No date
n.n.	No name
n.p.	No place
p., pp.	Page, pages
supra	Above
vol., vols.	Volume, volumes

DISCUSSION FOOTNOTES

In sharp contrast with source footnotes are discussion footnotes. Through discussion footnotes the writer strives to explain a part of the text, to amplify discussion on a phase of the presentation, to make cross-references to other parts of the report, and the like. The following examples illustrate some possibilities of this footnote type.

CROSS-REFERENCE:
[1] See the principle of focal points on page 72.

AMPLIFICATION OF DISCUSSION AND CROSS-REFERENCE:
[2] Lyman Bryson says the same thing: "Every communication is different for every receiver even in the same context. No one can estimate the variation of understanding that there may be among receivers of the same message conveyed in the same vehicle when the receivers are separated in either space or time." See *Communication of Ideas,* 5.

COMPARISON:
[3] Compare with the principle of the objective: Before starting any activity, one should make a clear, complete statement of the objective in view.

PLACEMENT OF QUOTED AND PARAPHRASED INFORMATION

You may use data obtained from secondary sources in two ways. You may paraphrase the information (cast it in your own words), or you may use it verbatim (exactly as the original author worded it). In typing paraphrased material, you need not distinguish it from the remainder of the report text. Material you use verbatim, however, must be clearly distinguished.

The procedure for marking this difference is simple. If the quoted passage is short (about eight lines or less), place it within the text and with quotation marks before and after it. Set off longer quotations from the margins, without quotation marks, as shown in the example below. If the text is double-spaced, further distinguish the quoted passage by single-spacing it.

Of those opposing the issue, Logan Wilson (1997) makes this penetrating observation:

> It is a curious paradox that academicians display a scientific attitude toward every universe of inquiry except that which comprises their own profession. . . . Lacking precise qualitative criteria, administrators are prone to fall back upon rather crude quantitative measures as a partial substitute. For example, student evaluations of teachers often lack acceptable reliability and validity statistics. And when they are administered is quite illogical. Moreover, most statements on them relate to contextual factors—office hours, fairness of tests, and such—and not to acquiring knowledge itself. Yet administrators use quantitative scores from these instruments to the minute fraction of a point to assess teaching quality. Multiple measures of teaching performance with an emphasis on student learning would bring a more rational approach to teaching as one dimension of academic responsibility. (201)

These logical, straightforward, and simple arguments of the critics of teacher evaluation appear to be irrefutable.

Frequently, you will find it best to break up or use only fragments of the quoted author's work. Because omissions may distort the meaning of a passage, you must clearly indicate them, using ellipsis points (a series of three periods typed with intervening spaces) where material is left out. If an omission begins after the end of a sentence, you must use four periods—one for final punctuation plus the ellipsis points. A passage with such omissions is the following:

Many companies have undertaken to centralize in the hands of specially trained correspondents the handling of the outgoing mail. Usually, centralization has been accomplished by the firm's employment of a correspondence supervisor. . . . The supervisor may guide the work of correspondents . . . , or the company may employ a second technique.

In long quotations it is conventional to show omission of a paragraph or more by a full line of periods, typed with intervening spaces (see example in Pd 3, Chapter 18).

THE BIBLIOGRAPHY

A bibliography is an orderly list of material on a particular subject. In a formal report the list covers references on the subject of the report. The entries in this list closely resemble footnotes, but the two must not be confused. The bibliography normally appears as an appended part of a formal report and is placed after the appendix. It may be preceded by a fly page containing the one word *Bibliography.* The page that begins the list bears the main heading *Bibliography,* usually typed in capital letters. Below this title the references are listed by broad categories and in alphabetical order within the categories. Such listed categories as *Books, Periodicals,* and *Bulletins* may be used. But the determination of categories should be based solely on the types of publications collected in each bibliography. If, for example, a bibliography includes a large number of periodicals and government publications plus a wide assortment of diverse publication types, the bibliography could be divided into these categories: *Periodicals, Government Publications,* and *Miscellaneous Publications.* As with footnotes, variations in bibliographic style are numerous. A simplified form recommended for business use follows the same procedure as described above for footnotes, with four major exceptions:

1. The author's name is listed in reverse order—surname first—for the purpose of alphabetizing. If an entry has more than one author, however, only the name of the first author is reversed.

2. The entry is generally typed in hanging-indention form. That is, the second and subsequent lines of an entry begin some uniform distance (usually about five spaces) to the right of the beginning point of the first line. The purpose of this indented pattern is to make the alphabetized first line stand out.

3. The entry gives the inclusive pages of articles, but not for books, and does not refer to any one page or passage.

4. Second and subsequent references to publications of the same author are indicated by a uniform line (see bibliography illustration). In typed manuscripts, this line might be formed by striking the hyphen six consecutive times. If you have high-end word processing,

you make 3 em dashes. But this line may be used only if the entire authorship is the same in the consecutive publications. For example, the line could not be used if consecutive entries have one common author but different coauthors.

Following is an example of a bibliography:

BIBLIOGRAPHY

Books

Burton, Helen. *The City Fights Back*. New York: Citadel Press, 1996.

Caperton, Hudson D. *The Business of Government*. Boston: Sherman-Kaufman Company, 1973.

Chapman, Kenneth W., Harvey H. Heinz, and Robert V. Martinez. *The Basics of Marketing*. 4th ed. New York: Barrow-Dore, Inc., 1939.

Kiernan, Gladys M. *Retailers Manual of Taxes and Regulation*. 12th ed. New York: Institute of Distribution, Inc., 1997.

Surrey, N.M.M. *The Commerce of Louisiana during the French Regime, 1699–1763*. New York: Columbia University Press, 1920.

Government Publications

U.S. Bureau of the Census. "Characteristics of the Population." *Twentieth Census of the United States: Census of Population*, Vol. 2, part 18. Washington, D.C.: U.S. Government Printing Office, 1991.

_____. *Statistical Abstract of the United States*. Washington D.C.: Government Printing Office, 1990.

U.S. Department of Commerce. *Business Statistics: 1990*. Washington, D.C.: U.S. Government Printing Office, 1996.

_____. *Survey of Current Business: 1997 Supplement,* Washington, D.C.: U.S. Government Printing Office, 1997.

Periodicals

Montgomery, Donald E. "Consumer Standards and Marketing." *Journal of Distribution* (May 1997). 141–49.

Phillips, Emily F. "Some Studies Needed in Marketing." *Journal of Marketing 9* (July 1980). 16–25.

_____. "Major Areas of Marketing Research." *Journal of Marketing 18* (July 1998), 21–26.

Miscellaneous Publications

Bradford, Ernest S. *Directory of Marketing Research Agencies in the United States*. New York: Bureau of Business Research, College of the City of New York, 1996.

Reference Sources on Chain Stores. New York: Institute of Distribution, Inc., 1997.

Smith, Lynn T. *Farm Trade Center in Louisiana, 1901 to 1990*. Louisiana Bulletin no. 234. Baton Rouge: Louisiana State University, 1998.

THE ANNOTATED BIBLIOGRAPHY

Frequently, in scholarly writing each bibliography entry is followed by a brief comment on its value and content. That is, the bibliography is annotated. The form and content of annotated bibliographies are illustrated in these entries:

Donald, W.T., ed. *Handbook of Business Administration*. New York: Shannon-Dale Book Co., Inc., 1996.

Contains a summary of the activities in each major area of business. Written by foremost authorities in each field. Particularly useful to the business specialist who wants a quick review of the whole of business.

Braden, Shelby M., and Lillian Como, eds. *Business Leader's Handbook*. 4th ed. New York: Mercer and Sons, Inc., 1993.

Provides answers to most routine problems of executives in explicit manner and with good examples. Contains good material on correspondence and sales letters.

DIFFERENCES IN APA AND MLA FORMATS

As noted previously, the APA and MLA systems differ somewhat from that presented in preceding pages. The primary differences are evident from the following illustrations.

Parenthetic References.

Chicago and MLA:

(Burton 1997)

APA:

(Burton, 1997)

Footnotes.

Books.

Chicago:

[2] Helen Burton, *The City Fights Back,* New York: Citadel Press, 1997, 17.

MLA:

[2] Helen Burton, *The City Fights Back* (New York: Citadel Press, 1997), 17.

APA: Does not use footnotes.

Periodicals.

Chicago:

[3] Donald E. Montgomery, "Consumer Standards and Marketing," *Journal of Distribution,* May 1996, 144.

MLA:

[3] Donald E. Montgomery, "Consumer Standards and Marketing," *Journal of Distribution,* May 1996: 144.

APA: Does not use footnotes.

Bibliography.

Books.

Chicago:

Burton, Helen. *The City Fights Back.* New York: Citadel Press. 1997.

MLA:

Burton, Helen. *The City Fights Back.* New York: Citadel Press, 1997.

APA:

Burton, H. (1997). *The city fights back.* New York: Citadel Press.

Periodicals.

Chicago:

Montgomery, Donald E. "Consumer Standards and Marketing." *Journal of Distribution,* (May 1996). 141–49.

MLA:

Montgomery, Donald E. "Consumer Standards and Marketing." *Journal of Distribution,* May 1996: 141–49.

APA:

Montgomery, D. E. (1996). Consumer standards and marketing. *Journal of Distribution,* 15(5), 141–149.

In place of the specific date of publication, APA style uses volume and number—in this example 15(5).

The Chicago system is used most in business, but any of these systems could be appropriate. Of course, you should use only one in a paper.

INDEX

Software tools—(*Cont.*)
    for presenting, 485–489
    for transmitting messages, 499–491
Sources of information, in reports, 358
Space, cultural views of, 501
Speaking, formal, 451–462
Speaking practices, summary of, 461
Special libraries, 539
Speed, of speaking, 459
Spelling, 532–534
Spelling checkers, 481–482
Spreadsheet software, 479
SPSS, 562–563
Stallard, John J., 3n
Standard and Poor's Corporation Records, 543
Standard and Poor's Register of Corporations, Directors, and Executives, 540
Standard and Poor's Statistical Service, 542
Statistical Abstract of the United States, 542
Statistical Reference Index, 542
Statistical Software, 479
Statistical Yearbook, 543
Stereotypes; *see* Rubber stamps
Structure; *see* Format
Style
    checkers, 483
    conversational, 58
    personal-impersonal, 240–241, 293
Subject line, 90, 583
Subject Directory of Special Libraries and Information Centers, 539
Subtopics, in organization, 279–280
Summary, of report, 359
Survey, 555–562
Survey of Current Business, 542
Survey Project Software, 556
Swanson, Jean C., and Neil, 3n
Symbols
    communication, 9–11
    outline, 284–285
Synchronous computer tools
    electronic meeting systems, 492
    Whiteborad systems, 492
Synopsis; *see* Executive summary

T

Tables, 402–403
Table of contents; *see* Contents, table of
Talking
    adaptation, 428
    definition of; 426
    style,427–428
    voice quality, 427
    word choice, 428
Talking headings; *see* Headings
Team presentations; *see* Collaboration, in speaking
Technology enabled communication
    collaborative writing, 491–492
    constructing messages, 474–485
    presenting, 485–489
    transmitting, 489–497
Telephone
    courtesy, 442–443
    procedures, 443–444
    voice mail techniques, 444
    voice quality, 442

Templates, 571–579
Tense, verb, 528–539
Test, diagnostic, 536, 568–69
Thank-you messages, 264
Thesaurus software, 482–483
Thomas Register of American Manufacturers, 541
Thoroughness, in speaking, 455
Thurstone, L. L., 561
Tie-in sentences; *see* Sentence, tie-in
Time
    attitude toward, 501
    as nonverbal communication, 436
    as organization basis, 285–286
    viewpoint, 293–294
Title fly, 352–353
Title page, 353
Title
    graphics, 401
    report, 352–353
Topic heading; *see* Headings
Topic selection, speech, 451
Topic sentence, 50–51
Transition, 71–72, 294–296
Transmittal, letter of, 353–355, 591
Trompenaars, Fons, 498
Truths, communication, 12–13
Two-word verbs, 506–508
Typography
    font, 487–488
    kerning, 487
    leading, 487
    points and picas, 487
    type style, 578–580
Twain, Mark, 23

U–V

United States Predicasts F & S Index, 548
Unity
    paragraph, 49–50
    sentence, 47–49
Validity, sample, 556
Value Line Investment Service, 543
Verbs
    action, 26–27, 238
    agreement, 525
    camouflaged, 27–28
    two-word, 506–508
Videoconferencing, 480
Video clips, 417
Virus, 481
Visuals; *see* Graphics
Voice
    active-passive, 26–27
    in speaking, 458–59
Voice messaging systems, 489–490
Voice recognition, 446, 485
Voice storage systems, 489–490

W–Z

Walking, in speaking, 458
Web; *see* Internet
Webster, 542
White space, 486
Whittenburg, G. E., 483n

Who's Who in America, 540
Who's Who in Computer Education and Research, 540
Who's Who in the East, 540
Who's Who in Economics, 540
Who's Who in Finance and Industry, 540
Who's Who in Insurance, 540
Who's Who in Labor, 540
Who's Who in the South and Southwest, 540
Who's Who in the World, 540
Wilsonline, 548
Word processing
    hidden text, 480
    table of contents, 481
Word processing software, 479–481
    basic math, 480
    footnoting, 480
    grammar checkers, 483–484
    hyphenation, 480
    index building, 481
    insert/delete, 480
    macros, 481
    merge, 481
    reference, 484, 521
    remark, 480
    search/place, 480
    simple sorting, 480
    style checkers, 483–484
    survey design project, 556
    tables, 480
Words
    abstract, 25–26
    action, 26–27
    choice, 21–34, 64
    concrete, 25–26
    conversational, 58
    correct use, 214, 529–530
    culturally derived, 508–509
    discriminatory, 30–33
    economical use of, 41–46
    effect of, 64
    familiar-unfamiliar, 22–23
    legal, 25
    length considerations, 23
    negative-positive, 64–65, 137–138, 143, 148, 163, 170–171
    precision of, 28–29
    racist, 32
    rubber stamps, 60–61
    selection of, 21–22
    short, 23
    slang, 508
    stereotyped, 33, 59
    strength of, 25
    surplus, 43–44
    technical, 24–25
    transition, 71–72
    unnecessary repetition, 44–45
Worldcasts, 543
Webster's New Collegiate Dictionary, 542
Who Owns Whom, 541
Yate, Martin, 262n
You-viewpoint, 62–63, 163, 170–171
Zero origin, violation of, 411
Zikmund, William, 556
Zinsser, William, 474
ZIP code, 586

PHOTO CREDITS

CHAPTER 1

1-1   David Joel/Tony Stone Images
1-2   Lee Snider/The Image Works
1-3   Andy Sacks/Tony Stone Images

CHAPTER 2

2-1   David Ash/Tony Stone Images
2-2   Keith Brofsky/PhotoDisc

CHAPTER 3

3-1   Larry Dale Gordon/The Image Bank
3-2   Dan Bosler/Tony Stone Images

CHAPTER 4

4-1   Walter Hodges/Tony Stone Images
4-2   ©PhotoDisc

CHAPTER 5

5-1   Superstock
5-2   Peter Cade/Tony Stone Images
5-3   Frank Herholdt/Tony Stone Images

CHAPTER 6

6-1   Comstock
6-2   Miro Vintoniv/Stock Boston

CHAPTER 7

7-2
Susan Buschman

CHAPTER 8

8-1a   Jon Riley/Tony Stone Images
8-1b   ©PhotoDisc
8-2   Mark Segal/Tony Stone Images
8-3   Jose L. Pelaez/The Stock Market

CHAPTER 9

9-1   Loren Santow/Tony Stone Images
9-2   Esbin-Anderson/The Image Works

CHAPTER 10

10-1   Michael Newman/PhotoEdit
10-2   David R. Frazier/Tony Stone Images
10-3   Superstock

CHAPTER 11

11-1   Steve Niedorf/The Image Bank
11-2   David Young Wolff/Tony Stone Images
11-3   Charles Gupton/Tony Stone Images

CHAPTER 12

12-1   Jose L. Pelaez/The Stock Market
12-2   Bryan F. Peterson/The Stock Market

CHAPTER 13

13-1   Matthew Borkoski/Index Stock

CHAPTER 14

14-1   Michael Newman/PhotoEdit
14-2   Bob Daemmrich/Stock Boston
14-3   Keith Wood/Tony Stone Images

CHAPTER 15

15-1   Courtesy Morris Massey Associates, Inc.
15-2   Tom Carroll/International Stock
15-3   John Madere/The Stock Market

CHAPTER 16

16-1   Jose L. Pelaez/The Stock Market
16-2   Dan Bosler/Tony Stone Images

CHAPTER 17

17-1   Will & Deni McIntyre/Tony Stone Images

CHAPTER 19

19-1   Loren Santow/Tony Stone Images
19-2   Bob Daemmrich/Tony Stone Images

PART OPENERS

PO-1   Terry Vine/Tony Stone Images
PO-2   Myrleen Ferguson/PhotoEdit
PO-3   Jose L. Pelaez/The Stock Market
PO-4   Mike Malyszko/FPG International LLC
PO-5   Terry Vine/Tony Stone Images
PO-6   Dan Bosler/Tony Stone Images
PO-7   © PhotoDisc